About the Authors

Ken Getz

Ken Getz is a programmer, technical writer, and educator. Formerly a member of the Ashton-Tate Framework III and IV development teams, he is an independent consultant, developing custom applications and tools using Microsoft Access, SQL Server, Visual C++, Visual Basic, and the rest of the Microsoft Office suite. He won Microsoft MVP awards in 1993 and 1994 by spending far too much spare time on CompuServe, learning while answering many of the questions posted there.

Ken has spent much of the past year traveling around the country, teaching Access developer training classes for the Application Developers Training Company, and is a frequent speaker at conferences (Microsoft's Tech*Ed '94 and Tech*Ed '95 in New Orleans, and the International Database Interchange conferences in Toronto and Palm Desert). He was chosen by Australia's PC Developer magazine to give two-day lectures in each of six Australian cities, preparing Access developers for their certification exam. He's also a Contributing Editor to Smart Access, a journal aimed at Access developers, published by Pinnacle Publishing. He's just released the *Microsoft Access 2 Developer's Handbook*, published by Sybex, Inc., along with co-authors Paul Litwin and Greg Reddick.

When not programming or writing, he turns his chair around and tickles the other keyboard, the grand piano that fills the other half of his office.

Helen Feddema

Helen Feddema was ready for computers when she was 12, but computers were not ready for her yet, so she got a B.S. in Philosophy from Columbia and an M.T.S. in Theological Studies from Harvard Divinity School, while working at various office jobs. She started with word processing and spreadsheets, went on to learn dBASE, and did dBASE development for six years.

Always looking for something new and better, Helen beta tested Access 1.0 and quickly decided that this was the database she had been looking for since the introduction of Windows 3.0. Since that time she has co-authored *Inside Microsoft Access* (New Riders, 1992), and written two books for Pinnacle's The

Pros Talk Access series, *Power Forms* and *Power Reports*. She is also a regular contributor to Pinnacle's *Smart Access* newsletter.

In July 1994 Helen joined Information Management Services, a Microsoft Solution Provider, as an Access developer. She is working on applications that link Access to other MS Office applications.

Mike Gunderloy

Mike Gunderloy is Development Partner at Pyramid Computers, a Brooklyn-based Microsoft Solution Provider. He specializes in Microsoft Access training and troubleshooting, small workgroup networking and integration, and end-user support on Microsoft Windows issues.

Mike is a Microsoft Certified Professional Product Specialist, with certifications in Windows, Windows for Workgroups, and Windows NT, among other products. He participated in the beta test programs for Access 2.0, the Access Distribution Toolkit for Access 2.0, and the Access Solutions Pack. He also maintains the monthly Access Frequently Asked Questions List (ACCFAQ) on CompuServe, and has been given the Microsoft Most Valuable Professional award for volunteer tech support several times.

Mike is the author of the Pinnacle Press research report "Developing Professional Access Applications," and has contributed to other Access books as well.

In previous lives, he was a fanzine editor, BBS sysop, finance manager for a food co-op, and clerk in a liquor warehouse. In his copious spare time, he helps run the House of Funny Noises in Brooklyn and raises cats that eat Cheetos.

Dan Haught

Dan Haught is a product manager with FMS, Inc. in Vienna, Virginia. He has been developing database applications and tools for over ten years on a variety of platforms and has been developing database tools for Microsoft Access for the last two years.

Dan wrote the Total Access Analyzer documentation program for Microsoft Access and continues to work on new add-in programs. He has written for Access Advisor magazine and is a contributing editor to Pinnacle's Smart Access journal. He has also written documentation for the Microsoft Access Developers Toolkit and has been a featured speaker at Microsoft's Tech*Ed and Borland International's Developers Conference.

When not at the keyboard, Dan spends time with his wife, Jayne and daughter, Hannah.

Table of Contents

Contents

Acknowledgments

I'd like to take this opportunity to thank several people who helped make this book possible.

First of all, Joe Ferrie, the editor of *Microsoft Access 2.0 How-To CD,* who kept me going through mounds of revisions, questions, and proofs. Even though Joe was working on several projects at the same time as we were rushing to finish this book, he always had time to work through the current problem, no matter how trivial. It often seemed to me that he was working only on our book.

Thanks to Andrew Miller, at Microsoft, for providing the three OLE Custom controls that we've included on the disk that comes with this book. Andrew is a real pioneer in the development of OCX controls, and we are indebted to him for his generosity and good will in making these available.

Thanks also to several folks who submitted ideas, reviewed existing How-To's, and provided feedback. Specifically, thanks to Jim Ferguson, Paul Litwin, and David Oxstein for their help. Thanks also to Kim Abercrombie and Heather Pacheco of Microsoft for their review of Chapter 5, and to Steve Alboucq and the rest of the CompuServe PSS crew, who constantly submitted ideas for the book, whether or not they were aware of it.

Finally, thanks to all our families, friends, and significant others. Without their understanding, patience, and motivation to find things to do to amuse themselves while we were working, we wouldn't have been able to put together this book.

Kenneth N. Getz

Foreword

Since its introduction two years ago, Microsoft Access has been a tremendous success in the desktop database market. With this success has come an enormous increase in demand for top quality technical support and answers to questions on development and design. Today Microsoft Access support engineers respond to well over 3000 phone calls per day. The Microsoft Access CompuServe forum (Go MSACCESS) handles more than 600 messages per day, and downloads of technical articles from the forum libraries and the Microsoft Internet ftp server number in the tens of thousands per month. People are putting Access to good use and they are demanding answers to questions that arise as they develop database applications.

Microsoft Access makes it easier than any other desktop PC database to solve tough database management challenges. However, because of the complexity and variety of our data management requirements, we all encounter involved problems as we develop our applications—and nothing brightens our day like finding a quick answer to a problem that is holding up progress.

There are numerous reference books on the market for Access 2.0, most focused on the lower- or mid-range user. The authors of this book have accomplished something significant—they've created a reference, the *Microsoft Access 2.0 How-To CD,* that is useful for the complete range of Access users. It is a convenient resource that belongs on the desk of the novice user as well as the Access Basic guru; in other words, it is a book for anyone who wants to find great solutions to common Access development problems.

The *Access How-To CD* is the kind of book that Microsoft Access support personnel enjoy seeing on bookstore shelves because it answers the frequently asked questions that cause customers to reach for their phone to call our support lines. It is an ideal resource for Access developers when they need an idea that will get them over a design hurdle, or when they want to add ease-of-use features to their application.

The four authors of this book are well known in the Access community for their creative ideas in solving the trickiest challenges of using Access. They have accumulated expansive knowledge of Access and they have kept in close touch with common problems and pitfalls that beset Access application developers. This book represents many of their best ideas, and answers to common questions compiled into one convenient place.

Our goal at Microsoft Access Product Support is to deliver the right answer, right now. This book supports our goal, and the goals of Access users, by providing solutions to common design and development problems in an easy-to-use format.

Steve Alboucq, Microsoft Access Support Team Manager

Introduction

This introduction provides a general overview of *Microsoft Access 2.0 How-To CD*. It also provides instructions on some basic procedures that you will need to understand before tackling the how-to's.

What This Book Is About

This is an idea book. It's a compendium of solutions, suggestions, and "neat stuff"—all devoted to making your work with Microsoft Access more productive. If you're using Access and you aspire to create database applications that are more than Wizard-created clones of every other database application, this is the book for you.

If, on the other hand, you're looking for a book that shows you how to create a form, or how to write your first Access Basic function, or how to use the Crosstab Query Wizard, this may *not* be the book you need. For those kinds of things we recommend one of the many Access books geared toward the first-time learner.

Promotes Creative Use of the Product

Rather than rehash the manuals, *Microsoft Access 2.0 How-To CD* offers you solutions to design problems you may have already encountered, have yet to encounter, or perhaps have never even considered. Some of the issues discussed in this book are in direct response to questions posted in the Microsoft Access forum on CompuServe; others are problems we've encountered while developing our own applications. In any case, our goal is to show you how to push the edges of the product, making it do things you might not even have thought possible.

For example, you'll learn how to create a query that joins tables based on some condition other than equality; how to size a form's controls to match the form's size; how to store and retrieve the locations and sizes of forms from session to session; and how to create a page range indicator on every report page. You'll see how to use some of the Windows common dialogs from your Access application; how to internationalize your messages; how to *really* control your printer; and how to create new table properties that allow you to store the user's name and the date last edited for each row. There are How-To's for creating a runtime execution profiler, for filling list boxes in a number of different ways, and for optimizing your applications. You'll find details on using Access in multi-user environments, creating transaction logs, adjusting database options depending on who's logged in, and keeping track of users and groups programmatically. There are instructions for using the Windows API to restrict mouse movement to a specific area of a form, for exiting Windows under program control, and for checking the status of and shutting down another Windows application. Finally, you'll see how, with OLE and DDE, you can use Access together with other applications such as Program Manager, Microsoft Graph, WinFax Pro, Excel, and Word.

Uses the Tools at Hand

This book focuses on using the right tool for the right problem. If at all possible, the solutions provided here use macros. (Given that the majority of Access users don't already use Access Basic, we wanted to make as many of these How-To's accessible to as many readers as possible.) On the other hand, some tasks just aren't well suited for macros and must be handled with Access Basic code. Sometimes even plain Access Basic code isn't sufficient, and we needed to use the Windows API or other libraries that all users have. In each case, we've tried to make the implementation of the technique as simple as possible, yet as generic as possible.

Question-and-Answer Format

The structure of this book is simple: Each How-To consists of a question and its solution. The chapters of questions and answers are arranged by categories: queries, forms, reports, application design, printing, data manipulation, Access Basic, optimization, user interface, multi-user applications, Windows API, and OLE/DDE. Each How-To contains a database with complete construction details, indicating which modules you need to import, what controls you need to create, and what events you need to react to. All the code, bitmaps, and sample data are included on the CD-ROM that accompanies the book.

Free Custom Controls

Also on the CD-ROM—in addition to the sample databases (one for each How-To)—you'll find OLE custom controls (often called OCX controls) that you can use in your Access applications, following the license agreement that you'll find in each control's directory. Chapter 12 demonstrates one of these controls. We hope you'll find these a useful addition to your Access bag of tools.

CUSTOM CONTROLS SUPPLIED AS IS
Each of these free OLE custom controls is provided as is. There's no implied or explicit support for these controls. Though Microsoft will provide support for the OLE controls that are shipped as part of its retail packages, it cannot provide technical assistance for the controls on the enclosed CD-ROM. Make sure you note the restrictions in each control's README.TXT file.

Expected Level of Reader

No, you don't have to be an Access Basic whiz to use this book. It's designed for all levels of readers: end users, power users, and developers. We've assigned each How-To a level of difficulty (Easy, Intermediate, or Advanced) based on the complexity of the solution. Problems that can be solved with a macro or two, or simple Access Basic code, are Easy. If a solution requires substantial Access Basic code, or even a little code that's nontrivial, it's Intermediate. Solutions that rely on advanced Access Basic techniques or on Windows API calls are Advanced.

In every case, we've made the steps to implement the solution as simple as possible. When Access Basic is involved, we recommend the modules to import from the sample database, with a discussion of the important features of the code within the text. You shouldn't have to retype any of the code unless you care to. What's more, you don't actually have to understand the solution to any of the problems covered in this book in order to make use of the solution. In each case, you'll find a sample database that demonstrates the technique and explicit instructions on how to implement the same technique in your own applications. If you do want to "dig in" and figure out how the samples work, feel free.

What You Need to Use This Book

In order to use this book you'll need a computer capable of running Windows 3.1 (or higher) and Microsoft Access 2.0. All of the example databases were prepared for display on a 640×480 (VGA) display. They'll work fine at a higher resolution, but you'll need at least standard VGA to run the examples well. A pointing device, (such as a mouse or pen), is highly recommended.

To demonstrate the topics in Chapter 12, you'll need copies of WinFax Pro from Delrina and Excel (5.0 or higher) and Word for Windows (6.0 or higher) from Microsoft. These items aren't necessary, of course, but will allow you to try out the example databases.

How This Book Is Organized

This book is organized into 12 chapters.

Chapter 1: Using the Power of Queries

In this chapter, you'll learn to create parameter queries, allowing you to control the selected rows at runtime, not at design time. You'll use this technique to control the available values in one combo box, based on the choice in another. You'll also see how to use the value of a particular column in a combo box as a parameter for a query and how to use Access Basic variables as parameters, too. You'll learn to control the output of cross-tab queries. A handy technique lets you group mailing labels by residence, to avoid sending multiple mailings to different members of a family. You'll study a query to create a random set of rows, in case you need to pull random sets of data from a data source, and a query that uses the Partition function to perform aging analysis. Finally, you'll find a group of topics dealing with more advanced uses of queries: "faking" a non-equijoin, using DDL (Data Definition Language) queries to create or alter tables, and using union queries to join tables or queries together. You'll also examine a suggested method for storing query information in a table, which can be protected and made invisible in applications, giving you complete control over which queries get run and when.

Chapter 2: Designing Creative and Useful Forms

You'll want to use the tips in this chapter to give a consistent "look" to your forms and to help users find exactly which control currently has the focus. You can control where users go on your forms by restricting their movement to another row, and you can give your forms custom navigation controls. Your understanding of controls will grow, too, as you learn to use option groups to collect and display non-numeric information and to control the display of multipaged forms. You'll also find a way to resize the controls inside your forms to match the size of the form. You'll see how to combine controls to create "hybrid" controls, by linking a text box and a list box to create a combination that works like a permanently opened combo box. Finally, you'll use the Windows API to save and restore application variables and to save and restore the size of your forms from one session to another.

Chapter 3: Reporting as an Art Form

Use the How-To's in this chapter to refine your reporting techniques. The first How-To's show you how to create an attractive multicolumn address list report; how to create a datasheet subreport for a report; how to make a report that looks just like a spreadsheet, using subreports for the columns; and how to work around the limitations of the CanGrow/CanShrink properties and prevent blank rows on reports, by combining an entire address into a single expression for a mailing labels report. A group of How-To's demonstrates how to print a message on a report only if certain conditions are met; how to create telephone book-style page range indicators; how to calculate page totals; and how to print a bar graph on a report using rectangle controls. You'll also learn to use advanced Access Basic to suppress printing a report if there are no records to print. Using an event procedure run from the report's Format event, you can print one set of headers and footers on odd pages and another (mirror-image) set on even pages. In two How-To's, the Line method is used to draw lines or rectangles on a report—in one case to make a line the same height as a variable-height text box, and in the other case to create gray bars overlaying every other row of the report. Finally, you'll find out how to prevent your report from breaking at an inappropriate place, such as right after a group header.

Chapter 4: Developing and Distributing Applications

This chapter is a compendium of tips and suggestions on making your application development go more smoothly, more professionally, and more internationally. You'll learn how to easily remove queries whose only purpose is to provide data for forms and controls, and how to build an object inventory so you can better document your applications. You'll find a way to *really* disable screen output (an improvement over the methods Access provides internally). There are tips on discerning the current language version of Access, and modifying text in error messages and on forms and reports to accommodate the current language. You'll see how to set and restore the Access caption, and how to set values in the MSACC20.INI that you probably didn't know about (unless you also use the Access runtime version). You'll use some of the tools in MSAU200.DLL, a library that's supplied with Access, to use the Windows common File Open/Save dialogs; to copy DOS files from place to place; and to use the Windows common color-choosing dialog. The final three topics deal with application distribution: clearing out test data before shipping your application, managing the use of forms to make the best use of resources versus speed, and packaging an add-in for distribution.

Chapter 5: Taming Your Printer

This chapter focuses on the three printer-related properties of forms and reports that are barely documented in other sources: prtMip, prtDevMode, and prtDevNames. We'll cover these properties in detail and show examples of their use. You'll be able to retrieve a list of all the installed printers and make a choice from that list, setting the new default Windows printer. You'll learn how to modify margin settings in forms and reports, thereby avoiding the use of Access's Print|Setup dialog in your applications. You'll get help on changing printer options, such as the number of copies to print, page orientation, and printer resolution. In particular, one How-To will demonstrate printing to paper sizes that your printer doesn't regularly support (if your printer supports variable-sized pages, of course). Finally, you'll see how to determine which device has been selected to print a report or form and whether it's the default device. If it is, you can change the destination from your application, provide your users with a choice of output devices, and print the object to a particular device. You'll also find a development tool that will run through all your reports and let you know which ones aren't set up to print to the default printer. By ensuring that all your reports print to the default printer, you will be able to send them to any output device just by changing what Windows thinks is the default printer.

Chapter 6: Managing Data

This chapter concentrates on working with data in ways that traditional database operations don't support. You'll learn how to filter your data, back it up, locate it on the file system, save housekeeping information, and more. All examples in this chapter use some form of Access Basic, but don't worry. They are clearly explained, and test-bed applications are supplied to show you how each technique works.

Chapter 7: Exploring Access Basic
The How-To's in this chapter cover some of the details of Access Basic that you might not find in the Access manuals. There's a complete explanation of embedding strings inside other strings, so you can build SQL strings and other expressions that require embedded values. One How-To is devoted to creating a procedure stack, allowing you to track the current procedure at all times. Another creates a profiling log file, helping you document where and for how long your code has wandered. You'll study the DoEvents statement, which gives Windows time to handle its own chores while your code is running. A group of four How-To's explain the details of creating list-filling functions, passing arrays as parameters, sorting arrays, and filling a list box with the results of a directory search. Finally, you'll find some details of *using* Access Basic: how to perform a global search-and-replace, even in closed form or report modules; and how to decide whether to use global or private modules.

Chapter 8: Optimizing Your Application
One immutable rule of application design is that your application will never run fast enough. Unless you and your application's users are equipped with the latest and most powerful workstations with huge amounts of memory, you can expect performance that is less than satisfying. There are many techniques for optimizing your application's performance, few of which are readily apparent in the Microsoft Access documentation. This chapter covers optimizations and accelerations for loading forms, adding and changing data, and running your Access Basic code, among others. Testing techniques are covered as well, so you can see which approaches to optimization are faster.

Chapter 9: Making the Most of Your User Interface
By implementing the ideas and techniques in this chapter, you'll be able to create a user interface that stands out and works well. You'll learn how to take full advantage of special keystrokes to help your user navigate through a complex application, and how to use a combo box to select from a list as well as actually maintain that list with new entries as they are needed. A map-based interface can help users jump to a set of records they need to work with; other techniques will help them choose a specific record to focus on. You'll dress up an application a bit with custom splash screens and animated buttons. Finally, you'll see how to hide some necessary complexity from users by allowing them to pick multiple items from a single list box and use an expanding dialog box to organize complex options.

Chapter 10: Addressing Multi-User Application Concerns
This chapter offers solutions to some of the common problems of networking and coordinating multiple simultaneous users. You can use a shared database table to help your users communicate with one another, and you can tell just which users are logged on at any given time. You can implement basic transaction logging. Several of the How-To's here tackle the problem of

updating a database that exists on hundreds of workstations around the world. Since multi-user applications also tend to use Access security, we'll explore the security system. You'll learn how to keep track of users and groups, how to find blank passwords, and how to enforce some additional password requirements beyond those that Access itself handles. You'll also go beyond Access's built-in security to actually set security on individual controls and menu options.

Chapter 11: Making the Most of the Windows API

No matter how much you've avoided using the Windows API from Access applications, in this chapter you'll discover that it's really not a major hurdle. We'll present some interesting uses of the Windows API, and other external libraries as well, with example forms and modules for each How-To. In most cases, using these examples in your own applications takes little more work than importing a module or two and calling some functions. You'll learn how to remove the Access system menu and the maximize and minimize buttons, how to restrict the user from moving to any other application (by making Access *system modal*), and how to restrict mouse movement to a specific area on the screen. We'll discuss language-independent classification of keypresses, so you can monitor exactly what keys and what kind of keys have been pressed. You'll learn how to run another program from your Access Basic code, and how to wait until that program is done before continuing. We'll demonstrate a method for exiting Windows under program control, and explore all the options involved with the associated API functions. You'll learn how to find and run an application, given a data file associated with the application, and how to check whether or not the application is already running. You'll see techniques for retrieving a list of all the top-level windows (generally, one per application) that are currently open, and for closing a window from your Access Basic code (allowing you to shut down another application). You'll learn how to retrieve file date and time stamp information, which can be useful if you're moving files around from within your applications, and to use some undocumented DLL calls to retrieve information about your disk drives. Finally, you'll create an About... box, listing information about your Access installation and the current Windows environment.

Chapter 12: Using OLE and DDE to Extend Your Applications

This chapter gives you examples of using OLE in each of the ways it interacts with Access, and a few examples of using DDE with applications that don't offer OLE Automation. You'll examine how to activate an embedded OLE object (a sound file, for example). One How-To uses a custom OLE control from its installation through its interactions with Access Basic; another How-To uses the statistical, analytical, and financial prowess of the Excel function libraries, directly from Access; and another uses Word for Windows to retrieve document summary information for any selected document. Using DDE, you'll control Delrina's WinFax Pro and Windows' Program Manager from Access Basic. Finally, you'll dig into OLE Automation, creating a form that allows you to alter properties of Microsoft Graph objects on a form.

Some Things You'll Need to Know

In order to keep this book to a reasonable length, we have made some assumptions about your skills. First and foremost, we take it for granted that you are interested in using Microsoft Access and are willing to research the basics in other resources. This isn't a reference manual or a "Getting Started" book, so we assume you have access to that information elsewhere. We expect that you've dabbled in creating the Access objects (tables, queries, forms, and reports) and that you've at least considered working with macros or perhaps Access Basic. We encourage you to look in other resources for answers to routine questions.

To get you started, though, the following sections provide some basic instructions that will help you use the How-To's in this book. For example, you'll encounter requests to "create a new event procedure." Rather than including specific steps for doing this in every How-To, we'll tell you how to do it just once here. For each instruction we've included a help topic name from the Access online help, so you can get more information there. By the way, none of the procedures here are the *only* way to get the desired results, but rather, a single method for achieving the required goal.

How Do I Create a New Macro?

To create a new macro object, which can contain a single macro or a group of related macros, follow these steps:

1. Make the Database Container the active window, if it's not already, by pressing the (F11) key.
2. Click on the Macro tab.
3. Click on the New button. Access will create a new, unnamed macro for you.
4. If you want to display (or turn off) the Macro Names column or the Conditions column, use the View|Macro Names and View|Conditions commands to toggle their state.
5. To add an action to your macro, choose it from the drop-down list in the Action column. Add one item per row, as shown in Figure I-1. Fill in the necessary information in the bottom pane (press (F6) to jump from pane to pane).

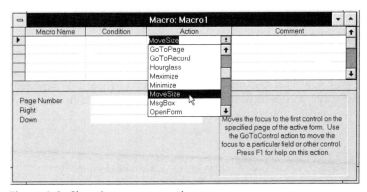

Figure I-1 Choosing a macro action

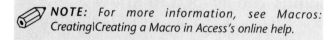

NOTE: For more information, see Macros: Creating|Creating a Macro in Access's online help.

How Do I Set Control Properties?

In the steps for many of the How-To's in this book, you'll be asked to assign properties to objects on forms or reports. This is a basic concept in creating any Access application, and you should thoroughly understand it. To assign properties to a control (or group of controls), follow these steps:

1. In design mode, select the control or group of controls. You can use any of the following methods. (Each of the items here refers to form controls, but works just as well with reports.)

   Single control: Click on a single control. Access will mark it with up to eight sizing handles—one in each corner and one in the middle of each side of the control, if possible.

   Multiple controls: Click on a single control. Then Shift-click on each of the other controls you want to select. Access will mark them each with sizing handles.

   Multiple controls: Drag the mouse through the ruler (either horizontal or vertical). Access will select each of the controls in the path you dragged over. If partially selected controls don't become part of the selection and you'd like them to, open View|Options|Form & Report Design and look at the Selection Behavior option. It should be set to Partially Enclosed.

   Multiple controls: If you need to select all but a few controls, select them all and then remove the ones you don't want. To do this, first select the form (choose Edit|Select Form, or just click on the white rectangle in the upper-left corner of the form, if rulers are visible). Then choose Edit|Select All. Finally, Shift-click on the controls you don't want included.

2. Make sure the properties sheet is visible. If it's not, use View|Properties (or the corresponding toolbar button).

3. If you've selected a single control, all the properties will be available in the properties sheet. If you've selected multiple controls, only the intersection of the selected controls' properties will be available in the properties sheet. That is, only the properties that all the selected controls have in common will appear in the list. As shown in Figure I-2, select a property group and then assign the value you need to the selected property. Repeat this process for any other properties you'd like to set for the same control or group of controls.

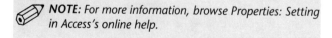

NOTE: For more information, browse Properties: Setting in Access's online help.

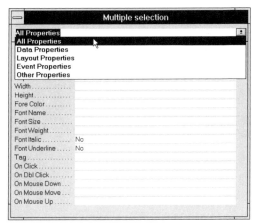

Figure I-2 Selecting a property group

How Do I Create a New Module?

Access Basic code is stored in containers called modules, each consisting of a single Declarations area, perhaps followed by one or more procedures. There are two kinds of modules in Access: global modules and form or report modules. Global modules are the ones you see in the Database Container, once you choose the Modules tab. Form or report modules (often referred to as CBF, or Code Behind Forms) are stored with the form or report itself, and never appear in the Database Container. There are various reasons to use one or the other of the two module types, but the major factor of concern is the availability of Access Basic procedures and variables. Procedures that exist in global modules can, for the most part, be called from any place in Access. Procedures that exist in a form or report's module can only be called from that particular form or report, and never from anywhere else in Access.

You'll never create a form or report module, since Access creates that kind of module when you create the object to which it's attached. To create a global module, follow these steps:

1. From the Database Container, click on the Modules tab to select the collection of modules, and then click on the New button, or just choose the File|New|Module menu item.

2. When Access first creates the module, it places you in the Declarations area. All the possible items in the Declarations area are beyond the scope of this Introduction, but you should always take one particular step at this point: Insert the Option Explicit instruction after the Option Compare Database instruction that Access has inserted. Without this statement, if Access encounters a reference to an unknown variable, Access will create the variable for you. With the Option Explicit statement, Access forces you to declare each variable before you use it.

> ## DON'T SKIP THIS STEP!
> Although this may seem like an unnecessary burden for a beginner, it's not. It's an incredible time-saver. With the Option Explicit statement in place, you can let Access check your code for misspellings. Without it, if you misspell a variable name, Access will just create a new one with the new name and go on about its business.

3. If you are asked to create a new function or subroutine, the simplest way to do that is to use Edit|New Procedure. For example, if the How-To instructs you to enter this new procedure,

```
Function SomeFunc(intX as Integer, varY as Variant)
```

you can use Edit|New Procedure, as shown in Figure I-3, to help you create the function.

4. Click OK in the New Procedure dialog, and Access creates the new procedure and places the cursor in it, ready to go. For the example in step 3, you must also supply some function parameters, so you'll need to move back up to the first line and enter the "intX as Integer, varY as Variant" between the two parentheses.

> **NOTE:** For more information on creating new modules and functions, see the online help topics Modules: Creating and Function|New Procedure command.

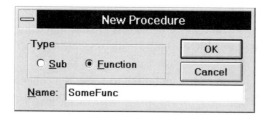

Figure I-3 The New Procedure dialog helps you create a new function or subroutine

How Do I Import a Module?

In this book's How-To's, you'll often be asked to import a module from one of the sample databases. The steps are the same, whether you're importing a module or any other database object.

1. With your database open on the Access desktop, select the Database Container by pressing (F11).
2. Choose File|Import. From the list of all the supported import types, choose Microsoft Access as the Import source.
3. From the Select Microsoft Access Database dialog, find the database from which you want to import a module, and click OK.
4. In the Import Objects dialog, choose the specific module or other object type that you want.

When importing modules, there's one possible problem to be concerned with: Access only allows one instance of a particular function or subroutine name throughout all the loaded modules, unless you've prefaced the procedure name with the "Private" keyword. If you attempt to load a module with duplicate procedure names, Access will complain and you'll need to rename the conflicting procedures in one or the other of the databases. You should also be aware of Windows API declarations, which can only appear once in all your global modules. A collision between API declarations won't cause trouble until you attempt to compile your Access Basic code. If Access complains about duplicate definitions at that point, find the offending declaration and comment it out.

If a How-To instructs you to import a module from one of the sample databases that you've already imported (for a different How-To), you can ignore the instruction. Any modules with matching names in the sample database contain the exact same code, so you needn't worry about trying to import it again.

 NOTE: *For more information on importing objects, see Import|Import Command (File menu) in online help.*

How Do I Create an Event Macro?

Programming in Access often depends on having macros or Access Basic procedures react to events that occur as you interact with forms. To create a macro that will react to a user event, follow these steps:

1. Select the appropriate object (report, form, or control) and make sure the properties sheet is displayed.
2. Either choose the Event Properties page on the properties sheet, or just scroll down the list until you find the event property you need.

> **PROPERTY NAMES VERSUS EVENT NAMES**
> The naming of event properties as opposed to the events themselves is rather ambiguous in Access. The event properties, in general, have an "On" prefix, as in OnClick, or OnActivate. The events themselves, however, are named without the "On" prefix, as in "the Click event" or "the Activate event". We've tried to be consistent throughout the book, but there are some places where the context just doesn't indicate which is the correct usage. You'll need to be aware that with or without the "On" prefix, when the event occurs, it activates the macro or procedure whose name is listed in the properties sheet for that event.

3. Click on the "..." button to the right of the event name, as shown in Figure I-4. This is the Builder button, and it appears next to properties sheet items that have associated Builders. In this case, clicking the Builder button displays the Choose Builder dialog, as shown in Figure I-5. Choose the Macro Builder item to create a new macro.

4. Give the macro a name, so Access can save it and place its name in the properties sheet. You can always delete it later if you change your mind. Give your new macro the name suggested in the How-To, and fill in the rows as directed. When you're done, save the macro and put it away.

5. Once you're done, you'll see the name of the macro in the properties sheet, as shown in Figure I-6. Whenever you cause the chosen event to occur (the Change event, in this case), Access will run the associated macro (mcrHandleChange).

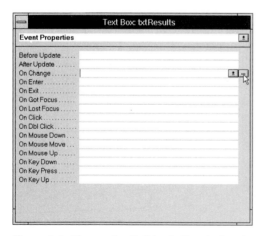

Figure I-4 Choose the Builder button to invoke the Choose Builder dialog

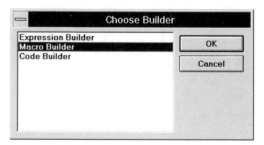

Figure I-5 The Choose Builder dialog—choose Macro Builder for macros and Code Builder for Access Basic

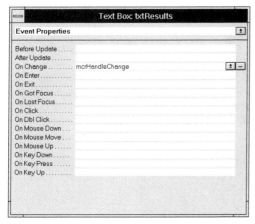

Figure I-6 The properties sheet with the selected macro assigned to the OnChange event property

6. If you want to call an existing macro from a given event property, click on the drop-down arrow next to the event name, rather than the Builder button. Choose from the displayed list of available macros (including macros that exist as part of a macro group).

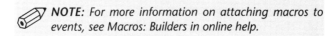

NOTE: For more information on attaching macros to events, see Macros: Builders in online help.

How Do I Create an Event Procedure?

To create an event property, follow steps 1, 2, and 3 above, for creating an event macro. In step 3, when you see the Choose Builder dialog, choose Code Builder instead of Macro Builder.

When you create a new event procedure, Access creates the subroutine name, fills in the parameters that it passes, and places the subroutine into the form or report's private module (also known as CBF, or Code Behind Forms). The name of the procedure is always the name of the object, followed by an underscore and the name of the event. For example, had you created the KeyPress event procedure for the cmdClose command button, you'd see a code skeleton like this:

```
Sub cmdClose_KeyPress(KeyAscii As Integer)

End Sub
```

Now follow these steps to complete the process:

1. If the How-To asks you to enter code into the event procedure, enter it between the lines of code that Access has created for you. Usually, the code

example in the How-To will include the lines between which you enter the new lines, so don't enter them again. When you're done, close the module window and save the form. By saving the form, you also save the form's module.

2. Another way to create an event procedure is to select an event property, pull down the list of choices for the property, and choose [Event Procedure]. When you click on the Builder button, Access takes you directly to the correct event procedure for the selected event, for the current object.

> ✎ **NOTE:** For more information, see Event Procedures|Creating an Event Procedure in online help.

How Do I Place Code in a Form or Report's Module?

When a How-To asks you to place a procedure in a form or report's module that isn't directly called from an event, follow these simple steps:

1. With the form or report open in design mode, choose View|Code (or click on the Code button on the toolbar, as shown in Figure I-7).

2. To create a new procedure, follow the steps for "How Do I Create a New Module?", starting at step 3.

3. Choose File|Save, close the module and then save the form, or click on the Save icon on the toolbar.

How Do I Know What to Do with Code Examples?

In most cases, the How-To's suggest that you import a module (or multiple modules) from the sample database for the particular How-To, rather than type in code yourself. In fact, code that isn't referenced as part of the discussion doesn't show up at all in the body of the How-To. Therefore, you should count on importing modules as directed. Then follow the instructions in the "Steps" and "How It Works" sections of each How-To to finish working with and studying the code.

If the How-To tells you to place some code in a form's module, follow the steps in "How Do I Place Code in a Form or Report's Module?" If you are instructed to place code in a global module, follow the steps in "How Do I Create A New Module?" In most cases, you'll just import an existing module and not type anything at all.

Figure I-7 Click on the Code toolbar button to view a form or report's module

About the CD

Please note this important information before using the CD.

What's on the Disk

The CD-ROM bundled with *Microsoft Access 2.0 How-To CD* includes every sample database, icon, bitmap, and external file needed to build and use the example projects in this book. All of these files are debugged and ready to run. The CD also includes several powerful utilities, add-ins, and help files that will enrich your use of Microsoft Access. On the CD you'll find

- three custom controls
- a shareware help file describing the naming conventions used in this book
- a freeware tool to help you find Windows API declarations, types, and constants
- a trial version of ClikBook, a highly-regarded print utility that installs itself directly on the Access add-in menu
- SuperSpy low-level spying utility
- Control Morph, a useful Access add-in for changing one control type to another, preserving its properties, and
- Microsoft's Security Wizard, an add-in for securing existing applications

The complete contents of the CD are shown in the CD Contents Table. All directories in the table are subdirectories of \AHT, on the CD's root.

DIRECTORY	FILES	DIRECTORY	FILES	DIRECTORY	FILES
\ACCSVC	LICENSE.TXT		01-02.MDB		05-04.MDB
\ACCSVC\DISK1			01-03.MDB		05-05.MDB
	COMPLINC.DLL		01-04.MDB		05-06.MDB
	BTRV200.DL_		01-05.MDB		05-07.MDB
	COMPOBJ.DL_		01-06.MDB		05-08.MDB
	CTL3D.DL_		01-07.MDB	\CH06	06-01.MDB
	MSACAHBB.DL_		01-08.MDB		06-02.MDB
	MSAJT200.DL_		01-09.MDB		06-03.MDB
	MSCPYDIS.DL_		01-10.MD		06-04.MDB
	MSJETERR.DL_		01-11.MDB		06-05.MDB
	MSJETINT.DL_		01-12.MDB		06-06.MDB
	MSSETUP.DL_	\CH02	02-01.MDB		06-07.MDB
	OLE2CONV.DL_		02-02.MDB	\CH07	07-01.MDB
	PDX200.DL_		02-03.MDB		07-02.MDB
	XBS200.DL_		02-04.MDB		07-03.MDB
	SETUP.EXE		02-05.MDB		07-04.MDB
	ACMSETUP.EX_		02-06.MDB		07-05.MDB
	MSSETUP.EX		02-07.MDB		07-06.MDB
	ACMSETUP.HL_		02-08.MDB		07-07.MDB
	SETUP.INI		02-09.MDB		07-08.MDB
	ADMIN.IN_		02-10.MDB		07-09.MDB
	SETUP.IN_	\CH03	03-01.MDB	\CH08	08-01.MDB
	SETUP.LST		03-02.MDB		08-03.MDB
	OLE2.RE_		03-03.MDB		08-04.MDB
	SETUP.STF		03-04.MDB		08-05.MDB
	STDOLE.TL_		03-05.MDB	\CH09	CHECK1.BMP
	READSRV.TXT		03-06.MDB		CHECK2.BMP
\ACCSVC\DISK2			03-07.MDB		CHECK3.BMP
	MSAJU200 DL_		03-08.MDB		CHECK4.BMP
	OLE2.DL_		03-09.MDB		CHECK5.BMP
	OLE2DISP.DL_		03-10.MDB		COPY1.BMP
	OLE2NLS.DL_		03-11.MDB		COPY2.BMP
	OLE2PROX.DL_		03-12.MDB		EXIT1.BMP
	STORAGE.DL_		03-13.MDB		EXIT2.BMP
	TYPELIB.DL_	\CH04	AHT.ICO		MINIMAL.BMP
	DECOMP.EXE		04-12.MDA		TEARDROP.BMP
	SETUPWIZ MD_		SYSAHT.MDA		TICK1.BMP
	JETVER TX_		04-01.MDB		TICK2.BMP
\APIHELP	README.1ST		04-02.MDB		TICK3.BMP
	API_CALL.DAT		04-03.MDB		TICK4.BMP
	API_CONS.DAT		04-04.MDB		TICK5.BMP
	API_TYPE.DAT		04-05.MDB		TICK6.BMP
	QPRO200.DLL		04-06.MDB		TICK7.BMP
	VBRUN200.DLL		04-07.MDB		TICK8.BMP
	APIHELP.EXE		04-08.MDB		USWEST.BMP
	API_CALL.IDX		04-09.MDB		09-01.MDB
	API_TYPE.IDX		04-10.MDB		09-02.MDB
	APIHELP.INI		04-11.MDB		09-03.MDB
	QPLIST.VBX	\CH05	05-01.MDB		09-04.MDB
	THREED.VBX		05-02.MDB		09-05.MDB
\CH01	01-01.MDB		05-03.MDB		09-06.MDB

DIRECTORY	FILES	DIRECTORY	FILES	DIRECTORY	FILES
	09-07.MDB		12-03.MDB		README.WR$
	09-08.MDB		12-04.MDB		CLIKBOOK.XL$
	09-09.MDB		12-05.MDB		IDGSAMP.XL$
	09-10.MDB		12-06.MDB	\CTLMORPH	CTLMORPH.MDA
\CH10	RECEIVE.BMP		12-07.MDB		CTLMORPH.TXT
	SEND.BMP	\CLIKBOOK	CLIKBTNS.DL$	\LRNAMG	LRNAMG.HLP
	SYSAHT.MDA		CLIKIO.DL$	\MSLB	MSAREG.EXE
	10-01BE.MDB		CLIKINST.DLL		MSLB.HLP
	10-01FE.MDB		CLKINST2.DLL		MSLB.LIC
	10-02BE.MDB		2WINE.DO$		MSLB.MDB
	10-02FE.MDB		CLIKBOOK.DO$		MSLB.OCX
	10-03.MDB		CBUNINST.DOC		README.TXT
	10-04.MDB		TRI-FLIP.DOT		MSLB.ZIP
	10-04A.MDB		TRI-FOLD.DOT	\OLEDLL	OC1016.DLL
	10-04B.MDB		CLIKBOOK.DR$		OC25.DLL
	10-04CH.MDB		CLIKAPP.EX$		MSAREG.EXE
	10-05BE.MDB		SETUP.EXE		REGSVR.EXE
	10-05FE.MDB		CLIKHELP.HL$		README.TXT
	10-06.MDB		CLIKRHLP.HL$	\POSITION	POSITION.TXT
	10-07.MDB		CLIKBOOK.INI	\SECWIZ	SECURE20.MDA
	10-08.MDB		CLIKHELP.INI		SECURE20.WRI
	10-09.MDB		CLIKWARE.INI	\SPINLB	MSAREG.EXE
\CH11	11-01.MDB		SETUP.INS		SPINLBL.HLP
	11-02.MDB		UNINST.INS		SPINLBL.LIC
	11-03.MDB		FILET.LIS		SPINLBL.MDB
	11-04.MDB		UNFILE1.LIS		SPINLBL.OCX
	11-05.MDB		CBINST.MD$		README.TXT
	11-06.MDB		CBINST2.MD$	\SUPERSPY	SBICTLW.DLL
	11-07.MDB		CLIKBOOK.MD$		SUPERSPY.DOC
	11-08.MDB		PHONE.MD$		SUPERSPY.EXE
	11-09.MDB		PRESENT.PP$	\TAB	REGSVR.EXE
	11-10.MDB		CLIKBOOK.SMM		TAB.HLP
	11-11.MDB		TRI-FLIP.STY		TAB.LIC
	11-12.MDB		TRI-FOLD.STY		TAB.MDB
	11-13.MDB		REPLACE.TXT		TAB.OCX
\CH12	12-01.MDB		TRI-FLIP.WPT		README.TXT
	12-02.MDB		TRI-FOLD.WPT	\VBAGRP	VBGAGRP.HLP

How to Install the Files

The following paragraphs explain how to install each of the different databases, utilities, and files you'll find on the CD.

Chapter Databases (\CH01 – \CH12)

All of the examples for each chapter are stored together in their own directory on the disk. For example, all the files for Chapter 2 are in directory CH02. Within each directory the database samples are numbered to match a specific How-To in the book. For example, the database for How-To 11.8 is named 11-08.MDB on the disk.

To use any of the sample databases, you'll need to copy all of the files from the specific directory on the CD to any directory you like on your hard disk. Since some of the examples require external files (bitmaps, icons, and so forth), you'll find it simplest to copy all of the files in the directory to your hard disk. If the directory contains only MDB files, you can be sure that they're all independent, unless they're marked as a group, as in 10-01BE.MDB and 10-01FE.MDB, where the BE stands for "back-end" and the FE stands for "front-end." To copy the directories you can use Windows' File Manager, another file-management utility, or DOS. If you use DOS, you may find it simplest to use the DOS XCOPY command to copy all the files at once. To do this, type the following at the DOS command prompt:

```
XCOPY I:*.* C:\AHT /S
```

replacing *I* with your CD-ROM drive letter, and C:\AHT with a destination drive and directory of your choice.

> **WARNING:** In general, you cannot run the sample databases directly from the CD. You'll need to copy them to a writable medium before you can use them.

The API Helper (\APIHELP)

APIHELP.EXE, written by Marshal Bostwick, is a freeware Visual Basic application, written to make it easy for you to find and place Windows API declarations directly into your Access Basic code. To install the API helper, just copy all the files from the APIHELP subdirectory on the CD to any directory on your hard disk. You can create a group and icon for it in Program Manager, add it to an existing group, or just run it from the Windows File|Run menu.

ClikBook Trial Version (\CLIKBOOK)

ClikBook (from Bookmaker Corp.) is a printing utility that makes it simple to print booklets, greeting cards, tri-fold brochures, or double-sided printouts of any data from almost any Windows application. It installs itself as a menu add-in in Access, so we've included a trial version here for you to experiment with. The trial version prints a dark watermark on each page, so its output isn't very useful, but it does show you the power of the program and what it can do.

To install the ClikBook trial version, run SETUP.EXE from the CLIKBOOK directory on the CD. This installs the software and places a file called README.WRI in an output directory that you choose. Read this file for late-breaking information on ClikBook.

Control Morph (\CTLMORPH)

Control Morph, written by Ken Getz and Paul Litwin, originally appeared in Pinnacle Publishing's Smart Access newsletter. It's an Access add-in that allows you to change a control's type while preserving the properties you've already set. For example, you can create a list box, set all its properties, and then convert it to a combo box, preserving all the properties you've set up.

To install Control Morph, use Access's Add-In Manager (choose the File|Add-In Manager menu item while you have a database loaded). Choose the Add New button to choose CTLMORPH.MDA from the CTLMORPH directory on the CD. This will copy the file to the Access directory on your hard disk. Look at the CTLMORPH.TXT file for more information on using Control Morph.

Naming Standards (\LRNAMG)

The programmers who wrote this book, along with many others, prescribe to a naming standard that was originally proposed by Stan Leszynski and Greg Reddick. This standard was originally published in the premier issue of *Smart Access* newsletter. All the code in this book adheres to this style.

Kwery Corporation has provided LRNAMG.HLP, a shareware Windows help file that documents this naming standard. If you find this tool helpful, they request that you register it, as documented in the help file itself.

To use LRNAMG.HLP, copy it to a directory on your hard disk. (Although it can be used directly from the CD, you'll most likely want it placed on your hard disk, so it's available at all times.) You can create an icon in an existing or new program group and then double-click on the icon to run WINHELP with LRNAMG.HLP loaded. (This assumes that you haven't changed the standard association for .HLP files.)

Microsoft Access Service Pack (\ACCSVC)

The Microsoft Access Service Pack provides you with the Jet database engine version 2.5, the OLE 2.02 DLLs, as well as installable ISAM drivers for Paradox, BTrieve, and xBase. Note that you must install this service pack in order to use the Tab OCX. For installation instructions please refer to the file READSRV.TXT in the \ACCSVC\DISK1 directory of the CD.

Multi-Select List Box OCX (\MSLB)
Spin-Label OCX (\SPINLB)
Tab OCX (\TAB)

These three custom controls, provided by Andrew Miller of Microsoft, extend the functionality of the normal set of Access controls. These three are the first in a wave of many, many OLE controls that will become available as OCX technology matures. At the time of writing, these are the only three controls available (besides the three that ship as part of the Access Developer's Toolkit).

- MSLB.OCX is an OLE custom control that provides a list box that allows you to select multiple items, unlike the standard single-select Access list box.
- SPINLBL.OCX allows you to rotate text and display it on forms or reports.
- TAB.OCX allows you to create tabbed dialog boxes, in the style of the Microsoft Word and Excel setup dialogs.

All three of these will help you to create interesting, powerful forms.

To install each of these, first copy the OCX file (and its associated licensing file, *.LIC) to a directory on your hard disk. Because OLE registration stores the full path to the OLE server (the OCX file), it's important that you first copy the files to your hard disk, and then register them in your system's OLE database. To register them, you must use either MSAREG.EXE or REGSVR.EXE (both of which are in the OLEDLL directory on your disk). Go to the OLEDLL directory on the CD and use File Manager's File|Run menu item to run the following command,

```
MSAREG C:\OCX\TAB.OCX
```

replacing the location and file name with the correct information for each of the OCX controls.

Once you've registered the controls, you'll need to register the OLE DLL's that provide the communications between Windows and Access. MSLB and SPINLBL use OC1016.DLL, and TAB uses OC25.DLL (both of which are in the OLEDLL directory). Copy the necessary DLL to your Windows SYSTEM directory. Once the DLL is on your hard disk, run MSAREG or REGSVR again to register the DLL, using the following command,

```
MSAREG C:\WINDOWS\SYSTEM\OC25.DLL
```

replacing the directory and file name with the appropriate information. Each control directory includes a help file describing this installation process in more detail, along with instructions on programming and using the controls.

Please note that you must install the Microsoft Access Service Pack in order to use the Tab OCX.

Positional Argument Information (\POSITION)

Microsoft Word's WordBasic supports named arguments, but Access only supports positional arguments. Using the WordBasic reference manuals will drive you crazy, since they list all the parameters to WordBasic actions by name, but in the wrong order. Without a road map listing the correct order for all the parameters, you won't be able to write any OLE Automation code from Access.

POSITION.TXT (a text document formatted to be displayed in Microsoft Word) lists all the parameter orders for each WordBasic action that you might try to execute from Access Basic. You can open POSITION.TXT directly from the CD, but you may just want to copy it to a convenient location on your hard disk (perhaps the Microsoft Word directory). To use it, load it as a document in Microsoft Word.

Security Wizard (\SECWIZ)

Security Wizard, supplied by Microsoft Access Product Support, secures and encrypts a database for you. To install it, use the Add-In Manager, following the procedure described previously in the section on Control Morph. For more information on Security Wizard, read the file SECURE20.WRI in the SECWIZ directory on the CD.

SuperSpy (\SUPERSPY)

SuperSpy from SoftBlox, Inc., is a freeware spying utility. You can use it to find class names (as we've done in the book), or to monitor Windows messages. You can run SuperSPY directly from the CD. If you want to place a copy on your hard disk, copy SBICTLW.DLL, SUPERSPY.EXE, and SUPERSPY.DOC to any directory.

Microsoft Graph 5 VBA Help (\VBAGRP)

VBAGRP.HLP is a help file, meant to be used with WINHELP.EXE. It includes information on OLE Automation with Graph 5. (We used this file as our only resource for creating the example in How-To 12.7.) Although it could be a lot more useful, it's the most concise resource for this information, so you'll probably need it if you plan to automate your graphs.

You can use it directly from the CD, but you'll most likely want to copy it to a directory on your hard disk and create an icon for it in a Program Manager group. Once you've done that, you can double-click on the icon and Windows will run WINHELP for you, loading the VBAGRP.HLP file (this assumes that you haven't changed the standard association for HLP files).

1

Using the Power of Queries

HOW DO I...

Access queries—the six types that can be created on the easy-to-use QBE grid plus the three SQL-specific query types—give you a tremendous amount of power and flexibility in selecting, sorting, summarizing, modifying, and outputting the data stored in your tables, before presenting it to the user on forms or printing it on reports. Access queries may be intimidating at first, especially if you are familiar with the more limited queries available in other database programs, but mastering queries will give you complete control over the appearance and functionality of your forms and reports. And Access queries are flexible—once you learn how to control them, you may start using them in places where you would have written program code in other applications.

In this chapter, you'll learn to create parameter queries, which allow you to control selected rows of a report at runtime, not at design time. You'll use this same technique to control the available values in one combo box, based on the choice in another. You'll also see how to use the value of a particular column in a combo box as a parameter for a query, and how to use Access Basic variables as parameters, too. You'll study ways to control the output of cross-tab queries, and learn a handy technique that lets you group mailing labels by residence, to avoid sending duplicate mailings to family members. In case you need to pull random sets of data from a data source, you'll see how to use a query to retrieve a random set of rows. You'll also examine a query that uses the Partition function to perform aging analysis.

Finally, you'll find a group of How-To's dealing with more advanced uses of queries. You'll learn how to create a join that's based on a comparison other than equality, how to use DDL (Data Definition Language) queries to create or alter tables, and how to use union queries to concatenate tables or queries. You'll also examine a suggested method for storing query information in a table, which can be protected and made invisible in applications, giving you complete control over which queries get run and when.

1.1 Let users specify query criteria when they run the query, not when they design it

This How-To will show you how you can use parameters in a query so that users can specify a start date and an end date to filter records selected for a report every time the report is run.

1.2 Use a query to limit the selections in one combo box based on a choice in another combo box

This How-To will demonstrate the use of a query with a form-based criterion as a row source for a combo box, in order to limit its drop-down list to items appropriate to the user's selection in the first combo box.

1.3 Use a specific combo box column as a query criterion

If you use the standard Column property to refer to a specific column in a combo box in a query criterion, you will get an error message. This How-To will demonstrate a workaround using a text box on a form to hold the column reference expression.

1.4 Override the default Access column headings and their orders in a cross-tab query

If you have a cross-tab query that uses functions to convert dates into text for column headings, Access sorts them alphabetically (Apr, Aug, and so on) rather than by date. This How-To will demonstrate the use of fixed column headings to specify the column heading you want for your query.

1.5 Group mailing labels by address

To avoid sending duplicate mailings to members of a family, you can use a totals query to group label data so that people with the same last name who live at the same address will only create one row in the output query. This How-To will also demonstrate the creation of a mailing label with different text for mailings to a family.

1.6 Use a variable to filter a query

Access queries won't accept variables in criteria expressions; this How-To will show you two alternatives for employing variables in query criteria, using functions or text boxes on a form.

1.7 Use a query to retrieve a random set of rows

This How-To will show you how you can build a new query returning a specified number of rows, randomly chosen from an existing data set.

1.8 Create a query that will show aging of receivables

When you're working with sales figures or any other dated values, you may need to perform aging analysis on the values. To gather information about transactions that occurred, for example, 1–30, 31–60, 61–90, or 91–120 days ago, this How-To will demonstrate the use of the Partition function, which will do all the work for you.

1.9 Create a relationship that's based on a comparison other than equality

In Access, relationships among tables are always based on equality—matching values in one table with those in another. Sometimes, though, you need to relate two tables on some other condition; perhaps the value from one table needs to be a substring of a value in another table. This How-To will demonstrate how you can relate two tables based on a condition other than equality.

1.10 Create or alter a table with a query

Sometimes you need to create a table that has fields of a specific data type and size, and/or with an index. This How-To will discuss the use of a data-definition query to create a table and its index programmatically.

1.11 Create a query to combine data from two tables with similar structures

If you have two tables with the same (or similar) structure, but completely different data, there is no way to link them in a standard Access query. If you want to send a mailing including records from both tables, you need the specialized union query. This How-To will demonstrate a union query that selects records from two tables and sorts them by zip code.

1.12 Save queries in a table for better programmatic access and security

Some queries exist only for use in your applications, not for user examination. You don't want users to be able to modify, or often even to see, these essential queries at all. This How-To will propose a solution to this problem, which involves storing the SQL string for each query in a table that your application controls and maintains.

1.1 HOW DO I... COMPLEXITY: EASY

Let users specify query criteria when they run the query, not when they design it?

Problem

I have a database with several years' worth of records in it, and I often want to print just some of the data, say, last month's or the current year's. I need a way to specify a range of data to include in a report when the query is run.

Technique

A parameter query is a handy way to specify different criteria every time a query is run, without having to change the query in design view. This How-To shows you how to set up a parameter query that lets you enter a start date and an end date for selecting the records included in a report. With this query as a data source, the report will be limited to data between the selected dates when it is printed.

Steps

Open 01-01.MDB, which contains rptSales, a simple sales report grouped by year and salesperson. The report is based directly on the sample table, tblSales, with no filtering, and it prints data for all years from 1990 through 1994. The all-inclusive report is shown in Figure 1-1.

Here are the steps to create a parameter query that will let you specify starting and ending dates.

1. In the database window, highlight the table you want to use as the report's source (in the sample, tblSales was used), and click on the New Query button on the toolbar to start a new query.

2. In the field list, highlight the fields you want to use in the report and drag them to the QBE grid. Include the date field (SalesDate in the sample database) among the fields dragged to the grid.

 TIP: This can be done quickly by clicking on the first field, then Ctrl-clicking on the remaining ones.

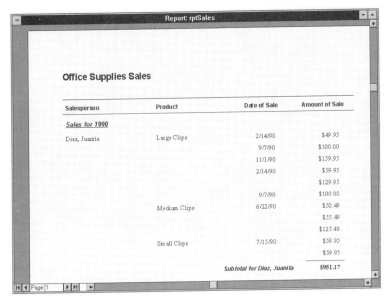

Figure 1-1 The all-inclusive sales report, rptSales

3. Type

```
Between [Enter start date] And [Enter end date]
```

   as the critera for the hidden date field. Note the brackets around "Enter start date" and "Enter end date". They tell Access to treat this text as a field when the query is run.

4. Select Query|Parameters to open the Query Parameters window and type

```
Enter start date
```

   as the first parameter and

```
Enter end date
```

   as the second. Note that brackets are *not* included in the parameter entries. Select Date/Time as the data type for both parameters.

5. Save the query (in the sample it's called qrySelectedSales), and switch to datasheet view to check that the parameter pop-ups work correctly. Figure 1-2 shows the query in design view, with the Query Parameters window open.

6. Open the report in design view and select the new query as its record source. Then save the report under another name, if desired. (In the sample database it's called rptSelectedSales.)

7. Open the report; two Enter Parameter Value pop-ups appear in turn, one for entering the start date and one for entering the end date. When the report appears in print preview, it is limited to dates within the range selected in the pop-ups.

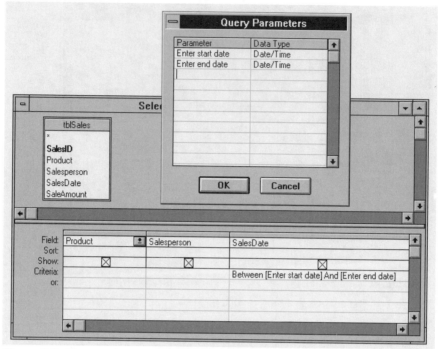

Figure 1-2 The sample query, qrySelectedSales, with parameters for start date and end date

How It Works

By placing brackets around the text (step 3), you force Access to treat the text as a field; and since no field of that name was found, Access pops up a window asking for the parameter. When a report includes a field that is not to be found in its record source, a parameter pop-up appears, asking for that field when the report is run (you can try this out by deleting a field from qrySelectedSales and running the report).

If you want to capture input for a text field, all you need to do is place the text in brackets in the Criteria line of the field's column. As an example of this technique, qrySelectedSalesperson (included in the sample database) is a query without an entry in the Query Parameters window. However, if you are entering parameters for a nontext field, or for an attached table, you may need to specify the data type in the Query Parameters window.

Comments

The parameter pop-up technique is easy to use and suitable for entering simple parameters such as dates, or first letters for alphabetic searches. However, if you want to limit parameter choices or do error checking, you need to make a form with combo boxes, list boxes, or option groups to limit user choices. The choices made on the form can then be picked up by the query that supplies the report's record source.

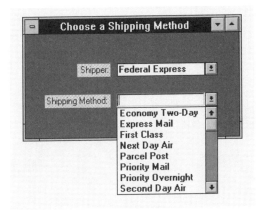

Figure 1-3 Original Shipping Method form, with a Shipping Method combo box displaying all methods for all shippers

1.2   HOW DO I...

COMPLEXITY: EASY

Use a query to limit the selections in one combo box based on my choice in another combo box?

Problem

I have a form that contains more than one combo box. When I make a choice from one combo box, I'd like it to limit the choices in the other. For example, when I choose the shipper, I'd like the combo box containing a list of shipping methods to include only items pertaining to the shipper I've chosen. Is there a way to do this?

Technique

This How-To shows you how to create row source queries for combo boxes, so you can make the contents of one combo box depend on the selection in another combo box. You will create lookup tables and a filter query for setting up a Shipping Method combo box with a list containing just the shipping methods used by the shipper selected in a Shipper combo box.

Steps

Open and run frmSelectShipperOriginal from 01-02.MDB. The combo boxes on this form are based on simple queries (qryShipper and qryDeliveryMethod) that sort the combo boxes' fields alphabetically, but do not filter them in any way. If you select a shipper in the Shipper combo box, and then open the Shipping Method list, you can see that it shows all the shipping methods for all the shippers (as shown in Figure 1-3) , which is not very helpful.

Follow these steps to create linked combo boxes:

7

Figure 1-4 Shipper and Shipping Method
lookup tables

1. Create two lookup tables; in the sample database one table contains shippers and one contains shipping methods (see Figure 1-4). Each shipper has a unique identifying code, which is used to link tblShipper to tblShippingMethod. Note that each Shipper Code in tblShipper has several matches in tblShippingMethod, representing the shipping methods used by that shipper.

2. Create a form with the combo boxes you want to link; in the following steps we'll use frmSelectShipper.

3. Create the row source query for the main combo box, using the Query Builder. From the row source property of the main combo box (cboShipper on the sample form), click on the Build button (...) to open the Query Builder, and select a table or query (the sample database uses qryShipper).

4. You need two fields for this query: a data field to display in the main combo box and a linking field to connect this combo box to the linked combo box. In the sample database, the data field is Shipper and the linking field is ShipperCode. Drag ShipperCode to the first column and Shipper to the second column, and save the query with a name of your choice (in the sample, it is qryShipperWithCode).

5. Set the ColumnCount and ColumnWidths properties to display the data field only. Change the ColumnCount property of the combo box to 2, since the query has two columns. Column widths are set by entering a semicolon-delimited list of desired widths in the ColumnWidths property. You don't need to display the linking ShipperCode field in the main combo box, so make it invisible by setting its column width to 0. You can enter a width for the second column, or leave it blank so that Access will automatically determine its width. In the sample database, "0in;1in" makes

the linking ShipperCode column 0 inches wide (in other words, invisible) and the Shipper column 1 inch wide.

6. Check that the BoundColumn property is set to 1 (the default). This ensures that column 1, the invisible ShipperCode column, is the bound column. When an expression in another control or a query criterion refers to a combo box, the expression picks up the value of the combo box's bound column. For a bound combo box, the bound column's value is saved to the underlying table.

7. Create or modify the query for the linked combo box's row source. This query needs a field to display in the combo box (ShippingType in the sample database) and a field that links it to the main combo box's ShipperCode field. Drag the data and linking fields (ShippingType and ShipperCode in the sample database) to the query grid.

8. The linking ShipperCode field needs a criterion to limit it to a match with the selection in the main combo box. Using the Expression Builder, if you wish (click on the Build button on the toolbar), enter an expression like the following as the criterion for the linking field:

`Forms![frmSelectShipper]![cboShipper]`

Save the modified query; in the sample it is called qryShippingMethodFiltered. This criterion links to the bound column of the main combo box, which in this case is the first (invisible) column.

9. Make the linking combo box's ColumnCount 2, and enter 1;0 in its ColumnWidths property (since the linking ShipperCode column is the second column in its row source query). The linking combo box's bound property does not matter in this case; the default setting of 1 makes the visible ShippingType column the bound column.

10. At this point, you can try dropping down the linking combo box after making a selection in the main combo box. The first time you try this, the linking combo box will display only the options for the chosen shipper. If you make another choice in the main combo box, and then open the linking combo box list again, it won't have the matching new values. Instead, it will still display the values for the previously selected item in the main combo box. Therefore, you'll need some way to force the linking combo box to requery every time you make a choice from the main combo box.

11. To force the linking combo box to requery itself each time you make a choice in the main combo box, use a simple macro with two macro actions, as in the sample macro (mcrShippingMethod) shown in Table 1-1. Then you can switch selections in the main combo box as often as you need to, and you will always see the appropriate selections in the linking combo box.

MACRO NAME	ACTION	PARAMETER	VALUE
cboShipper_AfterUpdate	SetValue Requery	cboShippingMethod cboShippingMethod	Null

Table 1-1 Macro settings to link two combo boxes

12. Finally, save the modified form; in the sample database it is frmSelectShipper.

How It Works

In the sample, the tblShipper lookup table uses a counter as a unique ID for shippers; it is matched by a long integer field in tblShippingMethod. A row source query for cboShipper includes the ShipperCode field but does not display it in the combo box. It is the first column of this query, but its width is set to 0 so it will be hidden. Because it is the bound column, a reference to the combo box will pick up the code.

The row source query for cboShippingMethod includes the code field from tblShippingMethod, with an expression on its Criteria row referring to cboShipper on the same form. This criterion limits the shipping methods displayed in this combo box to those with the same shipper code as the name chosen in cboShipper. After you choose a shipper, the macro attached to the AfterUpdate event will execute, first clearing out the value in cboShippingMethod, and then forcing it to requery. This way, the combo box will display only the rows you want when you open it.

Comments

Sometimes you need to refer to a column in a combo box other than the bound column. In that case, you can use the combo box Column property in an expression to pick up the value of a specific column of the combo box, rather than the value of the bound column. To refer to the second column of a combo box, for instance, use the following expression:

```
Forms![frmSelectShipper]![cboShipper].Column(1)
```

Note that the column count starts at 0 for the Column property, so the second column is Column(1). Oddly, the column count in the BoundColumn property of a combo box starts with 1, so you need to enter 2 in order to refer to the second column in the BoundColumn property.

In a real-life application, after selecting the shipper and shipping method on this form, you would probably want to use those selections elsewhere in the application. You could bind the form to a table so that the chosen values are saved to the table, and thus will be available after you close the form. Or you could hide the selection form by setting its Visible property to No, and then refer to controls on the form by the usual form syntax, such as:

```
Forms![frmSelectShipper].[cboShippingMethod]
```

In the sample database, you don't need to prevent the user from selecting an item in the linked combo box before the main, because each item in the Shipping Methods combo box has only one Shipper. However, in a more complex case, you might need to disable the second combo box until the user makes a choice from the first combo box. You could do this by setting the linked combo box's Enabled property to No on the form, and then resetting it to Yes in the main combo box's AfterUpdate macro or event procedure.

1.3   HOW DO I...   COMPLEXITY: EASY

Use a specific combo box column as a query criterion?

Problem

I made a two-column combo box on a form so I could display a more informative field for the user to select, and still have a more cryptic counter field available in a hidden column. I created a query with the counter field in the combo box's second column as a criterion, using the Column property, but I got an error message. How can I refer to a specific column of a combo box in a query?

Technique

If a query attempts to use the Column property of a combo box to reference the second column of that combo box, for example:

```
Forms![frmSelectCompany]![cboSelectCompany].Column(1)
```

you will get an "Undefined Function" error message when you attempt to run this query. This How-To demonstrates a simple method for bypassing this error, using an intermediate unbound control on a form.

Steps

Here are the steps for working around this limitation, so you can refer to a specific unbound column of a combo box in a query.

1. Open the form you want to work on in design view (in the sample database, you can use frmSelectCompanyOriginal).
2. Place a new text box on the form (no label is needed).
3. Enter an expression like the one below as the text box's ControlSource property:

```
=[cboSelectCompany].[Column](1)
```

   Note the count number; Access counts columns starting with 0.

4. Switch to form view. The text box displays the CompanyID counter field matching your selection in the combo box, as shown in Figure 1-5.
5. Return to the query and replace the CompanyID criterion with a reference to the new text box:

```
[Forms]![frmSelectCompany]![txtCompanyID]
```

Figure 1-5 Once you've set the ControlSource for the text box, it displays the chosen value from the combo box

6. Switch to datasheet view (no error message now!), and you will see that the query's output is limited to the company you selected in the combo box.

7. Return to the form and hide the CompanyID text box by setting its Visible property to No.

8. Finally, save the form. In the sample database, it is called frmSelectCompany.

How It Works

Curiously, Access does not detect a syntax error when you enter a column reference as a query criterion, but it can't process column references in query criteria. However, a control source expression for a text box on a form can refer to a particular column of a combo box, so you can construct the query criterion in two stages. You must first refer to the combo box column in the text box, and then refer to the text box in the query criterion.

Comments

Access is inconsistent in numbering query columns: Columns are counted from 1 up when specifying the bound column in a combo box's properties sheet, but from 0 up when counting columns for the Column property. So you have to enter 2 to specify that the second column is the bound column of cboSelectCompany, but you have to enter Column(1) when referencing this column from another control.

If you changed the combo box's bound column from 1 to 2, you could just refer to the combo box (without using the Column property) as

```
Forms![frmSelectCompany]![cboSelectCompany]
```

and pick up the value in the second column. A specific column reference is needed only when you want to pick up the value of an unbound column of a combo or list box.

This technique of using an invisible text box to pick up a reference to another control is also handy for dealing with complex main form or subform references, or for placing a field on a report when you need to refer to it in an expression, but don't want it to print.

Access will not accept variables as query criteria, either; working around this limitation is discussed in How-To 1.6.

1.4 HOW DO I...
COMPLEXITY: EASY

Override the default Access column headings and their orders in a cross-tab query?

Problem

I have a number of cross-tab queries, grouped by time periods, using expressions that convert date/time fields into month names or days of the week. But when I look at one of these queries in datasheet view, the months or days are sorted alphabetically instead of by date. I need a way to tell Access how to sort months and days correctly.

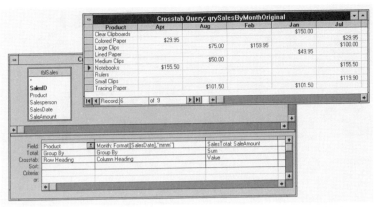

Figure 1-6 The original cross-tab query, qrySalesByMonthOriginal, with months sorted alphabetically

Technique

The Query Properties sheet allows you to specify fixed column headings for a query. This How-To illustrates how you can specify column headings that correctly sort the standard three-letter month abbreviations by date, for a cross-tab query that uses the Format function to extract month names from a date/time field.

Steps

Open 01-04.MDB and look at qrySalesByMonthOriginal, a simple cross-tab query using a Format function to extract three-letter month abbreviations for column headings. As you can see in Figure 1-6, in datasheet view, the month column headings are sorted Apr, Aug, Feb, and so on—not a very sensible sort!

Follow these steps to make Access sort the months correctly for a cross-tab query using a function to extract text labels from dates.

1. Open the query in design view.
2. Click on the Properties Sheet button on the toolbar, and then click in the background of the upper part of the query window to open the Query Properties sheet.
3. In the ColumnHeadings property enter the abbreviation for the month (or day, or other text date equivalent). Enclose each one in quotes and separate them with commas, as shown for three-letter month abbreviations in Figure 1-7. The items you type in this property must match the output of your date function exactly; a typo in the column headings list will result in missing data in the query's output.
4. Save the modified query; in the sample database, it is called qrySalesByMonth.
5. Switch back to datasheet view; now the months are in correct order by date.

How It Works

The ColumnHeadings property on the Query Properties sheet lets you specify the exact headings for each column of a query, in the order you want. Access

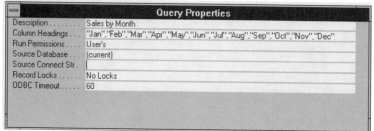

Figure 1-7 Entering the month abbreviations as column headings in the Query Properties sheet

uses these column headings when the query displays in datasheet view, in the order you specify, overriding the automatic (and possibly inappropriate) default Access column headings and sorting.

Comments

If you use the ColumnHeadings property to specify column headings for a query, then every month or day has a column, even if it has no data. This is helpful if you need to make a set of matching queries, say, for different regions' sales.

Headings must match the actual data; if they don't, you will get no data in the column with the mistyped heading.

> 🚫 **A WARNING ABOUT SETTING CRITERIA:** Beware of using criteria such as Between #7/1/93# And #7/21/93# on a date column in your query. This criteria won't work, because the date formatting won't match the column headings that have been converted into text. Similar problems can arise when using the Format function to format numbers with dollar signs and parentheses; the formatted numbers are now text, so they can't be matched by the usual mathematical criteria.

If you are making a new cross-tab query, you can avoid the problem of improperly sorted months or days by using the Crosstab Query Wizard. When you use this Wizard, Access automatically enters the standard three-letter month abbreviations as column headings in the query's properties sheet.

1.5 HOW DO I...   COMPLEXITY: EASY

Group mailing labels by address?

Problem

I need to print mailing labels for the general public. If my mailing list contains multiple occurrences of the same last name at the same address, I only want to print one label addressed to the entire family. Otherwise, I need to print one label for each person in my table. How can I accomplish this?

Technique

Using totals queries, you can group your label data so that people with the same last name who live at the same address will only create one row in the output query. If you count the number of occurrences of combinations of last name, address, and zip code, you can create the mailing label text based on that count.

Steps

In 01-05.MDB, open tblNames. The raw data appears as in Figure 1-8. Note that there are several examples of family members at the same address. Now open rptLabels (shown in Figure 1-9). This mailing label report has grouped the people with common addresses onto single labels, using the family name instead of the individual names.

To simulate this grouping in your own data, follow these steps:

1. Create a new query, based on your table (qryCountNames in the sample). Turn this query into a totals query by choosing the View|Totals menu item, or by clicking on the Sigma button on the toolbar. This query will group the data using one row for each unique combination of your grouping fields.
2. Add a column to the query grid for each column in your table on which you want to group rows. The example uses LastName, Address and Zip. For each column, set the Total field to be Group By. If you want to specify column names, place those names before the field names, separated with a colon, as shown in Figure 1-10.
3. Add a column to the query grid, in which Access will count the number of rows that it groups together to make a single row in the output. Choose any field, place it in the query grid, and set its Total row to be Count. (This field is called Residents in the example.) This instructs Access to count the number of rows in the same grouping. (See Figure 1-10.)

Table: tblNames

ID	LastName	FirstName	Address	City	State	Zip
1	Elliot	Cleo	135 Main St.	Arlington	MA	02174
2	Elliot	Steve	2435 Station St.	Cambridge	MA	02138
3	Elliot	Samuel	2435 Station St.	Cambridge	MA	02138
4	Lane	Edie	1354 Ocean Dr.	Santa Moni	CA	90401
5	Clark	Meredith	1111 5th Street	Santa Moni	CA	90401
6	Clark	Eric	1111 5th Street	Santa Moni	CA	90401
(Counter)						

Record: 1 of 6

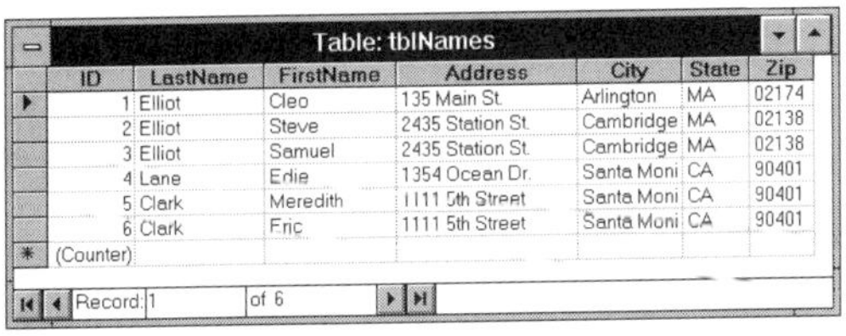

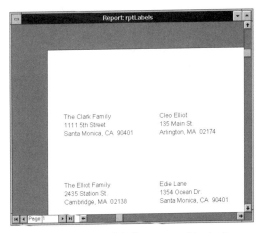

Figure 1-8 Sample data, including multiple people per address

Figure 1-9 Mailing labels, grouped by last name, address, and zip code

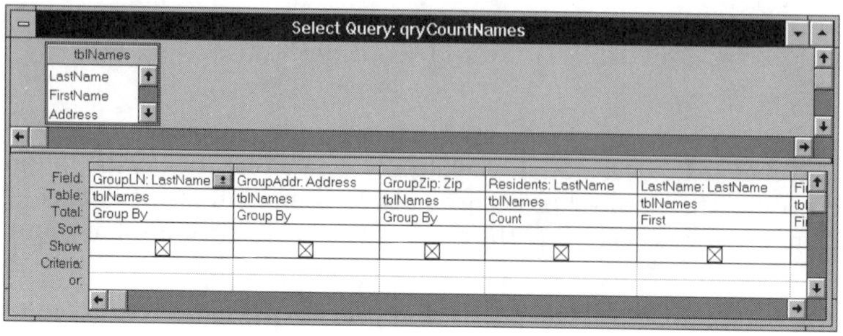

Figure 1-10 The grouping query, set up with new column headings

4. Add all other fields that you want to show on your labels to the query grid. For each, set the Total field to be First. For each column, you'll want to add a specific title; otherwise, Access will change each title to FirstOf*Column*. (See Figure 1-10.) When you run this query, its output will look something like that shown in Figure 1-11. Note that there's only one row in the output for each unique grouping of last name, address, and zip code.
5. To create the text for your labels, create a new query (qryLabels in the example) based on the previous query (qryCountNames). You'll base the mailing label name on the field in which you counted rows (Residents in the example), along with the FirstName and LastName fields. Pull in whatever columns you'll want in your label and add one more for the label name. For the example, the expression for this column (LabelName) was:

```
LabelName: IIf([Residents] > 1,"The " & [LastName] & " Family", ⇒
[FirstName] & " " & [LastName])
```

6. On the mailing label itself, use the LabelName field instead of the FirstName and LastName fields directly. This field (shown in Figure 1-12) shows either the family name, or the single individual's first and last name, depending on the value in the Residents column.

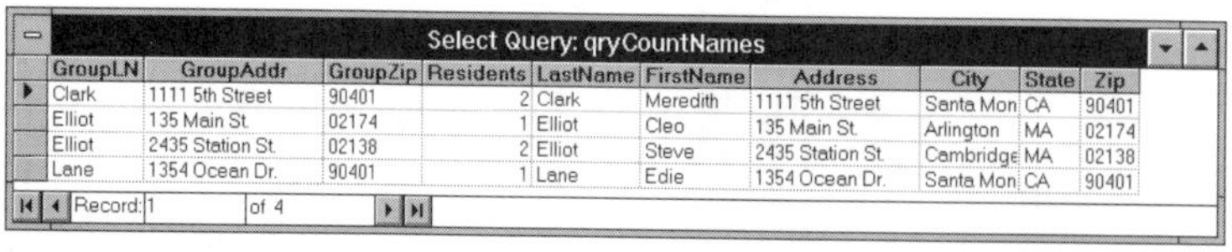
Select Query: qryCountNames

GroupLN	GroupAddr	GroupZip	Residents	LastName	FirstName	Address	City	State	Zip
Clark	1111 5th Street	90401	2	Clark	Meredith	1111 5th Street	Santa Mon	CA	90401
Elliot	135 Main St.	02174	1	Elliot	Cleo	135 Main St.	Arlington	MA	02174
Elliot	2435 Station St.	02138	2	Elliot	Steve	2435 Station St.	Cambridge	MA	02138
Lane	1354 Ocean Dr.	90401	1	Lane	Edie	1354 Ocean Dr.	Santa Mon	CA	90401

Record: 1 of 4

Figure 1-11 Output of the grouping query

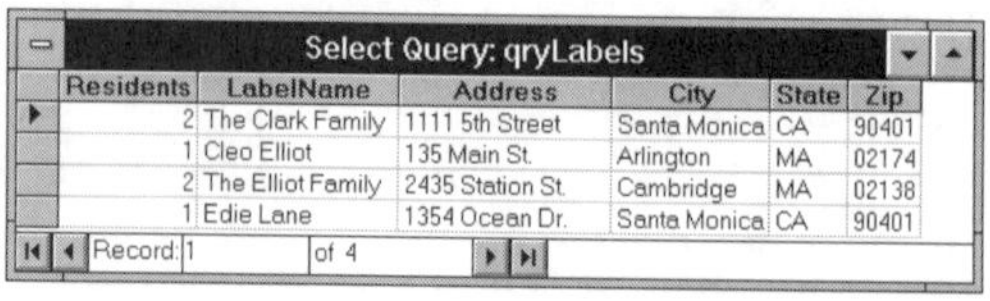
Select Query: qryLabels

Residents	LabelName	Address	City	State	Zip
2	The Clark Family	1111 5th Street	Santa Monica	CA	90401
1	Cleo Elliot	135 Main St.	Arlington	MA	02174
2	The Elliot Family	2435 Station St.	Cambridge	MA	02138
1	Edie Lane	1354 Ocean Dr.	Santa Monica	CA	90401

Record: 1 of 4

Figure 1-12 The LabelName field showing either the family name or individual's name

How It Works

By creating a totals query that groups on a combination of fields, you're instructing Access to output only a single row for each group of rows that have identical values in those columns. Since you're grouping on last name and address (zip was thrown in only to ensure that you wouldn't group on two families with the same name at the same address in different cities), you should end up with one output row for each household. You included one column for counting (the Residents field in the example), so Access will tell you how many rows collapsed down into the single output row. This way, the query can decide whether to list an individual's name or a family name on the label.

If the value in the counted field is greater than 1, the query builds an expression that includes just the family name:

```
"The " & [LastName] & " Family"
```

If the count is exactly 1, the query lists just the first and last names:

```
[FirstName] & " " & [LastName]
```

The immediate If function, IIf, does this for you, as shown in step 5. It looks at the value in the [Residents] field and decides which format to use based on that value.

Comments

Access does its best to optimize nested queries, so don't feel shy about basing one query on another. In this case, it simplifies the work. The first-level query groups the rows, and the second one creates the calculated expression based on the first. Though it might be possible to accomplish this same task in a single query, splitting the tasks makes this so much cleaner that it's worth the effort to use two separate queries.

1.6 HOW DO I...

COMPLEXITY: INTERMEDIATE

Use a variable to filter a query?

Problem

I'd like to be able to return rows in a query that have a test score greater than a specified value, which is stored in an Access Basic variable. When I try to use the variable in the query design grid, Access thinks it's a literal value. Is there some way to get queries to know about Access Basic variables?

Technique

There are two solutions to this issue, though one solves a different but related problem. To use an Access Basic variable in a query, you'll need to write an Access Basic function that returns the value of the variable as its return value. Functions are the only structural element of Access Basic that are globally available, and, just as with the properties sheet, they're the only type of Access Basic object you can use in queries. However, there's an alternative: You can filter a query based on the value on a form, too. This How-To demonstrates both methods.

Steps

In the sample database, 01-06.MDB, you'll find tblScores, a table of names and test scores. The goal of the sample is to allow you to specify a cutoff value and list everyone whose scores are greater than the cutoff value. The frmCriteria form allows you to specify that cutoff in one of two ways: either as a random value between 0 and 100, or by filling in a value on a text box. To view the scores, you'll use either qryScores, which shows all rows above a random value, or qryFormScores, which shows all values above the value you filled in on frmCriteria. Figure 1-13 shows the form and the query working together.

Choosing the Use Random Cutoff option on frmCriteria fills in an Access Basic variable in the module basCutoff, which is then used as the filter criteria for qryScores. The query retrieves the value of the Access Basic variable by calling a user-defined function, GetCutoff, that exists in basCutoff. Choosing the Use Specified Cutoff option causes qryFormScores to use the value in the form's text box as its filter criteria.

Try out frmCriteria, choosing both the random and the specified cutoff values, and notice that the query does indeed filter itself based on the criteria you've chosen. (Either close the query datasheet or press (SHIFT)-(F9) to requery it each time you make a new choice on the form.) Both of these methods may be used in your applications, and perhaps in the same application. To try them yourself, follow the procedures outlined below.

Using a Form Value as a Filter Criteria for a Query

If you've requested user input as part of your application, and would like to show rows from a query (or perhaps run a report based on that query) using the input as its criteria, you can reference the form control from within your query.

Use its full path reference,

Forms![*Your Form Name*]![*Your Control Name*]

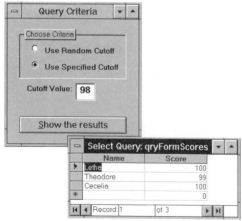

Figure 1-13 The sample form, frmCriteria, and the query, qryFormScores, that works with it

substituting actual form and control names for the placeholders. For example, Figure 1-14 shows qryFormScores in design mode, using a text box from frmCriteria as its criteria value. In this case, the query will show all rows whose value in the Score column is greater than the value in the txtCutoff text box on the frmCriteria form.

Using an Access Basic Variable as a Filter Criteria for a Query

Sometimes, you may need to filter the rows in your query based on the value of an Access Basic variable. Perhaps you've performed some calculation, or retrieved a value from a Windows INI file, or have used InputBox to request a value from a user. In any case, there's no direct way to use a variable as a criteria value, as there is with form controls.

To make a variable available to a query (or macro), write a simple function that returns the variable as its return value. For example, the sample query, qryScores, needs to filter its rows based on a previously calculated value, stored in the mintCutoff variable in basCutoff. To retrieve its value, you need a function like this:

```
Dim mintCutoff As Integer

Function GetCutoff ()
   ' Return the value of the module variable.
   GetCutoff = mintCutoff
End Function
```

The variable mintCutoff is only available to procedures within the same module as the variable, since it's declared in the module's declaration area and it's not global. By calling the GetCutoff function, you can retrieve that value from anywhere within Access. Therefore, you can use a query that calls this function to filter the rows. Figure 1-15 shows the sample query, qryScores, in design mode.

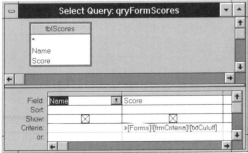

Figure 1-14 The sample query, qryFormScores, in design mode

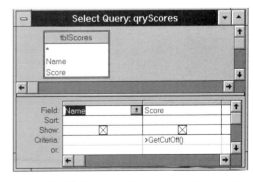

Figure 1-15 The sample query, qryScores, in design mode

> *NOTE: To call your function, you must either append empty parentheses if it accepts no parameters, or pass it appropriate parameters if it does expect them. The sample function expects no parameters.*

How It Works

Both solutions are based on the same principle: The query engine needs to be told where to look for filter criteria if the criteria are not parameters (like those discussed in How-To 1.1). To pull a value from a form, you must supply the entire path to the control that contains the value, in the format described in the first procedure, described above. To use an Access Basic variable, you must supply a function that returns the value of the variable. Since Access Basic variables are completely hidden from any portion of Access except Access Basic, the same rules apply for any other area in which you'd like to use a variable—on a form, in a macro, or on a report. In each case, you'll need to call the function you've created, rather than refer to the variable itself.

Comments

In this example, the sample form needs to place a value into the Access Basic variable, which presents another problem: You can neither read nor write Access Basic variables from the form's module, unless the variable happens to be global. Since most programmers try to avoid global variables, a good alternative is to provide a procedure to set the value of the variable. By working with variables this way, you *encapsulate* them in the module in which they're declared. No procedure outside that specific module can modify the variable without calling the procedure you've provided. This prevents accidental modifications to the variables that you want protected. Let's examine the code from the module basCutoff:

```
Option Compare Database    'Use database order for string comparisons
Option Explicit

' Store a cutoff score as a module variable
' The only way to set or get this value from
' outside this module is to call
' GetCutoff or SetCutoff

Dim mintCutoff As Integer

Function GetCutoff ()
    ' Return the value of the module variable.
    GetCutoff = mintCutoff
End Function

Sub SetCutoff (pintCutoff As Integer)
    ' Set the module variable to be
    ' the value passed in from externally.
    mintCutoff = pintCutoff
End Sub
```

As you can see, the only way to modify the value of mintCutoff from outside this module is to call the SetCutoff subroutine. The only way to retrieve the value from outside is to call the GetCutoff function. If you have multiple variables whose values you need to use in queries, you'll need to write a function to return the value of each one individually.

1.7 HOW DO I... COMPLEXITY: INTERMEDIATE

Use a query to retrieve a random set of rows?

Problem

I need to be able to retrieve a random set of rows from a table or query so I can identify a random sample for a research study. I can't find a way to make this happen in the normal query design grid. What's the trick to getting a random sample of a certain number of rows?

Technique

The solution to this problem is not quite as simple as it might at first appear. If you've been trying to figure this out on your own, you've probably been unsuccessful so far, because of the way Access attempts to optimize the use of function calls in queries. This How-To has the answer: You can write a tiny Access Basic function that, combined with Access 2.0's ability to retrieve a specified number of rows from a query, using Top N queries, can retrieve a random sample of rows for you.

Steps

In 01-07.MDB, open tblRandom. This table includes 50 rows of data. Your goal is to pull five randomly selected rows for this set of data. To do this, follow these steps:

1. Import the module basRandom from 01-07.MDB, or create your own, including this single function:

```
Function ahtGetRandom (varFld As Variant)

    ' Though varFld isn't used, it's the only
    ' way to force the query to call this function
    ' for each and every row.

    Randomize
    ahtGetRandom = Rnd
End Function
```

2. Create a new query or use an existing one. Set up the query as a simple Select query to pull in the fields you're interested in.

3. Add an extra column, with the following expression, replacing the reference to the [State] field with a single field in your query's underlying table or query. (This query won't run correctly unless you pass one of *your* field names to the function.)

```
ahtGetRandom([State])
```

4. Most likely, you'll want to clear this field's Show check box, since there's not much point in viewing a continually changing random number as part of your query output.

5. Set the Sort value for the new calculated field to Ascending (see Figure 1-16).

6. Open the query's properties sheet (make sure the View|Properties menu item is checked and click on the upper area of the query design surface, so the properties sheet says "Query Properties" in its title bar). Fill in the number of rows you'd like to return in the TopValues property. Figure 1-16 shows the sample query, qryRandom, in design view with the property filled in.

7. Run the query. Your query grid should show you as many rows as you specified in the properties sheet. If you press (SHIFT)-(F9), asking Access to requery the data, you will see a different set of rows. Repeating the process will return a different set of rows each time.

How It Works

The general concept behind this How-To is simple: You added a new column to your query, filled it with a list of random numbers, sorted on those random numbers, and retrieved the top *n* rows, where *n* is a number between 1 and the number of rows in your underlying data. There's only one complicating factor: To create the random number, you need to call a function for each row. Access tries to optimize such a function call, and will only call it once for the entire set of data—unless the function call involves a field in the data. That is, were you to replace the call to ahtGetRandom (in step 3) with a simpler call directly to Access's random number function (Rnd), you might be surprised to find that every value in every row would be exactly the same. Access' query engine thinks that the function has nothing to do with data in the query, so it only calls the function once. This will make the random number meaningless,

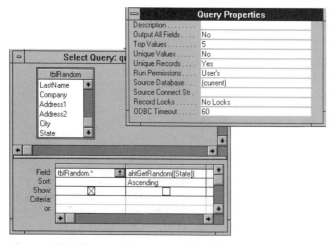

Figure 1-16 The sample query, qryRandom, set up to retrieve five random rows

since the whole point of using a random number was to generate a different number for each row.

The workaround, though, is simple: Just pass a field, any field, as a parameter to the function you call. That way, Access believes that the return value from the function is dependent on the data in each row, and will call the function once per row, passing to it the field you specified in the expression. The ahtGetRandom function doesn't really care about the value you pass it, since its only goal is to get a random number between 0 and 1 and return that to the query. Once you've successfully placed a random number in each row, Access will sort the data based on that number, since you've specified Ascending for the column's sorting. Unless you ask Access to sort on this column, you'll always get the same data, of course!

Finally, by specifying the TopValues property for the query, you're asking Access to only return that many rows as the result set of the query. If you wanted a certain percentage of the total rows, you could change it to be a percentage by adding the % sign after your number.

Comments

The ahtGetRandom function includes a call to the Access Randomize subroutine. By calling Randomize, you're asking Access to give you a truly random result every time you call the function. Omit this, and Access gives you the same series of random numbers each time you start it up and run this query. If you want a repeatable series of random rows, remove the call to Randomize. If you want a different set of rows each and every time you run the query, leave the Randomize statement where it is.

Since Access will be passing a field value to the ahtGetRandom function for each and every row of data in your data source, you'll want to optimize this function call as much as you can . If at all possible, use either a very short text field (zip code, for example) or, even better, an integer. You must pass some value, but you want it to be as small as possible to minimize the amount of information that must get moved around for each row of the data.

1.8 HOW DO I...   COMPLEXITY: INTERMEDIATE

Create a query that will show aging of receivables?

Problem
I want to use a cross-tab query to age my transactions, grouped by Account ID, into ranges of 1–30 days, 31–60 days, 61–90 days, and greater than 120 days. I know that I can group transactions by month using the standard query tools, but I can't find a way to group them by 30-day increments. How do I do this?

Technique
Access provides the Partition function, which allows you to take a range of values and partition it into even-sized chunks. By specifying a 30-day partition size, you can create a cross-tab query that will give you the information you need.

Steps

Load the sample database, 01-08.MDB. This database includes a very simple table, tblAccounts (see Figure 1-17), containing information about accounts and their activity. The qryAging query, shown in Figure 1-18, shows the final outcome: a cross-tab query including the aging information.

To create a comparable query in your own application, follow these steps:

1. Create a new query based on a table or query containing the appropriate account, date, and amount information.

2. Convert this query to a cross-tab query by choosing the Query|Crosstab menu item, or by clicking on the Crosstab button on the Query Design toolbar.

3. As when you create any cross-tab query, you'll need to specify at least three columns in the query grid: one for the column headings, one for the row headings, and one for the values that make up the cross-tab. In this case, choose the account number (or account name, depending on your data) as the Row Heading, and the amount (summed) as the Value. Figure 1-19 shows the sample query, qryAging, in design mode.

4. For the column headings, group the dates in 30-day increments, using the built-in Partition function. For this specific example, use the value,

```
Expr1:Partition(Now()-[Date],1,120,30)
```

for the column's expression. This tells the query to break the information into groups, based on the difference between today and the field named Date; starting with 1 day old, ending with 120 days old, and breaking every 30 days. Set the Total item to Group By, and the Crosstab item to Column Heading.

ID	Account	Date	Amount
1	100	6/30/94	$150.00
2	100	5/30/94	$250.00
3	100	4/30/94	$350.00
4	100	3/30/94	$450.00
5	100	2/20/94	$550.00
6	200	6/30/94	$250.00
7	200	5/30/94	$350.00
8	300	4/30/94	$350.00
9	300	3/30/94	$350.00
10	400	2/20/94	$450.00
(Counter)			$0.00

Figure 1-17 The table, tblAccounts, containing sample data to be used in an aging query

Account	1: 30	31: 60	61: 90	91:120	121:
100	$150.00	$250.00	$350.00	$450.00	$550.00
200	$250.00	$350.00			
300			$350.00	$350.00	
400					$450.00

Figure 1-18 The sample query, qryAging, showing the aging data grouped in 30-day increments

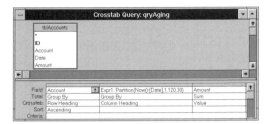

Figure 1-19 The sample query, qryAging, in
design mode

5. When you execute the query, you will see output similar to that shown in
Figure 1-18. Normally, you'd create a report based on this query, but you
can use this raw output to get an overview of the aging of your receivables.

How It Works

Except for the use of the Partition function, this cross-tab is really no different
from any other. It summarizes rows of data, summing the amount column,
grouped on a range of values in various columns. The only innovation, then, is
the use of the Partition function, which is most often used in situations just
like this one.

The Partition function returns a string, indicating where a value occurs
within a calculated series of ranges. That string (in the format *start:end)*
becomes the column heading in your query and is based on the starting value,
the ending value, and range size. You tell Access each of these values when you
call the Partition function. Table 1-2 shows the four parameters you'll use.

ARGUMENT	DESCRIPTION
number	Long integer to evaluate against your specified ranges.
start	Long integer, the start of the specified ranges. Can't be less than 0.
stop	Long integer, the end of the specified ranges. Can't be less than the value specified in start.
interval	Long integer, the interval spanned by each range in the series from start to stop. Can't be less than 1

Table 1-2 Parameters for the Partition function

For example, the expression

```
Partition( 42, 1, 120, 30)
```

would return the value "31: 60". This function call asks, "Where does the
number 42 occur within the range of 1 to 120, broken into 30-day ranges?"
Clearly, it falls in the 31 to 60-day range. That's what's indicated by the return
value:

```
" 31: 60"
```

In doing its calculation, Access formats the result for you in the format you see in the column headings in Figure 1-18.

If a value falls outside the requested range, Access returns an open-ended result. For example, the previous case will return

```
"121:    "
```

if the value is greater than 120, or

```
"    :  0"
```

if the value is less than 1. Access always includes enough spaces in the two halves of the result string for the largest possible value. This way, the result strings will sort correctly.

To see the Partition function doing its work, open qryShowAging from 01-08.MDB, in design mode (see Figure 1-20). This simple Select query will show the account number, amount due, date on which the transaction occurred, and the age range the transaction fits into, using the Partition function to calculate the ranges. Figure 1-21 shows the same query in datasheet view, using the data shown in Figure 1-17. The last column of the datasheet shows the output from the Partition function. When you group the rows on the values in this column, you end up with the cross-tab query you created earlier in the "Steps" section.

Comments

There are some limitations to the Partition function, of course. If you want uneven partitions, you'll need to write your own Access Basic function to do the work. For example, if you wanted your partitions to be 0–30 days, 31–60 days, 61–90 days, and 91–120 days, you'd be out of luck with the Partition function: All the partitions you've specified are 30 days except the first, which is 31. In addition, using Partition in a cross-tab query will omit ranges for which no values exist. For example, if no account had transactions between 31 and 60 days ago, there would be no column for this range in the output query.

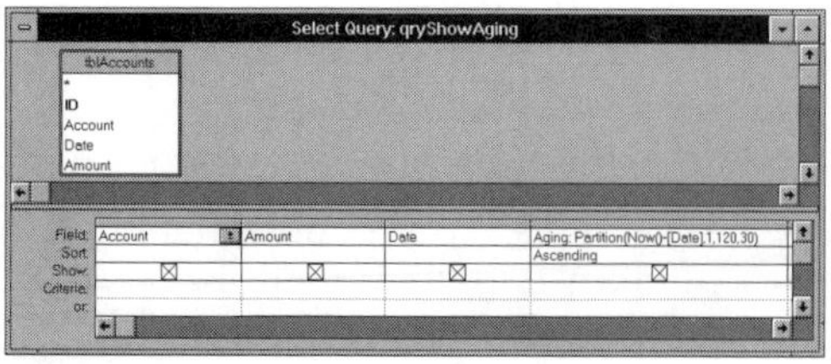

Figure 1-20 A simple Select query, qryShowAging, using the Partition function

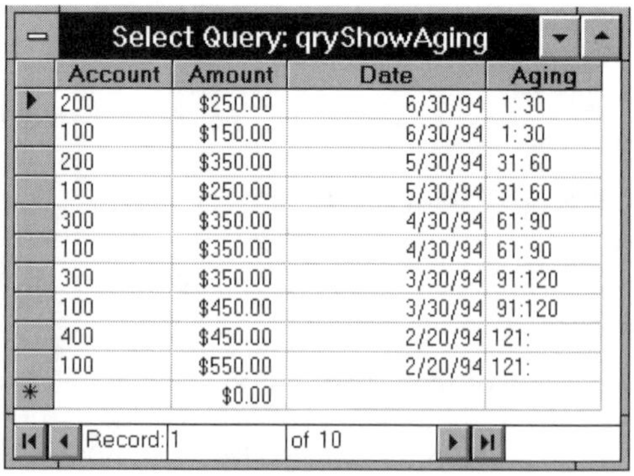

Select Query: qryShowAging

Account	Amount	Date	Aging
200	$250.00	6/30/94	1: 30
100	$150.00	6/30/94	1: 30
200	$350.00	5/30/94	31: 60
100	$250.00	5/30/94	31: 60
300	$350.00	4/30/94	61: 90
100	$350.00	4/30/94	61: 90
300	$350.00	3/30/94	91:120
100	$450.00	3/30/94	91:120
400	$450.00	2/20/94	121:
100	$550.00	2/20/94	121:
	$0.00		

Record: 1 of 10

Figure 1-21 The rows returned by qryShowAging

1.9   HOW DO I...

Create a relationship that's based on a comparison other than equality?

Problem

I need to relate two tables in a query on the Between operator. That is, I have a table of students and their grades, and a table of grade ranges and the matching letter grade. Though there are lots of ways to solve this problem with complex expressions and Access Basic, I *know* there has to be a solution involving just queries. What I need is a way to relate these two tables, finding matches when a value in the first table is between two values in the second table. Can I get this to work in Access?

Technique

Access really doesn't directly support relationships between tables that aren't based on equal values in the two tables, but you can "fake" the relationship by setting a criteria on the field in the first table and specifying that it must be between two fields in the second table. This method isn't limited to the Between operator, of course. You can use it for any operator.

Steps

From 01-09.MDB, open the tables tblGrades and tblLookup, both shown in Figure 1-22. The first table, tblGrades, includes a row for each student and his or her numeric grade. The lookup table, tblLookup, contains two columns for the range of numeric grades, and a third contains the corresponding letter

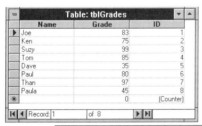

Figure 1-22 The two sample tables, tblGrades and tblLookup

grade. Your goal is to create a query listing each student along with his or her letter grade. To accomplish this goal, follow these steps:

1. Create a new query including both the sample tables. Don't attempt to use the standard Access methods to create a join between the tables, since there's no mechanism for creating the kind of join you'll need.

2. Drag the fields you'd like to include in your query to the query grid. Be sure to include the field that will link the two tables (Grade, from tblGrades, in this case).

3. In the criteria cell for the linking field, enter the expression that you'll use to link the two tables, using the syntax

```
TableName.FieldName
```

for any fields in the second table. Since you have not related the two tables, Access needs the table name to know what you're referring to. In the sample, the expression is:

```
Between [tblLookup].[LowGrade] And [tblLookup].[HighGrade]
```

Figure 1-23 shows the sample query in design mode.

4. Run the query. The output should look something like Figure 1-24. For each numeric grade, you've related the data in tblGrades to the values in tblLookup, matching one row in tblLookup for each numeric grade.

How It Works

In a normal join relating two tables, Access takes each value in the "left-hand" table (imagine the two tables laid out in the query design, one on the left and one on the right), finds the first matching value in the related field in the "right-hand" table, and creates a new row in the output set of rows containing information from the two, joined rows. In this case, however, you don't care to match the two tables on equality, but rather, on "betweenness." Since Access doesn't directly support this type of relation, you can get the same result by specifying that you only want values for the linking field in the left-hand table where it's between the two comparison values in the right-hand table, and not specifying a standard relationship at all. As it builds the output set of rows, Access looks up each value of the linking field in the right-hand table, looking

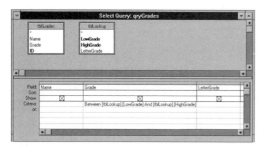

Figure 1-23 The sample query, qryGrades, in design mode

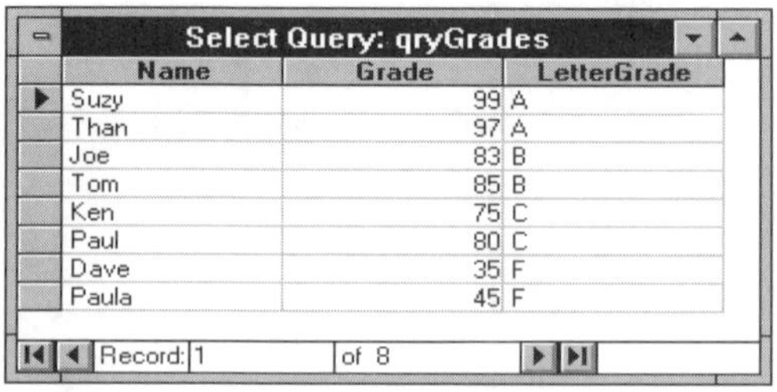

Figure 1-24 Data returned from running qryGrades

for the first match. It relates the rows in the two tables based on the value from the left-hand table being between the two values in the right-hand table.

> **BE CAREFUL WITH LARGE DATA SETS**
> The method described in this How-To can be slow and unwieldy for large data sets. Since you've not related the two tables, you're creating a combination of all the rows in both tables, normally called a "Cartesian Product," which includes an output row for each row in the first table, combined with each row in the second table. By specifying a WHERE condition, you limit the number of output rows, but you're counting on the query optimizer to figure this out before it creates the entire output set. Standard ANSI SQL does support non-equijoins, but Access 2.0 requires the workaround presented here.

Comments

This technique isn't limited to the Between operator. You can use any comparison operator (Between, In, >, <, >=, <=, < >) to perform a search in the second table, finding the first row that meets the required criterion. You can even relate two tables, using the InStr function (which indicates if and where one string occurs within another), to match words in a column of the first table with messages that contain that word in the second table.

As with any relationship between two tables, you'll get the best performance if the values in the matching fields in the right-hand table are indexed. This won't always help (in the InStr example just mentioned, for instance, there's really no way for an index to help Access find matches within a string), but in many cases it will. Consider indexing any fields used in the matching condition in either of the tables involved in your relationships, whether you build them yourself or use Access's built-in relationship mechanisms.

1.10 HOW DO I...   COMPLEXITY: INTERMEDIATE

Create or alter a table with a query?

Problem

I know how to create a table from a make-table query. But when I create a table in this way, it has no index, and the fields are all the same as in the source table, which doesn't always meet my needs. I need a way to create a table programmatically with fields of the data types and sizes I want, and with an appropriate index.

Technique

Access provides the data-definition query, which is used to create or modify tables programmatically. It is one of the SQL-specific queries, which can only be created as SQL statements. This How-To sets up a data-definition query to create a table whose fields are of specific data types and sizes, and with an index. It also shows how to delete a table with a data-definition query.

Steps

Open 01-10.MDB. The tblPersonalAddressOriginal table is created by a make-table query; it has no index. Follow these steps to create a table with an index, using a data-definition query:

1. Create a new query, and click on the Close button in the Add Table dialog box to cancel selecting a table.
2. Select Query|SQL Specific|Data Definition to open the Data Definition Query window.
3. As with other SQL-specific queries, you must type in the SQL statement; there is no way to compose such a query on the QBE grid.
4. Run the query. Figure 1-25 shows the data-definition query created with the SQL expression suggested above, and the resulting table. In the sample database, the query is called qryNewTable.

How It Works

When a data-definition query is run, Access reads through the query's clauses and creates a table according to their specifications. This allows you to precisely control the structure of the table and its indexes.

A data-definition query contains just a single data-definition statement. The five types of data-definition statements are:

- CREATE TABLE creates a table.

- ALTER TABLE adds a new field or constraint to an existing table (a constraint creates an index on a field or group of fields).

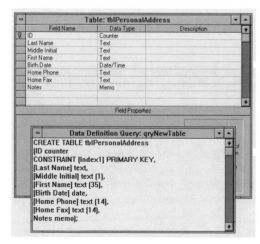

Figure 1-25 A sample data-definition query and the table it creates

⚷ DROP TABLE deletes a table from a database.

⚷ CREATE INDEX creates an index for a field or group of fields.

⚷ DROP INDEX removes an index from a field or group of fields.

For example, to create a simple personal address table, you could use the following SQL expression as a data-definition query:

```
CREATE TABLE tblPersonalAddress
(ID counter
CONSTRAINT [Index1] PRIMARY KEY,
[Last Name] text,
[Middle Initial] text (1),
[First Name] text (35),
[Birth Date] date,
[Home Phone] text (14),
[Home Fax] text (14),
Notes memo);
```

Note that most of the text fields in the sample code have their lengths specified to save space; by contrast, a make-table query replicates the field lengths in the source table, which may not always be what you want. If you don't specify a length for a text field in a data-definition query (as with the Last Name field), it will have the maximum length of 255 characters, which is rarely what you would want!

Field names that don't contain spaces don't need brackets, but those with spaces need to be enclosed in brackets so Access will know where the field begins and ends. In the sample code only field names with spaces are enclosed in brackets.

Comments

Like make-table queries, data-definition queries will not automatically overwrite an existing table. However, unlike make-table queries, you aren't offered the option of overwriting the existing table if you want to. If you need to overwrite an existing table when running a data-definition query, use one of these methods:

⚷ Use the DROP TABLE statement in another data-definition query, for instance:

```
DROP TABLE [tblPersonalAddress];
```

⚷ Run the query from a RunSQL action in a macro or an event procedure (as in the macro in Table 1-3). Use the SetWarnings action to turn off warnings before running the SQL statement, to avoid any unnecessary message boxcs.

MACRO NAME	ACTION	PARAMETER	VALUE
CreateTable	SetWarnings	Warnings On	No
	RunSQL	SQL Statement	CREATE TABLE tblPersonalAddress (ID counter CONSTRAINT [Index1] PRIMARY KEY, [Last Name] text, [Middle Initial] text (1), [First Name] text (35), [Birth Date] date, [Home Phone] text (14), [Home Fax] text (14), Notes memo);

Table 1-3 Macro settings for creating a table

After creating or deleting a table with a data-definition query, the new table won't immediately appear (nor will the deleted one disappear) in the database window. To refresh the display and see the change you have made, click on another tab in the database window (say, the Query tab) and then on the Table tab again.

> **WARNING:** As with other SQL-specific queries, be careful not to switch a data-definition query to another query type, such as a Select query. If you do, your SQL statement will be wiped out, because SQL-specific queries don't have a QBE equivalent.

1.11 HOW DO I...   COMPLEXITY: INTERMEDIATE

Create a query to combine data from two tables with similar structures?

Problem

I have two tables of addresses, one for Clients and one for Leads. Generally I send different mailings to these two groups, but sometimes I need to send the same letter to both. The problem is that I can't join them by any of the standard join types, because they lack fields with matching data. Is there a way to combine these two groups into a single dynaset, including just the U.S. addresses and sorted by zip code?

Technique

As you may have discovered, if two tables lack fields with matching data, you can't link them by any of the standard join types. However, Access provides a special type of query that can combine two tables into a single dynaset, providing they have similar structures. This is the union query, and it can only be constructed using SQL; there is no QBE equivalent for a union query.

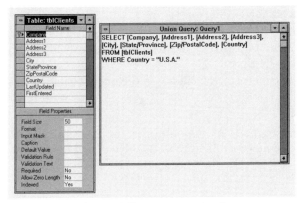

Figure 1-26 The partially constructed union query, with a table open for reference

Steps

Open 01-11.MDB. Open the two tables (tblClients and tblLeads) and examine their structure and data. They have the same field structure, but completely different data, so they cannot be linked by a standard query join. Follow these steps to construct a union query that combines data from two tables into a single dynaset limited to addresses in the United States and sorted by zip code.

1. Highlight tblClients in the database window, click on the New Query button on the toolbar, and then select the New Query button.

2. Select Query|SQL Specific|Union from the linked menus.

3. If you'd like, open tblClients in design view so you can see the field names while typing. Then type in the first part of the query:

```
SELECT [Company], [Address1], [Address2], [Address3], [City], [StateProvince], [ZipPostalCode],
[Country]
FROM [tblClients]
WHERE Country = "U.S.A."
```

(Yes, you do have to type it—there is no QBE equivalent to a union query.) Figure 1-26 shows the union query with the first component typed in and tblClients open for reference.

4. To save on keystrokes while entering the second clause of the query, copy what you have typed so far to the Clipboard.

5. Type UNION and then paste the contents of the clipboard. In the second SELECT statement, change tblClients to tblLeads.

6. Finally, to sort the query's dynaset by zip code, add an ORDER BY statement:

```
UNION SELECT [Company], [Address1], [Address2], [Address3], [City], [StateProvince],
[ZipPostalCode], [Country]
FROM [tblLeads]
WHERE Country = "U.S.A."
ORDER BY [tblClients].[ZipPostalCode];
```

Figure 1-27 shows the completed union query.

7. Switch to datasheet view to see the output of the query, as shown in Figure 1-28. Notice that the Canadian addresses have been excluded, and all the addresses are sorted by zip code.
8. Save the new query with a name of your choice; in the sample database, it's called qryBothLists.

How It Works

The UNION SQL statement simply joins the output of two or more SELECT statements into a single statement. Unlike the standard types of queries, no linking fields are needed.

Comments

While typing in the text of the union query, you may find it helpful to keep the source tables open in design view, so you can be sure that you are entering the field names correctly.

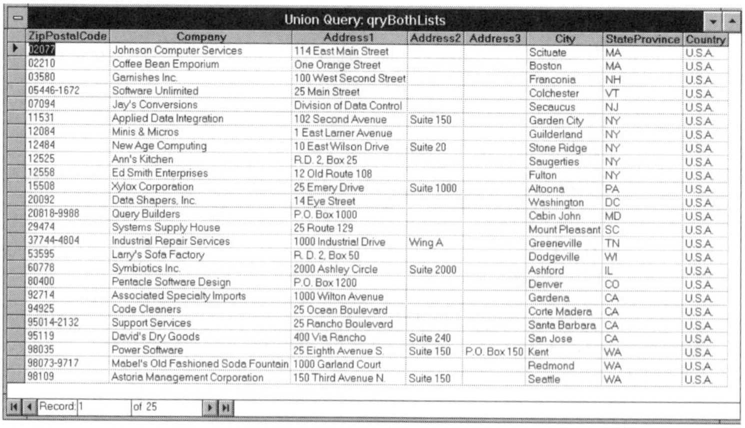

Union Query: qryBothLists

```
SELECT [Company], [Address1], [Address2], [Address3], [City], [StateProvince],
[ZipPostalCode], [Country]
FROM [tblClients]
WHERE Country = "U.S.A."

UNION SELECT [Company], [Address1], [Address2], [Address3], [City], [StateProvince],
[ZipPostalCode], [Country]
FROM [tblLeads]
WHERE Country = "U.S.A."
ORDER BY [tblClients].[ZipPostalCode];
```

Figure 1-27 The completed union query

Union Query: qryBothLists

ZipPostalCode	Company	Address1	Address2	Address3	City	StateProvince	Country
02077	Johnson Computer Services	114 East Main Street			Scituate	MA	U.S.A.
02210	Coffee Bean Emporium	One Orange Street			Boston	MA	U.S.A.
03580	Garnishes Inc.	100 West Second Street			Franconia	NH	U.S.A.
05446-1672	Software Unlimited	25 Main Street			Colchester	VT	U.S.A.
07094	Jay's Conversions	Division of Data Control			Secaucus	NJ	U.S.A.
11531	Applied Data Integration	102 Second Avenue	Suite 150		Garden City	NY	U.S.A.
12084	Minis & Micros	1 East Lamer Avenue			Guilderland	NY	U.S.A.
12484	New Age Computing	10 East Wilson Drive	Suite 20		Stone Ridge	NY	U.S.A.
12525	Ann's Kitchen	R.D. 2, Box 25			Saugerties	NY	U.S.A.
12558	Ed Smith Enterprises	12 Old Route 108			Fulton	NY	U.S.A.
15508	Xylox Corporation	25 Emery Drive	Suite 1000		Altoona	PA	U.S.A.
20092	Data Shapers, Inc.	14 Eye Street			Washington	DC	U.S.A.
20818-9988	Query Builders	P.O. Box 1000			Cabin John	MD	U.S.A.
29474	Systems Supply House	25 Route 129			Mount Pleasant	SC	U.S.A.
37744-4804	Industrial Repair Services	1000 Industrial Drive	Wing A		Greeneville	TN	U.S.A.
53595	Larry's Sofa Factory	R. D. 2, Box 50			Dodgeville	WI	U.S.A.
60778	Symbiotics Inc.	2000 Ashley Circle	Suite 2000		Ashford	IL	U.S.A.
80400	Pentacle Software Design	P.O. Box 1200			Denver	CO	U.S.A.
92714	Associated Specialty Imports	1000 Wilton Avenue			Gardena	CA	U.S.A.
94925	Code Cleaners	25 Ocean Boulevard			Corte Madera	CA	U.S.A.
95014-2132	Support Services	25 Rancho Boulevard			Santa Barbara	CA	U.S.A.
95119	David's Dry Goods	400 Via Rancho	Suite 240		San Jose	CA	U.S.A.
98035	Power Software	25 Eighth Avenue S.	Suite 150	P.O. Box 150	Kent	WA	U.S.A.
98073-9717	Mabel's Old Fashioned Soda Fountain	1000 Garland Court			Redmond	WA	U.S.A.
98109	Astoria Management Corporation	150 Third Avenue N.	Suite 150		Seattle	WA	U.S.A.

Record: 1 of 25

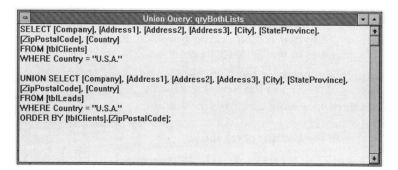

Figure 1-28 Output of the union query

Some dialects of SQL require the SQL statement to end with a semicolon. Access does not, but it doesn't hurt to use the standard syntax, especially if you program in other languages as well as Access.

Be careful not to convert a union query to another type of query; since union queries have no QBE equivalent, your union query will be wiped out.

A union query is a snapshot of the data in the underlying tables, and therefore it cannot be updated.

To sort a union query, add one ORDER BY clause at the end of the last SELECT statement, referring to a field name in the first SELECT clause (as in the sample query).

In the sample tables the field names are identical, but you can construct a union query for two tables whose fields don't match exactly. The following listing shows how two field names in the second table can be renamed to match their corresponding fields in the first table:

```
SELECT [Company], [Address1], [Address2], [Address3], [City], [StateProvince], [ZipPostalCode],
[Country]
FROM [tblClients]


UNION


SELECT [Company], [Address1], [Address2], [Address3], [City], [State] AS [StateProvince], [Zip] AS
[ZipPostalCode], [Country]
FROM [tblLeads]
```

A union query automatically screens out duplicate records (if any); if you want to include duplicates in the query's dynaset, use the UNION ALL statement instead of UNION.

1.12 HOW DO I...   COMPLEXITY: ADVANCED

Save queries in a table for better programmatic access and security?

Problem
My application uses a lot of queries, and I don't want these queries available or even visible to the users of my application. Also, I call my queries from Access Basic code. How can I hide the queries from users, as well as make them easier to retrieve, modify, and execute?

Technique
If you want more control over queries than Access provides, you can create a query management table that stores the SQL string of your queries in a memo field. Each query is named and contains a description. This technique has two immediate benefits. First, your queries are stored in a table rather than in the collection of queries. This table can be placed in a library database, making the queries accessible only to your Access Basic code. Second, by writing a simple Access Basic function, you can quickly retrieve the SQL string of any of your saved queries.

Steps

Open and run frmSavedQueries from 01-12.MDB. After a few moments of processing, the form shown in Figure 1-29 appears. This form is based on the tblQueryDefs table, which stores a record for each query you save. To add a new query to the table, you design and test the query using the Access Query designer. Then select the View|SQL menu item. When the query's SQL string is displayed, highlight it and copy it to the Clipboard. Open a new record in the frmSavedQueries form and paste the SQL string into the SQL Text text box. Type in a name and description. Notice that creation and modification times are automatically updated.

To use a saved query in your code, you search the tblQueryDefs table for the name of a query and get the value from the SQLText field. To use this technique in your application, follow these steps:

1. Import the tblQueryDefs table, the frmSavedQueries form, and the basSavedQueries module from 01-12.MDB into your database.
2. Populate the tblQueryDefs table using the frmSavedQueries form. Use the method described at the beginning of this section to create queries.
3. To get the SQL string of a saved query, use the GetSavedQuerySQL function located in the basSavedQueries module. The syntax for this function is

```
strSQL = GetSavedQuerySQL [ "QueryName"]
```

where strSQL is the string variable you want to store the query's SQL string in and *QueryName* is the name of the saved query you want to retrieve.

How It Works

The core of this technique is a simple function that retrieves a value from the tblQueryDefs table. The function uses the Seek method to find the supplied value and, if it finds a match, returns the record's SQLText field value.

```
Function GetSavedQuerySQL (strName As String) As String
    '
    ' Returns a SQL string from a saved query
    ' In  : strName - name of query to retrieve
    ' Out : SQL string
    '
    Dim dbCurrent As Database
    Dim rstQueries As Recordset

    Set dbCurrent = DBEngine.Workspaces(0).Databases(0)
    Set rstQueries = dbCurrent.OpenRecordset("tblQueryDefs")
    rstQueries.Index = "PrimaryKey"
    rstQueries.Seek "=", strName
    If Not rstQueries.NoMatch Then
        GetSavedQuerySQL = rstQueries![SQLText]
    End If

    rstQueries.Close
End Function
```

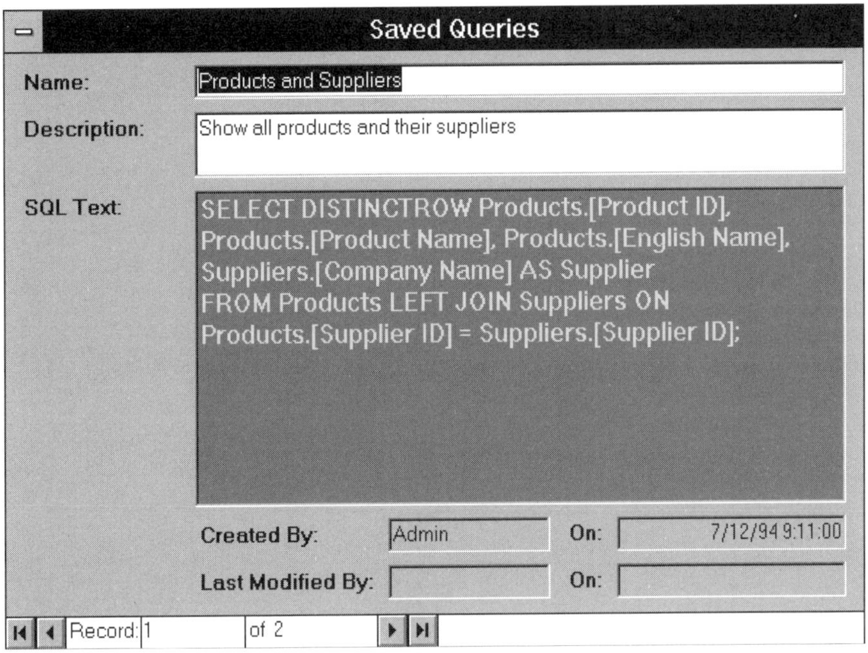

Figure 1-29 The saved queries form, frmSavedQueries

Comments

By extending this technique, you can create a complete replacement for saved queries in Access. Since you have full programmatic access to each query, you can load, modify, execute, and save queries at will, without having to open Querydef objects. Additionally, since you can store the queries table in a library database, you can completely remove a user's access to saved queries, except through your code. The one drawback is that you cannot base forms or reports on queries saved in tblQueryDefs without a little Access Basic code. But this is easily overcome by writing a function that retrieves a saved query's SQL string from tblQueryDefs and assigns the value to the form or report's RecordSource property before the form or report is run.

An enhancement to this technique would be a conversion routine that reads each of your database's saved queries and converts them to records in the tblQueryDefs table. Once this conversion is complete, you can delete the queries from the database window.

2

Designing Creative and Useful Forms

HOW DO I...

As far as users of your applications are concerned, your forms *are* the application. They're the windows into the data that make Access applications work. Access forms are incredibly flexible, and can take on as many different personalities as there are Access developers. The tricks and techniques covered in this chapter are not as complex as ones you might find in other chapters of this book, but they will help form the foundation of your entire application. You'll want to use these tips to help prepare a consistent "look" to your forms and to help your users find exactly which control currently has the focus. You'll also learn how to control where your users go on your forms by restricting their movement to another row, and how to give your forms custom navigation controls. Your understanding of controls will grow, too, as you learn to use option groups to collect and display non-numeric information, and to control the display of multipaged forms. You'll also find a way to resize the controls inside your forms to match the size of the form. You'll see how to combine controls to create new "hybrid" controls, by linking a text box and a list box to create a combination that works like a permanently opened combo box. Finally, you'll see how to use the Windows API to save and restore program settings or application variables, and to save and restore the size of your forms from one session to another.

2.1 Make custom templates for forms and reports
When you've decided upon a standard look for your forms and reports, you need not spend a lot of time setting the properties for each control. Access allows you to specify a particular form or report to be used as a template for all new forms or reports that you create. This How-To will examine the steps you take to create your own templates for form and report design.

2.2 Highlight the current field in data entry forms
As they move from field to field in data entry forms, users may want some visual clue as to which field has the cursor in it. This simple How-To will demonstrate some methods you can use to make sure the user can tell exactly which control on the form currently has the focus.

2.3 Restrict access to a single row on a form
As you press the (TAB) and (SHIFT)-(TAB) keys to move about on a form, Access will move from row to row as you move past the first and last controls on a form. If you want to have the cursor move from the last control back to the first, keeping the same row current, you'll have to do some work. This How-To will show how you can use two tab sentry controls to force the cursor to wrap around on the form.

2.4 Use an option group to collect and display text information
In Access, you can use option groups on a form to display numeric data only. Sometimes, you'll want to read and write data from a text field, instead, through an option group. This How-To will show straightforward expressions you can use to read and write text data using an option group.

2.5 Display multiple pages of information on one form
Many applications need to gather a large amount of information, divided into distinct categories, from the user. One method for doing this is to use

multipaged forms, but that requires that users go through the input form in the order you set up for them. Using a tabbed dialog format, you supply a group of tabs (or buttons) that allow users to choose the order in which they go through the data, and which pages they visit. This How-To will suggest a method for creating these useful forms.

2.6 Provide record navigation buttons on a form

Access provides navigation buttons for you to use on forms, allowing you to easily move from row to row. However, you can neither move nor resize these buttons, and they give no visible indication of whether or not pressing them will actually do anything, depending on your location in the recordset. This How-To will demonstrate the creation of customized navigation buttons. Using the information in this topic, you should be able to place your own navigation buttons on any form.

2.7 Size a form's controls to match the form's size

Windows users have become accustomed to resizing forms on their screen. A professional-looking application will resize the controls on a form proportionally when you stretch or reduce the size of a form. This How-To will demonstrate how to base the width and height of the controls in your form on the width and height of the form itself.

2.8 Make a simple "searching" list box

Combo boxes allow you to find matches as you type characters into their text box portion, but they roll up as soon as you leave them. List boxes stay open, but you can only match a single character as you type. By combining a text box and a list box, you can create a hybrid control that gives you the best of both worlds: You'll be able to enter as much text as you need to find a match, and the control will stay open. This How-To will show you how to link the two controls so that they act as a single control.

2.9 Save program settings or application variables to a file and retrieve them later

In many cases, you'll need to save and restore program settings or variable values between uses of your application. Windows provides functions to help you out, and this How-To will cover the use of the standard Windows API calls you'll need in order to read and write information in INI files: GetPrivateProfileInt, GetPrivateProfileString, GetProfileInt, GetProfileString, WritePrivateProfileString, and WriteProfileString. Several other How-To's throughout this book will rely on this information.

2.10 Store the sizes and locations of forms

This How-To builds on the previous one, showing you how to write particular characteristics about your form to an INI file. Not only will we use the Windows API calls presented in the previous How-To, but we'll use others to discern the exact size and location of the form in question. You'll be able to use the code in this How-To to preserve information about any form in your application. By attaching the code to the appropriate event procedure, you'll save and restore the necessary information when you close and later reopen the forms.

2.1 HOW DO I...

Make custom templates for forms and reports?

Problem

When I make a new blank form, the form properties and the properties of any control I place on it use the Access defaults. But I've decided upon a standard look for my forms and reports that is significantly different from these defaults, and I spend too much time changing control properties on every new form I create to make them match my look. I'd like some way to change the standard default values. Can I do this?

Technique

Access allows you to specify a particular form or report to use as a template for new forms or reports that you create. This How-To lists the steps in creating your own template for form design. The technique is the same for form templates and report templates.

Steps

Load 02-01.MDB and create a new form. Add controls of various types to the form. Notice that they look different from the defaults. To see where the properties are coming from, load the form named Normal from 02-01.MDB in design mode. Each of the controls on this form will act as templates for any new controls on any forms you create in this database. In addition, any new form you create will inherit its own properties from this template form.

To create your own template form, follow these steps:

1. To start, create a new blank form.

2. Make any general changes you want in the form properties, such as changing the GridX and GridY properties to different settings—many users may prefer 16×16, the smallest grid that will show dots. To access the form's properties sheet, click on the white square in the upper-left corner of the form, or select the Edit|Select Form menu item. If you don't want a record selector, navigation buttons, minimize or maximize buttons, a control box and/or scroll bars on your form template, turn them off too, in the Layout section of the form's properties sheet. In addition, you can choose to automatically center the form when it is opened by changing the AutoCenter property to Yes.

3. You may also wish to change the form's background color, by changing the background color for the form's Detail section (click on the Detail section bar in form design to select the section). If you want your forms to have page headers/footers or form headers/footers, activate them by checking Page Header/Footer or Form Header/Footer on the Format menu.

4. Once you have finished setting up the form's general properties as you wish, repeat the process to change the default settings for each control in turn. There are two ways you can do this:

   Click the tool for that control in the toolbox and change the properties in the control's properties sheet. Note that when you do this, the properties sheet's title bar says "Default Label" (or whatever control you have clicked), as shown in Figure 2-1.

⚷ Change the control directly, using the toolbar. Then select the Format|Change Default menu item, with that control highlighted.

5. Select all the sample controls, then select Format|Change Default. This will set the default properties for all the selected controls.

6. Verify that all the controls have the right properties by clicking on each tool in the toolbox in turn, and checking the appearance of the new control. Make sure you haven't inadvertently changed the properties of the control itself, rather than the default control.

7. Finally, open the View|Options dialog box, as shown in Figure 2-2. Select Form & Report Design from the Category list, and enter your form's name on the Form Template row.

How It Works

Access normally uses a hidden form named Normal for its form and report template. If you don't specify your own default properties, all your new forms will use Access's built-in form, report, and control properties. If you create a form named Normal and set the default control and form properties for that

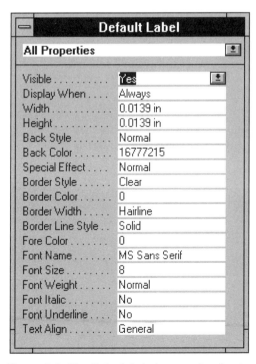

Figure 2-1 The Default Label properties sheet

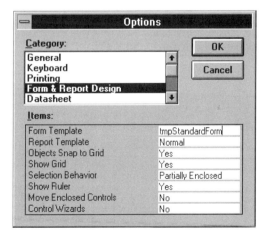

Figure 2-2 Specifying the form template name in the View\Options dialog box

form, Access will use that form as a template. If you name your form something besides Normal, you can instruct Access to use that form (or report) as the template by changing the values in the View|Options dialog box.

Comments
You might want to use different background colors for labels attached to text boxes or combo boxes, or for unattached labels, but Access won't let you save specific settings for different types of labels. There is just one type of label, as far as Access is concerned. The default label will have one background color, and you will have to change it as needed depending on its attachment.

To make a report template, follow the same procedure as for a form template, though you can omit controls that aren't useful on reports, such as combo boxes and command buttons.

A form or report template only supplies styles, such as color, presence of headers and/or footers, and grid granularity, to new forms; it doesn't supply controls. If you would like all your forms to contain standard controls at fixed locations, you'll need to make a copy of a standard form and work from that copy. If you copy the entire form, any code attached to the control's event procedures (in the form's module) will be copied also.

2.2   HOW DO I...   COMPLEXITY: INTERMEDIATE

Highlight the current field in data entry forms?

Problem
The text cursor is just too small in Access, and I can't always tell which text box on a form has the cursor. I need some way to *really* highlight the current field.

Technique
There are many visual cues you can use to tell the user which text box has the cursor in it. You could change the color of the text or the background, change the appearance of the text box, or change the appearance of the text box's label.

The simplest solution, which works quite well, is to change both the BackColor and SpecialEffect properties of the active control. This solution uses two simple macros, attached to each control's Enter and Exit events, to do the work. Figure 2-3 shows the sample form frmEffects in use, with the Address field currently selected.

Steps
Open 02-02.MDB and load frmEffects. As you move from field to field on the form, you'll note that the indents and background color of each control change when you enter and again when you leave the control. Follow these steps to create a form with this same sort of functionality.

1. Create a new macro (named mcrSpecialEffect in 02-02.MDB). Within the macro, turn on the macro names column (choose Macro Names from the View

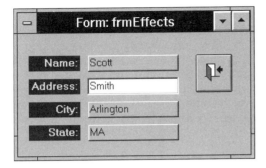

Figure 2-3 frmEffects in use, showing the active field

menu). Figure 2-4 shows the macro editing window as it ought to appear once you've followed all the steps outlined here. This macro will contain all the commands necessary to change the look of each control upon entry and exit.

2. Within the macro, enter the four commands shown in Table 2-1. You can leave a blank row between the two macros (as shown in Figure 2-4) if you like. You can also enter the comments, as shown in the figure, if you care to. They don't affect the workings of the macro, but they make it easier to interpret them later on. Once you're done, save this macro as mcrSpecialEffect.

MACRO NAME	ACTION	ITEM	EXPRESSION
Enter	SetValue	Screen.ActiveControl.SpecialEffect	2
	SetValue	Screen.ActiveControl.BackColor	16777215
Exit	SetValue	Screen.ActiveControl.SpecialEffect	1
	SetValue	Screen.ActiveControl.BackColor	12632256

Table 2-1 Contents of mcrSpecialEffect

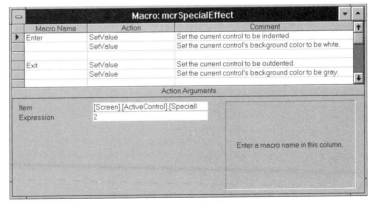

Figure 2-4 The completed mcrSpecialEffect macro

3. Create your input form, if you haven't already. In design mode, select all of the text boxes to which you'd like to attach this effect. (Shift-clicking with the mouse allows you to select multiple controls.) By selecting a group of controls, you can set properties for all of them at once. Set the properties of this group of controls as shown in Table 2-2. Figure 2-5 shows the design surface with all the text boxes selected. (Note that once you select multiple controls, the properties sheet's title can no longer display the name of the selected control, and it will only show "Multiple selection," as shown in Figure 2-5.)

PROPERTY	VALUE
SpecialEffect	Raised
BackColor	12632256
OnEnter	mcrSpecialEffect.Enter
OnExit	mcrSpecialEffect.Exit

Table 2-2 Property settings for the group of selected controls on frmEffects

4. Add the following code to the form's Load event procedure (see this book's Introduction for information on creating event procedures):

```
Sub Form_Open (Cancel As Integer)
    Me.SetFocus
End Sub
```

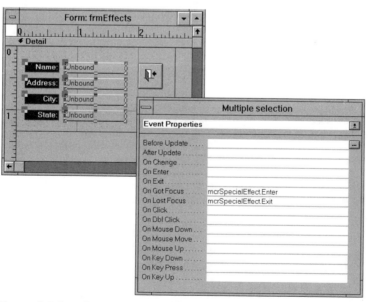

Figure 2-5 frmEffects in design mode, with all the text boxes selected

How It Works

These macros do their work by reacting to the events that occur when you enter or leave a control on the form. Every time you enter one of the text boxes to which you've attached a macro, Access executes that macro. Therefore, whenever you enter one of these special text boxes, Access will cause the text box to appear sunken and will change its background color to white. When you leave the control (by tab or mouse click) Access will set it back to being raised and will reset its background color to gray.

The pair of macros do their work for any control by using the built-in object, Screen.ActiveControl. This object always provides a reference to the currently active control. Therefore, when you enter a control, the macro acts on that particular control, setting the SpecialEffect and BackColor properties.

The only problem with this mechanism is that, when Access first opens a form, there *isn't* a current control. Attempting to refer to Screen.ActiveControl before the form is fully loaded will result in an Access error. Since Access will attempt to enter the first control on your form when it first opens the form, and there isn't yet a current control, the macro you've attached to that first text box's Enter event will fail. To work around this problem, you need to use the Access Basic code attached to the Open event, as shown in step 4 above. This tiny bit of code will force the form to load completely, before it attempts to enter the first text box on your form. You may find this technique useful in other applications you create that use Screen.ActiveControl.

Comments

These macros used in this How-To could be extended to include many other changes to the controls as you enter and leave them. You could change the font or its size, or the foreground color. It would be nice to change the color of the label attached to the text box, too, but that is quite difficult. Since Access provides no mechanism for linking a text box (or any other control) to its attached label, you have no programmatic way of referring to a control's label. You could accomplish the task with a careful naming convention (that way, you know a control's label name because you know the control name), but that method isn't reliable, and certainly can't be generalized.

2.3 HOW DO I...
COMPLEXITY: EASY

Restrict access to a single row on a form?

Problem

When I press (TAB) or (SHIFT)-(TAB), I can't keep Access from moving to the next or previous row of data, if I happen to be on the first or last control in a form's tab order. This often isn't what I want; I really want the cursor to wrap around to the first or last control on the form. Is there some way to keep Access from moving me right on to the next or previous row?

Technique

Though Access doesn't provide a built-in mechanism for keeping the current row current when you tab (or Shift-tab) past the last (or first) control on a form, you can easily make it happen yourself. You can always use the built-in navigation buttons (or provide your own, as shown in How-To 2.6), or use the (PGUP) and (PGDN) keys to move from row to row.

The solution is to use transparent controls, placed carefully in the form's tab order so that they force the focus to the correct control, no matter whether you've tabbed forward past the last control or Shift-tabbed backwards past the first control. As you enter each of these tab sentries, a tiny bit of Access Basic code will force the focus to go to the appropriate control on the form. All you need to do is set up the controls, set the tab order, and tell the controls what to do when you enter them.

Steps

Open and run frmTabAround from 02-03.MDB. Press (TAB) to move from field to field. When you get to the final field on the form, press (TAB) once more, and your cursor will move back up to the first control, rather than to the next row as it normally would. The same thing occurs when you press (SHIFT)-(TAB) to move backwards through the controls. When you reach the first control, the cursor will wrap around and go to the final control on the same row, rather than moving to the previous row. You can, of course, just press the (PGUP) or (PGDN) keys to move from row to row, or use the navigation buttons on the form.

Follow these steps to add this functionality to your own form:

1. Create two buttons. Set their properties as shown in Table 2-3.

CONTROL TYPE	PROPERTY	VALUE
Command button	Name	cmdTabFirst
	Transparent	Yes
	Width	0.1
	Height	0.1667
Command button	Name	cmdTabLast
	Transparent	Yes
	Width	0.1
	Height	0.1667

Table 2-3 Control properties for the two transparent buttons in Figure 2-6

2. Place the buttons on the form, one before the first control, and one after the last control. For both buttons, set the Transparent property, rather than the Visible property, to Yes. (This makes the button active, but invisible.) Figure 2-6 shows the sample form, frmTabAround, in design mode with one of the buttons selected.

3. Edit the tab order of the controls on the form by choosing Edit|Tab Order while your form is open in design mode. You'll need to make sure that cmdTabFirst and cmdTabLast are the final two items in the list. Figure 2-7 shows the Tab Order dialog box with those two buttons placed correctly, at either end of the list. To move an item within this dialog box, click once on the gray box to the left of the control name to highlight its row, and then

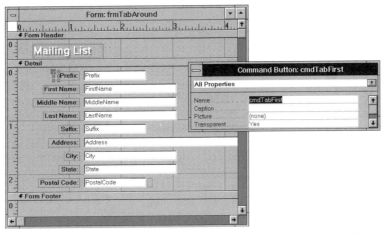

Figure 2-6 frmTabAround with two transparent buttons on either side of the form's controls

click and drag the selected row to its new location. Once you're done, the list should look somewhat like the list in Figure 2-7. You could also take this opportunity, before you place the transparent buttons in the correct locations, to choose the Auto Order button, which will place your other controls in a standard tab order: in increasing order from left to right, top to bottom.

4. Place the following function call in cmdTabFirst's OnEnter property, replacing FirstControlName with the name of the *first* control on your form. Leave the square brackets intact. This forces Access to send the focus to the first control on your form when you enter this button.

```
=ahtGotoControl([FirstControlName])
```

5. Place the following function call in cmdTabLast's OnEnter property, replacing LastControlName with the name of the *last* control on your form.

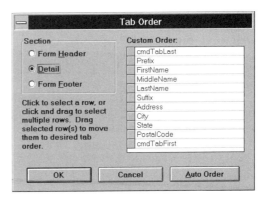

Figure 2-7 Tab Order editing dialog box, with the transparent buttons placed correctly

Leave the square brackets intact. This forces Access to send the focus to the last control on your form when you enter this button.

```
=ahtGotoControl([LastControlName])
```

6. Place the following function call in the form's OnLoad property, replacing FirstControlName with the name of the first control on your form. Leave the square brackets intact. This forces Access to send the focus to the first control on your form when loading the form. Otherwise, Access would go to the last control, since cmdTabLast is the first item in the tab order, and its Enter event sends the focus to the last editable control. Setting the control from the Load event forces Access to place the focus where you want it: on the first control.

```
=ahtGotoControl([FirstControlName])
```

7. Either import the module basControlTabs from 02-03.MDB or create a new global module in your application, and enter this code in your new module:

```
Function ahtGotoControl (ctl As Control)
    ctl.SetFocus
End Function
```

How It Works

Though the buttons used in this example are transparent, they still can react to clicks and other events. As you've set them up, as soon as you attempt to enter one of them (using either the (TAB) key or a mouse click), Access will set the focus to some other control. You specified exactly *which* control you want to receive the focus in each button's OnEnter event property.

Since the role of these transparent buttons is to move the focus to a specific control when you enter them via the (TAB) key, you must ensure that the tab order will force the focus to the correct transparent button as you tab around the form. Setting the tab order with the Tab Order dialog box took care of this.

For the example form, frmTabAround, as you press the (TAB) key, you move through the controls in order (see Figure 2-7). You'll get to City, State, and PostalCode, in that order. Once you press the (TAB) key to leave PostalCode, Access will take you to the next control in the list, which is cmdTabFirst. The moment Access tries to enter that button, though, the Enter event for the control immediately uses the SetFocus method to move the cursor to the control you specified (see step 3 above). Now, in the sample form, the cursor will be on Prefix.

As you press (SHIFT)-(TAB) to move backwards through the controls from the bottom of the form, you'll move through LastName, MiddleName, FirstName, and then Prefix. If you press (SHIFT)-(TAB) one more time, you'll hit cmdTabLast. As soon as Access tries to enter cmdTabLast, the code attached to its Enter event will move the focus to the last field on the form.

Comments

The effectiveness of the technique in this How-To depends on the exact placement of the transparent buttons in the form's tab order, and on the control to which each button forces you once you enter the command button.

Therefore, understanding the steps outlined above is crucial to your getting this technique to work. It all boils down to three ideas, though:

- The button that moves you to the *last* control on the form must appear *first* in the tab order.

- The button that moves you to the *first* control on the form must appear *last* in the tab order.

- You must move to the first control on the form manually, in the form's Open event. Otherwise, the form will open with the last control on the form selected.

In addition, the exact physical location of the two hidden buttons isn't important. It just makes sense to place them near the controls to which they'll move you, so that if you accidentally click on them during your use of the form, you won't find yourself in some control on the other end of the form.

2.4   HOW DO I...   COMPLEXITY: EASY

Use an option group to collect and display text information?

Problem
Option groups work great for collecting and displaying numeric values. But sometimes I need to use an option group bound to a column of values that isn't numeric. For instance, in each row I have a field that contains just one of four different alphabetic codes. I just want some way to let the user choose from those four codes on a form. How can I do that?

Technique
Most often, when you want a control on a form bound to a column in a table that contains just a few alphabetic items, you can use a list or combo box to display and collect the information. Other times, you really do want to use an option group, where you can have option buttons or even toggle buttons containing pictures. Option groups, though, as Access implements them, can only be bound to a numeric column.

The solution is to use an unbound option group. Rather than moving the data directly from the form to the underlying data, you'll make a pit stop along the way.

Steps
Open and run frmOptionExample in 02-04.MDB. This form, shown in Figure 2-8, pulls in two columns from the underlying table, tblCodes. Each row contains a Name field and a Code field. The Code field can be only one of four values: BT1, QRE, ARK, or UYE. The form displays the Name field in a text box and the Code field in an option group. In addition, it shows an extra text

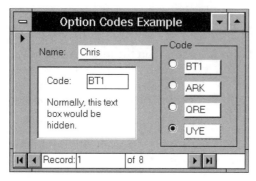

Figure 2-8 Example form using an option group to store character data

box control: the pit stop mentioned earlier. This (normally hidden) text box is the bound control, not the option group.

To create a minimal sample form that works with the same data, follow these steps:

1. In 02-04.MDB, create a new form. Choose tblCodes for the form's RecordSource property.

2. On your new form, create controls as shown in Table 2-4. Make sure you've selected the option group before you attempt to place any option buttons inside it. You should see the option group turn dark when you attempt to place an option button in it.

CONTROL TYPE	PROPERTY	VALUE
Option group	Name	grpCode
Option button (BT1)	Name	optBT1
	OptionValue	1
Option button (ARK)	Name	optARK
	OptionValue	2
Option button (QRE)	Name	optQRE
	OptionValue	3
Option button (UYE)	Name	optUYE
	OptionValue	4
Text box	Name	txtCode
	ControlSource	Code

Table 2-4 Control properties for your new sample form

3. Create a new macro. Turn on its Macro Name column (choose View|Macro Names or select the Macro Names button on the toolbar). Add actions as shown in Table 2-5, and then save it as mcrEvents.

MACRO NAME	ACTION	PARAMETER	VALUE
AfterUpdate	SetValue	Item Value	[txtCode] Choose([grpCode], "BT1", "ARK", "QRE", "UYE")
Current	SetValue	Item Value	[grpCode] Switch([txtCode]="BT1", 1, [txtCode]="ARK", 2, [txtCode]="QRE", 3, [txtCode]="UYE", 4, True, Null)

Table 2-5 Macro actions for the sample form

4. For the form's OnCurrent event property, choose mcrEvents.Current from the drop-down list of macros. This macro will set the correct value of the option group as you move from row to row.
5. For the option group's AfterUpdate event, choose mcrEvents.AfterUpdate from the drop-down list of macros. This macro will set the value in the bound text box, based on your choice in the option group.

How It Works

Using just two simple macros, you've managed to make the sample form store the data as required. The example works because of two distinct events and two distinct functions that you call from those events.

The Events

The form's Current event occurs every time you move from one row to another in the underlying data. In this case, you'll need to convert the data from its raw form (as three-character text strings) into a format that the option group on the form can display for each row, as you move to that row.

The option group's AfterUpdate event occurs whenever you make a change to its value. For this control, choosing any of the option buttons within it will trigger the event. You'll use this event to place a new value into the text box on the form, which is directly bound to the correct column in the underlying data.

The Functions

When you want to convert the raw data into an integer representation (so the option group can display the value), you'll use the Switch function. Its syntax is:

```
returnValue = Switch(expr1, value1 [,expr2, value2][, expr3, value3]...)
```

Access will evaluate *each* of the expressions but will return the value corresponding to the first one that returns a True value. In your example, the macro assigns the value of this expression,

```
Switch([txtCode]="BT1", 1, [txtCode]="ARK", 2, [txtCode]="QRE", 3, ⇒
[txtCode]="UYE", 4, True, Null)
```

to the option group. If the value of [txtCode] is BT1, then the option group gets the value 1. If [txtCode] is ARK, then the option group is 2, and so on. The final pair (the two Null values) ensures that if the value of [txtCode] is Null, the option group will be Null, too. Access calls this function from the form's Current event, so that every time you move from row to row, Access assigns the appropriate value to the option group, based on what it finds in the bound text box.

To convert a choice made in the option group into its appropriate text value to be stored in the table, you'll use the Choose function. Its syntax is:

```
returnValue = Choose(index, value1 [, value2][, value3]...)
```

Based on the value in *index*, the function will return the matching value from its list of values. In your example, the macro assigns the value of this expression,

```
Choose([grpCode], "BT1", "ARK", "QRE", "UYE")
```

to the bound text box, once you've made a selection in the option group. If you choose item 1 from the option group, it assigns BT1 to the text box. If you choose option 2, it assigns ARK, and so forth.

Comments

You can use the two events (AfterUpdate and Current) and the two functions described here to handle your conversions from integers (option group values) to text (as stored in the table). Be aware of a few limitations that apply to the Switch and Choose functions:

- Both functions support only a limited number of options. Switch can support up to 7 pairs of expressions/values. Choose can support up to 13 expressions. If you need more than that, you'll need to convert your event handlers to Access Basic. Of course, you also should avoid putting more than 7 items in an option group, anyway.

- Both functions evaluate *all* of the expressions they contain before they return a value. This can lead to serious errors unless you plan ahead. The following expression details the worst possible case:

```
returnVal = Choose(index, MsgBox("Item1"), MsgBox("Item2"), MsgBox("Item3"), ⇒
MsgBox("Item4"), MsgBox("Item5"), MsgBox("Item6"), MsgBox("Item7"), ⇒
MsgBox("Item8"), MsgBox("Item9"), MsgBox("Item10"), MsgBox("Item11"), ⇒
MsgBox("Item12"), MsgBox("Item13"))
```

You might assume that this expression would display the message box corresponding only to the value of *index*. You would be wrong. This expression will always display 13 message boxes, no matter what the value of *index* might be. Because Switch and Choose both evaluate all of their internal expressions before they return a value, they'll both execute any and all functions that exist as parameters. This could definitely lead to unexpected results, as Access runs each and every function used as a parameter to Switch or Choose.

In most cases you'd be better off using a list or combo box, with a separate lookup table, allowing users to choose from a fixed list. If you have only a small number of fixed values, and you need to store those values in your table (as opposed to an index value from a small lookup table), then the technique presented here should do.

To use the techniques outlined here in your own applications, you'll need to modify the screen display and the two macros. Once you've done that, you should be able to use an option group to gather text information.

2.5 HOW DO I... COMPLEXITY: INTERMEDIATE

Display multiple pages of information on one form?

Problem
I have a large number of fields that I need to display on a form. If I place them all on the form at once, it looks too complicated. I need some way to group them by category and only display the ones that correspond to each category, as the user works through all the groups. Is there some easy way to make this happen?

Technique
Because Access handles subforms so well, you'll use subforms to solve this problem. You can just divide your fields into categories, creating one form for each category. On a main form, you can create an option group and a subform. The option group's value will control which of the subsidiary forms is visible at any given time in the subform control.

Steps
Load 02-05.MDB and open frmMain. This sample form (shown in Figure 2-9) contains a text box and an option group in the form header and a single subform in the detail section. By selecting a button in the option group, you cause one of the four possible subforms (frmTime, frmCalendar, frmBooks, frmTravel) to be displayed in the detail section.

To create your own version of a form with subforms, follow these steps. In each case, the names and details of the subforms are just suggestions. Alter them to fit your own needs.

1. Create the table and/or query on which you want to base your form (tblSample in 02-05.MDB). Make sure your data includes a primary key (ID in 02-05.MDB).

2. On your main form (frmMain in 02-05.MDB), turn on the form header and footer by choosing Forms|Form Header/Footer.

3. Set at least the properties shown in Table 2-6 for the form itself. By setting the form's DefaultEditing property value to Can't Add Records, you won't be able to add new rows using this particular form, but it will make the whole package much simpler to handle. If you need to use the form to add new rows, you can later add an option (perhaps a new command button) to add the new row.

4. In the form's header section, create an option group (grpOptions) and place within it enough toggle buttons to handle all your categories. In addition, create one command button (cmdExit) to close the form. Figure 2-10 shows the sample form "exploded," so that you can see how the form's header has been laid out. Set the DefaultValue property to 1 (corresponding to the toggle button/subform that you'll want visible when your form first loads).

Once everything is placed correctly, you can collapse the size of the option group by pulling its right bottom corner in toward the upper-left of the option group as far as possible. Access will size the option group to fit the buttons inside it exactly.

PROPERTY	VALUE
RecordSource	tblSample (or the name of your table or query)
DefaultEditing	Can't Add Records
ViewsAllowed	Form
BorderStyle	Dialog

Table 2-6 Form property values for the main form, frmMain

5. Ensure that the OptionValue property for each of the toggle buttons has been set to a unique value. In the sample form, these range from 1 through 4. You'll want these values to be simple increasing values, starting at 1.

6. Add code like the following to the option group's AfterUpdate event procedure. This will select the appropriate subform, based on your choice from the option group. For more information on the Choose function, see the previous How-To.

```
Sub grpOptions_AfterUpdate ()
    Dim strSub As String

    strSub = Choose(grpOptions, "frmTime", "frmCalendar", "frmBooks", "frmTravel")
    subMain.SourceObject = strSub
End Sub
```

7. Add the following code to the OnClick event procedure for the command button (named cmdExit in the sample form):

```
Sub cmdExit_Click ()
    DoCmd Close
End Sub
```

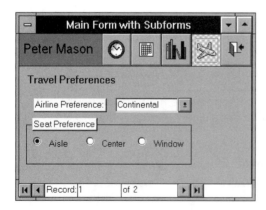

Figure 2-9 The sample form, frmMain, including the four subforms

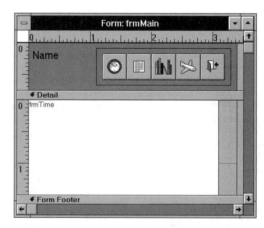

Figure 2-10 Sample form in design mode, "exploded" to show the option group

8. In the form's header section, place controls containing any data that you'd like to have appear no matter which "page" is selected. In this example, the Name field appears in the form header.

9. Create each of the subsidiary forms. Make sure they're all the same size, and each is bound to the same table or query (that is, the RecordSource property for each form is set to the same value). Figure 2–11 shows the four subsidiary forms for the sample.

10. Open just your main form (frmMain in the example) in design mode. From the Database Container, drag the form that you'd like displayed when the form first opens onto the main form. Figure 2–12 shows this step in action. Once you've placed the subform, you can remove its label and size it correctly. Set the subform's Name property to be subMain, so the code in step 6 can work correctly with this subform. When you're running the form, the code you attached to the option group's AfterUpdate event will replace this subform with the one you've chosen.

11. Set the LinkMasterFields and LinkChildFields properties of the new subform control to refer to the primary key value of the underlying data. This will link the main form and the subform to show the same row, even when you move from row to row on the main form.

How It Works

When you make a choice from the option group in the form's header, you trigger the control's AfterUpdate event. This causes the code listed in step 6, above, to change the subform control's SourceObject property. By changing this property, you force Access to reload the appropriate form into that subform control. This makes it look like you're moving from page to page on a single form.

This whole How-To relies on the fact that each member of an option group, whether it's a toggle button, option button, or check box, represents a unique value (the OptionValue property of each control). By choosing one of these internal controls, you supply the option group with a value. That value indicates which of the subforms you want to have displayed. Since each subform is bound to the same data source as the main form, you're effectively editing one row in the table, no matter which subform you display.

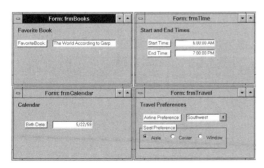

Figure 2-11 The four subsidiary forms, ready to be used by frmMain

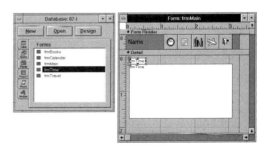

Figure 2-12 Drag a form onto the main form to create a subform

Comments

There are several other methods to create multipage forms, similar to what you've seen in this How-To.

You can place *each* of the subforms on the main form, setting all of them to be invisible except one. Then, in the AfterUpdate event of the option group, you can make the current subform invisible and the new one visible. This method is more difficult to set up than the one shown here, but it executes a bit faster, since all the subforms exist on the main form at all times. This method also consumes more system resources than the method shown in this How-To.

You can use multipaged forms, placing a page-break control between pages. This method is simple to implement, but it requires some work to keep users from moving from page to page with the arrow keys (unless you open the form in dialog mode, in which case Access disables the (PGUP) and (PGDN) keys). The code attached to the option group in the header could use the GotoPage macro action to jump to the appropriate page. Many developers find the subform method, as outlined in this How-To, simpler to create and maintain.

You can use Andrew Miller's custom control, TAB.OCX, available on the CD-ROM that accompanies this book, to implement your tabbed dialog boxes. For more information on using custom OLE controls, see Chapter 12. TAB.OCX provides an excellent solution, though the custom control solution can be unwieldy. It requires distributing and installing yet another file or two with your applications, and can use a measurable portion of your system resources.

> **WARNING:** *Neither Waite Group Press, Andrew Miller, nor Microsoft can supply support or warranties for the sample custom controls provided with this book. Please be aware that you use custom controls included with this book at your own risk, with no guarantees, explicit or implicit.*

2.6 HOW DO I...
COMPLEXITY: INTERMEDIATE

Provide record navigation buttons on a form?

Problem

I'd like to provide some mechanism for allowing users to move from row to row on my forms, but I think the navigation buttons Access provides are too small and unattractive. They also give no indication when you can or can't use them. If you're sitting on the first row and you click the first row button, it just doesn't do anything. I'd like it better if the buttons disabled themselves to indicate which were unavailable.

Technique

You can create your own buttons, place them on a form, and have each button use the GotoRecord macro action. Unfortunately, this has two severe drawbacks:

🔑   If you attempt to move to the previous or next row, and you're already at the end of the recordset, the macro will fail. The GotoRecord macro action just isn't smart enough to work in this case.

🔑   Your buttons will always be available, giving no indication as to when you can use them.

To avoid errors, you *must* use Access Basic. This How-To demonstrates the steps for adding the appropriate code to your application so that navigation buttons will move you safely from row to row, and will also disable the navigation buttons when they are unavailable. The frmNav form in 02-06.MDB (see Figure 2-13) works just this way. You can load it and give it a try before attempting to build your own. In Figure 2-13, note that the next and last buttons are disabled, because the form is currently displaying the last row in the table.

Steps

Open and run frmNav from 02-06.MDB. Use the navigation buttons to move from row to row (there are only a few rows in the table so far). Note that as you move around in the table, the appropriate buttons become enabled and disabled. Also try pressing the (PGUP) and (PGDN) keys. You'll see that the appropriate buttons still become disabled, as necessary.

Follow these steps to include this functionality in your own applications:

1. Set your form's properties as shown in Table 2-7, removing the form's scroll bars and built-in navigation buttons. (Of course, since this method only works for scrolling through rows of data, your form must also have its RecordSource property set so that the form displays rows of data.)

PROPERTY	VALUE
ScrollBars	Neither
NavigationButtons	No

Table 2–7 Property settings for forms to remove the built-in navigation buttons

2. Either copy the buttons from frmNav or create your own five buttons on your form. *Do not* use the Access Button Wizard to create your buttons, since that will add inappropriate Access Basic code to the buttons; you want to be able to supply the code yourself. By creating your own buttons, you can

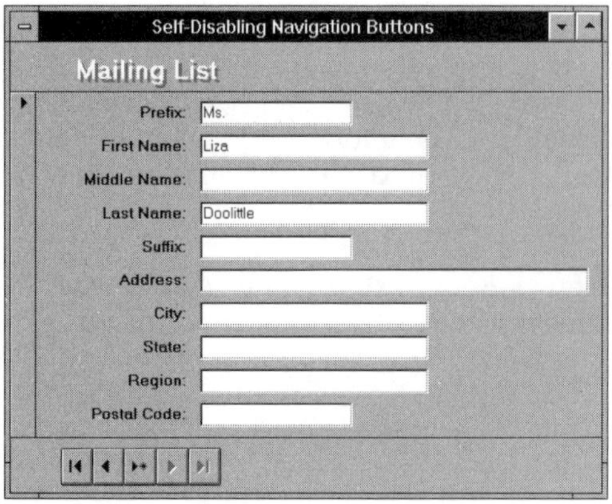

Figure 2-13 frmNav from 02-06.MDB,
demonstrating user-defined navigation buttons

add pictures from Access's selection of pictures. Click on the Builder button to the right of the Picture property on the properties sheet for each button.

3. Set the ControlName property for each of the buttons, based on the following list. The Access Basic code you'll use later depends on these particular names.

```
cmdFirst
cmdPrev
cmdNew
cmdNext
cmdLast
```

4. Add the following code to cmdFirst's Click event. (For information on adding code to a form event, see this book's Introduction.)

```
Sub cmdFirst_Click ()
    ahtMoveFirst Me
End Sub
```

5. Add the following code to cmdPrev's Click event:

```
Sub cmdPrev_Click ()
    ahtMovePrevious Me
End Sub
```

6. Add the following code to cmdNew's Click event:

```
Sub cmdNew_Click ()
    ahtMoveNew Me
End Sub
```

7. Add the following code to cmdNext's Click event:

```
Sub cmdNext_Click ()
    ahtMoveNext Me
End Sub
```

8. Add the following code to cmdLast's Click event:

```
Sub cmdLast_Click ()
    ahtMoveLast Me
End Sub
```

9. Add the following code to your form's Current event:

```
Sub Form_Current ()
    ahtHandleCurrent Me
End Sub
```

10. Import the basMovement module from 02-06.MDB into your own application.

How It Works

This How-To actually has two parts. The first deals with the record navigation (steps 1 through 8 above), and the second (step 9) handles the disabling of the unavailable buttons.

Handling Record Navigation

For each of the five buttons, you've attached Access Basic code that will call a common procedure whenever you press the button, thus reacting to the Click event. For each button, the subroutine you call ends up calling a procedure that handles all the motion. The subroutine,

```
Sub ahtMoveFirst (frm As Form)
    HandleMoveMent frm, A_FIRST
End Sub
```

calls the HandleMovement procedure:

```
Private Sub HandleMovement (frm As Form, intWhere As Integer)
    On Error Resume Next
    DoCmd GoToRecord A_FORM, frm.Name, intWhere
    On Error GoTo 0
End Sub
```

Every subroutine that calls HandleMovement passes to it a reference to a form and an Access constant that indicates to what row it wants to move (A_FIRST, A_PREVIOUS, A_NEWREC, and so on). HandleMovement disables error handling, so Access won't complain if you try to move beyond the edges of the record set. HandleMovement then uses the GotoRecord macro action to go to the requested row.

Disabling Buttons Depending on Your Location

The second, and more complex, part of this How-To handles the enabling/disabling of the buttons, depending on the current row. In step 9, above, you attached a subroutine call to the Current event of the form. This tells Access that every time you attempt to move from one row to another, Access should call this procedure before it displays the new row of data. This procedure, then, can do the work of deciding where in the record set the current row is, and based on that information, disable or enable each of the five navigation buttons. (This code, in basMovement, is completely optional. If you don't call ahtHandleCurrent, the only effect you'll see is that the buttons won't disable themselves according to the current row.)

A discussion of the full ahtHandleCurrent code is beyond the scope of this How-To (you can find the fully commented code in the basMovement module). It must, however, as part of its work, determine whether or not the current row is the "new" row. That is, if you press the (PGDN) key until you're on the last row of data, and then press the key once more (if your data set allows you to add rows), you'll be on the "new" row. Access doesn't include a specific function to determine whether or not you're currently on this row (and many Access Basic procedures require this information). Fortunately, you can use the code in the AtNewRecord function, below, to return a True value if the current row is the new row, and False otherwise. (See How-To 6.2 for more information on this technique.)

```
Private Function AtNewRecord (frm As Form)

    ' This function returns True if the
    ' current row on form frm is the "new" row.
    ' This function really only works from the
    ' Current event of a form, since Access 2.0
    ' now builds the new row (and assigns it a bookmark)
    ' as soon as you enter data.

    Dim strBM As String

Const NO_CURRENT_ROW = 3021

    On Error Resume Next
    strBM = frm.BookMark
    AtNewRecord = (Err = NO_CURRENT_ROW)
    On Error GoTo 0
End Function
```

AtNewRecord attempts to retrieve the bookmark for the current row on the form. The form's bookmark is a unique identifier indicating the current row. Every existing row in the form's recordset will have a bookmark, but the new row, before it's actually committed to the disk, will not. Therefore, attempting to retrieve the bookmark for the new row will trigger an Access Basic runtime error. AtNewRecord disables error trapping (using the On Error Resume Next statement), attempts to retrieve the bookmark, and then checks the value of the Err function. If it's been set to 3021, the code knows that it failed because there *was* no bookmark for the current row, and you therefore must be on the new row.

Comments

The code provided in basMovement makes it easy for you to move this functionality from one application to another, just by hooking the correct form and control events. On the other hand, you can get similar results by creating your own toolbar and using the record navigation buttons that Access provides. A toolbar you create will control whatever form happens to be the current form. Figure 2-14 shows a form/toolbar combination in action. You'll need to decide for yourself which technique you like best. Certainly, the toolbar approach is simpler, but it is difficult to move toolbars from one database to another, and they do clutter up the work area. You also have no programmatic control over the toolbars (except their visibility).

2.7 HOW DO I... COMPLEXITY: INTERMEDIATE

Size a form's controls to match the form's size?

Problem
I'd like to be able to resize my forms while the application is running and have the controls on the form react appropriately. For example, the Database Container window's list box expands when you expand the window. How can I do this on my own forms?

Technique
Because Access can notify your application when the user resizes a form, you can attach code to that particular form event property (OnResize) and react to the change in size. Access also triggers this event when it first draws the form, so you can place your controls correctly during that event, also. You'll want to key off of the form's WindowWidth and WindowHeight properties to do your calculations.

Steps
Load and run frmExpando in 02-07.MDB. Resize the form and watch the size of the large text box. Also, notice the positions of the two command buttons. Figure 2-15 shows the form in design mode, and Figure 2-16 shows two instances of the form, sized to different proportions. Though it's perfectly reasonable to change the size of all the controls, this form does not. It uses three different techniques:

➤ **Do nothing**. The label above the text box doesn't change at all as you resize the form.

➤ **Change position only**. The two command buttons move with the right edge of the form, but they don't change size.

➤ **Change size**. The large text box changes its size to match the size of the form.

The Access Basic code that does the work in this case is specific to the particular form. Follow these steps to create a form similar to frmExpando. Once you've gone through these steps, you should be able to expand on the concepts (pun intended) and create your own self-sizing forms.

1. Create a new form, and create controls and properties as shown in Table 2-8.

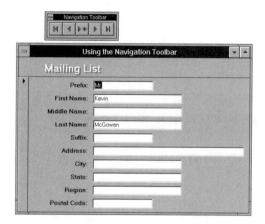

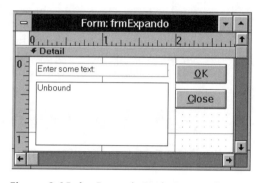

Figure 2-15 frmExpando in design mode

Figure 2-14 A Record Navigation toolbar can replace navigation buttons on the form

> 2. Place the following code in the form's OnResize event procedure (see this book's Introduction for more information on creating event procedures):

```
Sub Form_Resize ()
    Dim intHeight As Integer
    Dim intWidth As Integer
    Static fInHere As Integer

Const MINHEIGHT = 2000
Const MINWIDTH = 4000

    If fInHere Then Exit Sub
    fInHere = True

    On Error GoTo Form_Resize_Err

    ' Turn off the form's repainting.
    Me.Painting = False

    ' Get the current screen coordinates.
```

Figure 2-16 Two instances of frmExpando, with different proportions

CONTROL TYPE	PROPERTY	VALUE
Label	Name	lblSample
	Left	0.1 in
	Top	0.0833 in
	Width	1.7917 in
	Height	0.1667 in
	Caption	Enter some text:
Text box	Name	txtEntry
	Left	0.1 in
	Top	0.3333 in
	Width	1.8 in
	Height	0.8333 in
Command button (OK)	Name	cmdOK
	Caption	&OK
	Left	2 in.
	Top	0.0833 in
	Width	0.6979 in
	Height	0.25 in
Command button (Cancel)	Name	cmdCancel
	Caption	&Cancel
	Left	2 in.
	Top	0.4167 in
	Width	0.6979 in
	Height	0.25 in

Table 2-8 Controls and their properties for frmExpando

```
intHeight = Me.WindowHeight
intWidth = Me.WindowWidth

' Make sure the width and height aren't too small.
' If they are, resize the form accordingly.
' This could force Access to call this sub again,
' so use fInHere to avoid that extra overhead.
If intWidth < MINWIDTH Then
    DoCmd MoveSize , , MINWIDTH
    intWidth = MINWIDTH
End If
If intHeight < MINHEIGHT Then
    DoCmd MoveSize , , , MINHEIGHT
    intHeight = MINHEIGHT
End If

' Set the detail section's height to be the same
' as the form's.  Change this if you want to include
' header and footer sections.
Me.Section(0).Height = intHeight
```

(Continued on next page)

(Continued from previous page)

```
    ' Arbitrarily set the height of all the other
    ' controls.  You might want to deal with the width
    ' of the borders, but that involves the Windows API.
    '
    ' The numbers used here are all completely arbitrary.
    Me!txtEntry.Height = intHeight - 1000
    Me!txtEntry.Width = intWidth - Me!cmdOK.Width - 500
    Me!cmdOK.Left = intWidth - Me!cmdOK.Width - 250
    Me!cmdClose.Left = intWidth - Me!cmdClose.Width - 250

Form_Resize_Err:
    Me.Painting = True
    fInHere = False
    Exit Sub
End Sub
```

How It Works

The Access Basic code used in this How-To reacts to the Resize event that will occur when a user resizes a form in run mode. The code will retrieve the form's current size (its WindowWidth and WindowHeight properties) and resize controls accordingly.

This example starts out by checking a flag, fInHere, and causes the subroutine to exit if the variable's value is True. It's possible that the procedure itself might cause another Resize event (if the user has sized the form smaller than the preset minimum size), and this flag ensures that the routine doesn't do more work than it needs to do.

USING THE STATIC KEYWORD

The flag, fInHere, was declared with the Static keyword. This keyword indicates that Access will maintain the value of the variable between calls to the function. You could accomplish the same effect by making fInHere global; but if you make the variable static, it exists as long as the form is loaded, maintains its value from one call to another, and is local to the current procedure. The variable performs its task (as a sentry) without possible intervention from any other procedure.

Next, the code retrieves the current form size and stores it into local variables. By placing these values into variables, Access doesn't have to retrieve the value of the properties every time you need to use them. This speeds up the operation, since retrieving property values is a very "expensive" operation in terms of operating speed.

Once it has retrieved the sizes, the procedure verifies that the form hasn't been sized too small by the user. If so, it forces the form to be at least as large as the preset values of MINWIDTH and MINHEIGHT.

Finally, the procedure sets the sizes and locations of each of the controls, based on the new width and height of the form. First, it must set the height of the form's detail section, Section(0), so there'll be room for all of the controls at the new height. It then sets the width and height of the text box and the left coordinate of the command buttons. This will preserve their sizes, but reset their positions.

Comments
The values used as offsets in this example were all chosen arbitrarily. They work for this particular example, but you'll need to vary them for your own forms. Remember also that this example is quite simple. You'll be doing a great deal more calculations if you want to dynamically resize a multicolumn list box, for example. In any case, the concepts are the same: Just resize each of the controls based on the current size of the form.

2.8 HOW DO I... COMPLEXITY: ADVANCED

Make a simple "searching" list box?

Problem
I'd like to create a text box/list box combination, like the one in Windows Help. As users type into the text box portion of the control, I want the list box to scroll to match whatever has been typed so far. I know I could use a combo box for this, but the combo box keeps closing up. I want something that's permanently open.

Technique
Entering just a portion of the value you're looking for and seeing the matches displayed as you type is an excellent way to find specific values in a list. You get the best of both worlds: the functionality of a combo box, with the "permanently open" look of a list box.

The key to implementing this functionality is the text box's Change event. Every time the text in the text box changes, the code you'll use will automatically find the matching value in the associated list box. You'll be able to call a function that will handle all the work for you. In addition, since searching through indexed tables is so much faster than walking through dynasets (the results of running a query or an SQL expression), this How-To offers two solutions to this problem: one for list boxes that are bound to tables and another for list boxes that are bound to queries or SQL expressions. Figure 2-17 shows frmSearchFind in action.

The methods you'll find in this How-To apply only to bound list boxes.

Steps
To test out the functionality, open the database 02-08.MDB, and then open either frmSearchFind or frmSearchSeek. As you type into the text box, you'll see the associated list box scroll to match what you've typed. If you backspace to delete some characters, the list box will still match the characters that appear in the text box. When you either leave the text box or click on an item

in the list box, you'll see the full text of the chosen item in the text box. The functionality is the same, no matter which form you use. The frmSearchSeek form will look up items faster, though, since it's using indexes to do its work.

Follow these steps to build a form like frmSearchFind, which will use a query or SQL expression as the row source for the list box.

1. In your own database, create a new form that contains at least a text box and a list box. For the sake of this example, name the text box txtCompany and the list box lstCompany.

2. Set properties as shown in Table 2-9.

CONTROL TYPE	PROPERTY	VALUE
Text box	Name	txtCompany
	OnExit	[Event Procedure]
	OnChange	[Event Procedure]
List box	Name	lstCompany
	AfterUpdate	[Event Procedure]
	RowSource	qryCustomers
	ColumnCount	2
	ColumnWidths	0
	BoundColumn	2

Table 2-9 Controls and properties for search project form

3. Import the Customers table and the qryCustomers query from 02-08.MDB.

4. Put the following code in the lstCompany_AfterUpdate event procedure. (See this book's Introduction for more information on creating event procedures.)

```
Sub lstCompany_AfterUpdate ()
    ahtUpdateSearch Me!txtCompany, Me!lstCompany
End Sub
```

5. Put the following code in the txtCompany_Change event procedure:

```
Sub txtCompany_Change ()
    Dim intRetval As Integer

    intRetval = ahtDoSearchDynaset(Me!txtCompany, Me!lstCompany, "Company Name")
End Sub
```

Figure 2-17 Using Incremental Search on frmSearchFind

6. Put the following code in the txtCompany_Exit event procedure:

```
Sub txtCompany_Exit (Cancel As Integer)
   ahtUpdateSearch Me!txtCompany, Me!lstCompany
End Sub
```

7. Import the module basSearch from 02-08.MDB. This module contains the Access Basic code that does all the work.

How It Works

Every time you change the value in txtCompany, Access triggers txtCompany's Change event. The code attached to that event calls down into the common function, ahtDoSearchDynaset. In general, the syntax for calling ahtDoSearchDynaset is

```
intRetval = ahtDoSearchDynaset(textbox, listbox, "Field to search")
```

where *textbox* is a reference to the text box you're typing in, *listbox* is the list box you're searching in, and *"Field to search"* is the field in the list box's underlying record source through which you're going to search.

The function ahtDoSearchDynaset does its work by creating a dynaset-type recordset object, searching through it for the current value of the text box, and then setting the value of the list box to match the value the code just found in the underlying record source.

```
Function ahtDoSearchDynaset (ctlText As Control, ctlList As Control, ⇒
ByVal strBoundField As String) As Integer

   ' Search through a bound list box, given text to find from a text box.
   ' Move the list box to the appropriate row.
   ' The list box can have either a table or a dynaset
   ' (a query or an SQL statement) as its row source.

   Dim db As Database
   Dim rst As Recordset
   Dim intRetval As Integer

   On Error GoTo ahtDoSearchDynaset_Err

   Set db = DBEngine.Workspaces(0).Databases(0)
   Set rst = db.OpenRecordset(ctlList.RowSource, DB_OPEN_DYNASET)
   ' Use the .Text property, since you've not yet left the
   ' control. Its value (or its .Value property) aren't
   ' set until you leave the control.
   rst.FindFirst "[" & strBoundField & "] >= " & QUOTE & ctlText.Text & QUOTE
   If Not rst.NoMatch Then
       ctlList = rst(strBoundField)
   End If
   intRetval = ERR_NO_ERR

ahtDoSearchDynaset_Exit:
   On Error Resume Next
   rst.Close
   On Error GoTo 0
```

(Continued on next page)

(Continued from previous page)

```
    ahtDoSearchDynaset = intRetval
    Exit Function

ahtDoSearchDynaset_Err:
    intRetval = Err
    Resume ahtDoSearchDynaset_Exit
End Function
```

The example in this How-To is also set up so that if you leave the text box, it pulls in the currently selected item from the list box. That means you can press (TAB) to leave the text box, and the code will place the value that matches as much as you've typed so far in the text box.

You'll also notice that the list box's ColumnCount property is 2, and the ColumnWidths property is 0 in this example. This occurs because the query used, qryCustomers, contains two columns, with the first column hidden in the list box. Since it's the second column that you're searching for, that must be the bound column.

Comments

This example, as shown so far, uses a query as the data source for the list box. For large data sets, this method can really slow things down. If at all possible, you'll want to base your list box directly on a table instead, especially if your data set is much larger than a few hundred rows. In that case, you can use the Seek method, which can use an index and is much faster than the FindFirst method used in the previous example.

To make this happen, you'll need to change a few properties. To test it make a copy of your frmSearchFind and call the new form, frmSearchSeek. Change the RowSource property of your list box to be Customers, rather than qryCustomers.

In addition, you'll need to change the function that txtCompany calls from its Change event procedure:

```
Sub txtCompany_Change ()
    Dim intRetval As Integer

    intRetval = ahtDoSearchTable(Me!txtCompany, Me!lstCompany, "Company Name", "Company Name")

End Sub
```

In this case, you'll be calling the ahtDoSearchTable function, which searches through an indexed table instead of through an unindexed dynaset. In general, you'll call ahtDoSearchTable with the following syntax,

```
intRetval = ahtDoSearchTable(textBox, listBox, "BoundField", "IndexName")
```

where *textbox* is a reference to the text box you're typing in, *listbox* is the list box you're searching in, *"BoundField"* is the field in the list box's underlying record source through which you're going to search, and *"IndexName"* is the name of the index you're going to use. (Usually, it will just be "PrimaryKey", but in this example, use "Company Name". This table is indexed both on the Customer ID field (the primary key) and the Company Name field.)

The code for ahtDoSearchTable is almost identical to that in ahtDoSearchDynaset, except that the table search uses the Seek method to search through an indexed recordset, instead of the FindFirst method that ahtDoSearchDynaset uses. Since it can use the index, it should be able to find matches much more rapidly than ahtDoSearchDynaset.

> **NOTE:** Since ahtDoSearchTable requires that the list box's record source be a table, it will trap for that error and return a nonzero return value if you try to use it with some other data source. In addition, the function will not work correctly if you mismatch the bound field and the index. That is, the bound field must be the only field in the selected index.

The code for ahtDoSearchDynaset, ahtDoSearchTable, and ahtUpdateSearch is in the module basSearch. If you want to use this functionality in other applications, just import that single module into your application and follow the steps outlined above to set the properties on your text and list boxes.

2.9   HOW DO I...   COMPLEXITY: ADVANCED

Save program settings to a file and retrieve them later?

Problem
As part of my application, I need to be able to save some program settings (like serial numbers, colors, or sizes) in a file, so that I can read them back the next time I run the application. How can I do this?

Technique
Most Windows applications (Access included) store program initialization values in a text file with a standard format, usually with an extension of .INI. In general, every Windows program uses a format like this:

```
[Application1]
Topic1=Value1
Topic2=Value2

[Application2]
Topic1=Value1
Topic2=Value2
```

You can easily save and retrieve items from these files using a set of standard Windows API functions. You supply the file name, the application name, and the topic, and a function will return to you the value to the right of the equal sign. If you supply all those items, plus a value, you can have a function write the information to a file. Using the standard API functions relieves you of the burden of having to read the files line by line, looking for the topic you want within a specified group, and then parsing the line and breaking out the piece you need.

The Windows API supplies six procedures for use in this area:

- GetProfileString

- GetProfileInt

- GetPrivateProfileString

- GetPrivateProfileInt

- WriteProfileString

- WritePrivateProfileString

The functions that include the word Private can use any INI file. The ones that don't can only read and write to WIN.INI. Since your applications will very seldom deal with WIN.INI, this How-To will focus on the functions that can use any INI file.

Steps

From 02-09.MDB, load and run frmINITest. This form allows you to read and write to any INI file. In addition, it stores and retrieves the values it displays in its combo boxes from its own INI file (AHTAPI.INI, in your Windows directory). Figure 2-18 shows frmINITest in action.

To try this out yourself, enter the name of an INI file into the File combo box, the name of a section within that file into the Group combo box, and the name of a particular item into the Item combo box. Make sure you've selected the button next to the ahtGetINIString function label, and then click Execute. This will read the appropriate value from the file you indicated. If Windows can't find the file, the group, or the item, the frmINITest will display an empty string. Here is a combination that's guaranteed to work; it will return the name of your system database:

```
File: MSACC20.INI
Group: Options
Item: SystemDB
```

As you enter values into the combo boxes, code attached to each combo box will add your item to that list if it's not already there. When you close the form, code attached to the form's Close event writes the items in each of the combo boxes out to AHTAPI.INI. When you open the form, code attached to the form's Open event loads those items back into the combo boxes. Use the following steps to achieve this functionality in your own applications. These steps revolve around frmTestINI, but you can easily adjust them for your own forms.

1. Set the properties of the controls on your form as shown in Table 2-10.

CONTROL TYPE	PROPERTY	VALUE
Combo box (File)	Name	cboFile
	ControlSource	
	RowSourceType	Value List
	LimitToList	Yes
Combo box (Group)	Name	cboGroup
	ControlSource	
	RowSourceType	Value List
	LimitToList	Yes
Combo box (Item)	Name	cboItem
	ControlSource	
	RowSourceType	Value List
	LimitToList	Yes

Table 2-10 Control properties for your sample form

2. Add the following code to cboFile's NotInList event procedure. This code will handle the event that Access triggers when you attempt to add an item to the combo box that isn't already there (when you have the LimitToList property set to Yes). For more information on creating event procedures, see this book's Introduction.

```
Sub cboFile_NotInList (NewData As String, Response As Integer)
    HandleNewItem Me![cboFile], NewData
    Response = DATA_ERRADDED
End Sub
```

3. Add the following code to cboGroup's NotInList event procedure:

```
Sub cboGroup_NotInList (NewData As String, Response As Integer)
    HandleNewItem Me![cboGroup], NewData
    Response = DATA_ERRADDED
End Sub
```

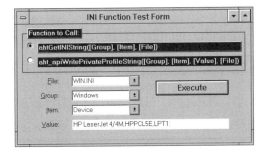

Figure 2-18 The sample form, frmINITest, after reading a value from WIN.INI

4. Add the following code to cboItem's NotInList event procedure:

```
Sub cboItem_NotInList (NewData As String, Response As Integer)
   HandleNewItem Me![cboItem], NewData
   Response = DATA_ERRADDED
End Sub
```

5. Place the following declarations in the Declarations area of your form's module:

```
Const ININAME = "AHTAPI.INI"
Const INISECTION = "Combos"
Const INIFILE = "File"
Const INIGROUP = "Group"
Const INIITEM = "Item"
```

6. Add the following code to the form's OnOpen event procedure. This code refills the combo boxes from the saved values in AHTAPI.INI.

```
Sub Form_Load ()

   ' Retrieve values from ININAME

Me!cboFile.RowSource = ahtGetPrivateINIString(INISECTION, INIFILE, ININAME)
Me!cboGroup.RowSource = ahtGetPrivateINIString(INISECTION, INIGROUP, ININAME)
Me!cboItem.RowSource = ahtGetPrivateINIString(INISECTION, INIITEM, ININAME)
End Sub
```

7. Add the following code to the form's OnClose event procedure. This code stores the values from the combo boxes into AHTAPI.INI.

```
Sub Form_Unload (Cancel As Integer)

   ' Copy values to ININAME for storage between instances
   ' of this form running.

   Dim strFile As String
   Dim strGroup As String
   Dim strItem As String
   Dim intRetval As Integer

   strFile = CStr(Me!cboFile.RowSource)
   strGroup = CStr(Me!cboGroup.RowSource)
   strItem = CStr(Me!cboItem.RowSource)

intRetval = aht_apiWritePrivateProfileString(INISECTION, INIFILE, strFile, ININAME)
intRetval = aht_apiWritePrivateProfileString(INISECTION, INIGROUP, strGroup, ININAME)
intRetval = aht_apiWritePrivateProfileString(INISECTION, INIITEM, strItem, ININAME)
End Sub
```

8. Add the following code to the form's module:

```
Sub HandleNewItem (ctl As Control, varValue As Variant)

   ' Add a new item to a combo box's RowSource.

   Dim varSource As Variant
```

```
    If TypeOf ctl Is ComboBox Then
        ' Retrieve the current value of the RowSource.
        varSource = ctl.RowSource

        If Not IsNull(varSource) Then
            ' If it's not null, then add a ";"
            ' and then the new value.
            varSource = varValue & ";" & varSource
        Else
            ' If it was null, just set it equal to
            ' the new value.
            varSource = varValue
        End If
        ' Set the new RowSource value.
        ctl.RowSource = varSource
    End If
End Sub
```

9. Import the module basIniFile from 02-09.MDB into your own application. This module contains the interface routines and declarations for the Windows API INI functions.

How It Works

Thankfully, the Windows API does most of the work in reading and writing INI files. Reading data is more complicated than writing it out, so you'll find a set of "wrapper" procedures in basIniFile that you can use to read data from INI files. If you look at the Declarations section in basIniFile, you'll find a series of statements like this:

```
Declare Function aht_apiGetPrivateProfileString Lib "KERNEL" ⇒
Alias "GetPrivateProfileString" (ByVal strAppName As String, ⇒
ByVal strKeyName As String, ByVal strDefault As String, ⇒
ByVal strReturned As String, ByVal intSize As Integer, ⇒
ByVal strFileName As String) As Integer
```

These statements provide a link between Access and the Windows DLLs. The statements must appear in any application that uses the external functions, and they must appear exactly as stated. Changing any facet of the Windows API declaration statement without knowledge of why you're making the change will most often lead to a crash—of either Access or Windows or both. This API declaration statement tells Access where to find the external function, the number and type of parameters it expects to receive, and the data type of the return value.

In this sample, you're retrieving information from AHTAPI.INI. The form's Load event calls code that does the work:

```
Me!cboFile.RowSource = ahtGetPrivateINIString(INISECTION, INIFILE, ININAME)
```

If you pass to ahtGetPrivateINIString (a wrapper function in basIniFile that handles some of the details for you) the name of the section, the specific item, and the INI file name, it will return the matching expression from the right-hand side of the = in the file.

When you close the sample form, you're writing information back out to the INI file. In this case, you're calling the WritePrivateProfileString Windows API function (aliased here) directly:

```
intRetval = aht_apiWritePrivateProfileString(INISECTION, INIFILE, strFile, ININAME)
```

Given the section, the item, the value, and the name of the INI file, this function will write the value out to the specified INI file.

These two functions, along with the others in basIniFile, will help you handle your INI file needs in any application.

Comments

Because of the way Windows handles INI files, bear in mind the following when using the functions discussed in this How-To:

- If you attempt to write to a file that doesn't exist, Windows will create it for you.

- If you attempt to write to a section that doesn't exist in a given file, Windows will create the section for you.

- If you write to an existing item within a section, Windows will overwrite the existing value with the new one. If the item doesn't already exist, Windows will add it to the specified section.

- The API functions that write to INI files will return zero, if they fail, and a nonzero value, if they succeed. They shouldn't fail, unless you're writing to a shared file that's currently locked or there was a disk error of some sort.

- The API functions that read from INI files return the length of the string that they read. The wrapper functions that call the API functions (ahtGetINIString, ahtGetPrivateINIString) return the actual string found, or an empty string if the file, section, or item was not found.

2.10 HOW DO I... COMPLEXITY: ADVANCED

Store the sizes and locations of forms?

Problem

My application uses a number of forms that I can move around the screen. I'd like it if the last location could be stored somewhere, so the forms will appear in the same location the next time I start the application.

Technique

Some Windows applications are "smart" and can save the locations of their windows when they exit. Your application can do this too, using a few Windows API calls to retrieve the position of a form. As mentioned in the previous How-To, you can store settings in an INI file when you close a form and read them back the next time you open it. Although you could write this information to the "master" INI file—WIN.INI—it makes more sense to write each application's settings to a different file. This keeps your WIN.INI file as small as possible and speeds up the save and restore steps.

Steps

Open and run frmSavePos in 02-10.MDB. Move it around the screen, and perhaps resize it. When you close the form, code attached to the Close event will save its coordinates in SAVESIZE.INI. When you reopen the form, if 02-10.MDB can find the INI file, it will reload the last set of coordinates and resize/position the form accordingly.

To use this technique with your own forms, follow these steps:

1. Import the modules basIniFile and basSaveSize from 02-10.MDB into your own application. The basIniFile module contains the declarations and wrapper functions for calling the INI file API functions, as described in the previous How-To; basSaveSize contains the API declarations and functions necessary to save and restore a form's size and location.

2. Add the following code to your form's OnLoad event procedure. (See this book's Introduction for more information on creating event procedures.) This will *restore* the size and location when you load the form.

```
Sub Form_Load ()
    ahtRestoreSize Me
End Sub
```

3. Add the following code to your form's OnUnload event procedure. This will *save* the size and location when you close the form.

```
Sub Form_Unload (Cancel As Integer)
    ahtSaveSize Me
End Sub
```

How It Works

Clearly, judging by the brief number of steps above, most of the work involved in saving and restoring the form size and location must happen in the imported module, basSaveSize. (The other module, basIniFile, handles reading and writing information to the INI file, as discussed in the previous How-To.) The two event procedures, called from the form's Load and Unload events, do nothing more than call procedures in the imported module, passing a reference to the current form. You'll need to investigate that module to see what's going on!

The procedures in basSaveSize hinge on two Windows API functions. GetWindowRect, aliased as aht_apiGetWindowRect, gets the coordinates of a screen window. MoveWindow, aliased as aht_apiMoveWindow, moves and sizes a window onscreen.

WHY USE MOVEWINDOW RATHER THAN MOVESIZE?
You might be wondering why you shouldn't use Access's built-in MoveSize macro action: It requires that you select a form first, and this causes the form to display at that point. This looks ugly onscreen and makes the procedure less generic. In addition, it requires some work to convert from screen coordinates (pixels), which GetWindowRect uses, to twips, which MoveSize uses.

The subroutine GetRelativeCoords, in basSaveSize, retrieves the coordinates of a given form. Since the MoveWindow function requires a position relative to that of the window's parent in order to move a window, GetRelativeCoords must find the coordinates of both the requested window and its parent window. It calls the Windows API function, GetParent, aliased as aht_apiGetParent, to find the parent, and retrieves the coordinates of both. It fills in a user-defined structure with the relative coordinates.

```
' Store rectangle coordinates.
Type ahtTypeRect
    intX1 As Integer
    intY1 As Integer
    intX2 As Integer
    intY2 As Integer
End Type


Private Sub GetRelativeCoords (frm As Form, rct As ahtTypeRect)

' Fill in rct with the coordinates of the window.
    ' Deal with the conversion from screen coordinates (pixels)
    ' to twips.

    Dim hwndParent As Integer
    Dim rctParent As ahtTypeRect

    ' Find the position of the window in question, in
    ' relation to its parent window (the Access desktop, most
    ' likely, unless the form is modal.)
    hwndParent = aht_apiGetParent(frm.hWnd)

    ' Get the coordinates of the current window and its parent.
    aht_apiGetWindowRect frm.hWnd, rct
    aht_apiGetWindowRect hwndParent, rctParent


    ' Subtract the left and top parent coordinates, since
    ' you need coordinates relative to the parent for the
    ' grl_apiMoveWindow function call.
    rct.intX1 = (rct.intX1 - rctParent.intX1)
    rct.intY1 = (rct.intY1 - rctParent.intY1)
    rct.intX2 = (rct.intX2 - rctParent.intX1)
    rct.intY2 = (rct.intY2 - rctParent.intY1)

End Sub
```

The ahtSaveSize procedure first retrieves the current coordinates for the requested form, and then saves those values to the INI file whose name is stored in the constant, INIFILE. A representative section from the INI file might look like this:

```
[frmSavePos]
Left=10
Top=67
Right=322
Bottom=244
```

The procedure uses the form name as the group heading and the property as the item name.

```
Const INIFILE = "SaveSize.INI"
Const INILEFT = "Left"
Const INIRIGHT = "Right"
Const INITOP = "Top"
Const INIBOTTOM = "Bottom"

Sub ahtSaveSize (frm As Form)
    Dim rct As ahtTypeRect
    Dim intRetval As Integer

    GetRelativeCoords frm, rct
    intRetval = aht_apiWritePrivateProfileString(frm.Name, INILEFT, CStr(rct.intX1), INIFILE)
    intRetval = aht_apiWritePrivateProfileString(frm.Name, INITOP, CStr(rct.intY1), INIFILE)
    intRetval = aht_apiWritePrivateProfileString(frm.Name, INIRIGHT, CStr(rct.intX2), INIFILE)
    intRetval = aht_apiWritePrivateProfileString(frm.Name, INIBOTTOM, CStr(rct.intY2), INIFILE)
End Sub
```

When it comes time to retrieve the saved coordinates, the ahtRestoreSize procedure retrieves the four coordinates and then, if the width and height of the new form would be greater than 0, resizes the form. Since ahtGetPrivateINIInt returns –1 on failure, and the most likely reason for failure in this case would be that the INI file just couldn't be found (in which case all of the values—top, left, right, and bottom—would be –1), checking the width and height for positive values provides a reasonable error check.

```
Sub ahtRestoreSize (frm As Form)
    Dim rct As ahtTypeRect
    Dim intRetval As Integer

    Dim intWidth As Integer
    Dim intHeight As Integer
    Dim intSuccess As Integer

    ' These will be -1 if they fail.
    rct.intX1 = ahtGetPrivateINIInt(frm.Name, INILEFT, INIFILE)
    rct.intY1 = ahtGetPrivateINIInt(frm.Name, INITOP, INIFILE)
    rct.intX2 = ahtGetPrivateINIInt(frm.Name, INIRIGHT, INIFILE)
    rct.intY2 = ahtGetPrivateINIInt(frm.Name, INIBOTTOM, INIFILE)

    intWidth = rct.intX2 - rct.intX1
    intHeight = rct.intY2 - rct.intY1
```

(Continued on next page)

(Continued from previous page)

```
' No sense even trying if either is less than 0.
  If (intWidth > 0) And (intHeight > 0) Then
     intSuccess = aht_apiMoveWindow(frm.hWnd, rct.intX1, rct.intY1, intWidth, intHeight, True)
  End If
End Sub
```

Comments

You might want to store other properties besides the size and location of the form—for instance, the current record number for a bound form, or perhaps even which control was last selected. In any case, the example in 02-10.MDB lets you store as many properties as you like, by adding to the section describing each form in the INI file.

3

Reporting as an Art Form

Certainly you devote days or weeks of work to designing tables and queries, creating forms and reports, and writing macros or code to put the application together behind the scenes; but the final output of your application is its reports. You see the queries, code, and macros; data entry operators see the forms—but since clients and customers see the reports you'll want to make them as clear and attractive as possible, to make a good impression.

The Report Wizards of Access 2.0 automate report creation, but the Wizards' formats are limited, and many common business reports have no Wizards. The first two How-To's in this chapter will show you how to create an attractive multicolumn address list report and a datasheet subreport. Next, you'll learn how to make a report that looks just like a spreadsheet, using subreports for the columns.

The next group of How-To's will teach you how to use Access Basic and macros to print a message on a report only if certain conditions are met; to create telephone-book-style page range indicators; to calculate page totals; and to print a bar graph on a report using rectangle controls.

Then you'll employ more challenging Access Basic to work around the limitations of the CanGrow/CanShrink properties, and prevent blank rows on reports by combining an entire address into a single expression for a mailing labels report. You'll see how to suppress printing a report if there are no records to print. Using an event procedure run from the report's Format event, you can print one set of headers and footers on odd pages and another (mirror-image) set on even pages. Two How-To's will demonstrate use of the Line method to draw lines or rectangles on a report, in one case to make a line the same height as a variable-height text box, and in the other case to create gray bars overlaying every other row of the report. Finally, you'll see how to prevent your report from breaking at an inappropriate place, such as right after a group header.

3.1   Create an attractive multicolumn report
This How-To will show you how to set up a report in a multicolumn format and group its data by the first letter of the grouping field.

3.2   Create a datasheet-type subreport
There is no datasheet view for reports, and a datasheet subform placed on a form displays and prints strangely; but you can use a subreport with some simple graphics to simulate the appearance of a datasheet subreport.

3.3   Create a report that looks like a spreadsheet
Sometimes you need to create a report that looks just like a spreadsheet, with unrelated data in each of the columns. There is no Report Wizard for such a report, but you can make one quite easily using subreports for the columns of data.

3.4   Print a message on a report only if certain conditions are met
This How-To will demonstrate the use of code attached to the OnFormat event property, to make a control or an entire report section visible only if the current record meets conditions you specify.

3.5   Create a page range indicator on each page
This How-To will suggest a macro to display the first and last items on each page in the page footer, as in a telephone book.

3.6   Create a page total
Access does not have a built-in page total, but you can construct one using two simple macros.

3.7   Create a simple bar graph on a report
This How-To will show you how you can place a rectangle control in the detail section of your report and use it to create a simple bar graph.

3.8   Avoid unwanted blank rows on mailing labels
Mailing label reports have special features that induce problems with the CanShrink and CanGrow properties of text boxes, resulting in blank rows in the addresses. This How-To will illustrate how you can combine the entire text of an address into a single expression to prevent these blank rows.

3.9   Suppress printing a report if there are no records to print
A simple Access Basic event procedure, using the DCount function, checks whether any records are found and suppresses printing the report if no records are found. This prevents reports from printing with just "#Error" in their detail section.

3.10   Print different headers or footers on odd and even pages
Double-sided printing requires different headers on odd and even pages for a symmetrical look, but Access lacks explicit Odd and Even footer properties. However, you can use two functions in an event procedure called from the header or footer section's Format event to print one of two sets of mirror-image header (or footer) controls, depending on whether the current page is odd or even.

3.11   Make a vertical line the same height as a CanGrow/CanShrink control
Graphic lines on reports won't grow or shrink to match the size of a text box with CanShrink and CanGrow set to Yes; but this How-To will show you how to use the Line method in Access Basic to create a line that will grow or shrink to match the varying height of a text box.

3.12   Create reports with altenating gray and white bars
Gray bars on alternate rows make a long report more readable. This How-To will illustrate the Line method technique to draw a rectangle every other row and fill it with a light gray shading.

3.13   Keep a report from breaking at an inappropriate place
Sometimes the built-in KeepTogether properties aren't enough to keep a report from breaking at inappropriate places, particularly when you want a group header to be followed by at least one line of detail text. This How-To will demonstrate how to attach a function to the OnFormat event property of a report's group header, ensuring that a new page will start unless there is enough room to print a line of text under a group heading.

3.1 HOW DO I...

Create an attractive multicolumn report?

Problem

I want to print a mailing list in an attractive multicolumn format, with large initial capital letters to set off each alphabetical grouping. There is no Report Wizard for creating such a report, and I don't see any Column property to set up the number of columns I want. How can I make a multicolumn report in Access?

Technique

There is a way to format a report for multiple columns, but it's not where you might look for it, on a report's properties sheet or the report design menu. Instead, you'll find it on the More drop-down panel of the Print Setup screen. This How-To guides you through setting up a multicolumn report and grouping it by the first letter of a group heading field.

Steps

Open 03-01.MDB. The tblCompanyAddresses table contains typical business addresses, and rptBusinessAddresses1 lists the addresses alphabetically, in a single-column format. As you can see, the addresses could be printed in a two-column format to save space. Follow these steps to format a two-column report, and group it by the first letter of the main grouping field:

1. Open the report you want to format for multiple columns in design view, and select File|Print Setup. The Print Setup dialog box opens.

2. Click the More button on the right to open the additional drop-down More section of the dialog box.

3. As shown in Figure 3-1, enter the desired number of columns (2 in the sample report) in the Items Across text box, and enter an appropriate column width (3 inches is good for a two-column report) in the Width text box.

4. Select the Horizontal or Vertical option button in the Item Layout option group. Horizontal positions records across a row, then down to the next row, and so on. Vertical (sometimes called *newspaper* or *snaking columns*) positions records in a column down the page, then goes up to the top of the next column. Click OK to save your selections.

5. If necessary, adjust the width of the controls on the report's detail section to fit within the column width you selected in the Print Setup dialog box (in the sample report, it's 3 inches).

6. Leave the report and page headers and footers as they are (if your report has these sections); they will still print across the entire report width.

7. To keep the addresses from breaking inappropriately, set the detail section's KeepTogether property to Yes.

8. Preview the report. Now it displays in two columns.

9. For grouping the addresses, add a large initial capital letter derived from the first character of the Company field. Open the Query Builder for the

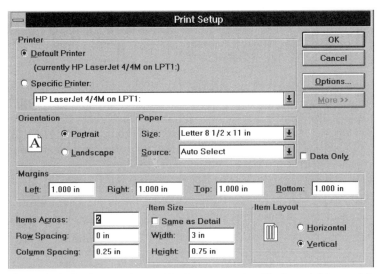

Figure 3-1 Setting up the multicolumn report rptBusinessAddresses2 in the Print Setup dialog box

report's data source and enter the following expression in an empty column (adjusting as necessary for your field name):

```
FirstLetter: Left([Company], 1)
```

10. Close the Query Builder and open the Sorting and Grouping window. Select the new FirstLetter field as the first group (make the Group Header and Group Footer both Yes for this group), and Company (or your field of choice) for the second group.

11. Place the FirstLetter field in the FirstLetter group header section, and make it large and bold, with a gray background if desired.

12. Print the formatted report. Figure 3-2 shows the completed report (rptBusinessAddresses3), with the a large first letter heading each alphabetical group of addresses.

How It Works

The Items Across selection in the Print Setup dialog box lets you specify the number of columns for the detail section of a report, and the Width selection lets you specify the column width. The Horizontal and Vertical options give you a choice for record layout.

Comments

The Mailing Labels Report Wizard creates a multicolumn report with a choice of Avery label formats. You may find this Wizard useful to get a multicolumn report started with the correct number of columns, though you will have to add page headers and footers yourself.

3.2 HOW DO I...
COMPLEXITY: EASY

Create a datasheet-type subreport?

Problem

When I create a form with a subform, using the Main Form/Subform Wizard, the subform appears in datasheet view. I would like to have a similar datasheet subreport on a report, but there is no Main Report/Subreport Wizard. I tried inserting a datasheet subform into a report, but it displayed and printed very strangely. How can I get the look of a datasheet subreport?

Technique

There is no datasheet view for reports, but you can simulate the look of a datasheet subreport by placing thin rectangles and lines on a subreport to create the datasheet's grid.

> **NOTE:** A subreport is not a special type of report, but just a report embedded on another report.

Steps

Open 03-02.MDB. This database contains tables of company addresses and employees (tblCompanyAddresses and tblEmployees) linked by the ID field. Take a look at frmCompanyAddresses to see a form with an embedded datasheet subform. The sample, rptCompanyAddressesSF, is a report based on the same main table, with the same subform embedded on it. It displays and prints poorly, as shown in Figure 3-3, with the grid lines overprinting the bottom of the text in the subreport. The following steps show you how to create a subreport that displays properly as a datasheet.

Figure 3-2 A mailing list report with each alphabetical group headed by a large initial capital letter

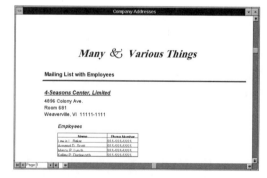

Figure 3-3 Report with an embedded datasheet subform illustrates problems with the grid lines

> ✔ **TIP:** *A form can have only embedded subforms, but a report can have both embedded subforms and embedded subreports.*

1. To create a report with an embedded subreport, you need two reports whose data sources have fields that can be linked because they contain matching data (they need not have the same names). The tblCompanyAddresses and tblEmployees tables in the sample database have linked ID fields.

2. Create the main report by using one of the Report Wizards or by placing controls on a new blank form.

3. Create another report as the subreport, based on the linked data source (generally this is the many side of a one-to-many relationship).

4. The subreport needs a detail section and (if desired) a report header section for column labels. Place the controls you want to display on the datasheet in the detail section.

5. If you want column headings, place the field labels in the report header section over their text boxes.

6. Make the borders of the text box controls transparent by clicking on the Clear button in the Palette, with the control highlighted. Then draw a thin rectangle around the text box controls.

WHY A RECTANGLE?

You might think it would be more efficient to just make the text box borders visible, instead of drawing a rectangle around them. However, Access does not allow you to specify the size of the internal margin around text in text boxes, nor to center text vertically within a text box. The default value for text box spacing places the text very close to the bottom of the text box border, regardless of the height of the text box. To achieve the effect of text positioned in the center of a box, with equal margins on all sides, you need to use a separate rectangle control as a border.

---

7. Draw a thin vertical line between the columns of the datasheet (in the report section too, if you have one for column headings).

8. Pull the bottom of the detail section up until it just touches the bottom of the rectangle.

9. Switch to preview to check the subreport's appearance, and adjust the size and/or thickness of the rectangles and text boxes as needed.

10. Save the subreport, and embed it on the main report, using one of these methods:

    Highlight the subreport in the database container, and drag it to the main report.

    Place a subform/subreport control on the main report, and enter the subreport's name as its SourceObject property.

11. Enter the linking Master and Child fields (ID for the tables in the sample database) in the LinkChildFields and LinkMasterFields properties of the subreport. Access may have filled in these fields automatically if you dragged the subreport to the main report.

12. Print the modified report. Figure 3-4 shows the completed sample report, rptBusinessAddressesSR, with a subreport that displays properly as a datasheet.

How It Works

This technique works around two difficulties in Access—the lack of a datasheet view for reports and the lack of control over positioning of text within a text box—by placing some simple graphic elements on a subreport and simulating the appearance of a datasheet.

Comments

If both the main report and the subreport are based on tables, and a relationship between the tables has been set up using Edit|Relationship, Access will use the linked fields for the LinkChildFields and LinkMasterFields properties of the subreport.

    If the main report is based on a table with a primary key, and the subreport's data source is a table or query that contains a field with the same name and the same (or compatible) data type as the primary key, Access will

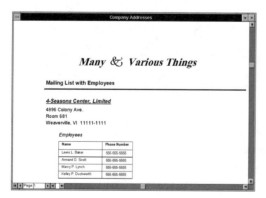

Figure 3-4 Report with a datasheet-type subreport

use the main report's primary key and the subreport's similarly named field as the linking fields.

3.3 HOW DO I... COMPLEXITY: EASY

Create a report that looks like a spreadsheet?

Problem

I want to create a report that looks just like a spreadsheet—with independent columns of information—to list data in different categories; but I can't find a suitable Access Report Wizard format. Is there a way to create a spreadsheet-type report in Access?

Technique

Although there is no built-in spreadsheet report format in Access, it is easy to construct such a report, using subreports for the spreadsheet columns and putting them together into a spreadsheet report. This How-To shows you how.

Steps

Open 03-03.MDB. This sample database contains two tables (tblProducts and tblCategories) imported from the Northwind sample database that comes with Access. To create a spreadsheet-type report listing products in columns by category, follow these steps:

1. Make a new blank report with only a detail section.

2. Click on the Build button (...) next to the RecordSource property to open the Query Builder.

3. Add the tables you need to the query (in the sample database they are tblCategories and tblProducts). If you need more than one table, Access will automatically link them if the tables have a relationship set up; otherwise, you need to link them by dragging the linking field from one table to the other.

4. Set up one field for the subreport's data and another field for selecting records. In the sample database the selection field is the Category Name field from tblCategories and the data field is Product Name from tblProducts. Drag your data and selection fields to the columns on the query grid, and sort them both in Ascending order.

5. On the Criteria line of the selection field column, type the matching text for the first column of report data. In the sample report it is "Beverages." Figure 3-5 shows the query in the Query Builder window.

6. Close the Query Builder window; the SQL statement appears as the report's RecordSource property.

7. Place the data field on the report, as its only field.

8. Save the report (but don't close it). The first subreport in the sample database is called rsubBeverages.

9. Open the report's Query Builder window again, and replace the criterion for the selection field column with matching text for the next column.

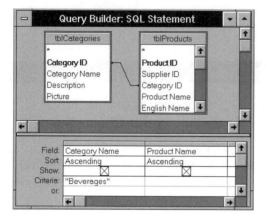

Figure 3-5 Query for the first column subreport, with a category entered as a criterion

10. Close the Query Builder window, and save the report under another name indicating the category of records selected for that subreport.
11. Repeat steps 9 and 10 as necessary until you have one subreport with an appropriate criterion for each column of the report. The sample database has five subreports—rsubBeverages, rsubCondiments, rsubDairyProducts, rsubProduce, and rsubSeafood.
12. Make a new blank report, with no record source, and place the subreports in its detail section. The easiest way to do this is to drag the subreports from the database container to the report. You can also place subreport controls on the report and select the subreports as their source objects. Leave the LinkChildFields and LinkMasterFields properties blank, since the subreports are not linked to the main report.
13. Modify the subreport label captions as desired (you may wish to move them to the page header area), and add a page or report title, if desired. Figure 3-6 shows the completed report in print preview.

How It Works

This technique makes use of unlinked subreports to place unrelated data in columns on a report, just like spreadsheet columns. Unlike a standard grouped report, the rows in each subreport are completely independent. Since each subreport has its own data source, it selects data that matches the text you specify for the subreport's single field. For practical purposes, a report of this type is a collection of separate reports that happen to be printed on the same page.

Comments

This Access report may look like a spreadsheet, but it does not have spreadsheet functionality. If you really need a spreadsheet, consider exporting your data to the Excel worksheet format so you can work on it in Excel. To export a query or table to Excel format, highlight it in the Database Container and click on

Figure 3-6 Spreadsheet-type report in print preview

the Excel button on the toolbar. Access converts the query or table into an Excel worksheet and opens it up immediately.

3.4 HOW DO I... COMPLEXITY: EASY

Print a message on a report only if certain conditions are met?

Problem

On a letter that I mail to all the customers on my mailing list, I want to print a message on only some customers' letters depending on (for example) their zip code, credit status, or past orders. How do I make a text box print only when certain conditions are met?

Technique

You can use code called from the Format event of a report section to make a single control—or the entire section—visible or invisible depending on a condition you specify. The expression in the event procedure is evaluated when you preview or print the report (actually, this happens when Access evaluates which data belongs in a section, but before it is printed). The message in the control prints when the condition is met, and otherwise does not print.

Steps

Open 03-04.MDB. The tblCompanyAddresses table contains typical customer address data, and rptMailingByZip is a letter report sorted by zip code, with a message in the page header that is appropriate only for zip codes starting with 98 (as a stand-in for whatever message and criterion you need on your report). If you preview rptMailingByZip, you will see the message on every page, even for addresses in locations far from Seattle. The following steps describe how to set up an event procedure to print a message only for customers with certain zip codes.

1. Click on the page header title band, and open its properties sheet (choose the All or Event Properties item from the combo box at the top).

2. Start a new event procedure for the Format event by clicking on the Build button next to the property and selecting the Code Builder.

3. Add standard error-trapping code if you wish (look at an event procedure created by the Command Button Wizard for sample code to copy).

4. Enter the following code to evaluate the zip code, and make the page header section visible if the condition is met, or invisible if it is not met:

```
If Mid(Me![ZipPostalCode], 1, 2) = "98" Then
    Me.Section(3).Visible = True
Else
    Me.Section(3).Visible = False
End If
```

5. Preview the report to check that the event procedure is working properly. Figure 3-7 shows an address with a zip code that fails to meet the condition, and Figure 3-8 shows an address that meets the condition; only the address that meets the condition has the message.

How It Works

The event procedure uses the report's Section property and the section's Visible property to make an entire section visible or invisible when the report is formatted. Whether or not the section is visible depends on its meeting the condition in the If expression. Only zip/postal codes starting with 98 meet this condition, so the message about the Seattle Expo will print only on pages for customers located in or near Seattle.

Comments

You could use a similar condition on a single control rather than a section, as in the code fragment below:

```
If Mid(Me![ZipPostalCode], 1, 2) = "98" Then
    Me![txtMessage].Visible = True
```

However, if you have several controls you want to print (or not print) as a unit, it is more convenient to place them all in a section and turn the entire section on or off from its Format event. In the sample report, there are four controls that need to be turned on or off together: the text box with the message, two text boxes with Wingdings pointing-hand graphics, and a

Figure 3-7 An address with a zip code that does not start with 98 has no message

Figure 3-8 An address with a zip code that starts with 98 has the message

rectangle surrounding the other controls. Thus turning the whole section on or off together is more efficient.

The invisible text box txtMid (if made visible) displays the first two digits of the Zip/Postal Code field, to check that the Mid expression is picking up the right data.

You might evaluate a currency field to print a message if the amount is over a certain figure, as in the following expression,

```
Me![YearlySales] > 1000
```

which selects customers with yearly sales over $1,000.

You could also use a date/time field as a condition for printing a control or section, as in the following expression,

```
Me![LastOrder] > Date - 60
```

which selects customers who ordered within the last 60 days.

The Section Property Help topic has a table of the Section property setting used to identify sections, reproduced in Table 3-1 here. You need to use these numbers in expressions referring to section properties.

SETTING	DESCRIPTION
0	Detail section
1	Form or report header section
2	Form or report footer section
3	Form or report page header section
4	Form or report page footer section
5	Group-level 1 header section (reports only)
6	Group-level 1 footer section (reports only)
7	Group-level 2 header section (reports only)
8	Group-level 2 footer section (reports only)

Table 3-1 Values used to identify form and report sections in expressions

3.5 HOW DO I... COMPLEXITY: EASY

Create a page range indicator on each page?

Problem

I'm creating a report that contains a large number of items. To make it easier to see the range of items on each page, I'd like to create a page range indicator. This would show the first and last items on the page, as in a telephone book. Is there a way to do this?

Technique

The answer to this question is a qualified yes. You can create such a page range indicator, but placing it anywhere other than the page footer is very difficult. Although you *can* place it in the page header, the method to do so is quite complex and is the subject of one of the topics in the Microsoft Access Solutions database, which ships with Access 2.0.

Since Access prints documents from top to bottom, by the time you know the last item on the page, it's too late to print it at the top of the page. The workaround involves forcing the report to format itself twice, and capturing the page ranges for all the pages during the first pass. When you make the second pass, you actually supply the values from the stored array of values. That solution requires Access Basic and is cumbersome. This How-To focuses on a simple method, placing the information you need in the page footer. If you can live with this placement, the solution is easy.

Steps

Load the rptPageRange report from 03-05.MDB in preview mode. At the bottom of each page you'll see a listing of the items printed on that page. Figure 3-9 shows that report in design mode. To create a page range indicator on your own reports, follow these steps:

1. Create a new macro named mcrPageRange. In it, create a single action, as shown in Table 3-2. Replace the [Product Name] reference with the name of the table field you'd like to keep track of. Figure 3-10 shows mcrPageRange in design mode.

ACTION	PARAMETER	VALUE
SetValue	Item	[txtFirstItem]
	Value	[Product Name]

Table 3-2 Macro information for tracking page ranges

2. Create a new report or use an existing one. Make sure that the report includes page header and footer sections (if it doesn't, choose Format|Page Header/Footer to add them). In the Page Header section, place a text box and set its properties as shown in Table 3-3. This text box will hold the first row's value when you print the page.

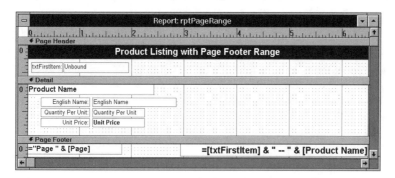

Figure 3-9 The sample report, rptPageRange, in design mode

PROPERTY	VALUE
Name	txtFirstItem
Visible	No

Table 3-3 Property values for the hidden text box in the report's page header

3. In the report's Page Footer section, add a text box. None of its properties are important to this technique except one, its ControlSource property. Set the text box's ControlSource property to be the expression,

```
=[txtFirstItem] & " — " & [Product Name]
```

replacing the [Product Name] reference with the name of the field you'd like to track in the page range indicator. This must match the field name you used in step 1.

4. Set the OnFormat event property for the report's page header section to be mcrPageRange. This tells Access to call the macro every time it formats the page header (once per page). To set the property, first select the divider bar labeled Page Header, then choose the OnFormat event property from the properties sheet. Finally, enter the correct macro name. Figure 3-11 shows the report and the properties sheet as they will look after you've assigned the property.

5. Save and run your report. You will see the page range indicator as in the sample report, rptPageRange.

How It Works

The technique presented in this How-To is based on the fact that when Access prints the page header (or the report header or group header), it gives you access to the row of data it's about to print. The same goes for footers, in reverse—it gives you access to the row of data that's just been printed.

When you call mcrPageRange from the Format event of the page header, you place the data from the first row of the page into the hidden text box, txtFirstItem. The data in that text box doesn't change until you reformat the page. When Access gets to the bottom of the page and attempts to print the page footer, it calculates the value of the text box you've placed there. That text box retrieves the value you previously stored in txtFirstItem and combines it with the data in the last row that printed on the page to create the page range indicator.

Figure 3-10 mcrPageRange in design mode

Figure 3-11 The sample report, rptPageRange, after setting the OnFormat event property

Comments

Though simple, this method does have its limitations:

☞ The page range indicator must go in the page footer. If you attempt to place it in the page header, the data it prints will always be off by a page in one direction or another, depending on how you're viewing the report. If you must have the page range in the page header, check out the method proposed in the Access Solutions database.

☞ For this method to work, you must include the page header section on every page. (The PageHeader property for the report must be set to All Pages.) Since you must fill in the hidden text box once for each page, the only place you can do that is in the page header. If you set up your report to skip the page header on the first page, for example, the page range will be incorrect for the first page, since the report won't have stored the first row's value in the page header. If you must remove some controls on the first page, add some code that sets the visibility of various controls depending on the Page property of the report.

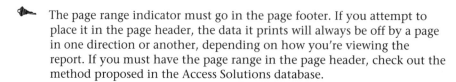

3.6 HOW DO I...

COMPLEXITY: EASY

Create a page total?

Problem

Access allows me to create a group total in the group footer on a report, or a report total on the report footer, but I can't find a way to create a page total in the page footer. I understand that this doesn't come up too often, but for my report, I really could use this element. Is there a way to sum up values over a single page?

Technique

It's true that Access only allows aggregate calculations in group or report footers. You can, however, easily create page totals using two simple macros. This How-To demonstrates this technique and shows how to add this capability to any of your own reports.

Steps

Load rptPageTotals from 03-06.MDB in preview mode. This report tracks orders and their freight costs. The items are grouped by month, and each group has a group total. At the bottom of each page, you'll see the total for all items on the current page. Figure 3-12 shows the sample report in design mode. To create page totals in your own reports, follow these steps:

1. Create a new macro and save it as mcrTotals. Within the macro group, create two macros as described in Table 3-4. Where the example refers to a field named [Freight], use any numeric field you would like to sum up in the page footer. Figure 3-13 shows the macro in design mode.

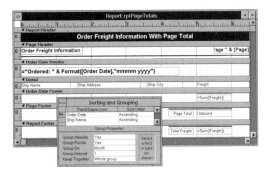

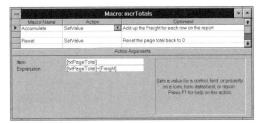

Figure 3-13 The macro group, mcrTotals, in design mode

Figure 3-12 Sample report with page totals, rptPageTotals, in design mode

MACRO NAME	ACTION	PARAMETER	VALUE
Accumulate	SetValue	Item	[txtPageTotal]
		Value	[txtPageTotal] + [Freight]
Reset	SetValue	Item	[txtPageTotal]
		Value	0

Table 3-4 Macro information for calculating page totals in mcrTotals

2. Create your report. Sort and group the data in any way you like. In the report's Page Footer section, include at least a text box. The macros you created in step 1 expect the name of the text box to be txtPageTotal. If you change the name in the macro, make sure the Name property for the text box control matches.

3. Attach the macros to the appropriate report events as shown in Table 3-5.

ITEM	EVENT PROPERTY	MACRO
Report header	OnFormat	mcrTotals.Reset
Page header	OnFormat	mcrTotals.Reset
Detail	OnPrint	mcrTotals.Accumulate

Table 3-5 Event property assignments to create page total

4. Save your report. Now, when you run it, you will see the total of the field you selected in the Accumulate macro (in step 1) in the page footer.

How It Works

Access makes it simple to sum values in group or report footers: Just use the Sum function in the ControlSource property for a text box. For example, to sum the freight costs in either a group footer or a report footer, you could use an expression like this,

```
=Sum([Freight])
```

and Access would perform the sum over the range included in the footer section (either the group or the entire report). To create a page total, however, you must dig a bit deeper in the way Access prints reports.

The Access Report Engine and Printing Events

The report printing engine in Access works as a forward-marching machine: The engine formats and then prints each section as it comes to the section. Each section is handled in the order it appears on the page. The report printing engine first deals with the report header, then any page header, then any group header, then each row of the detail section, and so on. At each point, Access allows you to hook into various events, doing work alongside its work.

The two events described in this How-To are the Format event and the Print event. Access formats each section before it prints the section. Normally, you'll attach a macro or an Access Basic procedure to the Format event of a section if you want to affect the section's layout on the page. You'll use the Print event to make calculations based on the data as you know it's going to print. When Access calls your macro or Basic code from the Print event, you are guaranteed that the current row is going to be printed. From the Format event, you can't assume this, since Access calls the code attached to the Format event before it decides whether or not the current row will fit on the current page. From either event, you have access to the current row of data that's about to be printed, and you can use that as part of your macro or procedure.

Using Events to Calculate the Page Total

In this case, calculating a page total requires two steps: You must reset the page total for each page (and before you start printing the report), and you must accumulate the value in each row as you print each row.

The accumulation part is simple: Every time you print a row, the macro attached to the detail section's Print event adds the current row's freight amount (or whatever field you're tracking on your own report) to the current value in txtPageTotal. When Access needs to print the page footer, that value is filled in and ready to print. You should call this macro from the Print event, and not the Format event, to ensure that you never add a value to the page footer unless you're sure the row will be printed on the current page. Calling the macro from the Print event guarantees this.

From the Format event of the page header section, you can reset the page total so it starts from 0. Since this is the first section that will print on every page, resetting the total in the page header should work. You *could* use the Print event here, but since you're guaranteed that the page header section will fit on its page, you might as well do the work as early as possible. The problem here arises from the fact that, in some reports, you may tell Access to only print the page header on pages where there isn't a report header (see the report's PageHeader property). If you do this, Access won't format the page header on the first page, and it therefore won't call the necessary macro. To make up for this, the example report (rptPageTotals in 03-06.MDB) also calls the macro from the report header's Format event. Since this event only occurs when Access prints the first page, there's no redundancy. You may not need to reset the page total from the report header, but it can't hurt.

Comments

Be very wary of performing any calculations during a section's Format event. Since you aren't guaranteed that the section will actually print on the current page, you could be calculating based on a value that won't be a part of the page. Making this mistake in the sample report, for example, would be a major error. Since this report is set up so that Access will only print a group if the entire group can fit on a page, it might format quite a number of rows, then decide that the whole group can't fit. Each time it attempted to format a row, it would call the code attached to the Format event, which would add the value to the total. To avoid this problem, perform calculations from a section's Print event only. Use the Format event to change the layout of a section—perhaps to make a specific control visible or invisible, depending on the data you find in the current row.

3.7 HOW DO I...   COMPLEXITY: EASY

Create a simple bar graph on a report?

Problem

I need to create a simple bar graph on a report. Microsoft Graph works, but it's far too complex and slow for my purposes. I just need a bar for each row, showing the relative score for each student. Can I do this with the standard Access controls?

Technique

You can place a rectangle control in the detail section of your report and set its width during the Format event that occurs as Access lays out each row of data. This How-To shows you how you can create a simple bar graph, setting the width of the rectangle control to be based on a numeric value in your data.

Steps

Open and run the rptGraph report in 03-07.MDB (see Figure 3-14). This report shows a list of students and their scores, along with a bar whose width represents the value of the score. The maximum width of a bar is four inches, so the widths of the bars are set to the score in the current row's percentage of four inches. To create a bar graph like this one in your own applications, follow these steps:

1. Create your report, including the text data you'd like to show for each row. (The sample report shows the Name and Score fields from tblScores.) Set the sorting and grouping as you require. (In the sample report, the names of these controls are txtName and txtScore.)

2. Add a rectangle control from the report toolbox, and place it next to the data in the detail section. Its width isn't important, since you'll be

adjusting that programmatically (the example report sets the width of the rectangle to be its maximum width for the report, four inches). You'll probably want to set its height to be the same as the height of the text boxes you've already placed on the report. Figure 3-15 shows the report in design mode, with the rectangle control selected. In the sample report, the rectangle's control name is rctBar.

3. If you want, you can place vertical lines at regular intervals along the maximum length of the bar. In the sample report, the vertical lines are placed at the 25%, 50%, and 75% locations. You can place these wherever you like, and if they're the same height as the detail section, they'll appear as continuous lines on the printed report. If you've used group headers and/or footers in your report, you'll need to place the vertical lines in those sections as well, to make them appear continuous.

4. To set the width of the rectangle for each row, you'll need to create a macro. (This could also be done in Access Basic, but since it's so simple, a macro seems reasonable for this task.) Create a new macro named mcrSetWidth and enter the single action shown in Table 3-6. (The final 4 in the macro indicates the maximum width of the rectangle. The 100 in the

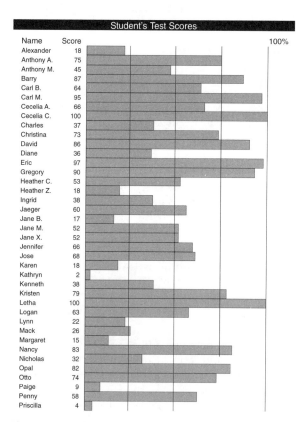

Figure 3-14 The sample report, rptGraph

same expression indicates the maximum value for the numeric field. You'll need to alter these values to match your own circumstances.)

ACTION	PARAMETER	VALUE
SetValue	Item	[rctBar].[Width]
	Value	([txtScore]/100)*(1440*4)

Table 3-6 The macro, mcrSetWidth, which sets the width of the rectangle for each row of data

5. Tell Access to run your new macro each time it formats a row of data. To do this, place the name of your macro in the OnFormat event property for the report's Detail section. Figure 3-16 shows the properties sheet for the detail section.

6. Save and run the report. It should look like Figure 3-14.

How It Works

As Access lays out the report and prepares to print it, it formats each row of data for presentation. As it does this, it runs any macro or Access Basic code attached to the OnFormat event property. In this case, for each row of data, you've told Access to set the width of the rectangle control, based on the value in a numeric field. When it prints that row, the rectangle has a width proportional to the value in that numeric field.

In the sample report, the maximum width of the rectangle is four inches. If a student has a score of 100%, you want the printed bar to be four inches wide. Therefore, the expression

[txtScore]/100 * 4

will evaluate to be the number of inches wide you'd like the bar to be. In order to set the width of the bar from the Format event, you'll need to specify the width in twips, not inches, since that's what Access expects. There are 20 twips in a point and 72 points in an inch, so there are 1440 twips in an inch. To convert the number of inches to twips, then, you must multiply the calculated value by 1440. The final expression in the sample report is:

([txtScore]/100) * (1440 * 4)

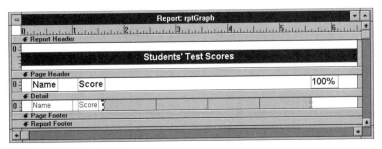

Figure 3-15 The sample report, rptGraph, in design mode

This expression will evaluate to be the width of the bar, in twips, which is what you need. If your report needs a scaling factor other than 100, or a maximum width other than 4, you'll need to adjust the expression accordingly.

Comments

Though the method presented in this How-To will only work for the simplest of cases, when it does work, it does a great job. It's quick, simple, and it produces very nice output. To achieve just the effect you need, you'll want to experiment with different shadings, border colors, and gaps between the rows.

3.8 HOW DO I...
COMPLEXITY: INTERMEDIATE

Avoid unwanted blank rows on mailing labels?

Problem

When I print mailing labels—especially when I use a small font size and place the address text boxes close together—I sometimes get unwanted blank rows in the addresses. And I can't use decorative lines or graphics at all on labels without causing blank rows. How can I get my labels to print correctly, without blank rows, even when I use graphics?

Technique

The Access CanGrow and CanShrink text box properties for reports should allow text boxes to grow or shrink vertically as needed. In a standard report, where text boxes are well separated, these properties generally work correctly. However, a mailing labels report has special features that are likely to interfere with text boxes' shrinking and growing.

A mailing labels report usually has one or more fields (a second and third address line, for example), which may remain empty. These fields need to have their CanShrink property set to Yes to prevent blank rows in the printed address.

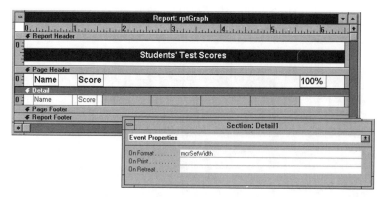

Figure 3-16 Properties sheet showing the event properties for rptGraph

Mailing labels reports frequently feature closely spaced text boxes and sometimes have a graphic line, rectangle, or image as decoration. Such a layout will most likely include one of the following features, all of which prevent CanGrow and CanShrink from working correctly:

☞ Text boxes are touching, or very close but not quite touching.

☞ There is another control (such as an OLE image) on the same row as a text box that needs to shrink.

When one of the above factors prevents the CanShrink property of a text box from working, the report will print with blank rows instead of closing up a row that doesn't have data.

To prevent this, you can combine the output of several text boxes into a single expression and use that expression as the row source of a single text box. This expression makes use of two functions to prevent printing blank rows: one inserts a carriage return/line feed at the end of each line of the label, and the other checks for null values. With only one text box containing the whole address, you won't have any problems with CanShrink.

Steps

Open 03-08.MDB. The tblCompanyAddresses table contains typical address data, with three address fields (Address1, Address2, and POBox). At least one of these fields is blank for every address, to simulate the normal layout of address information. The following steps guide you through creating a single expression that concatenates the contents of several address fields.

1. If you are working with your own database, import into it the basCRLF module from 03-08.MDB, to make the ahtCRLF and ahtMakeLine functions available.

2. Highlight the table containing the address data (tblCompanyInformation in the sample database), click on the New Report button on the toolbar, and select the Mailing Labels Report Wizard.

3. On the Report Wizard screens, select the fields you want to print on the labels, the sort field, and the label size. Figure 3-17 shows a plain mailing labels report, as produced by the Mailing Labels Report Wizard. Note that there are no blank rows in the addresses.

4. Add a line or an OLE graphic image to the label. Figure 3-18 shows the mailing labels report with a gray triangle (a Paintbrush image) to the left of the addresses. Here, the OLE control prevents the text boxes' CanShrink property from working, resulting in numerous blank rows in the addresses.

5. To eliminate the blank rows, first decide which lines you want to combine into a single expression—typically, all but the first line, which has the company or personal name. (Leaving the first line as a separate text box allows you to format it with a larger font or make it bold.) You may find it convenient to make a copy of the original report, so you will have the contents of the original text boxes available for cutting and pasting to the modified report.

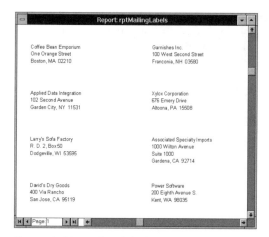

Figure 3-17 Mailing labels report produced with the Mailing Labels Report Wizard, with CanShrink working properly

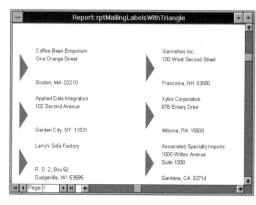

Figure 3-18 A simple Paintbrush image in the mailing labels report causes blank rows in the addresses

6. When you're ready, eliminate all the address text boxes on the report except the one for the first address line, and start creating the address expression as its row source.

> ✔ **TIP:** Press SHIFT-F2 *with your cursor in the text box's ControlSource property to open up the Zoom box, so you can see the whole expression as you work on it.*

For each text box that may be missing data, create an expression to wrap the field in the ahtMakeLine function (discussed in the "Comments" section below). Thus the first line of the label, containing the Address1 text box, becomes:

```
ahtMakeLine([Address1])
```

7. Concatenate the row expressions with ampersands (&) into a single long expression. Use the ahtCRLF function (listed in the "Comments" section) to insert a carriage return/line feed in lines with multiple fields. Here is a complete address expression, as used in the sample report rptMailingLabelsModified:

```
=ahtMakeLine([Address1]) & ahtMakeLine([Address2]) & ⇒
ahtMakeLine([POBox]) & [City] & ", " & ⇒
[StateProvince] & "  " & [ZipPostalCode] & ahtCRLF() & ⇒
IIf([Country]<>"U.S.A.",[Country])
```

Figure 3-19 shows the modified report, with no blank rows in the address lines.

Figure 3-19 Modified report with a Paintbrush image, using a single expression for the entire address

How It Works

When you combine several address fields into a single expression and use that expression as the row source of a single text box, you have only one text box to grow as needed. The elimination of multiple text boxes prevents problems with CanShrink/CanGrow that occur when a text box that needs to shrink is placed on the same row as a text box or other control (such as an OLE frame) that can't shrink.

Comments

The ahtMakeLine function (listed below) checks for nulls in a text field and yields a null value for the line if the varValue argument is null; otherwise, it adds the CRLF character to the field and yields the resulting value.

```
Function ahtMakeLine(varValue as Variant)
    If IsNull(varValue) Then
        ahtMakeLine = Null
    Else
        ahtMakeLine = varValue & ahtCRLF()
    End If
End Function
```

The ahtCRLF function concatenates the ANSI characters 13 and 10 to create a carriage return/line feed character to terminate a line:

```
Function ahtCRLF ()
    ahtCRLF = Chr$(13) & Chr$(10)
End Function
```

The Mailing Labels Report Wizard applies the Trim function to each address field; however, this function is not necessary (since Access stores the fields trimmed), and the labels print exactly the same without the Trim function.

If you use a concatenated expression for an address, you can accommodate more fields on a label than you could if you placed each address text box on a separate line. This method works fine as long as you know that each address will be missing at least one row of address data. If your labels only have room for four lines of data, for example, you could put five lines of data into a concatenated expression, if you know that no address will use all five lines.

Sometimes the CanShrink and CanGrow properties don't work correctly on reports, even when none of the text boxes touch and each is on a line by itself. When this happens, you may need to re-create the text boxes from scratch, or in extreme cases, re-create the entire report. This problem only occurs occasionally, and it appears to be a bug involving a subtle corruption of the report structure; the workaround involves re-creating report controls or entire reports with their original settings.

To make a Country field print only for addresses outside the United States, you can use the following expression as the text box's row source:

```
=IIf([Country]<>"U.S.A.", [Country])
```

This row will print only for other countries. If you leave the Country field blank for some or all domestic addresses (as in the sample table tblCompanyInformation), the expression will still work. It will print a blank row for blank Country fields, but since the blank row is at the bottom of the label, it won't cause any problems.

Unlike specialized label-printing programs, Access does not lock the report size to the label's dimensions, to prevent you from accidentally changing the size of labels after you have created them with the Mailing Labels Report Wizard. It is very easy to accidentally nudge the right edge or bottom edge of a mailing label report (by moving a control, for example), so that the report contents overprint the labels.

> **TIP:** When you first create a mailing labels report, make a note of its width and detail section height. This way you can quickly recover from any accidental resizing of the report, which could result in label text printing outside of the label's boundaries.

3.9 HOW DO I...

COMPLEXITY: INTERMEDIATE

Suppress printing a report if there are no records to print?

Problem

I have a report that prints records I select from a criteria form. Sometimes there aren't any records that match the criteria, and then the report opens with just "#Error" in the detail section, which is unattractive and confusing. Is there any way I can prevent the report from printing when it has no records to print?

Technique

You can use the DCount function in the Open event of the report to determine if any records meet the report's criteria, and suppress printing of the report, with a message box to let you know that no records match the specified criteria.

Steps

Open 03-09.MDB. The sample database contains a table of address data, with several fields suitable for report criteria, such as State, LastOrder, and OrderAmount. The frmReportCriteria1 form is a pop-up form for entering criteria to select records for a report. It is set to default values, which you can modify as desired.

1. Open frmReportCriteria1, select different criteria, and click the Go button. Note that if no records are found, the report opens with just the word "#Error" in its detail section. If records are found, the report opens in print preview, displaying the records that match its criteria.

2. To prevent the report from opening when it has no records to display or print, add the following code to an event procedure on the report's OnOpen property:

```
If Dcount("*", Me.RecordSource) = 0 Then
    MsgBox "Sorry, no records match these criteria!"
    Cancel = True
End If
```

3. Now try the report with the event procedure on its OnOpen property (use frmSelect2 in the sample database). If you enter criteria that don't find any matching records, you will get a message box telling you that no records meet the criteria.

How It Works

In its simplest form (as used in the sample event procedure), the DCount function examines the domain you specify (a table or query name) and counts the number of records with data in the specified field. If you use "*" for the expression indicating the field to count, DCount calculates the total number of records, including those containing null fields.

Using the DCount function requires running the report's data source query twice—once to count the number of records and once to print the rows. This slows down printing somewhat, but it's a good trade-off for a cryptic error message printing on a report if no matching records are found.

Comments

The report header contains controls to display the selection criteria, which are picked up from the criteria form, using expressions like this one:

```
=[Forms]![frmReportCriteria1]![txtLastOrderAfter]
```

The form disappears from view when the report opens in print preview, because the event procedure attached to the Go button sets its Visible property to False before opening the report. Making the form invisible (rather than closing it) ensures that the selection criteria are still available for the report's data source.

3.10 HOW DO I...

Print different headers or footers on odd and even pages?

Problem
Some of my reports are printed double-sided, and I would like to have mirror-image headers and footers on odd and even pages. How do I do that in Access?

Technique
This technique makes use of two sets of header and footer controls, one for odd pages and one for even pages. An event procedure run from the section's Format event uses the Page property and the Mod operator to determine whether the page is odd or even, and makes the appropriate controls visible or invisible.

Steps
Open 03-10.MDB. The simple business addresses report, rptBusinessAddresses1, has a header and footer that print the same on all pages. Follow these steps to convert this report (or one of your own) to print different headers and footers on odd and even pages.

1. Open the report you want to print double-sided.
2. Make a copy of the header control, and place one control on the left of the header and the other on the right. Make the left-hand control left-aligned (to print on even-numbered pages) and the right-hand control right-aligned (to print on odd-numbered pages). Figure 3-20 shows a page header in rptBusinessAddresses2 (in design view) with the two controls and a horizontal line that prints on all pages.
3. Open the page header's properties sheet, and start a new event procedure for the OnFormat property by clicking on the Build (...) button next to the property.
4. Enter the following code for the event procedure:

```
Sub PageHeader1_Format (Cancel As Integer, FormatCount As Integer)

On Error GoTo PageHeader1_FormatError

    Dim fIsOdd As Integer

    ' True for Odd pages, False for even
    fIsOdd = ((Me.Page Mod 2) = 1)

    Me![lblTitleLeft].Visible = fIsOdd
    Me![lblTitleRight].Visible = Not fIsOdd

PageHeader1_FormatExit:
    Exit Sub

PageHeader1_FormatError:
    MsgBox Error$
    Resume PageHeader1_FormatExit

End Sub
```

5. Make copies of the footer controls as well, and make a similar event procedure for the footer's OnFormat property, referencing its left and right controls. The event procedure code for the sample report's footer is listed in the "Comments" section below.

6. Figure 3-21 shows the report in print preview, with an odd page and an even page: The footer controls are reversed left/right on the odd and even pages.

How It Works

The Page property for a report yields the current page, and the Mod operator returns the remainder if you were to divide the page number by 2, yielding 0 for even pages, or 1 for odd pages. By setting fIsOdd to be True if the current page is Odd, you can set the visibility of the rest of the controls based on its value.

Comments

The footer's event procedure is as follows:

```
Sub PageFooter6_Format (Cancel As Integer, FormatCount As Integer)

On Error GoTo PageFooter6_FormatError

   Dim fIsOdd As Integer

   ' True for Odd pages, False for even
   fIsOdd = ((Me.Page Mod 2) = 1)

   Me![txtPageLeft].Visible = fIsOdd
   Me![txtPageRight].Visible = Not fIsOdd
   Me![txtPrintedOnLeft].Visible = Not fIsOdd
   Me![txtPrintedOnRight].Visible = fIsOdd

PageFooter6_FormatExit:
   Exit Sub

PageFooter6_FormatError:
   MsgBox Error$
   Resume PageFooter6_FormatExit

End Sub
```

Figure 3-20 Page header with two controls, one for printing on odd pages and one for even pages

Figure 3-21 Report in print preview, showing the appropriate footer for an odd page and an even page

3.11 HOW DO I...

Make a vertical line the same height as a CanGrow/CanShrink control?

Problem

I have a control on a report that has its CanShrink and CanGrow properties set to Yes, so it can grow or shrink to accommodate different amounts of text. I placed a vertical line to the left of the control, and I want it to be the same height as the control. Is there a way I can make the line conform to the control?

Technique

If you place a line on a report using the Line tool, it will always be the same size. To make a line change its height to match the height of another control (or group of controls), you need to use the Line method in a procedure attached to the Print event of a report section. This How-To will uses the Line method to make a line whose height varies to accommodate the changing height of a text box displaying a memo field.

Steps

Open 03-11.MDB. The rptBusinessAddresses1 report lists business addresses and contract conditions. The txtConditions text box in the group footer contains a memo field with its CanShrink and CanGrow properties set to Yes. Follow the steps below to construct a thick vertical line to the left of this box (or a control of your choice on your report), which will stretch down when the text box grows to accommodate larger amounts of text.

1. Open rptBusinessAddresses1. Preview the report, and note that the thick line to the left of the contract conditions stays the same height even though the text box varies in height, as shown in Figure 3-22. The line is thus too short for some conditions, and too long for others.

2. Remove the line from the report, and create an event procedure for the OnPrint property of the group footer section (or the section on your report where the variable-height control is located).

3. Enter the following code for the event procedure:

```
Dim sngLineTop As Single
Dim sngLineLeft As Single
Dim sngLineWidth As Single
Dim sngLineHeight As Single

Const SM_TWIPS = 1
Const DS_SOLID = 0

  Me.Scalemode = SM_TWIPS
  Me.DrawStyle = DS_SOLID
```

```
'Set coordinates for line
sngLineTop = Me![lblConditions].Top
sngLineLeft = 0
sngLineWidth = 100
sngLineHeight = Me![txtConditions].Top + Me![txtConditions].Height
```

`Me.Line (sngLineLeft, sngLineTop)-Step(sngLineWidth, sngLineHeight), , BF`

4. Preview the report, and notice that the thick line to the left of the conditions text box and label now varies in height to match the height of the conditions text box, as shown in Figure 3-23.

How It Works

The event procedure uses the Line method to create a line that starts at the top of the lblConditions label and extends down to the bottom of the txtConditions text box, growing and shrinking in proportion to the text box. The Line method draws lines or rectangles on reports, using the coordinates you specify (sngLineHeight through sngLineWidth in the sample procedure). The event procedure sets the sngLineTop argument to the top of the lblConditions label, sngLineLeft to 0, sngLineWidth to 100, and sngLineHeight to the bottom of the txtConditions text box. Since Access does not provide an Access Basic Bottom property for controls, this value is calculated by adding the text box's Height property to its Top property.

The line itself (actually, a rectangle) is drawn by the following line of code,

`Me.Line (sngLineLeft, sngLineTop)-Step(sngLineWidth, sngLineHeight), , BF`

where the variables in the first set of parentheses define the upper-left corner of the rectangle, and those in the second set of parentheses define its width and height. The reserved word Step allows you to use height and width values for the rectangle, instead of specifying the lower-right corner. The last argument, BF, indicates that the line will be a rectangle (B) instead of a line, and that it will be filled with the same color as its border (F).

Comments

The ScaleMode property specifies the unit of measurement. Since Access uses twips as its native measurement unit, this property is generally set to twips, as

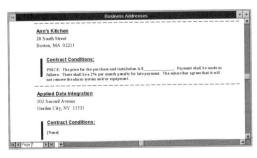

Figure 3-22 Fixed-height line next to a variable-height text box

Figure 3-23 Report with a programmatically created variable-length line

in the SM_TWIPS constant in the sample code. The available settings are listed in Table 3-7.

SETTING	DESCRIPTION
0	Custom values for ScaleHeight, ScaleWidth, ScaleLeft, and ScaleTop
1	(Default) Twip
2	Point
3	Pixel
4	Character
5	Inch
6	Millimeter
7	Centimeter

Table 3-7 ScaleMode property settings

The DrawStyle property specifies the line type; it is set to Solid in the sample code. The available settings are listed in Table 3-8.

SETTING	DESCRIPTION
0	(Default) Solid
1	Dash
2	Dot
3	Dash-dot
4	Dash-dot-dot
5	Invisible
6	Inside solid

Table 3-8 DrawStyle property settings

3.12 HOW DO I...

COMPLEXITY: INTERMEDIATE

Create reports with alternating gray and white bars?

Problem

I have some complex reports on which I'd like to print alternate rows with gray bars in the background. It makes the reports much easier to read, especially when there's lots of data or the report is very wide. Is there a way to create these bars in Access?

Technique

There are a number of ways to print rows with alternate gray and white backgrounds, but the simplest method isn't the most obvious: Use the Line method of a report to draw a rectangle the same size as the detail section of your report, with a very light gray fill pattern. By drawing or not drawing the rectangle for each row, you can achieve the effect you need.

Steps

Open 03-12.MDB and load the report rptGrayBar. If you view this report in print preview mode, it probably won't look very good on your screen. Printed, however, it looks something like Figure 3-24. (The exact output will depend on your printer, and you may need to modify the color setting for the gray bar to optimize it.)

To create your own reports with alternating gray bars in the detail section, follow these steps:

1. Create your report. Since this method will fill the entire detail section with gray shading, the effect will work best if your detail section is one line high. (It will work with taller detail sections, but it won't look as good.)

2. Edit the report's module (click on the Code button on the Report Design toolbar, or choose the View|Code menu option), and enter the following lines of code in the module's Declarations area:

```
' Shade this row or not?
Dim fShade As Integer
```

3. Create an event procedure attached to the OnPrint event property of your report's Detail section, and add the following code. This code must be attached to the OnPrint event property because the Line method for reports will not work when called during the Format event. (For more information on creating event procedures, see this book's Introduction.)

```
Sub Detail1_Print (Cancel As Integer, PrintCount As Integer)

    ' If it's time to draw a shaded row, set the
    ' drawstyle (so you don't get a border) and then draw
    ' the rectangle.

Const COLOR_SHADE = &HE8E8E8
Const DS_INVISIBLE = 5

    If fShade Then
        Me.DrawStyle = DS_INVISIBLE
        Me.Line (0, 0)-(Me.Width, Me.Section(0).Height), COLOR_SHADE, BF
    End If

    ' Alternate the value of fShade
    fShade = Not fShade
End Sub
```

4. If it matters whether the first row on a page is specifically shaded or not, you'll need to create an event procedure attached to the OnPrint property

of the report's page header. Replace the False value with True if you want the first row on each page to be shaded.

```
Sub PageHeader0_Print (Cancel As Integer, PrintCount As Integer)
    ' Make sure the first row on the page isn't shaded.
    ' Use True if you want the first row on each page shaded.
    fShade = False
End Sub
```

5. Print the report. Every other instance of the detail section will be printed with a gray background, the same size as the detail section.

How It Works

By attaching Access Basic code (or a macro) to a detail section's OnPrint property, you tell Access to execute the code every time it gets ready to print that particular section. Therefore, you've told Access to draw a rectangle over the entire detail section, every other time it prints the section. To make that happen, the code shown in step 3 relies on a module global variable, fShade, which alternates between True and False. If you followed the instructions for step 4, you set the value of fShade to be a particular value every time you print the page header. From then on, every time Access prints the detail section, it decides what to do based on the value in fShade. What's more, every time it prints the detail section, it alternates the value of fShade, using this line of code:

```
fShade = Not fShade
```

That is, if fShade was False, now it'll be True, and vice versa.

Once the code has decided whether or not to print the rectangle, it needs to draw it on the report. To draw a rectangle, you'll use the report's Line method. This method allows you to draw any rectangular shape, specifying the upper-left coordinate and the lower-right coordinate, as well as the color and the drawing style. You can also specify whether or not to draw a rectangle or just a line, and if it's a rectangle, whether or not to fill it in.

Before drawing the rectangle, you'll need to set the drawing style of the border (the DrawStyle property of the report). You have seven choices, as shown in Table 3-8 in the previous How-To. In this case, you'll probably want

Company	City	Last Order
Applied Data Integration	Garden City	6/15/94
Astoria Management Corporation	Seattle	2/4/93
Associated Specialty Imports	Gardena	8/22/93
Coffee Bean Emporium	Boston	9/19/93
Mabel's Old Fashioned Soda Fountain	Redmond	7/1/94
Pentacle Software Design	Denver	7/14/93
Power Software	Kent	2/2/93
Support Services	Santa Barbara	8/15/93
Amberley Enterprises Ltd.	Ottawa	1/12/92
David's Dry Goods	San Jose	5/17/94
Holography Inc.	Beaconsfield	4/7/93
Larry's Sofa Factory	Dodgeville	7/22/93
Software Unlimited	Colchester	4/14/94
Garnishes Inc.	Franconia	5/22/94
Query Builders	Cabin John	4/3/94
Xylox Corporation	Altoona	8/2/92
Ann's Kitchen	Boston	2/25/93

Figure 3-24 Report with gray bars on alternate rows

to choose DS_INVISIBLE (5), so the border doesn't show at all. If you do want a border around your gray areas, choose a different value.

To draw the rectangle, use the Line method. The Line method can be used in several ways, but here, you'll use it like this:

```
rpt.Line (ulx, uly) - (lrx, lry), color, BF
```

The two coordinates (ulx, uly) and (lrx, lry) are the coordinates of the upper-left and lower-right corners of the rectangle. For the report's detail section, those can be (0, 0) and (Me!Width, Me.Section(0).Height), since Section(0) is the detail section.

The color value has been preset at &HE8E8E8 (RGB(232, 232, 232)), but you may need to alter that value for your specific printer. Choosing three matching numbers for the three portions of the color will give you some variation on gray. You might try &HE0E0E0 or &HF0F0F0 if the current value doesn't look right on your printer.

The BF on the end of the Line method tells Access that you want it to draw a rectangle, rather than a line (the B does). The F, which isn't valid unless you're also using the B, tells Access to fill the rectangle.

For more information on the Line method and the DrawStyle property, see How-To 3.11.

Comments

If you have a color printer, consider altering the value of the COLOR_SHADE constant so that it actually prints out a green shading. You might also experiment with different border styles (changing the DrawStyle property of the report) to see their effect on the printed output. Most likely, your print preview will not be able to show the effects of changes to the DrawStyle property—you'll need to print the report to see those changes.

The settings you choose for your printer driver can affect the output of the gray bars. For example, using the HP LaserJet 4/4M driver, the bars looked much, much better after choosing the Line Art Images value for the HalfTones option (this option's default value is Photographic Images). You may find that settings like this for your own printer driver can make a marked difference in the appearance of grayscale colors.

3.13 HOW DO I... COMPLEXITY: INTERMEDIATE

Keep a report from breaking at an inappropriate place?

Problem

Access 2.0 introduced the KeepTogether property for report groups, which I can use to keep a whole group together or to ensure that a group header won't print without at least one detail item. However, when a single detail item requires many lines of print, I may not want to keep the entire detail item together, but I do want to have a reasonable number of lines under the header, so it won't be the last line on a page. How do I make a report start a new page while printing a single detail item rather than print the group header with just a single detail line at the bottom of a page?

Technique

You can use code called from a report's Format event to evaluate the length of a report page before it actually prints and take an action only if certain criteria are met (in this case, the action is activating a page-break control). This technique makes use of the ahtConditionalBreak function and a page break control.

Steps

Open 03-13.MDB and preview rptBusinessAddressesByCategory1. This typical business address report, which has its detail section's KeepTogether property set to Yes, occasionally prints a page with the Category group header as the last line of the page, as shown in Figure 3-25. Follow these steps to use ahtConditionalBreak to force a page break if there is not enough room to print at least one line of text from the detail section under a group header.

1. To make the ahtConditionalBreak function available to your database, import the basConditionalPageBreak module (03-13.MDB already contains this module).

2. Open the report in design view, and go to the group header you want to keep together with some text. Insert a page break control above any other controls in this group section (you may need to move some controls down a bit).

3. Open the group header properties sheet and set ForceNewPage to None and KeepTogether to Yes (this ensures that the group section itself won't be broken up).

4. Enter the following expression in the OnFormat property (substituting the name of your page break control for PageBreak1, if it is different):

```
=ahtConditionalBreak ([Report],12600,[PageBreak1])
```

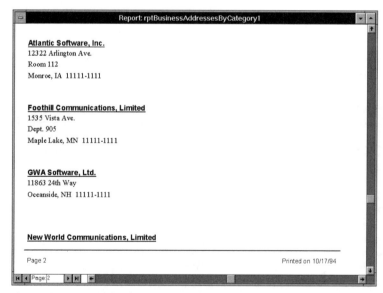

Figure 3-25 Report with a group header on the last line of a page

Use 12600 to indicate that you want a break at 8.75 inches (8.75 inches * 1440 twips/inch = 12600 twips).

5. Adjust the twips amount (the function's second argument) as necessary until the report is breaking appropriately (see the "Comments" section below).

6. Set the detail section's KeepTogether property to No, to allow it to break.

7. Print the report. Figure 3-26 shows the top of page 3 on the modified report (rptBusinessAddressesByCategory2), with the New World Communications header at the top of the page, together with its address.

How It Works

The ahtConditionalBreak function forces a page break if the section would print at or below the specified location on the page, in twips. This function has three arguments: the report name, the amount in twips, and the name of the page break to activate if the section's location is at or below the specified position.

Comments

Here is the ahtConditionalBreak function:

```
Function ahtConditionalBreak (rpt As Report, intBreak As Integer, ctl As Control)

On Error GoTo ahtConditionalBreakError

   ctl.Visible = (rpt.Top >= intBreak)

ahtConditionalBreakExit:
   Exit Function

ahtConditionalBreakError:
   MsgBox Error$
   Resume ahtConditionalBreakExit

End Function
```

Figure 3-26 Modified report, with the ahtConditionalBreak function keeping address lines together with their header

Don't let the expression

`ctl.Visible = (rpt.Top >= intBreak)`

confuse you. Access evaluates the expression to the right of the equal sign, (rpt.Top >= intBreak), as either True or False, and then assigns that value to the expression on the left of the equal sign. Therefore, the page break control's visibility is set to either True or False, depending on whether or not the current page top has gone beyond the value in intBreak.

You will need to experiment with different numbers for the twips argument until you get it working right for your report. Start by measuring the amount of vertical space needed to print a group header, together with the minimum number of lines you want to print under it. Add to this amount the height of the page footer. If you are measuring in inches, multiply this sum by 1440 to convert it to twips; if you are measuring in centimeters, multiply the amount by 567. Subtract the resulting amount from the total height of the page in twips (15,840 for a standard letter-sized sheet in portrait orientation). This will give you a starting point. Adjust as necessary until the report starts a new page, unless there is enough room to print the number of lines you want under a group heading.

The following calculations were used for the sample report:

```
Header + 1 address line = 1.25"
footer =                  1"
                          _____
                          2.25" = 3,240 twips

Page height =             15,840 twips
                          -3,240 twips
                          _____
                          12,500 twips
```

You can determine the amount of blank space to leave between the bottom of the last address on a page and the footer by changing the twips value in the ahtConditionalBreak function. The current value allows a generous amount; to save space, you can reduce the twips argument to a few hundred twips.

For many cases, you may find the built-in KeepTogether properties quite adequate. They work as follows:

- **To keep the contents of a section together:** Set the section's KeepTogether property to Yes in its properties sheet. This property can be set for report header, group header, detail, and report footer sections, regardless of whether or not they are also report groups.

- **To keep a group together:** Set the group's KeepTogether property to Whole Group in the Sorting and Grouping window.

- **To keep a group together with the first detail item:** Set the group's KeepTogether property to With first detail in the Sorting and Grouping window.

On a multicolumn report, KeepTogether does not work properly with group headers. Even when you have WholeGroup selected for a group header's KeepTogether property, the header will be separated from its detail items and placed in a different column. See rptBusinessAddressesByCategory3 in the sample database for an example of this problem.

4

Developing and Distributing Applications

HOW DO I...

This chapter is a compendium of tips and suggestions for making your application development go more smoothly and your applications more professional. You'll learn how to easily convert queries into embedded SQL strings that provide data for forms or reports. You'll learn how to build an object inventory so you can document your applications better, and how to disable screen output more effectively. You'll find tips on discerning the current language version of Access, and modifying text in error messages and on forms and reports to accommodate the current language. You'll see how to set and restore the Access caption, and how to set values in the MSACC20.INI that you probably didn't know about (unless you also use the Access runtime version). You'll learn to use some of the tools in the MSAU200.DLL library, which will allow you to use the Windows common File Open/Save dialogs, copy DOS files from place to place, and use the Windows common color-choosing dialog. The final three topics concern application distribution: clearing out test data before shipping your application, managing forms to make the best use of resources versus speed, and packaging an add-in for distribution.

Some of the techniques in this chapter use Windows API calls, and some use a library that's not part of Windows, but actually part of Access itself. This library, MSAU200.DLL, was written by the Access development team to help the Access Wizards perform some of their wizardry. The Wizards are Access Basic code, just like your applications, so nothing's keeping you from using this library yourself (except, of course, the fact that Microsoft didn't document it). How-To's 4.4 and 4.7 through 4.9 all use this library, and the sample databases for these topics include the necessary declarations for calling the functions included in the MSAU200.DLL library.

IMPORTING DUPLICATE MODULES

As in other chapters, many of the particular modules used in the example databases here are duplicated in multiple databases. In the instructions for implementing the functionality in your own applications, when the steps indicate that you should import one or more modules, import only the ones you don't already have. Modules with the same name in different sample databases all include the same code.

4.1 Convert Access 1.1 record or row source queries into SQL statements

Access 2.0 has removed the length limit that previously made it impractical to use SQL statements as sources for most combo boxes, forms, and reports. This How-To will demonstrate how to remove queries whose only purpose was to create row sources, and use SQL statements in the properties sheet instead.

4.2 Build an object inventory

As a developer, you often need to build an inventory of objects in your database. This How-To will show how to scan Access object collections and build a table containing information about each of the objects in your database.

4.3   *Really* hide Access screen activity
Sometimes you need more control over screen repainting than what you get with either Application.Echo or Form.Repaint. You can instruct Windows to stop updating a certain window and all its children. This How-To will demonstrate the use of the LockWindowUpdate API call, which almost always provides a clean way of disabling screen updates in Access.

4.4   Find out what language version of Access is installed
If you distribute applications to international users, certain parts of your code may depend on the specific version of Access that's installed at a site. If you're using SendKeys, for example, you may need to alter the strings you're using to accommodate a particular language. This How-To will show how you can determine which language version of Access is currently running, using a function in MSAU200.DLL.

4.5   Internationalize text in applications
This How-To will present some issues and some solutions to the problems involved in internationalizing your applications. This complex topic could take up several chapters, so we'll only cover some of the most important aspects, including message tables and altering forms and message boxes.

4.6   Change and reset the Access caption bar
As part of your application, you may need to change the Access caption bar (which normally contains the text "Microsoft Access") to something more appropriate for your application. This How-To will show how you can store the current caption, change it to match your preferences, and then put the caption back the way it was once you're done.

4.7   Use the Windows File Open/Save common dialogs
Windows provides common File Open and Save dialog boxes used by most applications. Access doesn't make these available to you directly, but you can get to them easily by using an interface function in MSAU200.DLL. This How-To will show you how to use this function, and the meaning of all the options that are available when you call the function.

4.8   Copy files within Access
You may need to copy files from one location to another as part of your applications, but Access doesn't make this possible without doing some work: You must either use the Shell function to have DOS do the work or write Access Basic code to do the copy for you. Or you can call a function in MSAU200.DLL, which makes a File Copy operation as simple as possible. This How-To will show you how to use this simple file-copying interface.

4.9   Use the Windows color-choosing common dialog
When you want to choose colors within your applications, you'll probably want to use the standard Windows common color-choosing dialog. Though Access doesn't make the common dialogs available to you directly,

MSAU200.DLL again comes to your aid. This How-To will show you how you can use this library to provide color-choosing capabilities for your applications.

4.10   Clean test data out of a database when it's ready to ship
In the process of designing and testing a database, you'll normally put in some simple test data to verify that everything is working right. When it's time to ship the database to a client, you'll need to remove this data. This How-To will demonstrate a method of automatically removing test data without worrying about referential integrity or losing permanent lookup table data.

4.11   Manage forms for fastest possible response time
If you switch frequently among forms in your application, the constant loading and unloading of forms will make the application appear to perform more slowly. This How-To demonstrates a method of switching quickly from form to form by manipulating their Visible properties. This will increase the perceived speed of your application at the expense of some additional memory and resource usage.

4.12   Package an add-in for distribution
Access 2.0 makes it much easier to load add-ins (Wizards, Builders, and other extensions to the core Access functionality). When your add-in is working correctly, you can add that last little bit of polish by packaging it for automatic Access installation. This How-To will show you how to make your add-in available via the Add-In Manager, as well as how to use Access security to hide the details of your work from other eyes.

4.1   HOW DO I... COMPLEXITY: EASY

Convert Access 1.1 record or row source queries into SQL statements?

Problem
Access 2.0's Query Builder makes it easy to create embedded SQL statements as row sources for combo boxes, or record sources for forms and reports. I now prefer to use SQL statements for row and record sources, since it reduces the number of unnecessary objects in my databases. I have converted a number of my databases from Access 1.1 to Access 2.0, and now I would like to convert all their row and record source queries to SQL statements. Is there an easy way to make these conversions?

Technique
There is no automatic conversion utility to transform queries into SQL statements, but you can use the View SQL button on the Query Design toolbar to display a query's SQL statement, copy it to the Windows Clipboard, and then paste it into the RecordSource or RowSource property of a form or combo box.

Steps

Open 04-01.MDB and look at frmCompanyAddresses. This form has a simple query as its record source, and the combo box in its header also has a query as its row source. Neither of these queries is needed elsewhere, so they are prime candidates for conversion into SQL statements. Take the following steps to convert a query into an SQL statement, using the form's record source query as an example. These steps have already been taken for the form frmCompanyAddresses1, both for the form's RecordSource property and for the combo box's RowSource property.

1. Open the form whose RecordSource you want to convert to an SQL statement in design view, and make sure that the properties sheet is open (Figure 4-1).
2. Click on the Build button (...) next to the RecordSource property to open the Query Builder for the record source query.
3. With the Query Builder open, click on the View SQL button on the toolbar or select View|SQL.
4. The SQL window opens, displaying the query as an SQL statement, as shown in Figure 4-2.
5. Highlight the entire SQL statement, and press (CTRL)-(C) or select Edit|Copy to copy it to the Clipboard.
6. Close the SQL window.
7. Highlight the query name in the RecordSource properties sheet, and press (CTRL)-(V) or select Edit|Paste to replace the query name with the SQL statement. Figure 4-3 shows the form's RecordSource property with the SQL statement in place.
8. Delete the original RecordSource query from the Database Container.

How It Works

Most Access queries can be converted back and forth between the graphical representation shown in the Query Builder window and the SQL representation of the query. The SQL window makes it easy to extract a query's SQL statement and use it directly as a record source or row source, or in Access Basic code. Since all queries in Access can be represented as an SQL statement, you have a choice—you can base a form or report on a query, or you can supply the SQL string directly in the properties sheet.

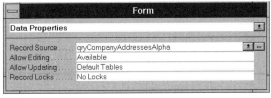

Figure 4-1 A form's properties sheet, with a query as its RecordSource property

Figure 4-2 SQL window for a simple query

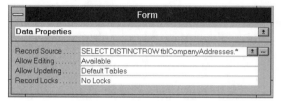

Figure 4-3 A form with an SQL statement as its
RecordSource property

Comments

By converting row source queries into SQL statements you eliminate many
trivial queries that have no purpose other than filling forms or combo boxes. In
addition, embedded SQL is much less likely to be inadvertently altered by end
users. In Access 2.0, if you have an SQL statement as a record source or row
source, you can open the Query Builder window to view or modify it, which
makes it much easier to use SQL statements in place of queries.

Two caveats: If you use the same complex query as a row source for several
different database objects, and especially if you anticipate changing the query,
it may be best to leave the query as a query object rather than converting it
into an SQL statement. If you use one query as a record source for several forms
or reports, when you change the query, the changes will be picked up by all
the forms or reports that use it. Also, Access can precompile queries. Once
you've set up a query in the Query Builder, Access compiles it and stores the
compiled version with the query itself. This can help speed query load times.
When you base a form or report on an SQL string instead of a query, you're
forfeiting the option of precompiling the query.

In some cases you may need to convert an SQL statement into a query (for
example, if you need to use it as a record source for several forms or reports). In
that case you can simply reverse the above steps: Open the SQL statement in
the Query Builder window, and then save it as a named query, which you can
use as a record source for other database objects.

4.2 HOW DO I...

COMPLEXITY: INTERMEDIATE

Build an object inventory?

Problem

In order to document my application, I'd like to be able to create a list of all
the objects in my databases, including their owners, date of creation, and date
of last update. I'm sure I can do it manually, but is there a better way to create
a table containing all this information?

Technique

Access's DAO (Data Access Objects) can give you the information you need. By
programmatically working your way through each of Access's container
collections, you can add a row to an inventory table for each object in your

application, storing away information about that object. Hopefully, you'll be able to use the techniques for this operation to write your own code, which you can use for enumerating other collections in Access. There are a few tricks along the way, and this How-To discusses those, but in general this is a very straightforward project.

Steps

To create an object inventory for your applications, you need take only two steps:

1. Import zsfrmInventory from 04-02.MDB into your own application.
2. Load and run the form. Once the form is open, click on the Create Object Inventory button. This creates the inventory table and fills it with information about all the objects in your database. Figure 4-4 shows the form, once it's been run on a sample database.

How It Works

In this topic, how it works is a lot more interesting than the final product. The object inventory itself can be useful, but the steps in creating the inventory may be more useful to you in the long run. All the code examples used in this section come from the form module attached to zsfrmInventory (in 04-02.MDB).

Starting the process

When you click the Create Object Inventory button on zsfrmInventory, you execute the following code. (The *zs* prefix, by the way, reminds you that zsfrmInventory is a system form, used only by your application. The *z* forces this form to sort to the bottom of the Database Container, so you won't get it confused with your "real" forms.)

```
Sub cmdCreateInventory_Click ()
    On Error GoTo CICError
    DoCmd Hourglass True

    CreateInventory
    Me!lstInventory.Requery

CICExit:
    DoCmd Hourglass False
    Exit Sub

CICError:
    Resume CICExit
End Sub
```

This code turns on the hourglass cursor, and then calls the CreateInventory subroutine. This procedure fills tblInventory with the object inventory and can take a few seconds to run. When it's done, the code requeries the list box that displays the list on the form, resets the cursor, and exits.

Documenting All the Containers

The CreateInventory subroutine first creates the tblInventory table. If CreateTable succeeds, CreateInventory then calls the AddInventory procedure for each of the Access containers (Tables, Forms, Reports, Scripts, and Modules) that represent user objects. (Tables and Queries are lumped together in one container. As you'll see, it takes a bit of extra effort to distinguish them.) Since each of the AddInventory procedure calls writes to the status bar, CreateInventory clears out the status bar once it's done, using the Access SysCmd function. The following code fragment shows the CreateInventory subroutine:

```
Sub CreateInventory ()
    Dim varRetval As Variant

    If (CreateTable()) Then
        ' These routines use the status line,
        ' so clear it once everyone's done.
        AddInventory "Tables"
        AddInventory "Forms"
        AddInventory "Reports"
        AddInventory "Scripts"
        AddInventory "Modules"

        ' Clear out the status bar.
        varRetval = SysCmd(SYSCMD_CLEARSTATUS)
    Else
        MsgBox "Unable to create tblInventory."
    End If
End Sub
```

Creating the Inventory Table

The CreateTable function prepares the tblInventory table to hold the current database's inventory. The function first checks to see whether the table already

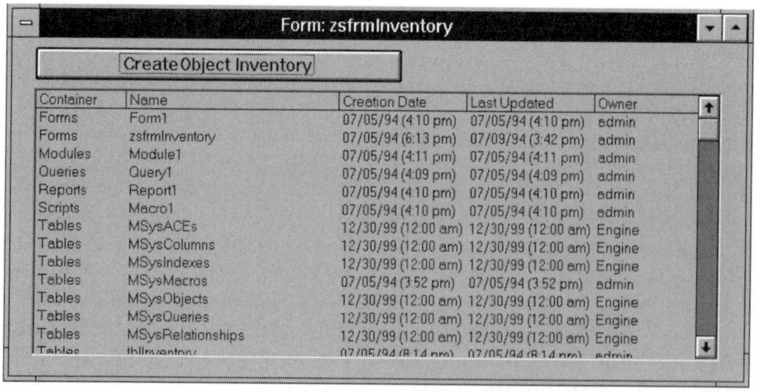

Figure 4-4 The inventory-creating form, zsfrmInventory, once it has done its work on a sample database

exists. To do this, it calls the isTable function. This function attempts to retrieve the Name property of the object from the database's TableDefs collection. If this doesn't trigger a runtime error, then that table must indeed exist. The code will also use this function later to distinguish a table from a query. Since attempting to retrieve a query's name from the TableDefs collection will certainly fail, you can use the isTable function to know whether or not an element of the Tables container (which contains both tables and queries) is a table.

```
Function isTable (ByVal strName As String)
    Dim db As Database
    Dim tdf As TableDef

    On Error Resume Next

    Set db = DBEngine.Workspaces(0).Databases(0)

    ' See the explanation below as to why
    ' this is commented out.
    'db.Tabledefs.Refresh
    Set tdf = db.TableDefs(strName)

    isTable = (Err = 0)
    On Error GoTo 0
End Function
```

USING THE REFRESH METHOD
Normally, before retrieving information about any Access persistent object collection (TableDefs, QueryDefs, and so on), you must refresh the collection. Since Access doesn't keep these collections up to date unless necessary, it's possible that a table recently added by a user in the user interface might not yet be added to the TableDefs collection. In this case, however, you'll be calling isTable repeatedly. In order to speed the operation of zsfrmInventory, the isTable function used here does not use the Refresh method each time it's called. It counts on the caller to have refreshed the collection. In almost any other use besides this one, you'd want to "uncomment" the call to the Refresh method in the code example and allow the code to refresh the collection before checking for the existence of a particular table.

Once the code has determined the presence or absence of tblInventory, it can decide what action it needs to take. If the table does exist, it just deletes all the rows. If not, it must create the table from scratch. The following code fragment, from CreateTable, does the work. If it needs to create the table, it uses a DDL (Data Definition Language) query, (new in Access 2.0) to do its work. CreateTable returns True if it succeeded and False if it failed.

```
' Refresh the TableDefs collection just
' once, before you use it the first time.
db.TableDefs.Refresh


' Empty out tblInventory if it exists,
' or create it if it doesn't.
If isTable("tblInventory") Then
    strSQL = "Delete * from tblInventory;"
Else
    strSQL = "CREATE TABLE tblInventory (Name Text (255), "
    strSQL = strSQL & "Container Text (50), "
    strSQL = strSQL & "DateCreated DateTime, "
    strSQL = strSQL & "LastUpdated DateTime, "
    strSQL = strSQL & "Owner Text (50), ID Counter "
    strSQL = strSQL & "Constraint PrimaryKey PRIMARY KEY)"
End If
' In either case, run the SQL string to empty
' or create the table.
Set qdf = db.CreateQueryDef("", strSQL)
qdf.Execute
```

Documenting Each Container

The AddInventory subroutine is the heart of the inventory-creating operation. In Access, each database maintains a group of container objects, each of which contains a number of documents. These documents are the saved objects of the container's type, such as tables, forms, reports, scripts (macros), or modules. Therefore, for each container, AddInventory looks at each document, adds a new row to tblInventory for each, and copies the information into the new row of the table. (All the code examples in this subsection come from AddInventory, in zsfrmInventory's module.)

The first step is to set up the necessary object variables:

```
Set wrk = DBEngine.Workspaces(0)
Set db = wrk.Databases(0)
Set con = db.Containers(strContainer)
Set rst = db.OpenRecordset("tblInventory")
```

The code then loops through each document in the given container, gathering information about each document:

```
For intI = 0 To con.Documents.Count - 1
...
Next intI
```

For each document the code must first determine, if this is the Tables container, whether the given document is a table or query. It does this by calling the isTable function mentioned earlier in this How-To. The result of this code fragment is to fill a string variable, *strType*, with the type of the current document (Tables,

Queries, Forms, Reports, Scripts, or Modules). This value will be written to tblInventory along with the document information, as shown here:

```
Set doc = con.Documents(intI)

' Handle the special queries case.
' Tables and queries are lumped together
' in the Tables container.
If strContainer = "Tables" Then
   strType = IIf(isTable(doc.Name), "Tables", "Queries")
Else
   strType = strContainer
End If
```

CACHING OBJECT REFERENCES

Note that the previous code sample sets up a variable, doc, to refer to the current document. Though this isn't necessary, it does accelerate the code. Since later code will refer to this particular document a number of times, it's more efficient to set up this direct reference than to ask Access to parse the general reference, con.Documents(intl), each time it needs to refer to the document. In general, any time you will need to refer to an object more than once, you can make your code run a little better by setting an object variable to refer to that object. This will save Access from having to look up the object each time.

Once AddInventory has determined the correct value for strType, it can add the information to tblInventory. AddInventory retrieves the various properties of the document, referred to by *doc,* and copies them to the current row in tblInventory, referred to by *rst.* Once that is done, AddInventory uses the recordset's Update method to commit the new row.

```
rst.AddNew
   rst!Container = strType
   rst!Owner = doc.Owner
   rst!Name = doc.Name
   rst!DateCreated = doc.DateCreated
   rst!LastUpdated = doc.LastUpdated
rst.Update
```

Using Transactions

If you look at the code in zsfrmInventory, you'll notice that the entire loop that was just discussed is surrounded by statements that begin and commit a transaction:

```
wrk.BeginTrans
.
.
.
wrk.CommitTrans
```

These methods of the workspace object are normally used to allow for rollbacks of failed transactions. In this case, however, they're being used to accelerate the operation. Since file activities inside a transaction are cached, and aren't actually written to disk until the code executes the CommitTrans method, wrapping disk-intensive activity inside a BeginTrans/CommitTrans pair can make a big difference in speed. For small applications, this speed difference won't be visible. For large applications that include many hundreds of objects, you should notice the difference.

Avoiding Errors

The list box on zsfrmInventory has the following expression as its RowSource property:

```
SELECT DISTINCTROW tblInventory.Container, tblInventory.Name, ⇒
Format([DateCreated],'mm/dd/yy (h:nn am/pm)') ⇒
AS [Creation Date], Format([lastUpdated],⇒
'mm/dd/yy (h:nn am/pm)') AS [Last Updated], ⇒
tblInventory.Owner FROM tblInventory WHERE ⇒
Name Not Like "~TMP*" ORDER BY tblInventory.Container, ⇒
tblInventory.Name;
```

There are two issues of note here. First, the SQL string used as the RowSource pulls data from tblInventory. It's quite possible, though, that when you load the form, tblInventory doesn't exist. To avoid this problem, the form's Error event catches and disregards this problem. The following code fragment, taken from zsfrmInventory's module, shows how you can check for a specific error, and if that's the particular error that triggered the Error event, tell Access to just disregard it.

```
Sub Form_Error (DataErr As Integer, Response As Integer)

    ' It's quite possible that the list box's row source
    ' (tblInventory) might not be there at this point.
    ' If that's the error, just keep going. It'll get
    ' there when you press the button.

Const ERR_NO_SOURCE = 3078

    If DataErr = ERR_NO_SOURCE Then
        Response = DATA_ERRCONTINUE
    End If
End Sub
```

The second thing to bear in mind is that Access doesn't always keep the collections completely up to date. You may find deleted objects in the collections. These deleted objects have a name starting with ~TMP. You'll most likely not want to include these objects in the inventory, so they are excluded by the SQL string used as the list boxes' RowSource. They'll still be in tblInventory, though, so if you create a report based on that table, you'll want to exclude them then, too.

Comments

A complete discussion of Access's Data Access Objects is far beyond the scope of this book. It could (and does) fill many more pages in manuals and online help than this book can incorporate. For more information, start with the diagram on the back of the Access "Building Applications" manual. This diagram shows the relationships between various collections and the objects they contain. From there, work through examples like this one (and others in this book that use DAO to do their work), and the examples in Access's online help. Once you get the hang of it, DAO is straightforward.

You might wonder why this application uses the Access containers to retrieve information about Tables and Queries, since this requires a great deal more effort than if the code had just used the TableDefs and QueryDefs collections. It makes more sense to use the Tables container instead because the TableDefs/QueryDefs collections don't contain information about the owner of the objects. Since that's the information this application is attempting to track, it must use the containers. That's the only way to gather the necessary information.

4.3 HOW DO I...   COMPLEXITY: INTERMEDIATE

Really hide Access screen activity?

Problem

I can use a form's Painting property to disable updates to that form, and the Application.Echo method to disable updates to the Access window, but some activities still seem to show through. For example, when I need to open reports in design mode to alter print settings, the screen flashes a lot. Is there any way to *really* hide screen activity?

Technique

You've already exhausted the alternatives in Access for controlling the screen display. There is one more alternative: Windows itself allows you to disable screen updates for a window and all its children. If you can get the handle for the main Access window (and you can, of course, using the ahtFindAccessHWnd function supplied in the example database 04-03.MDB), then you can disable all updates to that window. This How-To demonstrates a method of truly shutting off screen updates to the Access window. (Before you try it, however, be sure to read our cautions in the "Comments" section.)

Steps

Load and run frmLockScreen (Figure 4-5) from 04-03.MDB. This sample form does nothing more than open three reports in design mode, and then close them. (This is just the sort of thing you might do when changing the prtDevMode or prtMip property of a report; see Chapter 5.) The form includes a check box that allows you to run the test with screen updates enabled or disabled. Try it both ways, and you should see a clear difference between the two ways of running the test. With the check box set, the underlying code disables screen updates, so you shouldn't see the reports' icons pop up. Without the check box set, you will see the icons.

To use the Windows API to disable screen updates in your own applications, follow these steps:

1. Include the modules basGetHWnd and basLockScreen from 04-03.MDB. These modules include the API declarations and code to find the Access window handle and to disable updates to that window.

2. When you want to disable screen updates, call the ahtShowUpdates subroutine, passing a False value. To reenable screen updates, call the subroutine again, passing it a True value:

```
ahtShowUpdates False
' Do your work in here...
ahtShowUpdates True
```

How It Works

The ahtShowUpdates subroutine (in basLockScreen) does its work by calling the Windows API function, LockWindowUpdate (aliased as aht_apiLockWindowUpdate). This function takes as its only parameter a window handle. If that handle is nonzero, Windows just stops updating the contents of that window onscreen. If the handle is 0, Windows reenables screen updates to the locked window.

Since the only window you care about locking in Access is the main Access window itself, the ahtShowUpdates routine shields you from any of the details. If you pass it a False value, it blocks window updates. If you pass it a True

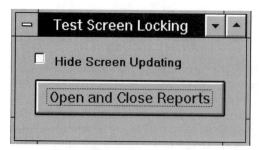

Figure 4-5 The sample form, frmLockScreen,
ready to run its tests

value, it reenables updates. It finds the Access window handle for you, if necessary, and then calls LockWindowUpdate.

```
Sub ahtShowUpdates (fShow As Integer)
   Dim hWnd As Integer
   Dim intRetval As Integer

   If fShow Then
      intRetval = aht_apiLockWindowUpdate(0)
   Else
      hWnd = ahtFindAccessHWnd()
      intRetval = aht_apiLockWindowUpdate(hWnd)
   End If
End Sub
```

Comments

Though effective, this method of disabling screen updates isn't perfect. Since Access has no idea that you've "turned it off," Access itself turns screen updates on, occasionally. For example, depending on how you open forms and reports in design mode, hiding the properties sheet completely may be very difficult. In the sample application, 04-03.MDB, as it was shipped, the properties sheet isn't showing. If you open one of the reports, then open the properties sheet, and then save the report, no combination of Application.Echo and calls to LockWindowUpdate will completely remove that properties sheet from the screen when you open the report in design mode.

Be aware that although setting Application.Echo to False does disable updates to the Access MDI Client window (the window that contains all the Access objects), setting it back to True causes a repaint of the entire Access MDI Client window. This is why, when you run the sample in 04-03.MDB with screen updates showing, you see the report icons appear at the bottom of the screen. Each time the code in ahtOpenReport opens a report, it sets Application.Echo back to True. As a generic routine, it must do this—any routine that turns off screen display should turn it back on. The subroutine that calls ahtOpenReport, then, must surround the code with calls to ahtShowUpdates, turning off the entire display before it opens the three reports, and turning it back on once it's closed all three reports.

```
If Me!chkHideUpdates Then
   ahtShowUpdates False
End If
For intI = 1 To 3
   intSuccess = ahtOpenReport("rptReport" & intI, A_DESIGN)
Next intI
'
' You could modify the reports in design mode, here.
'
For intI = 1 To 3
   DoCmd Close A_REPORT, "rptReport" & intI
Next intI
If Me!chkHideUpdates Then
   ahtShowUpdates True
End If
```

Throughout this book, we warn you of potential pitfalls involved in the techniques presented. Few actions have as much potential for disaster as turning off screen updates, so please heed the advice in the following box.

> ## NEVER TURN OFF THE SCREEN WITHOUT AN ERROR HANDLER!
>
> Though this same advice goes for using Application.Echo or Form.Painting, it's especially true for using LockWindowUpdate. Any time you've turned off the screen display, you absolutely must include an error handler in your routine that will immediately reenable the screen updates if an error occurs. Sooner or later, a runtime error *will* occur, and your code must react to this and clean up. Users tend to do unpleasant things, such as rebooting their computer, when their screens stop dead (and that's what would happen if an error occurred while you had screen updates turned off). This can be detrimental to their data and to your application, so never consider turning off the screen unless you also include an error handler to turn it back on.

As any example of an error handler that resets screen updates would, the code executed by frmLockScreen handles errors by using the normal exit route from the routine:

```
Sub cmdOpenReports_Click ()
    Dim intI As Integer
    Dim intSuccess As Integer

    On Error GoTo OpenReportsError
    If Me!chkHideUpdates Then
        ahtShowUpdates False
    End If
    For intI = 1 To 3
        intSuccess = ahtOpenReport("rptReport" & intI, A_DESIGN)
    Next intI
    For intI = 1 To 3
        DoCmd Close A_REPORT, "rptReport" & intI
    Next intI

OpenReportsExit:
    If Me!chkHideUpdates Then
        ahtShowUpdates True
    End If
    Exit Sub

OpenReportsError:
    Resume OpenReportsExit

End Sub
```

If an error occurs while this subroutine is active, the code will jump to the OpenReportsError label, and from there will resume at the OpenReportsExit label. The code will reenable screen updates and then exit the routine. Your own code may not look exactly like this, but you must handle errors so that the screen never locks up when an error occurs.

4.4 HOW DO I...   COMPLEXITY: INTERMEDIATE

Find out what language version of Access is installed?

Problem
I distribute my applications in several countries, and my users have different internationalized versions of Access installed. I'd like my applications to make decisions based on the installed version of Access. How can I find out which language version of Access is currently running?

Technique
It would be very helpful if Access's SysCmd function returned information about the national language version, but it does not. You can use SysCmd to tell you which version *number* is running and whether it's a runtime version or not, but you'll need to go outside of Access to find its national language version. Luckily, the Access Wizards need this information, and there's a convenient entry point in the MSAU200.DLL library (which ships with Access) that you can use to retrieve the information you need. This How-To demonstrates how you can gather the language information you need.

Steps
Load and run frmLanguage in 04-04.MDB. As it loads, it calls the necessary functions to determine the currently running version of Access. Figure 4-6 shows the form after it's been loaded into a retail German version of Access 2.0. To include this functionality in your own applications, follow these steps:

1. Import the module basAccessLanguage from 04-04.MDB into your own application. This module includes constants representing the seven most likely languages and related function definitions you'll need.

2. Create a module or global variable, intLanguage, somewhere in your code. When your application starts up, make a call to ahtAccessLanguage, which will return a constant representing the current running version of Access. You can use the value of that constant throughout your application to make decisions based on the current language version of Access:

```
intLanguage = ahtAccessLanguage()
```

How It Works
Retrieving language information directly from Windows requires calling a Windows API function that is both difficult to call and returns a great deal more information than you need. The function mentioned in step 2 above, ahtAccessLanguage, calls directly into the Access-supplied library, MSAU200.DLL, which calls the Windows API to retrieve the information it

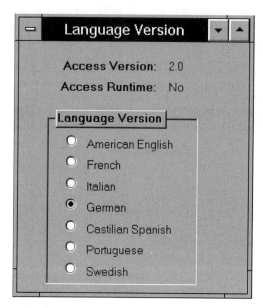

Figure 4-6 The sample form, frmLanguage, indicates the current language version of Access

needs. Though this library is not documented, several How-To's in this chapter will use it, and the Access Wizards use it to do their work. You have the rights to distribute this DLL along with any runtime applications you create.

The DLL function, aliased in the declaration as aht_apiGetLanguage, does most of the work for you and retrieves language version information that's stored with most Windows applications' executable files or DLLs. In this case, you'll use it to ask MSAIN200.DLL (one of the portions of Access itself that gets translated for national language versions) what it thinks the current version is.

Calling aht_apiGetLanguage

The call to aht_apiGetLanguage requires four parameters: two provide information about what you want, and two are filled in during the function call. The general syntax is as follows, and Table 4-1 lists the parameters and their uses.

```
intRetval = aht_apiGetLanguage(strModuleOrFile, fFileOrModule, intLang, intCharSet)
```

The following two uses are functionally equivalent:

```
Const LANG_MODULE = False
Const LANG_FILE = True

intRetval = aht_apiGetLanguage("MSAIN200.DLL", LANG_FILE, intLang, intCharSet)
intRetval = aht_apiGetLanguage("MSAIN200", LANG_MODULE, intLang, intCharSet)
```

In the first case, the function looks for MSAIN200.DLL wherever Windows normally looks for DLLs (the current directory, the Windows directory, the Windows/System directory, the DOS path, and so on). In the second case, the function looks through all the running application modules for a loaded library with the specified name. Either version will work, though the first version requires that MSAIN200.DLL be available on disk in a place Windows can find it. You could use this same mechanism to investigate the language version of any Windows executable or DLL.

PARAMETER NAME	DATA TYPE	DESCRIPTION	INPUT/OUTPUT
strModuleOrFile	String	Name of disk file or loaded module. . Specify the disk file (MSAIN200.DLL) or loaded module (MSAIN200).	Input
fFileOrModule	Integer	True if strModuleOrFile is a disk file name, False if it's a loaded module name.	Input
intLang	Integer	Filled in with the current language value.	Output
intCharSet	Integer	Filled in with the current character set.	Output

Table 4-1 Parameters for aht_apiGetLanguage and their usage

Return Values from aht_apiGetLanguage

The function fills in the values for both intLang, which tells you which language version the function found, and intCharSet, which tells you the Windows character set the application will use. Table 4-2 lists all the Windows languages and the ID values associated with them, though Access was available in only a few of these (English, German, French, Italian, Spanish, Swedish, and Portuguese) at the time of this writing.

Table 4-3 lists all the Windows character sets and their associated ID values. (The U.S. version of Access uses character set 1252, Windows Multilingual.)

The simple function in basAccessLanguage, ahtAccessLanguage, returns only the national language ID number (from Table 4-2) for the running copy of MSAIN200.DLL and disregards the character set value. Since you're likely to only need the language ID, that's all the function returns, for the sake of simplicity.

```
Function ahtAccessLanguage ()

  Dim intRetval As Integer
  Dim intLang As Integer
  Dim intCharSet As Integer

  ' Fill in intLang and intCharSet
  intRetval = aht_apiGetLanguage("MSAIN200.DLL", LANG_FILE, intLang, intCharSet)
  ahtAccessLanguage = intLang
End Function
```

LANGUAGE	ID	LANGUAGE	ID
Albanian	1052	Korean	1042
Arabic	1025	Mexican Spanish	2058
Bahasa	1057	Norwegian – Bokml	1044
Belgian Dutch	2067	Norwegian – Nynorsk	2068
Belgian French	2060	Polish	1045
Brazilian Portuguese	1046	Portuguese	2070
Bulgarian	1026	Rhaeto-Romanic	1047
Canadian French	3084	Romanian	1048
Castilian Spanish	1034	Russian	1049
Catalan	1027	Serbo-Croatian (Cyrillic)	2074
Croato-Serbian (Latin)	1050	Simplified Chinese	2052
Czech	1029	Slovak	1051
Danish	1030	Swedish	1053
Dutch	1043	Swiss French	4108
Finnish	1035	Swiss German	2055
French	1036	Swiss Italian	2064
German	1031	Thai	1054
Greek	1032	Traditional Chinese	1028
Hebrew	1037	Turkish	1055
Hungarian	1038	U.K. English	2057
Icelandic	1039	U.S. English	1033
Italian	1040	Urdu	1056
Japanese	1041		

Table 4-2 Windows languages and ID values

CHARACTER SET	ID
7-bit ASCII	0
Windows, Japan (Shift – JIS X-0208)	932
Windows, Korea (Shift – KSC 5601)	949
Windows, Taiwan (GB5)	950
Unicode	1200
Windows, Latin-2 (Eastern European)	1250
Windows, Cyrillic	1251
Windows, Multilingual	1252
Windows, Greek	1253
Windows, Turkish	1254
Windows, Hebrew	1255
Windows, Arabic	1256

Table 4-3 Windows character sets and ID values

If you find that you need the character set also, you can modify this function, or write your own, that calls aht_apiGetLanguage directly.

Comments

Once you know the ID for the national language, you can make choices in your application. As shown in the next two How-To's, you can modify labels on forms and reports, and modify the error messages that you display. For example, you'll need to be acutely cautious about the use of the SendKeys action in your applications. Because the Access menus are different in every version of Access (the position and action of each menu stays constant, but the text and the menu hotkeys change), you can't always count on your SendKeys statements to work. Most professional programmers using Access 2.0 do anything they can to avoid using SendKeys. It makes Access Basic code difficult to read and maintain, and it is prone to the troubles that can occur when you're running more than one application. If you find that you just can't avoid using SendKeys, at least make sure that you check the language and react accordingly. (Using the wrong keystrokes will, at best, do nothing. At worst, the keystrokes might do something completely different than what you intended. For example, you could use code like this to handle your SendKeys:

```
Dim strKeys as String
Select Case ahtAccessLanguage()
   Case lngEnglish
      strKeys = "%vo"
   Case lngFrench
      strKeys = "%ao"
   ' You fill in the rest...
End Select
SendKeys strKeys
```

If you find that you have several SendKeys instances in your application, consider storing the key strings in a table and using the lookup mechanism suggested in the next How-To to retrieve the strings, rather than using a Select Case statement each time.

4.5 HOW DO I... COMPLEXITY: INTERMEDIATE

Internationalize text in applications?

Problem

I'd like to pop up translated error messages in my applications, based on the currently running national language version of Access. I'd also like other text on my forms and reports to automatically adjust, based on the current language version. I know there are a number of ways to do this, but I can't decide which is best. What's the best way to store and retrieve messages in multiple languages?

Technique

The translated version of Access will handle its own error messages (in the German version, for example, the Access error messages appear in German). But you do need to translate your own messages if you want your application to run smoothly in other languages. Though there are several methods for handling text, a solution that can be applied in most cases uses a table of messages, which you can look up by ID number.

Steps

Load and run frmTestMessage from 04-05.MDB. This form, shown in Figure 4-7, allows you to choose from three different languages (English, French, and Spanish) in an option group. As you choose each language, code attached to the option group's AfterUpdate event changes the captions for labels on the form and the status bar text for text boxes accordingly. To try a sample error message in the chosen language, click the Test Message button.

In each case, the messages are coming from tblMessages. This table includes a column for the message identifier (the primary key) and one column for each of the languages your application supports. Figure 4-8 shows the table, filled in for the sample application.

To include similar functionality in your own applications, follow these steps:

1. From 04-05.MDB, import the modules basAccessLanguage (which includes the procedures from the previous How-To for obtaining the current language version of Access) and basGetMessages (which looks up particular messages in tblMessages).

2. From 04-05.MDB, import the table tblMessages. This is the table you'll use to hold your messages. Delete the existing rows, if you care to. Also, you can modify the structure and add more languages.

3. Add the necessary rows to tblMessages, filling in each column with the translated text, as shown in Figure 4-8.

4. On any form for which you'd like to have language-sensitive captions and status bar text, place the message ID (the MsgNum column from tblMessages) in the Tag property for the control whose text you'd like to change. For labels, the Access Basic code you'll call is currently set up to change the Caption property, and for text boxes, the StatusBarText

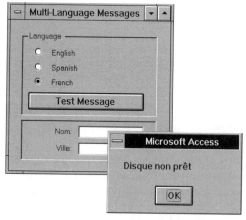

Figure 4-7 The sample form, frmTestMessage, showing the French test error message

Table: tblMessages

MsgNum	English	Spanish	French
1	The disk drive is not ready	El disco no está listo	Disque non prêt
2	Name:	Nombre:	Nom:
3	City:	Ciudad:	Ville:
4	Enter your name	Tecle su nombre	Tapez votre nom
5	Enter the address	Tecle su ciudad	Tapez votre ville
(Counter)			

Record: 1 of 5

Figure 4-8 The message table, tblMessages, filled in for the sample application 04-05.MDB

property. (If you want to include other control types, you can modify the code in the subroutine GetInfo, as described in the "How It Works" section.)

5. To set the captions for labels and the status bar text for text boxes when your form loads, place the following code in the Open event procedure for your form:

```
Sub grpLanguage_AfterUpdate ()
   ahtSetText Me.Name, A_FORM, ahtGetLanguage()
End Sub
```

The ahtSetText subroutine walks through all the controls on your form, searching for ones with a numeric value in the Tag property. For any such controls, it looks up the appropriate message and assigns it to the Caption or StatusBarText property.

How It Works

The technique presented in this How-To includes two basic pieces of functionality: retrieving the correct messages from the table of messages, and replacing all the required property values on your form or report. Together, these two operations accomplish your goals of changing labels and status bar text, and providing translated error messages.

The ahtGetMessage function retrieves the messages you need from tblMessages. You pass to it, as parameters, a long integer specifying the message number you want, and an integer specifying the correct language. This function starts by creating a table-type recordset based on tblMessages.

```
Set db = DBEngine.WorkSpaces(0).Databases(0)
Set rst = db.OpenRecordset(MSGTABLE, DB_OPEN_TABLE)
```

If there are any rows in tblMessages, the function seeks the row you've requested. If it doesn't find a match, you must have requested a message number that's not in the table, so the function returns a null value.

```
If rst.RecordCount Then
   ' Set the index, which is the message number
   rst.Index = "PrimaryKey"
   rst.Seek "=", lngMessage
   If rst.NoMatch Then
      varResult = Null
   Else
```

If it does find a match, it converts the language number into the table's column name for the language (using the GetLanguageName function). If it finds a language name, it retrieves the appropriate message from tblMessages.

```
varLanguage = GetLanguageName(intLanguage)
If Not IsNull(varLanguage) Then
   varResult = rst(varLanguage)
Else
   varResult = Null
End If
End If
```

If any error occurs along the way, ahtGetMessage returns a null value. If things work out, it returns the message it found in tblMessages.

You can call ahtGetMessage directly, perhaps to fill the text for a message box or to build up a more complex error string. In addition, the function that replaces the form text at load time calls it multiple times, once for each message. The ahtSetText subroutine does the work of replacing text when you load a form or report, and it uses ahtGetMessage to do its work.

The ahtSetText procedure takes three parameters, as shown in Table 4-4. This procedure will walk through all the controls on the requested form or report, calling the GetInfo function for each.

PARAMETER NAME	DATA TYPE	DESCRIPTION
strName	String	Name of the object to work with
intType	Integer	A_FORM or A_REPORT
intLanguage	Integer	One of the language ID's (see Table 4-2)

Table 4-4 The Parameters for ahtSetText

```
If intType = A_FORM Then
   Set frm = Forms(strName)
   For intI = 0 To frm.Count - 1
      Set ctl = frm(intI)
      GetInfo ctl, intLanguage
   Next intI
ElseIf intType = A_REPORT Then
   Set rpt = Reports(strName)
   For intI = 0 To rpt.Count - 1
      Set ctl = rpt(intI)
      GetInfo ctl, intLanguage
   Next intI
End If
```

The GetInfo subroutine does the actual work, and it is the procedure you'll need to change if you want to handle more than just labels' Caption properties and text boxes' StatusBarText properties. It checks the Tag property, and if it's numeric, looks up the associated text string in the appropriate language. Once it has the string, it checks the control type and places the string in the correct property for the given control type.

```
If IsNumeric(ctl.Tag) Then
   varCaption = ahtGetMessage(ctl.Tag, intLanguage)
   If Not IsNull(varCaption) Then
      If TypeOf ctl Is Label Then
         ctl.Caption = varCaption
      ElseIf TypeOf ctl Is TextBox Then
         ctl.StatusBarText = varCaption
      End If
   End If
End If
```

If you want to support more languages than just the three used in this example, you'll need to modify the structure of tblMessages, adding a new column for each new language. You'll also need to modify the GetLanguageName procedure in the basGetMessage module. As it is now, GetLanguageName looks like this:

```
Private Function GetLanguageName (ByVal intLanguage As Integer)
   ' Given a language identifier, get the
   ' column name in tblMessages that corresponds.

   ' This application only understands
   ' English, French and Spanish.

   Dim varLang As String

   Select Case intLanguage
      Case ahtUSEnglish
         varLang = "English"
      Case ahtFrench
         varLang = "French"
      Case ahtCastilianSpanish
         varLang = "Spanish"
   End Select
   GetLanguageName = varLang
End Function
```

Just add more Cases to the Select Case statement, matching the new columns in your messages table. The constants (ahtUSEnglish, ahtFrench, and so on) come from the module basAccessLanguage. You can add more, from Table 4-2, if you need to.

Comments

Clearly, the method suggested here will only work for forms that do not contain a large number of controls needing dynamic translation. Attempting to modify the properties of several hundred controls would increase load time for a form prohibitively. For forms that contain more than just a few controls, you might be better off creating multiple versions of the form, one per language, and distributing translated versions of your application.

Another problem you should consider when attempting to modify captions on the fly is that most non-English languages take more space to present the same information. You'll find that some languages require twice as much space (or more) as English for a given text string. This may mean that dynamic translation isn't feasible due to real estate problems. Again, the best solution is to carefully plan the translated versions and prepare a different set of forms and reports for each language.

Message boxes don't present such a problem, of course, since Access resizes them automatically to fit the data you send to them. Just call the ahtGetMessage function to provide the text for any text box you wish to fill, as in this example:

```
varRetval = MsgBox(ahtGetText(intLanguage, 1), MB_ICONSTOP, ahtGetText(intLanguage, 2))
```

4.6 HOW DO I...   COMPLEXITY: INTERMEDIATE

Change and reset the Access caption bar?

Problem
I'd like to change the caption of the main Access window as part of my application. Of course, I'd need to reset it to its original value when I'm done. Is there some way I can retrieve and set the Access caption, as I can with any of the windows within Access?

Technique
The Windows API comes to your rescue here. Retrieving and setting the Access caption both require a few steps, but neither process is terribly difficult. This How-To demonstrates the steps required to set the Access caption.

Steps
Load and run frmSetCaption from 04-06.MDB. The form displays the current Access caption. By filling in a new value in the New Access Caption text box and selecting the Set New Caption button, you can change the caption on the main Access window. Figure 4-9 shows the form once it has already done its work. Press the Reset Caption button when you're done.

To include this functionality in your own applications, follow these steps:

1. Import the modules basCaption (which supplies the necessary Windows API declarations and the interface routines) and basGetHWnd (which finds the main Access window's handle) from 04-06.MDB.

2. To retrieve the current Access caption, call the ahtGetAccessCaption function. For example:

```
strOldCaption = ahtGetAccessCaption()
```

3. To set a new Access caption, call the ahtSetAccessCaption subroutine, passing to it a string that holds your new caption:

```
ahtSetAccessCaption "Peter's Pet Palace"
```

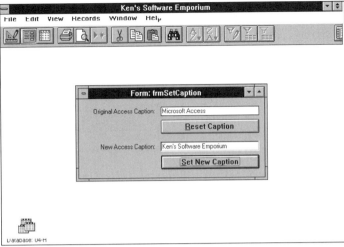

Figure 4-9 The sample form, frmSetCaption, after it has set the
new Access caption

How It Works

To retrieve the Access window caption, you call the ahtGetAccessCaption
function. Once it retrieves the Access window handle, this function in turn
calls the ahtGetWindowCaption function, which does its work in four steps:

🔑   It gets the length of the window caption, by calling the API function
GetWindowTextLength (aliased as aht_apiGetWindowTextLength).

🔑   Once it knows the length of the caption, it sizes a string buffer large
enough to hold all the characters, using the Access Basic Space function.

🔑   It calls the Windows API function, GetWindowText (aliased as
aht_apiGetWindowText), to fill the buffer with the actual window
caption. GetWindowText returns the number of characters it filled in.

🔑   It uses the Access Basic Left function to remove extra characters.

```
Function ahtGetWindowCaption (ByVal hWnd As Integer) As Variant

    ' Get any window's caption, given its hWnd.

    Dim intLen As Integer
    Dim strBuffer As String

Const MAX_LEN = 128

    If hWnd <> 0 Then
        strBuffer = Space(MAX_LEN)
```

(Continued on next page)

(Continued from previous page)

```
        intLen = aht_apiGetWindowText(hWnd, strBuffer, MAX_LEN)
        If intLen > 0 Then
            ahtGetWindowCaption = Left(strBuffer, intLen)
        End If
    End If

End Function
```

To set the Access caption, you call the ahtSetAccessCaption subroutine, passing to it the new caption you'd like to use. This procedure is much simpler than the previous one, and it requires only two steps:

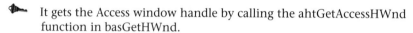 It gets the Access window handle by calling the ahtGetAccessHWnd function in basGetHWnd.

It sets the new caption, calling the SetWindowText API function (aliased as aht_apiSetWindowText), and passing as parameters the Access window handle and the new text.

```
Sub ahtSetAccessCaption (ByVal strCaption As String)

    ' Set the Access caption, to be the value in strCaption.

    Dim hWnd As Integer
    hWnd = ahtFindAccesshWnd()

    ' Set the window caption of the window you find.
    If hWnd <> 0 Then
        Call aht_apiSetWindowText(hWnd, strCaption)
    End If
End Sub
```

Comments

You can, of course, set the Access caption by specifying a value in the INI file you use when you start Access. For example, you can add a section titled "Run-Time Options" to the MSACC20.INI file and specify four different runtime settings in it, as shown in Table 4-5.

A Run-Time Options section in your MSACC20.INI might look like this:

```
[Run-Time Options]
TitleBar=Peter's Pet Palace
Icon=PETER.ICO
StartupScreen=PALACE.ICO
```

Though these items are only documented for the Access runtime version, they work just as well with the standard version of Access. By setting the title bar in the INI file, you needn't worry about setting it in your code. On the other hand, setting it in the INI file doesn't give you the opportunity to change it as your application is running.

To tell Access which specific INI file to use as it starts up, add the text

```
/ini YourFile.INI
```

to the command line. If you specify no INI file, Access uses MSACC20.INI.

OPTION	EXAMPLE	RESULT
TitleBar	TitleBar=Peter's Pet Palace	Display "Peter's Pet Palace" as Access's title bar when it starts up.
Icon	Icon=C:\ACCESS2\MYICON.ICO	Use your specified icon to represent Access when you minimize it.
HelpFile	HelpFile=C:\ACCESS2\MYHELP.HLP	Use your help file (based on your Help IDs) when a user requests help (via a menu or a keypress).
StartupScreen	StartupScreen=C:\ACCESS2\MYBMP.BMP	Display the specified bitmap as Access starts up.

Table 4-5 Available runtime options for MSACC20.INI

STARTING ACCESS WITHOUT ITS SPLASH SCREEN

Though there's no way to start Access without it showing some splash screen, you can avoid the large Microsoft Access screen if you like. To do this, specify your own bitmap in the INI file (either in MSACC20.INI or in your own). If you want to use a company logo, convert the logo into BMP format and specify that file in the INI file. If you want no splash screen at all, create a bitmap (using PaintBrush) that consists of a single white pixel. Specify this small bitmap as the StartupScreen, and you'll see no splash screen at all.

4.7 HOW DO I... COMPLEXITY: ADVANCED

Use the Windows File Open/Save common dialogs?

Problem

I need to allow users to choose file names for opening and saving files. I know that Windows supports a common way to get these names. How can I use this mechanism within Access?

Technique

Not only can you use the common File Open/Save dialogs, but the Access Wizard developers have again come to your rescue! A simple interface to these dialogs is provided in MSAU200.DLL. This How-To demonstrates the use of this interface, and lists all the options you have when using these common dialogs.

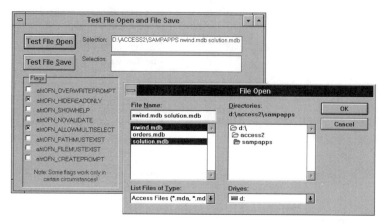

Figure 4-10 The sample form, frmTestOpenSave, showing the File Open dialog in use

Steps

Open and run frmTestOpenSave from 04-07.MDB. This sample form allows you to set various flags (described later in this How-To) and try out the settings. You can try both the File Save and File Open common dialogs. Try changing some of the settings. Figure 4-10 shows the File Open dialog, with the Read-Only check box hidden, and allowing for multiple selections.

To use this functionality within your own applications, follow these steps:

1. Import the modules basGetHWnd (if you haven't imported it already) and basCommonFile from 04-07.MDB into your own application. The basGetHWnd module provides the ahtFindAccessHWnd function, which retrieves the handle to the main Access window for you. The basCommonFile module just provides the type declarations you'll need to call the Wizard function, wlib_GetFileName, described later in this topic.

2. To use the File Open or File Save dialogs, you'll need to fill in a structure of the user-defined type, WLIB_GETFILENAMEINFO, with the values that are important to you. In the "How It Works" section, Table 4-6 lists and describes all the members of the WLIB_GETFILENAMEINFO structure, and Table 4-7 describes all the Flags options. The following sample demonstrates the minimal amount of work you'll need to do to call the dialogs yourself. This code could be used as part of a Click event procedure for a button, for example.

```
Dim gfni As WLIB_GETFILENAMEINFO
Dim lngFlags As Long
Dim strFilter As String
Dim intResult As Integer

' Set up the file filters in pairs: the first part
' of each shows the English description, and the
' second part lists the filespecs used to find files.
strFilter = "Access Files (*.mda, *.mdb)|*.MDA;*.MDB|"
```

```
strFilter = strFilter & "dBASE Files (*.dbf)|*.DBF|"
strFilter = strFilter & "Text Files (*.txt)|*.TXT|"

' Now fill in fields in the structure.
' Use the Access hWhnd as the parent for this
' dialog, so it'll be modal to Access.
gfni.hWndOwner = ahtFindAccessHWnd()
gfni.szFilter = strFilter
gfni.szTitle = "File Open"
gfni.Flags = ahtOFN_HIDEREADONLY Or ahtOFN_ALLOWMULTISELECT

intResult = wlib_GetFileName(gfni,True)
MsgBox "You chose: " & IIf(intResult = 0, Trim(gfni.szFile), Null)
```

How It Works

Though you can call directly into COMMDLG.DLL (which contains all the Windows common dialogs), the wlib_GetFileName function simplifies the work involved. The Access Wizard developers created this simple interface to relieve you of worrying about all the conversions from C-language strings to Basic strings. All you need to do is fill in the WLIB_GETFILENAMEINFO structure, call the wlib_GetFileName function, and then retrieve the results directly from the structure. Along the way, each string becomes a fixed-length string (usually 255 characters long), so you'll need to use the Trim function on any string returned as part of the WLIB_GETFILENAMEINFO structure.

The structure itself (named gfni in the example in step 2 above) contains a number of fields that you can fill in to specify how you want things to work once Windows pops up the dialog. Table 4-6 describes all the members of the structure.

Table 4-7 lists all the values you can use in the Flags member of the WLIB_GETFILENAMEINFO structure. You can use none, one, or more of these values, combined with the OR operator. For example, to hide the Read-Only check box and allow multiple files to be selected, use this code:

```
gfni.Flags = ahtOFN_HIDEREADONLY Or ahtOFN_ALLOWMULTISELECT
```

Not all of the flags make sense for both File Open and File Save operations, of course. Your best bet is to experiment with the flags, either using frmTestOpenSave from 04-07.MDB or your own code.

FIELD NAME	DATA TYPE	DESCRIPTION
hwndOwner	Integer	The handle of the dialog's owner (parent). Either the value returned from a call to ahtFindAccessHWnd, or 0 (or blank) to have Windows use 0 (the dialog will be owned by the screen, and you will be able to switch freely from this dialog to any other window in any application). Using the Access hWnd will keep you from switching to any other Access window while the dialog is up.
szFilter	String * 255	A string listing the available file filters. Leave blank to specify no filters, or use this standard format, Description1|FileSpec1|Description2|FileSpec2| placing a vertical bar (|) after each item. The items must be in pairs (description, filespec). See step 2 in the "Steps" section for an example.
szCustomFilter	String * 255	Either an empty string or a list of two items, as described in the szFilter item. This item provides the chosen filter when the dialog first opens, if it's not empty.
nFilterIndex	Long	The number of the file selection filter pair to use when the dialog first opens. The first pair is numbered 1. If 0, Windows will use the selection pair listed in szCustomFilter instead.
szFile	String * 255	The file name to use when the dialog is first displayed. After the dialog is closed, this field contains the name of the file that was chosen.
szFileTitle	String * 255	On output, the file name that was selected, without the drive and path information.
szInitialDir	String * 255	The initial directory that the dialog should use.
szTitle	String * 255	The title for the File Open/Save dialog.
Flags	Long	A combination of zero or more flags from Table 4-7 that control the operation of the dialog. Combine them using the OR operator.
nFileOffset	Integer	The number of characters from the start of the string in szFile to the location where the file name actually starts. The previous characters will contain the drive/path information.
nFileExtension	Integer	The number of characters from the start of the string in szFile to the location where the file extension starts.
szDefExt	String * 255	A default file extension to be appended to the file name if the user doesn't supply one. Don't include a period in the string.

Table 4-6 Members of the WLIB_GETFILENAMEINFO structure

CONSTANT NAME	ON INPUT	ON OUTPUT
ahtOFN_READONLY	Force the Read-Only check box to be checked.	Set if the user checked the Read-Only check box.
ahtOFN_OVERWRITEPROMPT	Issue a warning if an existing file for a File Save As operation is selected.	
ahtOFN_HIDEREADONLY	Hide the Read-Only check box.	
ahtOFN_NOCHANGEDIR	Prevent directories from being changed.	
ahtOFN_SHOWHELP	Show a Help button on the dialog. Though this option works, the button will not, so its use in Access is limited.	
ahtOFN_NOVALIDATE	Disable file name validation. Normally, COMMDLG.DLL checks the chosen file name to make sure it's valid.	
ahtOFN_ALLOWMULTISELECT	Allow selection of more than one file name (File Open only).	The szFile member will contain the chosen path followed by all the files within that path that were chosen, separated with spaces, as in: C:\ File1.TXT File2.TXT.
ahtOFN_EXTENSIONDIFFERENT		Set if the chosen file name has a different extension than that supplied in the szDefExt field.
ahtOFN_PATHMUSTEXIST	Force only valid path names to be supplied.	
ahtOFN_FILEMUSTEXIST	Force only existing file names to be supplied.	
ahtOFN_CREATEPROMPT	The dialog will prompt you if the selected file doesn't exist, allowing you to go on or make a different choice.	
ahtOFN_SHAREAWARE	Ignore sharing violations. Since Access code cannot handle the errors that occur when sharing violations occur in this code, you should not set this flag.	
ahtOFN_NOREADONLYRETURN	Force selection of files that aren't read-only and directories that aren't write-protected (File Save only).	
ahtOFN_NOTESTFILECREATE	Normally, COMMDLG.DLL tests to make sure that you'll be able to create the file when you choose a file name for saving. If set, it doesn't test, providing no protection against common disk errors.	

Table 4-7 Values that can be combined in the Flags member of the WLIB_GETFILENAMEINFO structure

Comments

The file filter (the szFilter member of the WLIB_GETFILEINFO structure) has a unique format: It consists of pairs of strings. Each item is terminated with a vertical bar (|). The first item in the pair supplies the text portion, which appears in the combo box in the lower-left part of the dialog. The second item supplies the file specifications that Windows uses to filter the list of files. Though it doesn't matter what you use in the first item, by convention, most applications use something listing the file description and then the file specification, like this:

```
Oogly Files (*.oog)
```

The full pair for this description might be something like this:

```
Oogly Files (*.oog)|*.oog|
```

If you need more items, just tack them onto the end of the list. See step 2 in the "Steps" section for an example.

Take the time to study all the fields in Table 4-6. There isn't room here to go into detail on each one, so your best bet is just to try them all out. See what happens when you place a value into one of them, and then experiment. Also, don't forget to use the Trim function on the results from the wlib_GetFileInfo function, since all strings will have been padded out to their maximum size with spaces.

Finally, remember that these dialogs don't actually *do* anything. They just supply you with the names of files: It's up to your application code to open or save the requested files.

4.8 HOW DO I...

COMPLEXITY: ADVANCED

Copy files within Access?

Problem

I'd like to copy files from one place to another, without leaving Access. Access Basic includes the ability to rename or delete files, but not to copy them. Is there a reasonable solution to this problem?

Technique

You could use the Shell function to run a DOS command to copy a file, or you could write an Access Basic routine to do the work. You don't need to do either, however, because the MSAU200.DLL library again comes to your rescue. This library contains two entry points that you might find useful: one to detect whether or not a specified file already exists, and one to copy a file from one place to another. This How-To focuses on copying files and demonstrates how to check for the existence of a file.

Steps

To try copying a file, load and run frmTestCopy in 04-08.MDB. Click on the Test File Copy button and choose an input file. If you select a file (rather than choosing the Cancel button on the File Open dialog), you'll get the opportunity to choose an output file name. If you choose a valid output file name, the code will copy the file from the input location to the output location, using the routine supplied in MSAU200.DLL. Figure 4-11 shows the sample form along with the common File Open dialog.

To copy files in your own applications, follow these steps:

1. Import the module basFileFuncs from 04-08.MDB. This module includes the necessary declaration statements and return value constants you'll need in order to use the functions in MSAU200.DLL. (The other two modules, basGetHWnd and basCommonFile, are there only to support the common File Open/Save dialog. If you're not going to use those dialogs, or if you've already imported them into your application, don't bother importing them now.)

2. To perform the Copy operation, call the aht_apiCopyFile function, passing to it the input file name and then the output file name. For example:

```
intRetval = aht_apiCopyFile("C:\AUTOEXEC.BAT", "D:\AUTOEXEC.SAV")
```

See Table 4-8 in the "How It Works" section for information on how to interpret the return value from the function.

3. To check for the existence of a file, use the aht_apiFileExists function. Pass to it the name of a file, and it will return 0 if the file doesn't exist, or a nonzero value if it does. For example:

```
intFileExists = aht_apiFileExists("DESCRIPT.ION")
```

Since Access treats 0 as False and any nonzero value as True, you can effectively treat the return value from this function as a True or False value. Be aware, however, that you cannot safely use the NOT operator or function on this return value, since it's not a true Access logical value.

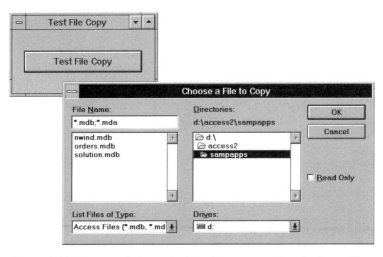

Figure 4-11 The sample form, frmTestCopy, requesting the input file name using the common File dialog

How It Works

The aht_apiCopyFile function does its work by creating a buffer in memory and then copying the input file to the output file, piece by piece. Along the way, errors might occur. The return value from your call to aht_apiCopyFile will tell you what happened during the copy operation. Table 4-8 lists all the possible return values, what they mean, and the matching Access Basic constant defined in basFileFuncs.

VALUE	CONSTANT NAME	MEANING
0	ahtFCOPY_OK	File successfully copied.
–101	ahtFCOPY_CANT_OPEN_SOURCE	Can't find or open the source file.
–102	ahtFCOPY_CANT_OPEN_DEST	Can't open the destination file (perhaps it already exists as a read-only file).
–103	ahtFCOPY_CANT_READ	An error occurred while reading from the source file.
–104	ahtFCOPY_CANT_WRITE	An error occurred while writing to the destination file.
–105	ahtFCOPY_NO_MEM	Not enough memory to copy the file.
–106	ahtFCOPY_NAME_TOO_LONG	One of the file name's lengths was too long.

Table 4-8 Possible return values from a call to aht_apiCopyFile

Though it wasn't the point of this particular How-To, the code in frmTestCopy uses the common file dialogs (see the previous How-To for more information) to get the input and output file names from you. The code looks like this:

```
Sub cmdTestCopy_Click ()
    ' Use the file open dialog to get the source and destination
    ' file names, and then copy the file from one to the other.

    Dim gfni As WLIB_GETFILENAMEINFO
    Dim strInFile As String
    Dim strOutFile As String
    Dim strFilter As String
    Dim intRetval As Integer

    ' Set up the file filters. Note the "|" character separating
    ' the pairs of options.
    strFilter = "Batch Files (*.bat)|*.BAT|"
    strFilter = strFilter & "Text Files (*.txt)|*.TXT|"
    strFilter = strFilter & "Access Files (*.mdb, *.mda)|*.mdb;*.mda|"
    gfni.szFilter = strFilter
    gfni.nFilterIndex = 3
```

```
' Set up the dialog's parent to be the
' main Access window.
gfni.hWndOwner = ahtFindAccesshWnd()

' Set the dialog box title.
gfni.szTitle = "Choose a File to Copy"

' Now get the input file name.
If (wlib_GetFileName(gfni, True) = 0) Then
    strInFile = Trim(gfni.szFile)

    ' Get the output file name.
    gfni.szTitle = "Choose a Place to Copy It"
    gfni.szFilter = strFilter
    gfni.nFilterIndex = 3
    gfni.Flags = ahtOFN_OVERWRITEPROMPT

    intRetval = wlib_GetFileName(gfni, False)
    If (intRetval = 0) Then
        strOutFile = Trim(gfni.szFile)

        ' Finally, copy the file.
        intRetval = aht_apiCopyFile(strInFile, strOutFile)
        If (intRetval = 0) Then
            MsgBox strInFile & " copied to " & strOutFile & " successfully!"
        End If
    End If
End If
End Sub
```

This subroutine fills in the nFilterIndex member of the WLIB_GETFILENAMEINFO structure, specifying which of the file filters the dialog should choose when it first appears. Also, note that you must use the Trim function to remove the excess blanks at the end of the file names returned by wlib_GetFileName. Otherwise, aht_apiCopyFile won't be able to find the file names, with all those trailing blanks. Finally, before retrieving an output file name, this code sets the Flags member of the gfni structure to be ahtOFN_OVERWRITEPROMPT. Without this flag, the code would quietly write the new file on top of an existing file. This way, if the output file exists, the dialog will ask you to verify that you want to write over an existing file.

Comments

You cannot copy a file if it's open and in use by an application. That is, you won't be able to copy the currently open database from within Access. If you try, aht_apiCopyFile will return ahtFCOPY_CANT_OPEN_SOURCE (–101), indicating that it wasn't able to open the source document.

4.9 HOW DO I...

Use the Windows color-choosing common dialog?

Problem

I'd like to be able to select colors for objects in my applications while the application is running. I know that Windows provides a standard interface for choosing colors. How can I use this standard interface within my applications? I'd also like to find a way that I can use the standard Windows system colors in my applications; that is, if the user changes the standard background color, I'd like my forms to use that same color.

Technique

Once again, the Access Wizard developers have made your life simpler. The MSAU200.DLL library includes a simple interface for you to use, allowing quick access to the standard Windows color-choosing dialog. This How-To demonstrates the use of this dialog, and explains all the options available to your application.

Color values, in Windows, are stored as the combination of their red, green, and blue (RGB) color values, ranging from 0 to 255 (&hFF in hexadecimal). For example, &hFF0000 (16711680) is solid blue, &h00FF00 (65280) is solid green, and &h0000FF (255) is solid red. Combining full red and blue, &hFF00FF (16711935), gives you bright purple. To try these out, enter either the hexadecimal values (preceded by the characters &h) or the decimal values just given into the BackColor property of a label control. When you call the common dialog, it returns the long integer representing the color you've chosen, and an array of 16 long integers representing the custom colors you've created.

Steps

To test the color-choosing dialog, load and run frmChooseColors in 04-09.MDB. This form, shown in Figure 4-12, allows you to choose the foreground and background colors for a test label, as well as the background color for the form. In addition, it shows you the custom colors you might have created and demonstrates the use of the standard Windows system colors. The following steps separate the use of color into three topics: retrieving colors using the dialog, using the custom colors, and setting colors to match the Windows system colors.

Retrieving Colors Using the Common Dialog

The Windows common color-choosing dialog allows you to select a color from 48 basic colors, or from up to 16 custom colors. Once you've opened the dialog, select the Define Custom Colors button. From these options, select the Hue, Saturation, and Luminosity (HSL) of a custom color, and then add the color to your selected list of up to 16 colors. (As you'll see in "How It Works," you can disable the creation of custom colors when you call the common dialog.) Figure 4-13 shows the dialog in action. To use the Windows common color-choosing dialog to retrieve color selections in your applications, follow these steps:

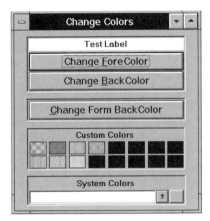

Figure 4-12 The sample form, frmChooseColors, which allows you to test the color-choosing common dialog

1. Import the two modules, basGetHWnd and basPickColors, from 04-09.MDB. The basGetHWnd module includes the ahtFindAccessHWnd function, which finds the handle of the current instance of Access for you. The basPickColors module includes the constant declarations and functions you'll need to access the code in MSAU200.DLL.

2. At the point in your application where you want to pop up the common dialog, call the ahtPickColor function, passing to it the color you'd like to

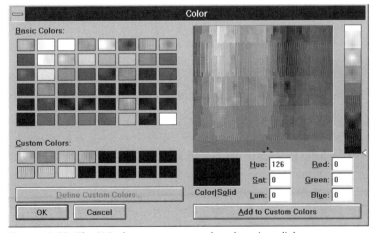

Figure 4-13 The Windows common color-choosing dialog

have chosen when the dialog first appears. For example, to call the dialog with the color of the current controls text selected, use this code:

```
Dim ctl as Control
Set ctl = Screen.ActiveControl
ctl.ForeColor = ahtPickColor(ctl.ForeColor)
```

If you need more control over options; or if, as the owner of the dialog you want to use a different window, you can call the function aht_apiGetColor yourself, rather than calling the ahtPickColor function. See the "How It Works" section for more information.

Using the Custom Colors

When you create custom colors in the common dialog, Windows sends those color values back to you as part of the data structure you passed in to the dialog. They are stored as an array of long integers, one for each of the 16 colors (with 0 representing black, or no choice at all).

If you've called ahtPickColor to select a color value, you can retrieve the custom color values by calling the ahtGetCustom subroutine in basPickColors. (If you've called aht_apiGetColor yourself, see "How It Works" for information on the data structure and the array of custom colors it contains.) To retrieve the custom colors after you've called ahtPickColor, follow these steps:

1. Create an array of long integers in your own code:

```
Dim alngCustom(16) As Long
```

2. Call the ahtGetCustom subroutine, passing to it your array:

```
ahtGetCustom alngCustom()
```

3. On return from the subroutine call, use the values in alngCustom as needed. The sample form displays them in the 16 text boxes on the form, using this subroutine in the form's module to place their values in the correct control's properties:

```
Sub FillInCustom ()
   ReDim alngColors(16) As Long
   Dim intI As Integer

   ahtGetCustom alngColors()
   For intI = 1 To 16
      Me("txtCustom" & intI).BackColor = alngColors(intI - 1)
   Next intI
End Sub
```

Setting Colors to Match the Windows System Colors

Windows supports 21 system colors (the active window colors, desktop colors, button colors, for example), which you can set by running the Colors applet on the Control Panel. Sometimes, you want to have your application match those standard Windows colors on any system. To allow this, Access supports special color numbers, one for each of the standard Windows colors.

To see these colors on an Access form, choose a color from the System Colors box at the bottom of frmChooseColors (see Figure 4-12). The code attached to this combo box's AfterUpdate event will place the appropriate color in the text box to the right of the combo box.

To use a Windows system color in your own applications, choose a value from the list shown in Table 4-9, filling in either the ForeColor or BackColor property of any form or report section, or any control. You can use either the decimal or the hexadecimal value to set the property.

DESCRIPTION	COLOR SETTING	HEX VALUE
Active border	−2147483638	&H8000000A&
Active title bar	−2147483646	&H80000002&
Active title bar text	−2147483639	&H80000009&
Application workspace	−2147483636	&H8000000C&
Button face	−2147483633	&H8000000F&
Button highlight	−2147483628	&H80000014&
Button shadow	−2147483632	&H80000010&
Button text	−2147483630	&H80000012&
Desktops	−2147483647	&H80000001&
Disabled text	−2147483631	&H80000011&
Highlight	−2147483635	&H8000000D&
Highlighted text	−2147483634	&H8000000E&
Inactive border	−2147483637	&H8000000B&
Inactive title bar	−2147483645	&H80000003&
Inactive title bar text	−2147483629	&H80000013&
Menu bar	−2147483644	&H80000004&
Menu text	−2147483641	&H80000007&
Scroll bars	−2147483648	&H80000000&
Window background	−2147483643	&H80000005&
Window frame	−2147483642	&H80000006&
Window text	−2147483640	&H80000008&

Table 4-9 Windows system colors and the properties sheet settings to use them in Access

How It Works

Though you can call directly into COMMDLG.DLL to use the color-choosing dialog, the interface in MSAU200.DLL is a lot easier. Using this simplified interface is just a matter of filling values into a user-defined data structure and calling the aht_apiGetColor function. This causes the dialog to pop up. When you're done with the dialog, the function returns the chosen value to you (along with some other information in the data structure).

The data structure itself (the type name is aht_tagGetColorInfo) has several fields that you can fill in and retrieve values from. Table 4-10 describes all the members of the structure.

FIELD NAME	DATA TYPE	DESCRIPTION
hWndOwner	Integer	The handle of the dialog's owner (parent). Either the value returned from a call to ahtFindAccessHWnd, or 0 (or blank) to have Windows use 0 (the dialog will be owned by the screen, and you will be able to switch freely from this dialog to any other window in any application). Using the Access hWnd will keep you from switching to any other Access window while the dialog is up.
rgbResult	Long	Color selection after the dialog's been dismissed. If the glrCC_RGBINIT flag is also set in the Flags field, then place the initial color setting in this field.
Flags	Long	A combination of zero or more flags from Table 4-11 that control the operation of the dialog box. Combine them using the OR operator.
rgCustColors(16)	Long	Storage for 16 custom colors, as defined by the user. To preserve the colors between invocations of your program, store the 16 colors in an INI file, and retrieve them at program startup.

Table 4-10 Members of the aht_tagGetColorInfo structure

The Flags member of the aht_tagGetColorInfo structure can contain combinations of different values (Table 4-11), controlling how the color-choosing dialog operates.

CONSTANT NAME	DESCRIPTION
ahtCC_RGBINIT	Use the color in the rgbResult field to initialize the dialog.
ahtCC_FULLOPEN	The full dialog, including the custom color portion, should be open when the dialog first appears.
ahtCC_PREVENTFULLOPEN	Only the left side of the dialog will be available (you won't be able to create custom colors).

Table 4-11 Values that can be combined in the Flags member of the aht_tagGetColorInfo structure

Retrieving Colors Using the Common Dialog

The function mentioned in the "Steps" section above, ahtPickColor, calls the DLL function aht_apiGetColor to do its work. First, ahtPickColor fills in the default color field, sets the owner's window handle, sets the Flags field, and then calls aht_apiGetColor. On return from the function call, the rgbResult field of the aht_tagGetColorInfo structure will hold the color you chose.

```
Function ahtPickColor (ByVal lngCurrentColor As Long) As Long
    ' Pick a color, and return its value, along with
    ' the current set of 16 custom colors.
    Dim lngRetval As Long

    gci.rgbResult = lngCurrentColor
    gci.hWndOwner = ahtFindAccessHWnd()
    gci.Flags = ahtCC_RGBINIT
    lngRetval = aht_apiGetColor(gci)
    ahtPickColor = IIf(lngRetval = 0, gci.rgbResult, -1)
End Function
```

If you need more control over the Flags field, or would like to use a different parent for the dialog (rather than the Access main window), you can rewrite this function for your own needs.

Using the Custom Colors

On return from the call to aht_apiGetColor, the aht_tagGetColorInfo's array of custom colors, the rgCustColors member, will hold a value for each of the 16 possible custom colors. The basPickColors module defines a module global variable, gci, of type aht_tagGetColorInfo, which it uses when it pops up the color-choosing dialog. Since the variable is global only in its module, however, it's not available from outside the module. To make the array of custom colors available to outside procedures, the module includes a subroutine, ahtGetCustom, that will copy the values from gci to an array you pass to the subroutine. (See step 3 in the "Using the Custom Colors" section of "Steps," above).

```
Sub ahtGetCustom (aCustomColors() As Long)

    ' Retrieve the custom color array from the module
    ' global variable, gci.

    Dim intI As Integer

    For intI = 0 To 15
        aCustomColors(intI) = gci.rgCustColors(intI)
    Next intI
End Sub
```

Comments

If you want to preserve the custom color choices for future sessions of your application, you can write them out to your application's INI file, using the techniques shown in Chapter 2. One solution might be to loop through them all, building up a single string, separating the values with a single space, and then storing that long string as a single item in your INI file, like this:

```
Custom Colors=255 0 1234567 34565778 ...
```

Changes made to controls' colors (as in the sample form, frmChooseColors) while the form is in any mode besides design mode won't be saved with the form. Access keeps two sets of control properties: one that's permanently set, at design time, and a temporary set, copied from the permanent values every time you run the form. If you want to save settings to your forms between sessions, you'll need to again place the values in your INI file, and load them when you restart your application. See How-To 2.9 for more information on saving and restoring program settings.

4.10 HOW DO I...

Clean test data out of a database when it's ready to ship?

Problem
I'm finished designing and building a database; it's ready to ship to my client. Before they can use it, I need to remove the artificial data I've put in, without destroying permanent lookup tables. Is there a simple way to do this without running into referential integrity problems?

Technique
One solution is to open every data table in datasheet view, select all records, press the (DELETE) key, and confirm the deletion. However, there are three problems with this simple method:

- You have to open tables in a particular order (many-side tables before their related one-side tables).

- You have to remember which tables contain test data and which ones contain production data.

- The task is tedious and repetitive.

Instead of clearing out your test data by hand, you can write a general-purpose Access Basic routine that uses a table of tables and a simple SQL statement to remove only the test data and do it in the correct order.

Steps
Open 04-10.MDB and view the tables in the database container. Open the tblFood table and try to delete some records. You'll get a referential integrity error, because there are related records in txrefFoodRestaurant. Figure 4-14 shows the relationships set up for the sample database. Now open frmDemo, and click on the Clear button to remove all of the test data from the database without any manual intervention.

To implement this technique in your own database, follow these steps:

1. Import the zstblDeleteOrder table (structure only, without data) into your own database, or create a new table with the fields shown in Table 4-12.

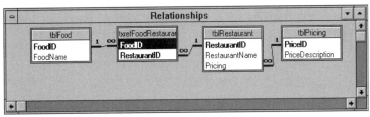

Figure 4-14 Relationships in the sample database

2. Import the module zsbasMaintain into your database, or create a new module with the single function shown here:

```
Const MB_ICON_STOP = 16

Function ahtClearData ()
' Remove all data from tables specified in zstblDeleteOrder
' Data is removed in the order specified to avoid
'   relational integrity violations
    On Error GoTo ahtClearData_Err

    Dim dbCurrent As Database
    Dim rstTables As Recordset

    Set dbCurrent = DBEngine.Workspaces(0).Databases(0)
    Set rstTables = dbCurrent.OpenRecordset("zstblDeleteOrder", DB_OPEN_SNAPSHOT)

    DoCmd SetWarnings False

    Do While Not rstTables.EOF
        DoCmd RunSQL "DELETE * FROM " & rstTables![TableName] & ";"
        rstTables.MoveNext
    Loop

    DoCmd SetWarnings True

    rstTables.Close

ahtClearData_Exit:
    On Error GoTo 0
    Exit Function

ahtClearData_Err:
    MsgBox "Error " & Err & ": " & Error$, MB_ICON_STOP, "ahtClearData()"
    Resume ahtClearData_Exit

End Function
```

FIELD NAME	DATA TYPE	FIELD SIZE	PROPERTIES
Order	Number	Integer	PrimaryKey
TableName	Text		

Table 4-12 Structure of zstblDeleteOrder

3. Open zstblDeleteOrder in datasheet view and add one record for each table you want to clear out before shipping. These tables must be listed in the order in which you want them cleared. Assign each table a unique order number, with the lowest number belonging to the first table to be cleared. Tables on the many side of a one-to-many relationship should be listed before tables on the one side of the relationship. Tables that you don't want to clear (including zstblDeleteOrder) should not be entered at all. Figure 4-15 shows the sample version of zstblDeleteOrder.
4. If you'd like a form to control the deletion process, create a new, blank form. Place one command button on the form and set the command button's OnClick property to:

```
=ahtClearData()
```

How It Works

The ahtClearData function automates the tedious task of selecting the delete order of your tables and then deleting the data table by table. You select the order when you build the zstblDeleteOrder table. The function works by opening a snapshot of this table and looping through the snapshot one line at a time. The line in the function that does the actual work is:

```
DoCmd RunSQL "DELETE * FROM " & rstTables![TableName] & ";"
```

This line concatenates the table name found in rstTables, using Structured Query Language keywords to form a complete SQL statement. If you specify tblFood as one of the tables to delete, for example, Access builds the SQL statement:

```
DELETE * FROM tblFood;
```

This is the SQL equivalent of a delete query that selects all rows from the table and deletes them. The DoCmd RunSQL statement turns this query over to the Jet engine for execution.

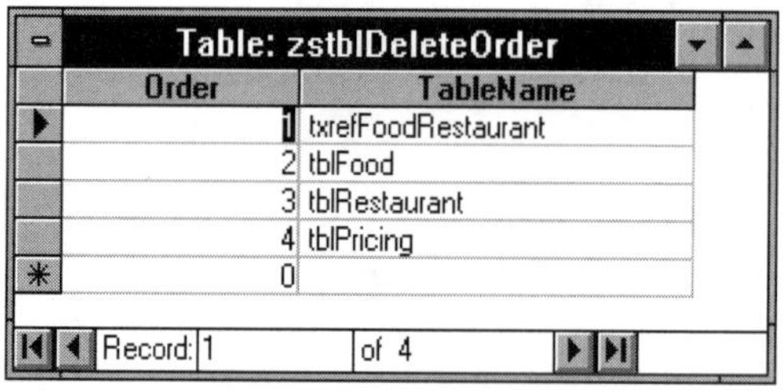

Order	TableName
1	txrefFoodRestaurant
2	tblFood
3	tblRestaurant
4	tblPricing
0	

Figure 4-15 Sample zstblDeleteOrder

Comments

The sample database has a second button, Restock, on the demo form. This button runs a macro that in turn runs four append queries, to take backup copies of the data and return them to the main data tables. This lets you test the function in the sample database more than once.

When you use this technique in your own database, be sure to compact the database before you distribute it to your users. To do this, select File|Compact Database when no database is currently open. There are two reasons to compact your database at this point:

🔑 Until you compact the database, the Access file won't shrink at all. When you delete data from tables, Access marks the data pages as empty, but it doesn't give them back to your hard drive as free file space. This only occurs when you compact.

🔑 When you compact a database, Access resets the next counter values for all counter fields. If you remove all the data from a table with a counter in it and compact the database, the next record added will have a counter value of 1.

4.11 HOW DO I...   COMPLEXITY: INTERMEDIATE

Manage forms for fastest possible response time?

Problem

My Access application is structured around forms, and users frequently have to move among forms. Access's performance seems a bit sluggish with this constant loading of forms from my disk. Is there anything I can do to decrease the forms' response time and thus accelerate my application?

Technique

Rather than opening and closing your forms, you can hide and show them. You can hide a form by setting the form's Visible property to False. Opening the form again will be very fast, because the form is still in memory. This How-To shows you how to choose which way to open each form in your application in order to better manage the trade-offs between response time and resources.

Steps

Load 04-11.MDB and open frmSwitchboardClose. This form has buttons to open five other forms, each of which has a Close button. When the forms are opened from frmSwitchboardClose, their Close buttons function normally, so reloading the form happens from your drive each time.

Now open frmSwitchboardHide and repeat the process of opening and closing forms. When the forms are opened from frmSwitchboardHide, their Close buttons are modified to hide the forms instead of closing them. Depending on the speed of your computer, you should see a difference in

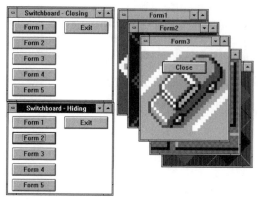

Figure 4-16 Closing versus hiding forms

response time, with forms opened from frmSwitchboardHide reopening faster than those loaded from frmSwitchboardClose. Figure 4-16 shows a sample session with both frmSwitchboardHide and frmSwitchboardClose.

To use this technique in your own applications, follow these steps:

1. Import the module basHideForms from 04-11.MDB to your own database, or create a new module (its name is irrelevant). If you've imported the module, you can skip to step 4.

2. Add a global variable to the Declarations section of your module:

```
Global fReallyClose As Integer
```

3. Add the three functions below to your new module:

```
Function ahtAutoExec () As Integer
' Runs from the AutoExec macro at startup
   On Error GoTo ahtAutoExec_Err

' Set hidable forms to hide instead of close
   fReallyClose = False

ahtAutoExec_Exit:
   On Error GoTo 0
   Exit Function

ahtAutoExec_Err:
   MsgBox "Error " & Err & ": " & Error$, MB_ICON_STOP, "ahtAutoExec()"
   Resume ahtAutoExec_Exit

End Function

Function ahtOpenForm (strFormName As String, fHide As Integer) As Integer
' Open strFormName in regular data entry mode. If fHide
' is true, initialize the form so that it hides instead of
' closes when the user tries to close it, for processing speed
   On Error GoTo ahtOpenForm_Err
```

```
    If fHide Then
        DoCmd OpenForm strFormName, A_NORMAL, , , A_EDIT, A_NORMAL, "Hide"
    Else
        DoCmd OpenForm strFormName, A_NORMAL, , , A_EDIT, A_NORMAL
    End If

ahtOpenForm_Exit:
    On Error GoTo 0
    Exit Function

ahtOpenForm_Err:
    MsgBox "Error " & Err & ": " & Error$, MB_ICON_STOP, "ahtOpenForm()"
    Resume ahtOpenForm_Exit

End Function

Function ahtQuit () As Integer
' Quit the application
    On Error GoTo ahtQuit_Err

' Set the form closing flag so that hidden forms don't
' force the application to stay open
    fReallyClose = True
    Application.Quit

ahtQuit_Exit:
    On Error GoTo 0
    Exit Function

ahtQuit_Err:
    MsgBox "Error " & Err & ": " & Error$, MB_ICON_STOP, "ahtQuit()"
    Resume ahtQuit_Exit

End Function
```

4. Create a macro with a single RunCode action, whose Function Name argument is:

```
=ahtAutoExec()
```

Save this macro as AutoExec.

5. Wherever you have a command button to open a form, call ahtOpenForm from the command button's Click event. If you want the form to be closed normally, the OnClick property should read

```
=ahtOpenForm("MyForm", False)
```

where MyForm is the name of the form to be opened. If you'd like the form to be hidden whenever the user tries to close it, use this expression in the OnClick property instead:

```
=ahtOpenForm("MyForm", True)
```

6. Wherever you have a command button to close down your application entirely, set its OnClick property to:

```
=ahtQuit()
```

7. For each form whose visibility you are managing, create an event procedure in the form's module (see this book's Introduction for more information on creating event procedures) for the form's Unload event. Enter this code in the module:

```
Sub Form_Unload (Cancel As Integer)

   If Me.OpenArgs = "Hide" And Not fReallyClose Then
      Me.Visible = False
      Cancel = True
   End If

End Sub
```

8. Save your forms. Any form opened with the ahtOpenForm function with the second argument set to True will now be hidden whenever you close it.

How It Works

When you open a form with the ahtOpenForm function and the second argument set to True, Access passes the text value "Hide" in to the form's OpenArgs property. This property, new in Access 2.0, has no direct effect on the Access user interface. Instead, it allows you to send arbitrary data to a form whenever it is opened.

When you close a form, the form's Unload event occurs. In the event procedure, the code checks to see whether the OpenArgs value of "Hide" was passed in, and whether a global flag has been set to override this value. If both the OpenArgs and the global variable agree, Access hides the form by setting its Visible property to False. It also sets the Cancel argument of the form's Unload event procedure to True. This prevents Access from continuing to close the form after it is hidden.

If you close a form and its OpenArgs property is set to anything other than "Hide", or the fReallyClose global variable is set to True, the form closes normally.

Comments

The fReallyClose global variable is necessary to provide a way to remove one of these resident forms from memory. Closing a form is not the only thing that triggers its Unload event. This event also happens whenever you switch the form from form mode to design mode, or when the application is closed with the form still open. If you didn't provide a way to override the hiding behavior, your application could not be closed.

This technique trades memory and resource usage for performance. Of the two, Windows resources are usually the more critical bottleneck. For simple forms, such as those used in the example, each open form (whether visible or hidden) takes up approximately one-half of one percent of the available system resources. More complex forms can take three to five percent. If you run too low on system resources, your computer will begin to behave strangely, and eventually it will crash. Since the technique presented in this How-To keeps forms open, you'll need to consider the speed versus memory usage issue carefully.

By using a function call to decide whether or not to hide a form when the user tries to close it, you can manage this resource usage very precisely. If you like, you can maintain a global list of open forms and open any forms beyond a certain limit in normal close mode. Alternatively, you could use the Windows GetFreeSystemResources API call to check the actual available resources before making use of this technique.

4.12 HOW DO I...   COMPLEXITY: ADVANCED

Package an add-in for distribution?

Problem
I've written an Access add-in that I'd like to distribute. I want it to install just as the built-in add-ins do, and I want to protect my source code from other developers. How can I accomplish this?

Technique
You can use Access security to protect your source code, so even people who can run your add-in can't open it in design view. To install your add-in, you can create a special table called USysAddIns, which is used to communicate information to the Add-in Manager.

Steps
The steps that follow will show you how to install and use the example builder in 04-12.MDA, how to open the builder so you can see how it works, and how to add similar features to your own add-ins.

Installing and Using the Sample Builder
1. Copy 04-12.MDA to your Access 2.0 directory.
2. Start Access and load any database. Select Add-Ins from the File menu, and then select Add-In Manager.
3. Scroll down the list of available add-ins until you find the entry for the Fragment Builder (your list will probably be different from that shown in Figure 4-17). Select the Fragment Builder, then click on Install and then Close.
4. Exit and restart Access.
5. Load any database.
6. Open a module and create a new function.
7. Click the Build button on the toolbar and select Code Fragment Builder from the list. Choose a fragment from the combo box and click the OK button to insert that fragment of code into your module. Figure 4-18 shows the Fragment Builder in use.

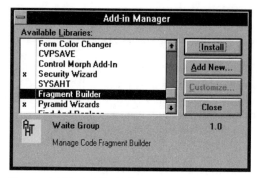
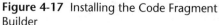

Figure 4-17 Installing the Code Fragment Builder

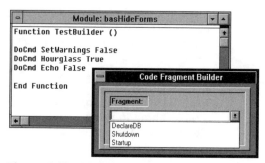

Figure 4-18 Using the Code Fragment Builder

Opening the Builder to Investigate It

The Code Fragment Builder is secured. We have included the appropriate system database so you can open the Builder's objects in design mode. To load the Code Fragment Builder with this system database, follow these instructions:

1. If you have loaded the Code Fragment Builder as a library, use the Add-In Manager to unload it.

2. Close Access.

3. Copy SYSAHT.MDA to your Access 2.0 directory.

4. Start the Microsoft Workgroup Administrator. Choose to join an existing workgroup and choose SYSAHT.MDA.

5. Start Access. In the Logon dialog box, shown in Figure 4-19, log on as user Reader with no password.

6. To load a file with an .MDA extension, you'll need to override Access's default file type in the File Open dialog. Either change the file specification to *.MDA, or just type in the name of the file you'd like to open.

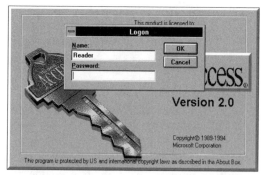

Figure 4-19 Logging on to Access once you've set the new system database

7. Since Reader is the owner of all the objects, you can now open any object in 04-12.MDA in design view.

Adding These Features to Your Own Add-in

To secure your database, you need to activate security and make sure the permissions on your database objects are properly set.

1. Run the Workgroup Administrator program that comes with Access. Click on the Create... button, and enter a unique Workgroup ID to create a secure system database.

2. Exit the Workgroup Administrator and start Access. Load any database and select Users... from the Security menu. Create a new user and add this user to the Admins group.

3. Select Security|Change Password. Change the Admin password from blank to any other password.

4. Close and restart Access. When prompted for a logon name, enter the new user that you just created. Load any database and select Security|Users to remove the Admin user from the Admins group.

5. At this point you are ready to create a secured database. You have two choices, depending on whether or not you have already created database objects that must be secured. If you have existing objects, the easiest way to secure them is to use the Microsoft Security Wizard to create a new database containing them. If you do not have existing objects, you can just secure them as you go along.

6. To secure an add-in, you need to ensure that the Admin user has no rights to any object, and the Users group has enough rights to run the add-in. Since the Admin user and the Users group are the same for every installation of Access, this will ensure that your code can be run while keeping unauthorized users away from your design. In general, most add-ins will require these permissions be given to the Users group:

🖝 **Tables:** No permissions.

🖝 **Queries:** Read Design and Read Data. If tables are to be modified, also Update Data, Insert Data, and Delete Data, as needed. All queries should have their Run Permissions property set to Owners.

🖝 **Forms and Reports:** Open/Run.

🖝 **Macros:** You should generally avoid macros in your add-ins.

🖝 **Modules:** No permissions.

7. To create an installation table for your add-in, import the USysAddIns table from one of the Microsoft Wizards. This will ensure that you get the right

definition for each field in the table. You will need to choose View|Options and set Show System Objects to Yes before this table will appear in the list of available tables to import.

8. Change the values in the imported installation table to the appropriate ones for your add-in. For the sample builder, which builds a code property, Table 4-13 shows the necessary settings.

PROPERTY NAME	VAL1	VAL2	VAL3	VAL9
AddInVersion	1.0			
CompanyName	Waite Group			
Description	Manage Code Fragment Builder			
DisplayName	Fragment Builder			
Logo				(picture)
IniFileEntry	Libraries	04-12.mda	rw	
IniFileEntry	Property Wizards	ahtCodeFragBuilder	Module, Code Fragment Builder, cf_BuildCodeFragment, rw	

Table 4-13 USysAddIns table for the Code Fragment Builder

9. Save the USysAddins table and close your database. Give it an MDA extension and it will install like any other add-in, as soon as it's copied into an Access 2.0 directory.

How It Works

Access security employs a two-part model, where users and groups have permissions on particular objects. Because the Users group is the same in every Access installation, you can assign permissions to this group knowing that anyone with Access will share in those permissions. But you can also limit all the design permissions to a unique user in your own system database so that your work is protected.

The Add-In Manager works by opening each file in your Access directory with the .MDA extension and looking in it for a USysAddins table. If it finds one, the entries in this table control the changes that the Add-In Manager makes to your MSACC20.INI file. By installing a USysAddins table in your own add-in, you can make use of this custom installation procedure.

Comments

Manipulating security in Access is complex, and covering it in detail would require far more space than we have available. The steps outlined here will work for an add-in, but for your own database systems, you'll need to dig a bit deeper. One place to start is the Security Wizard that's available from Microsoft. This tool will help you secure existing databases.

5

Taming Your Printer

HOW DO I...

Printing output is a major component of any database product, and Access gives you a great deal of control over the "look" of your forms and reports. Programmatic control over the printer itself, however, is somewhat complex in Access. Windows provides rich and intricate support for output devices, and Access attempts to shield you from most of that intricacy. Sometimes, however, you do need to take control over your output devices: You may need to change the particular device or change a setting pertaining to a particular device. Access makes this possible, but not easy. The topics in this chapter will make some of the details of handling your output devices more reasonable.

This chapter focuses on the three printer-related properties of forms and reports that are just barely documented: prtMip, prtDevMode, and prtDevNames. We'll cover these properties in detail and show examples of their use. You'll be able to retrieve a list of all the installed printers and make a choice from that list, setting the new default Windows printer. You'll learn how to modify margin settings in forms and reports, thereby avoiding the use of Access's Print|Setup dialog in your applications. You'll get help on changing printer options, such as the number of copies to print, page orientation, and printer resolution. In particular, How-To 5.5 will demonstrate how you can print to paper sizes that your printer doesn't regularly support (if your printer supports variable sized pages, of course). Finally, you'll learn how to determine which device has been selected to print a report or form and whether it's the default device. If it is, you can change the destination from your application, provide your users with a choice of output devices, and print the object to a particular device. You'll also find a development tool that will run through all your reports and let you know which of them aren't set up to print to the default printer. By ensuring that all your reports print to the default printer, you will be able to send them to any output device just by changing what Windows thinks is the default printer.

5.1   Retrieve a list of all the installed output devices

Windows stores the list of available output devices in WIN.INI. This How-To will describe how to retrieve that list and make it available on a form. The steps involve reading the information from WIN.INI a number of times, and they are a good exercise in using the Windows API functions that read from INI files.

5.2   Set and retrieve the name of the default output device

Windows stores information about the default output device in WIN.INI. This How-To will demonstrate steps for retrieving and setting the identity of the default output device.

5.3   Programmatically change margin and column settings for reports

Access provides a programmatic method for retrieving and setting margin and column settings for reports and forms: the prtMip property. Like the prtDevMode and prtDevNames properties explained in upcoming How-Tos, the prtMip property is unusual in that it's not a distinct value, but an entire data structure stored as a stream of bytes. This How-To will show how to move that unreadable stream of information into an editable data structure, and how to move it back. In addition, it will describe the prtMip property in detail.

5.4 Programmatically change printer options

Though you could use SendKeys to manipulate settings in Print|Setup dialog boxes, every printer works a bit differently and sooner or later, SendKeys will fail to perform the specific action you need. Access externalizes information about the print settings of each document that can be printed in the prtDevMode property. This How-To will show you how to change various print settings, such as the orientation and the number of copies, for any document you want to print from Access.

5.5 Print on odd-sized paper

Once you know how to analyze the printer settings stored in the prtDevMode property, you'll be able to change many of the printer settings. This How-To will demonstrate the use of this property to print on paper sizes your printer might otherwise not support. (This How-To will only work if your printer supports custom paper sizes. Most dot-matrix printers do, but most laser printers do not.)

5.6 Retrieve information about the selected printer of a form or report

Using the prtDevNames property, you can retrieve information about a form or report's selected output device. Access provides this property as a stream of bytes, like prtMip and prtDevMode, and you must take some care in "picking it apart." This How-To will provide the tools you need to crack the prtDevNames property and will tell you the device, the driver, and the output port for any form or report. In addition, you'll find out if an object is set to print to the default output device—crucial information if you want to change the output device in your applications.

5.7 Choose an output device at runtime

Given a list of available printers, this How-To will demonstrate how you can store away information about the currently chosen printer, set the default printer to be the chosen device, print your document, and then set the default printer back to its original setting. This method is particularly useful for sending documents to various fax drivers.

5.8 Determine which of my reports are not set to print to the default printer

In order to use the technique shown in How-To 5.7, the object you're trying to print must be configured to print to the default output device. If you have a large number of reports in your application, it can be difficult to track which ones may be configured to print to a specific printer. This How-To will provide a simple form and report that walks through all the reports in your application, and lists each report and whether it's been configured to print to the default output device. You'll recognize concepts from several earlier How-Tos and find some additional methods involving Data Access Objects to do the looping.

5.1 HOW DO I...   COMPLEXITY: ADVANCED

Retrieve a list of all the installed output devices?

Problem

I'd like to present my users with a list of all the installed printers, but I can't find a way to retrieve this information from Access. Is there some API call that will give me this list?

Technique

Windows stores a complete list of all the installed printing devices in WIN.INI. Retrieving the list is just a matter of using the INI-reading functions presented in Chapter 2. Windows provides a special feature, not discussed in Chapter 2, that allows you to retrieve an entire section of an INI file in one function call. This How-To uses this technique to read in the entire list of printers in one step. From there, it's a simple matter to break the resulting string into the various pieces that you'll need to provide the list of devices.

The steps involved in creating the list of printers and their output ports is, however, much more difficult because of the way Windows stores the information. This How-To presents data structures and techniques to retrieve the information that will be used throughout this chapter.

Steps

Load and run frmPrinterList from 05-01.MDB. Figure 5-1 shows the form displaying all the installed printers on a test machine. Note that one printer driver (HP LaserJet 4/4M, for example) can be installed on more than one printer port (LPT1: and LPT2:, in this case). The "How It Works" section describes, in detail, the techniques used in building the list in Figure 5-1.

To create your own list of installed printers, follow these steps:

1. Import the four modules from 05-01.MDB listed in Table 5-1.

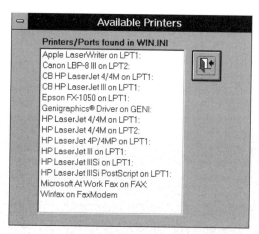

Figure 5-1 The sample form, frmPrinterList, showing the list of installed devices

MODULE NAME	PURPOSE	CONTAINS
basGetPrinters	Create an array of printers, fill a .list box with the array.	ahtGetPrinterList, ahtFillPrinterList
basINIFile	Read/write information in INI files.	ahtGetINIInt, ahtGetINIString, ahtGetPrivateINIInt, ahtGetPrivateIniString
basPrintTypes	Define data types and constants for all examples in this chapter.	
basToken	Retrieve pieces of a string: a utility module.	ahtGetToken

Table 5-1 Modules to import from 05-01.MDB

2. On a new or existing form, place a list or combo box. Set its properties as shown in Table 5-2, and set any other properties however you like.

PROPERTY	VALUE
RowSourceType	ahtFillPrinterList
ColumnCount	1
BoundColumn	1

Table 5-2 List/combo box property settings for displaying a list of output devices

How It Works

Though it's simple to use the example code we've provided (Table 5-1) to create your list of output devices, there's a lot of action going on underneath. This section is divided into subtopics, making it easier to follow the steps that ahtFillPrinterList goes through to fill that list or combo box with the list of installed devices. These subtopics focus on the code in the ahtGetPrinterList function, which ahtFillPrinterList must call to retrieve the list of devices, along with their drivers and output ports.

What's the Goal?

The goal of all the code in basGetPrinters is to fill an array with information about all the installed output devices. For each device, there are three bits of information that you're interested in: the device name, its device driver name, and the output port to which it will send its information. Since these three items are used so often as a group, basPrintTypes contains a structure definition that almost every How-To in this chapter will use to hold the information:

```
Type aht_tagDeviceRec
    drDeviceName As String
    drDriverName As String
    drPort As String
End Type
```

The first element, drDeviceName, holds the device name. The second, drDriverName, holds the name of the device driver (without its file name extension), and drPort holds the output port. Given an array of aht_tagDeviceRec structures, you can easily fill a list box (as in the sample form) or do anything else you'd like with the list.

What's in WIN.INI and How Do You Retrieve the Information?

The first step, then, is to retrieve the information from WIN.INI. Windows stores the entire list of installed devices in a section of WIN.INI, titled [devices]. In the WIN.INI that produced Figure 5-1, the section looked like this (most likely, you'll never run across a WIN.INI that contains this many different devices):

```
[devices]
Apple LaserWriter=PSCRIPT,LPT1:
Canon LBP-8 III=lbpiii,LPT2:
CB HP LaserJet 4/4M=ClikBook,LPT1:
CB HP LaserJet III=ClikBook,LPT1:
Epson FX-1050=EPSON9,LPT1:
Genigraphics" Driver=GENIGRPH,GENI:
HP LaserJet 4/4M=HPPCL5E,LPT1:,LPT2:
HP LaserJet 4P/4MP=HPPCL5E,LPT1:
HP LaserJet III=HPPCL5MS,LPT1:
HP LaserJet IIISi=HPPCL5MS,LPT1:
HP LaserJet IIISi PostScript=PSCRIPT,LPT1:
Microsoft At Work Fax=EFAXDRV,FAX:
Winfax=WinFax,FaxModem
```

Every line in the section is in this format,

DeviceName=DriverName,Port1[[*,Port2*]*, Port3*]*, ...*]

where *DeviceName* contains the string the user sees as the name of the device, *DriverName* contains the actual device driver name (without its file extension), and *Port1, Port2* (and so on) contain the output ports to which the device has been connected.

To retrieve the list from WIN.INI, you can call the GetProfileString API function, which was discussed in How-To 2.9. That particular topic focused on the functions that read information from private INI files, but in this case you'll need to read directly from WIN.INI, the standard file referred to by GetProfileString. Normally, you send GetProfileString a parameter that tells it which particular keyword you'd like to retrieve from the INI file. In this case, you want the entire list for the Devices topic.

Windows provides a special method of retrieving all keywords that are under a specific topic: You send GetProfileString a null value (0&) instead of the value of the particular keyword. This presents a problem, however, given the function declarations in basINIFile. That is, if you look in the Declarations section of basINIFile, you'll find this declaration for GetProfileString:

```
Declare Function aht_apiGetProfileString Lib "KERNEL" Alias "GetProfileString" ⇒
(ByVal strAppName As String, ByVal strKeyName As String, ByVal strDefault ⇒
As String, ByVal strReturned As String, ByVal intSize As Integer) ⇒
As Integer
```

The second parameter, strKeyName, is the one you'd like to replace with a null. Unfortunately, you can't. Access is quite particular about the data types you use, once you've set up a Declare statement like this. Access knows that the second parameter must be a string, and it passes the address of that string to the Windows DLL. You can *only* pass string values in that second parameter, but sending a string won't get you the results you need.

To solve this problem, the module basGetPrinters includes the following declaration for GetProfileString. (There's no reason not to maintain multiple declarations for the same API function, each with different parameter lists, if the function can take different kinds of parameters.)

```
Declare Function aht_apiGetProfileSection Lib "KERNEL" Alias ⇒
"GetProfileString" (ByVal strAppName As String, ByVal ⇒
strKeyName As Long, ByVal strDefault As String, ByVal ⇒
strReturned As String, ByVal intSize As Integer) As Integer
```

The new declaration, now aliased as aht_apiGetProfileSection, allows you to pass a Long value as the second parameter. Then, when you pass it the required null value, Access doesn't complain. It calls GetProfileString, passing a null value and retrieving the full list of values. Given a buffer to fill, aht_apiGetProfileSection fills the buffer with a list of all the strings to the left of the equal signs, strung together in one string. Each item has a 0 (Chr$(0), not the digit "0") separating it from the next item. The code you could use to retrieve the string might look like this:

```
Const MAX_SIZE = 255
Const STR_DEFAULT = ""
Const APINULL = 0&

Dim strPrinters As String
Dim intCount as Integer

strPrinters = Space(MAX_SIZE)

    ' Get complete section labelled [Devices] from Win.INI
    intCount = aht_apiGetProfileSection("DEVICES", APINULL, ⇒
STR_DEFAULT, strPrinters, MAX_SIZE)
```

Now That I Have the List of Names, What Do I Do?

Having a 0-delimited list of device names doesn't do you much good. You must first find some way to split them apart into an array of strings. The example code uses the SplitDevices function in basGetPrinters to take on this job.

```
intCount = SplitDevices(strPrinters, intCount, astrPrinters())
```

SplitDevices breaks up the long string containing device names *(strPrinters)* into an array of strings *(astrPrinters)*. To do its work, it uses a utility function, ahtGetToken (in basToken), which you may find useful for other tasks. The general syntax for calling ahtGetToken is,

```
varToken = ahtGetToken (strValue, strDelimiter, intPiece)
```

where *strValue* is the string you want to search through, *strDelimiter* holds the delimiter character, and *intPiece* tells the function which token you want to extract from the list.

For example, to retrieve the third word from the sentence, "Hello, my name is John!", you could use this function call:

```
varWord3 = ahtGetToken("Hello, my name is John!", " ", 3)
```

Since the sentence uses space characters as word delimiters, this example uses a space character in quotes as the second parameter.

When breaking up the list of printers, SplitDevices first walks through the list, counting the number of 0s:

```
For intI = 1 To intLen
   If Mid$(strPrinters, intI, 1) = Chr$(0) Then
      intCount = intCount + 1
   End If
Next intI
```

Once SplitDevices knows how many pieces there are, it just calls ahtGetToken repeatedly, pulling out all the device names. It makes sure the array to hold them contains enough rows and returns the number of rows as the function's return value.

```
' Reserve enough space in the array for them all.
ReDim astrPrinters(1 To intCount)

For intI = 1 To intCount
   astrPrinters(intI) = ahtGetToken(strPrinters, Chr$(0), intI)
Next intI
SplitDevices = intCount
```

Using the Array of Names

At this point, the code has an array of strings, each row of which contains the name of an output device from the [Devices] section in WIN.INI. The next step is to call the GetDevices function in basGetPrinters, which will fill in the real array of devices:

```
If intCount > 0 Then
   intCount = GetDevices(astrPrinters(), atagDevices())
End If
```

GetDevices requires two parameters: astrPrinters, the array of printer device names that you built in the previous section, and atagDevices, an empty array of aht_tagDeviceRec structures. GetDevices fills in that second array and returns the number of rows in that array as its return value.

To fill the output array, GetDevices loops through all the elements of astrPrinters, retrieving the information from WIN.INI about each item (the part to the right of the =):

```
strBuffer = ahtGetINIString("Devices", astrPrinters(intI))
```

In each case, strBuffer will contain a string containing driver and port information, like this:

```
HPPCL5E,LPT1:,LPT2:
```

It's quite possible, as in this example, that the string might contain more than one port name. GetDevices must add a row to the output array for each device/port combination. In this case, then, GetDevices would add two rows to atagDevices, as shown in Table 5-3.

drDeviceName	drDriverName	drPort
HP LaserJet 4/4M	HPPCL5E	LPT1:
HP LaserJet 4/4M	HPPCL5E	LPT2:

Table 5-3 Rows added to atagDevices by HPPCL5E,LPT1:,LPT2: in strBuffer

The following code from GetDevices does the work here:

```
strBuffer = ahtGetINIString("Devices", astrPrinters(intI))
If Len(strBuffer) > 0 Then
    ' Add rows as necessary to atagDevices()
    ParseDriverInfo astrPrinters(intI), strBuffer, atagDevices()
End If
```

The ParseDriverInfo subroutine adds the rows to atagDevices, adding multiple rows if necessary. It does its work by brute force—breaking up the comma-delimited list of items and adding at least one row to the atagDevices array. You can study ParseDriverInfo in basGetPrinters, if you're interested. This subroutine uses ahtGetToken to dissect the string retrieved from WIN.INI, looking for one or more output ports and adding rows to atagDevices as necessary.

Using the Array of aht_tagDeviceRec Structures

To fill the list box, frmPrinterList uses the ahtFillPrinterList function, a list-filling callback function (for information on using such functions, see How-To 7.5). In its initialization step, ahtFillPrinterList calls ahtGetPrinterList to fill its array of aht_tagDeviceRec structures.

```
Case LB_INITIALIZE
    intCount = ahtGetPrinterList(atagDevices())
```

Then, when Access requests data items from ahtFillPrinterList, it returns a string constructed from two elements of the aht_tagDeviceRec structure:

```
Case LB_GETVALUE
    varRetval = atagDevices(varRow).drDeviceName & " on " & atagDevices(varRow).drPort
```

Comments

It's true: This seems like an awful lot of work just to retrieve a list of installed output devices. But How-To topics later in the chapter will build on these ideas, allowing you to select a new default printer, for example. Since all the code you need in order to retrieve the list of printers is so neatly encapsulated in the single function, ahtGetPrinterList, you shouldn't even need to worry about how the items all got into their array. By calling this function to provide the array, you should be able to use the list any way you'd like.

5.2 HOW DO I...
COMPLEXITY: INTERMEDIATE

Set and retrieve the name of the default output device?

Problem

Windows allows me to install a number of printer drivers, but one of them must always be denoted as the default printer. I'd like to be able to control which printer Windows thinks is the default printer, perhaps even choosing from a list of all the installed printers. Is there a way to do this from Access?

Technique

Just as Windows stores the full list of available printers in the WIN.INI file (see How-To 5.1 for information on retrieving the full list of installed devices), it also stores information about the default printer in WIN.INI. This How-To shows how you can retrieve and change the default printer setting.

Steps

Load and run frmDefaultPrinterList from 05-02.MDB. This form, shown in Figure 5-2, includes a combo box from which you can select a new default printer. When you first load the form, the combo box should already have the current default output device selected. If you make a choice, the code attached to the AfterUpdate event for the combo box will write the changed value for the default printer to WIN.INI. This change will affect any program that counts on retrieving the default output device from WIN.INI (and most do).

To create a combo box in your own application like the one on frmDefaultPrinterList, follow these steps:

1. Import the modules listed in Table 5-4 into your own application. Skip any modules that you've previously imported. These modules supply the

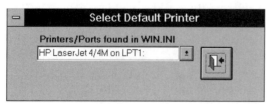

Figure 5-2 The sample form, frmDefaultPrinterList, from which you can choose a new default printer

support routines you'll need to provide the list of devices, and to retrieve and set the default printer in WIN.INI.

MODULE NAME	PURPOSE	CONTAINS
basDefaultPrinter	Retrieve and set default printer setting.	ahtGetDefaultPrinter, ahtSetDefaultPrinter
basGetPrinters	Create an array of printers, fill a list box with the array.	ahtGetPrinterList, ahtFillPrinterList
basINIFile	Read/write information in INI files.	ahtGetINIInt, ahtGetINIString, ahtGetPrivateINIInt, ahtGetPrivateIniString
basPrintTypes	Define data types and constants for all examples in this chapter.	
basToken	Retrieve pieces of a string: a utility module.	ahtGetToken

Table 5-4 Modules to import from 05-02.MDB

2. Create a combo box on a new or existing form. Set the properties as shown in Table 5-5 (other properties may be set as you see fit).

PROPERTY	VALUE
Name	cboPrinters
RowSourceType	FillPrinterList
ColumnCount	4
ColumnHeads	No
ColumnWidths	;0 in;0 in;0 in
BoundColumn	1
AfterUpdate	[Event Procedure]

Table 5-5 Properties to be set for cboPrinters

3. Place the following code in the form's Open event procedure. (For more information on creating event procedures, see this book's Introduction.) This code retrieves the current default printer from WIN.INI and sets cboPrinters to show the name and output port for the default printer.

```
Sub Form_Open (Cancel As Integer)
   Dim dr As aht_tagDeviceRec
   Dim strBuffer As String

   If ahtGetDefaultPrinter(dr) Then
      Me!cboPrinters = BuildName(dr)
   End If
End Sub
```

4. Place the following code in the combo box cboPrinters' AfterUpdate event procedure (in the form's module). This code writes the chosen value back to WIN.INI.

```
Sub cboPrinters_AfterUpdate ()
    Dim dr As aht_tagDeviceRec
    Dim intRetval As Integer
    Dim ctl As Control

    ' Retrieve the pieces needed by dr from
    ' the combo box.
    Set ctl = Me!cboPrinters
    dr.drDeviceName = ctl.Column(1)
    dr.drDriverName = ctl.Column(2)
    dr.drPort = ctl.Column(3)
    intRetval = ahtSetDefaultPrinter(dr)
End Sub
```

5. Add the following function to the form's module (*not* to a global module). This function fills the combo box.

```
Function FillPrinterList (ctl As Control, varID As Variant, ⇒
varRow As Variant, varCol As Variant, varCode As Variant)

    Static atagDevices() As aht_tagDeviceRec
    Static intCount As Integer
    Dim varRetval As Variant

    Select Case varCode
        Case LB_INITIALIZE
            intCount = ahtGetPrinterList(atagDevices())
            varRetval = True

        Case LB_OPEN
            varRetval = Timer

        Case LB_GETROWCOUNT
            varRetval = intCount

        Case LB_GETCOLUMNCOUNT
            varRetval = 4

        Case LB_GETCOLUMNWIDTH
            varRetval = -1

        Case LB_GETVALUE
            Select Case varCol
                Case 0
                    varRetval = BuildName(atagDevices(varRow))
                Case 1
                    varRetval = atagDevices(varRow).drDeviceName
                Case 2
                    varRetval = atagDevices(varRow).drDriverName
```

```
        Case 3
            varRetval = atagDevices(varRow).drPort
        End Select

    Case LB_END
        Erase atagDevices
    End Select
    FillPrinterList = varRetval
End Function
```

6. Add the following function to the form's module (*not* to a global module). This function builds up the string that appears in the combo box, and it is called by several procedures in the form.

```
Function BuildName (dr As aht_tagDeviceRec)
    BuildName = dr.drDeviceName & " on " & dr.drPort
End Function
```

How It Works

The important actions of this example take place in the two support functions, ahtSetDefaultPrinter and ahtGetDefaultPrinter (in the basDefaultPrinter module). Each function takes, as a parameter, an aht_tagDeviceRec structure (see How-To 5.1 for details on the aht_tagDeviceRec structure). The ahtGetDefaultPrinter function looks in WIN.INI, in the [Windows] section, for a line with the keyword Device. A sample WIN.INI section might look like this:

```
[Windows]
spooler=yes
load=
run=
Beep=Yes
NullPort=None
CursorBlinkRate=530
DoubleClickSpeed=452
Programs=PIF EXE BAT COM
Documents=doc txt wri xls xlc sam jw jwt tg1 qw qwt
CoolSwitch=1
Device=HP LaserJet 4/4M,HPPCL5E,LPT1:
```

The final line with Device as the keyword indicates the name, driver, and output port of the default output device. The ahtGetDefaultPrinter function uses the ahtGetINIString function to read from WIN.INI, and then uses the ahtGetToken function to separate the comma-delimited pieces. It places the values in the appropriate fields of the aht_tagDeviceRec structure.

```
Function ahtGetDefaultPrinter (dr As aht_tagDeviceRec)
    Dim strBuffer As String

    strBuffer = ahtGetINIString("Windows", "Device")
    If Len(strBuffer) > 0 Then
        dr.drDeviceName = ahtGetToken(strBuffer, ",", 1)
        dr.drDriverName = ahtGetToken(strBuffer, ",", 2)
        dr.drPort = ahtGetToken(strBuffer, ",", 3)
        ahtGetDefaultPrinter = True
```

(Continued on next page)

(Continued from previous page)

```
   Else
      ahtGetDefaultPrinter = False
   End If
End Function
```

The ahtSetDefaultPrinter function performs almost the same set of steps as ahtGetDefaultPrinter, in reverse. It builds up a comma-delimited string, pulling the pieces from the passed-in aht_tagDeviceRec structure. It then calls aht_apiWriteProfileString to write the new value back out to WIN.INI.

```
Function ahtSetDefaultPrinter (dr As aht_tagDeviceRec)

   Dim strBuffer As String
   Dim intRetval As Integer

   ' Build up the appropriate string.
   strBuffer = dr.drDeviceName & ","
   strBuffer = strBuffer & dr.drDriverName & ","
   strBuffer = strBuffer & dr.drPort

   ' Now write that string out to WIN.INI.
   ahtSetDefaultPrinter = (aht_apiWriteProfileString("Windows", "Device", strBuffer) <> 0)
End Function
```

For information on the mechanisms of providing the list of available printers, see How-To 5.1. The details here are all the same except for one: In this combo box, there are four columns (instead of just one, as in How-To 5.1). This example shows one column, containing a string with the device name and its output port, but stores all three pieces from the aht_tagDeviceRec structure in hidden columns in the combo box. Thus it's much easier to retrieve the values for all the fields when you need to set the new default printer. The LB_GETVALUE case (from step 5) shows the details:

```
Case LB_GETVALUE
   Select Case varCol
      Case 0
         varRetval = BuildName(atagDevices(varRow))
      Case 1
         varRetval = atagDevices(varRow).drDeviceName
      Case 2
         varRetval = atagDevices(varRow).drDriverName
      Case 3
         varRetval = atagDevices(varRow).drPort
   End Select
```

Now, when you need to retrieve the values from the combo box to write out to WIN.INI, you can just pull them from the selected row in the combo box, using the Column property, as shown in this code from step 4:

```
Set ctl = Me!cboPrinters
dr.drDeviceName = ctl.Column(1)
dr.drDriverName = ctl.Column(2)
dr.drPort = ctl.Column(3)
intRetval = ahtSetDefaultPrinter(dr)
```

Comments

Access uses the default output device for printing unless you specify otherwise, in Access's Print|Setup dialog. Later, How-To 5.7 will combine methods from this topic and others to show you how to send a report to the printer you choose at runtime. The methods shown there will allow you to direct a report to the printer today, and to the fax modem tomorrow.

Though it's possible to remove the default printer name from WIN.INI, you should not do this. Access (and many other Windows programs) will complain and request that you select a default printer if you attempt to print without one. You can, of course, use the code presented here to let users set the default printer if your application determines that none is currently selected.

5.3 HOW DO I... COMPLEXITY: ADVANCED

Programmatically change margin and column settings for reports?

Problem

I'd like to give users of my applications some control over report layout, especially in designating column and margin settings. I could just "turn them loose" in report design mode, but I'd like to maintain a little more control over their actions. Is there some way to modify these layout settings from Access Basic?

Technique

Access provides three underdocumented properties for forms and reports: prtMip, prtDevMode, and prtDevNames. This How-To will focus on prtMip, How-To 5.4 on prtDevMode, and 5.6 on prtDevNames.

You can use the prtMip property to retrieve and set layout properties of reports and forms, though it's not easy. This How-To provides some wrapper functions to hide the details of the property, which will make the process a bit easier for you. The prtMip property is actually a data structure containing information about the layout of your object. It contains fields representing the left, top, bottom, and right margins; the number of columns; and the size, spacing, and item order of the columns. In addition, it contains the Data Only option in the Print|Setup dialog. In order to use the prtMip property, you'll need to retrieve it, copy it to a user-defined structure, set new values, and then copy it back to the property. The "How It Works" section of this How-To explains all the details.

Steps

Load and run frmPrintSettings from 05-03.MDB. Figure 5-3 shows the form (which emulates Access's Print|Setup dialog) after rptReport3 has been selected from the list of reports. Choose a report from the drop-down list, and the form will load that report in design mode. By typing new values into the text boxes, you can change the settings for the selected report. Some of the items on the form are only available if you've specified more than one column for the Items

Across value, so you'll want to use a number greater than 1 in that field. To save the changes back to the selected report, click the Save Settings button. This writes the new prtMip property back to the report. If you view the chosen report in print preview mode once you've reset its prtMip property, you will see your changes in effect. The following sections explain both how to use the sample form from 05-03.MDB, and how to read and write the prtMip property of your own objects.

Using the Sample Form

To use the sample form in your own applications, follow these steps:

1. Import the modules listed in Table 5-6 from 05-03.MDB into your own application. Skip any modules you have already imported. These modules supply the support routines you'll need in order to generate the list of reports, and to retrieve and set the prtMip property.

MODULE NAME	PURPOSE	CONTAINS
basOpenReport	Open a report in design mode, or do nothing if it's already open.	ahtOpenReport
basPrintTypes	Define data types and constants for all examples in this chapter.	
basPrtMip	Get and set prtMip values.	ahtGetMip, ahtSetMip

Table 5-6 Modules to import from 05-03.MDB in order to use the frmPrintSettings

2. Import frmPrintSettings into your application. This form allows you to choose from the existing reports in your database. Once you've chosen the report (which the form will open in design mode), you can alter print layout settings. Once you're done, you'll need to save the report using the Access menus or your own code: The sample form will not save the reports for you.

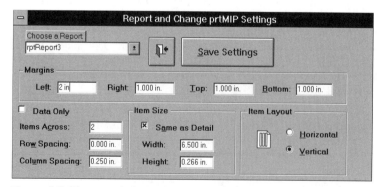

Figure 5-3 The sample form, frmPrintSettings, was modeled after Access's Print|Setup dialog

Using the Routines to Read and Write the prtMip Property

To use the routines that read and write the prtMip property *without* the sample form, follow these steps:

1. Import the modules listed in Table 5-7 from 05-03.MDB into your own application. These modules supply the support routines you'll need in order to retrieve and set the prtMip property.

MODULE NAME	PURPOSE	CONTAINS
basPrintTypes	Define data types and constants for all examples in this chapter.	
basPrtMip	Get and set prtMip values.	ahtGetMip, ahtSetMip

Table 5-7 Modules to import from 05-03.MDB in order to modify an object's prtMip property

2. To retrieve an object's prtMip property, call the ahtGetMip function. It takes three parameters: the name of an object, that object's type (either A_FORM or A_REPORT), and an aht_tagMip structure to hold the values. For example, the following code fills the variable named *mip* with the requested report's or form's prtMip property information.

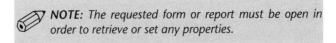

> **NOTE:** *The requested form or report must be open in order to retrieve or set any properties.*

```
Dim mip As aht_tagMip
Dim fSuccess as Integer

fSuccess = ahtGetMip("rptYourReport", A_REPORT, mip)
' or, for a form:
' fSuccess = ahtGetMip("frmYourForm", A_FORM, mip)
```

3. To modify the prtMip values, you need to modify values in the aht_tagMip structure. The "How It Works" section just below explains this. Once you're done, you must write the prtMip value back to the original object for it to take effect. To do that, call the ahtSetMip function. It takes the same parameters as the ahtGetMip function: the name of an object, that object's type (either A_FORM or A_REPORT), and an aht_tagMip structure that holds the new values. For example, the following code replaces the selected object's prtMip property with the values stored in *mip*:

```
fSuccess = ahtSetMip("rptYourReport", A_REPORT, mip)
' or, for a form:
' fSuccess = ahtSetMip("frmYourForm", A_FORM, mip)
```

How It Works

Using the code we've supplied here is quite simple, although the code itself is quite complex. The following sections describe the prtMip property in detail, how to retrieve the prtMip setting, how to modify its data, and how to place the changed data into your form or report. In addition, we'll introduce the wrapper functions that shield you from most of this level of detail.

The prtMip Data Structure

The prtMip property, as well as the prtDevMode and prtDevNames properties, (discussed in later How-To's) are unique in that they're not directly readable. As stored and retrieved from an object, these properties are just a stream of bytes: To peruse them or modify their values, you must copy them into a user-defined data structure that's been declared in just the right way. The information is the same either way you look at it, but it's impossible to view or edit it as an unbroken stream of bytes. Once you copy it to a data structure, though, it's easy to access any of the pieces of the property.

To use the prtMip property, copy its value into a data structure (as defined in basPrintTypes) of type aht_tagMip:

```
Type aht_tagMIP
    xLeftMargin As Integer
    yTopMargin As Integer
    xRightMargin As Integer
    yBotMargin As Integer
    fDataOnly As Integer
    xFormSize As Integer
    yFormSize As Integer
    fDefaultSize As Integer
    cxColumns As Integer
    xFormSpacing As Integer
    yFormSpacing As Integer
    radItemOrder As Integer
End Type
```

Table 5-8 describes the fields in the aht_tagMip structure.

FIELD NAME	DESCRIPTION	COMMENTS
xLeftMargin	Left margin	Distance between the left edge of the paper and the object to be printed (in twips: 1 twip = 1/1440 inch).
yTopMargin	Top margin	Distance between the top edge of the paper and the object to be printed (in twips).
xRightMargin	Right margin	Distance between the right edge of the paper and the object to be printed (in twips).
yBotMargin	Bottom margin	Distance between the bottom edge of the paper and the object to be printed (in twips).
fDataOnly	Print data only?	If True (–1), Access should print just data, not labels, control borders, grid lines and display graphics. If False (0), Access prints all elements.

Table 5-8 Members of the aht_tagMip structure and their meanings

FIELD NAME	DESCRIPTION	COMMENTS
xFormSize	Column width	Width of the detail area. If the fDefaultSize element is False and cxColumns is greater than 1, the width of each column (in twips).
yFormSize	Column height	Returns the height of the detail section (read-only).
fDefaultSize	Use default size?	If True (–1), use the width and height of the design mode detail section when printing. If False (0), use the values specified in the xFormSize and yFormSize members.
cxColumns	Items across	Integer that specifies the number of columns across the page, for multicolumn reports.
xFormSpacing	Column spacing	Distance between detail section columns (if cxColumns > 1) in twips.
yFormSpacing	Row spacing	Distance between detail sections vertically (in twips).
radItemOrder	Item order	Horizontal (1953) or vertical (1954) layout for multi-column reports.

Table 5-8 Members of the aht_tagMip structure and their meanings

> ✎ *NOTE: The names of the members of this data type don't match the normal naming style used in this book. In order to standardize, we've left the names the same as those used in the matching data type in the Access Wizards. That way, if you dig into the Access Wizard code, the names will match what you'll find there.*

Retrieving prtMip Settings

Retrieving prtMip settings is trivial: Just copy the value of the property from an open report or form into a string variable.

```
Dim strMip As String
strMip = Reports!rptReport1.prtMip
```

At this point, strMip will contain an unformatted stream of bytes, representing all the information in Table 5-8. You'll need some way of separating all the data into a data structure of type aht_tagMip. Although you could do this by brute force, copying the data one byte at a time, Access Basic provides a method for copying data from one data type to another, converting the individual bytes as necessary. A form of the LSet command lets you move the data from the prtMip property directly into an aht_tagMip data structure. LSet's general syntax is,

```
LSet Data1 = Data2
```

where *Data1* and *Data2* are variables of user-defined data types—and therein lies the catch. The data types on both sides of the equal sign must be user-defined types. So you can't copy the data directly from the prtMip property using the LSet command.

The trick, then, is to use a second user-defined type. You'll find one of these "helper" types defined in basPrintTypes for each of the prtMip, prtDevMode, and prtDevNames properties. The type aht_tagMIPStr is defined as just a single 24-byte string:

```
Type aht_tagMIPStr
   MIPStr As String * 24
End Type
```

This may be a cheap trick to get around a limitation in the LSet command, but it does solve the problem. Therefore, to retrieve a report's prtMip property, you'll use code like this:

```
Dim mipStrTemp As aht_tagMIPStr
Dim mip As aht_tagMIP

mipStrTemp.MIPStr = Reports!rptReport1.prtMip
LSet mip = mipStrTemp
```

After you execute those lines of code, *mip* contains all the data from the report's prtMip property, all neatly parsed out into the correct fields. The same technique will work for each of the prtMip, prtDevMode, and prtDevNames properties: Using the correct "helper" data structure, you'll copy data from the property into the helper structure, and then use the LSet command to move the data into the appropriate "real" data structure.

Modifying the Data

Once you've got the data into the data structure, you can change the values as you would with any other user-defined structure. For example, given a variable containing prtMip data, you would set the left margin to be 3 inches using code like this:

```
' Don't forget to convert to TWIPS!
mip.xLeftMargin = 3 * 1440
```

Putting Data Back

To place the changed aht_prtMip structure back into a form's or report's prtMip property, follow the steps outlined above in "Retrieving prtMip Settings," except in reverse:

```
Dim mipStrTemp As aht_tagMIPStr

' mip is the structure containing your changed values
LSet mipStrTemp = mip
Reports!rptReport1.prtMip = mipStrTemp.MIPStr
```

You first use the LSet command to copy the data from the aht_tagMIP structure into the helper structure, and from there, you copy the string in the helper structure directly to the prtMip property.

Making It a Bit Easier

To make things a bit simpler, we've supplied ahtGetMip and ahtPutMip in the module basPrtMip in 05-03.MDB. These two functions, used in the example form for this How-To, make it easy to retrieve and set an object's prtMip property. These functions follow the steps in this How-To, doing it all for you. For information on calling these functions, see steps 2 and 3 under "Using the Routines to Read and Write the prtMip Property" in the foregoing "Steps" section. To see examples of using ahtGetMip and ahtSetMip, look at the cboReportList_AfterUpdate and cmdSaveSettings_Click event procedures in the frmPrintSettings module (in 05-03.MDB).

Comments

The prtMip, prtDevMode, and prtDevNames properties are all read/write in design mode, but they are *read-only* at runtime. This means you must open an object in design mode if you need to change any of these properties. The example database 05-03.MDB contains a function, ahtOpenReport (in basOpenReport) that will ensure that the report whose name you pass is open and in design mode. You might find this function useful in your own applications.

> **NOTE:** Don't forget that all the measurements in the aht_tagMip structure are stored in twips. To convert from inches to twips, multiply by 1440. (A twip is defined as $\frac{1}{20}$ of a point. There are 72 points per inch and 20 twips per point; therefore, 72 * 20 = 1440 twips per inch.) To convert from twips to inches, divide by 1440.

The combo box with the list of reports uses a common but undocumented technique. The Access system tables (set View|Options|General|Show System Objects to Yes to see the system tables in the database container) contain information about the current database. One table in particular, MSysObjects, contains a row for each object in the database. To fill the combo box with a list of reports, you can use this SQL expression:

```
Select Name from MSysObjects where Type = -32764 Order By Name;
```

The Name column includes the name for each object, and the Type column contains –32764 for reports (it contains –32768 for forms). Microsoft suggests not querying against the system tables to retrieve lists of items, but using Data Access Objects instead; however, our method is much faster and much simpler for filling lists. Since the Access Wizards use this technique, it's probably safe for the short run.

5.4 HOW DO I...

Programmatically change printer options?

Problem

I've tried using SendKeys to change printing options in the Print|Setup dialog, but this really isn't satisfactory. Sometimes it works, and sometimes it doesn't, depending on the circumstances and the printer driver that's loaded. Isn't there some way to modify printer options without using SendKeys?

Technique

Windows makes many of the printer driver settings available to applications, including the number of copies, page orientation, and page size. Though Access makes it rather difficult to retrieve and modify these values, you can get at them through the prtDevMode property of forms and reports. This How-To focuses on the prtDevMode property and demonstrates how to read and write values in it.

Steps

Load and run frmPrintSettings in 05-04.MDB. Figure 5-4 shows the sample form in action. This form allows you to choose a report from a combo box. Once you've made your choice, the form loads the report in design mode, and retrieves the number of copies, page size, and page orientation from the report's prtDevMode property. You can change any of these values, and once

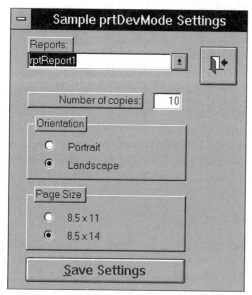

Figure 5-4 The sample form, frmPrintSettings, showing prtDevMode information for rptReport1

you press the Save Settings button, the form writes the values back to the report's prtDevMode property. If you save the report, those settings will still be there the next time you open the report.

To modify prtDevMode settings for reports or forms in your own application, follow these steps:

1. Import the modules from 05-04.MDB listed in Table 5-9 into your own application. Skip any modules you may have previously imported.

MODULE NAME	PURPOSE	CONTAINS
basOpenReport	Open a report in design mode, or do nothing if it's already open.	ahtOpenReport
basPrintTypes	Define data types and constants for all examples in this chapter.	
basPrtDevMode	Get and set prtDevMode values.	ahtGetDevMode, ahtSetDevMode, various constants

Table 5-9 Modules to import from 05-04.MDB in order to access the prtDevMode property

2. To retrieve the prtDevMode property values from a given open report or form, call the ahtGetDevMode function, as shown in the following code example. If the return value from the function call is True, then you can use the information that the function filled in for you in the aht_tagDevMode structure. For example, the following code fragment retrieves the prtDevMode property for a report whose name is stored in strReport:

```
Dim DM as aht_tagDevMode
Dim fSuccess as Integer

' Pass ahtGetDevMode the name of the object, the type of the
' object (either A_FORM or A_REPORT), and a structure to
' fill in (type aht_tagDevMode)
fSuccess = ahtGetDevMode(strReport, A_REPORT, DM)
```

3. To change values in the prtDevMode property, you manipulate values in the aht_tagDevMode structure. You must also tell Windows that you've changed the field, by changing the value in the dmFields member. See the "How It Works" section for details on filling in the various fields of the aht_tagDevMode structure. For example, to set the number of copies to 2, you would use code like this:

```
' Change the value
DM.dmCopies = 2
' Make sure and tell Windows that you changed the value!
DM.dmFields = dm.dmFields Or ahtDM_COPIES
```

4. To write the prtDevMode value back to the object, call the ahtSetDevMode function.

```
fSuccess = ahtSetDevMode(strReport, A_REPORT, DM)
```

How It Works

The following sections discuss the prtDevMode data structure and how to use it in your code. Just like the prtMip property discussed in How-To 5.3, the prtDevMode property is actually an entire data structure, stored as a stream of bytes. To read values from it, you need to move it into a user-defined data structure. If you haven't read the "How It Works" section in How-To 5.3, do it now, so that you understand the LSet command used there. Unlike the prtMip property, however, the structure stored in the prtDevMode property is not specific to Access. Windows supplies the DEVMODE data structure, which contains the same information that is stored in the prtDevMode property. The settings in the prtDevMode property, then, are not determined by Access, but by your selected printer driver.

The Data Structure

The module basPrintTypes contains a definition for a data structure, type aht_tagDevMode, that can contain all the information stored in an object's prtDevMode property:

```
Type aht_tagDEVMODE
    dmDeviceName As String * 32
    dmSpecVersion As Integer
    dmDriverVersion As Integer
    dmSize As Integer
    dmDriverExtra As Integer
    dmFields As Long
    dmOrientation As Integer
    dmPaperSize As Integer
    dmPaperLength As Integer
    dmPaperWidth As Integer
    dmScale As Integer
    dmCopies As Integer
    dmDefaultSource As Integer
    dmPrintQuality As Integer
    dmColor As Integer
    dmDuplex As Integer
    dmYResolution As Integer
    dmTTOption As Integer
End Type
```

Any time you need to work with an object's prtDevMode property settings, move the property into a structure of this type, make your modifications, and then move the structure back into the prtDevMode property, just as in How-To 5.3. Table 5-10 describes each of the items in this structure and their range of values. Notice that some items in this structure cannot be changed by your code.

FIELD NAME	READ-ONLY?	CONTAINS	DATA TYPE	VALUES (from basPrtDevMode)
dmDeviceName	Yes	Device supported by the selected driver.	32-character string	For example, HP LaserJet 4/4M.
dmSpecVersion	Yes	Version number of this structure itself.	Integer	For Windows 3.1, this value must be 778 (&H30A).
dmDriverVersion	Yes	Version of the driver, as assigned by the driver developer.	Integer	
dmSize	Yes	Size, in bytes, of the DEVMODE structure.	Integer	
dmDriverExtra	Yes	Size, in bytes, of the optional driver-specific data, which can follow this structure.	Integer	
dmFields	No	Indication of which fields have been initialized or changed in the structure. If you modify a value in this structure and then write the structure back to the form or report, this value must reflect the fields you've changed.	Long	None or more of the values in Table 5-11, added together.
dmOrientation	No	Paper orientation.	Integer	ahtDMORIENT_PORTRAIT (1) or ahtDMORIENT_LANDSCAPE (2).
dmPaperSize	No	Size of the physical page to print on.	Integer	A value from Table 5-12 (depending on which paper sizes the printer supports). If you choose ahtDMPAPER_USER, the width and length of the paper are specified by the dmPaperWidth and dmPaperLength members of this structure.
dmPaperLength	No	Paper length (measured in tenths of a millimeter.) Used only if the value in the Paper Size member is 256 (user-defined).	Integer	Limited by data storage to 328 centimeters.
dmPaperWidth	No	Paper width (measured in tenths of a millimeter.) Used only if the value of the Paper Size member is 256 (user-defined).	Integer	Limited by data storage to 328 centimeters.

Table 5-10 Members of the aht_tagDevMode structure

(continued on next page)

FIELD NAME	READ-ONLY?	CONTAINS	DATA TYPE	VALUES (from basPrtDevMode)
(continued from previous page)				
dmScale	No	Factor by which the printed output is to be scaled. The apparent page size is scaled from the physical page size by a factor or Scale/100.	Integer	
dmCopies	No	If the printing device supports multiple copies, the number of copies to be printed.	Integer	
dmDefaultSource	No	Default bin from which paper is to be fed.	Integer	A value from Table 5-13.
dmPrintQuality	No	Printer resolution. If you specify a positive value, it's treated as the x-resolution, in dots per inch (DPI) and is device-dependent.	Integer	A device-independent value from Table 5-14 or a device-dependent value of your choosing, in dots per inch. In this case, the dmYResolution field must contain the y-resolution in DPI.
dmColor	No	Color usage, if the printer supports color printing.	Integer	ahtDMCOLOR_COLOR (1) or ahtDMCOLOR_MONOCHROME (2).
dmDuplex	No	Duplex usage, if the printer supports duplex printing.	Integer	ahtDMDUP_SIMPLEX (1), ahtDMDUP_HORIZONTAL (2), or ahtDMDUP_VERTICAL (3).
dmYResolution	No	Y-resolution for the printer, DPI. If this value is specified, you must also specify the x-resolution in the dmPrintQuality member. These values are device-specific.	Integer	If the dmPrintQuality field is positive, a device-dependent value in DPI.
dmTTOption	No	Specifies how TrueType fonts should be printed.	Integer	A value from Table 5-15.

Table 5-10 Members of the aht_tagDevMode structure

Since Access makes all this information available to you through the prtDevMode property, you can retrieve and modify any of the property settings that aren't read-only. The prtDevMode property for reports and forms provides the only programmatic access to these aspects of printing.

Table 5-11 shows the flags you need to use when setting or retrieving information from the dmFields member. To see if a specific field has been initialized in the structure, you can use code like this:

```
If DM.dmFields AND ahtDM_COPIES 0 Then
   ' Now you know that the dmCopies member
   ' member has been initialized.
End If
```

To make sure Access knows that your code has modified one of the fields in the aht_tagDevMode structure, set the value in the dmFields member like this:

```
' Tell Access that you've changed the dmCopies member.
DM.dmFields = DM.dmFields OR ahtDM_COPIES
```

FLAGS	VALUE
ahtDM_ORIENTATION	&H0000001
ahtDM_PAPERSIZE	&H0000002
ahtDM_PAPERLENGTH	&H0000004
ahtDM_PAPERWIDTH	&H0000008
ahtDM_SCALE	&H0000010
ahtDM_COPIES	&H0000100
ahtDM_DEFAULTSOURCE	&H0000200
ahtDM_PRINTQUALITY	&H0000400
ahtDM_COLOR	&H0000800
ahtDM_DUPLEX	&H0001000
ahtDM_YRESOLUTION	&H0002000
ahtDM_TTOPTION	&H0004000

Table 5-11 Constants for the dmFields member flags

Table 5-12 shows a list of all the defined paper sizes. You can use one of these constants in the dmPaperSize member to set a new paper size, or you can use ahtDMPAPER_USER (256). This latter alternative will tell Windows that you want to use the values in the dmPaperLength and dmPaperWidth members to specify the paper size.

CONSTANT	VALUE	DESCRIPTION
ahtDMPAPER_LETTER	1	Letter (8.5 x 11 in.)
ahtDMPAPER_LETTERSMALL	2	Letter, small (8.5 x 11 in.)
ahtDMPAPER_TABLOID	3	Tabloid (11 x 17 in.)
ahtDMPAPER_LEDGER	4	Ledger (17 x 11 in.)
ahtDMPAPER_LEGAL	5	Legal (8.5 x 14 in.)
ahtDMPAPER_STATEMENT	6	Statement (5.5 x 8.5 in.)
ahtDMPAPER_EXECUTIVE	7	Executive (7.25 x 10.5 in.)
ahtDMPAPER_A3	8	A3 (297 x 420 mm)
ahtDMPAPER_A4	9	A4 (210 x 297 mm)
ahtDMPAPER_A4SMALL	10	A4 Small (210 x 297 mm)
ahtDMPAPER_A5	11	A5 (148 x 210 mm)
ahtDMPAPER_B4	12	B4 (250 x 354)
ahtDMPAPER_B5	13	B5 (182 x 257 mm)
ahtDMPAPER_FOLIO	14	Folio (8.5 x 13 in.)
ahtDMPAPER_QUARTO	15	Quarto (215 x 275 mm)
ahtDMPAPER_10X14	16	10 x 14 in.
ahtDMPAPER_11X17	17	11 x 17 in.
ahtDMPAPER_NOTE	18	Note (8.5 x 11 in.)

Table 5-12 Constants and descriptions for the dmPaperSize member   *(continued on next page)*

CONSTANT	VALUE	DESCRIPTION
(continued from previous page)		
ahtDMPAPER_ENV_9	19	Envelope #9 (3.875 x 8.875 in.)
ahtDMPAPER_ENV_10	20	Envelope #10 (4.125 x 9.5 in.)
ahtDMPAPER_ENV_11	21	Envelope #11 (4.5 x 10.375 in.)
ahtDMPAPER_ENV_12	22	Envelope #12 (4.25 x 11 in.)
ahtDMPAPER_ENV_14	23	Envelope #14 (5 x 11.5 in.)
ahtDMPAPER_CSHEET	24	C size sheet (17 x 22 in.)
ahtDMPAPER_DSHEET	25	D size sheet (22 x 34 in.)
ahtDMPAPER_ESHEET	26	E size sheet (34 x 44 in.)
ahtDMPAPER_ENV_DL	27	Envelope DL (110 x 220 mm)
ahtDMPAPER_ENV_C5	28	Envelope C5 (162 x 229 mm)
ahtDMPAPER_ENV_C3	29	Envelope C3 (324 x 458 mm)
ahtDMPAPER_ENV_C4	30	Envelope C4 (229 x 324 mm)
ahtDMPAPER_ENV_C6	31	Envelope C6 (114 x 162 mm)
ahtDMPAPER_ENV_C65	32	Envelope C65 (114 x 229 mm)
ahtDMPAPER_ENV_B4	33	Envelope B4 (250 x 353 mm)
ahtDMPAPER_ENV_B5	34	Envelope B5 (176 x 250 mm
ahtDMPAPER_ENV_B6	35	Envelope B6 (176 x 125 mm)
ahtDMPAPER_ENV_ITALY	36	Envelope (110 x 230 mm)
ahtDMPAPER_ENV_MONARCH	37	Envelope, Monarch (3.875 x 7.5 in.)
ahtDMPAPER_ENV_PERSONAL	38	6¾ Envelope (3.625 x 6.5 in.)
ahtDMPAPER_FANFOLD_US	39	U.S. std. fanfold (14.875 x 11 in.)
ahtDMPAPER_FANFOLD_STD_GERMAN	40	German std. fanfold (8.5 x 12 in.)
ahtDMPAPER_FANFOLD_LGL_GERMAN	41	German legal fanfold (8.5 x 13 in.)
ahtDMPAPER_USER	256	User-defined

Table 5-12 Constants and descriptions for the dmPaperSize member

Table 5-13 shows possible values for the dmDefaultSource member of the structure, and Table 5-14 shows the predefined, device-independent choices for the dmPrintQuality field of the aht_tagDevMode structure. You can use a positive value instead, which will then represent a device-dependent x-resolution value, measured in dots per inch. If you choose this method, you must also specify a device-dependent positive value in the dmYResolution member.

CONSTANT	VALUE	DESCRIPTION
ahtDMBIN_UPPER	1	Upper bin
ahtDMBIN_ONLYONE	1	Only one bin
ahtDMBIN_LOWER	2	Lower bin
ahtDMBIN_MIDDLE	3	Middle bin
ahtDMBIN_MANUAL	4	Manual bin
ahtDMBIN_ENVELOPE	5	Envelope bin
ahtDMBIN_ENVMANUAL	6	Envelope manual bin
ahtDMBIN_AUTO	7	Automatic bin
ahtDMBIN_TRACTOR	8	Tractor bin

Table 5-13 Constants and descriptions for the dmDefaultSource member

CONSTANT	VALUE	DESCRIPTION
ahtDMBIN_SMALLFMT	9	Small-format bin
ahtDMBIN_LARGEFMT	10	Large-format bin
ahtDMBIN_LARGECAPACITY	11	Large-capacity bin
ahtDMBIN_CASSETTE	14	Cassette bin
ahtDMBIN_USER	256	Device-specific bins start here

Table 5-13 Constants and descriptions for the dmDefaultSource member

CONSTANT	VALUE	DESCRIPTION
ahtDMRES_HIGH	−4	High resolution
ahtDMRES_MEDIUM	−3	Medium resolution
ahtDMRES_LOW	−2	Low resolution
ahtDMRES_DRAFT	−1	Draft

Table 5-14 Constants and descriptions for the dmPrintQuality member

Table 5-15 lists the possible ways that the printer can handle TrueType fonts. The dmTTOption member of the aht_tagDevMode structure will contain one of these values.

CONSTANT	VALUE	DESCRIPTION
ahtDMTT_BITMAP	1	Print TrueType fonts as graphics
ahtDMTT_DOWNLOAD	2	Download TrueType fonts as soft fonts
ahtDMTT_SUBDEV	3	Substitute device fonts for TrueType fonts

Table 5-15 Constants and descriptions for the dmTTOption member

Using the prtDevMode Property

The "Steps" section above shows how to use the ahtGetDevMode and ahtSetDevMode functions to retrieve and set the prtDevMode property for a form or report. The two functions work exactly like their counterparts in How-To 5.3: They use the LSet command to move data to and from the raw property value.

In between calls to ahtGetDevMode and ahtSetDevMode, however, you need to do a bit more work with the aht_tagDevMode structure than you did with the aht_tagMip structure. Specifically, you must set the dmFields member of the structure, indicating to Access which fields you've modified. For example, to set the number of copies, the orientation, and the page size, you would need code like this:

```
Sub SetDevMode ()

    ' Set rptReport1 to print 5 copies in landscape mode on
    ' normal letter paper.

    Dim dm As aht_tagDEVMODE
    Dim intSuccess As Integer

    ' rptReport1 must be open in design mode for this to succeed.
        If ahtGetDevMode("rptReport1", A_REPORT, dm) Then
            dm.dmCopies = 5
            dm.dmOrientation = ahtDMORIENT_LANDSCAPE
            dm.dmPaperSize = ahtDMPAPER_LETTER
            ' Tell Access which fields you changed!
            dm.dmFields = ahtDM_COPIES Or ahtDM_ORIENTATION Or ahtDM_PAPERSIZE
            intSuccess = ahtSetDevMode("rptReport1", A_REPORT, dm)
        End If
End Sub
```

Comments

By using the functions supplied here—ahtGetDevMode and ahtSetDevMode—you can at least be assured that you're getting the data copied in and out of the prtDevMode property correctly. On the other hand, this property is very "raw." That is, if you set it incorrectly, chances are that Access and/or Windows will crash when you try to preview or print the form or report. Just as when working with the Windows API, be careful to save everything before you first run any code dealing with the prtDevMode (or prtMip or prtDevNames) property.

5.5 HOW DO I... COMPLEXITY: INTERMEDIATE

Print on odd-sized paper?

Problem

My printer driver supports user-defined paper sizes. I can see that option in the list of available paper sizes, on the Print|Setup dialog. But when I choose it, I can't find a way to tell Access how big the page should be. Is there a way to control this from Access Basic?

Technique

Some printers support user-defined paper sizes. Most laser printers do not, but the new HP LaserJet 4P/4MP (for example) does. If you're printing an odd-sized report, you must set up your printer so that it knows what paper size to expect. This information is especially crucial on continuous-feed printers, since the printer must eject just enough paper once it has finished printing the current page to get to the top of the next.

To find out if your printer supports custom page sizes, open the Access Print|Setup dialog, and scroll through the values available in the Paper Size combo box (see Figure 5-5). If you see a User Defined Size or Custom Size option, you know your printer supports custom paper sizes. If not, you won't be able to use the technique in this How-To.

This How-To uses the prtDevMode property, presented in detail in How-To 5.4, to allow you to choose custom page sizes for printing. Although Access won't complain if you run this example code with a printer selected that doesn't support custom paper sizes, the code will appear to be broken: It will do nothing at all to your reports.

Steps

This section covers two ways to manipulate page sizes—using the example form, frmPrintSettings, and in your own applications. Before trying the sample, you'll need to load Access's Print|Setup dialog, and take note of the supported paper sizes. Then, load and run frmPrintSettings in 05-05.MDB (Figure 5-6).

Using the Example Form

1. With frmPrintSettings loaded, choose a report from the Reports combo box. This opens the report in design mode, minimized.

2. If your printer supports user-defined sizes, choose that value from the Page Size combo box. If not, you can choose one of the other paper sizes from the sample form's combo box.

> ✎ NOTE: This example provides a list of all the available paper sizes in Windows, no matter which printer driver you've selected. If you select a paper size that your printer doesn't know about, Access will disregard your selection.

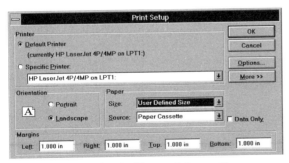

Figure 5-5 Access's Print|Setup dialog, with a user-defined page size selected

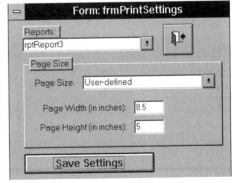

Figure 5-6 The sample form, frmPrintSettings, showing rptReport3's page size settings

3. If you chose User-defined in step 2, the two text boxes on frmPrintSettings will be available. Enter a reasonable page width and height (in inches) into the text boxes. If you choose a size that makes it impossible for Access to print the report, given the report's margin settings, the driver will substitute a page size, based on its own internal calculations.

4. Choose the Save Settings button. The code attached to this button's Click event will write a new aht_tagDevMode structure to the chosen report's prtDevMode property. (See How-To 5.4 for more information on the prtDevMode property.) Unless you click this button, the form will make no changes to the report.

5. Select the report, click on it to open it, and switch into print preview mode. It will be displayed using the page dimensions you selected. Figure 5-7 shows rptReport3 set up to print on a 5×5-inch square of paper.

Using the Code in Your Own Application

To use this technique in your own application, import the objects listed in Table 5-16 from 05-05.MDB into your database. With these objects in your application, you can use code from the module attached to frmPrintSettings, along with the routines in the global modules (as shown in "How It Works"), to set the paper size for any report or form in your application.

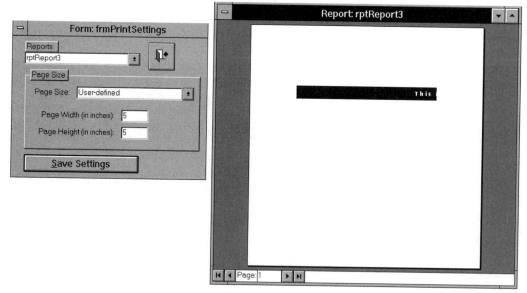

Figure 5-7 rptReport3 in print preview mode, set up for printing on a 5×5-inch square

OBJECT TYPE	OBJECT NAME
Form	frmPrintSettings
Module	basOpenReport
Module	basPrintTypes
Module	basPrtDevMode

Table 5-16 Objects to import from 05-05.MDB, allowing you to change paper sizes

How It Works

As mentioned in How-To 5.4, you can set an object's page size (among many other values) using the object's prtDevMode property. In this case, you're working with the dmPaperSize member of the user-defined aht_tagDevMode structure. The value of this member can be any of the items from the first column in Table 5-12. If its value is ahtDMPAPER_USER (256), for example, you must supply the exact paper size, in 1/10 millimeters, in the dmPaperWidth and dmPaperLength elements of the structure.

On the frmPrintSettings sample form, once you choose a specific report, the code attached to the Reports combo box's AfterUpdate event executes this fragment:

```
If ahtOpenReport(strReport, False) Then
    If ahtGetDevMode(strReport, A_REPORT, dm) Then
        Me!cboPaperSize = dm.dmPaperSize
        Me!txtPaperWidth = dm.dmPaperWidth / INCHES_TO_MM
        Me!txtPaperLength = dm.dmPaperLength / INCHES_TO_MM
    End If
    ' Enable the two text boxes if the user chose
    ' a user-defined page size.
    EnableItems
End If
```

Once the code succeeds in opening the selected report in design mode, it attempts to retrieve the prtDevMode property for that report, in the aht_tagDevMode structure named *dm*. If it succeeds, it pulls the dmPaperSize, dmPaperWidth, and dmPaperLength values from that structure and places them in controls on the form. Note that the code converts the width and length values to inches from tenths of millimeters by dividing by the INCHES_TO_MM constant (254). Finally, if the report is to be printed on paper with a user-defined size, this code enables the width and length text boxes on the form.

Once you enter the width and height values you want, clicking the Save Settings button executes this code fragment:

```
dm.dmPaperSize = Me!cboPaperSize
If dm.dmPaperSize <> ahtDMPAPER_USER Then
    dm.dmPaperWidth = 0
    dm.dmPaperLength = 0
Else
    dm.dmPaperWidth = Me!txtPaperWidth * INCHES_TO_MM
    dm.dmPaperLength = Me!txtPaperLength * INCHES_TO_MM
```

(Continued on next page)

(Continued from previous page)

```
End If
dm.dmFields = ahtDM_PAPERSIZE Or ahtDM_PAPERLENGTH Or ahtDM_PAPERWIDTH
intSuccess = ahtSetDevMode(Me!cboReportList, A_REPORT, dm)
```

This code retrieves the selected paper size from the combo box on the form. If you selected anything besides a user-defined size, the code sets the dmPaperWidth and dmPaperLength members to be 0. Otherwise, it converts the values you entered from inches to tenths of millimeters (multiplying by INCHES_TO_MM (254)) and stores the new values in the dmPaperWidth and dmPaperLength members.

Before it replaces the report's prtDevMode property, it must take one final action: setting the dmFields member to reflect the fields that have changed. The code uses the OR operator to add together the three constants from Table 5-11 that indicate which fields have been changed, and places the sum in the dmFields member of the structure. Once done, the code can call the ahtSetDevMode function to replace the prtDevMode property.

> ### OR VS. ADDITION
> Programmers normally use the OR operator to add together constants, like the ahtDM_* constants in Table 5-11. The constants in that table tell the dmFields member of the aht_tagDevMode structure which fields have been changed in the structure. Each constant consists of a 16-bit hexadecimal value that has exactly one bit set to 1. All the rest of the bits in the value are 0. Using this technique, you can store up to 16 different pieces of information in one 16-bit number. You could use the + to add the values, but using the OR operator instead makes it clear, in context, that you're not so much adding ordinary values as setting the bits in a flag field.

Comments

The technique presented in this How-To will only work if the object whose prtDevMode property you're modifying is opened in design mode. If you switch the report into print preview mode, and then select the Save Settings button on frmPrintSettings, you'll see no error message: The code attached to the button will just fail in its attempt to set the prtDevMode property. In production code, you'd either want to handle that error or ensure that the object was open in the correct mode before attempting to set the property.

To help you check the mode, you can use one of two methods:

- For forms, you can check the CurrentView property. This will tell you if the form is in design, form, or datasheet view.

- For reports, there's no such convenient test. To check and see whether the report is in design view (which is all that really matters for your purposes here), you can use the isReportInDesignMode function, in the basOpenReport module. You'll find it set up as a private function, but you can easily remove the Private keyword and use it as is, or copy it to your own application. It returns True if the report you specify is open in design mode and False otherwise.

Paper size is just one of many options you can change using the prtDevMode property. Since it's more involved than most, we chose it as the topic for this How-To. You may want to combine the information in this topic with all the detail in How-To 5.4 to create your own form that will allow your applications to change any or all of the prtDevMode properties for reports or forms.

5.6 HOW DO I...   COMPLEXITY: ADVANCED

Retrieve information about the selected printer of a form or report?

Problem

Access's Print|Setup dialog allows me to specify either the default printer or a specific printer for each printable object. I'd like to be able to find out, programmatically, which printer has been selected for an object and whether or not the object is set to print to the default printer. How can I retrieve that information?

Technique

The Windows DEVNAMES structure keeps track of the three pieces of information Windows must know about an output device: the device name (HP LaserJet 4/4M), the driver name (HPPCL5E), and the output port (LPT1:). In addition, the DEVNAMES structure keeps track of whether the specific printer happens to be the default Windows printer. The DEVNAMES structure is too complex to be very useful to Basic programmers, so Access provides the prtDevNames property, which mirrors the data in the DEVNAMES structure for forms and reports. The goal of this How-To is to get the information from an object's prtDevNames property into an aht_tagDeviceRec structure, which is far simpler to manage but carries the same information.

Steps

Load and run frmSelectedPrinters in 05-06.MDB. Figure 5-8 shows the form after rptReport3 is selected, and the report's output device, driver, and port are filled in on the form. In addition, since this report was set up to print to the default printer, the Printing to Default Printer check box is selected.

To retrieve printer information about forms or reports in your own applications, follow these steps:

1. Import the modules listed in Table 5-17 from 05-06.MDB into your own application. Skip any modules that you have previously imported.

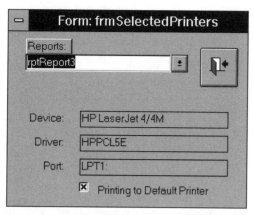

Figure 5-8 The sample form, frmSelectedPrinters, after selecting rptReport3

MODULE NAME	PURPOSE	CONTAINS
basOpenReport	Open a report in design mode, or do nothing if it's already open.	ahtOpenReport
basPrintTypes	Define data types and constants for all examples in this chapter.	
basPrtDevNames	Get and set prtDevName values, copying them into an aht_tagDeviceRec structure.	ahtGetDevNames, ahtSetDevNames

Table 5-17 Modules to import from 05-06.MDB in order to access the prtDevNames property

2. To retrieve prtDevNames information about a particular form or report, call the ahtGetDevNames function, with the following syntax. Table 5-18 lists the parameters for ahtGetDevNames and their data types.

```
fSuccess = ahtGetDevNames (strObject, intType, dr, fDefault)
```

PARAMETER NAME	DATA TYPE	DESCRIPTION
strObject	String	Name of the object in question
intType	Integer	A_FORM or A_REPORT
dr	aht_tagDeviceRec	On return, the prtDevNames info
fDefault	Integer	On return, True if this is the default printer, False otherwise

Table 5-18 Parameters for the ahtGetDevNames function

For example, the following code fragment, from frmSelectedPrinters, displays the chosen report's device name, driver name, and output port in text boxes on the form. In addition, it sets the value of the chkDefault check box if the selected printer is also the default printer.

```
If ahtGetDevNames(strReport, A_REPORT, dr, fDefault) Then
   Me!txtDevice = dr.drDeviceName
   Me!txtDriver = dr.drDriverName
   Me!txtPort = dr.drPort
   Me!chkDefault = fDefault
End If
```

How It Works

Just like the prtMip and prtDevMode properties discussed previously in How-To's 5.3 and 5.4, the prtDevNames property consists of a stream of bytes, not distinct values. To retrieve the values, you must use the LSet command to overlay the data from the prtDevNames property onto a user-defined type. The prtDevNames property is a bit more complex, however, than was explained in How-To 5.3, since it contains variable-length text. Unlike prtMip and prtDevMode, the prtDevNames property includes two parts: The first part contains integers acting as pointers into the second part. Three integers in the first part give the offsets, within the second part, of the three null-delimited strings contained in the property (the device name, the driver name, and the output port). One extra integer contains either a 1 or a 0, indicating whether or not the object was set up to print to the default printer (1) or to a specific printer (0).

The following paragraphs explain how ahtGetDevNames extracts the necessary three strings from an object's prtDevNames property. (All the following code fragments are from ahtGetDevNames, in basPrtDevNames.) First, it copies the prtDevNames property of an object to a string variable:

```
Dim strNames As String

If intType = A_FORM Then
   strNames = Forms(strObject).prtDevNames
Else
   strNames = Reports(strObject).prtDevNames
End If
```

Since *strNames* now holds a stream of bytes containing all the information you need, you must use the LSet command to copy it to a structure where you can break it down into its component. Remember, though, LSet requires that both operands be user-defined data types. (See How-To 5.3 for information on using LSet.) In this case, you just want the first 8 bytes of the prtDevNames property (three offsets plus the default flag), so you'll use a helper structure defined like this:

```
Type aht_tagDEVNAMEStr
   DNStr As String * 8
End Type
```

You'll need to use the LSet command to copy just the first 8 bytes from the string (comprising the four integers you need, since each one takes up 2 bytes) into the structure where you really want the four integers, of user-defined type aht_tagDevNames. As usual, basPrintTypes contains all the type definitions you'll need:

```
Type aht_tagDEVNAMES
    dnDriverOffset As Integer
    dnDeviceOffset As Integer
    dnOutputOffset As Integer
    dnDefault As Integer
End Type
```

The code, then, looks like this:

```
Dim dnStrTemp As aht_tagDevNameStr
Dim dn As aht_tagDevNames

dnStrTemp.dnStr = Left(strNames, 8)
If Err = 0 Then
    LSet dn = dnStrTemp
End If
```

Once you've gotten the four integers into the aht_tagDevNames structure, you can pull apart the three strings that follow the integers in the original data. To make this as simple as possible, basPrtDevNames includes a function, GrabDevName, whose purpose it is to pull pieces out of the prtDevNames string, given a starting position. The code in ahtGetDevNames calls GrabDevName like this:

```
dr.drDeviceName = GrabDevName(strNames, dn.dnDeviceOffset)
dr.drDriverName = GrabDevName(strNames, dn.dnDriverOffset)
dr.drPort = GrabDevName(strNames, dn.dnOutputOffset)
```

This code fills in all three pieces of dr, the aht_tagDeviceRec structure that ahtGetDevMode is attempting to fill in.

To finish up, ahtGetDevNames copies the value from dn.dnDefault into the integer parameter you passed to ahtGetDevNames:

```
fDefault = dn.dnDefault
```

Comments

Notice that basPrtDevNames does include a function named ahtSetDevNames. This function exists only for the sake of completeness, and you should be wary about using it. Normally, you can't use it to set the values in the prtDevNames property, since changing the output device in the prtDevNames property also requires changing it in the prtDevMode property. But if you change the output device without also retrieving reasonable data for the rest of the prtDevMode property, you're likely to cause Access, Windows, and/or your computer to crash, since Windows and Access will be at odds as to the current output device and its characteristics. Though it's possible to make this work using an additional user-supplied DLL, you're better off just setting up your reports to print to the default printer, and changing that value.

If you can't use the prtDevNames property without an added library to change the selected printer for an object, you might be tempted to believe that prtDevNames doesn't do you any good. That's not true, as you'll see in How-To's 5.7 and 5.8. The first one (5.7) discusses how you can choose a new default printer at runtime, so that reports configured to print to the default device will now go to the new default printer. You can (and should) set the default printer back to its original state when you're done. The second How-To (5.8) shows you how to use the prtDevNames property to create a report that lists all the reports in your database and whether or not they're configured to print to the default printer. Using this tool, you can ensure that all your reports are set up correctly before delivering your application. As long as all your reports print to the default printer, you can use the technique from How-To 5.7 to change the default printer, print the report, and then switch the default printer back to its original state.

5.7 HOW DO I... COMPLEXITY: INTERMEDIATE

Choose an output device at runtime?

Problem
I'd like to be able to select an output device while my application is running, without having to pop up the Print|Setup dialog. Is there a way to present a list of available printers and have the chosen report print to the chosen device? For example, sometimes I'd like to print my reports to the printer, and other times to the fax device.

Technique
Though this topic sounds complex, its solution is really just a combination of previous How-To's in this chapter. How-To 5.2 showed how to retrieve a list of available print devices, and retrieve and set the default device. How-To 5.6 showed how to determine if a given report or form was configured to print to the default printer. Given those two techniques, this How-To shows you how to retrieve and store the current default output device, set a new output device, print the Access object (using the new default device), and then restore the original default device. This process will only work for Access objects that print to the default printer, and the sample form takes that into account.

Steps
Load and run frmDefaultPrinterList from 05-07.MDB. Figure 5-9 shows the form in use, with the report rptReport3 selected and ready to print. Since rptReport3 has been configured to print to the default printer (you can open the Print|Setup dialog to confirm this), the Default Printer? check box on the sample form is checked. In addition, if the chosen object will print to the default printer, you can choose a different output device from the combo box on the bottom of the form (of course, this will only work in your test case if you have more than one output device installed). If the report you choose is set up to print to a specific printer, you won't be able to choose a new output device. (In the sample database, only rptReport3 is configured to print to the default printer.) If you choose a different output device (a fax driver, for example), the sample form will send the selected report to that output device, saving, modifying, and restoring the default print device.

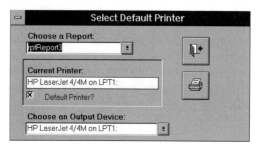

Figure 5-9 The sample form,
frmDefaultPrinterList, ready to choose a new
output device

To print a report to a specific output device in your own applications,
follow these steps:

1. Import the objects listed in Table 5-19 from 05-07.MDB.

OBJECT TYPE	OBJECT NAME
Form	frmDefaultPrinterList
Module	basDefaultPrinter
Module	basGetPrinters
Module	basINIFile
Module	basOpenReport
Module	basPrintItem
Module	basPrintTypes
Module	basPrtDevNames
Module	basToken

Table 5-19 Objects to import from 05-07.MDB, allowing you to choose output devices at runtime

2. When you're ready to print, open frmDefaultPrinterList. If you select a
    report that's set up to print to the default printer, you'll be able to specify a
    new output device.

How It Works

The sample form, frmDefaultPrinterList, consists of three items, all of which
have been covered previously in this chapter. The list of reports was used in
How-To's 5.3, 5.4, 5.5, and 5.6, and the method for filling the list was discussed
in How-To 5.3, in the "Comments" section. Once you've chosen a report from
the combo box, the sample form shows the selected printer for that report and
whether or not the report is to be printed on the default printer. The combo
box on the bottom of the sample form allows you to choose an output device,
if the selected report is destined for the default printer.

The only outstanding issue, then, is the code for printing the report: storing
away the current default printer, setting the new printer, printing the report to

the new printer, and then resetting the original device. These activities are well supported by the routines you'll find in the 05-07.MDB modules.

When you click on the printer button on the sample form, you execute this code in the form's module:

```
Sub cmdPrint_Click ()

    Dim dr As aht_tagDeviceRec
    Dim ctl As Control

    ' Retrieve the pieces needed by dr from
    ' the combo box.
    Set ctl = Me!cboPrinters
    dr.drDeviceName = ctl.Column(1)
    dr.drDriverName = ctl.Column(2)
    dr.drPort = ctl.Column(3)
    If Not PrintItem(Me!cboReportList, A_REPORT, dr) Then
        MsgBox "Unable to print " & Me!cboReportList
    End If
End Sub
```

The first step in cmdPrint_Click is to gather up the information about the new printer. Since the combo box showing the list of printers contains all the necessary information (device name, driver name, and output port) in hidden columns, it's simple to fill in the required aht_tagDeviceRec structure, using the Column property of the combo box:

```
Set ctl = Me!cboPrinters
dr.drDeviceName = ctl.Column(1)
dr.drDriverName = ctl.Column(2)
dr.drPort = ctl.Column(3)
```

Once you've filled the data structure, cmdPrint_Click calls the PrintItem function (in the basPrintItem module) to do the work of storing the current printer, setting the chosen output device, printing the report, and then resetting the output device to its original status:

```
Function PrintItem (ByVal strName As String, intType As Integer,dr As aht_tagDeviceRec)

    ' Return True if successful, False otherwise.

    Dim drOld As aht_tagDeviceRec
    Dim intRetval As Integer

    intRetval = False

    ' Store away the previous default printer
    If (ahtGetDefaultPrinter(drOld)) Then
        If ahtSetDefaultPrinter(dr) Then
            ' Turn off error checking, so cancelling the
            ' report doesn't trigger a runtime error.
            On Error Resume Next
            Select Case intType
```

(Continued on next page)

(Continued from previous page)

```
            Case A_REPORT
                DoCmd OpenReport strName, A_NORMAL
                DoCmd Close A_REPORT, strName
            Case A_FORM
                DoCmd OpenForm strName
                DoCmd Print
                DoCmd Close A_FORM, strName
        End Select
        On Error GoTo 0

        ' Put the original printer information back in
        ' WIN.INI.
        If ahtSetDefaultPrinter(drOld) Then
            ' If you got all the way to here,
            ' you succeeded!
            intRetval = True
        End If
      End If
   End If
   PrintItem = intRetval
End Function
```

This is the procedure that does all the work, and you can call this from any application in which you need this functionality—it's not dependent on the form. Pass it an object name, the object type (A_FORM or A_REPORT), and a filled-in structure with information about the printing device, and you're all set.

To change the default printer, PrintItem first preserves the original default printer:

```
If ahtGetDefaultPrinter(drOld) Then ...
```

Then, it sets the new output device:

```
If ahtSetDefaultPrinter(dr) Then ...
```

Then, it's time to print. PrintItem opens the object and prints it, using macro actions that depend on the object type:

```
' Turn off error checking, so cancelling the
' report doesn't trigger a runtime error.
On Error Resume Next
Select Case intType
   Case A_REPORT
      DoCmd OpenReport strName, A_NORMAL
      DoCmd Close A_REPORT, strName
   Case A_FORM
      DoCmd OpenForm strName
      DoCmd Print
      DoCmd Close A_FORM, strName
End Select
On Error GoTo 0
```

Finally, PrintItem restores the original printer:

```
' Put the original printer information back in WIN.INI.
If ahtSetDefaultPrinter(drOld) Then
    ' If you got all the way to here,
    ' you succeeded!
    intRetval = True
End If
```

Comments

There are many changes you can make to this sample application. You might, for example, want to supply the report name without providing a combo box for it on the form. In that case, you would use a form like the sample form in How-To 5.2, showing only the list of output devices. You would modify the cmdPrint_Click procedure, shown in the "How It Works" section above, to take the report name from a variable instead of from the form's combo box.

You might also want to add some error handling. For the sake of simplicity, the routines here include minimal, if any, error handling. Though it's unlikely that your application will be unable to write or read WIN.INI, it could certainly happen. Production code would enable error handling and check the error value any time you read or write disk files, and react accordingly should an error occur.

5.8 HOW DO I...   COMPLEXITY: INTERMEDIATE

Determine which of my reports are not set to print to the default printer?

Problem

I am about to distribute my application to other Access users. I want to ensure that all my reports are set to Default Printer so they will work with the user's installation of Windows. How do I create a list of all my reports and show whether or not they have been saved with the Default Printer setting?

Technique

Building on the code examples in this chapter, you can use the functionality of the ahtGetDevNames procedure to determine if a report has Default Printer selected. This How-To uses this function, along with some simple Data Access Objects code, to get a list of reports in your database, check the Default Printer setting, and save the results to a table. This table feeds a report that you can print, rptReportPrinters. Once you have this list, you can set the output device for each report that has been set to print to a specific printer, rather than to the Windows default printer.

Steps

Open and run frmShowReports from 05-08.MDB. Figure 5-10 shows the form once it has done all its calculations. It will show the name of every report in your database, along with the Default Printer setting for each. You can obtain a

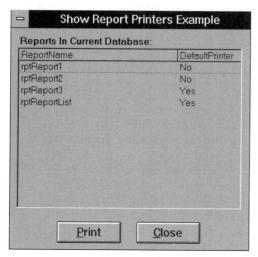

Figure 5-10 Report Printers Example form

printout of this information by pressing the Print button, which prints the rptReportPrinters report (Figure 5-11).

To use this form in your own applications, follow these steps:

1. Import the objects listed in Table 5-20 from 05-08.MDB. (Skip any of the modules that you might have imported already.)

2. Once you've imported the objects, open frmShowReports to create the list of reports in your application, along with their output status.

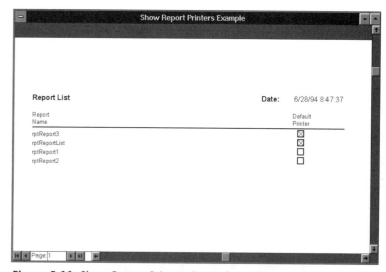

Figure 5-11 Show Report Printers Example report

OBJECT TYPE	OBJECT NAME
Table	tblReportPrinters
Form	frmShowReports
Report	rptReportPrinters
Module	basOpenReport
Module	basPrintTypes
Module	basPrtDevNames

Table 5-20 Objects to import from 05-08.MDB, allowing the creation of output status report

How It Works

To see how this technique works, open the frmShowReports form in design view, then open the form's module window and locate Form_Open. This subroutine calls the GetReports subroutine, which does most of the actual work. By iterating through the Documents collection of the Reports container, GetReports has access to each report in your database. Notice that the subroutine calls the Refresh method before it actually uses the collection; this ensures that the collection is up to date.

```
Sub GetReports ()
    '
    ' Get a list of reports from the current database,
    ' and write the name, along with the default printer
    ' status, to the output table
    '
    Dim db As Database
    Dim rst As Recordset
    Dim conReports As Container
    Dim intCounter As Integer
    Dim strName As String

    On Error GoTo GetReportsError

    Call EmptyTable("tblReportPrinters")
    Set db = DBEngine.Workspaces(0).Databases(0)
    Set rst = db.OpenRecordset("tblReportPrinters")
    Set conReports = db.Containers("Reports")

    Application.Echo False

    ' Refresh to get latest list
    conReports.Documents.Refresh

    ' Loop through all the reports in the container's
    ' documents collection, opening each report in turn,
    ' and checking to see if that report is formatted to
    ' send its output to the default printer.
    For intCounter = 0 To conReports.Documents.Count - 1
        strName = conReports.Documents(intCounter).Name
        rst.AddNew
```

(Continued on next page)

(Continued from previous page)

```
          rst![ReportName] = strName
          rst![DefaultPrinter] = GetDefaultPrinter(strName)
      rst.Update
   Next intCounter

GetReportsExit:
   Application.Echo True
   On Error Resume Next
   rst.Close
   Exit Sub

GetReportsError:
   Resume GetReportsExit
End Sub
```

The core of this technique is the ahtGetDevNames function, introduced in How-To 5.6. By calling this function and checking the value of the passed fDefault parameter, you can quickly tell if a report is set to print to the Windows default printer. This function only works on an open report, so the technique must first open the report. (Since, in this case, you won't be writing to the report but just retrieving its prtDevNames property, you can open it in preview mode. This will minimize the screen flashing.) It opens the report by calling ahtOpenReport, obtaining the output status by calling GetDefaultPrinter, and then closing the report. GetDefaultPrinter is the function that determines whether or not a report is set to print to the default printer.

```
Function GetDefaultPrinter (ByVal strReport As String) As Integer
   '
   ' Determine if the named report is set to 'Default Printer'
   '
   ' In  : strReport - name of report to check
   ' Out : True/False
   '
   Dim dr As aht_tagDeviceRec
   Dim fDefault As Integer

   If ahtOpenReport(strReport, A_PREVIEW) Then
      If ahtGetDevNames(strReport, A_REPORT, dr, fDefault) Then
         GetDefaultPrinter = fDefault
      End If
   End If

   ' ahtOpenReport() leaves the report open,
   ' so close it now.
   DoCmd SelectObject A_REPORT, strReport, False
   DoCmd Close

End Function
```

This routine is passed a report name, which passes it in turn to ahtOpenReport. The ahtOpenReport function, used throughout this chapter, handles opening the report. Next, the routine calls the ahtGetDevNames function to determine whether or not the report has been set to print to the Windows default printer. Finally, the routine closes the report and returns the value stored in fDefault to the GetReports subroutine. GetReports fills in the table named tblReportPrinter's which contains a record for each report containing the report name and a Yes/No field for the Default Printer setting of that report.

Comments

This How-To loads every report, in turn, to retrieve the prtDevNames property of each. When you open a report, there is some screen painting involved. When you open a report in design view, the toolbars and properties sheet associated with report design also open. When you open a report in print preview mode (as in this How-To) there's still a bit of screen flashing as the code loads each report. Even if you turn off the screen display using Application.Echo before opening the report, you will still see activity on your monitor. Although this is not a problem in a development process like the technique shown here, it can be a real eyesore when presented to your users. Unfortunately, Access has no built-in functionality to completely disable screen painting. On the other hand, if you are willing to do a little Windows API programming, you can easily call the LockWindowUpdate function to completely disable screen painting, as shown in How-To 4.3.

6

Managing
Data

HOW DO I...

The point of a database program is to handle data. Access provides a majority of the tools you'll need, but there are many tasks for which you'll have to "roll your own." This chapter concentrates on working with data in ways that traditional database operations don't support. You'll learn how to filter your data, back it up, find where it's located on the file system, and save housekeeping information.

All examples in this chapter use some form of Access Basic, but don't worry. They are clearly explained, and "test-bed" applications are supplied to show you how each technique works.

6.1 Save, with each record, the name of the person who last edited it and the date

Access keeps track of when an object is created and last modified. However, it does not track this information at the record level. This How-To will show how to use the CurrentUser and Now functions to retrieve record modification information and then use form events to write this information to the form's record whenever it is changed or added.

6.2 Identify a new record in a form

There is no inherent functionality in Access to programmatically determine whether you are on a new record while in a form. In this How-To you'll see how to use the Bookmark property to identify whether you are on a new record.

6.3 Create an automated backup procedure

Since Access saves all database objects in a single DOS file, it can be difficult to save and restore selected objects from backups. This How-To will demonstrate routines to selectively save Access objects to another Access database. Using the CopyObject action and a variety of support routines, you can create an easy-to-use form that allows you to select and back up objects.

6.4 Create and use flexible counter fields

Access counter fields provide an easy way to add unique key values to records. But the value in a counter field is "informationless"—it is not useful on its own for sorting or identifying a record. This How-To will illustrate the use of custom counter fields that are multi-user aware and contain characters from another identifying field (such as LastName) to create unique keys that sort intuitively.

6.5 Get a complete list of field information from a table or query

Through the Data Access Objects model, Access maintains a list of all objects in your database, and you can use this model to easily get a list of structure information from a table or query. This information can be used in other functions, such as the generic Query By Form example discussed in this chapter.

6.6 Create a Query By Form filter

There are many ways to filter data on a form. You can base the form on a query that selects the desired record, modify the form's embedded query, or dynamically change the form's query parameter values. However, all of these methods require either hard-coded changes to the form, or a lot of form-specific references. In this How-To, you will create a generic form that prompts you for filter criteria and filters the data in your form.

6.7   Determine the name and path of Access databases

Often you need to know the physical location of various files that make up your Access application. This How-To will use Data Access Objects and Windows API calls to return file names and paths of the current database, a library database, any open database, the currently active workgroup database (SYSTEM.MDA), and the currently active utility database (UTILITY.MDA).

6.1   HOW DO I...   COMPLEXITY: EASY

Save, with each record, the name of the person who last edited it and the date?

Problem

My application is used in a multi-user environment with users regularly adding and editing records. I want to save information in each record about the record's creation and modification. How do I save the data and time of edits and updates, along with the user's name, in each record?

Technique

Access has no built-in functionality to log changes to table data. Often, you need this information to track changes and additions to your database. This How-To demonstrates a technique for saving user information with each record. Using the BeforeUpdate event and the Now and CurrentUser functions, you can easily add this functionality to your application.

Steps

Load frmUserInfoExample from 06-01.MDB. In this form, shown in Figure 6-1, you can enter and edit data in the form's record source (the tblSample table). Make a change to an existing record, and the DateModified and UserModified

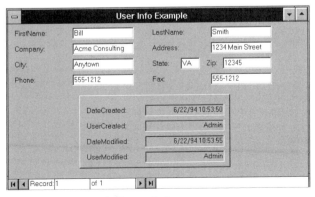

Figure 6-1 User Info Example form

fields are updated with the current date, time, and user's name. Add a new record, and the DateCreated and UserCreated fields are updated.

To add this functionality to your application, follow these steps:

1. Modify your table to include four new fields as shown in Table 6-1.

FIELD NAME	FIELD TYPE
DateCreated	Date/Time
UserCreated	Text (20)
DateModified	Date/Time
UserModified	Text (20)

Table 6-1 New fields to add to your table

2. Open your form in design view. Add new text box controls as shown in Table 6-2.

CONTROL NAME	CONTROL SOURCE
txtDateCreated	DateCreated
txtUserCreated	UserCreated
txtDateModified	DateModified
txtUserModified	UserModified

Table 6-2 New controls to add to your form

3. Set the Enabled property of these new fields to No and the Locked property to Yes. This prevents users from modifying the user information fields.
4. Create an event procedure for the form's BeforeUpdate property by selecting [Event Procedure] in the form's properties sheet under Before Update. Then click on the Builder button on the right of the properties sheet. The form's module appears.
5. Type the following code into the new event procedure:

```
Sub Form_BeforeUpdate (Cancel As Integer)

  If IsNull(Me!txtDateCreated) Then
     Me!txtDateCreated = Now
     Me!txtUserCreated = CurrentUser()
  Else
     Me!txtDateModified = Now
     Me!txtUserModified = CurrentUser()
  End If

End Sub
```

6. Save the form, then run it to test your new code.

How It Works

This simple technique uses a form's BeforeUpdate event, which is executed by Access every time you make a change to a record or create a new record. You attach Access Basic code to the event by creating an event procedure for the BeforeUpdate event. The code then looks at the value of the txtDateCreated control, and if it's null (meaning it contains no value), the code assumes it is a new record and writes the current date and time and the name of the current user to the two creation fields. If the txtDateCreated control is not null, the code assumes this is a modification to an existing record and writes to the two modification fields.

Comments

By tying code to a form's events, you gain complete control over how data is managed. In this example, the BeforeUpdate event is used because it allows you to make changes to the record before it is committed to the table. Notice that the AfterUpdate event is not used. If you tied your Access Basic code to the AfterUpdate event, the code would retrigger the AfterUpdate event when you write to the user information controls. This would leave Access in a state where you cannot move off the current record without first discarding your changes to the record.

6.2 HOW DO I...
COMPLEXITY: INTERMEDIATE

Identify a new record in a form?

Problem

I frequently need to perform an action based on whether or not the current row is the "new" row on a form. For example, I might want to disable a command button that allows the user to move to the new row. Access doesn't provide a means of determining whether the current row is the new row. How can I do this?

Technique

You can use an underdocumented feature in Access to check whether or not the current row of a form is the new row. By attempting to gather some information about the form that doesn't yet exist when on the new row, you'll trigger a runtime error. By checking for the particular error, you'll know that you were on the new row. This solution requires a tiny bit of Access Basic code but is really quite simple.

Steps

Load and run frmContacts from 06-02.MDB. Move from row to row, using the (PGUP) and (PGDN) keys or the navigation buttons on the form. Either way, when you reach the end of the recordset and move to the new row, you'll see a brightly colored message pop up on the form, as shown in Figure 6-2.

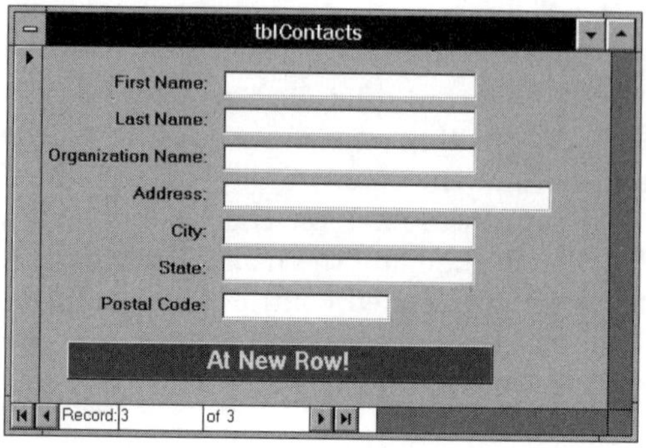

Figure 6-2 The sample form, once it has reached the new row

To implement this functionality in your own forms, follow these steps:

1. Create a new module or use an existing one. Enter this code into the module:

```
Function ahtAtNewRow (frm As Form)
Const ERR_NO_CURRENT_ROW = 3021

    Dim strBM As String

    On Error Resume Next
    strBM = frm.Bookmark
    ahtAtNewRow = (Err = ERR_NO_CURRENT_ROW)
    On Error GoTo 0
End Function
```

2. Check the returned value of the ahtAtNewRow function from your form's Current event. If it returns True, you are on a new row. If it returns False, you are not on a new row. In the sample form, the event procedure code makes a label visible or invisible, depending on the return value from the ahtAtNewRow function. Note that you must pass a form reference to the function. The reference can be the Me object available only in a form's module, an explicit form reference (Forms!SomeForm), or the Form property, when called directly from the properties sheet. The following example shows how the function is called from the Current event of the sample form. It sets the Visible property of a label control to the return value of the function:

```
Sub Form_Current ()
    Me!lblMainNew.Visible = ahtAtNewRow(Me)
End Sub
```

How It Works

The ahtAtNewRow function first disables error trapping, with the On Error Resume Next statement. This way, should a runtime error occur, the code will continue without so much as a complaint.

> **WARNING:** *Bear in mind that you should only use this technique when you're checking for specific errors in your code immediately after each line of code that does any work. Disabling error handling in general is a very bad idea.*

With error handling disabled, ahtAtNewRow attempts to gather a piece of information that it knows will trigger an error if the current row is the new row. If that error occurs, the function knows that you were on the new row. To trigger the error, the code attempts to retrieve the current row's bookmark. For each existing row on a bound form, Access maintains a unique value, the row's bookmark, which you can use to refer to this row. Since the new row is not yet written to disk, it doesn't have a bookmark. Attempting to retrieve this nonexistent bookmark triggers a runtime error.

The function returns True or False, depending on the evaluation of this expression:

```
ahtAtNewRow = (Err = ERR_NO_CURRENT_ROW)
```

That is, if the current error number (Err) is equal to the ERR_NO_CURRENT_ROW constant, then it returns True (you're on the new row). If it's not equal to that constant, then it returns False.

Comments

Although it's not explicitly stated in the documentation, you must reset the error handler (On Error Goto 0) as you exit ahtAtNewRow. Normally, if you have an error handler set up in your code, you only jump to the error handler if an error occurs. Once you get there, you use a Resume statement to jump to an exit point. Doing this clears the Err value, so the calling procedure doesn't know that the error occurred. On the other hand, this function disables error handling, and if an error occurs (as it will in this function if you move to the new row), the code just "falls out" of the function. If you neglect to reset the error handler, the calling procedure will see the error value and might react to it, if the code in that procedure checks the value of Err for some reason. It's also just good programming form: If you set the error handler, you ought to clear it. In most cases, you can safely leave this step out. However, where the code might be called from many different procedures, forgetting to reset the error handler can be disastrous.

6.3 HOW DO I...   COMPLEXITY: INTERMEDIATE

Create an automated backup procedure?

Problem

I use a standard backup program to save my databases. However, because the backup is at the DOS level, the entire database is saved. This is fine for archival purposes, but I want more control over which objects are saved. How can I get

Access to display a list of objects and allow me to save selected ones to the output database I specify?

Technique

Most backup programs work at the DOS level. You specify the files and directories to be saved, and the program compresses and writes the files to the specified destination. When you need to restore data, you can selectively restore files and directories. But Access stores all database objects in one DOS file, which complicates saving and restoring specific database objects. For example, you may inadvertently delete records from a table and want to restore the original table from a backup. Using a typical backup program, you would restore the entire MDB file to a temporary location and then use Access to import the saved table.

This How-To shows you how to create routines to selectively save Access objects to another Access database. Using the CopyObject action and a variety of support routines, you can create an easy-to-use form that allows you to select and back up objects.

Steps

The 06-03.MDB database contains a table named USysBackup, a form named frmAutomatedBackup, and a module named basAutomatedBackup. The table holds a list of objects in the current database and their types. The form is used to select objects and start the backup process. The module contains the code that fills the list of available objects and does the object copying. Some sample objects have been copied into this database from the Northwind Traders example database that ships with Access. You can use these sample objects to test the automated backup procedure.

To see the process in action, open and run frmAutomatedBackup from 06-03.MDB (Figure 6-3). Click the Refresh List button to display a list of all of the objects in your database. To select an object for backup, click on the Selected? check box. Once all desired objects are selected, type in a name of a database in which you want the objects backed up. Be sure to specify the .MDB extension. Click the Make Backup button, and the backup database is created and all selected objects are copied to it.

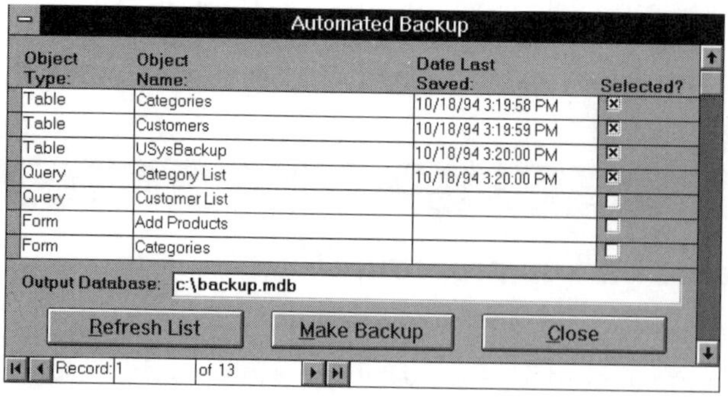

Object Type:	Object Name:	Date Last Saved:	Selected?
Table	Categories	10/18/94 3:19:58 PM	X
Table	Customers	10/18/94 3:19:59 PM	X
Table	USysBackup	10/18/94 3:20:00 PM	X
Query	Category List	10/18/94 3:20:00 PM	X
Query	Customer List		
Form	Add Products		
Form	Categories		

Output Database: c:\backup.mdb

Refresh List   Make Backup   Close

Record: 1 of 13

Figure 6-3 Automated Backup form, frmAutomatedBackUp, with objects selected for archiving

To add this functionality to your database, follow these steps:

1. From 06-03.MDB, import the USysBackup table, the frmAutomatedBackup form, and the basAutomatedBackup module into your database.
2. Call the automated backup procedure from anywhere in your application by opening the frmAutomatedBackup form. For example, you can place a command button on your application's main menu form. In the command button's OnClick event procedure, type the following code:

```
DoCmd OpenForm "frmAutomatedBackup"
```

How It Works

To see how this technique works, open frmAutomatedBackup in design view. Open the form's module window. The form has three command buttons that initiate actions.

The first, cmdRefresh, refreshes the list of available objects by calling the ahtGetObjects subroutine. The ahtGetObjects subroutine uses Data Access Objects (DAO) methods and properties to build a table containing an inventory of all objects in your database. It works by looping through each collection of objects and writing the object's name and type to the USysBackup table. Notice that the writing process is handled by a separate subroutine called WriteObject. This allows you to write an object in one line of code. Finally, you see that all writes are encased in a BeginTrans...CommitTrans pair. This technique allows you to perform buffered writes, which are much faster (see Chapter 8).

Next, frmAutomatedBackup is requeried to display the current values from the USysBackup table. To make the backup, you click the cmdBackup button. The event procedure for this button's OnClick property calls the ahtMakeBackup subroutine, passing the name of the output database you selected. The ahtMakeBackup subroutine is the heart of the technique. It creates the new database and performs the actual copying:

```
Sub ahtMakeBackup (strOutputDatabase As String)
'
' Makes a backup of objects identified in USysBackup table
' using the CopyObject action
'
' In:
' strOutputDatabase - name of database to output to
'
Dim dbCurrent As Database
Dim dbOutput As Database
Dim rstSelected As Recordset
Dim intCounter As Integer
Dim intType As Integer

Const MB_ICONQUESTION = 32
Const MB_YESNO = 4
Const ID_YES = 6

' Check to see if the output database exists
If Len(Dir(strOutputDatabase)) > 0 Then
   Beep
```

(Continued on next page)

(Continued from previous page)

```
        If MsgBox("Output Database exists. Overwrite?", MB_ICONQUESTION + MB_YESNO) = ID_YES Then
            Kill strOutputDatabase
        Else
            Exit Sub
        End If
    End If

    DoCmd Hourglass False
    Set dbCurrent = DBEngine.Workspaces(0).Databases(0)
    Set rstSelected = dbCurrent.OpenRecordset("SELECT * FROM USysBackup WHERE [Selected]=Yes;")
    Set dbOutput = DBEngine.Workspaces(0).CreateDatabase(strOutputDatabase, DB_LANG_GENERAL)
    dbOutput.Close

    If Not (rstSelected.EOF And rstSelected.BOF) Then
        Do Until rstSelected.EOF
            If Not IsNull(rstSelected![ObjectName]) Then
                Select Case rstSelected![ObjectType]
                    Case "Table": intType = A_TABLE
                    Case "Query": intType = A_QUERY
                    Case "Form": intType = A_FORM
                    Case "Report": intType = A_REPORT
                    Case "Macro": intType = A_MACRO
                    Case "Module": intType = A_MODULE
                End Select

                ' Don't try and export the current form
                If Not (intType = A_FORM And rstSelected![ObjectName] = "frmAutomatedBackup") Then

                    ' If export fails, let the user know
                    On Error Resume Next
                    DoCmd CopyObject strOutputDatabase, rstSelected![ObjectName], ⇒
intType, rstSelected![ObjectName]
                    If Err  0 Then
                        Beep
                        MsgBox "Unable to backup " & rstSelected![ObjectType] & ": " ⇒
& rstSelected![ObjectName]
                    Else
                        ' Update Date Last Saved
                        rstSelected.Edit
                        rstSelected![DateLastSaved] = Now
                        rstSelected.Update
                    End If
                End If
            End If
            rstSelected.MoveNext
        Loop
    End If

    ' Cleanup
    rstSelected.Close
    DoCmd Hourglass False

End Sub
```

This subroutine first uses the CreateDatabase method to create the output database. If the database already exists, you are asked if you want to overwrite it. Next, the recordset is opened on the USysBackup table, selecting only those records where the Selected field is set to True. A loop then walks through each record and uses the CopyObject action to copy the current object to the output database. An error trap is set to check the status of each CopyObject action. There are some cases where you cannot copy an object, such as when the object is open in design view, or when an object is based on other objects that don't exist. For example, the 06-03.MDB database contains two reports that are based on tables that don't exist. Since the CopyObject action can't copy these objects, a runtime error occurs. The subroutine's error handling, initiated by the On Error Resume Next statement, allows the runtime error to be ignored until the code is ready to deal with it. If an error occurs, the subroutine presents a message box explaining that the object could not be copied, along with the name and type of the object.

Comments
The name of the backup table, USysBackup, is somewhat unusual. Each Access database contains a set of tables called system tables. These are the tables that begin with the characters Msys. These objects only appear when you have Show System Objects set to Yes in the View|Options menu. You can hide these objects by setting Show System Objects to No. Access 2.0 provides the undocumented ability to hide your own tables by prefixing the table's name with Usys. By calling the backup table USysBackup, you can hide the table in the database window by setting the Show System Objects option to No.

Notice that this technique uses the CopyObject action instead of the more traditional TransferDatabase action. CopyObject, which was added in Access 2.0, offers you the same functionality as TransferDatabase, but since it only supports Access objects, it requires fewer arguments. CopyObject also allows you to specify a new name for the object in the destination database. This is useful if you want give the object's copy a name different from the source object.

6.4 HOW DO I...
COMPLEXITY: INTERMEDIATE

Create and use flexible counter fields?

Problem
I use counter fields in my tables to ensure that I have unique values for my key fields. But a key based on the numeric counter field doesn't sort my tables in a useful order. Also, counter fields always start at 1, and I want my counter values to start at another number. Can I create a replacement for Access counter fields that gets around these limitations?

Technique
Access makes it easy to add unique value key fields to a table using the counter data type. Counters, which are automatically maintained by Access, ensure a unique value for each record. Since they are just numbers, counter fields are

"informationless." Viewing data sorted on a counter field often shows data out of its natural order. Additionally, counter fields always start at 1, thereby limiting their usefulness when your application needs to start counting at another value. This How-To shows you how to create your own counter fields that are multi-user ready and to combine these counter values with other fields in the table to make your data sort more intuitively.

Steps

This example shows two techniques in action: getting a unique counter value and appending it to the first five characters of the LastName field. The resulting value is then written to the ContactID field. This serves two purposes. It guarantees you a unique key value and creates a key field that contains information that is useful for sorting. To see the Flexible Counter Fields technique in action, open and run frmFlexibleCounterExample from 06-04.MDB (Figure 6-4). Add a new record by pressing (END) and then (PGDN). Type in some data and be sure to put a value in the LastName field. Move to a new record to cause the form's BeforeUpdate event to fire. The form will automatically put the new value in the ContactID field.

You can easily add this technique to your application by following these steps:

1. From 06-04.MDB import the tblCounters table and the basFlexibleCounters module into your database.
2. Prepare your table by adding a new field to become the key value. If you only want to store a numeric counter value, set the field's type to Number, Long Integer. To add information for sorting, set the new field's type to Text and set its length long enough to accommodate the numbers returned by the flexible counter routine, plus the length of the characters you want to add to the field.
3. Open the tblCounters table and edit the CounterValue field to start at the desired value.
4. Open the data entry form for your application in design view. In the form's BeforeUpdate event procedure, write code that calls the flexible counter

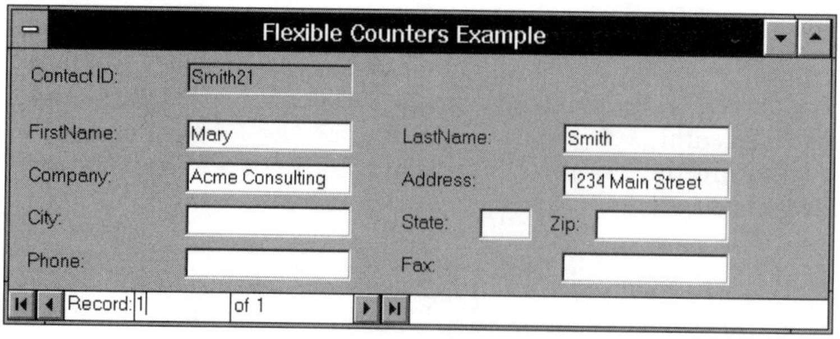

Figure 6-4 Flexible Counters Example form, frmFlexibleCounterExample

routine and writes the returned value to your key field. To call the routine, use the following syntax:

```
Dim LngCounter As Long
LngCounter = ahtGetCounter()
If LngCounter > 0 Then
   Me![MyKeyField] = LngCounter
End If
```

This code will run whenever a new record is added to the form, but before the new record is actually written to the form's table. The lngCounter variable is assigned to the value returned by the ahtGetCounter value. If the value is greater than 0, it is written to the MyKeyField field.

If you want to add information to the key field, use the same technique but concatenate the counter value to text from another field, as in this example:

```
Dim LngCounter As Long
LngCounter = ahtGetCounter()
If LngCounter > 0 Then
   Me![MyKeyField] = Left$(Me![LastName],5) & LngCounter
End If
```

Note that if you are basing your key value on another field, your code should ensure that a value exists in that field. The best way to assure this is to set the Required property on the field to Yes in the table's design.

How It Works

The heart of this technique is the ahtGetCounter function. In a nutshell, the function tries to open the tblCounters table exclusively and, if it succeeds, gets the value in the CounterValue field and increments it. This value is then returned to the procedure that called it.

```
Function ahtGetCounter ()
   '
   ' Get a value from the counters table and
   ' increment it
   '
   ' Out:
   '     Long Integer
   '
   Dim dbCurrent As Database
   Dim rstCounter As Recordset
   Dim intLockOptions As Integer
   Dim intLocked As Integer
   Dim intRetries As Integer

   Const MB_ICONQUESTION = 32
   Const MB_YESNO = 4
   Const ID_YES = 6

   ' Set number of retries
   Const MAXRETRIES = 30
   Set dbCurrent = DBEngine.Workspaces(0).Databases(0)
   intLockOptions = DB_DENYWRITE + DB_DENYREAD
```

(Continued on next page)

(Continued from previous page)

```
    intLocked = False

  Do While (True)
    For intRetries = 0 To MAXRETRIES
      On Error Resume Next
      Set rstCounter = dbCurrent.OpenRecordset("tblCounters", DB_OPEN_TABLE, intLockOptions)
      If Err = 0 Then
        intLocked = True
        Exit For
      End If
    Next intRetries

    If Not intLocked Then
      Beep
      If MsgBox("Could not get a counter: " & Error$ & " Try again?", ⇒
MB_ICONQUESTION + MB_YESNO) = ID_YES Then
        intRetries = 0
      Else
        Exit Do
      End If
    Else
      Exit Do
    End If
  Loop

  On Error GoTo 0
  If intLocked Then
    ahtGetCounter = rstCounter![CounterValue]
    rstCounter.Edit
    rstCounter![CounterValue] = rstCounter![CounterValue] + 1
    rstCounter.Update
    rstCounter.Close
  Else
    ahtGetCounter = -1
  End If

  DBEngine.Idle DB_FREELOCKS

End Function
```

After assigning some variable, the function tries to open a recordset object on the tblCounters table. By specifying the DB_DENYREAD and DB_DENYWRITE constants as the Options argument to the OpenRecordset method, you are trying to exclusively lock the table by preventing other users from reading from or writing to the table. If the function cannot lock the table after the number of retries specified by the MAXRETRIES constant, it displays a message box allowing the user to retry or cancel. If the user chooses to cancel, a −1 value is returned. If the lock succeeds, the value of the counter field is saved and the counter field is incremented.

At the end of the function, the Idle method with the DB_FREELOCKS constant is used to give Access processing time to explicitly remove any locks the function placed.

Comments
This technique employs a few helpful multi-user tricks that are worth noting. First, you have precise control over how a table is locked, by specifying options for the OpenRecordset method (see Table 6-3). It's necessary to understand these options if your application is to be effective in a multi-user environment.

OPTION/CONSTANT	DESCRIPTION
DB_DENYREAD	Prevent other users from reading records.
DB_DENYWRITE	Prevent other users from modifying or adding records.
DB_READONLY	Prevent your code from modifying or adding records (other users can still modify or add records).
DB_APPENDONLY	Prevent your code from modifying existing records; it can only add new records.

Table 6-3 Multi-user options for the OpenRecordset method

Second, it is important to understand the correct use of the Idle method. In a multi-user environment with heavy activity, Access will not always have enough time to unlock objects immediately and write pending data to tables. By using the Idle method, you force Access to take the time to write all pending requests to disk. With the DB_FREELOCKS constant, you force Access to stop other processing and immediately update the lock table.

6.5   HOW DO I...   COMPLEXITY: INTERMEDIATE

Get a complete list of field information from a table or query?

Problem
I want to get a list of fields in a table or query. The ListFields method is fine for certain situations, but it does not return all of a field's properties. How can I create a replacement for ListFields that supplies all the available information on fields?

Technique
In Access 1.x, the ListFields method was the only supported way to return a list of fields. Its usefulness is limited by the fact that it only returns some of the field information, and it always returns a snapshot. Through Data Access Objects (DAO), Access 2.0 provides you with all the properties of field objects. You can use DAO to write a more robust replacement for ListFields that returns all of a field's information in the form of an Access table. Because the resulting object is a table rather than a snapshot, you can modify its records.

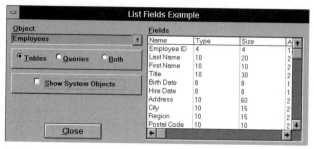

Figure 6-5 ListFields Example form, frmListFieldsExample, showing field information for the Employees table

Steps

The 06-05.MDB database contains the ahtListFields function and a sample form to demonstrate how it works. Also included are several sample tables and queries from the Northwind Traders example database. To see the technique in action, open and run the frmListFieldsExample form from 06-05.MDB (see Figure 6-5). Select Tables, Queries, or Both to specify the object types you want to view. Select an object from the Object combo box. After a moment, the form will display a list of fields and their properties in the Fields list box. Scroll left and right to see additional properties and up and down to see additional fields.

To use this technique in your application:

1. Import basListFields into your database.
2. To call the subroutine, use the following syntax with the parameters described in Table 6-2.

ahtListFields (*strName, intTable, strOutputTable*)

PARAMETER NAME	DESCRIPTION	EXAMPLE
strName	The name of the table or query you want a list of fields for.	"Customers"
intTable	True if strName is a table, False if it is a query.	True
strOutputTable	The name of the table to hold the field list.	"tmpOutputFields"

Table 6-4 Parameters for the ahtListFields function

3. The ahtListFields function creates a table with the name specified by strOutputTable and fills it with one record for every field in the specified table or query. The table is similar in structure to a snapshot returned by the ListFields method, except that it has additional fields to hold the values of other field properties. Table 6-5 describes the structure of the table. Note that the first seven fields are identical to those returned by Access's ListFields method. The remaining fields are additional information supplied only by the ahtListFields function.

FIELD NAME	DATATYPE	DESCRIPTION
Name	String	Name of the field.
Type	Integer	Data type of the field as represented by an integer. Search Access' online help under ListFields to decode this value.
Size	Integer	Size of the field.
Attributes	Long Integer	Field's attributes. Search Access's online help under Attributes to decode this value.
SourceTable	String	Name of the field's underlying table. If the table is an attached table, this field will contain the name of the table as it exists in the real table.
SourceField	String	Name of the field's underlying field. If the table is an attached table, this field contains the name of the field as it exists in the real table.
CollatingOrder	Integer	Collating order of the table. Search Access's online help under CollatingOrder to decode this value.
AllowZeroLength	Integer	True if zero length strings are allowed in the field, False otherwise.
DataUpdatable	Integer	True if the field is updatable, False otherwise.
DefaultValue	Text	Field's default value.
OrdinalPosition	Integer	Field's position in the table starting at 0.
Required	Integer	True if the field requires an entry, False otherwise.
ValidationRule	String	Field's Validation Rule property.
ValidationText	String	Field's Validation Text property.
Caption	String	Field's Caption property.
ColumnHidden	Integer	True if the field is hidden in datasheet view, False otherwise.
ColumnOrder	Integer	Order that the field appears in datasheet view.
ColumnWidth	Integer	Width of the field as it appears in datasheet view.
DecimalPlaces	Integer	Field's number of decimal places.
Description	Text	Field's description.
Format	Text	Field's format string.
InputMask	Text	Field's input mask string.

Table 6-5 The ahtListFields table structure

How It Works

The ahtListFields function stores its results in a table, so the first thing the subroutine does is to create a table. By calling the MakeListTable subroutine, it creates a table using an SQL MAKE TABLE command. It does this by constructing an SQL string that equates to an SQL MAKE TABLE command along with all of the field definitions, and then it passes this string to the CreateQueryDef method:

```
Set dbCurrent = DBEngine.Workspaces(0).Databases(0)
Set qdTmp = dbCurrent.CreateQueryDef(DBEngine.Workspaces(0).Databases(0), strSQL)
qdTmp.Execute
```

Once the output table is created, ahtListFields opens an object variable on the table or query you specified. (If your source object is a table, a Tabledef object is opened. If your source object is a query, a QueryDef object is opened.) The function then reads the value of each of the Tabledef or QueryDef object's fields and their properties and writes them to the output table.

```
Set tdfInput = dbCurrent.Tabledefs(strName)
For intCounter = 0 To tdfInput.Fields.Count - 1
    Set fld = tdfInput.Fields(intCounter)
    rstOutput.AddNew
    rstOutput![Name] = fld.Name
    rstOutput![Type] = fld.Type
    rstOutput![Size] = fld.Size
    rstOutput![Attributes] = fld.Attributes
    rstOutput![SourceTable] = fld.SourceTable
    rstOutput![SourceField] = fld.SourceField
    rstOutput![CollatingOrder] = fld.CollatingOrder

    ' Some DAO properties may not yet exist, so disregard errors.
    On Error Resume Next
    rstOutput![AllowZeroLength] = fld.Properties("AllowZeroLength")
    rstOutput![DataUpdatable] = fld.Properties("DataUpdatable")
    rstOutput![DefaultValue] = fld.Properties("DefaultValue")
    rstOutput![OrdinalPosition] = fld.Properties("OrdinalPosition")
    rstOutput![Required] = fld.Properties("Required")
    rstOutput![ValidationRule] = fld.Properties("ValidationRule")
    rstOutput![ValidationText] = fld.Properties("ValidationText")
    rstOutput![Caption] = fld.Properties("Caption")
    rstOutput![ColumnHidden] = fld.Properties("ColumnHidden")
    rstOutput![ColumnOrder] = fld.Properties("ColumnOrder")
    rstOutput![DecimalPlaces] = fld.Properties("DecimalPlaces")
    rstOutput![Description] = fld.Properties("Description")
    rstOutput![Format] = fld.Properties("Format")
    rstOutput![InputMask] = fld.Properties("InputMask")
    rstOutput.Update
Next intCounter
```

Notice the On Error Resume Next statement about halfway through the code. This is necessary because some properties do not exist until they are assigned a value. If the error-handling statement is not in effect, a runtime error will occur when the code tries to read the value of one of these properties. By telling the code to resume after an error, you are allowing the subroutine to execute without stopping for runtime errors.

Finally, now that ahtListFields has populated the new table with field information, it closes the recordset and object variables. You can use this table to get a complete list of information about the specified object's fields. This information can be useful when your program needs to display a list of fields for user selection, or perform a specific action depending on a table's field properties.

Comments

This technique is easy to implement and offers more functionality than the built-in ListFields method. All of a field's properties are returned, and since it returns a table instead of a snapshot, you can use indexes to search the table and modify the table's records if necessary. You'll find useful example code in the frmListFieldsExample. Look at the GetTables function to see how to get a list of tables and queries, and at the FillTables function for a sample of a list-filling function.

6.6 HOW DO I...   COMPLEXITY: ADVANCED

Create a Query By Form filter?

Problem

I would like to create a generic Query By Form utility that I can call from my forms, allowing users to filter the records shown. I want users to be able to type in criteria for multiple fields. I also want to implement this technique in my forms with a minimum of modifications. How can I do this using Access?

Technique

There are many ways to filter data on a form. You can base the form on a query that selects the desired record, modify the form's embedded query, or dynamically change the form's query parameter values. However, all of the methods require either hard-coded changes to the form or a lot of form-specific references. To make a more generic Query By Form, the ApplyFilter action is the best answer. This action allows you to limit the records a form displays based on either an existing saved query, or a string expression equivalent to the WHERE clause in an SQL Select statement. This How-To demonstrates how to create a generic form that prompts the user for filter criteria, and then constructs a WHERE clause and applies it to the current form using the ApplyFilter action.

Steps

To see this technique in action, open and run frmQueryByFormExample from 06-06.MDB (Figure 6-6). This is a sample data entry form that is based on the Customers table (also in 06-06.MDB). Initially, there is no filter applied, so all records are visible. To apply a filter, click the Filter Records button, and the Query By Form dialog appears (Figure 6-7).

In the Fields combo boxes, select the fields for which you want to specify criteria. In the Criteria text boxes, type in the filter criteria. If the selected field is a numeric field, click the field's corresponding Numeric check box. Notice that as you select fields and type in criteria, the Filter SQL String text box displays the filter string. This string will be passed back to your form when you click OK.

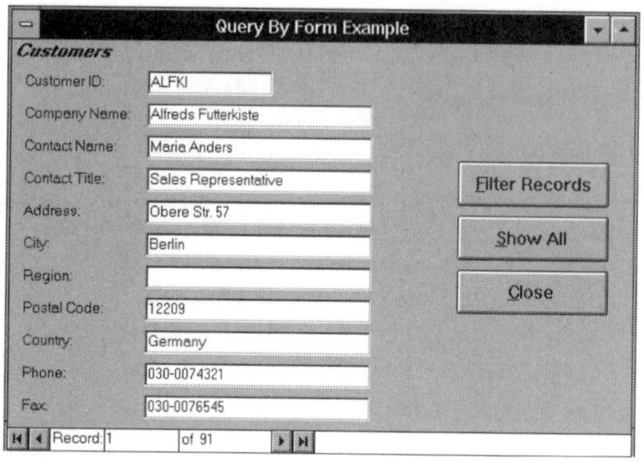

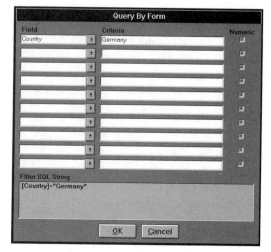

Figure 6-6 Query By Form Example form, frmQueryByFormExample, in use

Figure 6-7 Query By Form dialog, frmQueryByForm

When you have finished filling in the Query By Form dialog, click OK to return focus to the Query By Form Example form, with the new filter in place. To remove the filter and show all records, click the Show All Records button.

To call the Query By Form from your application, follow these steps:

1. From 06-06.MDB, import frmQueryByForm and basQueryByForm into your database.

2. Select the form from which you want to call the Query By Form routine and open it in design view.

3. Place a command button control on your form called cmdFilter. This button calls the Query By Form dialog. Set the button's caption to something descriptive, such as Query By Form or Filter Records. In the button's OnClick event property, select [Event Procedure].

4. Click the Builder button to create an event procedure for the Click event. The form's module appears with a skeleton subroutine defined. In the subroutine, type the following code:

```
Sub cmdFilter_Click ()
  Dim strFilter As String

  strFilter = GenericFilter(Me)
  If strFilter <> "" Then
    On Error Resume Next
    DoCmd ApplyFilter , strFilter
    If Err <> 0 Then
      MsgBox "Could not apply filter '" & strFilter & "'"
    End If
  End If

End Sub
```

5. Place another command button control on your form and name it cmdShowAll. This button is used to remove the filter and show all records. In the button's OnClick property, select [Event Procedure].

6. Click the Builder button to create an event procedure for the Click event. The form's module appears with a skeleton subroutine defined. Inside the subroutine, type the following code:

```
DoCmd ShowAllRecords
```

7. Save and close the form. To test the Query By Form routine, open your form and click the cmdFilter button. Try some filters on various fields to get a feel for how it works. To return to viewing all records, click the cmdShowAll button.

How It Works

If all you had to do was call the ApplyFilter action to create a filter, this would be a substantially shorter How-To! The truth is, to create a more generic Query By Form, there is some work involved. Keep in mind that your ultimate goal is to construct an SQL WHERE clause that you can pass to the ApplyFilter action.

The process starts when you click the cmdFilter button, which contains the following code:

```
Sub cmdFilter_Click ()
   Dim strFilter As String

   strFilter = GenericFilter(Me)
   If strFilter <> "" Then
      On Error Resume Next
      DoCmd ApplyFilter , strFilter
      If Err <> 0 Then
         MsgBox "Could not apply filter '" & strFilter & "'"
      End If
   End If

End Sub
```

This routine calls the GenericFilter function, passing a reference to the current form. The GenericFilter function does the actual work of generating a filter string. Once it returns the string, the cmdFilter_Click subroutine tries to apply the string as a filter, and it displays a message if it fails. Looking at the GenericFilter function in the basQueryByForm module, you see the following code:

```
Function GenericFilter (frmCurrent As Form) As String

' Opens the Query By Form form as a dialog, suspending
' execution until focus returns
'
' Returns a string containing a SQL WHERE clause
'
DoCmd OpenForm "frmQueryByForm", , , , , A_DIALOG, frmCurrent.RecordSource

If Not IsNull(Forms![frmQueryByForm]!txtSQL) Then
```

(Continued on next page)

(Continued from previous page)

```
      GenericFilter = Forms![frmQueryByForm]!txtSQL
   End If


   DoCmd Close A_FORM, "frmQueryByForm"

End Function
```

This function starts by opening frmQueryByForm as a Dialog form, passing your form's RecordSource property as an Open Argument. There are two things happening here. First, by opening the form as a Dialog form, you are suspending execution of the GenericFilter function until the frmQueryByForm closes or becomes hidden. This is important because you don't want the GenericFilter function to attempt to return a value to your form until the user has finished selecting a filter condition. Second, by setting the OpenArgs argument of the OpenForm action to the value of your form's RecordSource property, you are passing information to frmQueryByForm that it can use to generate a list of available fields.

Now that frmQueryByForm is open, look at how the lists of available fields are generated. This may appear to be a simple task at first, but given the possibility that your form may be based on a complex multitable query or SQL string, this becomes a difficult proposition. You may even have two or more fields with the same name from different tables. Since Access doesn't expose a field's underlying table to you as a programmer, there is no way your code can generate such a list. The trick is to let Access do the work for you.

Access combo boxes have built-in functionality to display a list of fields in a table. By setting a combo box's RowSourceType property to FieldList, you are telling Access to look at a table's structure instead of its data. This causes Access to populate the combo box with a list of fields specified in the combo box's RowSource property. The OnOpen subroutine in frmQueryByForm reads the value passed to it by the GenericFilter function, which happens to be the record source of your form. By assigning this value to the combo box's RowSource property, you end up with a list of fields.

The ten text boxes on the form allow users to type in the criteria for the corresponding selected field. You will also notice that each field has a Numeric check box. Because you are going to be constructing an SQL string, the parser needs to know how to delimit the fields. Apostrophes will be placed around the text fields, and nontext fields will not be delimited. Since Access does not provide you with the fields' underlying table names, there is no method for generically determining the data type of a field. To get around this, you ask the user to specify whether or not the field is numeric.

As the user makes changes to each control, the control's AfterUpdate event fires, calling the MakeFilter function. This function reads the values of each of the combo boxes, text boxes, and check boxes, constructs an SQL WHERE clause, and displays it in the txtSQL text box. MakeFilter is one of the simpler functions in this How-To. It steps through each control and, depending on its value, adds it to the SQL WHERE clause:

```
Function MakeFilter ()
    '
    ' Construct an SQL WHERE clause based on the value
    ' of the form's controls
    '
    Dim intCounter As Integer
    Dim varValue as Variant

    Const QUOTE = """"
    strFilter = ""

    For intCounter = 1 To 10
        If Not IsNull(Me("cbo" & intCounter)) Then
            If Not IsNull(Me("txtField" & intCounter)) Then
                If Len(strFilter) > 0 Then
                    strFilter = strFilter & " AND "
                End If
                strFilter = strFilter & " [" & Me("cbo" & intCounter) & "]="

                varValue = Me("txtField" & intCounter)
                If Me("chk" & intCounter) Then
                    strFilter = strFilter & varValue
                Else
                    strFilter = strFilter & QUOTE & varValue & QUOTE
                End If
            End If
        End If
    Next intCounter

    Me!txtSQL = strFilter

End Function
```

The real action begins when the user clicks the OK button. Looking at the code behind the cmdOK button for the Click event, you see that the form's Visible property is set to False. How does this cause anything to happen? Remember that the GenericFilter function opened the Query By Form form as a Dialog form. Doing this caused the GenericFilter code to suspend execution and the code in the Query By Form form's module to begin execution. To return control from a Dialog form, you either close the form or do something to cause it to lose focus. You want focus to return to the GenericFilter function, but you want to leave the Query By Form dialog open so you can read the value of the SQL WHERE clause it generated. Obviously, closing the dialog is not the way to go. Instead, use the DoCmd Hide action. This hides the Dialog form, causing control to return to the GenericFilter function, but it leaves the Dialog form open so you can get values from its controls.

The GenericFilter function now resumes execution and reads the value of the txtSQL text box. If it is not blank, it tries to apply it as a filter to your form. Finally, it closes the Query By Form form.

Comments

As you can see, there are some limitations to implementing a truly generic routine, the most significant being the inability of Access to supply you with the name of the table underlying a control's field. It is thus impossible to check the data type of a field, forcing the user to explicitly identify numeric fields. However, on most single-table forms, this Query By Form technique works quite well. You can extend the concept to determine field data types if the calling form is based on a single table, or a single-table query. You can also extend the searching capability by adding user-selectable operators, such as greater than and less than, and a case-matching option.

6.7 HOW DO I...

COMPLEXITY: ADVANCED

Determine the name and path of Access databases?

Problem

In my application, I need to know the path and file names of various databases. Specifically, I want a function that can return the name and path of the current database, of an attached table's parent database, the currently executing library database (if applicable), the currently active workgroup database, the currently active utility database, and for good measure, the current working directory and the directory where Access 2.0 resides. Is there a way to write a reusable function that will return this information?

Technique

When you start Access and load your database, you actually have at least three databases loaded. Access automatically loads a workgroup database and a utility database every time it starts. In addition, library databases may be loaded to support the Access Wizards and any third-party add-ins you have installed. Often, it is useful in application design to know the actual file names and paths of these databases. Also, when you are using attached tables you need to know the name and path of the attached table's parent database.

There is no single method for getting a database's name and path. The process you use depends on the database you are interested in. This How-To shows you how to write a single function that encompasses all the needed methods. For determining the name and path of the current or library database or an attached table's parent database, you use Data Access Objects. For the system and utility database, a few Windows API calls return the desired information. Built-in Access functions return the current working directory and the Access directory.

Steps

Open the 06-07.MDB database, and open the frmViewFilePaths form (Figure 6-8), which shows all the information that the GetFilePaths function can return. This form works its magic by calling a fairly simple function called ahtGetFilePath.

This form's Open event calls code that in turn calls the ahtGetFilePath function for each of the seven items on the form. The name and path of the

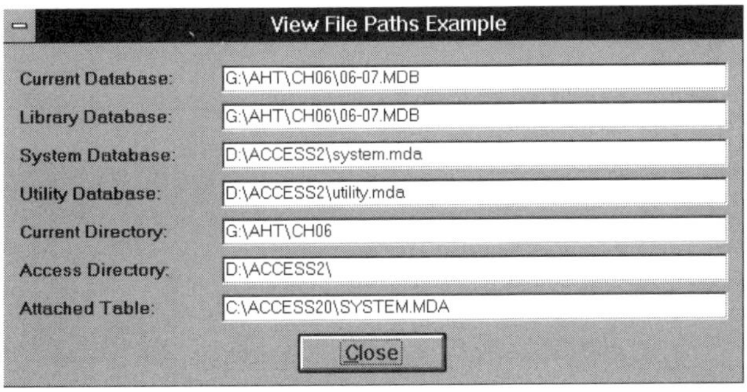

Figure 6-8 View File Paths Example form, showing various directory information

current database are displayed first. This is the database that is currently loaded through the Access user interface. (In our example, it is 06-07.MDB, preceded by the path where it is located.) Next the name of the library database is displayed. If this form was located in a library database that you invoked through your MSACC20.INI file, the name and path of the library database will be shown here. Because you are currently executing the form from the current database, the name and path of the "library" database is equivalent to the name and path of the current database. Next, the system database name and path are displayed. Your system database (the workgroup database you are logged into) is defined in MSACC20.INI. Unless you have implemented security and created your own workgroup database, this will most likely be SYSTEM.MDA in your Access directory. The utility database containing financial functions, some Access forms, and a few other objects necessary for running Access name and path comes next. The name and path of your utility database are also defined by an entry in MSACC20.INI. The current directory and the directory where the MSACCESS.EXE executable is stored are displayed next. Finally, the form displays the path of an attached table's underlying database.

To add this functionality to your application, follow these steps:

1. Copy the following function declarations from the basGetFilePath module to the declarations section of a module in your database:

```
Declare Function aht_apiGetWindowsDir Lib "Kernel" Alias "GetWindowsDirectory"⇒
(ByVal strBuf As String, intLen As Integer) As Integer
Declare Function aht_apiGetPrivProfileStr Lib "Kernel" Alias ⇒
"GetPrivateProfileString" (ByVal strAppName As String, ByVal strKeyName⇒
As String, ByVal strDefault As String, ByVal strReturned As String, ByVal⇒
intSize As Integer, ByVal strFileName As String) As Integer
```

2. Copy the ahtGetFilePath, GetPrivProfile, and GetWindowsDir functions from the basGetFilePath module to a module in your database. To call the function, you need to supply a string describing the type of information you want and, if you are looking for the name and path of an attached

table, a table name. Use the following syntax with the parameters supplied in Tables 6-6 and 6-7.

```
strPath = ahtGetFilePath (strType, strTable)
```

PARAMETER NAME	DESCRIPTION
strType	Specifies the path you are looking for. See Table 6-7.
strTable	If you specified "Attached" for the strType argument, set strTable to the name of the attached table.

Table 6-6 Parameters for the ahtGetFilePath function

VALUE	RETURNS THE PATH OF
"CurrentDB"	Current database
"LibraryDB"	Library database
"SystemDB"	Current workgroup database
"UtilityDB"	Current utility database
"CurrentDir"	Current working directory
"AccessDir"	Access directory
"Attached"	Attached table's underlying database

Table 6-7 Values for the strType parameter

How It Works

The ahtGetFilePath function uses a variety of techniques to get the desired information. The function evaluates the strType argument in a Select Case statement and runs the appropriate code.

Getting the Current and Library Databases

To determine the current database, the function sets a database variable to the current database and references the Name property of the database object. The library database code is similar, but instead of using the DBEngine.Workspaces(0).Databases(0) syntax to assign a database variable, the CodeDB function is used. CodeDB returns a reference to the library database in which the code is executing. As mentioned previously, if this code is called from a library database installed through the MSACC20.INI file, it will return the name and path of the database containing the library code.

Getting the Workgroup and Utility Databases

To get the name and path of the workgroup database, a little more work is involved. First, Access doesn't maintain the workgroup database in the Data Access Objects (DAO) hierarchy. Because of this, you can't use DAO to retrieve information about the workgroup database. The only way you can programmatically find the name of the current workgroup database is to look in the INI file that was used when Access loaded.

Most Windows applications use INI (initialization) files to specify options for the application's behavior, and Access is no exception. The MSACC20.INI file specifies a wide variety of options, some of which can be configured by the user. The INI files are divided into sections. The Options section of the Access INI file contains the name of the workgroup database and is identified by this SystemDB= line:

```
[Options]
SystemDB=C:\ACCESS20\SYSTEM.MDA
UtilityDB=C:\ACCESS20\UTILITY.MDA
AllowCustomControls=1
AllowOLE1LinkFormat=0
```

Typically, this file is named MSACC20.INI and is located in your Windows directory. In an ideal world, you could simply get the value from C:\WINDOWS\MSACC20.INI. However, Access allows you to specify an alternate INI file by using the /INI parameter on the Access command line.

To further complicate matters, Windows may not be installed in C:\WINDOWS. Fortunately, Access will supply the name of its INI file, and you can use a Windows API call to get the directory from which Windows is executing. The first step is to get the name of the INI file. Using the SysCmd function with an action constant of SYSCMD_INIFILE returns the name of the INI file. If the INI file is the standard MSACC20.INI file, only the name of the file is returned. If the name is different from MSACC20.INI, the full path and name of the file are returned. This undocumented behavior can be tricky at first, but once you understand the way it works, it becomes quite easy to locate the INI file. If the SysCmd function returns MSACC20.INI, the function then gets the path of the Windows directory, using a Windows API call, and appends that path to the beginning of the INI file name.

Next, the function calls the GetPrivateProfileString Windows API function. By passing the name of the INI file, the section name, and the value you are looking for, you can use GetPrivateProfileString to return any value in an INI file. The function returns a string value, which is trimmed and passed back to your function.

The process for obtaining the name and path of the utility database uses the same technique, differing only in that it asks the GetPrivateProfileString function to look for UtilityDB instead of SystemDB.

Getting the Current Directory and the Access Directory

Getting the current directory and Access directory is very simple. The ahtGetFilePath function maps them to the built-in CurDir and SysCmd functions. CurDir returns the name of the current directory; and SysCmd, with an argument of SYSCMD_ACCESSDIR, returns the path of the directory that contains the MSACCESS.EXE executable.

Getting the Path of an Attached Table

Finally, the athGetFilePath returns the path of the attached table's underlying database by setting a database variable to the current database and looking at the value of the attached table's TableDef object's Connect property. The Connect property contains a string that tells Access where to look for a file and what type of file it is. Typically, the Connect string is in the format:

databasetype ;DATABASE=

The function gets the Connect property for the attached table, strips the identifying information, and returns the path and name of the database.

Comments

Since there is no all-encompassing function in Access to return the path of a database, you have to employ some more sophisticated techniques. As you can see from the above example, to get the name and path of the workgroup database, you have to perform some additional steps. However, since Access 1.x provided absolutely no way to determine database paths, the functionality in Access 2.0, along with a little work on your part, can yield reliable results.

7

Exploring Access Basic

HOW DO I...

Most applications that are distributed to end users include at least some Access Basic code. Since Access Basic provides the only mechanism for performing some tasks (using variables, building SQL strings on the fly, handling errors, and using the Windows API, among others), most developers sooner or later must delve into its intricacies. The topics in this chapter cover some of the details of Access Basic that you might not find in the Access manuals. You'll first find a complete explanation of embedding strings inside other strings, allowing you to build SQL strings and other expressions that require embedded values. Two How-To's here are devoted to creating a procedure stack, allowing you to keep track of the current procedure at all times. The second of the two also creates a profiling log file, helping you document where and for how long your code wandered. You'll learn about the DoEvents statement, which gives Windows time to handle its own chores while your code is running. A group of four How-To's will cover the details of creating list-filling functions, passing arrays as parameters, sorting arrays, and filling a list box with the results of a directory search. The final two How-To's cover some details of *using* Access Basic: how to perform a global search-and-replace, even in closed form or report modules; and how to decide whether to use global or private modules.

7.1 Build string references that include other strings
Many times throughout your work with Access, you'll need to build string expressions that, in turn, include other strings; for example, when calling the domain functions, building SQL expressions, or using the FindFirst or Seek methods. This How-To will show in detail how to create these complex expressions.

7.2 Retrieve the name of the current procedure
Access supplies no function for returning the name of the current procedure. This information can be very useful in error-handling routines. If an error occurs, the user can be presented with an error message and the name of the procedure that was executing at the time. This simple How-To will demonstrate a method you can use to implement your own Access Basic call stack.

7.3 Track the execution order and timing of procedures
Many programming languages such as C and Pascal have profilers that allow the developer to see execution times of each component of an application. Using an extension of the procedure stack discussed in the previous topic, this How-To will show how to implement a profiler in Access Basic. This profiler creates a log file of each procedure executed and its execution time.

7.4 Multitask my Access Basic code
Because of the way Windows handles multitasking, it's quite possible for your Access Basic code to tie Windows up completely for the duration of your procedure. This How-To will demonstrate how you can inadvertently bring Windows to a halt, and how you can solve the problem using the DoEvents statement.

7.5 Add items to a list or combo box programmatically
Unlike Visual Basic, Access Basic doesn't support the simple AddItem method for adding new items to a combo or list box. Because of its datacentric

viewpoint, Access's controls are geared toward pulling data in from tables or queries. Sometimes, however, you must fill a list or combo box with data that isn't stored in a table. This How-To will provide two methods for dynamically filling a control with data.

7.6 Pass a variable number of parameters to a procedure

Access Basic supports passing of arrays to functions and subroutines. Unfortunately, the syntax is not clearly documented. This How-To will give examples of how to pass arrays to procedures as parameters. Using this technique, you'll be able to supply a variable number of parameters to an Access Basic procedure. This capability isn't available by any other means in user-defined procedures.

7.7 Sort an array in Access Basic

A glaring omission from Access is support for a method of sorting arrays. This How-To will demonstrate a general-purpose algorithm you can use to sort arrays in your applications.

7.8 Fill a list box with a list of files

Using the concepts from the previous three topics, this How-To will demonstrate how you can fill a control with a sorted list of file names, given a file specification. In addition, it will demonstrate how to use the built-in Dir function to retrieve the list of names.

7.9 Perform search-and-replace operations on my form and report modules' code

Although form and report modules add many new features to Access 2.0, they complicate matters because they're not always available. If a form isn't loaded, neither is its code. That means that if you're attempting to perform a global search-and-replace operation, Access will find no matches in form modules that aren't currently loaded. This How-To will demonstrate a tool you can use to help you in this process. Studying the tool itself will provide some insights into how to encapsulate code along with its form.

7.10 Decide whether to use form and report modules or general modules

As demonstrated in the previous How-To, using private modules adds to the overhead involved in developing an application. This How-To will enumerate the questions you must answer in deciding whether to use form/report or global modules when adding Access Basic code to your application.

7.1 HOW DO I... COMPLEXITY: INTERMEDIATE

Build string expressions that include other strings?

Problem

I need to use the DLookup function, specifying a search criteria based on an Access Basic variable. No matter what I do, I can't get Access to understand what I'm trying to do. What am I doing wrong?

Technique

Any place in Access where you're required to provide a string expression that contains other strings, you're going to face this problem. That might be (as in the above problem) in using the domain functions (DLookup, DMax, DMin, and so on), in building an SQL expression on the fly, or in using the Find methods (FindFirst, FindNext, FindPrevious, and FindLast) on a recordset. Many programmers agonize over these constructs, but it needn't be that difficult. Since all strings must be surrounded with quotation marks, and you can't embed quotes inside a quoted string, you can quickly find yourself in trouble. This How-To explains the problem and shows you a somewhat generic solution.

Steps

To see an example of building expressions on the fly, load and run frmQuoteTest in 07-01.MDB. This form, shown in Figure 7-1, allows you to specify criteria. Once you press the Find button, the code attached to the button will build the SQL expression shown in the text box and will set the RowSource property for the list box at the bottom of the form accordingly.

To try all the features of the form, follow these three steps:

1. In the First Name text box, enter A. When you press (RETURN), the form builds the appropriate SQL string and filters the list box. Note, in the SQL string, that the value you entered is surrounded by quotation marks. (This is the state in which Figure 7-1 was captured.)

2. In the Birth Date text box, enter 3/13/60. Again, the form should filter the data (down to a single row). Note that the SQL expression must have # signs around the date value you entered, since all dates must be surrounded by # signs.

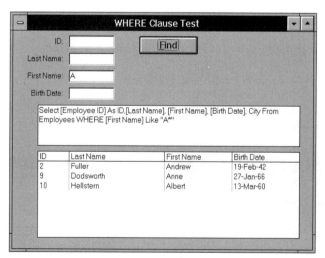

Figure 7-1 The test form, frmQuoteTest, with a subset of the data selected

3. Delete all the data from the four text boxes, and then press the Find button. That should fill the list box with all the rows again. Enter the value 8 in the ID text box, and then press (RETURN). Note that the SQL string this time has no delimiter around the value that you entered.

How It Works

The point of the foregoing exercise is to alert you to the fact that different data types require specific delimiters when they become part of an expression. For example, to use DLookup to find the row in which the LastName field was Smith, you'd need an expression like this:

```
[LastName] = "Smith"
```

Certainly, leaving those quotation marks off would confuse Access, since it would be looking for some variable named Smith.

Date values don't require quotes. Instead, they require # delimiters. To find the row in which the BirthDate field is May 16, 1956, you'd need an expression like this:

```
[BirthDate] = #5/16/56#
```

If you left off the delimiters, Access would think you were trying to numerically divide 5 by 16, and then by 56.

Numeric values require no delimiters. If you were searching for the row where the ID value was 8, you could use this expression,

```
[ID] = 8
```

and Access would know exactly what you meant.

Building Search Criteria

Many situations in Access require that you create strings that supply a search criteria. Since the Jet database engine has no knowledge of Access Basic or its variables, you must supply the actual values before you apply any search criteria or perform lookups. That is, you must create a string expression that contains the *value* of any variable involved, not the variable name.

You could use any of the three examples in the previous section as search criteria, and you would have to surround the string values with quotes. The next few paragraphs show you how to create these search criteria strings.

To build expressions that involve variables, you must supply any required delimiters. For numeric expressions, there is no required delimiter. If the variable named *intID* contained the value 8, then you could use this expression to create the search string that you need:

```
"[ID] = 8"
```

As part of an SQL string, or as a parameter to DLookup, this string is unambiguous in its directions to Access.

To create a search criteria that includes a date variable, you need to include the # delimiters. For example, if you have a variant variable named *varDate* that contains the date May 22, 1959, and you want to end up with this expression,

```
"[BirthDate] = #5/22/59#"
```

you have to insert the delimiters yourself. The solution might look like this:

```
"[BirthDate] = #" & varDate & "#"
```

The complex case occurs, of course, when you must include strings. For those cases, you'll need to build a string expression that contains a string itself, surrounded by quotes, with the whole expression also surrounded by quotes. The rules for working with strings are as follows:

- An expression that's delimited with quotes can't itself contain quotes.

- Two quotes ("") inside a string are seen by Access as a single quote.

- You can use an apostrophe (') inside a string to represent a quote character.

- An expression that's delimited with an apostrophe can't itself contain an apostrophe.

- You can use the value of Chr$(34) inside a string expression to represent the quote character (34 is the ANSI value for the quote character).

Given these rules, you can create a number of solutions to the same problem. For example, if the variable *strLastName* contained "Smith", and you wanted to create a WHERE clause that would search for that name, you must end up with this expression:

```
"[LastName] = "Smith" "
```

That expression, of course, isn't allowed, since it includes internal quotes. An acceptable solution would be the following:

```
"[LastName] = " "Smith" " "
```

The problem here is that the literal value "Smith" is still in the expression. You're trying to replace that with the name of the variable, *strLastName*. You might try this expression,

```
"[LastName] = " "strLastName" " "
```

but that will search for a row with the last name of "strLastName". You probably won't find a match.

One solution, then, is to break that up into three separate pieces—the portion before the variable, the variable, and the portion after the variable (the final quote):

```
"[LastName] = " " " & strLastName & " " " " "
```

Although that may look confusing, it's correct. The first string,

```
"[LastName] = " " "
```

is just a string containing the name of the field, an equal sign, and two quotes. The rule is that two quotes inside a string are treated as one. The same logic works for the portion of the expression after the variable (""""). That's just a string containing two quotes, which Access sees as one quote. Although this solution works, it's quite confusing.

To make things simpler, you can just use apostrophes inside the string:

```
"[LastName] = '" & strLastName & "'"
```

This is somewhat less confusing, but there's a serious drawback: If the name itself contains an apostrophe ("O'Connor", for example), you'll still be in trouble. Access doesn't allow you to nest apostrophes inside apostrophe delimiters, either. So this solution only works when you're sure that the data in the variable can never itself include an apostrophe.

The simplest solution, then, is to use Chr$(34) to embed the quotes for you. An expression such as the following would do the trick:

```
"[LastName] = " & Chr$(34) & strLastName & Chr$(34)
```

If you don't believe this works, go to the Immediate Window in Access and type this:

```
? Chr$(34)
```

Access will return to you by typing the value of Chr$(34)—a quote character.

To make this solution a little simpler, you could create a string variable at the beginning of your procedure and assign it the value of Chr$(34):

```
Dim strQuote As String
Dim strLookup As String

strQuote = Chr$(34)
strLookup = "[LastName] = " & strQuote & strLastName & strQuote
```

This actually makes the code almost readable!

Finally, if you weary of defining that variable in every procedure you write, you might consider using a constant instead. You might be tempted to try this:

```
Const QUOTE = Chr$(34)
```

But, alas, Access won't allow you to create a constant whose value is an expression. If you want to use a constant, your answer is to rely on the "two-quote" rule:

```
Const QUOTE = " " " "
```

Although this expression's use is not immediately clear, once you understand the "two-quote" rule, it works just fine.

Comments

To encapsulate all these rules, you might want to use the function named FixUp in the basFixUpValue module in 07-01.MDB. This function takes as a parameter a variant value and surrounds it with appropriate delimiters.

```
Function FixUp (ByVal varValue As Variant) As Variant

' Add the appropriate delimiters, depending on the data type.
' Put quotes around text, "#" around dates, and nothing
' around numeric values.

    Dim strQuote As String
```

(Continued on next page)

(Continued from previous page)

```
' strQuote contains the ANSI representation of
' a quote character.
strQuote = Chr$(34)

Select Case VarType(varValue)
    Case V_INTEGER, V_SINGLE, V_DOUBLE, V_LONG, V_CURRENCY
        FixUp = CStr(varValue)
    Case V_STRING
        FixUp = strQuote & varValue & strQuote
    Case V_DATE
        FixUp = "#" & varValue & "#"
    Case Else
        FixUp = Null
End Select
End Function
```

Once you've included this function in your own application, you can call it, rather than formatting the data yourself. The sample code in frmQuoteTest uses this function. For example, here's how to build the expression you labored over in the previous example:

```
"[LastName] = " & FixUp(strLastName)
```

FixUp would do the work of figuring out the data type and surrounding the data with the necessary delimiters.

7.2 HOW DO I...   COMPLEXITY: INTERMEDIATE

Retrieve the name of the current procedure?

Problem

Often, when I'm writing an application, I need to know the name of the current procedure from within my code. For example, if an error occurs, I'd like to have a generic function handle the error and display the name of the procedure in which it occurred. Access Basic doesn't include a way to retrieve this information. How can I accomplish this?

Technique

By maintaining a list of active procedures, adding the current name to the list on the way into the procedure, and removing it on the way out, you can always keep track of the current procedure. There are many other uses for this functionality (see the next How-To, for example), but one simple use is to retrieve the name of the current procedure in a global error-handling procedure.

Generally, the kind of data structure that you'll need for maintaining your list is called a stack. That is, as you enter a new procedure, you "push" its name onto the top of the stack. When you leave the procedure, you "pop" the name off the stack. Figure 7-2 shows a graphical representation of a procedure

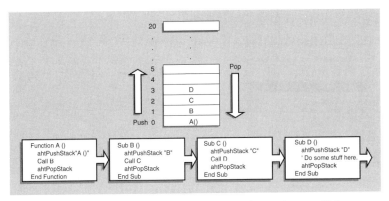

Figure 7-2 The procedure stack and the sample routines to fill it

stack in action. The arrows indicate the direction in which the stack grows and shrinks as you add and remove items.

Steps

To see the procedure stack in action, load 07-02.MDB. Open the module basTestStack in design mode. Open the Immediate Window (choose View|Immediate Window). In the Immediate Window, type

```
? A()
```

which will execute the function named A. Figure 7-2 shows A and the procedures it calls. At each step, the current procedure pushes its name onto the procedure stack, and then calls some other procedure. Once the calling procedure gets control again, it pops its name off the stack. In addition, each procedure prints the name of the current procedure (using the ahtCurrentProc function, discussed in the "How-It Works" section) to the immediate window. Once all execution has finished, you should see output like that shown in Figure 7-3 in the Immediate Window.

Follow these steps to incorporate this functionality into your own applications:

1. Import the module basStack into your application. This includes the procedures that initialize and maintain the procedure stack.

2. Insert a call to the ahtInitStack subroutine into code that executes when your application starts up. Consider adding this procedure call to the code in your main form's OnLoad event procedure. You'll want to call ahtInitStack any time you restart your program during development, so you probably don't want to call it from the Autoexec macro, which only executes when you first load the database. (This is one of the reasons that ahtInitStack is set up as a subroutine, rather than as a function. Since you can't call subroutines from macros, this is an incentive to have you call the

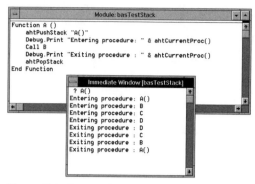

Figure 7-3 Output from running the sample procedure

procedure from some startup Access Basic code.) To call ahtInitStack, either place its name alone on a line of code, or use the Call construct:

```
ahtInitStack
```

or

```
Call ahtInitStack
```

3. For each procedure in your application, place a call to ahtPushStack as the first statement. This procedure will place the value passed to it on top of the stack. As the single argument for each call, pass the name of the current procedure. The example places a pair of parentheses after function names, and nothing after subroutine names, just as a matter of style. As the last line in each procedure, add a call to ahtPopStack, which will remove the current name from the top of the stack.

4. At any time in your application, to retrieve the name of the currently executing procedure, call the ahtCurrentProc function. This function looks at the top of the stack and returns the string it finds there. You can use this as part of an error handler or, as in the next How-To topic, to help track procedure performance.

How It Works

The module you imported from 07-02.MDB, basStack, includes code for maintaining the procedure stack and a module-local variable that is the stack itself. There are just four entry points (nonprivate procedures) in the module. Table 7-1 lists those procedures. By encapsulating all the code for the stack in that one module, you never really have to know how it all works. On the other hand, it's all quite simple.

PROCEDURE NAME	PURPOSE	PARAMETERS
ahtInitStack	Initialize the stack.	
ahtPushStack	Add an item to the stack.	A string to push
ahtPopStack	Remove an item from the stack.	
ahtCurrentProc	Retrieve the name of the current procedure.	

Table 7-1 The four entry points into basStack

BasStack includes two module-global variables: mastrStack, the array of strings that is the stack itself, and mintStackTop, an integer that holds the array slot into which the next stack item will be placed. When you begin your work with the stack, mintStackTop must be 0, so the first item will go in the slot numbered 0. The ahtInitStack procedure does nothing besides initialize mintStackTop:

```
Sub ahtInitStack ()

    ' Resets the stack top to be 0.
    mintStackTop = 0
End Sub
```

At any time, you can add an item to the stack by calling ahtPushStack. You pass to this subroutine the item you want pushed. To push the item, the code places the item in the array, at the location stored in mintStackTop, and then increments the value of mintStackTop.

```
Sub ahtPushStack (strToPush As String)

    ' Handle the error case first.
    If mintStackTop > MAX_STACK Then
        MsgBox MSG_STACK_OVERFLOW
    Else
        ' Store away the string and time.
        mastrStack(mintStackTop) = strToPush

        ' Set mintStackTop to point to the NEXT
        ' item to be filled.
        mintStackTop = mintStackTop + 1
    End If
End Sub
```

The only problem that might occur is that the stack might be full. The constant MAX_STACK is originally set to 20, which ought to be enough levels. (Remember that mintStackTop only goes up one when a procedure calls another procedure. If you have 20 levels of procedure calling, then you might consider rethinking your application, instead of worrying about procedure stacks!) If the stack is full, ahtPushStack will pop up an alert and will not add the item to the stack.

When leaving a procedure, you'll want to remove an item from the stack. To do so, you call the ahtPopStack procedure:

```
Sub ahtPopStack ()

    ' Handle the error case first.
    If mintStackTop = 0 Then
        MsgBox MSG_STACK_UNDERFLOW
    Else
        ' Since you're removing an item, not adding one,
        ' set the stack top back to the previous row. Next time
        ' you add an item, it'll go right here.
        mintStackTop = mintStackTop - 1
    End If
End Sub
```

Just as in ahtPushStack, this code first checks to make sure that the stack integrity hasn't been violated: You can't remove an item from the stack if there's nothing to remove! If you try, ahtPopStack will just pop up an alert and exit. If the stack is intact, the procedure will decrement the value of mintStackTop. By decrementing that value, you've set up the next call to ahtPushStack so that it will place the new value where the old one used to be.

To retrieve the value at the top of the stack without pushing or popping anything, call the ahtCurrentProc function:

```
Function ahtCurrentProc () As String
    ahtCurrentProc = IIf(mintStackTop > 0, mastrStack(mintStackTop - 1), "")
End Function
```

This function retrieves the value most recently placed on the stack (at the location one less than mintStackTop, since mintStackTop always points to the next location to be filled). You can't look at mastrStack yourself, since it's local to basStack. And that's the way it *ought* to be. By keeping you from the details of how the stack works, you can replace just basStack, using a different architecture for the stack's data structure, and the rest of your code won't have to change at all.

Comments

In order for the procedure stack to work, you have to religiously place calls to ahtPushStack and ahtPopStack on entry and exit from *each and every* procedure call. Good coding practice supports the concept of only one exit point from each of your procedures, but even the best programmer sometimes breaks this rule. In order to use the call stack, however, you must catch each and every exit point with a call to ahtPopStack. Keep this in mind as you retrofit old code to use this mechanism, and when devising new code to use it. You can always code for a single exit point, and you will find code maintenance much more reasonable if you do.

7.3   HOW DO I...   COMPLEXITY: INTERMEDIATE

Track the execution order and timing of procedures?

Problem

I'd like to optimize my Access Basic code, but it's almost impossible to tell how long Access is spending inside any one routine, and it's very difficult to track which procedures get called by my code most often. I'd like some way to track which routines get called, in what order, and how much time each takes to run. Can I do this in Access Basic?

Technique

As outlined in How-To 7.2, you can create a code profiler using a stack data structure to keep track of the execution order and timing of the procedures in your application. Though the Access Basic code involved here is a bit more advanced than in How-To 7.2, it's still not terribly difficult to create the profiler. Using it is simple, since all the work is wrapped up in a single module.

Steps

Open 07-03.MDB and load the module basTestProfiler in design mode. In the
Immediate Window, type

? A()

to run the test procedures. Figure 7-4 shows the profile stack and the code in A.
As you can see, A calls B, which calls C, which calls D, which waits 100
milliseconds and then returns to C. C waits 100 milliseconds, and then calls D
again. Once D returns, C returns to B, which waits 100 milliseconds and then
calls C again. This pattern repeats until the code gets back to A, where it finally
quits. The timings in the profile stack in Figure 7-4 are actual timings from one
particular run of the sample.

As the code is set up now, the profiler writes to a text file named
LOGFILE.TXT in your Access subdirectory. You can read this file in any text
editor. For a sample run of function A, the file contained this text:

```
*******************************
Procedure Profiling
10/14/94 4:58:07 PM
*******************************
+ Entering procedure: A()
   + Entering procedure: B
      + Entering procedure: C
         + Entering procedure: D
         - Exiting procedure : D                   109 msecs.
         + Entering procedure: D
         - Exiting procedure : D                   110 msecs.
      - Exiting procedure : C                 329 msecs.
      + Entering procedure: C
         + Entering procedure: D
         - Exiting procedure : D                   110 msecs.
         + Entering procedure: D
         - Exiting procedure : D                   110 msecs.
      - Exiting procedure : C                 330 msecs.
   - Exiting procedure : B               824 msecs.
   + Entering procedure: B
      + Entering procedure: C
         + Entering procedure: D
         - Exiting procedure : D                   110 msecs.
         + Entering procedure: D
         - Exiting procedure : D                   110 msecs.
      - Exiting procedure : C                 330 msecs.
      + Entering procedure: C
         + Entering procedure: D
         - Exiting procedure : D                   110 msecs.
         + Entering procedure: D
         - Exiting procedure : D                   109 msecs.
      - Exiting procedure : C                 329 msecs.
   - Exiting procedure : B               769 msecs.
- Exiting procedure : A()           1702 msecs.
```

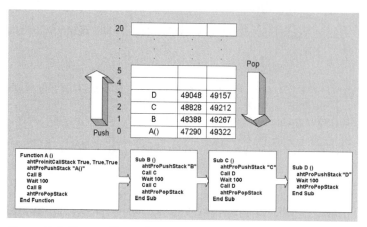

Figure 7-4 The profile stack and the sample routines used to fill it

To incorporate this sort of profiling into your own applications, follow these steps:

1. Import the module basProfiler into your own application. This module includes all the procedures to initialize and use the profiling stack.

2. Insert a call to ahtProInitStack into code that executes when your application starts up. In How-To 7.2, you might have gotten by without calling the initialization routine. In this situation, however, you must call ahtProInitStack each time you want to profile your code, or the profile stack will not work correctly. To call ahtProInitStack, you must pass it three parameters, all of which are logical values (True or False). Table 7-2 lists the question answered by each of the three parameters.

PARAMETER NAME	DESCRIPTION
fDisplay	Display message box if an error occurs?
fLog	Write to log file or just track items in the array in memory?
fTimeStamp	If writing to the log file, also write out time values?

Table 7-2 Parameters for ahtProInitStack

The procedure initializes some global variables and, if you're writing to a log file, writes a log header to the file. A typical call to ahtProInitStack might look like this:

```
ahtProInitStack False,True,True
```

3. For each procedure in your application, place a call to ahtProPushStack as the first statement. This procedure places the value passed to it on top of the stack, along with the current time. As the single argument for each call, pass the name of the current procedure. The example places a pair of parentheses after function names, and nothing after subroutine names, just

as a matter of style. As the last line in each procedure, add a call to ahtProPopStack, which will remove the current name from the top of the stack and record the current time.

4. At any time in your application, to retrieve the name of the currently executing procedure, call the ahtProCurrentProc function. This function looks at the top of the stack and returns the string it finds there.

5. To review the outcome of your logging, view the file LOGFILE.TXT (in your Access directory) in any text editor. If you followed the previous steps carefully, you should see matching entry and exit points for every routine. Nested levels are indented in the printout, and entry and exit points are marked differently (entry with a + and exit with a –).

How It Works

The module you imported from 07-03.MDB, basProfiler, includes all the code that maintains the profiler. There are just four public entry points to the module, as shown in Table 7-3.

PROCEDURE NAME	PURPOSE	PARAMETERS
ahtProInitStack	Initialize the profile stack.	
ahtProPushStack	Add an item to the profile stack.	A string to push
ahtProPopStack	Remove an item from the profile stack.	
ahtProCurrentProc	Retrieve the name of the current procedure.	

Table 7-3 The four entry points into basProfiler

In general, the profiler works almost exactly like the simpler procedure stack shown in How-To 7.2. As a matter of fact, the code for this How-To was written first and was then stripped down for use in the simpler example. This example includes the code necessary to write to the file on disk, as well as to gather timing information. The next few paragraphs outline the major differences and how they work.

Storing Information

Whereas How-To 7.2 used a simple array of strings to hold the stack information, the profiler must also store starting and ending times for each routine. Therefore, it uses a user-defined type, ahtStack, defined as follows, to create the stack.

```
Type ahtStack
    strItem As String
    lngStart As Long
    lngEnd As Long
End Type
Dim maStack(0 To MAX_STACK) As ahtStack
```

Gathering Time Information

Access provides the Timer function, which returns the number of seconds since midnight; but for measuring the duration of procedures in Access Basic, this resolution won't give you enough information. Windows provides the GetTickCount function, which returns the number of milliseconds since you started Windows. In addition, GetTickCount (aliased as aht_apiProGetTickCount in the code) resets itself back to 0 every 48 days, whereas Timer resets once every day. So if you need to time a lengthy operation, GetTickCount provides a mechanism for measuring time spans longer than a single day. (Of course, if you're timing an operation that takes more than a day, you're probably not going to care about millisecond accuracy, but that's what you get!) The code in basProfiler calls GetTickCount to retrieve the current "time" whenever you push or pop a value, and stores it in the stack array. You can call GetTickCount in any application, once you include this declaration in a global module:

```
Declare Function aht_apiProGetTickCount Lib "USER" Alias "GetTickCount" () As Long
```

The code in basTestProfiler also uses GetTickCount, in the Wait subroutine. This procedure does nothing but wait for the requested number of milliseconds, calling DoEvents inside the loop, giving Windows time to do its work.

```
Sub Wait (intWait As Integer)
   Dim lngStart As Long
   lngStart = aht_apiProGetTickCount()
   Do While aht_apiProGetTickCount() < lngStart + intWait
      DoEvents
   Loop
End Sub
```

Writing to the Log File

The code in basProfiler opens and closes the output file each time it needs to write a piece of information. Although this slows down your application, it ensures that if your machine crashes for some reason, your log file will always be current. Although you'll never actually call this routine directly, you might find it interesting to see how it does its work, if you've never used Access to write directly to a text file.

The procedure, ahtProWriteToLog, first checks to see if an error has ever occurred in the logging mechanism (that is, if mfLogErrorOccurred has been set to True). If so, it doesn't even try to write anything to the file, since it's possible that something is wrong with the disk. Otherwise, it gets a free file handle, opens the log file for appending, writes the item to the file, and then closes it.

```
Private Sub ahtProWriteToLog (strItem As String)

   On Error GoTo LogIt_Err

   ' If an error has EVER occurred in this session,
   ' then just get out of here.
   If mfLogErrorOccurred Then Exit Sub
```

```
    Dim intFile As Integer
    intFile = FreeFile
    Open LOG_FILE For Append As intFile
    Print #intFile, strItem
    Close #intFile
    Exit Sub

LogIt_Err:
    mfLogErrorOccurred = True
    MsgBox "Error: " & Error & " (" & Err & ") while writing to log."
    Exit Sub
End Sub
```

Comments

As in How-To 7.2, you'll find that you must be conscientious about the place-ment of your calls to ahtProPushStack and ahtProPopStack for the procedure stack profiler mechanism to be of any value. If you have multiple exit points from routines, this is a good time to try and consolidate them. If you can't, you'll need to make sure that you've placed a call to ahtProPopStack before every exit point in a procedure.

If you attempt to decipher the log file, you'll notice that the elapsed time for each procedure must also include any procedures it happens to call, as in the example of A calling B, which calls C, which calls D. The elapsed time for function A was 1702 milliseconds. That's the time that elapsed between the calls to ahtProPushStack and ahtProPopStack in function A, including the time it took to run all the calls to B, C, and D. This isn't necessarily a problem, nor is it wrong, but you should be aware that there's no way to "stop the clock" while in subsidiary procedures.

The code for the profiler includes a public entry point, ahtProLogString, which wasn't mentioned earlier. The profiler doesn't actually call this procedure, but your own code can. Pass it a single string, and the profile will send that string to the log file for you. For example, the following code will append "This is a test" to the log file:

```
ahtProLogString "This is a test"
```

Finally, make sure that you turn off logging (in your call to ahtProInitStack) in finished applications. Repeated writing to disk will slow down production applications.

7.4 HOW DO I...

COMPLEXITY: INTERMEDIATE

Multitask my Access Basic code?

Problem

If my Access Basic code includes a loop that runs for more than just a second or two, Windows seems to come to a halt. I can't move the windows on the screen, and I can't use the (ALT)-(TAB) key combination to move to any other application. Why is this happening? Is there something I can do to relinquish some control?

Technique

You may have noticed that it's quite possible to completely tie up Windows with a simple bit of Access Basic code. Since Windows relies on cooperative multitasking, it can only multitask if all the running applications are "well behaved" and yield time for other applications to do their work. You should make a conscious effort, if your code contains loops that run for a while, to give Windows time to catch up and do its own work. Access Basic includes the DoEvents statement, which effectively yields time to Windows, so that Windows and other running applications can perform whatever tasks they must. Effective use of DoEvents can make the difference between an Access application that hogs the system, and one that allows Windows and other applications to run smoothly at the same time.

Steps

To see the problem in action, load and run frmMoveTest (in 07-04.MDB). Figure 7-5 shows the form in use. The form includes three command buttons, each of which causes the label, "Watch Me Grow!," to change its width from 500 to 2000 twips (in Figure 7-5, you can only see a portion of the label), in increments of 5, in a loop like this:

```
For intI = 0 To 1500 Step 5
    Me!lblGrow1.Width = Me!lblGrow1.Width + 5
    ' Without this call to Repaint, you'll
    ' never see any changes on the screen.
    Me.Repaint
Next intI
```

To test the effects of DoEvents, try these steps:

1. Press the Run Code Without DoEvents button. The code attached to this button (as seen in Figure 7-5) will change the width of the label inside a loop without yielding time to Windows. While the code is running, try to click on another button on the form, to move or size the active window, or use (ALT)-(TAB) to switch to a different application. You will find that any of these tasks is impossible while the label is expanding. Once the label has finished its growing, Windows will display any actions you attempted to take during the process.

2. Try the same loop with DoEvents inserted. Click the second button, Run Code With DoEvents 1. This time, as the code executes, you will be able to move or size the active window, and use (ALT)-(TAB) to switch to other applications. In addition, you can click on any of the form's buttons while the code is running. The next step tests this situation.

3. While the label is growing, click on the Run Code With DoEvents 1 button many times in quick succession. Sooner or later (it might take 30 or more clicks) Access will greet you with the message box shown in Figure 7-6. Every time you click the button, Access is starting up another instance of the Click event procedure, and each instance of the procedure eats up some

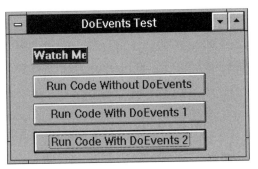

Figure 7-5 The sample DoEvents Test form, frmMoveTest, in action

Figure 7-6 Multiple instances of procedures will consume all of Access's stack space

of the limited stack space Access maintains. Sooner or later, you'll consume it all. The next step offers a solution to this problem.

4. Click the third button, Run Code with DoEvents 2. While the label is expanding, try clicking on the button again. You'll see that this time your clicks won't have any effect. The code attached to this button checks to see if it's already running, and if so, just exits the code. This method will solve the problem of recursive calls to DoEvents.

How It Works

The code attached to the first button does its work without any concern for Windows or other running applications. When you press it, it executes this code:

```
Sub cmdNoDoevents_Click ()
    Dim intI As Integer

    Me!lblGrow1.Width = 500
    For intI = 0 To 1500 Step 5
        Me!lblGrow1.Width = Me!lblGrow1.Width + 5
        ' Without this call to Repaint, you'll
        ' never see any changes on the screen.
        Me.Repaint
    Next intI
End Sub
```

Because the code never gives Windows time to "catch up," you must include the call to Me.Repaint in order to make sure the form repaints itself after each change. To see for yourself how this works, comment out that line and press the first button again. You'll see that the screen won't repaint until the entire operation is done.

The code attached to the second button does the same work, but it calls DoEvents within the loop. With that statement added, you no longer need the call to Me.Repaint, since DoEvents allows Windows to take care of the pending repaints. In addition, it allows you to use the mouse and other applications while this loop is running. The code attached to the second button looks like this:

```
Sub cmdDoEvents1_Click ()
   Dim intI As Integer

   Me!lblGrow1.Width = 500
   For intI = 0 To 1500 Step 5
      Me!lblGrow1.Width = Me!lblGrow1.Width + 5
      DoEvents
   Next intI
End Sub
```

The problem with this code, as mentioned above in step 2, is that nothing keeps you from initiating it while it's still running. That is, if you press the same button while the code is in the middle of the loop, Access will start up the same procedure again. Every time Access starts running an Access Basic routine, it stores information about the routine and its local variables in a reserved area of memory, called its stack. The size of this area is fixed and limits the number of procedures that can be running concurrently. If you press that button over and over again, in quick succession, it's quite possible you'll overrun Access's stack space (as demonstrated in Figure 7-6). The third button on the form demonstrates the solution to this problem. It ensures that its code isn't already running before it starts the loop. If it's already in progress, the code exits. The code attached to the third button looks like this:

```
Sub cmdDoEvents2_Click ()
   Dim intI As Integer
   Static fInHere As Integer

   If fInHere Then Exit Sub
   fInHere = True
   cmdDoEvents1_Click
   fInHere = False
End Sub
```

It uses a static variable, fInHere, to keep track of whether the routine is already running. If fInHere is currently True, then it exits. If not, it sets the variable to True, and then calls cmdDoEvents1_Click (the previous code fragment). Once cmdDoEvents1_Click returns, cmdDoEvents2_Click sets fInHere back to False, clearing the way for another invocation.

Comments

DoEvents is one of the most misunderstood elements of Access Basic. No matter what programmers would *like* DoEvents to do, it does nothing more than yield time to Windows. It has no effect on the Access database engine itself and can't be used to slow things down or help timing issues, other than those involving Windows. When used in Access Basic code, DoEvents will release control to the operating environment, which won't return control until it has processed the events in its queue and handled all the keys in the SendKeys queue. Access will ignore DoEvents in:

- A user-defined procedure that calculates a field in a query, form, or report

⚷ A user-defined procedure that creates a list to fill a combo or list box, or an OLE object

As you can see from the second button on the sample form, calling DoEvents recursively can lead to trouble. You should take steps, as in the example of the third button, to make sure that this won't occur in your applications.

7.5 HOW DO I...   COMPLEXITY: ADVANCED

Add items to a list or combo box programmatically?

Problem
Getting items into a list or combo box from a data source is elementary in Access. Sometimes, though, I need to put things into a list box that I don't have stored in a table. In Visual Basic, this is simple: I just use the AddItem method. But Access list boxes don't support this method. How can I add items to a list box that aren't stored in a table?

Technique
It's true: Access list boxes (and combo boxes) don't support the AddItem method that Visual Basic programmers are used to. In order to make it easy for you to get bound data into list and combo boxes, the Access developers had to forego a simple method for loading unbound data. To get around this limitation, there are two methods you can use to place data into an Access list or combo box: You can programmatically build the RowSource string yourself, or you can call a list-filling callback function. The RowSource string method is easy, but it only works in the simplest of situations. A callback function will work in any situation. This How-To demonstrates both methods.

One important question is, why would you ever need either of these methods for filling your list or combo box? Since you can always pull data from a table, query, or SQL expression directly into the control, why bother with all this work? The answer is simple. Sometimes, you just don't know ahead of time what data you're going to need, and the data isn't stored in a table. Or, perhaps you need to load the contents of an array into the control, and you don't need to store the data permanently.

Steps
The following steps walk you through both methods for modifying the contents of a list or combo box while your application is running. The first example modifies the value of the RowSource property, given that the RowSourceType property is set to Value List. The second example covers list-filling callback functions.

Filling a List Box by Modifying the RowSource Property

1. Open frmRowSource in 07-05.MDB.

2. Change the contents of the list box by choosing either Days or Months from the option group on the left. Try both settings, and change the number of columns, to get a feel for how this method works. Figure 7-7 shows the form set to display month names in three columns.

Filling a List Box By Creating a List-Filling Callback Function

1. Open frmListFill in 07-05.MDB.
2. Select a weekday from the first list box, and the second list box will show you the date of that day this week, plus the next three instances of that weekday. Figure 7-8 shows the form with Saturday, June 18, 1994 selected.
3. To use this method, you set the control's RowSourceType property to be the name of a function (without an equal sign and without parentheses). Functions called this way must meet very strict requirements, as discussed in the next section. In Figure 7-9 the properties sheet for the list box on frmListFill shows the RowSourceType property with the name of the list-filling function.

How It Works

This section explains the two methods for filling list and combo boxes programmatically. The text refers only to filling list boxes, but the same techniques apply to combo boxes. You may find it useful to open the form module for each form as it's being discussed.

Modifying the RowSource Property

If you set a list box's RowSourceType property to be Value List, then you can supply a list of items, separated with semicolons, that will fill the list. By placing this list in the control's RowSource property, you tell Access to display the items one by one in each row and column that it needs to fill. Since you're placing data directly into the properties sheet, you're limited by the amount of space available in the properties sheet: 2048 characters.

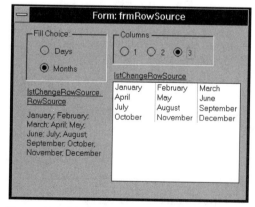

Figure 7-7 The sample form, frmRowSource, displaying months in three columns

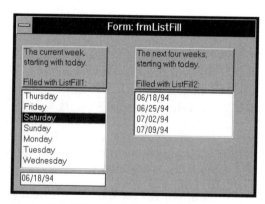

Figure 7-8 Using list-filling callback functions to fill the lists on frmListFill

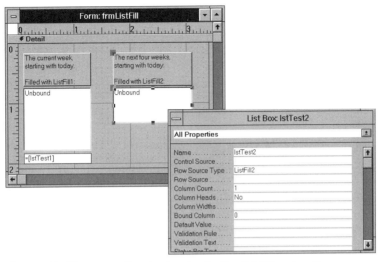

Figure 7-9 The properties sheet entry for the list-filling function

At any time, you can modify the RowSource property of a list box, placing into it a semicolon-delimited list of values. The ColumnCount property plays a part, in that Access fills the rows first and then the columns. You can see this for yourself if you modify the ColumnCount property on the sample form (frmRowSource).

The sample form creates a list of either the days in a week or the months in a year, based on the value of an option group on the form. The code that performs the work looks like this:

```
Select Case Me!grpChoice
   Case 1  ' Days
      ' Get last Sunday's date.
      varStartDate = Now - Weekday(Now)
      ' Loop through all the week days.
      For intI = 1 To 7
         strList = strList & Format(varStart + intI, "dddd") & "; "
      Next intI
   Case 2  ' Months
      For intI = 1 To 12
         strList = strList & Format(DateSerial(1995, intI, 1), "mmmm") & "; "
      Next intI
End Select

' Get rid of the extra "; " on the end.
strList = Left(strList, Len(strList) - 2)
```

Depending on the choice in grpChoice, you'll end up with either a string of days,

```
Sunday; Monday; Tuesday; Wednesday; Thursday; Friday; Saturday; Sunday
```

(the extra spaces are included only so the displayed version will wrap correctly—Access disregards the extra space), or a string of months:

January; February; March; April; May; June; July; August; September; October; November; December

Once you've built the string, just ensure that the RowSourceType property is set correctly, and then insert the new RowSource string:

```
LstChangeRowSource.RowSourceType = "Value List"
LstChangeRowSource.RowSource = strList
```

Creating a List-Filling Callback Function

You may have overlooked this technique, which involves creating a special Access Basic function that provides the information Access needs to fill your list box. It was underdocumented in the first release of Access and appears to be totally undocumented (except in the online help file) in Access 2.0. List filling using a callback function provides a great deal of flexibility, and it's not very difficult.

The concept is quite simple: You provide Access with a function that, when requested, returns information about the control you're attempting to fill. Access "asks you questions" about the number of rows, number of columns, width of the columns, column formatting, and the data itself. Your function must react to these requests and provide the information, so Access can fill the control with data. This is the only situation in Access where you provide a function but you never call it. Access calls your function as it needs information in order to fill the control. The sample form frmFillList uses two of these functions to fill its two list boxes.

In order to communicate with Access, your function must accept five specific parameters. Table 7-4 lists those parameters and explains their purpose.

ARGUMENT	DATA TYPE	DESCRIPTION
ctl	Control	A reference to the control being filled.
varId	Variant	A unique value that identifies the control being filled (you assign this value in your code). Although you could use this value to let you use the same function for multiple controls, this is most often not worth the extraordinary trouble it causes.
varRow	Variant	The row currently being filled (0-based).
varCol	Variant	The column currently being filled (0-based).
varCode	Variant	A code that indicates the kind of information Access is requesting.

Table 7-4 Required parameters for all list-filling functions

The final parameter, varCode, is how Access lets you know what information it is currently requesting. Access places a particular value in that variable, and it's up to your code to react to that request and supply the necessary information as the return value of your function. Table 7-5 lists the possible values of varCode, the meaning, the predefined constant, and the value your function must return to Access in response to each.

VARCODE	CONSTANT	MEANING	RETURN VALUE
0	LB_INITIALIZE	Initialize data	Nonzero if the function will be able to fill the list; null or 0 otherwise.
1	LB_OPEN	Open the control	Nonzero unique ID if the function will be able to fill the list; null or 0 otherwise.
2	(not used)		
3	LB_GETROWCOUNT	Get rows	Number of rows in the list; –1 if unknown (see the text for information).
4	LB_GETCOLUMNCOUNT	Get column count	Number of columns in the list (cannot be 0).
5	LB_GETCOLUMNWIDTH	Get column widths	Width (in twips) of the column specified in the varCol argument (0-based); specify –1 to use the default width
6	LB_GETVALUE	Get a value to display	Value to be displayed in the row and column specified by the varRow and varCol arguments.
7	LB_GETFORMAT	Get column formats	Format string to be used by the column specified in varCol.
8	LB_CLOSE	(Unknown)	
9	LB_END	End (when the form is closed)	Nothing.

Table 7-5 Values of varCode, their meanings and return values

You'll find that almost all of your list-filling functions will be structured the same. Therefore, you may find it useful to always start with the ListFillSkeleton function, listed below. It's set up to receive all the correct parameters and includes a Select Case statement handling each of the useful values of varCode. All you need to do is change its name and make it return some real values.

```
Function ListFillSkeleton (ctl As Control, varId As Variant, ⇒
varRow As Variant, varCol As Variant, varCode As Variant)

    Dim varRetval As Variant

    Select Case varCode
        Case LB_INITIALIZE
            ' Could you initialize?
            varRetval = True
```

(Continued on next page)

(Continued from previous page)

```
    Case LB_OPEN
        ' What's the unique identifier?
        varRetval = Timer

    Case LB_GETROWCOUNT
        ' How many rows are there to be?

    Case LB_GETCOLUMNCOUNT
        ' How many columns are there to be?

    Case LB_GETVALUE
        ' What's the value in each row/column to be?

    Case LB_GETCOLUMNWIDTH
        ' How many twips wide should each column be?
        ' (optional)

    Case LB_GETFORMAT
        ' What's the format for each column to be?
        ' (optional)

    Case LB_END
        ' Just clean up, if necessary.
        ' (optional, unless you use an array whose
        ' memory you want to release)

    End Select
        ListFillSkeleton = varRetval
End Function
```

For example, the following function from frmListFill fills in the first list box on the form. This function fills in a two-column list box, with the second column hidden (its width is set to 0 twips). Each time Access calls the function with LB_GETVALUE in varCode, the function calculates a new value for the date and returns it as the return value.

```
Function ListFill1 (ctl As Control, varId As Variant, ⇒
varRow As Variant, varCol As Variant, varCode As Variant)

    Select Case varCode
        Case LB_INITIALIZE
            ' Could you initialize?
            ListFill1 = True

        Case LB_OPEN
            ' What's the unique identifier?
            ListFill1 = Timer

        Case LB_GETROWCOUNT
            ' How many rows are there to be?
            ListFill1 = 7
```

```
Case LB_GETCOLUMNCOUNT
   ' How many columns are there to be?

   ' The first column will hold the day of the week.
   ' The second, hidden, column will hold the
   ' actual date.
   ListFill1 = 2

Case LB_GETCOLUMNWIDTH
   ' How many twips wide should each column be?

   ' Set the width of the 2nd column to be 0.
   ' Remember, they're 0-based.
   If varCol = 1 Then ListFill1 = 0

Case LB_GETFORMAT
   ' What's the format for each column to be?

   ' Set the format for the first column so
   ' that it displays the day of the week.
   If varCol = 0 Then
      ListFill1 = "dddd"
   Else
      ListFill1 = "mm/dd/yy"
   End If

Case LB_GETVALUE
   ' What's the value for each row in each column to be?

   ' No matter which column you're in, return
   ' the date varRow days from now, and Access
   ' will format it for you.
   ListFill1 = Now + varRow

   End Select
End Function
```

The next example, which fills the second list box on the sample form, fills an array of values in the initialization step (LB_INITIALIZE) and returns items from the array when requested. This function displays the next four instances of a particular day of the week. That is, if you choose Monday in the first list box, this function will fill the second list box with the date of the Monday in the current week, along with the dates of the next three Mondays.

```
Function ListFill2 (ctl As Control, varId As Variant, ⇒
varRow As Variant, varCol As Variant, varCode As Variant)

Const MAXDATES = 4

   Static varStartDate As Variant
   Static avarDates(0 To MAXDATES) As Variant
```

(Continued on next page)

(Continued from previous page)

```
    Dim intI As Integer
    Dim varRetval as Variant

    Select Case varCode
        Case LB_INITIALIZE
            ' Could you initialize?
            varStartDate = Me!lstTest1
            If Not IsNull(varStartDate) Then
                For intI = 0 To MAXDATES - 1
                    avarDates(intI) = DateAdd("d", 7 * intI, varStartDate)
                Next intI
                VarRetval = True
            Else
                VarRetval = False
            End If

        Case LB_OPEN
            ' What's the unique identifier?
            VarRetval = Timer

        Case LB_GETROWCOUNT
            ' How many rows are there to be?
            VarRetval = MAXDATES

        Case LB_GETCOLUMNCOUNT
            ' How many columns are there to be?
            VarRetval = 1

        Case LB_GETFORMAT
            ' What's the format for each column to be?
            VarRetval = "mm/dd/yy"

        Case LB_GETVALUE
            ' What's the value for each row in each column to be?
            VarRetval = avarDates(varRow)

        Case LB_END
            ' Just clean up, if necessary.
            Erase avarDates

    End Select
    ListFill2 = varRetval
End Function
```

Note that the array this function fills, avarDates, is declared as a Static variable. Declaring it this way makes it persistent: Its value remains available between calls to the function. Since the code fills the array in the LB_INITIALIZE case, but doesn't use it until the multiple calls in the LB_GETVALUE case, avarDates must "hang around" between calls to the function. If you fill an array with data for your control, it's imperative that you declare the array as Static.

You should also consider the fact that Access only calls the LB_INITIALIZE case once, but it calls the LB_GETVALUE case at least once for every data item to be displayed. In this tiny example, that barely makes a difference. If you're doing considerable work to calculate values for display, however, you should put all the time-consuming work in the LB_INITIALIZE case, and have the LB_GETVALUE case do as little as possible. This optimization can make a big difference if you have a large number of values to calculate and display.

Two more things to note about this second list box example:

- In the LB_END case, the function clears out the memory used by the array. In this small example, this hardly matters. If you'd been filling a large array with data, you'd want to make sure that the data gets released at this point. For dynamic arrays (where you specify the size at runtime), Erase will release all the memory. For fixed-size arrays, Erase empties out all the elements.

- This example didn't include code for all the possible cases of varCode. If you don't need a specific case, don't bother coding for it. Here, there was no need to set the column widths, so there's no code handling LB_GETCOLUMNWIDTH.

Comments

If you intend to use the first method presented in this How-To, modifying the RowSource property, make sure you understand its main limitation: Since it writes the string containing all the values for the control into the control's properties sheet, it's limited by the number of characters the properties sheet can hold. You can use, at most, 2048 characters in the RowSource property. If you need more data than that, use a different method.

In the list-filling callback function method, when Access requests the number of rows in the control (when it passes LB_GETROWCOUNT in varCode), you'll most often just return the number of rows as the return value from your function. Sometimes, however, you won't know the number of rows or won't be able to get the information easily. For example, if you're filling the list box with the results of a query that returns a large number of rows, you won't want to perform the MoveLast method, which you use to find out how many rows the query returned. This requires Access to walk through all the rows returned from the query and would make the load time for the list box too long. Instead, respond to LB_GETROWCOUNT with a –1. This tells Access that you'll tell it later how many rows there are. Then, in response to the LB_GETVALUE case, return data until you've reached the end. Once you return a null in response to the LB_GETVALUE case, Access understands that there's no more data.

This method has its pitfalls, too. Although it allows you to load the list box with data almost immediately, it means that the vertical scroll bar can't operate correctly until you've scrolled down to the end. If you can tolerate this side effect, returning –1 in response to LB_GETROWCOUNT will significantly speed the loading of massive amounts of data into list and combo box controls.

To provide values for the LB_GETCOLUMNWIDTH case, you can specify a different width for each column based on the varCol parameter. To convert from inches to twips, multiply the value by 1440. For example, to specify a half-inch column, return 0.5 * 1440.

> ### THE MISSING LB_GETFORMAT OPTION
> The documentation in the Access 2.0 online help file was incorrect when discussing the LB_GETFORMAT case for the list-filling function. It indicated that you could specify a different format for each row and column. At the time this book was written, Access always passed a –1 in the varRow parameter when requesting the format. This may change in future versions to match the documentation. At this point, though, you can only specify a format on a column-by-column basis.

7.6 HOW DO I...
COMPLEXITY: INTERMEDIATE

Pass a variable number of parameters to a procedure?

Problem
Some applications allow you to pass a variable number of parameters to a procedure, as Excel does with its Sum function, but Access Basic does not. I need a routine that will work on a list of items, and I don't know ahead of time how many items there will be. How can I accomplish this?

Technique
Although it's true that Access Basic will not support variable numbers of parameters to procedures, you can get around this problem by passing an array. An array (an ordered list of items) must contain a single data type. By using the variant data type, though, you can pass a list of varying types into your procedure. Unfortunately, the Access documentation contains very few examples of passing arrays as parameters to procedures.

Steps
From 07-06.MDB, load the module basArrays in design mode.

1. Open the Immediate Window (choose the Immediate Window button on the toolbar, or choose the View|Immediate Window menu item).

2. Perhaps you need a procedure that will take a list of words and convert each to uppercase. The UCaseArray procedure can do this for you. To test it, type the following in the Immediate Window:

TestUCase 5

You can replace the 5 in the command line with any value between 1 and 20. The procedure will create as many strings as you request, place them into an array, and then call the UCaseArray procedure. This procedure will convert all the strings in the array to uppercase. The test procedure will display the original version, followed by the altered version of the array. As you can see, no matter how many items you specify for the UCaseArray procedure to work on, it will convert them all to uppercase. Figure 7-10 shows this procedure in use.

3. Here's another case: a procedure that can accept any number of numeric arguments and perform some operation on them. The sample procedure, SumThemUp, accepts an array of integers, calculates their sum, and returns the total. To try it, type

TestSum 15

in the Immediate Window. (You can use any number between 1 and 20.) The sample routine, TestSum, will generate an array full of random integers between 1 and 9 and will send the array to SumThemUp for processing. Figure 7-11 shows TestSum working with 15 values.

How It Works

Both procedures, UCaseArray and SumThemUp, accept an array as a parameter. To send or receive an array as a parameter, you must add the trailing () characters, indicating to Access that the variable represents an array. Therefore,

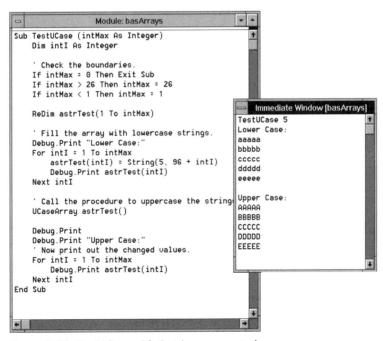

Figure 7-10 TestUCase with 5 strings converted

to pass the array named aintValues to SumThemUp, you call the function like this, making sure to include the () on the array name:

```
varSum = SumThemUp(aintValues())
```

To receive a parameter that is an array, the procedure declaration must also include the parentheses:

```
Function SumThemUp (aintValues() As Integer) As Variant
```

Once the procedure has received the array, it needs some way to know the bounds of the array: the lowest and highest element number. Access provides the two functions LBound and UBound to retrieve the lowest and highest element numbers. Therefore, both sample procedures include loops like this,

```
For intI = LBound(avarArray) To UBound(avarArray)
   avarArray(intI) = UCase(avarArray(intI))
Next intI
```

which loop through all the elements in the array no matter what the starting and ending items are. In Basic, you can declare an array with any positive integer as its start and end points. For example, in

```
Dim avarArray(13 To 97) as Integer
```

you need to loop from 13 to 97 to access each element of the array. The LBound and UBound functions make it possible for your generic routines to loop through all the elements of an array, even though they don't know ahead of time how many elements there will be.

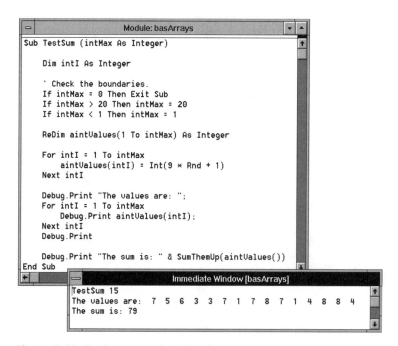

```
Module: basArrays
Sub TestSum (intMax As Integer)

    Dim intI As Integer

    ' Check the boundaries.
    If intMax = 0 Then Exit Sub
    If intMax > 20 Then intMax = 20
    If intMax < 1 Then intMax = 1

    ReDim aintValues(1 To intMax) As Integer

    For intI = 1 To intMax
        aintValues(intI) = Int(9 × Rnd + 1)
    Next intI

    Debug.Print "The values are: ";
    For intI = 1 To intMax
        Debug.Print aintValues(intI);
    Next intI
    Debug.Print

    Debug.Print "The sum is: " & SumThemUp(aintValues())
End Sub
```

```
Immediate Window [basArrays]
TestSum 15
The values are:  7  5  6  3  3  7  1  7  8  7  1  4  8  8  4
The sum is: 79
```

Figure 7-11 TestSum summing 15 values

The UCaseArray procedure is quite simple: It just loops through all the elements of the passed-in array, converting each to uppercase.

```
Sub UCaseArray (avarArray() As Variant)

   ' Convert the entire passed-in array to uppercase.
   Dim intI As Integer

   For intI = LBound(avarArray) To UBound(avarArray)
      avarArray(intI) = UCase(avarArray(intI))
   Next intI
End Sub
```

The SumThemUp function is no more complex. It just maintains a running sum as it loops through all the elements of the array you sent it.

```
Function SumThemUp (aintValues() As Integer) As Variant

   ' Find the sum of the values passed in.

   Dim intI As Integer
   Dim lngSum As Long

   For intI = LBound(aintValues) To UBound(aintValues)
      lngSum = lngSum + aintValues(intI)
   Next intI
   SumThemUp = CVar(lngSum)
End Function
```

Comments

In order to use this method of passing parameters to procedures effectively, always be aware that Access creates arrays with the first element numbered 0, unless told otherwise. Some programmers insist on starting all arrays with 1, and so use the Option Base 1 statement in their modules' Declarations area. Others are happy with 0 as their starting point. You must never assume anything about the lower or upper bounds on arrays, or sooner or later your generic routines won't work. In addition, some programmers leave the Option Base setting at 0 (its default), but they disregard the element numbered 0. If you're writing code that will be called by other programmers, you need to be aware of these possible variations on the normal usage.

7.7 HOW DO I...   COMPLEXITY: ADVANCED

Sort an array in Access Basic?

Problem

Amazingly, although it's a database product, Access doesn't include a way to sort an array. I need to present sorted arrays in an application and can't find a reasonable way to sort them without saving them to a table first. I know I've seen array-sorting methods in other languages. Can I write a sorting routine that executes quickly?

Technique

It's true. Access doesn't provide a built-in sorting mechanism for arrays. There are entire volumes in libraries devoted to the study of various sorting and searching algorithms, but you don't have to dig too deep for Access array sorting. Since you'll probably place any large data sets into a table, most arrays in Access aren't very large. Therefore, most any sort will do. This How-To uses a variant of the standard quicksort algorithm. (For more information on various sorting and searching algorithms, consult your computer library. This is a *big* topic!)

Steps

To try out the sorting mechanism, load the module named basSortDemo in 07-07.MDB. From the Immediate Window, type

TestSort 6

where the 6 can be any integer between 1 and 20, indicating the number of random integers between 1 and 99 that you want the routine to sort. The sample routine, TestSort, will create the array of integers and send it off to VisSortArray, a special version of the sorting routine ahtSortArray that shows what it's doing as it works. Figure 7-12 shows the output from a sample session.

To use this sorting code in your own application, follow these steps:

1. Import the module named basSortArray into your own application.

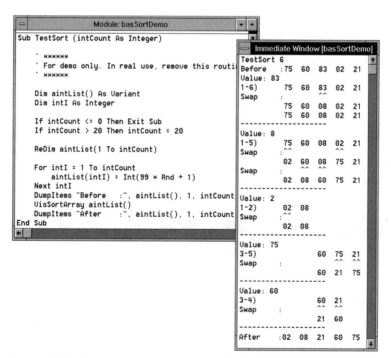

Figure 7-12 Output from a sample run of TestSort

2. Create the array you'd like to have sorted. This must be an array of variants, but those variants can hold any data type: This How-To uses an array of integers, and How-To 7.8 uses an array of strings.

3. Call ahtSortArray, passing to it the name of the array you'd like to sort. For example, to sort an array of named avarStates, use the following call:

```
ahtSortArray avarStates()
```

After the call to ahtSortArray, your array will be sorted. Remember that ahtSortArray is sorting your array in place: Once it's sorted, there's no going back! If you don't want to sort your only copy of the array, make a duplicate first.

How It Works

The quicksort algorithm works by breaking the array into smaller and smaller chunks, sorting each one, until all the chunks are just one element in length. The ahtSortArray procedure calls the main sorting routine, QuickSort, passing to it the array and the start and end points for sorting. The QuickSort routine breaks the array into two chunks, then calls itself twice to sort each of the two halves.

You might be grumbling, at this point, about recursive routines and how they use lots of memory. Normally, that's true. This version of the sorting algorithm, however, tries to be conservative about how it uses memory. At each level, it always sorts the smaller of the two chunks first. This means that it will have fewer recursive levels: The small chunk will end up containing just a single element much quicker than would the large chunk. By always working with the smallest chunk first, this method avoids calling itself more often than it has to.

Following are the basic steps of the QuickSort procedure. These steps use intLeft to refer to the beginning sort item and intRight for the ending item:

```
Private Sub QuickSort (varArray() As Variant, intLeft As Integer, intRight As Integer)
    Dim i As Integer
    Dim j As Integer
    Dim varTestVal As Variant
    Dim intMid As Integer

    If intLeft < intRight Then
        intMid = (intLeft + intRight) \ 2
        varTestVal = varArray(intMid)
        i = intLeft
        j = intRight
        Do
            Do While varArray(i) < varTestVal
                i = i + 1
            Loop
            Do While varArray(j) > varTestVal
                j = j - 1
            Loop
            If i <= j Then
                SwapElements varArray(), i, j
```

(Continued on next page)

(Continued from previous page)

```
                i = i + 1
                j = j - 1
            End If
        Loop Until i > j
        ' To optimize the sort, always sort the
        ' smallest segment first.
        If j <= intMid Then
            QuickSort varArray(), intLeft, j
            QuickSort varArray(), i, intRight
        Else
            QuickSort varArray(), i, intRight
            QuickSort varArray(), intLeft, j
        End If
End If
End Sub
```

1. If intLeft isn't less than intRight, the sort is done.
2. The sort takes the value in the middle of the subset of the array that's being sorted as the "comparison" value. Its value is going to be the dividing factor for the two chunks. There are different schools of thought on how to choose the dividing item. This version of the sort just uses the item that's physically in the middle of the chosen list of items.

```
intMid = (intLeft + intRight) \ 2
varTestVal = varArray(intMid)
```

3. The sort starts from the left, walking along the array until it finds an item that isn't less than the dividing value. This search is guaranteed to stop at the dividing value, which certainly isn't less than itself.

```
Do While varArray(i) < varTestVal
    i = i + 1
Loop
```

4. The sort starts from the right, walking backwards through the array until it finds an item that isn't more than the dividing value. This search is guaranteed to stop at the dividing value, which certainly isn't more than itself.

```
Do While varArray(j) > varTestVal
    j = j - 1
Loop
```

5. If the position from step 3 is less than or equal to the position found in step 4, the sort swaps the elements at the two positions, then increments the pointer for step 3 and decrements the pointer for step 4.

```
If i <= j Then
    SwapElements varArray(), i, j
    i = i + 1
    j = j - 1
End If
```

6. The sort repeats steps 3 through 5 until the pointer from step 3 is greater than the pointer from step 4 (i > j). At this point, every item to the left of the dividing element is less than or equal to it, and everything to the right is greater than or equal to it.

7. Choosing the smaller partition first, the sort repeats all these steps on each of the subsets to either side of the dividing value, until step 1 indicates that it's done.

```
If j <= intMid Then
    QuickSort varArray(), intLeft, j
    QuickSort varArray(), i, intRight
Else
    QuickSort varArray(), i, intRight
    QuickSort varArray(), intLeft, j
End If
```

Comments

There are probably sort algorithms that are simpler than the quicksort algorithm, but for arrays that aren't already sorted, quicksort's speed is hard to beat. (For presorted arrays, it doesn't do as well as some other sorts. But most arrays don't come to the QuickSort subroutine in order.) As it is, the QuickSort subroutine is only capable of handling single-column arrays. If you need to sort multicolumn arrays, you'll need to modify the code to handle those cases, or you'll need to move the data into a table and let Access do the sorting for you.

See the next How-To for an example of using QuickSort.

7.8 HOW DO I...   COMPLEXITY: ADVANCED

Fill a list box with a list of files?

Problem

I need to present my users with a sorted list of files in a particular directory, with a specific file name extension. I found the Dir function, but I can't find a way to get this information into a list box. Is there a way to do this?

Technique

The answer to this question is the perfect opportunity to use the past three How-To's. It involves creating a list-filling callback function, passing arrays as parameters, and sorting an array. In addition, you fill that array with a list of files matching a particular criteria, using the Dir function.

Steps

Load frmTestFillDirList from 07-08.MDB. Enter a file specification into the text box, perhaps something like D:\WINDOWS*.INI. Once you leave the text box (by pressing either TAB or RETURN), the code attached to the AfterUpdate event will force the list box to requery. When that happens, the list box will fill with the matching file names. Figure 7-13 shows the results of a search for D:\WINDOWS*.INI.

To include this same functionality in your own applications, follow these steps:

1. On a form, create a text box and a list box, with properties set as shown in Table 7-6.

CONTROL TYPE	PROPERTY	VALUE
Text box	Name	txtFileSpec
	AfterUpdate	[Event Procedure]
List box	Name	lstDirList
	RowSourceType	FillList
	AfterUpdate	[Event Procedure]

Table 7-6 Property settings for the controls on the directory list form

2. Enter the following code in the text box's AfterUpdate event procedure. (See this book's Introduction for more information on creating event procedures.) This code will force the list box to requery itself when you enter a value in the text box and then move to some other control.

```
Sub txtFileSpec_AfterUpdate ()
    Me!lstDirList.Requery
End Sub
```

3. Enter the following code in the list box's AfterUpdate event. This is just sample code that pops up a message box indicating which file you chose.

```
Sub lstDirList_AfterUpdate ()
    MsgBox "You chose: " & Me!lstDirList.Value
End Sub
```

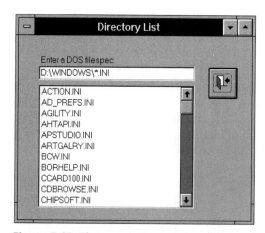

Figure 7-13 The sample form, frmTestFillDirList, searching for *.INI in the Windows directory

4. Enter the following code into the form's module. This is the list-filling function for the list box.

```
Function FillList (ctl As Control, varID As Variant, varRow As ⇒
Variant, varCol As Variant, varCode As Variant)
   Static avarFiles() As Variant
   Static intFileCount As Integer

   Select Case varCode
      Case LB_INITIALIZE
         If Not IsNull(Me!txtFileSpec) Then
            intFileCount = FillDirList(Me!txtFileSpec, avarFiles())
         End If
         FillList = True

      Case LB_OPEN
         FillList = Timer

      Case LB_GETROWCOUNT
         FillList = intFileCount

      Case LB_GETCOLUMNCOUNT
         FillList = 1

      Case LB_GETCOLUMNWIDTH
         FillList = -1

      Case LB_GETVALUE
         FillList = avarFiles(varRow)

      Case LB_END
         Erase avarFiles
   End Select
End Function
```

5. Enter the following code into a global module. (Though this code would work fine in a form's module, it is general enough to serve you best as part of a global module that can be copied from one database to another.)

```
Function FillDirList (ByVal strFileSpec As String, avarFiles() As Variant) As Integer

   ' Given the file specification in strFileSpec, fill in the
   ' dynamic array passed in avarFiles().

   Dim intNumFiles As Integer
   Dim varTemp As Variant

   On Error GoTo FillDirList_Err
   intNumFiles = 0

   ' Set the filespec for the dir() and get the first filename.
   varTemp = Dir(strFileSpec)
```

(Continued on next page)

(Continued from previous page)

```
   Do While Len(varTemp) > 0
       intNumFiles = intNumFiles + 1
       ReDim Preserve avarFiles(intNumFiles - 1)
       avarFiles(intNumFiles - 1) = varTemp
       varTemp = Dir
   Loop

FillDirList_Exit:
   If intNumFiles > 0 Then
       ahtSortArray avarFiles()
   End If
   FillDirList = intNumFiles
   Exit Function


FillDirList_Err:
   FillDirList = intNumFiles
   Resume FillDirList_Exit
End Function
```

6. Import basSortArray from 07-08.MDB. This is the same sorting code that was covered in How-To 7.7.

How It Works

The list box in this example uses a list-filling callback function, FillList, to supply its data. (See How-To 7.5 for information on callback functions.) In FillList's LB_INITIALIZE case, it calls the FillDirList function to fill in the avarFiles array, based on the value in the text box, txtFileSpec. FillDirList fills in the array, calling ahtSortArray along the way to sort the list of files, and returns the number of files it found. Given that completed array, FillList can just return the value from the array that it needs, when requested in the LB_GETVALUE case. It uses the return value from FillDirList, the number of files found, in response to the LB_GETROWCOUNT case.

There's also an interesting situation you should note in the two routines, FillList and FillDirList. FillList declares a dynamic array, avarFiles, but doesn't give a size. It can't, because it doesn't yet know the number of files that will be found. FillList passes the array off to FillDirList, which adds file names to the array, based on the file specification, until FillDirList doesn't find any more matches. FillDirList returns the number of matching file names, but with the side effect of having set the array's size and filled it in. Here's the code that does the work. This code fragment uses the ReDim Preserve keywords to resize the array every time it finds a matching file name.

```
' Set the filespec for the dir() and get the first filename.
varTemp = Dir(strFileSpec)
Do While Len(varTemp) > 0
   intNumFiles = intNumFiles + 1
   ReDim Preserve avarFiles(intNumFiles - 1)
   avarFiles(intNumFiles - 1) = varTemp
   varTemp = Dir
Loop
```

To create the list of files, FillDirList uses the Dir function. This function is unusual in that you call it multiple times. The first time you call it, you send it the file specification you're trying to match, and Dir returns the first matching file name. If it returns a non-empty value, you continue to call it, with no parameters, until it *does* return an empty value. Each time you call Dir, it returns the next matching file name.

Once FillDirList has finished retrieving the list of file names, if there are names in the array, it sorts them. It returns the number of files it found as its return value. The following code shows how this is done:

```
If intNumFiles > 0 Then
    ahtSortArray avarFiles()
End If
FillDirList = intNumFiles
```

Comments
FillDirList declares its first parameter, strFileSpec, by value, using the ByVal keyword. Normally, procedures declare their parameters ByVal if they intend to use the parameter internally and might change its value, but they don't want the calling procedure to know that they've changed the value. In this case, and in many procedures like this one, it's possible that the parameter might be sent directly from the value of a control. Since Access can only pass control values by value, and never by reference, adding the ByVal keyword here makes it possible to use an expression like this:

```
intFileCount = FillDirList(Me!txtFileSpec, avarFiles())
```

Try this without the ByVal keyword, and Access will complain with a "Parameter Type Mismatch" error.

Note that when Access calls the list-filling callback function, values for the varRow and varCol parameters are always zero-based. Therefore, when you use arrays within callback functions, you should consider always using zero-based arrays to hold the data you'll display in the control. If you don't, you'll always be dealing with "off by one" errors. Using a 0-based array will mean that the row values (sent to your code in varRow) will match your array indices.

7.9 HOW DO I...   COMPLEXITY: EASY

Perform search-and-replace operations on my form and report modules' code?

Problem
My application contains Access Basic code in form and report modules. When I perform a search-and-replace operation, it affects only global modules and modules attached to forms or reports that are currently open. I want the search-and-replace to see *all* my form and report modules. How do I do this?

Technique
When you perform a Replace operation from a module's Edit menu, Access allows you to choose the scope of the replacement by choosing Current

Procedure, Current Module, or Loaded Modules. Figure 7-14 shows the Access module's Replace dialog.

Unfortunately, the Loaded Modules option only considers modules that are actually open. This includes all modules that you can see from the database window when you press the Module button, and any forms or reports that are open. If you want the Replace operation to work on all your form and report modules, you must open each form and report in design view in order for Replace to include it. Because you must explicitly open each form or report, then perform the Replace, and then explicitly close and save each object, this can be a tedious process.

This How-To illustrates a technique that opens all of your database's forms and/or reports in design view, allows you to run the Replace operation, and then saves all changes and closes the forms and reports it opened.

Steps

This How-To includes a form you can use to implement global search-and-replace. You can use this form in any of your databases by importing the frmGlobalReplace form. Since it contains all its own code, the form is completely encapsulated and is simple to move from application to application.

1. Load the frmGlobalReplace form (Figure 7-15) from 07-09.MDB.

2. Select Forms and/or Reports to specify which type of objects you want opened.

3. Press the Open Objects button, and the form will open all your forms (and reports if selected) in design view.

4. Press the Replace button, and the module's Replace dialog will appear. Fill in the desired values and execute the Replace operation by pressing the Verify or Replace All button.

5. Once your search is complete, return to the Global Replace form. This is easily accomplished by selecting the form from the Window menu. If you

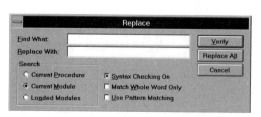

Figure 7-14 The module's Replace dialog

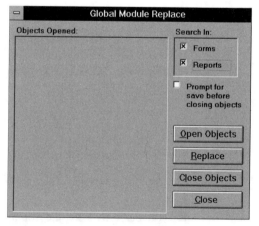

Figure 7-15 The Global Replace form

want the form to automatically save all your changes, clear the Prompt for Save Before Closing Objects check box.

6. Finally, press the Close Objects button, and all your forms and reports will be closed.

How It Works

The technique is implemented in a single form that contains both the interface controls and the Access Basic code. The code starts executing when you press the Open Objects button. The Click event of this button calls the OpenModules subroutine, which uses the Forms and Reports collection to get a list of all the forms and reports in your database. Each object is opened in design view, added to an array, and minimized to avoid screen clutter. The array is then used by the FillObjects list-filling function, which fills the lstObjects list box on the form. Finally, the Me.SetFocus method returns focus to the frmGlobalReplace form. Notice that the array is declared at the module level to allow other procedures to access its contents. The form uses the values in the array later when you close all the forms and reports.

When you press the Replace button, the form sets focus to the first form or report module that was opened by the OpenModules subroutine and uses the SendKeys command to select the object's module window (if a module window is not active, you cannot invoke the Replace dialog). Finally, the form uses the SendKeys action to call the Replace dialog from the Edit menu. No code can execute after this line. This is due to the peculiar way in which Access compiles Access Basic. If you perform a Replace operation while any code is executing, and the Replace causes Access to think it needs to recompile your modules, the executing code will be halted. This happens mainly when you change the name of a global variable, or the type of a variable. Because executing code will be halted in these circumstances, the frmGlobalReplace code simply calls the Replace dialog and ends.

Finally, when you press the Close Objects button, the CloseModules subroutine is called. This subroutine loops through the array it created earlier and closes each object. If you have the Prompt for Save Before Closing Objects check box cleared, the subroutine turns the SetWarnings option off. This tells Access to automatically select the default button on all dialog boxes that Access displays. Because the default button on the close dialog boxes will be yes for save, this has the effect of automatically saving your changes without prompting. Focus then returns to the frmGlobalReplace form.

Comments

Even though this technique automates most of the process of replacing module text in form and report modules, you still must reselect the frmGlobalReplace form manually after the Replace operation is complete. However, given the fact that Access halts program execution when you change module text, there is no practical workaround for this problem.

7.10 HOW DO I...

COMPLEXITY: EASY

Decide whether to use form and report modules or general modules?

Problem

Access 2.0 allows me to place code directly into a form or report. These form and report modules seem to be an excellent way to make self-contained objects. But putting code in a form or report's module makes all the code private. Global modules seem to make coding simpler. How do I decide where to put my code?

Technique

Form and report modules are one of the more powerful improvements in Access 2.0. Their use, though, can cause unexpected behavior. There are certain things you cannot do in form and report modules that you can do in global modules. And Access treats the memory used by form and report modules differently from that used by global modules. Given these factors, determining which type of module to use is not always an easy decision. The steps in this How-To will help you decide on the best approach for your application.

Steps

Access does not support the use of certain programming constructs in form and report modules that are available in global modules. This can make the decision very easy. If your program needs to use these constructs, you must use global modules. Ask the following questions about your application and proceed with the steps as indicated.

1. Does your program need to declare user-defined types like the following:

```
Type MyRecord
   intRecords As Integer
   strName As String
   lngType As Long
End Type
```

If the answer is yes, use a global module: Access does not support the declaration of user-defined types in form or report modules. If the answer is no, go on to step 2.

2. Does your program need to declare global variables? If the answer is yes, use a global module: Access does not support the declaration of global variables in form or report modules. If the answer is no, go on to step 3; there are no basic restrictions on using form or report modules for your code.

> NOTE: Although you cannot declare global variables in form and report modules, you can access global variables declared in global modules from form and report modules. Also consider that all form and report module variables are automatically private to that form or report, so their use can make it easier to create and maintain self-contained objects.

3. Is the load time of your form more important than the memory used by your application as a whole?

   If the answer is yes, consider using a global module. Form and report modules are loaded and compiled when you open the form or report, which can slow down the loading process. For reports, this is usually not a concern because the speed of the printer is the limiting factor. But for forms, load time can be crucial. If you keep your code in a global module, it is precompiled and is immediately ready whenever you load a form or report.

   If the answer is no, and the overall memory usage of your application is more important (you frequently run out of memory), consider putting your code in form and report modules. Because form and report modules are loaded and use memory only when their form or report is opened, you can minimize the amount of memory in use at any given time. Using form and report modules gives you one extra advantage: Because Access doesn't have to load all the code at load time, as it does with global modules, Access will load your application faster.

4. Does your Access Basic code have to be completely secure against unwanted viewing? If the answer is yes, move your code to global modules. Form and report modules cannot be completely protected against snooping like global modules can. This is especially true when you use library databases to distribute your code. Even if the underlying form or report is completely secured by removing the Read Definitions permission, an untrapped runtime error will immediately allow the user access to your form or report module's source code when called from a library database.

How It Works

Access loads global modules differently from form and report modules. Using what is known as the Global namespace, Access loads each global module when it starts. Each of these modules is loaded into memory and is available to your application. This means two things: Access needs to load each module into memory, so it takes longer to load a database with a lot of global modules than it does to load a database with fewer global modules. Second, it uses up memory a lot more quickly.

Form and report modules, on the other hand, are loaded into memory only when you open the form or report. This also means two things: Access doesn't have to load the code when it starts, so it loads faster and uses less memory. Second, when the form or report is opened, its code has to be loaded into memory, increasing the time it takes to load the form.

Comments

Fortunately, choosing between form or report modules and global modules is not an all-or-nothing proposition. You should design your application to take advantage of each approach's strengths and weaknesses. You may find that the best balance involves putting code that directly relates to the form's user interface in the form's module, and all other code in global modules. Since load time is generally not an issue in reports, and you probably don't need to declare global variables in report code, report modules are good for code that relates to a specific report. Finally, you can perform benchmark tests to determine whether the overhead that Access introduces into form loading is acceptable for your application.

8

Optimizing Your Application

HOW DO I...

One unavoidable fact of application design is that your application will never run as fast as you would like it to. Unless you and your application's users are equipped with the latest and most powerful workstations with huge amounts of memory, you should expect performance that is less than satisfying. There are, nevertheless, many techniques you can use to optimize your application's performance, few of which are readily apparent in the Access documentation. Although your application will never run "fast enough," you can certainly make it run faster.

This chapter covers several ways to optimize your applications, including loading forms faster, adding and changing data faster, and making your Access Basic code run faster. It also describes methods to test the speed gains of these techniques.

8.1   Make forms load and display faster
Access 2.0 adds a wealth of new form and control events and properties; however, this power exacts a price on performance. In many cases, forms in version 2.0 load more slowly than they did in previous versions. This How-To will discuss various techniques to improve form loading performance, including optimizing control references and optimizing multipage forms. There is also a discussion of the performance drawbacks of form modules.

8.2   Make more memory available to an application
The single most important factor in Access application performance is the availability of system memory. The more RAM available to your application, the faster it will run. By disabling unneeded Access library code, you can reclaim memory for use by your application. This How-To will show you how much memory each of the Microsoft Wizard libraries uses and how to disable the libraries.

8.3   Accelerate Access Basic code
Access Basic is an interpreted language and, as such, does not run as fast as compiled languages. This How-To will offer various techniques for accelerating your code execution. Topics include using correct variable types, referring to objects, optimizing loops and conditions, and using comments.

8.4   Accelerate routines that add, edit, and change data in tables
Many of your Access Basic procedures work with data stored in tables. Table access can be one of the slower operations of your application because it is bound to physical reads and writes of your storage device. Although Access employs sophisticated buffering and memory management, it does not always provide optimum resources for programmatic table access. This How-To will suggest the use of transactions to buffer table writes and greatly enhance the performance of your application.

8.5   Test the comparative benefits of various optimization techniques
In order to find the best optimization technique for a particular operation, you need to compare two or more approaches. In this How-To you will learn how to implement a test-bed utility that shows the comparative timings of two different functions. The utility runs two functions that you specify and shows

the elapsed time of each function and the difference in times. A discussion of accurate testing and elimination of outside variables is also provided.

8.6 Accelerate client/server applications

Access, through the ODBC (Open Database Connectivity) interface, provides a robust front-end tool for developing client/server applications. Many of the issues involved in working with a back-end database are not obvious. This How-To will cover techniques for improving the performance of applications that attach to server data through ODBC drivers. Special attention is given to optimization of forms based on server data.

8.1   HOW DO I...   COMPLEXITY: INTERMEDIATE

Make forms load and display faster?

Problem

I'm not happy with the speed at which my forms load and display. Forms that I converted from the previous version of Access load more slowly in version 2.0, and the performance in general is not what I expected. How can I change my forms so they will load and display faster?

Technique

Access 2.0 adds substantial new properties and events for forms and controls. But this extra power has a price. Because Access has to manage a larger number of properties and trigger the new events, your forms will probably load more slowly than they did in Access 1.x. Even if you are starting fresh with Access 2.0, you probably would like to decrease the amount of time your forms take to load. There is no panacea in form optimization. Rather, this How-To offers a set of individual optimizations that you can apply to your form; taken together, they will decrease the load time.

Steps

The sample database 08-01.MDB contains two versions of the same form, one optimized and the other unoptimized. The unoptimized version, shown in Figure 8-1, takes an average of 17 seconds to load in test cases. The optimized version, shown in Figure 8-2, takes 3 seconds to load. These two forms show two extremes of optimization. To see the forms in action, load frmBadExample from 08-01.MDB. Note how long it takes to load and for Access to display the Form View prompt. Now load frmGoodExample from the same database and notice how much quicker it loads.

To optimize your own forms, follow these steps:

1. If your form is based on a query, ensure that only the necessary columns are returned. This is a common query optimization: The more columns a query has to return, the longer it takes to fill its dynaset. Since the form loading process must run the form's underlying query, any performance problems with that query are evident when the form is loaded.

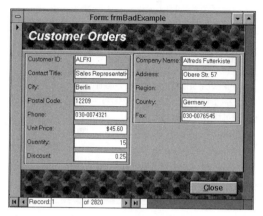

Figure 8-1 The frmBadExample form (unoptimized), which takes longer to load

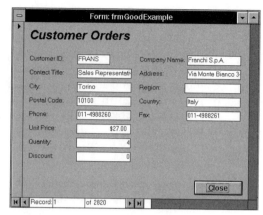

Figure 8-2 The frmGoodExample form (optimized), which loads much more quickly

2. Try to minimize the amount of code in your form modules. Form modules differ from regular modules in one important way: They are loaded and compiled when the form loads. If the form's module contains a large amount of code, this compilation adds to loading time. You may want to consider moving parts of your form module's code to a regular module, which is compiled when Access itself loads. By leaving the form-specific event procedures in the form module (to take advantage of Code Behind Forms and local scoping) and moving the more generic code to a regular module, you enjoy the best balance of speed and convenience.

3. Try to minimize the number of graphic objects on your form, such as OLE objects and bitmaps. Each graphic object takes up storage space in the form and increases the load time, especially when your form loads on a workstation containing an unaccelerated video card. Weigh the graphic's contribution to your form's usability against the performance drawbacks.

4. If you are using a multipage form, prepare controls only when the user moves to a page, not when the form loads. On multipage forms, users may reach later pages, so it makes sense to set properties on controls and bind controls to data only when the user actually moves to a specific page.

   For example, if you have a query-driven list box on page 3 of your form, Access runs the query when the form loads, even though page 3 is not yet displayed. A better approach is to save the form with that list box's RowSource property left blank so the query will not run when the form is loaded. Then, when the user actually moves to page 3, set the RowSource property from an Access Basic routine.

   Note that this type of optimization doesn't apply to combo box controls. Access only retrieves a combo box's underlying dynaset when the combo box is first activated. An example of this concept is shown in the frmShowQueriesRun form in 08-01.MDB. Load and run the form. A message box appears while the query for the list box control runs. The query for the combo box doesn't run until you actually click on the combo box.

> ## WHEN YOU CAN'T GO ANY FASTER
> If you can't make your forms load faster, at least give the user the impression that something is happening. This technique can range from a simple control on the form that reads "Loading..." to a status meter displaying the progress of an operation that is preparing the form. For example, if your form executes a lengthy Access Basic procedure when it loads, you might add code for a status meter to the procedure, as described in How-To 9.10.

How It Works

The techniques presented here show specific ways to accelerate your form's loading. By understanding what Access is doing when it loads a form, you can create and test your own optimization techniques.

When Access loads a form, it must read all the form's properties and trigger the events that occur when a form loads. Access also loads each control and each control property from the database. Thus, the most obvious optimization involves reducing the number of things that Access has to load. Anything you can do to reduce the number of controls will enhance performance.

Since forms are usually based on some type of data set, the second thing to examine is how you are telling Access to retrieve the data. If your form is based on a table and you don't need all the table's fields, consider using a query instead, which only returns the fields you need. If your form is already based on a query, look for ways to optimize that query. Copy the form's query to a regular query and test it there. This allows you to closely examine the speed of the data loading process.

Next, look at the tasks performed by your code or macros as the form loads. Could you postpone data retrieval actions until after the form is loaded? Can you reduce load time by moving some of the form module's code to a regular module? Finally, if your form uses Access Basic code as it loads, try the Access Basic optimizations discussed in How-To 8.3.

Comments

Unfortunately, there is no programmatic way to measure the time a form takes to load. Although you can set timers at each of the form's events, Access does some things internally after the last loading event has fired. The only way to measure a form's loading time is to manually test and average the time using a stopwatch. Most of the optimizations shown in this How-To should yield dramatic results, eliminating the need to precisely test each approach. See How-to 8.5 later in this chapter for more information on optimization testing.

8.2 HOW DO I...

Make more memory available to an application?

Problem

I'm sure that my application would run faster if I had more memory. But when I load Access by itself, a lot of my system memory is already used up. Is it possible to reclaim some of the memory and make it available to my application?

Technique

Access includes Wizards that provide help in everything from designing tables to creating buttons. These tools are very useful in development, but are often not needed in the final application. By disabling unneeded Wizard library databases, you can reclaim the memory used by the Wizards and make it available to your application.

Steps

First determine which Wizard functionality you do need to use. Wizards are split into five library databases; use Table 8-1 to determine which library databases you can eliminate.

LIBRARY DATABASE	MEMORY USED	DESCRIPTION
WZLIB.MDA	27K	The main Wizard library database. Contains the code and objects for the Database Documenter, Attachment Manager, Menu Builder, and Add-in Manager. Also contains support procedures for the other Wizards, so if you use any other Wizard library databases, you must also enable this library database.
WZTABLE.MDA	5.8K	Table Wizard.
WZQUERY.MDA	3.8K	Query Wizard.
WZFRMRPT.MDA	17.3K	Form and Report Wizards.
WZBLDR.MDA	3.2K	Miscellaneous Builder routines, such as the Command Button Builder and the Option Group Builder.

Table 8-1 Wizard library databases and their memory requirements

1. To disable the library databases you don't need, edit the Access initialization file (MSACC20.INI) located in your Windows directory. Using Windows Notepad or your favorite text editor, find the section entitled [Libraries].
2. At the beginning of each line containing a library database you want to disable, place a semicolon (;). This comments out the line.
3. Restart Access and you will have more memory available.

How It Works

Every time Access starts, it reads each library database specified in the initialization file (MSACC20.INI) and loads the library database code into a central area of memory. The memory used by the library databases cannot be reclaimed and is "lost" as far as your application is concerned. Overall, the amount of memory is small, but in complex applications, every kilobyte counts. After a few months of development, you may find that you are using a substantial portion of memory by keeping many library databases loaded.

There are several commercial library databases as well as a good number of public domain and shareware offerings; however, most of these are for development work. You probably won't distribute your application with these library databases. So if you don't need them, reclaim the memory and make your application run faster.

Comments

Continually disabling and reenabling library databases during development can be a real chore. You may find yourself enabling library databases to do development work and then disabling them when you test your application. You can ease this process by keeping two copies of the Access initialization file on disk and loading Access with the specific INI file you need. Name one MSACRUN.INI (for running the application) and the other MSACDEV.INI (for developing the application). In MSACRUN.INI, disable the library databases you don't need. In MSACDEV.INI, enable the library databases you need for development. Then create two Program Manager icons, one for running the application and one for developing it. In the command line of each, point to the correct initialization file using the /INI command line option. You can now easily switch between the testing and development environments.

8.3 HOW DO I...   COMPLEXITY: ADVANCED

Accelerate Access Basic code?

Problem

I have optimized my forms and queries, but this isn't enough in terms of my entire application which contains a lot of Access Basic code. I'm sure there is something I can do to make it run faster. What optimizations can I perform?

Technique

Access Basic is an interpreted language that has much in common with any other interpreted language. This How-To demonstrates seven specific programmatic techniques you can apply to accelerate your code. The improvement will range from modest increases to two times faster.

Steps

To see the seven optimizations in action, open and run frmShowOptimizations from 08-03.MDB, shown in Figure 8-3. Click the Run Tests button and each test will run, one by one. The tests compare two different methods of using

Access Basic to achieve a result. You will quickly notice that the techniques on the right take much less time to run.

Here are the instructions for using all seven optimizations in your application:

1. *When dividing integers, use integer division.* A good percentage of the division operations performed by your application are probably done on integer values. Many developers use the / (slash) operator to divide two numbers, without knowing that it is optimized for floating-point division. If you are dividing integers, you should use the \ integer division operator (backslash) instead. With \, Access only has to work at the integer level instead of the floating-point level, and the computation will be faster. (Of course, this is only useful if you're assigning the results of the division operation into an integer. If you care about the fractional portion of the division, you'll need to use floating-point math, and the / operator, to do your work.) For example, instead of

```
intX = intY / intZ
```

use:

```
intX = intY \ intZ
```

2. *Use specific data types instead of variants.* Variants offer convenience at the expense of performance. Every time you refer to a variant, Access needs to perform type conversion to ensure that the data is in the correct format. By using the data type that matches your variable, you explicitly eliminate the need for this type conversion, and your code runs faster. In addition, a variant variable is four times larger than an integer (on a 16-bit operating system) and thus takes longer to move around. (Remember that only variant variables can constrain Null values, however. When moving data to and from tables, you *must* use the variant data type.)

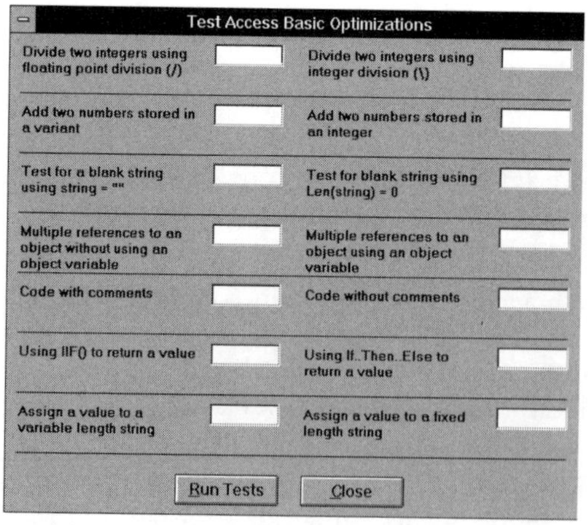

Figure 8-3 The Test Access Basic Optimizations form, frm ShowOptimization, ready to run

3. *Test for blank strings using the Len function.* You probably have code that tests for blank strings by comparing the string to an empty string (""). However, because Access stores the length of the string as the first byte in the string, testing for a length of 0 using the Len function is always faster. Instead of

```
If strTemp = "" Then
   MsgBox "The string is blank"
End If
```

use:

```
If Len(strTemp) = 0 Then
   MsgBox "The string is blank"
End If
```

4. *If you refer to an object more than once in a section of code, assign it to an object variable.* Every time you reference an object, Access has to perform some work to figure out which object you are referring to. This adds overhead to your code each time the object is referenced. But if you assign the object to an object variable, Access "finds" the object once and caches the reference in memory. In the remainder of the code, you can refer to the object through the object variable, and your code will run faster. For example, instead of

```
Dim intCount As Integer
For intCount = 0 To Forms![MyForm].Count - 1
   Debug.Print Forms![MyForm](intCount).Name
   Debug.Print Forms![MyForm](intCount).Caption
Next intCount
```

use:

```
Dim intCount As Integer
Dim intControls As Integer
Dim frmCurrent As Form
Dim ctl As Control

Set frmCurrent = Forms![MyForm]
intControls = frmCurrent.Count

For intCount = 0 To intControls - 1
   Set ctl = frmCurrent(intCount)
   Debug.Print ctl.Name
   Debug.Print ctl.Caption
Next intCount
```

5. *Use as few comment lines as possible.* This may go against everything you have been taught about programming, but the fact remains that Access Basic is an interpreted language. Each line of your code is interpreted regardless of its contents. And every comment line is another line of code that the interpreter has to parse. Code with no comments will always run faster than code with comments. One approach is to write your code with your normal comments. Then, before you distribute the application, strip all the comments out. Be sure to keep an unstripped version of your code.

Your development system can use the code with comments, and your user's system can use the code without comments.

Another suggestion is to never place comments inside loops. Your program spends a lot of its time in these repetitive control structures, and removing comments inside them can make a measurable difference.

6. *Use If...Then...Else instead of the IIf function.* Access Basic does not employ short-circuit evaluation in the IIf function. If you use an immediate if statement (IIf), both result expressions are evaluated regardless of the test value. By replacing IIf statements with the equivalent If...Then...Else statement, your code will run faster. For example, instead of

```
MsgBox IIf(intX = 1, "One", "Not One")
```

use:

```
If intX = 1 Then
    MsgBox "1"
Else
    MsgBox "Not 1"
End If
```

7. *If you know the length of a string beforehand,* use fixed length strings. By declaring a string variable with no qualifier, you are creating a variable length string. This data type has two advantages: You don't have to know beforehand how much space to allocate, and less memory is used because you are not wasting space on smaller strings. But variable length strings exact a price on performance. If you know ahead of time that a specific string will be an exact number of characters, declare the variable to hold that string as a fixed length string. For instance, instead of

```
Dim strZipCode As String
strZipCode = "22202-1234"
```

use:

```
Dim strZipCode As String * 10
strZipCode = "22202-1234"
```

How It Works

Remember two important things when you are trying to optimize your Access Basic code. First, Access Basic is an interpreted language. In most interpreted languages, each line is read and parsed regardless of content. Therefore, less verbose code is generally faster code. Keep this in mind as you write, and reduce the number of lines that need to be interpreted. Second, Access Basic is very similar to other languages, compiled and otherwise, in its interaction with the computer at the lowest level. Many optimizations that apply to other languages could also apply to Access Basic. For example, the technique of checking for a blank string using the Len function is a common optimization in other languages. Don't be afraid to try new techniques.

Comments

Optimization techniques for programming languages are a vital part of your toolbox. But don't sacrifice other vital elements for the sake of speed. First, make sure your code works correctly before you optimize. Second, write your code so it is easy to explain. It can be very difficult to optimize code you don't understand. Finally, don't break working code by optimizing it. By optimizing code that works correctly (albeit slowly), you may introduce bugs. Follow the three rules of optimization:

☛ Make it right before you make it faster.

☛ Make it clear before you make it faster.

☛ Keep it right as you make it faster.

Finally, you may find that there are no easy optimizations for a particular piece of code. No matter what you do, it just won't run fast enough. A favorite saying in software design is "Don't diddle code to make it faster; find a better algorithm." Often you need to step back from a piece of slow code. There may be a better overall approach or a better algorithm you can employ.

8.4   HOW DO I...   COMPLEXITY: INTERMEDIATE

Accelerate routines that add, edit, and change data in tables?

Problem
I have Access Basic routines that add, edit, and change data in tables using recordset objects. It seems the code I write to edit and delete data in tables runs more slowly than an equivalent Access query. How do I make these operations run faster?

Technique
When you programmatically access table data using recordset objects, you are not automatically getting the best performance from Access. You can do better by minimizing the number of times that Access reads to or writes from the physical disk. This How-To uses Access transactions to buffer reads and writes in memory (as much as possible), giving you much better performance.

Steps
Open and run frmTestTransactions in 08-04.MDB, as shown in Figure 8-4. This form tests adding, changing, and deleting records in the tblContacts sample table. To see it in action, type in the number of records you wish to add, change, or delete (100 records is a good test) and click the Start Test button. The form runs each of the operations, first without using transactions, then with transactions, and displays the number of milliseconds each method takes. You will see how using transactions greatly reduces the amount of time taken by table access operations.

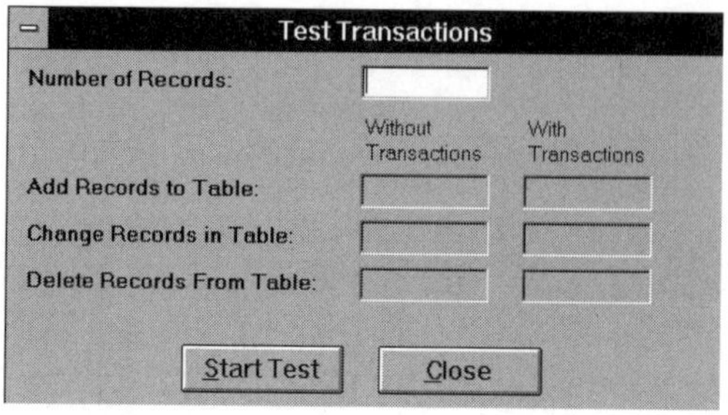

Figure 8-4 The Test Transactions form, frmTestTransactions

To use this technique in your code, insert a BeginTrans method before you start accessing records and a CommitTrans method when you are finished. Follow these steps:

1. In your code, locate a point when the needed objects are open, but *before* you access any table data. At that location, start a transaction using the BeginTrans method of the current workspace object. For example, in the code that follows step 2, the transaction is started after the database and recordset variables are opened, but before any records are accessed.

2. Locate a point in your code *after* all table accesses are finished, but before you close the objects involved. At this point, use the CommitTrans method of the current workspace object to commit the changes to disk, as shown here:

```
Sub DeleteLastNames()

    Dim dbCurrent As Database
    Dim rstContacts As Recordset
    Dim wrk As Workspace

    Set wrk = DBEngine.Workspaces(0)
    Set dbCurrent = wrk.Databases(0)
    Set rstContacts = dbCurrent.OpenRecordset("Contacts")

    ' Start Transaction
    wrk.BeginTrans

    Do Until rstContacts.EOF
        rstContacts.Edit
        rstContacts![LastName] = ""
        rstContacts.Update
        rstContacts.MoveNext
    Loop

    ' Commit the transaction
    wrk.CommitTrans

    ' Cleanup
    rstContacts.Close

End Sub
```

How It Works

Transactions are crucial in any database product. By using a transaction, you can group a set of operations as a logical unit. At any point within a transaction you can commit or roll back the transaction. This allows you to save the changes only if all necessary changes were made. Access uses transactions at many levels. When you perform action queries, Access automatically wraps the operation in a transaction, allowing the operation to roll back all changes if an error is encountered.

What does this have to do with performance? A useful side effect of transactions is that changes made to data during a transaction are not actually written to tables. Instead, the changes are buffered in memory until a CommitTrans method causes them to be written or a RollBack method causes them to be discarded. Since memory access is much faster than disk access, the end result is a faster operation.

Comments

The performance benefits of transactions are related to the amount of system RAM available to Access at the time the transaction is executed and how many rows of data are involved in the transaction. A large number of changes may reduce the amount of available RAM. In this case, Access will start swapping to disk, negating some of the performance gains.

Also note that in Access 1.x, transactions only made a difference when you opened your database in nonexclusive mode. In Access 2.0, transactions make a difference regardless of how you open your database. By using transactions in your Access Basic code, you can almost always increase performance.

8.5 HOW DO I... COMPLEXITY: INTERMEDIATE

Test the comparative benefits of various optimization techniques?

Problem

Now that I've tried the optimization techniques in this chapter, how do I recognize the improvement achieved by a particular approach? I want to know exactly how much faster one approach is compared to another. How do I test and compare optimizations?

Technique

By using a Windows API call, some simple math, and a cover function, you can easily compare the performance of two optimization techniques with relatively high accuracy. This How-To shows you how to create a form in which you can type in two functions for comparison. It runs the functions, shows you how long each takes to execute, and shows you which of the two is faster and by how much.

Steps

Open and run frmTestOptimize from 08-05.MDB. The form shown in Figure 8-5 allows you to type in the name of two functions and test their performance relative to each other. The 08-05.MDB database contains two test functions that show the comparative performances of integer division and float division. To run the test, type

```
FloatDivision()
```

into the Function 1 text box, type

```
IntegerDivision()
```

into the Function 2 text box, and click the Test button. The form will run each function, show the time taken by each function, and which function is faster and by how much.

To use the frmTestOptimize form to test your own functions, follow these steps:

1. Import frmTestOptimize from 08-05.MDB into your database. This form is completely self-contained and requires no other objects.

2. Open frmTestOptimize and type in the name of the two functions you wish to test, along with any required parameters. Type the entries in the Function 1 and Function 2 text boxes exactly as if you were calling the functions in your Access Basic code, but omit the assignment operator and assignment object. For example, for a function that is called in your Access Basic code like this,

```
intReturned = MyTestFunction ("MyTable")
```

you would type the following into the frmTestOptimize text box:

```
MyTestFunction ("MyTable")
```

How It Works

There are two key components to this technique. The first is the use of a Windows API call to the GetTickCount function. GetTickCount returns the number of milliseconds elapsed since Windows was started. This number, which has no intrinsic value for optimization purposes, is extremely useful for

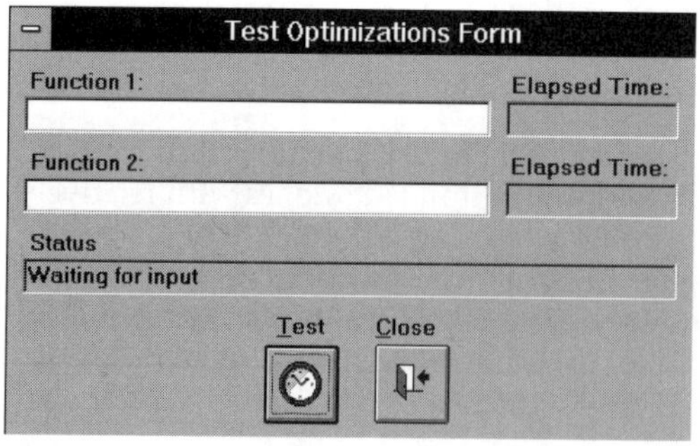

Figure 8-5 The Test Optimizations form, frmTestOptimize, ready to run a timing test

comparing two points in time. You may wonder if you can use Access's built-in Timer function instead, or even the Now function. Both of these functions return time values that are only accurate to within one second. Even though many of your optimization tests will perform operations that run longer than a second, you will lose a great deal of accuracy with these methods. Because the GetTickCount function returns time measurements in milliseconds, it is one thousand times more accurate than using the built-in functions.

The second key component of this optimization test technique is the use of the Eval function. This function is one of the least understood functions in Access Basic, yet one of the most powerful. You can use Eval to execute a function that is named in a variable or some other expression. If you have programmed in a lower-level language such as C or Pascal, you probably miss not having pointers to functions. You can use the Eval function to simulate this by passing a function name as a parameter to Eval. This technique calls Eval for both of the functions you type into the form.

Finally, a little math is used to compare the milliseconds used by each function. The end result is a string stating that Function X is faster by a factor of Y.

Comments

When you are testing optimization techniques you need to watch out for a couple of things that can yield false results.

- Access employs a sophisticated caching algorithm that keeps as much information in memory as possible. Any tests you perform that access objects from the database must take this into account. For example, if you are testing an optimization on form loading time, your results can be erroneous if you perform the comparison of the two methods one after the other. The first time you load the form, Access caches it in memory if possible. The second time you load the form, it will invariably load faster because Access is retrieving it from memory rather than the disk, skewing your test results. This is also true of disk caching software such as Microsoft's SmartDrive and Windows For Workgroups. To test optimizations that involve disk activity, you should disable any disk-caching software. Removing the Access cache variable from your tests requires a little more work. Perform the test on your first optimization method, note the results, and exit Access to clear its cache. Then restart Access to perform the test on your second optimization method.

- Windows is a multitasking operating system. Because of this, your test results may be further skewed if Windows is performing some other operation in the background while one of your tests is running. The best way to minimize this is to ensure that no other Windows programs are running when you perform your tests. It is also usually a good idea to run the test several times and average the results.

8.6   HOW DO I...

Accelerate client/server applications?

Problem

I am using Access as a front end by attaching to remote tables using ODBC. I'm not satisfied with the response time of my client/server application. What can I do to make it run faster?

Technique

There are a variety of optimization techniques you can use when developing client/server applications. If you are attaching remote tables in databases such as SQL Server or Oracle, you access data through the Microsoft ODBC drivers. Typically, client/server applications using ODBC require more horsepower on the part of your workstations and network. By knowing how data is retrieved from the server, you can make your application run faster.

Steps

Here are suggestions to consider when optimizing your client/server application:

1. *Your forms should retrieve as few records as possible when loading.* Fetching data is one of the more significant bottlenecks in client/server applications. Design your form to retrieve few or no records by setting the RecordSource property of the form to a blank string. If the RecordSource is an SQL string or form query, change its WHERE clause to WHERE FALSE. This causes no records to be selected. So users can see data, you create an interface to allow them to select a small subset of records. See How-To 6.6 for an example of this technique. You can also speed up form loading by forcing Access to use a snapshot recordset instead of a dynaset recordset. If your form is read-only, and the data retrieved is less than 500 records, set the AllowUpdating property of the form to NoTables. This tells Access to use a read-only snapshot instead of a dynaset. Finally, you can set the form's DefaultEditing property to DataEntry, which tells Access not to retrieve any records when the form is loaded.

2. *Optimize the way your application connects to the server.* When the user starts your application, log the user into the server using the OpenDatabase method. This establishes a connection and caches it in memory. Subsequent data access is faster because the connection has already been established.

```
Sub ConnectUser (strUser As String, strPass As String)
    Dim wrk As Workspace
    Dim db As Database
    Dim strConnect As Database

    strConnect = "ODBC;DSN=MyServer;DATABASE=dbCustomers;"
    strConnect = strConnect & "UID=" & strUser & ";"
    strConnect = strConnect & "PWD="  & strPass & ";"
    Set wrk = DBEngine.Workspaces(0)
    Set db = wrk.OpenDatabase("", False, False, strConnect)
End Sub
```

3. *Reduce connections by limiting dynasets to 100 records or less.* Most servers (such as SQL Server) require two connections for dynasets of more than 100 records. By limiting the size of the dynaset, you reduce the number of connections that need to be made, speeding up your application.

4. *Offload as much processing in queries as possible to the server.* Generally, your server will search and process data faster than the local Access engine (this is probably the reason you moved to client/server in the first place). Design your queries to eliminate expressions or functionality not supported by the server such as user-defined functions. If it isn't supported by the server, Access will process the query locally and performance will suffer. Read the documentation that comes with your database server to determine which functionality is supported.

5. *Be sure to use transactions when updating records.* In How-To 8.4 you learned how to use Access transactions to optimize updates and additions to data in Access Basic code. This becomes even more important in client/server applications. It is usually significantly faster to have Access buffer updates in transaction memory rather than sending all changes across the network. Note that although Access supports five levels of transaction nesting on local tables, it does not support nesting on ODBC tables. Only the top-level transaction is passed to the server.

6. *Add a timestamp field to a table to improve update and deletion performance.* If a table has a timestamp field, Access can use it to quickly see whether a record has changed. Without this field, Access must check and compare the contents of every field. Obviously, checking a single field is a lot faster. To add a timestamp field to a table on the server, create and execute an SQL-specific query using the ALTER TABLE statement:

```
ALTER TABLE Customers ADD TimeStampCol TIMESTAMP
```

7. *Avoid using server data to fill list box and combo box controls.* The performance of these controls is generally poor when accessing server data. Consider, instead, storing the data for the list box or combo box in a local database. This approach works if the data does not change frequently and can be easily copied from the server.

8. *Explicitly cache server data in your Access Basic code.* Datasheets and forms automatically cache server data, but recordsets created by your Access Basic code do not. In addition to using transactions to cache data, use the FillCache method of the recordset object. For example, say you have code that finds all customers with a specific value in a field and updates another field accordingly. You can make the code run faster by finding the first matching records and starting a cache at that point in the dynaset, as shown here:

```
Dim wrk As Workspace
Dim db As Database
Dim strConnect As Database
Dim rstCustomers As Recordset

strConnect = "ODBC;DSN=MyServer;DATABASE=dbCustomers;"
```

(Continued on next page)

(Continued from previous page)

```
strConnect = strConnect & "UID=" & strUser & ";"
strConnect = strConnect & "PWD="  & strPass & ";"
Set wrk = DBEngine.Workspaces(0)
Set db = wrk.OpenDatabase("", False, False, strConnect)
Set rstCustomers = db.OpenRecordset("tblCustomers", DB_OPEN_DYNASET)

rstCustomers.FindFirst "[OrdersToDate] > 100000"
If Not rstCustomer.NoMatch Then
    rstCustomers.FillCache rstCustomers.Bookmark, 100
    Do Until rstCustomer.EOF
        If rstCustomers![OrdersToDate] > 100000 Then
            rstCustomers.Edit
                rstCustomers![Status] = "Priority Customer"
            rstCustomers.Update
        End If
        rstCustomers.MoveNext
    Loop
End If
```

In this code, the FillCache method does two things: It initializes a cache to hold 100 records, and then it loads 100 records into the cache starting at the first matching record. Experiment with the cache size to determine the optimal balance between memory use and performance. Obviously a large setting may make the code run slower, since more records are being retrieved.

9. *If you are making a single pass through read-only data, use a forward-scrolling snapshot recordset.* For example:

```
Set rstCustomers = db.OpenRecordset ("tblCustomers", _DB_OPEN_SNAPSHOT, DB_FORWARDSCROLL)
```

By specifying this option, you are telling Access to eliminate the scroll buffer that is usually created. This scroll buffer is a mechanism that stores previously accessed records in a cache. Bear in mind that while this improves the performance of operations that need to scroll backwards through data, it penalizes operations that only scroll forward through data.

How It Works

Understanding how client/server applications differ from single-user and file-server applications is crucial to optimizing their performance. The key is in deciding when to let Access do the work and when to let the server do the work. With a few exceptions, you want the server to perform queries and Access to perform the user-interface issues. Concentrate on minimizing the traffic across the network by reducing the data retrieved from the server and written to the server. If your application uses Access Basic code, remember that the automatic optimizations and caching employed by datasheets and forms is not available. You must explicitly write your code to optimize and cache data access operations.

Comments

You can also optimize performance of your client/server applications by modifying settings in your MSACC20.INI initialization file. There are settings specific to ODBC data access that you should be familar with. To find more information on these settings, search in the Access online help for initialization files.

9

Making the Most of Your User Interface

No matter how much database design you do in the background, what matters to the outside world is your user interface. Certainly, perfecting the database design is crucial—but once that's done it pays to devote considerable time to designing a user interface that is workable, aesthetically pleasing, and helps users get their work done. By implementing the ideas and techniques in this chapter, you'll be able to create an interface that stands out and works well.

You'll learn how to take full advantage of special keystrokes to help users navigate through a complex application. You'll see how to use a combo box not just to select from a list but to maintain that list with new entries as they are needed. A map-based interface will let users jump to a particular set of records they need to work with; other techniques will help them choose a specific record to focus on. You'll also learn how to dress up your application with custom splash screens and animated buttons. You'll see how to hide some necessary complexity from your users by allowing them to pick multiple items from a single list box and use an expanding dialog box to organize complex options. You'll learn how to emulate the interface used by the built-in Wizards to move a group of items from one list box to another, and how to create a custom status meter that's more attractive than the default status bar.

9.1 Change the AutoKeys macro to match the current form
The AutoKeys macro allows you to assign special keystrokes to perform specific tasks, but you may run out of special keystrokes and need to reuse them. This How-To will demonstrate new version 2.0 functions that let you use a nearly limitless number of AutoKeys macros as the form changes.

9.2 Create a combo box that accepts new entries
It's easy to program a combo box that lets users add new entries to a record instead of limiting them to the prepared list. But what happens when you want to support the addition of the new entry to the underlying list? This How-To will use the new NotInList event to trap for a new entry and pop up a form to gather more information.

9.3 Create a geographical map interface
Many applications manage large amounts of data organized around states or regions, and users work on records for one region at a time. The simplest way to allow selection of a state or region to work with is to use a combo box. This How-To will illustrate a more visual, map-based interface, in which users can just click on the map and have Access know which state they selected.

9.4 Jump quickly to specific records
Often, you'll want to jump to a specific record on your form to inspect information there. The ApplyFilter action, the FindFirst method in Access basic, and the RecordSource property of your forms provide several ways to do this. This How-To will demonstrate the various possibilities and discuss the pros and cons of each.

9.5 Create a splash screen
The first chance you have to impress users is when you display your splash screen. This How-To will show you how to design a splash screen that displays

quickly while your application finishes loading, and how to dress it up with a bit of simple animation.

9.6 Create multiple-selection list boxes

The Add-In Manager uses a clever new design to display multiple selections in limited space: a list box with two columns, one with *x*'s to indicate loaded items. In this How-To you will learn how to implement this space-saving paradigm on your own forms.

9.7 Create animated buttons

Animated buttons add a touch of class to your application. This How-To will explain the use of the new PictureData property to create animated buttons. You'll learn how to create two-state buttons that look different when you click them, and cyclic buttons that run a continuous animation for as long as the form is open.

9.8 Design an expanding dialog box

One way to keep your application easy to use is to hide unnecessary information from your users until it's needed. The Access Print Setup dialog box demonstrates one technique for information hiding: It keeps some of its controls on a section of the form that is normally invisible. This How-To will show you how to design a similar expanding dialog box for your own applications, and how to manage the switch from compressed to expanded form and back again.

9.9 Use two list boxes to select records

Many of the Access Wizards employ a pair of list boxes, side by side, with four buttons in between them for selecting items. Users can select any or all items from the left-hand list box and use the buttons to move them to the right-hand list box. In this How-To, you'll see how to emulate this interface using a combination of a hidden field, update queries, and appropriate macros.

9.10 Create a customized status meter using Access Basic

You can control the built-in status meter using the SysCmd functions. You can't, however, move this status meter to a custom position on your screen or change its color. This How-To will demonstrate using a form to build a custom status meter that can be personalized with your own interface.

9.1 HOW DO I... COMPLEXITY: EASY

Change the AutoKeys macro to match the current form?

Problem

I want to use an AutoKeys macro to assign special keystrokes to perform specific tasks. But there are only a limited number of special keystrokes available. Is there a way to reuse keys so that I don't have to write complex branching macros to interpret the keystrokes differently based on the particular form or other situation?

Technique

In Access 2.0, there are two new methods of the Application object that let you change the value of any of the database options at runtime. Although you normally change database options by selecting Options from the View menu (see Figure 9-1), your program can use the SetOption method to make similar changes under programmatic control. Combining this functionality with the OnActivate property of your forms allows you to set a new group of key assignment macros for each form.

Steps

Open 09-01.MDB. This sample database contains information on units, assemblies that make up parts, and parts that make up assemblies. Open frmUnit in form view. At any time you can press (CTRL)-(D) to "drilldown" to the next level of detail or (CTRL)-(R) to revert to the previous level of detail. Figure 9-2 shows the sample database after pressing (CTRL)-(D) twice.

To add unique AutoKeys macros to each form in your own application, follow these steps:

1. Create a key assignment macro for each form in your application (you can use the same macro for more than one form if you like). Follow all of the design rules for an AutoKeys macro, but give your macro a unique name when you are done. In the sample application, for instance, the three key assignment macros are called mcrUnitAutoKeys, mcrAssemblyAutoKeys, and mcrPartAutoKeys, so that the macro name immediately reminds you of its function. Table 9-1 shows the settings for the mcrUnitAutoKeys macro.

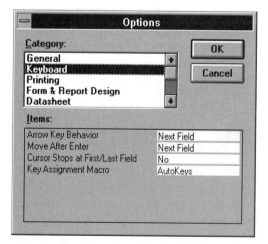

Figure 9-1 The database Options dialog, allowing you to change the Key Assignment macro

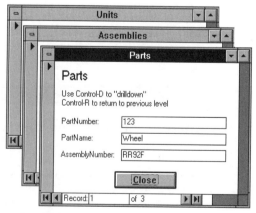

Figure 9-2 The sample database after pressing (CTRL)-(D) twice

MACRO NAME	ACTION	ARGUMENT	VALUE
^D	OpenForm	Form Name	frmAssembly
		View	Form
		Where Condition	[UnitNumber]=[Forms]![frmUnit]![UnitNumber]
		Data Mode	Edit
		Window Mode	Normal
^R	Close	Object Type	Form
		Object Name	frmUnit

Table 9-1 Macro actions for mcrUnitAutoKeys

You will probably want to add comments to your macro for easy maintenance, as illustrated in Figure 9-3.

2. Import the basOptions module from 09-01.MDB into your own application.

3. Add a RunCode action to your AutoExec macro (or create a new macro named AutoExec containing only this one action). Set the action's function name argument to:

```
=ahtStoreOriginalAutoKeys()
```

4. In the OnActivate property of each of your forms, add a call to the function ahtSetAutoKeys. This function takes a single argument: the name of the key assignment macro to use while that form is active. For example, on the frmUnit form in the sample application, this property is set to:

```
=ahtSetAutokeys("mcrUnitAutokeys")
```

5. In the OnClose event of the *last* form to be closed in your application (typically, this is your main switchboard form), add a call to the function ahtRestoreOriginalAutokeys. If there is more than one possible last form in your application, you'll need to add this function call to *every possible*

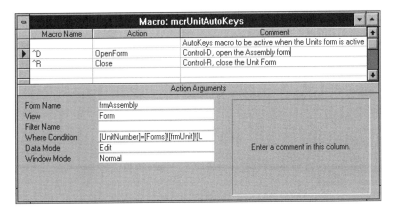

Figure 9-3 The mcrUnitAutoKeys macro

last form. The ahtRestoreOriginalAutokeys function takes no arguments. Figure 9-4 shows these calls in the sample application.

How It Works

The special built-in Application object refers to your entire Access application. The GetOption method of this object lets you read any of the options stored under Options in the View menu, and the SetOption method lets you write new values for any of those options. Since the database options are stored in the user's system database, any changes you make to them will affect not only the current database, but also any other database the user runs. It's best to always store the original value of any option you change and restore it when your application is closed.

The ahtStoreOriginalAutokeys function uses the GetOption method to read the original Key Assignment macro name when your application is loaded:

```
Function ahtStoreOriginalAutokeys ()
'
' Store the user's original Autokeys macro name
' so we can restore it when we're done
'
On Error GoTo ahtStoreOriginalAutokeys_Err

    strOriginalAutokeys = Application.GetOption("Key Assignment Macro")
```

The ahtRestoreOriginalAutokeys function uses this stored value to reset the option when you close your application:

```
Function ahtRestoreOriginalAutokeys ()
'
' Put the Autokeys macro setting back the way we found it.
'
On Error GoTo ahtRestoreOriginalAutokeys_Err

    Application.SetOption "Key Assignment Macro", strOriginalAutokeys

ahtRestoreOriginalAutokeys_Exit:
    Exit Function
```

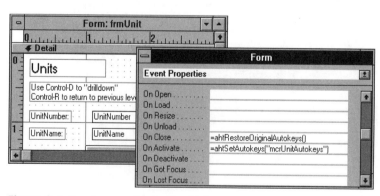

Figure 9-4 Event properties for frmUnit

Each form passes the name of its preferred key assignment macro to the ahtSetAutokeys function when the form is activated. This function uses the SetOption method to take the form's macro name and place it in the Key Assignment Macro option. This macro then becomes the active key assignment macro, replacing whatever was there before.

```
Function ahtSetAutokeys (strMacroName As String)
'
' Set a new Autokeys macro. Takes the name of the
' macro to use for keyboard reassignment.
'
On Error GoTo ahtSetAutokeys_Err

    Application.SetOption "Key Assignment Macro", strMacroName

ahtSetAutokeys_Exit:
    Exit Function

ahtSetAutokeys_Err:
    MsgBox "Error " & Err & ": " & Error$, MB_ICON_STOP, "ahtSetAutokeys()"
    Resume ahtSetAutokeys_Exit

End Function
```

Comments

You can generalize this technique of using GetOption and SetOption to control many properties of your application at runtime, for example, to turn the status bar and toolbars on or off, selectively refuse DDE requests, and allow the user to pick a new font for datasheets from a list you supply. You should always follow the same basic three steps:

1. Use GetOption to read the current option value and save it in a module-level variable.
2. Use SetOption to set your new value. Be sure to use the name of the option exactly as it appears in the database options window.
3. Use SetOption to restore the original value when your application is closed.

DETECTING WHEN THE USER CLOSES YOUR APPLICATION
There is no built-in way to have Access always run a cleanup routine when the user closes your application. The final event you can trap is the last form's closing. If there are multiple possible last forms, you must make sure you check when any of them closes to see whether it is actually the last form. As an alternative, you can open a hidden form in your AutoExec and place your cleanup processing in this form's OnClose property. Access will automatically close this form when the user exits, and since it's the first form opened, it will be the last form closed.

The individual calls to the ahtSetAutoKeys function are attached to the forms' OnActivate events rather than their On Got Focus events for a very good reason. Unless there are no controls on a form that can get the focus, the form itself will *never* get the focus. Only forms consisting strictly of graphic objects and disabled controls will ever trigger a form-level GotFocus event.

9.2 HOW DO I...   COMPLEXITY: INTERMEDIATE

Create a combo box that accepts new entries?

Problem

I'm using combo boxes for data entry on my forms. Sometimes I want to allow users to add a new entry to the list of values allowed in the combo box. Is there a better way to do this than by closing the data entry form, opening a new form using the combo box's table, and then going back to my main form?

Technique

You can use the NotInList event to trap the error that occurs when users type a value into a combo box that isn't in the underlying list. Then you can pop up a separate form to gather any necessary data for the new entry, add it to the list, and put users back where they started.

This How-To also demonstrates using the new OpenArgs property to pass information to a form, as well as how to stop code execution by opening a form in dialog mode.

Steps

Open the sample database 09-02.MDB and open frmDataEntry, which allows you to select a state from the combo box (only a few states are included with the database). To enter a new state, just type its abbreviation in the form and answer yes when it asks whether you want to add a new record. A form will pop up, as shown in Figure 9-5, to collect the other details (in this case, the state name), and then you'll be returned to the main data entry form, with your new selection already in the combo box.

To add this functionality to your own combo boxes, follow these steps:

1. Import the basNotInList module from 09-02.MDB into your application.

2. On your form, create the combo box to which you want to add records. Set the combo box properties as shown in Table 9-2.

PROPERTY	VALUE
RowSourceType	Table/Query
RowSource	*Any table or single-table query*
LimittoList	Yes
OnNotInList	[Event Procedure]

Table 9-2 Property settings for combo box to take new records

3. Put the following code in the NotInList event procedure (shown here for a control named cboState):

```
Sub cboState_NotInList (NewData As String, Response As Integer)
    Response = ahtAddViaForm("frmState", "txtAbbreviation", NewData)

End Sub
```

Replace the arguments to ahtAddViaForm with the appropriate arguments for your own database: the name of the data entry form used to add new records to the combo box and the name of the control on the data entry form that matches the first displayed column of the combo box.

4. Create the data entry form. Set the form properties as shown in Table 9-3.

PROPERTY	VALUE
RecordSource	*The same table or query that is the combo box source*
DefaultEditing	Data entry
OnLoad	=ahtCheckOpenArgs([Form])

Table 9-3 Property settings for data entry form

5. Add controls to the data entry form for all table fields that you need the user to fill in. Be sure that one of them is the field that corresponds to the first visible column of the combo box, and that this field's name is the one you supplied in step 3.

6. Save the data entry form, using the name you supplied in step 3. Now open the main form with the combo box on it. Type a new value into the combo box. You should be prompted with a message box asking if you want to add a record (see Figure 9-6). Answer yes, and your data entry form will appear, with the information you typed in the proper control. Fill in the rest of the required information and close the data entry form. Your new information will be added to the combo box list and the new value selected in the combo box.

How It Works

When you have a combo box with its Limit To List property set to yes, Access generates an event when the user types in a value that's not in the list. By

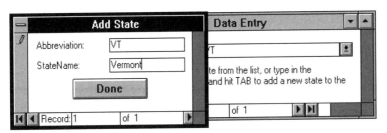

Figure 9-5 Adding a new record to the underlying table

default, this merely displays an error message. However, with the NotInList event, you can intercept this message before it occurs and add the record to the list yourself.

When you're done processing the event, you set the Response argument provided by Access to one of three possible symbolic constants:

- DATA_ERRDISPLAY tells Access to display the default error message and not add the new value to the underlying list.

- DATA_ERRCONTINUE tells Access not to display a message or add the value to the list.

- DATA_ERRADDED tells Access not to display the error message and to requery the underlying list. This is the return value to use when you add the value yourself.

This How-To uses a generic function, ahtAddViaForm, to handle the record adding.

```
Function ahtAddViaForm (strAddForm As String, strControlName As ⇒
String, strNewData As String) As Integer
'
' Add a new record to a table by calling a form, and then
' requery the calling form. Designed to be called from On
' NotInList event procedures
'
'   strAddForm - the form to be opened to add a record
'   strControlName - the control on the add form that matches
'        the displayed info in the calling combo box
'   strNewData - the data as supplied by the calling combo box
'
On Error GoTo ahtAddviaForm_Err

    Dim varRet As Variant
```

Figure 9-6 Prompt for new record

To allow for the possibility that the user may not want to enter a new value (perhaps she mistyped the entry), the function displays a simple message box and quits if the user selects the no button. You also have to tell the original event procedure what to do with the data. The DATA_ERRCONTINUE symbolic constant tells Access to suppress the default error message, but not to try to add the new value to the combo box.

```
' First, confirm that the user really wants to enter a new record
  varRet = MsgBox("Add new value to List?", MB_ICON_QUESTION + MB_YESNO, "Warning")
  If varRet = IDNO Then
      ahtAddViaForm = DATA_ERRCONTINUE
      Exit Function
  End If
```

If the user does want to add a new record, the function opens the data entry form in dialog mode. This pauses the function at this point (since a dialog mode form, once opened, won't give up the focus) and lets the user enter the required data to fill out the record.

However, this leads to another issue. You can't fill in controls on the form before it's open, and you can't fill them in afterwards since the function is suspended. The ahtAddViaForm function gets around that by using the OpenArgs property of the form, which allows you to pass a text string to the form itself. You'll see in this How-To how this property is used by the form to fill in its key field.

```
' Open up the data add form in dialog mode, feeding it
' the name of the control and data to use
  DoCmd OpenForm strAddForm, A_NORMAL, , , A_ADD, A_DIALOG, strControlName & ";" & strNewData
```

After the data entry form is closed, all you have to do is set the appropriate return value. In this case, DATA_ERRADDED tells Access that you've added the value to the underlying table and it can be used as the value for the combo box.

```
' Before control returns to the calling form,
' tell it we've added the value
  ahtAddViaForm = DATA_ERRADDED
```

The data entry form uses its OnOpen event to process the OpenArgs argument passed in. This can be done generically by the ahtCheckOpenArgs function, which takes a form variable from the active form as its only parameter.

```
Function ahtCheckOpenArgs (frm As Form)
'
' Designed to be called on loading a new form
' Checks the OpenArgs and if it finds a string of
' the form
'   controlname;value
' loads that value into that control
On Error GoTo ahtCheckOpenArgs_Err

   Dim strControlName As String
   Dim strControlValue As String
   Dim intSemi As Integer
```

(Continued on next page)

(Continued from previous page)

```
If IsNull(frm.OpenArgs) Then
    Exit Function
Else
    intSemi = InStr(1, frm.OpenArgs, ";")
    If intSemi = 0 Then
        Exit Function
    End If
    strControlName = Left$(frm.OpenArgs, intSemi - 1)
    strControlValue = Mid$(frm.OpenArgs, intSemi + 1)
' Possibly this OpenArgs belongs to someone else and just looks
' like ours. Set the error handling to just ignore any errors
' on the next line
    On Error Resume Next
    frm.form(strControlName) = strControlValue
End If
```

Note that ahtCheckOpenArgs has to be careful to avoid errors, since it's called every time the form is opened. First, it's possible that no OpenArgs argument was passed in. Second, the OpenArgs might be there for another reason; if it doesn't parse out properly as ControlName;Value, then it has to be ignored.

Comments
The solution presented in this How-To is designed to be generic. You may find that you need a more specific function for some particular combo box. For example, you could allow for abort processing via the data entry form, in case the user decides against adding a new record; or you could use unbound text boxes on the data entry form to display pertinent information from the main form, adding context for data entry.

9.3 HOW DO I...
COMPLEXITY: EASY

Create a geographical map interface?

Problem
I want to display a map and allow users to click on regions of the map. I want the form to react based on the selected region. The regions aren't necessarily rectangular. How can I do this in Access?

Technique
You can accomplish this task using a combination of bitmaps and buttons. Depending on how far from rectangular your shapes are, this task can be trivial or quite complex: You'll use command buttons to react to mouse clicks, and buttons can only be rectangular. By making the command buttons transparent, you make the application appear to react directly to mouse clicks on the map.

Steps
Open frmWesternUS in 09-03.MDB (see Figure 9-7). This form has been created with an imported bitmap file as the background. Above each state's image on

the map, there's at least one command button with its Transparent property set to yes. Figure 9-8 shows the form named frmWesternUSDesign, in which the buttons haven't yet had their Transparent property set to yes. Here you can see the actual layout of the command buttons.

To implement similar functionality on your own form, follow these steps:

1. Create your map form, and choose the Unbound OLE Object from the Form Design toolbar. Once you release the mouse button, Access displays a dialog box requesting information about the OLE object (see Figure 9-9). Your Insert Object dialog box may look slightly different, depending on your configuration. Choose the appropriate image for the map background. For the example form, use WEST.BMP.

2. Set the bitmap's SizeMode property to Clip. This disallows resizing of the bitmap, because you'll be overlaying the bitmap with command buttons.

3. Overlay each rectangular area of the bitmap with a command button, naming each as desired. Figure 9-8 shows this process completed for the sample form. You'll find that for odd-shaped regions, you'll need to use multiple buttons, as demonstrated for Idaho, Texas, and Nevada on the map.

> ✔ **TIP:** The (SHIFT)- and (CTRL)-arrow keys are helpful in achieving exact placement of the command buttons. Use the (SHIFT)-arrow keys to expand and contract the size of a control, one pixel at a time; use the (CTRL)-arrow keys to move the control, one pixel at a time.

4. Select all the command buttons (hold down the (SHIFT)-key and click on each). On the properties sheet, set the Transparent property to yes, making the selected controls invisible, yet still active. Figure 9-10 shows the sample

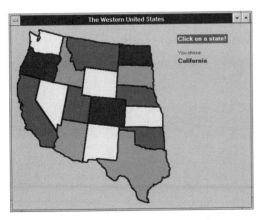

Figure 9-7 The finished map form with transparent buttons

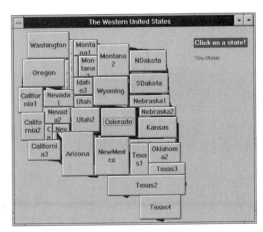

Figure 9-8 The bitmap form with buttons showing

329

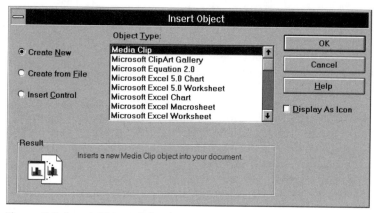

Figure 9-9 Insert Object dialog box

form in design mode; note that in design mode you can still see a faint outline for each button.

5. For each transparent command button, attach code to the OnClick event property. (You can also do this in step 3, if you like.) In the example form, each button calls the HandleStateClick function, passing to it the state name. Obviously, you'll want your own form to do something more useful.

```
Function HandleStateClick (strState As String)
    Dim frm As Form

    Set frm = Screen.ActiveForm
    frm!txtChosenState = strState
End Function
```

How It Works

It's very simple: Because each button has its Transparent property set to yes, which is very different from having its Visible property set to no, it's still

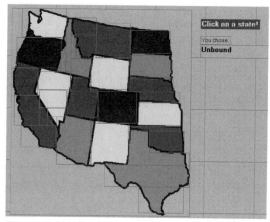

Figure 9-10 The map sample in design mode

active. You can click on transparent buttons, and they can react to events. Each transparent button corresponds to some physical region on the bitmap, so you can have the buttons' Click event procedures react according to their location on the bitmap. Now, if only Windows supported irregularly shaped command buttons!

Comments

The size of the bitmap is extremely important to the effectiveness of this technique. If you lay out the buttons all over the bitmap, and then decide to resize it, all your buttons' locations will no longer be correct. Make sure you've fixed the size of the bitmap before you start laying down your buttons. Although you can select all the buttons and resize them as a group, this is still not a perfect solution.

Don't spend too much time on getting the transparent buttons placed exactly. On the example form the buttons' placement is fairly concise, but that only works because most of the states in the west are generally rectangular (you'll notice that there's no eastern seaboard on that map). Users will typically click in the center of the region, so covering each pixel on the edge isn't a serious concern.

9.4 HOW DO I...   COMPLEXITY: INTERMEDIATE

Jump quickly to specific records?

Problem

I need to navigate through large amounts of data quickly. I'd like to type in a search key, or even part of a field, and have my form instantly display the matching records.

Technique

There are three different methods you can use to jump quickly to records, depending on your requirements:

- When the user chooses a key from an unbound combo box, apply a filter to your form to restrict it to records having that key value.

- When the user enters a partial key value, use the FindFirst and FindNext methods on a clone of the form's recordset to move directly to the matching records.

- When the user enters a search value, combine this with standard Access SQL keywords to revise the form's RecordSource on the fly.

Steps

All three of these techniques are demonstrated in 09-04.MDB.

Applying a Filter

To see a form that lets you jump to a record using the ApplyFilter technique, open 09-04.MDB and open frmArticleComboSearch. You can flip through all of the records in the database. To jump quickly to an individual record, select an article number from the combo box in the form's header (see Figure 9-11). To return to the original state, showing all the records, click on the Show All button.

To implement this technique on your own forms, follow these steps:

1. Create a new form based on your data table (tblArticle in the sample database). Add controls to the detail section of the form to display all the data in the table. In the form's header, create an unbound combo box that draws on the column in your table that has the key values you want to search. In the sample form, this combo box is named cboArticleNumber. Set its properties as shown in Table 9-4.

PROPERTY	VALUE
Name	cboArticleNumber
ControlSource	*leave blank to create an unbound control*
RowSourceType	Table/Query
RowSource	tblArticle
ColumnCount	1
BoundColumn	1
LimitToList	Yes
AfterUpdate	mcrComboFilter.Apply

Table 9-4 Property settings for search combo box

2. Place a command button in the form header. Set its OnClick property to mcrComboFilter.Remove. It's a good idea to name your command buttons as well, in case you should ever want to use Code Behind Forms (CBF) instead of macros for them. In the sample database, this button is named cmdShowAll.

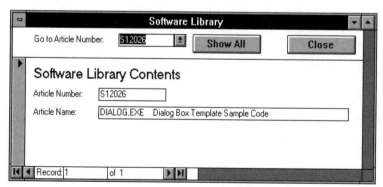

Figure 9-11 Searching by selecting a key value from a combo box

3. Save the form as frmArticleComboSearch.

4. Create a new macro and add the actions in Table 9-5 to it. Save the macro as mcrComboFilter.

MACRO NAME	ACTION	ARGUMENT	VALUE
Apply	ApplyFilter	Filter Name Where Condition	[ArticleNumber]=[Forms]![frmArticleComboSearch]![cboArticleNumber]
Remove	ShowAllRecords		

Table 9-5 Macro actions for mcrComboFilter

5. Open the form in form view and choose a value from the combo box. The form will display the matching record. Click the Show All button to return the form to showing all records.

Using FindFirst and FindNext

The form frmArticleFindMethods demonstrates using Access Basic's FindFirst and FindNext methods to search for matching records. Open this example in form view, and enter part of an article number (for example, S120) in the text box on the form's header. Then use the Find First and Find Next buttons to navigate to matching records (see Figure 9-12.)

To create a similar find form in your application, follow the steps below. You will need to substitute the names of your own data, unless you're working in the sample database.

1. Create a new form based on your data table (tblArticle in the sample database). Add controls to the detail section of the form to display all the

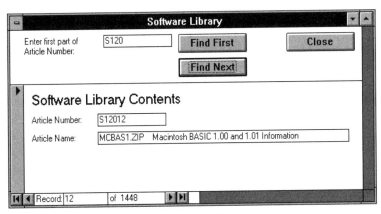

Figure 9-12 Find form after several Find Next actions

data in the table. In the form's header, create an unbound text box for the user to enter the partial key in. Name the box txtSearch.

2. Create two command buttons in the form header. Set their properties as shown in Table 9-6.

CONTROL NAME	PROPERTY	VALUE
cmdFindFirst	OnClick	=FindFirstArticle([txtSearch])
cmdFindNext	OnClick	=FindNextArticle([txtSearch])

Table 9-6 Properties for buttons on frmArticleFindMethods

3. Save the form as frmArticleFindMethods.
4. Import the module basFindMethod into your database or create a new module with the two functions ahtFindFirstArticle and ahtFindNextArticle.
5. Open frmArticleFindMethods in form view and enter a partial key in the text box. As you click on the Find First and Find Next buttons, the form will display matching records.

Changing the RecordSource

To explore changing a form's RecordSource as a means of locating records, open frmArticleRecordSourceSwitch in form view. Enter any keyword that appears as part of an article name (for example, dialog, as shown in Figure 9-13) in the text box on the form's header. When you tab out of the text box, the form will reset to display only matching records. You can switch keywords as often as you wish, or use the Show All button to return to the original set of all records.

Follow the steps below to create a similar wildcard searching form in your application. You will need to substitute the names of your own data fields, unless you're working in the sample database.

1. Create a new form based on your data table (tblArticle in the sample database.) Add controls to the detail section of the form to display all the

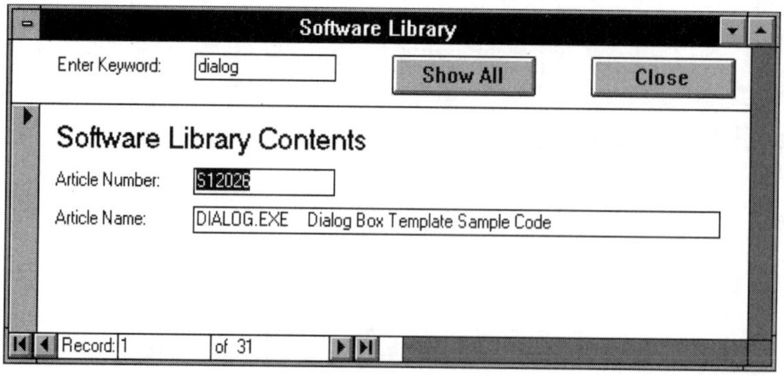

Figure 9-13 Using a keyword to display a partial list of records

data in the table. In the form's header, create an unbound text box. Set its properties as shown in Table 9-7.

PROPERTY	VALUE
Name	txtKeyword
AfterUpdate	mcrSwitchRecordSource.Apply

Table 9-7 Properties for unbound text box on frmArticleRecordSourceSwitch

2. Place a command button in the form header. Set its OnClick property to mcrSwitchRecordSource.Remove. Name this button cmdShowAll.
3. Save the form as frmArticleRecordSourceSwitch.
4. Create a new macro and add the actions in Table 9-8 to it. Save the macro as mcrSwitchRecordSource.

MACRO NAME	ACTION	ARGUMENT	VALUE
Apply	SetValue	Item	[Forms]![frmArticleRecordSourceSwitch].[RecordSource]
		Expression	"SELECT * FROM tblArticle WHERE tblArticle.ArticleName Like ""*" & [Forms]![frmArticleRecordSourceSwitch]![txtKeyword] & "*"";"
Remove	SetValue	Item	[Forms]![frmArticleRecordSourceSwitch].[RecordSource]
		Expression	"SELECT * FROM tblArticle;"

Table 9-8 Macro actions for mcrSwitchRecordSource

5. Open frmArticleRecordSourceSwitch in form view. Enter a keyword in the unbound text box and press (TAB). You'll see matching records on the form.

How It Works

The first example works by using a combo box to apply a filter to the form. A filter is the equivalent of an Access query that works to limit the records actually displayed without changing the underlying RecordSource. In this case, the filter is called whenever the combo box changes values (as determined by its After Update event firing) and uses an ApplyFilter macro action to apply the filter. The filter itself is expressed as an Access SQL WHERE clause:

```
[ArticleNumber]=[Forms]![frmArticleComboSearch]![cboArticleNumber]
```

Here the [ArticleNumber] refers to the field in the underlying table, while [Forms]![frmArticleComboSearch]![cboArticleNumber] is the standard Access syntax for referring to the cboArticleNumber control on the open form, frmArticleComboSearch.

The Show All command button on this form invokes a ShowAllRecords macro action, which is the inverse of ApplyFilter. It removes any filters that have been applied.

The second form takes user input and uses it as an argument to an Access Basic function to find the right records. The first thing the function does is create a *clone* of the form's recordset. Although every bound form has an associated set of records, you can't do much in Access Basic that will operate directly on this recordset. By using the form's RecordsetClone method, however, you can get an exact duplicate of the recordset to search.

```
Set rstForm = Forms![frmArticleFindMethods].RecordSetClone
```

The code, from ahtFindFirstArticle, uses the input from the user to construct a search string, and then uses the FindFirst method of the recordset clone to locate the first matching record.

```
strCriterion = "ArticleNumber Like ""*" & strSearch & "*"""
rstForm.MoveFirst
rstForm.FindFirst strCriterion
```

The FindFirst method sets the NoMatch property. If NoMatch is False, then there is a matching record, and the recordset is positioned at this record. You can then use the recordset's Bookmark property to transfer this location to the form's recordset. Reading the Bookmark from the code recordset captures the location of the found record; writing that same value to the form's recordset moves the form to that record.

```
' Move there on the form if there is a match
  If Not rstForm.NoMatch Then
     Forms![frmArticleFindMethods].Bookmark = rstForm.Bookmark
  End If
```

The FindNext code is very similar to the FindFirst code. The only difference is that it sets the clone recordset's pointer to the form's current record before starting the search, by reading the form's Bookmark and writing the recordset's Bookmark. This means that the search will start from the current record instead of the first record.

```
' And look for records to match, starting at the current spot
  rstForm.Bookmark = Forms![frmArticleFindMethods].Bookmark
  rstForm.FindNext strCriterion
```

> **NOTE:** The only time you can transfer bookmarks between two recordsets is when one is a clone of the other. In all other cases, even when both recordsets are based on the same query, bookmarks in one are not equivalent to bookmarks in the other.

The third technique takes advantage of your ability to change a form's RecordSource property at runtime in Access. As long as the field names returned match those displayed on the form, you can set the RecordSource to any table, query, or SQL statement. When you enter a new value into the unbound text box, it triggers the AfterUpdate event of the text box. This runs the macro mcrSwitchRecordSource.Apply, which sets the form's record source to be:

```
"SELECT * FROM tblArticle WHERE tblArticle.ArticleName Like """*"⇒
& [Forms]![frmArticleRecordSourceSwitch]![txtKeyword] & "*""";"
```

This expression uses the value of the txtKeyword control to construct an appropriate SQL WHERE clause.

For example, if you enter "dialog" into the text box, this expression evaluates to:

```
SELECT * FROM tblArticle WHERE tblArticle.ArticleName Like "*dialog*";
```

To show all records in this case, the macro sets the record source for the form back to the default record source of:

```
SELECT * FROM tblArticle;
```

Comments

When making a choice among the three techniques presented here, consider these differences:

- The ApplyFilter method can be implemented entirely in macros. You can use either a WHERE clause or an actual query as your filter. If you're most comfortable using the QBE grid to select records, this is the best technique for you.

- The FindFirst/FindNext method can only be implemented in Access Basic code. However, it is the only method of the three presented here that jumps to a record while keeping all records as part of the form's record source. The other two methods both remove records from the set being displayed, which may confuse some users.

- The RecordSource method can be implemented using macros or Access Basic code. This is the only method that allows you to swap in a completely different set of records if you need to. The ApplyFilter method only sorts particular records out of a form's recordset, not put more records into it.

9.5 HOW DO I...   COMPLEXITY: INTERMEDIATE

Create a splash screen?

Problem

I need to load several forms and perform calculations when my application is launched, but I don't want to leave users staring at the Access database container while this is happening. How can I create a professional splash screen to catch their attention while the application finishes loading?

Technique

A custom form can act as a splash screen for your application. By coupling this form with a timer event and a bit of Access Basic, you can even animate the splash screen. If you give users something animated to look at, they won't notice the delays in loading as much. As Figure 9-14 shows, this splash screen need not even look like a form.

Steps

Open 09-05.MDB and run the macro mcrSampleAutoExec. As you watch the splash screen with a small animation, Access is loading five forms in hidden mode. You can verify this by choosing Unhide from the Window menu (see Figure 9-15).

Here are the steps to add this capability to your database:

1. Create a new, unbound form in your database. Set its properties to match those in Table 9-9.

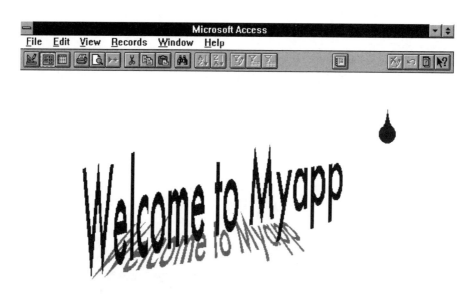

Figure 9-14 Custom splash screen for Access

Figure 9-15 Forms loaded while the splash screen was displayed

PROPERTY	VALUE
Caption	*a single space character*
DefaultView	Single form
ScrollBars	Neither
RecordSelectors	No
NavigationButtons	No
AutoResize	Yes
AutoCenter	Yes
BorderStyle	None
ControlBox	No
MinButton	No
MaxButton	No
Width	6.7 in
OnTimer	[Event Procedure]
TimerInterval	60

Table 9-9 Properties for splash form

2. Click anywhere in the detail section of the form. Set the back color of the detail section to white (or whatever color you prefer). Set the Height property of the detail section to 4.25 in. (This size is appropriate for VGA screens running in 640x480 resolution. If you use a higher resolution, you'll need to experiment to find a size that works properly with your monitor.)

3. Add a command button control anywhere in the detail section of the form. Set the properties of this button as shown in Table 9-10.

PROPERTY	VALUE
Transparent	Yes
StatusBarText	Loading application, please wait...

Table 9-10 Properties for command button

4. Insert an unbound object frame roughly in the center of the form. Select Create New from the Insert Object dialog and use whatever OLE server you like to create a picture or caption for your splash form. For the sample form, we used Microsoft WordArt 2.0, which ships with Microsoft Word and Microsoft Publisher. You could also use Paintbrush.

5. Right-click on your new object in design view. The fourth choice on the list will be a submenu headed Paintbrush Picture Object, WordArt Object, or the like. Choose this item, and from the submenu select Change to Picture.

6. Insert another unbound object frame in the upper-right corner of the form. Select Create From File from the Insert Object dialog box and insert TEARDROP.BMP (or another bitmap). Right-click on this new object and change it to a picture as well. Name this object objTeardrop.

7. Insert the following code for the OnTimer event procedure of the form:

```
Sub Form_Timer ()
   Static i As Integer

   Me![objTeardrop].Top = Me![objTeardrop].Top + 60

   i = i + 1
   If i >= 70 Then
      DoCmd Close
   End If
End Sub
```

8. Save the form as frmSplash. Open this form as the first action in your application's AutoExec macro.

How It Works

The splash form has properties that are carefully chosen to make it blend into the background. Leaving off the border, scroll bars, and record selectors makes it impossible to tell where the form ends and the background starts. Leaving off the control box, minimize button, maximize button, and caption tells Access not to allocate any space for a caption bar and not to display a blank caption bar.

By putting a single command button on the form, you give Access a place to set the focus when it opens the form. The control that gets the focus controls the status bar, so this gives you an easy way to set status bar text that appears while the rest of your application is loading.

Turning the OLE objects into pictures makes them load faster, since Access doesn't need to open an OLE session to load them. When you turn an OLE object into a picture it also becomes static rather than editable, but in this case you'll never need to edit the object.

The OnTimer loop animates the teardrop and closes the form when the animation is finished. By looping every 60 milliseconds, it provides relatively smooth motion yet allows plenty of time for other events to happen in the background.

Comments

Once you remove the control box, it's gone from both form and design views. This can make editing the form a bit tricky—once you open it in design mode, you have to remember to select File|Close to close it, since you'll no longer have a control menu to close the form.

If you have control over the user's MSACC20.INI file you can also suppress the default Access splash screen (with the large key) that displays when Access opens by supplying your own bitmap. See How-To 4-6 for more information.

The sample disk includes MINIMAL.BMP, a bitmap consisting of a single white pixel, which should blend into most backgrounds as if there were no splash screen at all.

9.6 HOW DO I...   COMPLEXITY: ADVANCED

Create multiple-selection list boxes?

Problem

I need to be able to select several items from a list at one time and use the selections in Access Basic. I like the interface used by the built-in Add-in Manager for doing this, with a column of *x*'s next to a column of choices. How do I implement this interface in my own application, to achieve the look shown in Figure 9-16?

Technique

You can emulate the dual-column selection list interface on your own forms by combining a custom list-filling function with code attached to the OnClick property of the list box. The code maintains the contents of the list box in an array in memory, together with an array of check marks. When you click on the list, the list box senses which item you clicked and adjusts its check mark accordingly. You also need to manipulate the form's Painting property to get it to display the results correctly.

Steps

Load 09-06.MDB and open frmMultiListboxDemo in form mode. You'll get a list of animals in a scrolling list box (see Figure 9-17). Click on any animal, and you'll see an *x* appear next to its name. Click again on the same animal, and the *x* will vanish. Click on OK, and the form will display a list of all the animals that you picked.

To create a similar list box, follow these steps:

1. Create a new form. Because this type of interface is most often used in Wizards, the sample form has typical Wizard properties, as shown in Table 9-11.

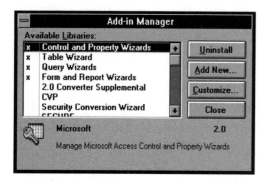

Figure 9-16 Add-in Manager selection list

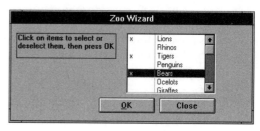

Figure 9-17 A dual-column selection list

PROPERTY	VALUE
RecordSource	
Caption	Zoo Wizard
DefaultView	Single Form
ViewsAllowed	Form
ShortcutMenu	No
ScrollBars	Neither
RecordSelectors	No
NavigationButtons	No
AutoResize	No
AutoCenter	Yes
PopUp	Yes
Modal	Yes
BorderStyle	Dialog
ControlBox	No
MinButton	No
MaxButton	No

Table 9-11 Properties for a Wizard form

2. Add an unbound list box control to the form and give it the properties shown in Table 9-12.

PROPERTY	VALUE
Name	lboAnimals
ControlSource	
RowSourceType	ahtFillWithAnimals
RowSource	
BoundColumn	1
DefaultValue	1
OnClick	[Event Procedure]

Table 9-12 List box properties for multiple-selection list

3. Right-click on the list box control, select Build Event, and then Code Builder. Use the Procedure combo box in the toolbar to switch to the control's OnClick event procedure and enter the following code:

```
Sub lboAnimals_Click ()

    Me.Painting = False
    If avarAnimal(2, lboAnimals.ListIndex) = "x" Then
        avarAnimal(2, lboAnimals.ListIndex) = " "
    Else
        avarAnimal(2, lboAnimals.ListIndex) = "x"
    End If
    Me.Painting = True

End Sub
```

4. Add a command button to the form and name it cmdOK. Right-click on the button and enter this code in its OnClick event procedure:

```
Sub cmdOK_Click ()
    Dim i As Integer
    Dim strResult As String
    Dim intAnimalsSelected As Integer

    intAnimalsSelected = 0
    strResult = "You selected "

    For i = 0 To UBound(avarAnimal, 2)
        If avarAnimal(2, i) = "x" Then
            intAnimalsSelected = intAnimalsSelected + 1
            If intAnimalsSelected > 1 Then
                strResult = strResult & "and "
            End If
            strResult = strResult & avarAnimal(3, i) & " "
        End If
    Next i
    If intAnimalsSelected > 0 Then
        MsgBox strResult
    End If

End Sub
```

5. Save and close the form.
6. Create a new module with a list box callback function for your list box. The one in the sample database is called ahtFillWithAnimals, and can be used as a template for your own function.
7. Open your new form and click on several items in the list. Then click the OK button. You will see a message box listing the items you clicked, as shown in Figure 9-18.

How It Works

When you open the sample form, Access uses your custom list box function to populate the list box. (Custom list box functions are explained in Chapter 7.)

This particular function uses a global array to maintain three columns of information: The first column contains the primary key of each record in the table; the second column is initially blank, and is reserved for the *x*'s; and the third column contains the data to display in the list box

When you click on any particular record in the list box, Access uses its ListIndex property to determine which record you clicked. Then it switches the state of the second column, placing or removing an *x* as appropriate. To force Access to redisplay the list, the code turns the form's Painting property off before changing the state of the column, and turns it back on afterwards. (You can't requery the list box, because this will make Access discard the contents of the global array and start over.)

When you click the OK button, Access looks down the array for rows where the second element of the array is an *x*. In the sample database, the values from these rows are read back into a message box. In your code, you can do whatever further processing is necessary, perhaps putting the selected rows into a recordset.

Comments

In this simple case, it's not really necessary to set the form's AutoResize property to no, since the form consists of a single page. Most Wizard forms are several pages long and use GoToControl actions to step from page to page. In these forms, you must be sure to turn AutoResize off and open the form in dialog mode to prevent accidentally displaying multiple pages to users at the same time.

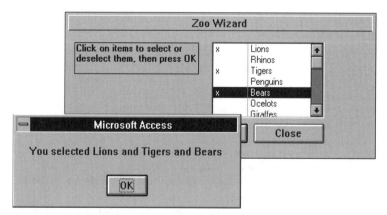

Figure 9-18 Results from the multiple-selection list box

9.7 HOW DO I...   COMPLEXITY: ADVANCED

Create animated buttons?

Problem

My application works, but it isn't dressy enough. I'd like to add some animation to it. How do I create animated buttons on my forms?

Technique

Access command buttons have an undocumented PictureData property, which stores the actual bitmap that's displayed on the button face. This How-To examines two ways to use this property. First, you can create "two-state" buttons with pictures that change when you click on them. In this case, you can trap mouse events to know when to change the pictures. Or you can create fully animated buttons that cycle through a set of pictures at all times to attract attention, using the form's Timer events to force display of a smooth succession of bitmaps.

Steps

Load 09-07.MDB and open frmAnimateDemo (see Figure 9-19). The top two buttons are two-state buttons whose pictures change when you click them. The Copy button shows a second document, and the Exit button shows the door closing just before it closes the form. The bottom two buttons are examples of animated button faces. (Only the Exit button on this form actually does anything when you press it.)

Creating "Two-State" Buttons

To create the two-state buttons, follow these steps:

1. Open the form where you want the button. Place two command buttons on this form. The first button should be sized correctly for your pictures and be located where you want the button to be displayed. The second button can

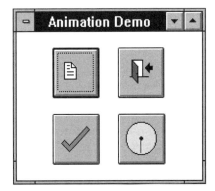

Figure 9-19 frmAnimateDemo

be located anywhere and be any size. Name the first button cmdMyButton and the second button cmdMyButton2. Set the Visible property of cmdMyButton2 to No.

2. Click on cmdMyButton, select the Picture property on the properties sheet, and click the Builder button next to the property. On the button face form, select the face you want your button to have in its unpressed state. (You can use the Browse button to select from bitmap files on your disk.)

3. Click on cmdMyButton2, select the Picture property, and load the face you want your button to have when it is pressed.

4. Attach the following code to the MouseDown property of cmdMyButton:

```
Sub cmdMyButton_MouseDown (Button As Integer, Shift As Integer, X As Single, Y As Single)

    Dim varTemp As Variant
    varTemp = Me![cmdMyButton].PictureData
    Me![cmdMyButton].PictureData = Me![cmdMyButton2].PictureData
    Me![cmdMyButton2].PictureData = varTemp
    Me.Repaint

End Sub
```

5. Attach the following code to the MouseUp property of cmdMyButton:

```
Sub cmdMyButton_MouseUp (Button As Integer, Shift As Integer, X As Single, Y As Single)

    Dim varTemp As Variant
    varTemp = Me![cmdMyButton].PictureData
    Me![cmdMyButton].PictureData = Me![cmdMyButton2].PictureData
    Me![cmdMyButton2].PictureData = varTemp

End Sub
```

Continuously Animated Buttons

To create the animated buttons, follow these steps:

1. Import tblButtonAnimation, frmButtonFaceChooser, and basAnimate from 09-07.MDB to your own database.

2. Open frmButtonFaceChooser (see Figure 9-20) and select eight images for use on your animated button. You can either type the file names directly into the text boxes or click on the blank buttons to select files from the common file dialog box. The pictures will appear on the command buttons as you choose them. The buttons are sized to accept standard 32×32-pixel icons or bitmaps, but you may use any size.

3. When you have selected eight bitmaps, enter an animation name to refer to this set of pictures (for example, "clock") and click on the Save button.

4. Create a new blank form and place a command button on it. Name the button cmdClock. Set the form's properties as shown in Table 9-13.

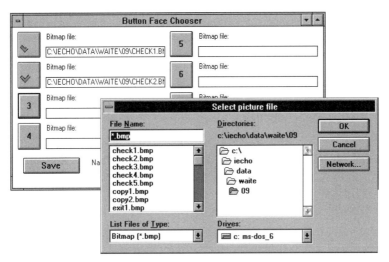

Figure 9-20 frmButtonFaceChooser

PROPERTY	VALUE
OnLoad	[Event Procedure]
OnTimer	[Event Procedure]
TimerInterval	250

Table 9-13 Form properties for animated button form

5. Click on the Code button on the Form Design toolbar. Enter the following code in the (declarations) section:

```
Option Compare Database    'Use database order for string comparisons
Option Explicit

Dim i As Integer
Dim abinAnimation(8) As Variant
```

6. Enter the following code for the form's Load event:

```
Sub Form_Load ()

Dim dbCurrent As Database
Dim rstAnimation As Recordset

i = 1

Set dbCurrent = DBEngine.Workspaces(0.)Databases(0)
Set rstAnimation = dbCurrent.OpenRecordset("tblButtonAnimation", DB_OPEN_DYNASET)

rstAnimation.MoveFirst
rstAnimation.FindFirst "AnimationName='clock'"
    abinAnimation(1) = rstAnimation![Face1]
```

(Continued on next page)

(Continued from previous page)

```
        abinAnimation(2) = rstAnimation![Face2]
        abinAnimation(3) = rstAnimation![Face3]
        abinAnimation(4) = rstAnimation![Face4]
        abinAnimation(5) = rstAnimation![Face5]
        abinAnimation(6) = rstAnimation![Face6]
        abinAnimation(7) = rstAnimation![Face7]
        abinAnimation(8) = rstAnimation![Face8]
    rstAnimation.Close
End Sub
```

7. Enter the following code for the form's Timer event:

```
Sub Form_Timer ()
    i = i + 1
    If i = 9 Then
        i = 1
    End If
    Me![cmdClock].PictureData = abinAnimation(i)
End Sub
```

8. Save the form and open it in form view. You will see your animation running on the face of the button.

How It Works

Access stores the picture displayed on a command button in the undocumented PictureData property. This property is a binary representation of the bitmap displayed and is read/write in all views. To store such a bitmap elsewhere, you have three choices: on another button, in a variable of the Variant data type, or in a table field of the OLE object data type.

In this How-To you use all three of these techniques. The two-state buttons work by storing the normal image on the button you can see and parking the second image in an invisible button. You can still read and write the PictureData property of an invisible button. When you click the visible button, its MouseDown event gets called, which swaps the pictures in the visible and invisible buttons. The MouseUp event code does the same swap again to return the original picture to the button face.

> **NOTE:** To see the effects of the MouseDown event you must call the form's Repaint method, which tells Access to complete any pending screen updates. On the other hand, you don't need to do this in the MouseUp event—for some reason, Access automatically repaints the screen after a MouseUp event.

In the animated button technique, the eight different button faces are stored in a table as Long Binary Data (which is what Access will tell you if you open the table in datasheet view) in OLE object fields. The form's Load event procedure reads these button faces into an array of variants, and its Timer event is used to fetch the next button face every 250 milliseconds, in round-robin fashion.

In frmButtonFaceChooser you'll find an easy way to load bitmaps into the table of animations. You can load a button's PictureData property by setting its Picture property to the name of any bitmap or icon file. The command buttons on this form use a function from UTILITY.MDA, wlib_GetFileName, to invoke the common file dialog box.

Comments

You could extend the animated button technique in several directions.

☞ By including multiple hidden buttons on your form, you can create three-state buttons that change their picture when they are the current default button, as well as when they are pushed.

☞ You can modify the event procedure to allow for animated buttons with more or less than eight frames of animation. To do this, break the table of frames up into two related tables, one holding the name of the animation and the number of frames, the other holding the actual picture data.

☞ The sample form shows how to use two arrays and some more code to have two animated buttons on the same form. You might generalize this code as well, but watch out—almost any form will start to look busy with more buttons animated.

If you open the sample form and hold down any button, you'll see that the animations stop for as long as you keep the button held down. This prevents the form's Timer events from firing.

9.8 HOW DO I...
COMPLEXITY: ADVANCED

Design an expanding dialog box?

Problem

I have a dialog box with a lot of options, most of which are only needed in specific situations. I'd like to set this up as an expanding dialog box, similar to Access's Print Setup, as shown in Figures 9-21 and 9-22. How can I do this with my own form?

Technique

You can resize a form at runtime by executing a MoveSize action, either in a macro or in Access Basic code. However, to get the expanding dialog box effect, you must accommodate the width of the borders and the height of the caption bar on the form. In addition, you must be careful to restrict users from opening the expanded section by accident.

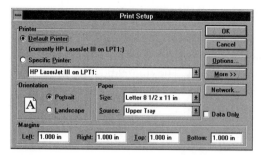

Figure 9-21 Access's Print Setup dialog in its initial state

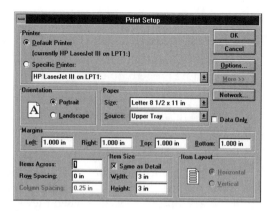

Figure 9-22 Access's Print Setup dialog in its expanded state

Steps

Load the sample database 09-08.MDB, and use mcrOpenAsDialog to open the frmExpandDemo form. Click on the Expand button to see the controls that are hidden when the form is first opened. Click on the Contract button to hide these controls again. To create a similar form in your database, follow these steps:

1. Create a new form. Click and drag the lower-right corner of the design surface (the white area where you can place controls) and until the form is three inches high and three inches wide on screen. Set the properties of the form as shown in Table 9-14. (Except for the functions, these are the standard properties for a dialog box form.)

PROPERTY	VALUE
DefaultView	Single Form
ScrollBars	Neither
RecordSelectors	No
NavigationButtons	No
BorderStyle	Dialog
MaxButton	No
MinButton	No
OnOpen	=ahtInitializeExpand([Form])
OnLoad	=ahtResizeForm(3,1)
OnActivate	=ahtInitializeExpand([Form])

Table 9-14 Form properties for expanding dialog box

2. Place a command button somewhere in the upper inch of the form. Name this button cmdExpand and set its OnClick property to =ahtResizeForm(3,3).

3. Place a command button somewhere in the lower two inches of the form. Name this button cmdContract and set its OnClick property to =ahtResizeForm(3,1).

4. Add other controls as desired and save the form.

5. Import the module basExpandForm to your database.

6. Open your new form in form view. The OnLoad code will size it to be one inch high and three inches wide. Click Expand and the form will grow to three inches high. Click Contract and it will shrink back to one inch high.

How It Works

When you open or activate the form, it calls Windows API functions to set a pair of global variables, intBorderWidth and intCaptionHeight. This is the purpose of the ahtInitializeExpand function shown below, which takes the calling form as its only argument. You have to reset these global variables whenever a form that uses them becomes active, since they might be different in each form. This function uses the GetDeviceCaps and GetSystemMetrics Windows API calls to find out two things: How many pixels there are per inch on this particular display device and the size of the caption bar and borders of the current form.

```
Function ahtInitializeExpand (frm As Form)
'
' Call the Windows API to get metrics for the current form
'
On Error GoTo ahtInitializeExpand_Err

    Dim intDC As Integer
    Dim intPixelsX As Integer
    Dim intPixelsY As Integer

' Determine number of pixels per inch in each
' direction on this screen.
    intDC = aht_apiGetDC(frm.hwnd)
    intPixelsX = aht_apiGetDeviceCaps(intDC, WU_LOGPIXELSX)
    intPixelsY = aht_apiGetDeviceCaps(intDC, WU_LOGPIXELSY)

' Store the caption height and border width in module
' scope variables. This makes for faster access, since
' we will be using them repeatedly as we work.
    intCaptionHeight = ((aht_apiGetSystemMetrics(SM_CYCAPTION) + ⇒
(2 * aht_apiGetSystemMetrics(SM_CYFRAME))) / intPixelsY) * TWIPS_PER_INCH
    intBorderWidth = ((2 * aht_apiGetSystemMetrics(SM_CXFRAME)) / intPixelsX) * TWIPS_PER_INCH

' Clean up before exiting
    intDC = aht_apiReleaseDC(frm.hwnd, intDC)

ahtInitializeExpand_Exit:
    On Error GoTo 0
    Exit Function

ahtInitializeExpand_Err:
```

(Continued on next page)

(Continued from previous page)

```
    MsgBox "Error" & Err & ": " & Error$, MB_ICON_STOP, "ahtInitializeExpand()"
    Resume ahtInitializeExpand_Exit

End Function
```

When the form loads, or when you click on the Expand or Contract button, the ahtResizeForm function sets the size of the form. This function is mainly a wrapper around the MoveSize action, but it also adds on the appropriate border and caption sizes as determined by the ahtInitializeExpand function.

```
Function ahtResizeForm (sngWidth As Single, sngHeight As Single)
'
' Resize a form without moving it, taking into account
' the border width and caption height
'
On Error GoTo ahtResizeForm_Err

    DoCmd MoveSize , , (TWIPS_PER_INCH * sngWidth) + intBorderWidth, ⇒
(TWIPS_PER_INCH * sngHeight) + intCaptionHeight

ahtResizeForm_Exit:
    On Error GoTo 0
    Exit Function

ahtResizeForm_Err:
    MsgBox "Error " & Err & ": " & Error$, MB_ICON_STOP, "ahtResizeForm()"
    Resume ahtResizeForm_Exit

End Function
```

Comments

When you use these functions, ahtInitializeExpand and ahtResizeForm on your own forms, be aware that some users prefer the keyboard to the mouse. To keep (PGUP) and (PGDN) keystrokes from moving around in the form's window, open the form in dialog mode, which automatically disables these keystrokes. To keep the (TAB) key from bringing up controls in the expanded part of the form, set the Tab Stop property of all of those controls to no. You might want to set it to yes when the form is expanded and return it to no when the form is contracted. You can do this by calling a macro that executes a series of SetValue actions, or by writing Code Behind Forms to do the equivalent assignments.

These functions use all three of the measuring systems that are involved in Access programming:

- Users measure things in inches (or centimeters), and the Access user interface displays size settings in inches.

- Device capacities are given in pixels—for example, a VGA resolution screen is 640 pixels wide and 480 pixels high. If you pass in the proper parameters, the GetDeviceCaps API function will return conversion factors from pixels to inches.

🗝 The internal storage system of Access (and Windows generally) uses twips. A twip is ¹⁄₂₀ of a typesetting point, or ¹⁄₁₄₄₀ of an inch. When you execute the MoveSize action in Access Basic, you give it arguments in twips.

9.9 HOW DO I...   COMPLEXITY: INTERMEDIATE

Use two list boxes to select records?

Problem
I want to let users select a group of records to be shown on a report. I'd like to use an interface similar to that of the Access Wizards, where available items in one list box can be moved to a second list box, using command buttons. How can I emulate this interface in my own application?

Technique
Although the Access Wizards use a more flexible technique developed in Access Basic, you can do a single-purpose dual list box with a combination of macros, update queries, and a hidden field. When you click on one of the buttons on the form, Access runs an update query to move the appropriate record or group of records from one list box to another.

Steps
Load 09-09.MDB and open frmDualBox in regular form mode (see Figure 9-23). You'll be presented with a list of available menu items in the left-hand list box and a blank list on the right. At any time, you have these options:

🗝 Select an item in the left-hand list box and click the > button to move just that item to the right-hand list box.

🗝 Click the >> button to move all remaining items from the left-hand list box to the right-hand list box.

🗝 Select any item in the right-hand list box and click the < button to move just that item to the left-hand list box.

🗝 Click the << button to move all items from the right-hand list box back to the left-hand list box.

When you are satisfied with your selections, click the OK button. Access will close the selection form and show you a report based on only the items you selected, as illustrated in Figure 9-24.

To re-create this example, follow these steps:

1. Create a new table and add three fields to it, with the properties shown in Table 9-15. Select MenuItem as the primary key of this table and save the table as tblMenu.

FIELD NAME	DATA TYPE	SIZE
MenuItem	Text	50
Selected	Yes/No	
Calories	Number	Integer

Table 9-15 Fields in tblMenu

2. Create a new blank form and name it frmMenu. Set the form properties as shown in Table 9-16.

PROPERTY	VALUE
Caption	Build Menu
DefaultView	Single Form
ScrollBars	Neither
RecordSelectors	No
NavigationButtons	No
AutoResize	Yes
AutoCenter	Yes
ControlBox	Yes
MinButton	No
MaxButton	No
OnOpen	mcrRemoveAll

Table 9-16 Properties for frmMenu

3. Place a list box on the left-hand side of the form. Click on the Build button to the right of the RowSource property. Select tblMenu from the table list and click OK. Drag all three fields from the field list to the query grid. Set the sort order of the MenuItem field to Ascending. Set the Criteria of the Selected field to no. Figure 9-25 shows this process of building a Row Source with the Query Builder.

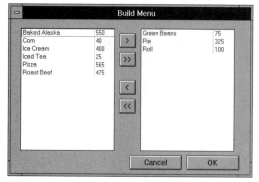

Figure 9-23 A dual list box interface

Figure 9-24 Report generated from selected items

Close the Query Builder window and answer yes when Access asks whether you would like to save changes to the record source. Set the other properties of this list box as shown in Table 9-17.

PROPERTY	VALUE
Name	lboAvailable
ColumnCount	3
ColumnHeads	No
ColumnWidths	1.4 in;0.35 in;0 in
BoundColumn	1

Table 9-17 Properties for lboAvailable

4. Select the lboAvailable list box and choose Duplicate from the Edit menu. Use the mouse to move the duplicate control to the right-hand side of the form. Change the name of the duplicate to lboSelected and edit the RowSource property of the duplicate to:

```
SELECT DISTINCTROW tblMenu.MenuItem, tblMenu.Calories, ⇒
tblMenu.Selected FROM tblMenu WHERE ((tblMenu.Selected=Yes)) ORDER BY tblMenu.MenuItem;
```

5. Place four command buttons on the form between the list boxes. Set their properties as shown in Tables 9-18 through 9-21.

PROPERTY	VALUE
Name	cmdAddOne
Caption	>
OnClick	mcrAddOne

Table 9-18 Properties for cmdAddOne button

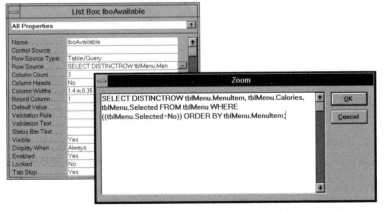

Figure 9-25 Building the Row Source for the lboAvailable control

PROPERTY	VALUE
Name	cmdAddAll
Caption	>>
OnClick	mcrAddAll

Table 9-19 Properties for cmdAddAll button

PROPERTY	VALUE
Name	cmdRemoveOne
Caption	<
OnClick	mcrRemoveOne

Table 9-20 Properties for cmdRemoveOne button

PROPERTY	VALUE
Name	cmdRemoveAll
Caption	<<
OnClick	mcrRemoveAll

Table 9-21 Properties for cmdRemoveAll button

6. Place two command buttons at the bottom of the form. Set their properties as shown in Tables 9-22 and 9-23.

PROPERTY	VALUE
Name	cmdCancel
Caption	Cancel
Cancel	Yes
OnClick	mcrClose

Table 9-22 Properties for cmdCancel button

PROPERTY	VALUE
Name	cmdOK
Caption	OK
Default	Yes
OnClick	mcrOpenrptMenu

Table 9-23 Properties for cmdOk button

7. Save the form as frmDualBox and close it.

8. Create a new query based on the tblMenu table. Bring the Selected field down to the query grid. Click on the Update button on the toolbar to transform the query into an update query. Enter yes in the Update To row for the Selected field. Save the query as qupdAddAll and close it.

9. Create a new query based on the tblMenu table. Bring the Selected and MenuItem fields down to the query grid. Click on the Update button on the toolbar to transform the query into an update query. Enter yes in the Update To row for the Selected field. Enter [Forms]![frmDualBox]![lbo Available] in the Criteria row for the MenuItem field. Save the query as qupdAddOne and close it.

10. Create a new query based on the tblMenu table. Bring the Selected field down to the query grid. Click on the Update button on the toolbar to transform the query into an update query. Enter no in the Update To row for the Selected field. Save the query as qupdRemoveAll and close it.

11. Create a new query based on the tblMenu table. Bring the Selected and MenuItem fields down to the query grid. Click on the Update button on the toolbar to transform the query into an update query. Enter no in the Update To row for the Selected field. Enter [Forms]![frmDualBox]![lbo-Selected] in the Criteria row for the MenuItem field. Save the query as qupdRemoveOne and close it.

12. Create a new macro with the actions shown in Table 9-24. Save this macro as mcrAddAll.

ACTION	ARGUMENT	VALUE
SetWarnings	Warnings On	No
Open Query	Query Name	qupdAddAll
	View	Datasheet
	Data Mode	Edit
Requery	Control Name	lboSelected
Requery	Control Name	lboAvailable

Table 9-24 Actions for mcrAddAll

13. Create a new macro with the actions shown in Table 9-25. Save this macro as mcrAddOne.

ACTION	ARGUMENT	VALUE
SetWarnings	Warnings On	No
Open Query	Query Name	qupdAddOne
	View	Datasheet
	Data Mode	Edit
Requery	Control Name	lboSelected
Requery	Control Name	lboAvailable

Table 9-25 Actions for mcrAddOne

14. Create a new macro with the actions shown in Table 9-26. Save this macro as mcrRemoveOne.

ACTION	ARGUMENT	VALUE
SetWarnings	Warnings On	No
Open Query	Query Name	qupdRemoveOne
	View	Datasheet
	Data Mode	Edit
Requery	Control Name	lboSelected
Requery	Control Name	lboAvailable

Table 9-26 Actions for mcrRemoveOne

15. Create a new macro with the actions shown in Table 9-27. Save this macro as mcrRemoveAll.

ACTION	ARGUMENT	VALUE
SetWarnings	Warnings On	No
Open Query	Query Name	qupdRemoveAll
	View	Datasheet
	Data Mode	Edit
Requery	Control Name	lboSelected
Requery	Control Name	lboAvailable

Table 9-27 Actions for mcrRemoveAll

16. Create a new macro named mcrClose consisting of a single Close action with no argument.

17. Create a new macro with the actions shown in Table 9-28. Save this macro as mcrOpenrptMenu.

ACTION	ARGUMENT	VALUE
Close	Object Type	Form
	Object Name	frmDualBox
Open Report	Report Name	rptMenu
	View	Print Preview

Table 9-28 Actions for mcrOpenrptMenu

18. Create another new query based on tblMenu. Drag down all three fields to the query grid. Set the Criteria row of the Selected field to yes. Save the query as qryMenuSelected and close it.

19. Create a new report based on qryMenuSelected. Drag text fields for MenuItem and Calories to the detail section. Add a calculated control with a Control Source of =Sum([Calories]) to the Report footer section. Add whatever labels and formatting you prefer. Save the report as rptMenu and close it. The final report is shown in Figure 9-26.

20. Open the frmDualBox form and select items from the left-hand list box, clicking > after clicking on each item. When you have selected several items, click on the OK button. The form closes and the report opens, containing only the items that you selected.

How It Works

When you open the dual list box form, Access runs the mcrRemoveAll macro, which calls the qupdRemoveAll query to set the Selected field of all the records to no. This means that the control source for the lboAvailable list box will return all records, and the control source for the lboSelected list box will return no records, so the form starts off with all the records on the left-hand side.

As you click the selection buttons, Access uses macros to run update queries that change the Selected fields of one or more records, depending on which button you pushed. After each change, the macros requery the list boxes to keep their contents up to date.

When you click the OK button, Access uses a query to find the selected records and return them in a report.

Comments

To use this technique on your own data, you will need to:

⚷ Add a Selected field with a data type of yes/no to flag which records are displayed in each list box at any given time.

⚷ Write appropriate update queries to maintain the Selected flag.

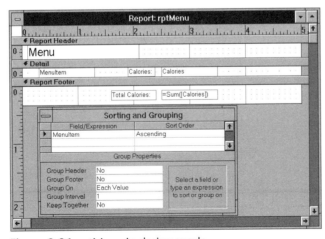

Figure 9-26 rptMenu in design mode

➤ Call these queries from the mcrAddOne, mcrAddAll, mcrRemoveOne, and mcrRemoveAll macros.

➤ Write appropriate macros and other objects to use the selected items after the user is done choosing them.

To generalize this technique, you could write an Access Basic function to change the RecordSource of the dual list boxes to reflect a new table each time you open the form, depending on how you open it.

9.10 HOW DO I...   COMPLEXITY: INTERMEDIATE

Create a customized status meter using Access Basic?

Problem
Access allows me to control the built-in status meter using the Syscmd function, but I have no control over the location or appearance of this status meter. How do I create a status meter that I can control?

Technique
You can create a status meter based on an Access form and control it using Access Basic routines. The status meter is composed of a rectangle control and a label control. By updating the Width property of the rectangle, you can control the meter's progress. Additionally, by updating the Caption property of the label, you can insert messages such as "50% complete." Figure 9-27 shows the sample status meter form, starting at 0%.

Steps
Open 09-10.MDB and run frmStatusMeter. To start the status meter, click the Start button. The status meter will increment to 100% and then stop. To reset it, click the Reset button. To create a status meter for your own application, follow these steps:

1. Create a form and set its properties as shown in Table 9-29.

PROPERTY	VALUE
DefaultView	Single Form
RecordSelectors	No
ScrollBars	Neither
NavigationButtons	No
MinButton	No
MaxButton	No
BorderStyle	Thin

Table 9-29 Properties for the status meter form

2. Place a rectangle on the form, name it recStatus, and set its Width property to 0. Set its background color to the color you want the status meter to be.

3. Place a label on the form, name it lblStatus, and set its Width property to the total width you want the status meter to be. Set its Background to Clear. In the Label property, type in 0% Complete.

4. Save the form as frmStatusMeter and close it.

5. Import the module basStatus from 09-10.MDB. This module includes these two procedures, which control the display of the status bar:

```
Sub ahtInitStatus (frm As Form, strTitle As String)
   frm!recStatus.Width = 0
   frm!lblStatus.Caption = "0% complete"
   frm.Caption = strTitle
   DoCmd RepaintObject
End Sub

Sub ahtUpdateStatus (frm As Form, intValue As Integer)
   frm!recStatus.Width = CInt(frm!lblStatus.Width * (intValue / 100))
   frm!lblStatus.Caption = Format$(intValue, "##") & "% complete"
   DoCmd RepaintObject
End Sub
```

6. To call the status meter from your application, open the form and call the ahtInitStatus subroutine, passing it a reference to the current form along with the title you want to appear in the form's title bar. For example, to open the status meter with the title "Deleting Records," type:

```
DoCmd OpenForm "frmStatusMeter"
Call aht_InitStatus (Me, "Deleting Records")
```

7. To update the status meter, call the ahtUpdateStatus subroutine with a reference to the form and the percentage value desired. For example, to update the status meter to 50%, type:

```
Call ahtUpdateStatus(Me, 50)
```

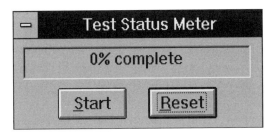

Figure 9-27 Example status meter form, frmStatusMeter

How It Works

By manipulating the Width property of the rectangle, you can cause the rectangle to "grow." The rectangle control is placed behind a transparent label control that defines the boundaries of the status meter and contains the status text. In the above example, there are two management routines. The first, ahtInitStatus, initializes the Status meter by setting the Width property of the recStatus control to 0, setting the Caption property of lblStatus to "0% Complete", and updating the form's Caption property with a user-defined string. The RepaintObject action causes these updates to be reflected on the form.

Next, the ahtUpdateStatus subroutine updates the status meter with a supplied value. It does this by changing the width of the recStatus control relative to the width of the lblStatus control. This relative change ensures that the status meter rectangle never exceeds the limits as defined by the width of the lblStatus control. The routine then updates the Caption property of the lblStatus control to contain the current status value as a string. Using the Format function ensures that the text will be formatted correctly. Finally, the RepaintObject action causes the form to be updated.

The code tied to the buttons manages the display of the status meter. The test procedure, cmdStart_Click, calls the ahtInitStatus subroutine to initialize the status meter and display a custom title. Then it enters a loop that calls the ahtUpdateStatus subroutine, passing the current value of the intCounter variable. This causes the label control to grow wider and wider. When you press the Reset button, the cmdReset_Click event procedure calls the ahtInitStatus subroutine to reinitialize the status meter.

Comments

Since the status meter is implemented using Access controls, you have complete control over its appearance and behavior. You may want to experiment with different form settings. For example, if you want the status meter to "float" over other forms, try setting the form's Frame property to None and its Popup property to yes. This will eliminate the border and title bar, causing the status meter form to open above all other forms.

Note that the value you send to the UpdateStatus subroutine must be between 0 and 100. It is up to your calling routine to calculate the boundaries of your operation and send UpdateStatus the appropriate values.

10

Addressing Multi-User Application Concerns

HOW DO I...

Access offers native support, right out of the box, for multi-user applications. But this additional power brings with it some additional problems, chiefly those of coordinating multiple users who may be spread across a large network. This chapter explores some solutions to problems common to multi-user applications. You'll learn how to use a shared database table to help your users communicate with one another, and how to find out which users are logged in at any given time. You'll learn how to implement basic transaction logging. Several of the How-To's here tackle the problem of updating a database that exists on multiple workstations, perhaps even worldwide. Since multi-user applications often use Access security, we also explore the security system. For instance, you'll learn how to keep track of users and groups, how to check to see whether they have blank passwords, and how to enforce some additional password requirements beyond those that Access itself handles. You'll also learn how to go beyond the Access built-in security and set security yourself on individual controls and menu options.

10.1   Send messages to other users without using e-mail

If your network uses Microsoft Mail or another MAPI-compliant mailer, Access 2.0 offers easy connectivity to other users via the SendObject action. Even if you use a different mailer, or you don't want the overhead of an e-mail interface, you can still let users communicate with one another. This How-To will show how to share a data table on a server as a sort of electronic bulletin board, and to check it at regular intervals from each logged-on user.

10.2   Show which users have a shared database open at any given time

Although Access 2.0 provides much more system information to the programmer than previous versions did, there is still no built-in way to find out which users are logged in to a particular shared database. This How-To will work around the problem by initializing and maintaining a table of active users in the shared database. You can also use this method to limit the number of simultaneous logins that users are allowed.

10.3   Create a transaction log

Full-blown client-server databases offer the ability to record the actions of users and replay them later on a copy of the database. This How-To will help you set up a simple transaction log within Access to track additions, edits, and deletions, so you'll have a permanent record of these events.

10.4   Find and transfer objects that changed between two versions of a database

Upgrading a shared database can be tricky, since you need to make the update on multiple computers. There are times when you'll upgrade a database by creating new objects for it and then need to install these new objects in an older version. Although you can track these changes by hand, it's a lot of work. This How-To includes a routine for identifying the changes between two versions of a database and automatically importing new objects from the newer copy to the older one.

10.5 Automatically update objects at login
When you have multiple copies of an application on a network, it can be a great nuisance to update them all. Why not let them update themselves? This How-To will demonstrate how to track version numbers of your application and move out the latest objects to update them to the current version whenever an obsolete version logs in to the shared network database.

10.6 Keep track of users and groups programmatically
If you're in charge of an Access workgroup, you'll need to keep track of your security layout, and you can use the tools Access provides to print out such a listing. But if you need to create tables to contain this information, so you can use them as part of your applications, you'll need to do a little work. This How-To will demonstrate the steps you take to retrieve and store user and group information in tables.

10.7 List all users with blank passwords
If you're maintaining a workgroup using Access, you may need to get a list of all users without passwords. Though this is not a difficult task, it's also not obvious how to implement it. This How-To will show how to use simple Access Basic and Data Access Objects to retrieve this type of information.

10.8 Implement password aging and minimum length requirements
Although Access security is good, it isn't perfect. This How-To will help you implement two features that are missing from the built-in security: tracking the age of passwords and ensuring that users periodically change their passwords, and preventing users from establishing passwords that are too simple and easy to guess.

10.9 Adjust database options depending on who's logged in
There's no need to create multiple database objects for users at different security levels so that they can have their own settings present when they work in your application. This How-To will illustrate how to store custom settings and retrieve them when a user logs in.

10.1 HOW DO I...   COMPLEXITY: INTERMEDIATE

Send messages to other users without using e-mail?

Problem
When I have multiple users logged in to my application, I'd like them to be able to communicate quickly and easily with one another. I need a simple interface for sending notes back and forth, so users can check whether anyone else is editing a particular entry, compare notes on work flow, and so forth. How can I implement this in Access?

Technique
You can keep notes in a table in a shared database that all users have access to. Whenever someone writes a note to another user, that note is added as another

record in this table. By using a form that implements the new Timer event, you can monitor the status of this table from any Access application and notify users when new messages have arrived.

Steps

This How-To employs two files, 10-01FE.MDB and 10-01BE.MDB. Before you can try it, you'll need to attach the data tables from 10-01BE.MDB (the "back-end," or data database) to 10-01FE.MDB (the "front-end," or application database). Attaching a data table allows you to use a table from one Access database within another Access database. Start Access and load 10-01FE.MDB. Choose File|Attach Table and select Microsoft Access as your data source. Select 10-01BE.MDB as the Access database to attach a table from. Access will show you a list of the tables in the remote database. Select tblMessage and click Attach, as shown in Figure 10-1.

Now you can test-drive this How-To by sending a message to yourself. Open both frmSendMail and frmReceiveMail. Minimize the Receive Mail form. Enter your user name in the To box. If you haven't changed your Access security settings at all, your user name is Admin. Enter any message and click the Send button. Figure 10-2 shows this process from the sending end.

The Send Mail form will clear as soon as the message is sent. Within ten seconds, the Receive Mail form will pop up with the message. Figure 10-3 shows this process for the message sent in Figure 10-2. Click on the Mark as Read button to clear the Receive Mail form. If there is more than one message waiting, each one will show up on the form in turn.

To use this technique in your own applications, follow these steps:

1. Identify the shared database you'll be using to hold the messages. This can be an existing shared database or a new one designed expressly for this purpose. Create a new table with the fields shown in Table 10-1. Make MessageID the Primary Key of this table, and save it as tblMessage.

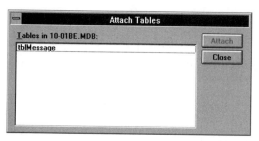

Figure 10-1 Attaching a data table

Figure 10-2 Sending a message to yourself

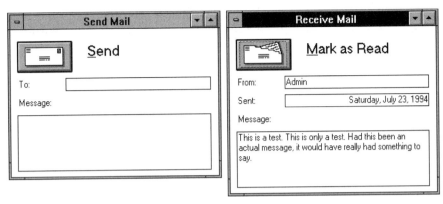

Figure 10-3 Receiving the message

FIELD NAME	DATA TYPE
MessageID	Counter
From	Text
To	Text
DateSent	Date/Time
DateReceived	Date/Time
Message	Memo

Table 10-1 Fields in tblMessage

2. Close the shared database and open the database you want to use to send and receive messages. This is where you'll create the remaining objects.
3. Create a new form, with the properties shown in Table 10-2.

PROPERTY	VALUE
Caption	Send Mail
DefaultView	Single Form
ScrollBars	Neither
RecordSelectors	No
NavigationButtons	No

Table 10-2 Properties for frmSendMail

4. Add two unbound text box controls to the form. Name the first one txtTo, and size it to hold the recipient's address. Name the second one txtMessage, and size it to hold the text of your message. Set the EnterKeyBehavior property of the second control to New Line in Field.
5. Add a command button to the form with the properties shown in Table 10-3. In the sample database, this button is dressed up with a bitmap, which is

included on your disk as SEND.BMP. You can add this bitmap to your own button by typing its path and file name into the Picture property of the button. The &S caption makes the button respond to the ⒜ᴸᵀ-Ⓢ accelerator key combination, even though the caption is hidden by the bitmap.

PROPERTY	VALUE
Name	cmdSend
Caption	&S
OnClick	=ahtSendMail ( )

Table 10-3 Properties for cmdSend

6. Save this form as frmSendMail.
7. Select File|Attach Table, and attach the tblMessage you created in your shared database to this front-end database.
8. Create a new query based on tblMessage. Drag all of the fields from the field list to the query grid. Set query criteria as shown in Table 10-4. Save this query as qryNewMail.

FIELD NAME	CRITERIA
To	CurrentUser ( )
DateReceived	IsNull

Table 10-4 Criteria for qryNewMail

9. Create another new form with the properties shown in Table 10-5.

PROPERTY	VALUE
RecordSource	qryNewMail
Caption	Receive Mail
DefaultView	Single Form
ScrollBars	Neither
RecordSelectors	No
NavigationButtons	No
OnTimer	=ahtCheckMail ( )
TimerInterval	10000

Table 10-5 Properties for frmReceiveMail

10. Add three bound text box controls to the form. Name the first one txtFrom, set the control source to From, and size it to hold the sender's address. Name the second one txtSent, set the control source to DateSent, and size it

to hold the time the message was sent. Name the third one txtMessage, set the control source to Message, and size it to hold the message text.

11. Add a command button to the form with the properties shown in Table 10-6. In the sample database, this button is dressed up with a bitmap, which is included on your disk as RECEIVE.BMP. You can add this bitmap to your own button by typing its path and file name into the Picture property of the button.

PROPERTY	VALUE
Name	cmdReceive
Caption	&M
OnClick	=ahtReceiveMail ()

Table 10-6 Properties for cmdReceive

12. Save this form as frmReceiveMail.
13. Import basMail from 10-01FE.MDB to your database.

How It Works

This technique works by passing messages back and forth through tblMessage. The sending form is unbound, because when you send a message, you don't want to have to flip through all previous messages. The ahtSendMail function takes whatever you type into the form and puts it into this table. It also uses the CurrentUser function to put your name into the From field of the table and the Now function to timestamp the message.

```
Set rstMail = dbCurrent.OpenRecordset("tblMessage",DB_OPEN_DYNASET, DB_APPENDONLY)
Set frmMail = Forms![frmSendMail]

rstMail.AddNew
    rstMail![From] = CurrentUser()
    rstMail![To] = frmMail![txtTo]
    rstMail![DateSent] = Now
    rstMail![Message] = frmMail![txtMessage]
rstMail.Update
```

Opening the recordset with the DB_APPEND_ONLY flag accelerates the process of adding a new record, because it avoids reading in the existing records that the Send function doesn't care about.

The Receive Mail form is based on a query that finds all messages directed to the current user that do not have anything in their DateReceived field. By default, new records added from elsewhere in a network do not show up on a form that is already open; you must explicitly requery the form for this to happen. The ahtCheckMail function automatically performs this requery once every ten seconds to check for new mail, by looking at the RecordsetClone property of the form. This property returns an exact duplicate of the form's underlying recordset. If there are any records to be shown, this RecordsetClone will not be at its EOF, so the function sets the focus to the form and restores it to full size.

```
Dim rstClone As Recordset
Dim frmMail As Form

Set frmMail = Forms![frmReceiveMail]
frmMail.Requery
Set rstClone = frmMail.RecordsetClone

rstClone.MoveFirst
If Not rstClone.EOF Then
   frmMail.SetFocus
   DoCmd Restore
End If
```

Comments

This method uses the Access user name to track mail senders and recipients. In order to use it in production, you'll need to activate Access security (otherwise, everyone is signed on as the Admin user at all times). To activate security, simply use Security|Change Password to assign a password to the Admin user. Then you can select Users from the Security menu and create as many new users as you like.

To test this How-To with multiple users, you'll need to have several machines available on a network, since only one Access user can be signed on to a single machine at one time. Make a copy of 10-01FE.MDB for each computer, and use File|Attach Tables to attach the same copy of tblMessage to each one. Log in as a different user at each computer, and you'll be able to send messages back and forth.

You can adjust the performance impact of this technique by changing the TimerInterval property of frmReceiveMail. This property measures the number of milliseconds between each execution of the OnTimer event. In the sample database, the TimerInterval property is set to 10,000 milliseconds, or ten seconds; its highest possible value is 65,535, or just over a minute. If you want a longer delay than this, you can add a static integer variable to ahtCheckMail and increment it more than once before you check for new mail. For example, changing the TimerInterval to 60,000 and using the replacement ahtCheckMail, as follows, will give you a five-minute delay.

```
Function ahtCheckMail () As Integer
' Check for new mail, and if there is any,
' restore the received mail form
   On Error GoTo ahtCheckMail_Err

   Dim rstClone As Recordset
   Static intMinutes As Integer
   Dim frmMail as Form

   intMinutes = intMinutes + 1
   If intMinutes < 5 Then
      Exit Function
```

```
Else
    intMinutes = 0
End If

frmMail.Requery
Set rstClone = frmMail.RecordsetClone

rstClone.MoveFirst
If Not rstClone.EOF Then
    frmMail.SetFocus
    DoCmd Restore
End If

rstClone.Close

ahtCheckMail_Exit:
    On Error GoTo 0
    Exit Function

ahtCheckMail_Err:
    If Err <> 3021 Then   'No current record
        MsgBox "Error " & Err & ": " & Error$, MB_ICON_STOP, "ahtCheckMail()"
    End If
    Resume ahtCheckMail_Exit

End Function
```

10.2 HOW DO I...

COMPLEXITY: ADVANCED

Show which users have a shared database open at any given time?

Problem

I need better control over a networked Access application. Sometimes users log in and leave a form open while they go to lunch, locking other users out. Also, some users have a habit of logging in from multiple workstations at the same time. How can I keep track of who is logged in to an Access database, and set limits on the number of simultaneous connections they can have?

Technique

Although Access keeps track of who has records locked, this information is internal to your application's LDB file, and the format of that file is undocumented. Access has no built-in tools to limit logins. You can work around both of these shortcomings by constructing your own table of active users in the shared database and maintaining its contents as people open and close your application.

Steps

This How-To employs two files, 10-02FE.MDB and 10-02BE.MDB. Before you can try it, you'll need to attach the data tables from 10-02BE.MDB to 10-02FE.MDB. Load 10-02FE.MDB while holding down the (SHIFT) key to prevent the AutoExec macro from executing. Now use File|Attach Tables to attach tblCurrentUsers and tblUserLimits from 10-02BE.MDB to this database. Close and reopen the database, this time letting the AutoExec macro execute. Open frmCurrentConnection, and you will be the only connected user, as shown in Figure 10-4.

To see the login limiting process, open tblUserLimits and change the LoginLimit for Admin from 1 to 0. Close the table, and then close and reopen the database. This time you'll see the error message (Figure 10-5). Click on OK and Access will unload. You can get back in by reopening the database with the (SHIFT) key depressed.

To add login tracking to your own project, follow these steps:

1. Create two new tables in your shared database, with the field definitions shown in Tables 10-7 and 10-8.

FIELD NAME	DATA TYPE	DESCRIPTION
UserName	Text	Primary Key
NumberOfLogins	Number	Integer

Table 10-7 Fields in tblCurrentUsers

FIELD NAME	DATA TYPE	DESCRIPTION
UserName	Text	Primary Key
LoginLimit	Number	Integer

Table 10-8 Fields in tblUserLimits

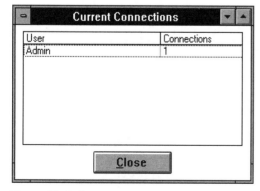

Figure 10-4 Current users

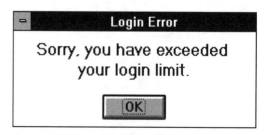

Figure 10-5 Login limit message

2. Open tblUserLimits, and add a new record for each user of your database. Enter the user's name and the maximum number of simultaneous logins for that user.

3. Close your shared database, and open the database that will be used to access the shared data. To this database, attach both new tables from the shared database.

4. Create a new macro named AutoExec, or add a RunCode action that calls the following function to your existing AutoExec macro:

```
=ahtAddLogin()
```

5. Create a new query based on tblCurrentUsers. Set the first field name to User: UserName and sort it in ascending order. Set the second field name to Connections: NumberOfLogins. Save this query as qryCurrentConnections.

6. Create a new form with the properties shown in Table 10-9.

PROPERTY	VALUE
Caption	Current Connections
DefaultView	Single Form
ScrollBars	Neither
RecordSelectors	No
NavigationButtons	No

Table 10-9 frmCurrentConnections properties

7. Place an unbound list box control on the form with the properties shown in Table 10-10.

PROPERTY	VALUE
Name	lboConnections
RowSourceType	Table/Query
RowSource	qryCurrentConnections
ColumnCount	2
ColumnHeads	Yes
ColumnWidths	1.75 in; 1 in

Table 10-10 lboConnections properties

8. Place a command button on the form. Name it cmdClose, and enter this event procedure for its OnClick property:

```
Sub cmdClose_Click ()
   DoCmd Close
End Sub
```

9. Save this form as frmCurrentConnections.

10. Create another new form. Set its OnUnload property to:

```
=ahtRemoveLogin()
```

Place a single button on this form, name the button cmdClose, and enter this event procedure for its OnClick property:

```
Sub cmdClose_Click ()
    DoCmd Close
End Sub
```

Save this form as zsfrmCloseProcessing. You don't have to worry about any of the form's other properties because it will never be seen by the user.

11. Create another new form with the properties shown in Table 10-11, and save this form as zsfrmLoginError.

PROPERTY	VALUE
Caption	Login Error
DefaultView	Single Form
ScrollBars	Neither
RecordSelectors	No
NavigationButtons	No
AutoCenter	Yes
BorderStyle	Dialog
OnClose	=ahtQuitApplication()

Table 10-11 zsfrmLoginError properties

12. Import the basUserLog module from 10-02FE.MDB.

How It Works
In order to track logins, this How-To runs one function whenever a user starts the database and another when they leave the database. The startup function, ahtAddLogin, gets called by the AutoExec macro, which runs whenever the database is opened. In a production database, you would employ the Access Distribution Toolkit to create a runtime environment where users could not override this macro with the (SHIFT) key.

The ahtAddLogin first determines whether there are any users listed in the login table at all. If not, then the current user can't be exceeding the limit, and a record is added for this user.

```
strSQL = "SELECT * FROM tblCurrentUsers WHERE UserName='" & CurrentUser() & "'"
Set rstUsers = dbCurrent.OpenRecordset(strSQL,DB_OPEN_DYNASET)

If rstUsers.EOF Then
    rstUsers.AddNew
        rstUsers![UserName] = CurrentUser()
        rstUsers![NumberOfLogins] = 1
        intRet = 1
    rstUsers.Update
...
End If
```

For users already listed in the login table, it compares the existing login count (if any) with their limit in tblUserLimits. If this login will not put the user over that limit, the login count is increased. Otherwise the count is left unchanged.

```
strSQL = "SELECT * FROM tblUserLimits WHERE UserName='" & CurrentUser() & "'"
Set rstLimits = dbCurrent.OpenRecordset(strSQL, DB_OPEN_DYNASET)
If Not rstLimits.EOF Then
    If rstUsers![NumberOfLogins] >= rstLimits![LoginLimit] Then
        intRet = -1
    Else
        rstUsers.Edit
            rstUsers![NumberOfLogins] = rstUsers![NumberOfLogins] + 1
        rstUsers.Update
        intRet = rstUsers![NumberOfLogins]
    End If
Else
    rstUsers.Edit
        rstUsers![NumberOfLogins] = rstUsers![NumberOfLogins] + 1
    rstUsers.Update
    intRet = rstUsers![NumberOfLogins]
End If
rstLimits.Close
```

Depending on whether this is a legal login, the ahtAddLogin function opens one of two forms. If the login is disallowed, the zsfrmLoginError form displays the error message and waits for a user response. Otherwise, the zsfrmCloseProcessing form opens in hidden mode and remains loaded while the rest of the application proceeds.

If the user is not allowed to log in, the only possible action is to close the form with the error message. No matter whether this is done with its control menu or its OK button, the ahtQuitApplication function runs and uses the Quit method of the Application object to force this instance of Access to unload.

Whenever the user unloads Access by any means, the last form to close will be the hidden zsfrmCloseProcessing that was opened during the startup processing. This automatically runs the ahtRemoveLogin function to decrease the user's count of active logins, with the code shown here:

```
Set dbCurrent = DBEngine.Workspaces(0).Databases(0)
strSQL = "SELECT * FROM tblCurrentUsers WHERE UserName='" & CurrentUser() & "'"
Set rstUsers = dbCurrent.OpenRecordset(strSQL, DB_OPEN_DYNASET)

rstUsers.Edit
    rstUsers![NumberOfLogins] = rstUsers![NumberOfLogins] - 1
    ahtRemoveLogin = rstUsers![NumberOfLogins]
rstUsers.Update

rstUsers.Close
```

Comments

If you try to streamline the ahtAddLogin function by dropping the error message form and automatically closing the application if the login count would be exceeded, you will find that the Application.Quit statement is not legal in any function that runs while your AutoExec macro is still processing. The sample database works around this limitation by opening a form and placing this method in the form's OnClose processing. This works because form processing and module processing are asynchronous with regard to one another. When you open a form, the module continues processing without waiting for the form, and in this case finishes the login procedure before the user can possibly click the OK button.

If you do want to close the database without user intervention, you can modify the error form to unload itself in response to a Timer event, and open it in hidden mode.

If you have sufficient memory (at least 12 megabytes), you can test the login limit feature of this sample without a second machine. Open two copies of Access and load the same database into each copy. When you load the database, make sure to load it in shared mode by leaving the Exclusive box unchecked on the Open Database dialog box (as shown in Figure 10-6).

10.3 HOW DO I...   COMPLEXITY: INTERMEDIATE

Create a transaction log?

Problem

I want to keep a permanent record of activities in my database. With multiple users changing data in my application simultaneously, how can I keep track of who made which changes?

Technique

Full-blown databases such as SQL Server offer built-in transaction logging to handle this task, with a separate file that tracks all data activity. This provides both a permanent record and a way to recover from disasters by replaying the

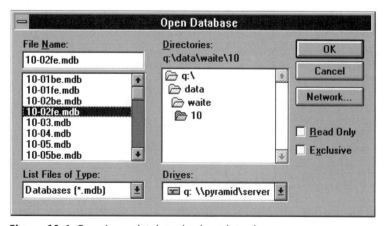

Figure 10-6 Opening a database in shared mode

transaction log. This How-To demonstrates a simpler transaction log in Access that will track users and their edits, without saving all the detail that would be necessary to re-create the edits entirely.

Steps

Start Access and load 10-03.MDB. Open frmBook, and add a few records, update some existing records, and delete some records. Then review the information in tblLog; you'll find a record in this table for each change you made, as illustrated in Figure 10-7.

To add this simple logging capability to your own database, follow these steps:

1. Create a new table, tblLog, with the fields shown in Table 10-12.

FIELD NAME	DATA TYPE
UserName	Text
TableName	Text
RecordPK	Text
ActionDate	Date/Time
Action	Number (integer)

Table 10-12 Fields in tblLog

2. Import the module basLogging from 10-03.MDB to your own database.

3. Add three event procedures to each form on which users can make changes that you want to track. In the sample database, these event properties are attached to frmBook, and are shown in Table 10-13. Substitute the name of your own table for tblBook, and the Primary Key of the table for [BookID].

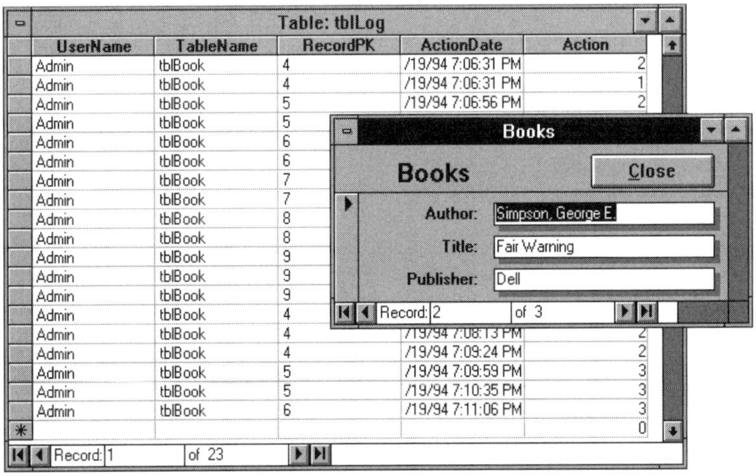

Figure 10-7 Logging changes to tblBook

PROPERTY	VALUE
AfterInsert	=ahtLogAdd("tblBook", [BookID])
AfterUpdate	=ahtLogUpdate("tblBook", [BookID])
OnDelete	=ahtLogDelete("tblBook", [BookID])

Table 10-13 Logging properties for frmBook

How It Works

Changing data through a form triggers a series of events. This technique assigns code to each event that indicates a change has been executed, and uses that code to append a record to a logging table. You can use the CurrentUser function to keep track of who made the change and the Now function to record when it was made.

Since the three types of records in the logging table are similar, the functions are just wrappers for a single general-purpose function that actually adds the records. This function depends on symbolic constants that are defined in the declarations section of the module:

```
Const ACT_ADD = 1
Const ACT_UPDATE = 2
Const ACT_DELETE = 3
```

The ahtLog function accepts as arguments all of the information that needs to be stored, opens a recordset on the logging table, and then saves the information in a new record of that recordset.

```
Function ahtLog (strTableName As String, varPK As Variant, intAction As Integer) As Integer
' Log a user action in the log table
    On Error GoTo ahtLog_Err

    Dim dbCurrent As Database
    Dim rstLog As Recordset

    Set dbCurrent = DBEngine.Workspaces(0).Databases(0)
    Set rstLog = dbCurrent.OpenRecordset("tblLog", DB_OPEN_DYNASET, DB_APPENDONLY)

    rstLog.AddNew
        rstLog![UserName] = CurrentUser()
        rstLog![TableName] = strTableName
        rstLog![RecordPK] = varPK
        rstLog![ActionDate] = Now
        rstLog![Action] = intAction
    rstLog.Update

    rstLog.Close

    ahtLog = True
ahtLog_Exit:
    On Error GoTo 0
    Exit Function
```

```
ahtLog_Err:
    MsgBox "Error " & Err & ": " & Error$, MB_ICON_STOP, "ahtLog()"
    ahtLog = False
    Resume ahtLog_Exit

End Function
```

Comments

This technique demonstrates one reason why you should allow users to interact with your application only via Access forms: Forms alone generate events that you can trap. If you let users edit data directly on either a table datasheet or a query datasheet, you cannot track the edits.

You could extend this technique to capture additional detail about the records being added, updated, or deleted. You might even add extra fields to the logging table to capture the actual data, rather than just the Primary Key that identifies the changed record. This leaves you in a position to completely reconstruct the table at any time by inspecting the logging file and making or removing changes. The drawback to enabling this capability is that it requires substantially more storage space, because you'll be storing a full copy of the data every time any part of it changes.

The ahtLog function opens a recordset on the logging table with the DB_APPENDONLY argument. This returns an initially blank recordset ready to receive new records, instead of a full dynaset where existing records can be edited. This accommodates much faster data access when all you are trying to do is add new records to a table without regard for what is already there.

10.4 HOW DO I...   COMPLEXITY: ADVANCED

Find and transfer objects that changed between two versions of a database?

Problem

I've made a number of changes to an Access front-end database since it was originally installed. I'd like to update the existing copies without having to replace them entirely and reattach all of the back-end tables. Is there a way in Access to get a list of objects and the last date they were modified, and use this list to drive an update procedure?

Technique

Every object in Access has a LastUpdated property, so it's relatively easy to collect a list of change dates using DAO (Data Access Objects). However, since Access can create new objects, right up to whole databases, you can do more than just list this information. This How-To compares the LastUpdated properties of objects in two copies of the same database, and then uses that information to create a third database that will automatically update the older copy to match the newer one.

Steps

Load Access and open 10-04.MDB. Open zsfrmMain in regular form view. You will need to fill in the names of three databases on this form to look something like Figure 10-8, as follows:

➤ The Old Database is the older of the two copies you want to compare. On the sample disk, we've provided 10-04A.MDB to use as an old database.

➤ The New Database is the newer of the two copies you want to compare. On the sample disk, we've provided 10-04B.MDB to use as a new database. This is a copy of 10-04A.MDB with some objects changed, some new objects added, and some objects left untouched.

➤ The Changes Database is the new database that this application will create, containing all of the changed items and a way to install them. Use any valid name for this, as long as it's not a preexisting file.

Click OK when you've filled in all three database names. The hourglass appears while Access processes the databases. When the cursor returns, close the reconciliation form and the database. Load your New Changes database, and it automatically loads a form asking for the target database. As shown in Figure 10-9, fill in the location of 10-04A.MDB and click OK, and that database will be updated with the new and changed objects from the more recent copy.

The following steps describe the construction of each object in 10-04.MDB. Unlike most of the other How-To's in this book, this is a self-contained utility that you can use as is to reconcile any pair of your own databases. Rather than rebuilding the utility, you should use these steps as a guide to understanding it.

1. Create a new table with the fields shown in Table 10-14.

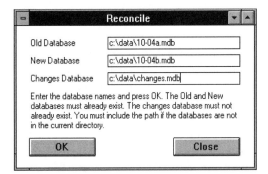

Figure 10-8 Reconciling two databases

Figure 10-9 Exporting the changes

FIELD NAME	DATA TYPE
ObjectName	Text
ObjectType	Text
LastUpdated	Date/Time

Table 10-14 Fields in zstblChangedObjects

2. Save this table as zstblChangedObjects. Use the copy and paste functions to make two more copies of this table, one named zstblNew and one named zstblOld. You don't need to put any data into these tables, since they'll be maintained entirely in code.

3. Create a new query based on zstblNew. Add zstblOld to the query as well. Drag the ObjectName field from zstblNew, and drop it on the ObjectName field of zstblOld. Click on this join line, and select the option to include all records from zstblNew and matching records from zstblOld. Drag the ObjectType field from zstblNew, and drop it on the ObjectType field of zstblOld. Click on this join line, and select the option to include all records from zstblNew and matching records from zstblOld.

4. Drag the ObjectName and ObjectType fields from zstblNew to the query grid. Drag the LastUpdated field from zstblOld to the query grid. Set the criteria on the LastUpdated field to:

```
Is Null Or <[zstblNew].[LastUpdated]
```

5. Click on the Make Table button on the toolbar or select Query|Make Table. Enter zstblChangedObjects as the name of the table to make. Save this query as zsqmakChangedObjects (see Figure 10-10).

6. Create a new form with the properties shown in Table 10-15.

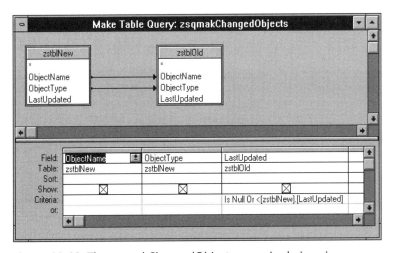

Figure 10-10 The zsqmakChangedObjects query in design view

PROPERTY	VALUE
Caption	Export
DefaultView	Single Form
ScrollBars	Neither
RecordSelectors	No
NavigationButtons	No
AutoCenter	Yes

Table 10-15 Properties of zsfrmExport

7. Add an unbound text box control to the form and name it txtOldDB.
8. Add two command buttons to the form. Name one cmdOK and set its caption to OK. Name the other cmdClose and set its caption to Close. Set the OnClick property of both buttons to [Event Procedure], and enter the event procedures shown below in the form's module.

```
Sub cmdClose_Click ()

    DoCmd Close

End Sub

Sub cmdOK_Click ()

    Dim intRet As Integer

    If IsNull(Me![txtOldDB]) Then
        intRet = MsgBox("You must enter a database name", MB_ICON_STOP, "Entry Error")
    Else
        intRet = ahtFinalExport( CStr(Me![txtOldDB]))
    End If

End Sub
```

9. Save this form as zsfrmExport.
10. Create a new form and set its properties to those in Table 10-16.

PROPERTY	VALUE
Caption	Reconcile
DefaultView	Single Form
ScrollBars	Neither
RecordSelectors	No
NavigationButtons	No
AutoCenter	Yes

Table 10-16 Properties of zsfrmMain

11. Place three unbound text boxes on this form. Name them txtOldDB, txtNewDB, and txtRecDB.

12. Add two command buttons to the form. Name one cmdOK and set its caption to OK. Name the other cmdClose and set its caption to Close. Set the OnClick property of both buttons to [Event Procedure], and enter the event procedures shown below in the form's module.

```
Sub cmdClose_Click ()

    DoCmd Close

End Sub

Sub cmdOK_Click ()

    Dim intRet As Integer

    If IsNull(Me![txtNewDB]) Or IsNull(Me![txtOldDB]) Or IsNull(Me![txtRecDB]) Then
        intRet = MsgBox("You must fill in all three database names", MB_ICON_STOP, "Entry Error")
    Else
        intRet = ahtReconcileDatabases(CStr(Me![txtOldDB]), CStr(Me![txtNewDB]), CStr(Me![txtRecDB]))
    End If

End Sub
```

13. Create a new macro containing a single OpenForm action. Set the action arguments as shown in Table 10-17. Save this macro as zsmcrAutoExec.

ARGUMENT	VALUE
Form Name	zsfrmExport
View	Form
Data Mode	Edit
Window Mode	Normal

Table 10-17 Arguments for zsmcrAutoExec

How It Works

To reconcile two databases you must take several steps, which are described in the following sections.

1. Clear out the temporary storage tables.
2. Fill zstblOld with a list of all objects in the old database.
3. Fill zstblNew with a list of all objects in the new database.
4. Compare the two tables and identify the changed objects.
5. Import those changed objects to this database.
6. Create a reconciliation database and send those changed objects to the reconciliation database.
7. Send other objects to the reconciliation database to run the update process.
8. Delete the changed objects from this database.

When you run ahtReconcileDatabases from the main form, it executes each of these steps in turn, checking for errors along the way.

Clearing the Temporary Storage Tables

You can clear a table quickly without changing its structure by executing a simple SQL statement that is the equivalent of a delete query. To do this in code, you have to use the DoCmd keyword and set SetWarnings to False to prevent warning messages from interrupting smooth processing.

```
DoCmd RunSQL "DELETE * FROM zstblOld;"
DoCmd RunSQL "DELETE * FROM zstblNew;"
```

Filling zstblOld and zstblNew with Lists of Database Objects

The ahtListObjects function takes the name of a database and the name of a table and fills the table with a list of all queries, forms, reports, and macros in that database, together with the date and time of their last modification. It does this by iterating through the collections of those objects that Access maintains internally. For example, here's the code that lists the forms:

```
Set cnt = dbList.Containers("Forms")
For i = 0 To cnt.Documents.Count - 1
    rstStore.AddNew
        rstStore![ObjectName] = cnt.Documents(i).Name
        rstStore![ObjectType] = "Form"
        rstStore![LastUpdated] = cnt.Documents(i).LastUpdated
    rstStore.Update
Next i
```

The *cnt* variable is an object variable of type Container. A Container object is the internal code structure that is represented by one of the Database Container tabs onscreen. Each container has a specific name, as defined in Table 10-18. The code snippet just above shows how to point to a container once you know its name. Each container in turn contains a collection of documents, where each document is an individual Access object. The Count property of the collection tells you how many items are in the collection, numbered from 0 to Count-1. The function looks at each of these objects in turn and retrieves its .Name and .LastUpdated properties, which tell you what the object is called and when it was last changed.

CONTAINER NAME	HOLDS
Databases	Information on the database itself
Tables	Tables and queries
Relationships	Relations between tables
Forms	Forms
Reports	Reports
Scripts	Macros
Modules	Modules
SysRel	Layout of the relationships window

Table 10-18 Containers and their contents

To retrieve the list of queries, this function uses the QueryDefs collection, since there is no Queries container (queries and tables are both stored in the Tables container).

Comparing the Two Tables and Identifying the Changed Objects

The Make Table query, zsqmakChangedObjects, does all the work of identifying new and updated objects and saving their details to a separate table. In general, action queries are more efficient for this sort of chore than opening up recordsets and stepping through them in code. Creating an outer join between the two tables provides a way to identify both new and updated objects. New objects are ones that don't have a LastUpdated property in the list of old objects. Updated objects are those where the LastUpdated property is more recent in the new database than it was in the old one.

Importing Changed Objects to this Database

Access does not provide a function for moving objects directly between two databases, neither of which is open. Instead, this technique works by first importing the objects to this database and then exporting them to another database. In both cases, the movement of objects is handled by the TransferDatabase action. For example, here's the code line that exports a single query from the current database to the database named in strDBName:

```
DoCmd TransferDatabase A_EXPORT, "Microsoft Access", strDBName, ⇒
A_QUERY, rstCh![ObjectName], rstCh![ObjectName]
```

Creating a Reconciliation Database and Sending It the Changed Objects

The lines of code

```
Set wsCurrent = DBEngine.Workspaces(0)
Set dbRec = wsCurrent.CreateDatabase(strRecDB, DB_LANG_GENERAL)
```

create a new database within the current workspace. To create a database, you must specify the sort order for the database. DB_LANG_GENERAL is the standard English sorting order. If the database needs to be owned by a user with a password, you also have to specify the user name and password in the CreateDatabase statement. This version assumes that the current user has no password.

Sending Other Objects to the Reconciliation Database to Run the Update Process

The ahtExportChangedObjects function does the actual work of moving the objects listed in zstblChangedObjects from the current database to the reconciliation database. After the new and changed objects are moved, it transfers the following additional objects to that database. These are the macro, table, form, and module that make the Export form function.

```
' And now export the objects to make the other database work
DoCmd TransferDatabase A_EXPORT, "Microsoft Access", strDBName, A_MACRO, "zsmcrAutoexec", "AutoExec"
DoCmd TransferDatabase A_EXPORT, "Microsoft Access", strDBName, A_TABLE, "zstblChangedObjects", ⇒
"zstblChangedObjects"
DoCmd TransferDatabase A_EXPORT, "Microsoft Access", strDBName, A_FORM, "zsfrmExport", "zsfrmExport"
DoCmd TransferDatabase A_EXPORT, "Microsoft Access", ⇒
strDBName, A_MODULE, "zsbasExport", "zsbasExport"
```

Deleting the Changed Objects from this Database

The final step is to delete the transferred objects from the utility database. Once again, this requires stepping through the zstblChangedObjects table. This time the function ahtDeleteObjects uses the DeleteObject action to remove each one in turn.

Comments

This version of this utility does not transfer either updated tables or updated modules. To properly move tables, you would have to inspect the relations as well as the table and write procedures to change them as necessary, and provide a means to transfer data from the old table to the new one if a table were updated.

In a well-designed database, changes to the table schema are unlikely after the initial installation, so the lack of this capability should not be a major problem.

Access Basic modules present another problem. There is no easy way to identify the functions contained within any given module (the only method available to do this is to export the module as text and then parse the text file). Allowing the utility to automatically transfer modules raises the risk of putting a duplicate procedure name into the target database and rendering it nonfunctional. If you are willing to take this risk, adding code to iterate the Modules collection to each procedure is simple.

The last thing to watch out for is object naming. If any object in the new database has the same name as an object in 10-04.MDB, it will not be properly transferred (the object from 10-04.MDB will be transferred instead). Worse, the utility itself will stop functioning when it deletes one of its own objects.

10.5 HOW DO I...   COMPLEXITY: INTERMEDIATE

Automatically update objects at login?

Problem

I maintain a multi-user database on a central server that's used at numerous networked computers. How do I deliver upgraded objects automatically to these network users so that they are always running a current copy, without my having to travel from desk to desk with update disks?

Technique

This How-To demonstrates an alternative strategy for maintaining multiple copies of the same database. You set up a table of objects on the server and have those objects imported automatically to any network copy of the database with a previous version stamp.

Steps

This How-To employs two files, 10-05FE.MDB and 10-05BE.MDB. Before you can try it, you'll need to attach the data tables from 10-05BE.MDB to 10-05FE.MDB. Load 10-05FE.MDB, and use File|Attach Tables to attach both zstblNewObjects and zstblServerVersion from 10-05BE.MDB to this database.

> ✐ *NOTE: For demonstration purposes, this How-To requires both of these files to be in the same directory. In an actual production setting you could place them in different directories.*

Run the macro mcrUpdate. Two new objects (a form and a table) will be imported from the back-end database to this front-end database. If you run the macro a second time, nothing happens, because the first run updates the local version stamp.

Follow these steps to implement this function in your own database:

1. Create a new back-end database to hold objects waiting to be distributed. This database should reside on a server drive where it is visible to all copies of your application. Place any objects to be distributed in this database.

2. Create two tables in this back-end database. The first, zstblNewObjects, should have an ObjectName field and an ObjectType field, both text. Place one record in this table for each object waiting to be copied. The second table, zstblServerVersion, should have a single field called ServerVersion. Add one record to this table with a version number in it. Figure 10-11 shows a sample set of these control tables. In the sample database, the ServerVersion field is text, to allow for version numbers such as 3.2A. You may want to make the field numeric instead, so that a simple comparison will correctly return 1.1 as being less than 9.5.

3. Close the back-end database, and open your front-end application database. Create a new table with two fields, each of type Text, named LocalVersion and ServerPath. Save the table as zstblLocalVersion and add a single record to it. Give it a version number *less than* the server version number, and place the full path and file name of the back-end database in the ServerPath field. Figure 10-12 shows one possible local version table.

4. Create a new macro with a single RunCode action. Set the action's Function Name argument to:

```
=ahtUpdateVersion()
```

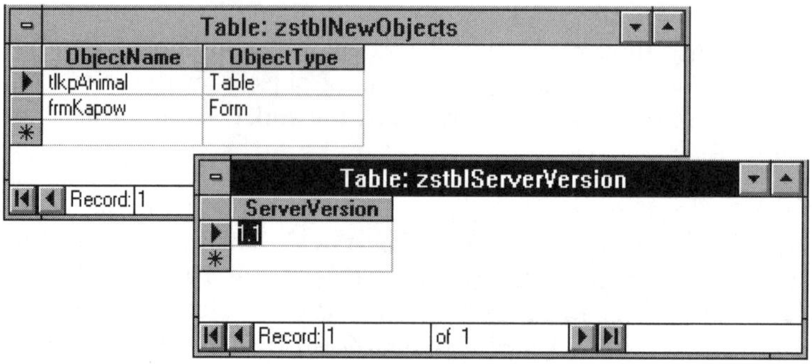

Figure 10-11 Control tables in the back-end database

Save the macro as mcrUpdate. Alternatively, you can add this action to your AutoExec macro so that version numbers are compared each time your application is run.

5. Import the basUpdate module from 10-05FE.MDB.

How It Works

The ahtUpdateVersion function listed in part below starts by comparing the first record in the LocalVersion table to the first record in the ServerVersion table (if you properly secure your database, these tables will never contain more than a single record). If the local version number is below the server version, the function opens the table listing changed objects. For each object, the function first tries to delete any existing copy, so that you won't end up with a serialized copy of an existing object. (For example, if you try to import frmMenu when there is already a frmMenu in your database, you'll end up with frmMenu1 instead.) If this action causes any error, the function just ignores the error and proceeds, since the overwhelmingly likely error is that the object does not exist.

After deleting any existing object, the function imports the new one, using the ServerPath entry in zstblLocalVersion to know where to get it. When all of the objects have been imported, the local version is set equal to the server

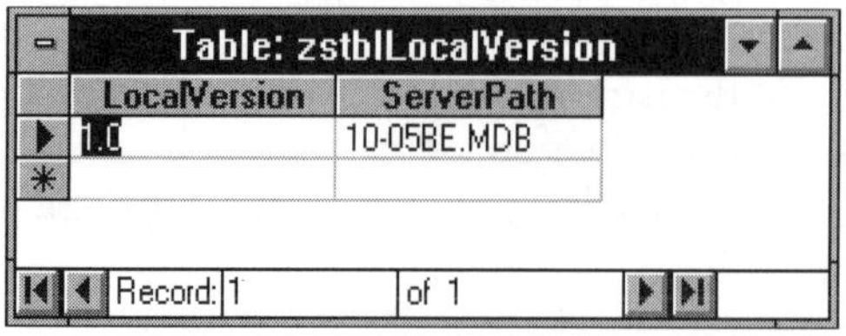

Figure 10-12 Local version table

version, to prevent the function from running again before the server version number is changed again.

```
Function ahtUpdateVersion () As Integer
' Update by importing new objects from the server
' if the version there is later than the version here
    On Error GoTo ahtUpdateVersion_Err

    Dim dbCurrent As Database
    Dim rstLocal As Recordset
    Dim rstServer As Recordset
    Dim rstObjects As Recordset
    Dim intType As Integer

' Compare versions
    Set dbCurrent = DBEngine.Workspaces(0).Databases(0)
    Set rstLocal = dbCurrent.OpenRecordset("zstblLocalVersion", DB_OPEN_DYNASET)
    Set rstServer = dbCurrent.OpenRecordset("zstblServerVersion", DB_OPEN_DYNASET)
    If rstLocal![LocalVersion] < rstServer![ServerVersion] Then
' For each object in the new objects table, delete any
' existing copy and import a new one
    Set rstObjects = dbCurrent.OpenRecordset("zstblNewObjects", DB_OPEN_DYNASET)
    Do Until rstObjects.EOF
        Select Case rstObjects![ObjectType]
            Case "Table"
                intType = A_TABLE
            Case "Query"
                intType = A_QUERY
            Case "Form"
                intType = A_FORM
            Case "Report"
                intType = A_REPORT
            Case "Macro"
                intType = A_MACRO
            Case "Module"
                intType = A_MODULE
        End Select
        On Error Resume Next
        DoCmd DeleteObject intType, rstObjects![ObjectName]
        On Error GoTo ahtUpdateVersion_Err
        DoCmd TransferDatabase A_IMPORT, "Microsoft Access", ⇒
rstLocal![ServerPath], intType, rstObjects![ObjectName], rstObjects![ObjectName]
        rstObjects.MoveNext
    Loop

' Update the local version
    rstLocal.Edit
        rstLocal![LocalVersion] = rstServer![ServerVersion]
    rstLocal.Update

    End If
```

(Continued on next page)

(Continued from previous page)

```
    rstLocal.Close
    rstServer.Close
    rstObjects.Close

ahtUpdateVersion_Exit:
    On Error GoTo 0
    Exit Function

ahtUpdateVersion_Err:
    MsgBox "Error " & Err & ": " & Error$, MB_ICON_STOP, "ahtUpdateVersion()"
    Resume ahtUpdateVersion_Exit

End Function
```

Comments

Obviously, the function can't update its own code, so if you have to update basUpdate you'll have to make those changes by hand. As written, the function also presumes that every copy of the database on your network will be updated before you change the server database again. If you expect some copies to be updated less frequently than others, add a version number field to zstblNewObjects and check the version number of each object before importing it.

10.6 HOW DO I...
COMPLEXITY: ADVANCED

Keep track of users and groups programmatically?

Problem

As the database administrator, I'd like to track users and their groups within my workgroup. I know I can use Security|Print Security to print a report of users and groups, but I'd also like to use that information as part of applications I write. How can I gather the information I need?

Technique

Using Data Access Objects (DAO), you can retrieve all the information you need about users' names and groups. As the database administrator, you have the necessary rights to retrieve the information about the current session's security. Once you have that information, you can use it to create lists of users and/or their groups.

Steps

The sample form frmUserGroups, in 10-06.MDB, fills tables with the information you need and presents it in a list box. To test it, open and run frmUserGroups. Figure 10-13 shows the form in use for a sample workgroup.

To gather this information in your own applications, follow these steps:

1. Create the tables you'll need to hold the information. Either import the three tables from 10-06.MDB or use the information in Table 10-19 to create your own. Figure 10-14 shows the three tables in design mode.

TABLE NAME	FIELD NAME	DATA TYPE	PRIMARY KEY?
tblGroups	Group	Text	No
	GroupID	Counter	Yes
tblUserGroups	UserID	Number (Long Integer)	Yes
	GroupID	Number (Long Integer)	Yes
tblUsers	UserName	Text	No
	UserID	Counter	Yes

Table 10-19 Table layouts for gathering user/group information

2. If you created your own tables in step 1, you'll also need to add an index to tblGroups. In the Indexes properties sheet (available by choosing View|Indexes when tblGroups is open in design mode), add a row as described in Table 10-20. Use the default settings for the index properties. Table 10-20 also shows the Primary Key row that should already exist in the Indexes properties sheet.

Figure 10-13 The sample form, frm UserGroups, shows users and their groups for a sample workgroup

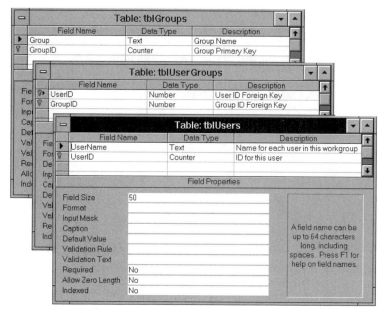

Figure 10-14 The three tables, tblGroups, tblUserGroups, and tblUsers, in design mode

INDEX NAME	FIELD NAME	SORT ORDER
Group	Group	Ascending
PrimaryKey	GroupID	Ascending

Table 10-20 Index settings for tblGroups

3. Either import the module basListUsers from 10-06.MDB or enter the following code into either a global or a form module. This is the code you'll use to fill the three tables you just created.

```
Sub ahtListUsers ()

' Create tables containing all
' the users and groups in the current
' workgroup.
'
' The results will be in:
'    tblUsers, tblGroups and
'    tblUserGroups.
' Run qryUserGroups to see sorted list.

Dim db As Database
Dim wrk As WorkSpace
```

```
Dim intI As Integer
Dim intJ As Integer

Dim rstUsers As Recordset
Dim rstGroups As Recordset
Dim rstUserGroups As Recordset

Dim usr As User

' Clear out the old values.
DoCmd SetWarnings False
DoCmd RunSQL "Delete * From tblUserGroups"
DoCmd RunSQL "Delete * From tblUsers"
DoCmd RunSQL "Delete * From tblGroups"
DoCmd SetWarnings True

' Set up object variables.
Set wrk = DBEngine.Workspaces(0)
Set db = wrk.Databases(0)

Set rstUsers = db.OpenRecordset("tblUsers")
Set rstGroups = db.OpenRecordset("tblGroups")
Set rstUserGroups = db.OpenRecordset("tblUserGroups")

' Buffer the disk writes, so the operation
' runs quicker.
wrk.BeginTrans

' Build up a list of all the groups in tblGroups
For intI = 0 To wrk.Groups.Count - 1
   rstGroups.AddNew
      rstGroups!Group = wrk.Groups(intI).Name
   rstGroups.Update
Next intI

' Loop through all the users, adding
' rows to tblUsers and tblUserGroups.
For intI = 0 To wrk.Users.Count - 1
   ' Add a user to tblUsers.
   Set usr = wrk.Users(intI)
   rstUsers.AddNew
      rstUsers!UserName = usr.Name
   rstUsers.Update
   rstUsers.Move 0, rstUsers.LastModified

   ' Now loop through all the groups
   ' that user belongs to, hooking up the rows
   ' in tblUserGroups.
   For intJ = 0 To usr.Groups.Count - 1
      rstGroups.Index = "Group"
```

(Continued on next page)

(Continued from previous page)

```
            rstGroups.Seek "=", usr.Groups(intJ).Name
            If Not rstGroups.NoMatch Then
                    rstUserGroups.AddNew
                        rstUserGroups!UserID = rstUsers!UserID
                        rstUserGroups!GroupID = rstGroups!GroupID
                    rstUserGroups.Update
            End If
        Next intJ
    Next intI
    wrk.CommitTrans
    rstUsers.Close
    rstGroups.Close
    rstUserGroups.Close
End Sub
```

4. Either import the query qryUserGroups from 10-06.MDB or create a new query, as follows: When Access asks you to add a table, just close the dialog box. Once in design mode, click on the SQL button on the toolbar and enter the following expression:

```
SELECT DISTINCTROW tblUsers.UserName, tblGroups.Group
FROM tblUsers INNER JOIN (tblGroups INNER JOIN tblUserGroups ON tblGroups.GroupID =
tblUserGroups.GroupID) ON tblUsers.UserID = tblUserGroups.UserID
ORDER BY tblUsers.UserName, tblGroups.Group;
```

Then save the query as qryUserGroups.

5. To produce the current list of users and groups, execute the code in ahtListUsers. You call it directly, or use a button whose Click event calls the procedure, or call it from the Immediate Window. (The sample form calls ahtListUsers from the Click event of the button on the form.) Executing that code fills in the three tables. You can use qryUserGroups to retrieve the information you need or create your own queries based on the three tables.

How It Works

This How-To relies on Access's object model to gather its information. The object hierarchy is diagrammed on the back of the Access "Building Applications" manual, among other places. Study that diagram, and notice in the hierarchy that the DBEngine object (the root of all DAO references) has, as its only collection, the Workspaces collection. The default workspace contains information about the collection of open databases (only one is open in the user interface—all others must be opened via Access Basic code) along with the available user and group collections. These are the collections you'll need for filling tables with the user names and their groups. The code in the ahtListUsers subroutine does all the work, so let's take a look at the details of that procedure.

The ahtListUsers function starts out by deleting all the existing rows in the three tables, using the RunSQL macro action:

```
DoCmd SetWarnings False
DoCmd RunSQL "Delete * From tblUserGroups"
DoCmd RunSQL "Delete * From tblUsers"
DoCmd RunSQL "Delete * From tblGroups"
DoCmd SetWarnings True
```

The SetWarnings macro action is required to disable warnings, or Access would pop up an alert, telling you how many rows will be deleted from each table. Once these lines of code have executed, the three tables will all be empty.

The procedure then sets up object variables to refer to the correct database objects and opens a transaction. This transaction, though not used in the normal sense (allowing for rollbacks if an error occurs), accelerates the process by buffering disk writes.

```
' Set up object variables.
Set wrk = DBEngine.Workspaces(0)
Set db = wrk.Databases(0)

Set rstUsers = db.OpenRecordset("tblUsers")
Set rstGroups = db.OpenRecordset("tblGroups")
Set rstUserGroups = db.OpenRecordset("tblUserGroups")

' Buffer the disk writes, so the operation
' runs quicker.
wrk.BeginTrans
```

The next step is to build a list of all the groups. Since an object variable *(wrk)* that refers to the current workspace already exists, the function loops through all the elements of the workspace's Groups collection. Just like all other collections in Access, Groups provides its Count property, indicating how many elements it contains. These items are numbered from 0 through Count –1, and we loop through them all, adding a row to tblGroups for each group in the collection.

```
' Build up a list of all the groups in tblGroups
For intI = 0 To wrk.Groups.Count - 1
    rstGroups.AddNew
        rstGroups!Group = wrk.Groups(intI).Name
    rstGroups.Update
Next intI
```

Once tblGroups is filled in, we do the same for users. Just as the workspace contains a collection of groups, it contains a collection of users. We can walk through the users collection, adding a row at a time to tblUsers, as shown here:

```
' Loop through all the users, adding
' rows to tblUsers and tblUserGroups.
For intI = 0 To wrk.Users.Count - 1
    ' Add a user to tblUsers.
    Set usr = wrk.Users(intI)
    rstUsers.AddNew
        rstUsers!UserName = usr.Name
```

(Continued on next page)

(Continued from previous page)

```
    rstUsers.Update
    rstUsers.Move 0, rstUsers.LastModified
    '
    ' See the following code example...
    '
Next intI
```

Once a user is added, rows are added to tblUserGroups for each group that contains the current user. This is accomplished by enumerating through the Groups collection for the current user. (There was a choice here: Each member of the workspace's Users collection has its own Groups collection, listing the groups to which it belongs, and each member of the workspace's Groups collection has its own Users collection, listing the member. The code can either walk through the users, looking at the Groups collection in each, or walk through the groups, looking at the Users collection in each. This example walks through the workspace's Users collection, one at a time, studying the Groups collection in each one.) The following code loops through every item in the user's Groups collection, finding the matching name in tblGroups, and then adding a row to tblUserGroups containing both the user's UserID field (from tblUsers) and the GroupID field (from tblGroups). This way, tblUserGroups contains a single row for every user/group pair.

```
' Now loop through all the groups
' that user belongs to, hooking up the rows
' in tblUserGroups.
For intJ = 0 To usr.Groups.Count - 1
    rstGroups.Index = "Group"
    rstGroups.Seek "=", usr.Groups(intJ).Name
    If Not rstGroups.NoMatch Then
        rstUserGroups.AddNew
            rstUserGroups!UserID = rstUsers!UserID
            rstUserGroups!GroupID = rstGroups!GroupID
        rstUserGroups.Update
    End If
Next intJ
```

Once the code has looped through all the users and all the groups to which each user belongs, it commits the transaction (writing all the changes to disk) and closes all the objects:

```
wrk.CommitTrans
rstUsers.Close
rstGroups.Close
rstUserGroups.Close
```

Now tblUsers, tblGroups, and tblUserGroups contain information about each user and the groups to which he or she belongs. Figure 10-15 shows the three tables, filled in for the sample workgroup.

Comments

Once you've filled the three tables, you can easily perform lookups in your Access Basic code or create reports like the one you get with Security|Print

Security. You could also just lift pieces of the code from ahtListUsers, once you understand it, for use in your own applications.

The ahtListUsers procedure is not production quality code. In order to keep it simple, there's no error-handling code. Certainly, any procedure of this nature that manipulates tables must include sufficient error handling. Though it's not likely, some other user may have the output tables locked, or you may not have permissions for the system tables you need in order to gather this information. In a production environment, it's best to trap errors and handle them.

In the list of users in Figure 10-15, notice there are two users that you might never have seen before: Creator and Engine. These two users are created by Access itself and cannot be used or manipulated by Access Basic code. As you'll see in the next How-To, you can create a Workspace object for any normal user, allowing that user to log in to a new session of the Access engine, but you can't use Creator or Engine to create new workspace objects. It's a good thing, too! Since neither can have a password (their passwords are always blank), this would otherwise provide a security breach: Your code could log on as Creator or Engine, without a password. Because you can neither log on manually as

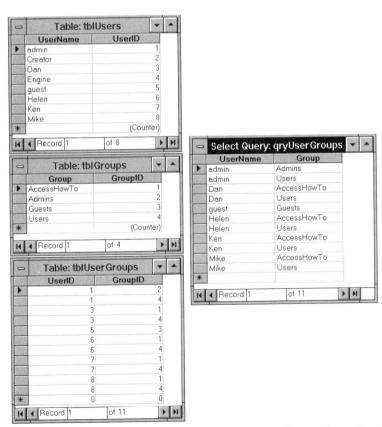

Figure 10-15 The three user/group tables, filled in, along with qryUserGroups

Creator or Engine, nor log on using the CreateWorkspace method with them, these two special users don't pose a security risk.

Once you know how to enumerate through collections, as shown in this How-To, you should be able to apply the same techniques to other database collections and their objects. For more information, see Chapter 4.

10.7 HOW DO I...   COMPLEXITY: ADVANCED

List all users with blank passwords?

Problem

As database administrator, I need to ensure that every member of my workgroup has an Access password. As far as I can tell, a user's Password property is *write-only!* I can use the NewPassword method to create a new password, and I understand why I can't retrieve the value of a user's password, but I need a way to find out if a user hasn't yet established a password. I'd like to create a list of all users, indicating which ones don't have a password. How can I do this?

Technique

You're right: You can't retrieve users' passwords. Access does provide a way for you to find out, however, whether a user has a password set up or not. When you attempt to create a new Workspace object in Access Basic, you must supply a user name and a matching password. By attempting to create a Workspace object for each user in turn, supplying a blank password, you can find out which users don't yet have passwords; these will be the users for which this attempt *doesn't* fail! Just as in the previous How-To, you'll use DAO to walk through the list of users in the workgroup.

Steps

The sample form frmUserPasswords, in 10-07.MDB, fills tables with the information you need and presents it in a list box. To test it, open and run frmUserPasswords. Figure 10-16 shows the form in use for a sample workgroup.

To use this information in your own applications, follow these steps:

1. Create the table you'll need to hold the information. Either import the table tblUsers from 10-07.MDB or use the information in Table 10-21 to create your own. Figure 10-17 shows the table in design mode.

FIELD NAME	DATA TYPE	PRIMARY KEY?
UserName	Text	No
UserID	Counter	Yes
PasswordSet	Yes/No	No

Table 10-21 Table layouts for gathering users' password information

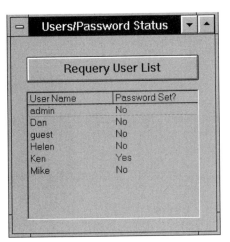

Figure 10-16 The sample form, frm UserPasswords, shows users and their password status for a sample workgroup

Figure 10-17 The table, tblUsers, in design mode

2. Either import the module basFindBlank from 10-07.MDB or enter the following code into either a global or a form module. (If you intend to call the routine from anywhere besides an event procedure, you'll want it in a global module.) This is the code you'll use to fill the table you just created.

```
Sub ahtFindBlankPasswords ()

  ' Fill tblUsers with list of users, and
  ' whether or not their password is blank.

  Dim intI As Integer
  Dim usr As User

  Dim db As Database
  Dim wrk As WorkSpace
  Dim wrkTest As WorkSpace

  Dim rst As Recordset
  Dim fPwdUsed As Integer

  Const ERR_INVALID_PASSWORD = 3029

  DoCmd SetWarnings False
  DoCmd RunSQL "Delete * From tblUsers"
  DoCmd SetWarnings True

  ' Set up object variables.
  Set wrk = DBEngine.Workspaces(0)
  Set db = wrk.Databases(0)
  Set rst = db.OpenRecordset("tblUsers")
```

(Continued on next page)

399

(Continued from previous page)

```
' Loop through all the users.
For intI = 0 To wrk.Users.Count - 1
    Set usr = wrk.Users(intI)
    ' Skip the two special users, since you can't log on
    ' as either of them via CreateWorkspace().
    If usr.Name <> "Creator" And usr.Name <> "Engine" Then
        ' Try to log on with a blank password. If this
        ' doesn't fail, the user has a blank password.
        On Error Resume Next
        Set wrkTest = DBEngine.CreateWorkspace("Test", usr.Name, "")
        fPwdUsed = (Err = ERR_INVALID_PASSWORD)
        On Error Goto 0

        ' Add a new row to tblUsers, storing the
        ' user's name and whether or not they have a
        ' password.
        rst.AddNew
                rst!UserName = usr.Name
                rst!PasswordSet = fPwdUsed
        rst.Update
        wrkTest.Close
    End If
Next intI
rst.Close
End Sub
```

3. To produce the list of all users whose passwords are blank, execute the code in ahtFindBlankPasswords. You can call it from the Immediate Window, or from a click event, as in the sample form, frmUserPasswords. (If you decide to use frmUserPasswords, you must also create a query, qryUserPasswords, which sorts the rows in tblUsers in ascending order on the UserName field. This query fills the list box on the sample form.) You could create a report that pulls its rows from tblUsers, as well, allowing you to prepare a regular report listing all users with blank passwords.

How It Works

The ahtFindBlankPasswords procedure uses Data Access Objects (DAO) to do most of its work. It starts by clearing out the previous contents of tblUsers, so later code can fill in the table with the current list of users and their password status.

```
DoCmd SetWarnings False
DoCmd RunSQL "Delete * From tblUsers"
DoCmd SetWarnings True
```

Next, the code sets up the object variables it will need to retrieve and store the password information. It uses the Workspace object to loop through all the users (since the Workspace object provides the Users collection that you'll use), and the Recordset object refers to the table into which you'll write the new data.

```
Set wrk = DBEngine.Workspaces(0)
Set db = wrk.Databases(0)
Set rst = db.OpenRecordset("tblUsers")
```

The next step is to loop through the Users collection of the default Workspace object. For each user, the code attempts to create a new workspace, as shown here:

```
For intI = 0 To wrk.Users.Count - 1
   Set usr = wrk.Users(intI)
   '
   ' See the next code sample
   '
Next intI
```

Finally, the important step: For each user, the code calls the CreateWorkspace method of the DBEngine object. To call this method, you must supply three parameters: the name for the new workspace (since you only need the results of attempting to create the workspace, you don't care about its name); the user name; and the user's password. An empty string ("") is passed for the password. An error indicates that the current user had a password; the attempt to create a new workspace, logging in that user, failed. If there is no error, that user did not have a password. The code checks whether an error occurred, comparing the Access built-in Err value with the known error value that occurs when you attempt to create a workspace with an invalid password. Whether or not an error occurred, the code adds a new row to tblUsers and stores the user name along with the password status in the table. Here is the code for all these steps:

```
' Skip the two special users, since you can't log on
' as either of them via CreateWorkspace().
If usr.Name <> "Creator" And usr.Name <> "Engine" Then
    ' Try to log on with a blank password. If this
    ' doesn't fail, the user has a blank password.
   On Error Resume Next
   Set wrkTest = DBEngine.CreateWorkspace("Test", usr.Name, "")
   fPwdUsed = (Err = ERR_INVALID_PASSWORD)
   On Error GoTo 0

    ' Add a new row to tblUsers, storing the
    ' user's name and whether or not they have a
    ' password.
   rst.AddNew
      rst!UserName = usr.Name
      rst!PasswordSet = fPwdUsed
   rst.Update
   wrkTest.Close
End If
```

As discussed in the previous How-To, the Users collection contains two users that are not actually part of your workgroup: Creator and Engine. Access creates these two users but doesn't allow you to log on as either one, from the command line or by creating a new workspace. Therefore, your code should just skip these two users, since you don't really care whether their passwords are blank or not.

Comments

If you intend to use ahtFindBlankPasswords in a production environment, you should add some error-handling code to the procedure. Any time you write to tables, you must include some method of dealing with errors. At the very least, alert the user (which could very well be yourself) that an error has occurred, and what that error was.

10.8 HOW DO I...
COMPLEXITY: INTERMEDIATE

Implement password aging and minimum length requirements?

Problem

I'm using Access security to enforce login names and passwords for each user of my application. I'd like to tighten up the default security a bit, to disallow one-character and blank passwords. I'd also like to require users to change their passwords on a regular basis. How can I add these features to my database?

Technique

This How-To shows you how to maintain a table of password change dates and check it each time the user logs on to the system. If the password is too old, you can require the user to change it immediately via a custom form. Using a form instead of Security|Change Password also gives you the opportunity to enforce minimum length restrictions on new passwords.

Steps

Open 10-08.MDB and run the macro mcrSampleAutoExec. Since the Admin user's password is already flagged as expired in this database, you'll see the warning shown in Figure 10-18.

When you dismiss this dialog box, the Change Password form shown in Figure 10-19 opens and asks for a new password. If you enter an incorrect old password, or neglect to change the password, or don't type the new password the same way twice, or use a new password that's too short, you'll get an error message when you click the Change button. Otherwise, your password will be changed.

> **WARNING:** If you do this with your original SYSTEM.MDA file, you'll change your default Admin password. Make sure you immediately change it back to an empty password (using the Security|Change Password menu option), or remember the new one.

Figure 10-18 Password expiration message

Figure 10-19 Password change form

To implement a password-aging strategy in your own application, follow these steps.

1. Create a new table with the fields shown in Table 10-22.

FIELD NAME	DATA TYPE	DESCRIPTION
UserName	Text	Primary Key
PasswordChangeDate	Date/Time	

Table 10-22 Fields in tblPasswordAging

2. Save this table as tblPasswordAging. Switch the table to datasheet view, and enter one record for each user in your database, with their user name and date of last password change.

3. Create a new form with the properties shown in Table 10-23.

PROPERTY	VALUE
Caption	Change Password
DefaultView	Single Form
ScrollBars	Neither
RecordSelectors	No
NavigationButtons	No

Table 10-23 Properties of frmChangePassword

4. Place three unbound text boxes on the form, named txtOldPassword, txtNewPassword, and txtConfirmPassword. Set the InputMask property of each of these fields to Password, so that the text typed by the user appears as asterisks.

5. Add a command button to the form. Name the command button cmdChange and set its OnClick property to:

```
=ahtChangePassword()
```

Save the form as frmChangePassword.

6. Create a new macro with a single RunCode action, or add the action to your existing AutoExec macro. The RunCode action should call the function:

```
=ahtCheckPasswordAge()
```

7. Import the basChangePassword module from 10-08.MDB, which includes the necessary Access Basic code, as well as the MIN-LENGTH and MAX-AGE constants.

How It Works

The password-aging check compares the stored password change date with the date returned by the built-in Access Basic date function. If the password is older than allowed by the constant MAX_AGE, the change form is opened in dialog mode (the user must deal with this box before the rest of the application can proceed).

The ahtChangePassword function does the actual work of changing the password, making four separate checks to the data the user entered.

First, the function confirms that the old password was entered correctly by using it to open a new workspace for the current user:

```
' Check for correct old password
If IsNull(frmPW![txtOldPassword]) Then
    strPassword = ""
Else
    strPassword = frmPW![txtOldPassword]
End If
Set wsNew = DBEngine.CreateWorkspace("Check", strUserName, strPassword)
If Err Then
    Debug.Print Err
    MsgBox "Invalid Old Password", MB_ICON_STOP, "Change Password"
    Exit Function
End If
```

Second, it confirms that the old and new passwords are different by comparing their values.

Third, it confirms that the new password is longer than the MIN_LENGTH constant:

```
' Make sure new password is long enough
If Len(frmPW![txtNewPassword]) < MIN_LENGTH Then
    MsgBox "New Password is Too Short", MB_ICON_STOP, "Change Password"
    Exit Function
End If
```

Fourth, it confirms that the new password was entered the same way twice to guard against an unintentional typographical error:

```
' Make sure new password was entered twice the same
If frmPW![txtNewPassword] <> frmPW![txtConfirmNewPassword] ⇒
Or IsNull(frmPW![txtConfirmNewPassword]) Then
   MsgBox "New Password Entered Incorrectly", MB_ICON_STOP, "Change Password"
   Exit Function
End If
```

Finally, if the new password passes all of these tests, the function uses the .NewPassword method of the User object to assign the new password to the user. The function checks for an error here, since it would still be possible to enter a password that was unacceptable to the Access security system.

```
DBEngine.Workspaces(0).Users(strUserName).NewPassword strPassword, frmPW![txtNewPassword]
If Err Then
   MsgBox "Invalid Password", MB_ICON_STOP, "Change Password"
   Exit Function
End If
```

Comments

In the sample database, the password change is not forced. The user can simply close the Change Password form without entering anything or clicking the Change button. You can prevent this if you like, and force a password change, by checking the value of the global constant fPasswordOK in the OnClose event of the password change form. The code sets this flag variable to True if the password was successfully changed and False otherwise.

Users might still fool the password-aging check by setting the system clock to a date after the day they are running your program. To prevent this, your best bet may be to take advantage of whatever features your network offers for time synchronization between its server and the individual workstations.

10.9 HOW DO I...   COMPLEXITY: INTERMEDIATE

Adjust database options depending on who's logged in?

Problem

I'm using Access security on my application, but this security is not fine-grained enough for me. For instance, if I want to show a specific user a menu with a unique list of options, or remove a single button from a form when this user has it open, I have to design a whole new form and give that user permissions on that form. Is there a way I can reuse a single form with individual settings based on which user is logged in?

Technique

With the Access Basic CurrentUser function, you can check your database at startup to see who is logging in. Based on the value this function returns, you can change any runtime property of any form before the user takes an action.

Steps

Because this How-To makes use of Access security, before you can try the sample database, you'll need to join the supplied workgroup. As shown in Figure 10-20, run the Workgroup Administrator application from your Microsoft Access Program Manager group. (You may need to run Access Setup again and choose to install this application if it's not part of your current setup.) Click the Join button on the first screen and the Browse button in the second dialog box. Locate the supplied SYSAHT.MDA file and choose to join it. Exit from the Workgroup Administrator after you acknowledge the confirmation message.

Now start Access and load 10-09.MDB. Open the frmSimpleMenu form. You have your choice of two different login names with this SYSTEM.MDA file; neither one has a password set. Member has user-level security and will only see the options shown in Figure 10-21. Reader has Admin-level security and will see the (slightly) richer set of options in Figure 10-22.

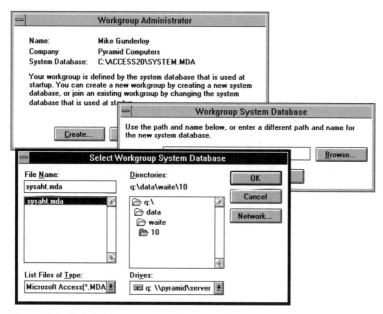

Figure 10-20 Joining a new workgroup

To re-create the sample database, follow these steps:

1. Create a new form. Set the form's properties as shown in Table 10-24.

PROPERTY	VALUE
Caption	Simple Menu
DefaultView	Single Form
ScrollBars	Neither
RecordSelectors	No
NavigationButtons	No
MenuBar	UserMenu
On Open	mcrCheckUser

Table 10-24 Properties of frmSimpleMenu

2. Add two command buttons to the form. CmdExit should run mcrExit, and cmdClose should run mcrClose. Set the .Visible property of cmdClose to no. Save the form as frmSimpleMenu.

3. Import the macros from 10-09.MDB to your own database. (All of the menu macros were created with the Access Menu Builder add-in.) The Exit and Close macros run Quit and Close actions, respectively. The remaining macro, mcrCheckUser, has the settings shown in Table 10-25.

CONDITION	ACTION	ARGUMENT	VALUE
CheckUser ( ) ="Reader"	SetValue	Item Expression	[Forms]![frmSimpleMenu]![MenuBar] "AdminMenu"
...	SetValue	Item Expression	[Forms]![frmSimpleMenu]![cmdClose].[Visible] True

Table 10-25 Macro mcrCheckUser

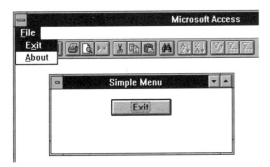

Figure 10-21 Database for user Member

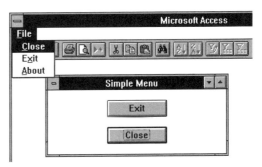

Figure 10-22 Database for user Reader

How It Works

By default, the form is saved with the least secure options set; if anything goes wrong, this provides a little extra assurance. When any user opens frmSimpleMenu, the mcrCheckUser macro runs automatically in response to the Open event and checks the user name. Only if the user name is Reader does the macro turn on the additional control and make the additional menu items visible.

Comments

You can use this technique to alter any runtime property in response to the user name. This gives you a selection of settings to make on a user-by-user basis, including

- Whether certain menu items appear

- Whether certain controls are visible, and therefore active

- What query a form is based on—some users can see more records than others

- What data entry controls are visible—some users can enter more fields than others

- What toolbars are shown

11

Making the Most of the Windows API

HOW DO I...

The Windows API has a "bad rap" among many Access programmers who think it's too hard to figure out, or too hard to call, or "mysterious." We're here to prove that none of these ideas is correct—even if you've never seen the Windows API programmer's reference, you can use the Windows API, given some help. In this chapter, we'll present some interesting uses of the Windows API and other external libraries within Access, with example forms and modules for each How-To. In most cases, using these in your own applications takes little more work than importing a module or two and then calling the functions. We've divided the How-To's in this chapter into three broad categories: Windows user interface, Windows shell, and hardware information.

User Interface Issues

You'll learn how to remove the Access system menu and maximize and minimize buttons; and how to make sure you can't move to any other application (by making Access *system modal).* We'll discuss language-independent classification of keypresses, so you can monitor exactly what keys have been pressed. We'll also show how to restrict the mouse movement to a specific area on the screen.

The Windows Shell

You'll learn how to have your Access Basic code (which runs asynchronously) run another program and pause until the other program is done before continuing. We'll demonstrate a method for exiting Windows under program control that covers all the options of the associated API functions. You'll learn to find and run an application, given an associated data file, and how to determine if the application is already running. You'll see how to retrieve a list of all the open top-level windows (generally, one per application), and how to close a window from your Access Basic code.

Files, Drives, and Hardware

You'll learn how to retrieve file date and time stamp information—useful if you're moving files around from within applications. You'll use some undocumented DLL calls to retrieve information about your disk drives, and see how to create an About... box, concerning your Access installation and the current Windows environment.

A NOTE ABOUT THE EXAMPLE DATABASES

Most of the How-To's in this chapter instruct you to import one or more modules from the example databases. In each case, the module contains the Windows API user-defined types and function declarations you need for the example. If you've already imported a module with the specified name for a previous How-To, you can skip it, since all modules with matching names contain the same code.

11.1 Remove the Access system menu and maximize and minimize buttons

Access 2.0 makes it easy to remove a specific form's system menu and its maximize and minimize buttons, but there's no matching functionality for the main Access window. The code in this How-To will let you remove and replace these items for the main Access window, too.

11.2 Make a window system modal

You may need to give an Access form the focus in your application and not let the user move to any other Windows application while it has the focus. Although this isn't a wise thing to do very often, when you need this functionality, it's there for you. This How-To will demonstrate how you can harness this power in your own applications.

11.3 Classify keypresses in a language-independent manner

The Windows API includes a number of functions you can call to categorize characters. The isCharAlpha and isCharAlphaNumeric functions are both faster than Access Basic, and they deal with international issues. This How-To will demonstrate how you can use these functions to classify characters.

11.4 Restrict mouse movement to a specific region

You may find that you need to have strict control over mouse movement in your application. This How-To will demonstrate the ClipCursor API call, which limits the region available to the mouse.

11.5 Run another program and pause until it's done

You may need to run another program as part of an application. Since Access Basic runs asynchronously, it just keeps on going while your program is running. If you need to stop and wait until the other program has finished its work, investigate this How-To, which will show a method for pausing Access Basic until the application has finished.

11.6 Exit Windows under program control

The Windows API allows you to call one of two functions and quit Windows: quit Windows and then return; or quit, run a DOS program, and then return. This How-To will explain the steps necessary to call this Windows API.

11.7 Run an application associated with a given data file

In Windows, many file name extensions are associated with the application that created them. Use the information in this How-To to locate the particular application associated with a given data file, if such an association exists.

11.8 Check to see if an application is already running

You can use the Shell function to start a foreign application, such as Excel, but there's no built-in function to determine whether Excel is already running. This How-To will show how to detect whether Excel (or any other application) is already running, to avoid starting up a second copy.

11.9   Retrieve a list of all the top-level windows

When you need to know what other applications are also running, this How-To will demonstrate walking through the list of windows, starting with the Windows desktop, to fill an array with information about each running application's main window.

11.10   Close a running Windows application

If you start an application from Access Basic code, most likely you'll also want to shut it down when your program terminates. This How-To will use the PostMessage Windows API function to close the other application's main window.

11.11   Retrieve file date and time stamps

The Windows API provides the OpenFile function, which can be used to retrieve information about a specified file. In this How-To we'll use the function to retrieve the time and date stamp information for the file you specify.

11.12   Retrieve information about the disk drives in my computer

If you need to know how much space is free on a disk drive, or how much total space is available on that drive, you'll need some external help. Access itself doesn't include such a function. Though not part of the Windows API, the MSSETUP.DLL library ships with each Microsoft desktop application, so you and your users already have a copy. It's also part of the Access Developer's Toolkit, and can be shipped with runtime applications. This How-To shows how you can call into this library from Access to retrieve disk information.

11.13   Collect and display information about the system and the Access installation

The Windows API, and Access itself, include a number of function calls you can use to retrieve information about your application's environment (the version of Windows that's running, the amount of memory, and so on). This How-To will show you how to gather this information for your own About... box or other information display.

11.1 HOW DO I...   COMPLEXITY: ADVANCED

Remove the Access system menu and maximize and minimize buttons?

Problem

Access makes it easy to remove the control box (often called the system menu) and the minimize and maximize buttons when I design forms, but there doesn't seem to be a way to do this for the main Access window or for forms at runtime. I'd like to be able to remove these buttons and replace the standard menus to control how users interact with my application. Is there a way to remove these items and then replace them later?

Technique

Removing or replacing these window controls requires changing the style bits for the particular window. Every window maintains a 32-bit value that describes its physical characteristics: its border type and the existence of scroll bars, a system menu, and the minimize and maximize buttons, for example. The values are stored as bit flags, in which the state of a single bit in the 32-bit value indicates the value of some characteristic of the window. In general, you can't change the state of many of these flags without re-creating the window, but by setting or clearing the bits in the window's style value, you can force the system menu and the minimize/maximize buttons to appear or disappear. This How-To demonstrates how to control these features of the main Access window.

Steps

Load and run frmSystemItems in 11-01.MDB. This form, shown in Figure 11-1, allows you to add or remove the system menu, the minimize button and/or the maximize button, from the main Access window, and from the current form. Select items on the form to make the corresponding items visible, or deselect to remove them. Once you've made your choices, click on the Execute button, and the Access Basic code will remove or replace the items you've chosen.

To include this functionality in your own applications, follow these steps:

1. Import the modules listed in Table 11-1 from 11-01.MDB.

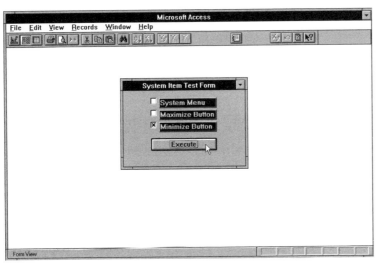

Figure 11-1 The sample form, frmSystemItems, allows you to remove or replace any of the system items

MODULE NAME	CONTAINS
basControl	ahtAccessSystemItems, ahtFormSystemItems, type declarations
basGetHWnd	ahtFindAccessHWnd
basLockScreen	ahtShowUpdates

Table 11-1 Modules to import from 11-01.MDB, for controlling system items

2. To remove or replace Access system items, call the subroutine ahtAccessSystemItems, passing to it three parameters, as shown in Table 11-2.

PARAMETER NAME	DATA TYPE	VALUE
fSystemMenu	Integer	True = show system menu; False = hide
fMaxButton	Integer	True = show maximize button; False = hide
fMinButton	Integer	True = show minimize button; False = hide

Table 11-2 Parameters for ahtAccessSystemItems

For example, the following statement will hide the system menu and the maximize button, but will show the minimize button:

```
ahtAccessSystemItems False, False, True
```

3. To remove or replace a form's system items, call the subroutine ahtFormSystemItems, passing to it four parameters, as shown in Table 11-3.

PARAMETER NAME	DATA TYPE	VALUE
frm	Form	Reference a form
fSystemMenu	Integer	True = show system menu; False = hide
fMaxButton	Integer	True = show maximize button, False = hide
fMinButton	Integer	True = show minimize button, False = hide

Table 11-3 Parameters for ahtFormSystemItems

For example, the following statement, called from a button's Click event in a form's module, will show the system menu, but will hide the minimize and maximize buttons:

```
ahtFormSystemItems True, False, False
```

Though Access does provide the ControlBox, MaxButton, and MinButton properties for forms, they are read-only once your form is in use: If you need to alter these properties at runtime, you'll have to use ahtFormSystemItems to do your work, rather than changing the properties directly.

How It Works

The bulk of the work in controlling these system items takes place in the private subroutine, HandleStyles, in the basControl module. This function accepts a window handle (either the Access handle or the hWnd property of a form) and three True/False values indicating which options you'd like to see and which you'd like removed. Like every window, the window you want to alter maintains a 32-bit value, its style value. Within that long integer, each of the 32 positions represents one of the possible styles for the window. If the bit is 1, the style is set on; if it's 0, the style is set off. HandleStyles builds up two long integers, each containing a series of 32 bits. The first, lngStylesOn, contains all 0s, except for the bits representing the styles you want turned on, which contain 1s. The other, lngStylesOff, contains all 1s except the bits representing the styles you want turned off, which contain 0s.

Using the AND operator to combine the current window style with lngStylesOff sets each style whose bit contains 0 in lngStylesOff to be 0. Using the OR operator to combine the current window style with lngStylesOn sets each style whose bit contains 1 in lngStylesOn to be 1. For example, suppose the current window style value is this:

10001000 10001010 10101011 01101101

The value in lngStylesOff contains 1s in all positions except the ones you want turned off, which contain 0s. If the value of lngStylesOff is this:

11111111 11111111 11111111 11111011

the result of using the AND operator with the original style and lngStylesOff will be this:

10001000 10001010 10101011 01101001

The value in lngStylesOn contains 0s in all positions except the ones you want turned on, which contain 1s. If the value of lngStylesOn is this:

00000000 00000000 00010000 10000000

the result of using the OR operator with lngStylesOn and the result of ANDing the original style with lngStylesOff will be this:

10001000 10001010 10111011 11101001

This final result will have three changed values: one bit that was 1 is now 0 due to the settings in lngStylesOff, and two bits that were 0 are 1 due to the settings in lnStylesOn.

To retrieve and replace the window's style information, the code uses the GetWindowLong and SetWindowLong API functions. Given a window handle and a flag (GWL_STYLE) indicating which 32-bit value to retrieve or set about the window, these functions allow you to get the current value, do your work with it, and then reset it. This is the line of code that does all the work:

```
HandleStyles = aht_apiSetWindowLong(hWnd, GWL_STYLE, ⇒
(aht_apiGetWindowLong(hWnd, GWL_STYLE) And lngStylesOff) Or lngStylesOn)
```

It sets the window style to be the value that GetWindowLong retrieved, combined with the two style flags the code previously built up based on your choices.

The entire procedure looks like this:

```
Private Function HandleStyles (ByVal hWnd As Integer, ⇒
fSystemMenu As Integer, fMaxButton As Integer, fMinButton As Integer) As Integer

    Dim lngStylesOn As Long
    Dim lngStylesOff As Long

    On Error GoTo HandleStylesExit

    ' Set all bits off.
    lngStylesOn = 0

    ' Set all bits on. -1 is represented,
    ' internally, as all bits set.
    lngStylesOff = -1

    ' Turn ON bits to set attribute, turn them OFF to turn
    ' attribute off.
    If fSystemMenu Then
        lngStylesOn = lngStylesOn Or WS_SYSMENU
    Else
        lngStylesOff = lngStylesOff And Not WS_SYSMENU
    End If
    If fMinButton Then
        lngStylesOn = lngStylesOn Or WS_MINIMIZEBOX
    Else
        lngStylesOff = lngStylesOff And Not WS_MINIMIZEBOX
    End If
    If fMaxButton Then
        lngStylesOn = lngStylesOn Or WS_MAXIMIZEBOX
    Else
        lngStylesOff = lngStylesOff And Not WS_MAXIMIZEBOX
    End If

    ' Set the attributes as necessary.
HandleStyles = aht_apiSetWindowLong(hWnd, GWL_STYLE, ⇒
(aht_apiGetWindowLong(hWnd, GWL_STYLE) And lngStylesOff) Or lngStylesOn)

HandleStylesExit:
    Exit Function
End Function
```

Comments

After the style bits are set, there's still one issue left: You must coerce the window into repainting itself, so the changes become visible. Just changing the styles isn't enough, since they don't become visible until the next time the window repaints its border.

For forms, this is easy. All you need to do is turn off the form's Painting property before you make the changes, and then turn it on again once you're done. This forces the entire form, including its border, to repaint. The ahtFormSystemItems subroutine does exactly that:

```
Sub ahtFormSystemItems (frm As Form, ByVal fSystemMenu As ⇒
Integer, ByVal fMaxButton As Integer, ByVal fMinButton As Integer)
    Dim hWnd As Integer
    Dim intRetval As Integer

    hWnd = frm.hWnd
    frm.Painting = False
    intRetval = HandleStyles(hWnd, fSystemMenu, fMaxButton, fMinButton)
    frm.Painting = True
End Sub
```

With the main Access window, however, it's not so simple. Access doesn't know that you've changed anything, so it doesn't know that it needs to repaint itself. As a matter of fact, using the normal Windows API methods to *force* Access to repaint itself will all fail. The solution presented here uses the GetWindowPlacement/SetWindowPlacement Windows API functions to effectively swap the restored/maximized setting of the main Access window. If it has been maximized, this code "unmaximizes" it, and vice versa. Then, the code immediately puts the window back the way it was. By disabling screen updates around the API calls, you won't see any of the action on the screen. Here is the code that does this work, the private subroutine ForceUpdate:

```
Private Sub ForceUpdate (hWnd As Integer)
    Dim typWP As aht_tagWindowPlacement
    Dim intRetval As Integer

    ' Turn off screen updates.
    intRetval = aht_apiLockWindowUpdate(hWnd)

    ' Set the length of the data structure. Windows will
    ' not return the window placement unless you do this.
    typWP.length = Len(typWP)

    ' Get the current window placement.
    intRetval = aht_apiGetWindowPlacement(hWnd, typWP)

    ' Set the opposite window placement, then set it back.
    ' This forces Access to repaint itself.
    typWP.ShowCmd = IIf(typWP.ShowCmd = SW_SHOWMAXIMIZED, SW_RESTORE, SW_SHOWMAXIMIZED)
    intRetval = aht_apiSetWindowPlacement(hWnd, typWP)
    typWP.ShowCmd = IIf(typWP.ShowCmd = SW_SHOWMAXIMIZED, SW_RESTORE, SW_SHOWMAXIMIZED)
    intRetval = aht_apiSetWindowPlacement(hWnd, typWP)

    intRetval = aht_apiLockWindowUpdate(0)
End Sub
```

11.2 HOW DO I...   COMPLEXITY: INTERMEDIATE

Make a window system modal?

Problem

Sometimes it is critical to restrict users to Access. That is, I don't want to allowing switching to any other application (using ALT-TAB, ALT-ESC, or any other method) while a critical activity is occurring. How can I prevent users from switching to any other process?

Technique

When a window programmatically retains the user's focus and won't relinquish it until your program tells it to, its state is *modal*. In Access, you set a form to be modal by setting its Modal property to True. When a window is modal throughout all of Windows, its state is *system modal*. You can't switch away from a system modal window to any other application; nor can you move or size it.

Though you won't use this technique in every application, you can make any window in Access a system modal window. Windows provides the SetSysModalWindow API function for this purpose, and you can use this function in your own applications. Only one window can be system modal at once (of course), and that window can be either a specific form or the Access main window. All children of the system modal window are still available for use.

Steps

To try out the system modal functionality, load and run frmTestSysModal from 11-02.MDB. This form, shown in Figure 11-2, allows you to make either the main Access window or the current form system modal. While either is system modal, you won't be able to switch to a different application. However, if the Access window is system modal, you can still select a different window within Access (but you can't move or resize any child of Access). When a system modal window is active, the form changes color, to remind you that you need to remove the system modal form.

To make any window system modal from your own applications, follow these steps:

1. Import the modules basGetHWnd and basSystemModal from 11-02.MDB.

2. To make the Access main window system modal, call the ahtAccessSystemModal function. This function finds the Access window handle for you, and then calls the Windows API SetSysModalWindow function. Call ahtAccessSystemModal with a True parameter to make Access system modal, and with a False parameter to clear the system modal state. That is,

```
fSuccess = ahtAccessSystemModal(True)
```

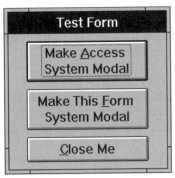

Figure 11-2 The sample form, frmTestSysModal, allows you to set Access or the current form to be a system modal window

will make Access system modal if possible (there's not much reason for it to fail) and will return True if it succeeded; False if it didn't. Call the function as

```
fSuccess = ahtAccessSystemModal(False)
```

to reset the system modal state.

3. To make an Access form system modal, you'll just call the Windows API function directly, passing it the hWnd property of the form. For example, in the form's Open event, you could call code like this:

```
fSuccess = aht_apiSetSysModalWindow(Me.hWnd)
```

For more examples, see the example form module for frmTestSysModal in 11-02.MDB.

How It Works

As Windows API calls go, this is a simple one. Only one window can be system modal at a time, and by specifying a window handle when you call the SetSysModalWindow API function, you're telling Windows which window will be system modal. Once you've designated a system modal window, you won't be able to switch from it to any other running application, and you won't be able to move or size it or any of its children. To release the system modal state, you call SetSysModalWindow, passing it a value of 0, which is an invalid window handle.

Comments

The Windows documentation states that once a window is system modal, the only way to remove that status is to close the window. Based on our experience, that doesn't appear to be the case. As with any other undocumented behavior, however, be wary when setting and releasing system modal windows throughout your application. If at all possible, close a window that's system modal rather than calling the API function to reset the status, just to be safe.

11.3 HOW DO I...

COMPLEXITY: INTERMEDIATE

Classify keypresses in a language-independent manner?

Problem

I need to be able to classify a keypress as a character, a digit, or neither. I also need to know if a character is uppercase or lowercase. I know I can write Access Basic code to handle this, but if I do that, I'm limiting myself to a single language, and languages classify their characters differently. Since Windows knows all these things about various character sets, is there some way I can use Windows to do this work for me?

Technique

You could write Access Basic code to classify characters, but it certainly wouldn't be language independent. For example, the ANSI character 65 is an uppercase character in the standard multinational character set, but that doesn't guarantee anything about any other character set. If you want your applications to work in various languages, you must not assume specific character ranges. Windows provides a set of simple functions that will classify characters for you, based on their ANSI values. Luckily, this is exactly what the KeyPress event procedure in Access sends you, so you can use these functions from within KeyPress event procedures that you write.

Steps

In addition to the necessary function declarations, the sample database 11-03.MDB includes a demonstration form, showing all the ANSI characters and their classifications. Load and run frmCharClasses from 11-03.MDB, and you'll see a display like that in Figure 11-3. By scrolling through the form, you'll be able to see all 255 ANSI characters (in the Arial font) and their classifications.

To use this functionality in your own applications, follow these steps:

1. Import the module basClassifyChars from 11-03.MDB into your application.

2. To classify an ANSI value, call one or more of the functions in Table 11-4. Each of these functions takes as its parameter a value between 1 and 255. Each function returns a nonzero value if the character code you passed is a member of the function's tested group, or 0 if it's not. (As you can see from Table 11-4, some of the functions come directly from the Windows API, and others return values based on those functions.) These functions will return correct values, no matter which language version of Windows is running.

For example, imagine that you need to limit the number of characters typed into a text box, and the number of allowable characters isn't known until runtime. On top of that, you want to allow only alphabetic or numeric values, and that choice, too, isn't known until runtime. Although you could programmatically control the input masks, creating a new one each time conditions change, it is simpler to handle this problem using the KeyPress

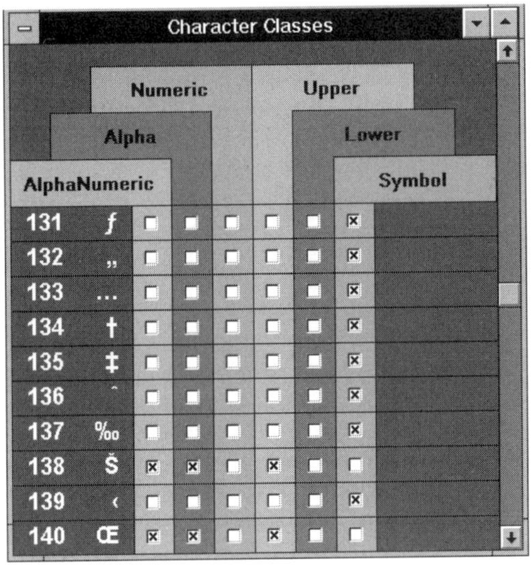

Figure 11-3 The sample form, frmCharClasses, shows all the ANSI characters and their classifications

event and some code that checks the state of the current keypress. The sample form, frmInputTest, (Figure 11-4), shows a simple test form. The code attached to txtCharTest's KeyPress event looks like this:

```
Sub txtCharTest_KeyPress (KeyAscii As Integer)

    ' Always allow a backspace.
    If KeyAscii = 8 Then Exit Sub

    ' If txtChars is non-null and greater than 0,
    ' and txtCharTest is non-null and has too many
    ' characters, then set KeyAscii to 0.
    If Not IsNull(Me!txtChars) Then
        If Me!txtChars > 0 Then
            If Not IsNull(Me!txtCharTest.Text) Then
                If Len(Me!txtCharTest.Text) >= Me!txtChars Then
                    KeyAscii = 0
                End If
            End If
        End If
    End If
    ' In any case, if the keypress isn't the correct
    ' type, set KeyAscii to 0.
    If Me!grpCharType = 1 Then
        If (aht_apiIsCharAlpha(KeyAscii) = 0) Then KeyAscii = 0
    Else
        If (ahtIsCharNumeric(KeyAscii) = 0) Then KeyAscii = 0
    End If
End Sub
```

In the KeyPress event, Access sends to you a parameter, KeyAscii, which contains the ANSI value of the key that was just pressed. To tell Access to disregard this key, modify its value to 0 during the event procedure. In this case, if there's no room left in the field (based on the number in Me!txtChars) or if the character is not the right type (based on calls to aht_apiIsCharAlpha and ahtIsCharNumeric), the code sets the value of KeyAscii to 0, causing Access to disregard the keypress. Play with the sample form, changing the values, to see how the code works.

FUNCTION NAME	API?	INCLUSION CLASS
aht_apiIsCharAlphaNumeric	Yes	Language-defined alphabetic or numeric characters
aht_apiIsCharAlpha	Yes	Language-defined alphabetic characters
ahtIsCharNumeric	No	Alphanumeric, but not alpha
ahtIsSymbol	No	Not alphanumeric
aht_apiIsCharUpper	Yes	Language-defined uppercase characters
aht_apiIsCharLower	Yes	Language-defined lowercase characters

Table 11-4 The character classification functions in basClassifyChars

How It Works
Windows maintains, internally, information about the currently selected language and character set. For each language, there are certain characters that are treated as uppercase and others that aren't. Some characters in the character set represent alphabetic characters, and others don't. It would be impractical to maintain this information for each possible language your application might use. Luckily, you don't have to manage this. The Access functions, UCase and LCase, handle case conversions for you, but Access doesn't include case-testing functions. That's the role of the functions introduced in this How-To—they allow you to test the classification of characters, no matter what the language. Attempting to perform this task in Access Basic will sooner or later cause you trouble, if you plan on working internationally.

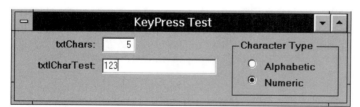

Figure 11-4 The sample input form, frmInputTest, uses character classifications to disallow keypresses

Comments

You may not need these routines often, but when you do, the API versions are both faster and more reliable than hand-written code would be. Don't ever count on specific ANSI values to be characters, uppercase or lowercase, since these values change from version to version of internationalized Windows.

11.4 HOW DO I...   COMPLEXITY: INTERMEDIATE

Restrict mouse movement to a specific region?

Problem

I'd like to be able to restrict mouse cursor movement to certain areas of the current form. I think I can help users of my application by making sure the mouse stays where it needs to be until I'm done with it. How can I limit mouse movement in Access?

Technique

The Windows API's ClipCursor subroutine will limit the movement of the mouse, just as you require, to a single form or region on a form, as you'll see in this How-To.

Steps

To try out this technique, load and run frmClip in 11-04.MDB. This form, shown in Figure 11-5, limits the mouse movement to the area of the form once you click the large button. If you click the button again or close the form, code attached to either event frees the mouse cursor to move anywhere on the screen.

To use this technique in your own applications, follow these steps:

1. Import the module basClipCursor from 11-04.MDB. This module contains the function declarations and user-defined types that you'll need.

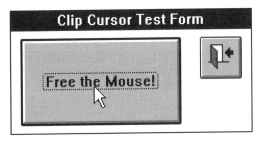

Figure 11-5 The sample form, frmClip, limits mouse movement to the area of the form

2. To limit the mouse to a single form, you'll need to get the form coordinates, and then tell Windows to use those coordinates as limits for the mouse. To do this, you'll need code something like this (since this code fragment uses "Me," it must be in a form's module, not a global module):

```
Dim typRect as aht_tagRect

GetWindowRect Me.hWnd, typRect
ClipCursor typRect
```

3. To free the mouse cursor, call the ahtFreeCursor procedure. This subroutine takes no parameters and can be called from anywhere in Access. See the "How It Works" section for an example.

How It Works

The ClipCursor API routine expects as its only parameter a user-defined data type consisting of four integers, representing coordinates of a rectangle. This data type has been declared for you in basClipCursor, as aht_tagRect. This is a very common data structure, used often with API routines that interact with the screen or printer.

```
Type aht_tagRect
    intLeft As Integer
    intTop As Integer
    intRight As Integer
    intBottom As Integer
End Type
```

When you want to restrict mouse movement, you'll need to retrieve the coordinates of the current form. You can accomplish this by calling the GetWindowRect API function (aliased as aht_apiGetWindowRect in the code), which will fill in an aht_tagRect structure with the left, top, right, and bottom coordinates of the window whose handle you pass it. Therefore, by calling GetWindowRect with the handle of the current form, you'll retrieve the coordinates of that form, in pixels.

```
Dim typRect as aht_tagRect
aht_apiGetWindowRect Me.hWnd, typRect
```

Once you've got a structure containing the coordinates of the current form, you can call ClipCursor (aliased as aht_apiClipCursor in the code) and pass to it that filled-in structure. The sample form combines these API calls, as shown below:

```
Sub cmdClip_Click ()
    Dim typRect As aht_tagRect
    Static sstrCaption As String

    ' Static variable to keep track of
    ' clipping.
    Static fClip As Integer

    If fClip Then
        ahtFreeCursor
```

```
        Me!cmdClip.Caption = sstrCaption
    Else
        sstrCaption = Me!cmdClip.Caption
        Me!cmdClip.Caption = "Free the Mouse!"
        aht_apiGetWindowRect Me.hWnd, typRect
        aht_apiClipCursor typRect
    End If
    fClip = Not fClip
End Sub
```

In the sample routine, which is executed each time you click the large button on frmClip, fClip alternates between True and False, keeping track of whether mouse clipping is currently in effect. If it is, the routine calls ahtFreeCursor to disable clipping and resets the button's caption. If clipping was not in effect, it stores away the original caption, sets a new one ("Free the Mouse!"), retrieves the form's coordinates, and finally, calls ClipCursor to restrict the cursor's movement.

Since the only way to end the mouse cursor restrictions is to restrict the mouse movement to the entire screen, the ahtFreeCursor routine must find the size of the screen and restrict the mouse to that region. To find the size of the screen, ahtFreeCursor calls the GetSystemMetrics API function (aliased as aht_apiGetSystemMetrics in the code), requesting first the width and then the height. (See How-To 11.13 for more information on the GetSystemMetrics function.) Given a rectangle with the coordinates (0, 0, Width, Height), ahtFreeCursor can call ClipCursor to free the mouse, as shown here:

```
Sub ahtFreeCursor ()

    ' Free the cursor to move anywhere on the screen,
    ' by setting it to clip at the screen borders.

' Windows API Constants
Const SM_CXSCREEN = 0
Const SM_CYSCREEN = 1

    Dim typRect As aht_tagRect

    typRect.intLeft = 0
    typRect.intTop = 0
    typRect.intRight = aht_apiGetSystemMetrics(SM_CXSCREEN)
    typRect.intBottom = aht_apiGetSystemMetrics(SM_CYSCREEN)
    aht_apiClipCursor typRect
End Sub
```

Comments

The method presented in this How-To is not foolproof in Access. Once again, you're taking control of a feature that Access normally controls itself, and sometimes the interaction is unpredictable. In this case, if you restrict the mouse movement to a single form, but you use the mouse to move or resize the form, Access will free the mouse for you. So if you're using this technique to *force* users to stay on a single form, you're better off using a modal form, instead. If, on the other hand, you're just trying to ensure that the mouse remains in the area of the form where the users need it to be, the method described here is more appropriate. Restricting the mouse movement is not meant for every application, but if you want to help your users out a little, try it.

Don't forget that the mouse is a shared resource: If you limit its use in Access, it's limited in every other application, too. Therefore, keep the mouse restricted for the shortest possible periods. You should make sure that any event that closes your form releases the mouse as well.

11.5 HOW DO I...   COMPLEXITY: INTERMEDIATE

Run another program and pause until it's done?

Problem

From my application, I occasionally need to run a DOS batch file or utility program that requires some time to do its job. There are also times when I'd like to run some other Windows application. In both cases, I'd like my Access application to pause until the other program has finished its work. Every time I try this, the Access Basic code starts up the other application but then just keeps on going. Is there a way to make Access wait until the other application has completed before moving on?

Technique

The Shell function in Access Basic (and the ShellExecute function mentioned in How-To 11.7) returns a unique integer value representing the running task. You can use this value, the *instance handle* for the running application, to track the state of the application. The GetModuleUsage API function will return a nonzero value for the particular instance handle until the application's window is closed. Since this happens automatically once a DOS application has finished running, you can use this technique to wait until a DOS window has closed before moving on in your application.

Steps

The sample form, frmTestWait, in 11-05.MDB, allows you to start both a DOS application and a Windows application and wait for either to complete. There's also a button that allows you to start a DOS application but continue the attached code. In any of these three cases (see Figure 11-6), the sample code attempts to load the text file C:\AHTTEST.TXT into a text box on the form once the application you've started finishes its work. (In the case where the code doesn't wait for the other application, of course, there's nothing to load.) Use frmTestWait, trying each of the command buttons to test the functionality demonstrated in this How-To.

To use this functionality in your own applications, follow these steps:

1. Import the module basRunApp from 11-05.MDB into your application.

2. To run another application, waiting for it to finish before going on with your code, call the ahtRunAppWait subroutine, passing it two parameters: a

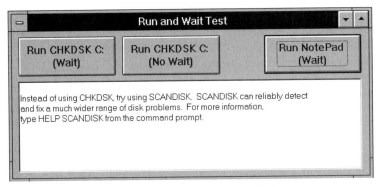

Figure 11-6 The sample form, frmTestWait, after it has run an application

command string telling it what to run and an integer designating the window mode you'd like to use (see Table 11-5). These are essentially the same values that you can use when calling the ShellExecute API function, in How-To 11.7 (though these examples use the Access Basic Shell function, which doesn't support hidden windows, option 0).

VALUE	WHAT HAPPENS TO THE WINDOW
1	Restored to its previous state (neither minimized nor maximized)
2	Made visible and minimized
3	Made visible and maximized
4	Displayed, but doesn't gain the input focus
5	Made visible
6	Minimized (as an icon) when started
7	Made visible and minimized, but it doesn't receive the input focus
8	Displayed without any change to the window's state (remains minimized, normal, or maximized)
9	Restored to its previous state (neither minimized nor maximized); same as ahtSW_SHOWNORMAL

Table 11-5 Window display options, using Shell

For example, to start the Windows calculator maximized, use a statement like this:

```
ahtRunAppWait "CALC.EXE", 3
MsgBox "Done with the calculator."
```

You won't see the message box until you finish with the calculator.

How It Works

The secret to the ahtRunAppWait subroutine is its use of the Windows API function, GetModuleUsage (aliased as aht_apiGetModuleUsage in the code). This function takes as a parameter the instance handle of an application, started here with the Access Basic Shell command. It returns the number of instances of that application that are currently active. As long as the value is 1, the application is running. As soon as the value becomes 0, you know that it has stopped running.

Consider the following code, which will check for the existence of a running application:

```
hInstance = Shell(strCommand, intMode)
Do While GetModuleUsage(hInstance)
   ' Do nothing until the application has closed.
Loop
```

Though this will almost do what you need, it won't quite succeed. You've left Access running a tight loop, waiting for the new application to finish. Unfortunately, Access is grabbing all of the clock cycles in Windows, looping and waiting for the other application to be done. It won't be possible to quit the other application, because it will never get enough attention from Windows to even let you pull down a menu!

The solution, then, is to be a good Windows citizen, allowing other applications their processing time. To do this, you must add a DoEvents statement inside the loop. This allows other applications to do their own work as Access loops, waiting for the application you started to be finished. (See How-To 7.4 for more information on DoEvents.) Thus, the ahtRunAppWait subroutine looks like this:

```
Sub ahtRunAppWait (strCommand As String, intMode As Integer)

   ' Run an application, waiting for its completion
   ' before returning to the caller.
   Dim hInstance As Integer

   hInstance = Shell(strCommand, intMode)
   Do While aht_apiGetModuleUsage(hInstance)
      DoEvents
   Loop
End Sub
```

Comments

To use the Shell command, you must specify an executable file. If you need to run a DOS internal command, or if you need to redirect the output from a program to a text file, you'll have to load a second copy of COMMAND.COM to do your work. In addition, you'll have to use the /C parameter, indicating to COMMAND.COM that you just want a temporary instance and that it should quit when the program you run finishes. For example, to run the CHKDSK.EXE program directly, you could use the following function call. (All these examples assume that the necessary programs are available in the DOS PATH.)

```
hInstance = Shell("CHKDSK.EXE", 6)
```

To run DIR, on the other hand, you'll need to start COMMAND.COM first:

```
hInstance = Shell("COMMAND.COM /C DIR C:\*.BAT", 6)
```

To redirect the output from a program to a text file, you'll also need to use COMMAND.COM:

```
hInstance = Shell("COMMAND.COM /C CHKDSK C: > C:\AHTTEST.TXT", 6)
```

In our test cases, it was impossible to make a DOS application started with the Shell command run transparently. If we used mode 7, the application would run invisibly, but would not complete until we switched to it with (ALT)-(TAB). If we used mode 6, the DOS application would complete, but there was some screen updating as it swapped in and out. You might try replacing the 6 with 7 in the sample form's module, to see if it works better in your environment:

```
ahtRunAppWait "COMMAND.COM /C CHKDSK C: > C:\AHTTEST.TXT", 6
```

You may also want to investigate using the ShellExecute API function, as discussed in the How-To 11.7, to run your DOS application in a hidden window (which the Shell command in Access Basic doesn't support).

> ✏️ NOTE: You may want to study the FileRead subroutine in the sample form's module, which demonstrates how to open a text file and read its contents directly into a control on a form.

11.6 HOW DO I...   COMPLEXITY: INTERMEDIATE

Exit Windows under program control?

Problem
I'd like to be able to control what happens once I quit my applications. Sometimes I want to exit Windows at the same time or even perhaps reboot the machine. How can I do that from Access?

Technique
The Windows API provides two functions that grant you control over exiting Windows, and you have a choice of four different things you can do once you quit: stay in DOS, return to Windows directly, reboot the computer, or run a DOS program and when it's finished return to Windows. This How-To demonstrates these simple functions, and it will suggest situations in which you'd use each.

Steps
To try exiting Windows under program control, load and run frmExitWindows in 11-06.MDB. This sample form, shown in Figure 11-7, allows you to choose from the four exit options. Two of the options allow you to specify additional information: Choosing the Quit to DOS button lets you input the return code you want to send back to whatever process started Windows in the first place

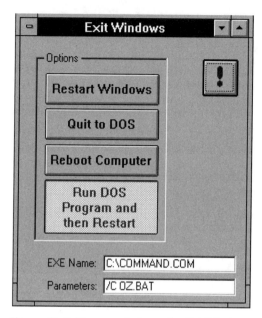

Figure 11-7 The sample form, frmExitWindows

(perhaps a DOS batch file). Choosing the Run DOS Program and then Restart Windows button lets you specify the DOS executable you'd like to run, along with any parameters you want to send to it. Figure 11-7 shows the form about to use this option. In this case, once the application quits Windows, it will run a batch file named OZ.BAT, and when that program is done, Windows will restart. Make your choice and click on the ! button, which will execute the necessary code to quit in the manner you've specified.

To use this functionality within your own applications, follow these steps:

1. Import the module basExitWindows from 11-06.MDB.
2. Call the function, chosen from Table 11-6, that best suits your needs. The table lists the function names and the necessary parameters. In each case, if the function returns at all, it indicates that some Windows process wasn't able to shut down, and your function call failed. This won't happen often.

   For example, to exit Windows and return a value of 1 to the calling process, you can use a function call like this one:

```
intRetval = ahtExitWindows(1)
```

Then, suppose you called Windows with a batch file like this:

```
:LabelTop
win myapp.mdb
if ErrorLevel 1 goto LabelTop
```

Though not terribly useful, this batch file will start Windows, run Access with your database loaded, and then wait for Windows to exit. Once the batch file regains control, if the ErrorLevel value is 1 or greater, it will loop back up to the label labelTop. For more information on batch file programming, refer to a DOS manual or reference book.

To exit Windows, run a DOS program, and then restart Windows, you'll need to call aht_apiExitWindowsExec, specifying the executable file and any parameters. If the program you want to run is an EXE program, just place its name in the first parameter, and any parameters for the program you're running as a string value in the second parameter to aht_apiExitWindowsExec. For example, to run the command line

```
ProFax /1
```

the function call would be this:

```
intRetval = aht_apiExitWindowsExec("ProFax.EXE", "/1")
```

If you need to run a batch file, however, you have to use COMMAND.COM with the /C option:

```
intRetval = aht_apiExitWindowsExec("C:\COMMAND.COM", "/C ProFax.BAT")
```

FUNCTION NAME	DESCRIPTION	TYPE	PARAMETERS
ahtExitWindows	Exit Windows, returning a return code value to the calling process (usually a batch file).	Access Basic	intRetCode (integer), an arbitrary return code
ahtReboot	Exit Windows, then reboot the computer.	Access Basic	None
ahtRestartWindows	Exit Windows, then immediately restart.	Access Basic	None
aht_apiExitWindowsExec	Exit Windows, run a DOS program, then restart Windows once that DOS program has finished.	API	strEXE (string), the DOS executable to run strParams (string), the parameters to send to that executable

Table 11-6 Available functions for exiting Windows

How It Works

When you quit Windows by your normal means, it sends a message around to check with every running application before shutting down. If other applications have any unsaved data files that require user intervention, you'll usually be asked if it's OK to save the files. Once all the applications have agreed to shutting down, Windows shuts itself down and returns to DOS.

Windows will follow the same shutdown procedures when you use any of the functions listed in Table 11-6. The only difference between the functions listed in the table is what happens after Windows shuts down.

Comments

Each of the four functions listed in Table 11-6 has its own role. You're most likely to use ahtExitWindows in a situation where your application is meant for users who *only* use Access. When they're done with your application, they're done with Windows! The other functions have more usefulness in utility applications rather than Access, but if you use your imagination, you may think of reasons why you'd need to reboot—perhaps you've changed a setting in CONFIG.SYS for the user, and you'd like it to take effect now. The same goes for ahtRestartWindows—perhaps you've made a change to SYSTEM.INI for the user, and now you'd like to restart Windows so it takes effect.

Certainly, these are not functions that every application will need or that you will use every day. But if you need to control what happens once your application has done its work, there's no replacing them!

11.7 HOW DO I...

COMPLEXITY: ADVANCED

Run an application associated with a given data file?

Problem

I'd like to provide a list of existing files and allow users to select a file and automatically run the appropriate application to edit that file. Windows knows how to do this—for instance, when I double-click on a file with a .TXT extension in File Manager, Windows runs Notepad with that file. How can I provide this sort of functionality in my own applications?

Technique

Windows provides two API functions, FindExecutable and ShellExecute, which make running a related application possible from within an Access application. They both rely heavily on the Windows registration database, REG.DAT, which tracks the relationships between file name extensions and related executable programs. Figure 11-8 shows the results of running the REGEDIT.EXE program, which ships as part of Windows. REGEDIT allows you to add, edit, modify, or delete file associations.

In this How-To, you use the FindExecutable function to get the name of the executable file associated with a selected data file. You also use the ShellExecute function to run the executable file, with the selected data file opened and ready to edit.

Steps

Load and run frmTestExecute, shown in Figure 11-9, from 11-07.MDB. To use this form, first select a path (it defaults to your Windows directory when it first loads). Once the list box has been filled with all the files in the specified directory, click on one of the files with the mouse. If there's an active file association in REG.DAT for the selected file, the form will display that executable file name in a text box. If there's an associated executable, you can run it and load your chosen file by double-clicking on the list box or by clicking on the check mark button.

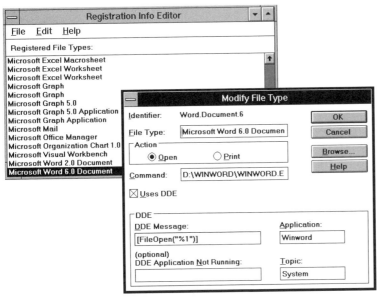

Figure 11-8 REGEDIT.EXE, showing file types registered on a typical system

To use this functionality in your own applications, follow these steps:

1. Import the module basShellAPI from 11-07.MDB into your application.
2. To find the executable file associated with a given document, use the FindExecutable function (aliased as aht_apiFindExecutable in the code). Call it with three parameters, as described in Table 11-7.

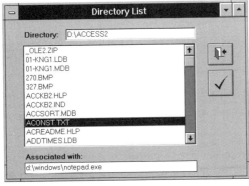

Figure 11-9 The sample form, frmTestExecute, from 11-07.MDB

PARAMETER NAME	DATA TYPE	DESCRIPTION
strFile	String	The file name that has an association in the registration database.
strDir	String	The drive letter and path for the default directory. (You can use "." to indicate the current directory.)
strResult	String	A buffer to contain the returned executable name.

Table 11-7 Parameters for the FindExecutable API function

The FindExecutable function returns an integer error code. If the value is greater than 32, the function succeeded. Otherwise, it returns one of the error codes in Table 11-8 (note that these error codes are shared by several functions). If the function succeeded, strResult will be a null-terminated string containing the associated executable file. You'll need to trim off that trailing null character, and one easy way to do it is by using the TrimNull function in basShellAPI:

```
Private Function TrimNull (strValue As String)

    ' Trim strValue at the first
    ' null character you find.

    Dim intPos As Integer
    intPos = InStr(strValue, Chr$(0))
    If intPos > 0 Then
        TrimNull = Left$(strValue, intPos - 1)
    Else
        TrimNull = strValue
    End If
End Function
```

VALUE	DESCRIPTION
0	System error occurred.
2	File not found.
3	Path not found.
5	Sharing violation occurred.
6	SHELL.DLL requires separate segments for each task.
8	Not enough memory to start the task.
10	Wrong Windows version used.
11	The EXE file is not a Windows application or is corrupted.
12	The EXE file is an OS/2 file or some other EXE format

Table 11-8 Shared error codes for FindExecutable and ShellExecute

VALUE	DESCRIPTION
13	The EXE file is an MS-DOS 4.0 application.
14	An unrecognized EXE file format was used.
15	The EXE file is a Windows 2.0 or Windows 3.0 "real mode" application that will not run under Windows 3.1.
16	The EXE file is already loaded into memory and only allows on instance to operate.
19	The EXE file is stored in compressed form.
20	A DLL required to run the EXE file is corrupted.
21	The EXE file requires 32-bit extensions, which were not located.
31	No association in the registration database for the file extension.

Table 11-8 Shared error codes for FindExecutable and ShellExecute

For example, the following code will find the executable file associated with MyFile.OOG:

```
Dim strBuffer As String
Dim strResult As String

strBuffer = Space(128)
strResult = ""

intRetval = aht_apiFindExecutable("MyFile.OOG", ".", strBuffer)
If intRetval > 32 Then
    ' Use the TrimNull() function, in basShellAPI,
    ' to remove the trailing Null character
    strResult = TrimNull(strBuffer)
End If
' Now, strResult holds either "" or the
' name of the executable you need.
```

To make this simpler, basShellAPI includes the ahtFindExecutable function. This function requires the same parameters and returns the same values as aht_apiFindExecutable, but it handles the details of initializing the string buffer and trimming off the trailing null for you. You'll want to use this function, rather than calling the Windows API directly, since it will ensure that you use the correct methods for sending and receiving strings.

3. Once you know the name of the executable file associated with the selected document, you'll want to execute it with the ShellExecute API function. You could, of course, use the Access Basic Shell command, but ShellExecute gives you a bit more flexibility. Specifically:

✎ ShellExecute returns an error code if something goes wrong, but Shell requires that you write Access Basic error-handling code to trap and deal with errors. Using ShellExecute is far simpler in the long run.

🔑   ShellExecute can load applications hidden; Shell can only load applications visibly.

To use this function, you'll need to call it with six parameters as shown in Table 11-9.

PARAMETER NAME	DATA TYPE	DESCRIPTION
hWnd	Integer	The handle of the window to be used as the parent for message boxes that may appear.
strOp	String	The operation to perform; normally, only "open" or "print."
strFile	String	Name of the program to start.
strParams	String	Command line arguments for the executable program; normally, the name of the file to load into the application.
strDir	String	The default drive/directory for the application when it starts up.
intShowCmd	Integer	Specification of how to show the new window when the application starts up. For a list of values, see Table 11-10.

Table 11-9 Parameters for the ShellExecute API function

Table 11-10 lists all the possible values you can use for the intShowCmd parameter. These values control how the new application's window appears on the Windows desktop.

CONSTANT NAME	VALUE	DESCRIPTION
ahtSW_HIDE	0	The window is hidden when started.
ahtSW_MINIMIZE	6	The window is minimized (as an icon) when started.
ahtSW_SHOWNORMAL	1	The window is restored to its previous state (neither minimized nor maximized).
ahtSW_RESTORE	9	The window is restored to its previous state (neither minimized nor maximized). (Same as ahtSW_SHOWNORMAL.)
ahtSW_SHOW	5	The window is made visible.
ahtSW_SHOWMAXIMIZED	3	The window is made visible and maximized.
ahtSW_SHOWMINIMIZED	2	The window is made visible and minimized.
ahtSW_SHOWMINNOACTIVE	7	The window is made visible and minimized, but it doesn't receive the input focus.
ahtSW_SHOWNA	8	The window is displayed without any change to the window's state (remains minimized, normal, or maximized).
ahtSW_SHOWNOACTIVATE	4	The window is displayed, but doesn't gain the input focus.

Table 11-10 Window display options for the intShowCmd parameter to ShellExecute

For example, to run the program C:\OOGLY\MKOOGLE.EXE, (which created MyFile.OOG), maximized on the screen, you could run code like this from a form's module:

```
intRetval = aht_apiShellExecute(Me.hWnd, "open", ⇒
"C:\OOGLY\MKOOGLE.EXE", "MyFile.OOG", "C:\OOGLY", ahtSW_SHOWMAXIMIZED)
```

How It Works

Normally, you'll use the FindExecutable function to retrieve an associated executable file for a given document, and then you'll pass both the executable name and the document name to ShellExecute to load them. For example, you might use code like this in your application:

```
Dim intRetval As Integer
Dim strBuffer As String

strBuffer = Space(255)
intRetval = ahtFindExecutable("MyFile.XXX", ".", strBuffer)
strBuffer = TrimNull(strBuffer)
If intRetval > 32 Then
    ' You're only here if you found the executable.
    intRetval = aht_apiShellExecute(Me.hWnd, "open", strBuffer, ⇒
    "MyFile.XXX", "C:\NewDocs", ahtSW_SHOWMAXIMIZED)
    If intRetval <= 32 Then
        MsgBox "Unable to load application. Error " & intRetval & "."
    End If
Else
    MsgBox "Unable to find executable. Error " & intRetval & "."
End If
```

Comments

You may find it interesting to work your way through the sample form, frmTestExecute. It borrows code presented in other chapters to provide the list of files, but once you've selected a file it uses code very similar to the previous code sample to find and load the associated executable.

The methods presented in this How-To rely heavily on the Windows registration database, which wasn't included in Windows 3.0. Clearly, these methods won't work with that version of Windows. You're not likely to be running Access on Windows 3.0, so this shouldn't be a problem. It could be, however, that you or users of your applications may have incorrectly registered applications, or are using a damaged REG.DAT file. The Windows application registration is prone to errors, so be prepared to manually edit registration information (using REGEDIT.EXE), if things don't appear to be working correctly when you use FindExecutable and ShellExecute.

11.8 HOW DO I...   COMPLEXITY: INTERMEDIATE

Check to see if an application is already running?

Problem

I need to start other Windows programs from my Access application—for instance, to send data to Excel or to format a report in Word for Windows. If I just use the Shell command to start them, it's quite possible I'll end up with multiple instances of the application. How can I tell if an application is already running before I attempt to start it?

Technique

There are a number of solutions to this problem, and none, unfortunately, is as easy as you'd like. In order to ask Windows, "Is Excel currently running?" and get an answer, you must know the Windows class name for the main window of the application. This How-To explains the format of the question and how to ask it. In addition, this How-To will demonstrate how to switch to a running application from your Access application.

Steps

Normally, you need to know whether a specific application is currently running so that you can either activate that application or use it as part of a DDE conversation (see Chapter 12 for more information on DDE). The sample form, frmAppsRunning (Figure 11-10), asks Windows the question, "Is this app running?" for each of six predefined window classes, and you can add one more of your own. For each application that frmAppsRunning finds, it fills in the hWnd (window handle column) and Window Caption column on the

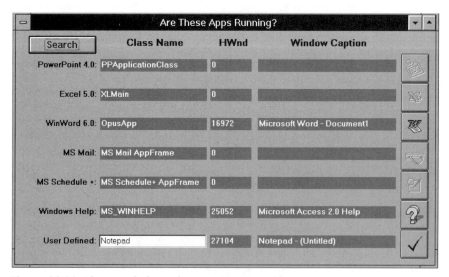

Figure 11-10 The sample form, frmAppsRunning, shows the state of certain applications

form. The AppActivate command in Access requires that you know the exact title of the window, so the form uses code from Chapter 4 (in basAccessCaption) to retrieve the caption for each running application. Finally, you can click on any of the enabled buttons in the right-hand column to switch to the running application.

Try the sample form with Microsoft applications that you have installed. Press (F1) to bring up Help, and then switch back to Access and click on the Search button on the sample form. This will reinitiate the search for active applications, and it will find WINHELP.EXE running. Click on the question mark icon to switch back to WinHelp.

Follow these steps to include this functionality in your own applications:

1. Import the modules listed in Table 11-11 from 11-08.MDB into your application.

MODULE NAME	CONTAINS
basCaption	ahtGetAccessCaption, ahtGetWindowCaption, ahtSetAccessCaption
basGetHWnd	ahtFindAccessHWnd
basUsage	ahtIsAppLoaded

Table 11-11 Modules to import from 11-08.MDB

2. To be able to ask Windows the question, "Is <some Application> running?", you'll need to know the Windows class name for the main window of the application. Table 11-12 lists the names for several Windows applications. As you can see from the table, the class names appear to be somewhat arbitrary. Since they're assigned not by the marketing or documentation departments, but rather by the development staff, they often reflect the project's code name or the state of mind of the developer.

FINDING CLASS NAMES

If you need the names of other applications, you'll have to do some digging. Contact the manufacturer, or use a tool that will tell you the class name. We've supplied such a tool, the freeware SUPERSPY.EXE, on the disk that comes with this book. SuperSpy, among other things, will tell you the class name for a selected window. To determine the class name for the main window of an application, run the application, then run SuperSpy. Choose the Select button on SuperSpy's main screen, and move the question mark cursor around the screen until you've highlighted your application's main window. The Class text box will tell you the class name you need. Figure 11-11 shows SuperSpy retrieving information about the Word for Windows main window.

APPLICATION	CLASS NAME
Access	OMain
Calculator	SciCalc
Excel	XLMain
File Manager	WFS_Frame
MS Mail	MS Mail AppFrame
MS Schedule +	MS Schedule+ AppFrame
Notepad	Notepad
Paintbrush	pbParent
PowerPoint	PPApplicationClass
Print Manager	PrintManager
Program Manager	Progman
Windows Help	MS_WINHELP
Windows Write	MSWRITE_MENU
Word for Windows	OpusApp

Table 11-12 Class names for some Windows applications

3. To check and see whether a given application is currently running, use the ahtIsAppLoaded function, in basUsage. You pass a class name to this function as a parameter, and it returns the window handle of the application if it's running or 0 if it's not. For example,

```
hWnd = ahtIsAppRunning("ms_winhelp")
```

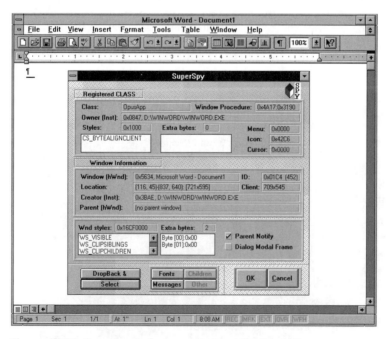

Figure 11-11 SuperSpy (a freeware spying utility) in action

will return a nonzero value if Windows Help is currently running. (Note that the class names are not case-sensitive.)

4. Once you know the window handle for the application, if you want to make that application active, you can use the AppActivate command in Access. To switch to the application, though, you'll need to know the exact window caption. To make that easier, you can call the ahtGetWindowCaption function, in basCaption, *before* attempting to activate the application. For example, this code will switch to Excel, if it's running:

```
Dim hWnd as Integer

hWnd = ahtIsAppLoaded("XLMain")
If hWnd <> 0 Then
     AppActivate ahtGetWindowCaption(hWnd)
End If
```

5. If the application you want to activate isn't currently running (ahtIsAppLoaded returned 0), you'll want to use the Shell command. In this case, you need to know the DOS executable file name for the given application (EXCEL.EXE, for example). The example form doesn't attempt to load the applications if they aren't already loaded, because that would require them to be in your DOS path.

How It Works

The ahtIsAppLoaded function couldn't be simpler: It calls a single Windows API function. The entire routine looks like this:

```
Function ahtIsAppLoaded (ByVal varClassName As Variant) As Integer
   If IsNull(varClassName) Then
      ahtIsAppLoaded = False
   Else
      ahtIsAppLoaded = aht_apiFindWindow(CStr(varClassName), 0&)
   End If
End Function
```

It allows you to pass in a class name, which might be null. If the class name isn't null, the function calls the FindWindow (aliased as aht_apiFindWindow) API function, which takes a class name and returns the window handle of the first instance it finds of that class. AhtIsAppLoaded returns that handle back to its caller.

Comments

Don't expect ahtIsAppLoaded to distinguish between multiple copies of the same application. That is, if you have two copies of Notepad running, you can't count on ahtIsAppLoaded to return the handle to a specific instance of Notepad. It will return the handle of the first one it comes across.

There are other ways to determine whether an application is currently running. One method uses an application's module name to find its main window. The module name is the name applied to the application when the programmer puts the whole thing together. The problem with module names is that they're harder to find—often, they're the same as the name of the executable file, but sometimes they're not. Since SuperSpy does such a great job of digging up window class names, and since it's free, we recommend you use the method in this How-To.

11.9 HOW DO I...   COMPLEXITY: INTERMEDIATE

Retrieve a list of all the top-level windows?

Problem

I know I can determine if specific applications are currently running (I learned how to do that in How-To 11.8), but I'd like to obtain just a list of all the running applications. That way, I could decide, as part of my application, what to present to my users. Is there a way to walk through all the open main windows and build up a list?

Technique

Windows is nothing if not hierarchical: It includes API functions that allow you to walk down and around the tree of open windows, starting with the main desktop window. This How-To provides a function that will do that for you, filling an array with information on each top-level window. You can then use that array to list applications, switch to them, or close them (see the How-To 11.10 for information on closing other windows).

Steps

Load and run frmListWindows from 11-09.MDB. This sample form fills a list box with all the top-level windows and provides a button that will use the AppActivate command in Access Basic to display the selected window. You'll find that some top-level windows are hidden, and you won't be able to display them (Dde Common, for example, on the test system). Figure 11-12 shows the sample form in action.

Figure 11-12 The sample form, frmListWindows, allowing you to select and display any of the top-level windows

To include this functionality in your own applications, follow these steps:

1. Import the module basWindowList from 11-09.MDB. This module includes the API declarations, constants, and wrapper functions you'll need to list and select top-level windows.

2. In your code, declare an array of type aht_tagWindowInfo to hold the list of open windows, like this:

```
Dim atypWindowList() As aht_tagWindowInfo
```

3. Call ahtWindowList, passing your array to be filled in. The function returns the number of windows it found. After the function call, your array will have *intCount* rows, with each row containing information about a specific top-level window.

```
intCount = ahtWindowList(atypWindowList())
```

4. In your application, decide which (if any) window you'd like to display, perhaps by looping through all the elements of the array. Use the AppActivate command, along with the window name, to activate the selected window:

```
AppActivate atypWindowList(intI).strCaption
```

How It Works

Windows provides three functions, used in ahtWindowList, for navigating through its hierarchy of windows. Table 11-13 describes the three functions (all are aliased with the "aht_api" tag in the code).

FUNCTION NAME	DESCRIPTION
GetDesktopHWnd	Retrieve the window handle for the main desktop window. All applications are children of this window.
GetWindow	Find a window, in a specified relation to a specified window. In this case, you'll be looking for the first child window of the desktop window.
GetNextWindow	Given a window handle, and a direction (next or previous), find the requested sibling of the specified window.

Table 11-13 Windows API navigation functions

The ahtWindowList function first retrieves a handle to the main desktop window, using GetDesktopHWnd. Once it knows that, it can find the handle for the desktop's first child window, using GetWindow. From then on, as long as the handle for the current window isn't 0, the code loops, filling in the array with information about the current window and then moving on to the next window with the GetNextWindow function. You'll note that the loop skips windows without captions (of which there are quite a few). Windows maintains a number of top-level hidden windows without captions for its own use.

```
Type aht_tagWindowInfo
    strCaption As String
    hWnd As Integer
End Type

Function ahtWindowList (atypWL() As aht_tagWindowInfo) As Integer

    ' Fill an array with a list of all the currently
    ' open top-level windows.

    Dim hWnd As Integer
    Dim strCaption As String
    Dim intCount As Integer

    ' Get the desktop window, and from there,
    ' the first top-level window.
    hWnd = aht_apiGetDesktopHwnd()
    hWnd = aht_apiGetWindow(hWnd, GW_CHILD)

    ' Loop through all the top-level windows.
    Do While hWnd <> 0

        strCaption = ahtGetCaption(hWnd)
        If Len(strCaption) > 0 Then
            ' If you got a caption, add one element
            ' to the output array, and fill in the
            ' information (name and hWnd).
            ReDim Preserve atypWL(0 To intCount)
            atypWL(intCount).strCaption = strCaption
            atypWL(intCount).hWnd = hWnd
            intCount = intCount + 1
        End If
        ' Move to the next top-level window.
        hWnd = aht_apiGetNextWindow(hWnd, GW_HWNDNEXT)

    Loop

    ' Return the number of windows.
    ahtWindowList = intCount
End Function
```

Comments

You may find it instructive to study the code in the sample form's module. It calls ahtWindowList, and then uses a list-filling callback function to fill the list box on the form with the window captions and hWnds. This is a perfect example of when you'd use such a function: when you need to fill a control with data from an array that couldn't be gathered until the application is running.

Some of the windows on the list exist at the time the form is filling its list, but they aren't available (the Access Immediate Window, for example). You can attempt to switch to them, but the attempt will fail. The code attached to the check mark button's Click event disregards errors, so it just keeps going if an error occurs when it tries to switch the active window. See the next How-To for information on deleting windows in this list.

11.10 HOW DO I... COMPLEXITY: INTERMEDIATE

Close a running Windows application?

Problem
As part of some of my large Access applications, I often allow users to start other Windows tools (Notepad, Calculator, Calendar, and so on), and once those tools are open, my application doesn't touch them. Some users have been complaining about all the "junk" left over once my application closes. Is there some way I can close another window from my Access application? That way, on the way out, I can attempt to close any tools my application has opened.

Technique
How-To 11.9 demonstrated retrieval of a list of all the running Windows applications' captions and window handles. Once you know that information, it's a trivial task to close an application: Given a window handle, just tell it to close. Using the Windows API PostMessage function, you can close any window at any time. Note that newer applications such as Excel 5 and Word for Windows 6 support OLE Automation to the extent that you can close them from Access Basic without using the Windows API. Other applications that don't support OLE Automation will either require the API method described here or SendKeys, which is, at best, unreliable.

Steps
Load and run frmListWindows from 11-10.MDB. This form, shown in Figure 11-13, is the same sample form as in How-To 11.9, with the addition of the stop sign button, which lets you close the selected window. Try a few (you can even close Access this way, if you want).

> ### DON'T TRY THIS AT HOME
> Some top-level windows shouldn't be closed—you should never include a form like this as part of an end-user application. On the other hand, given an array of window captions and handles, you could programmatically decide which window to close and close it yourself from within your application. This form is a demonstration of the power of the method, not a tool you'd actually use.

To use this functionality in your own applications, follow these steps:

1. Import the modules basWindowList (if you didn't do that for How-To 11.9) and basCloseWindows.

2. Follow the steps listed in How-To 11.9 to create and fill in the array of top-level windows.

3. Decide which window you want to close, if any. Since Windows sometimes appends document names to the application name (such as "Microsoft Word - 11-10.DOC"), you'll need to check against just the first portion of the window name in your array. For example:

```
For intI = 0 To intCount - 1
   If Left$(atypWindowList(0).strCaption, 14) = "Microsoft Word" Then
      ' You found a match. Do something.
   End If
Next intI
```

4. When you've found the item you want to close, use the ahtCloseWindow function, passing to it the handle of the window you care about:

```
If ahtCloseWindow(atypWindowList(intI).hWnd) = 0 Then
   ' If you got 0 back, it got the message!
End If
```

How It Works

The ahtCloseWindow function calls the PostMessage API function. By posting a message to a particular window, you send it a message telling it to do something, but you don't bother waiting for a result (the corresponding API function, SendMessage, *does* cause you to wait for a response). The ahtCloseWindow function sends the WM_CLOSE message to your chosen window, telling it to shut down. It's as if you had quit your Windows Shell program with some applications still running. Your shell sends a message to

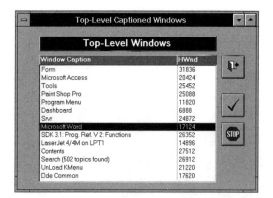

Figure 11-13 The revised frmListWindows, including a "kill" button to close top-level windows

each main application window to shut down because Windows is shutting down. The ahtCloseWindow function, then, looks like this:

```
Function ahtCloseWindow (ByVal hWnd As Integer)

Const APINULL = 0&
Const WM_CLOSE = &H10

   ahtCloseWindow = aht_apiPostMessage(hWnd, WM_CLOSE, 0, APINULL)
End Function
```

The purpose of this Access Basic wrapper function that calls PostMessage is just to shield you from having to remember how to post a message to a window. It's a lot simpler to call ahtCloseWindow than to call PostMessage directly.

Comments
Sending a WM_CLOSE message to a window doesn't necessarily close it. If that application has an unsaved document that needs saving, it will pop up its own dialog box asking what you want to do with that unsaved document. In the sample form, if this happens, the list box won't be updated correctly. Once you return from your duties with the foreign application, press the Requery button on the form to force it to search again for all open applications.

11.11 HOW DO I...   COMPLEXITY: ADVANCED

Retrieve file date and time stamps?

Problem
I need to retrieve the modification date and time for files on disk. One of my applications is a document-handling system, and I want to display on a form the last date and time of modification for each document in the system. I know I can do some ugly tricks with DOS batch files, redirecting directory listings to text files, but there has to be a better way. Is there a Windows API call to retrieve this information?

Technique
Though there's no function that does specifically what you want here, the solution is buried in the OpenFile API function. Rather than actually opening a file, you'll need to use one of the function's special capabilities: It determines whether a file exists, and if so, retrieves information about the file. This How-To shows you how to retrieve information about DOS files programmatically.

Steps
The sample form, frmTimeStamp, allows you to select a file name. Then the function displays the date and time of last modification for the file, as shown in Figure 11-14.

To retrieve file date and time information in your own applications, follow these steps:

1. Import the module basTimeStamp from 11-11.MDB. This module includes the type definitions and Windows API declarations you'll need. It also includes an Access Basic function to convert dates and times as retrieved from the API call into a date/time value that Access can understand.

2. To retrieve the modification date information about a specific file, call the ahtGetTimeStamp function, passing it a file name as a parameter. For example, the following code will place the modification time and date for C:\AUTOEXEC.BAT into the variant variable, varDate:

```
varDate = ahtGetTimeStamp("C:\AUTOEXEC.BAT")
```

How It Works

Though the steps involved in using this functionality don't appear to be very complex, there's a lot of work going on behind the scenes, both in the Access Basic routines you call (ahtGetTimeStamp) and in Windows itself. When you call ahtGetTimeStamp, you're actually using the OpenFile function from the Windows API (aliased as aht_apiOpenFile in the code), which does most of the work. It requires three parameters: a file name, a structure of type aht_tagOFSTRUCT (see below for more information on this structure), and a flag telling it what to do with the specified file name. In this case, OpenFile is being sent the value OF_EXIST in the final parameter, telling it that all you want to do is verify that the file exists. If the file does exist, OpenFile fills in the aht_tagOFSTRUCT value with information about the specified file, and it's from this structure that you'll extract the modification date and time. If OpenFile can't find the file you specified, it returns HFILE_ERROR (–1).

If you specify only a file name and extension for the first parameter, OpenFile will look through a series of documented locations for your file. It looks through these locations in this order:

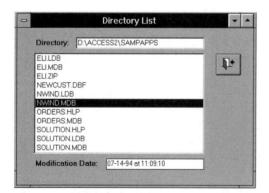

Figure 11-14 The sample form, frmTimeStamp, showing the modification date and time of a selected file

⚿ The current directory

⚿ The Windows directory (the directory containing WIN.COM)

⚿ The Windows system directory (the directory containing such system files as GDI.EXE)

⚿ The directory containing MSACCESS.EXE (or MSARN200.EXE)

⚿ Directories listed in the PATH environment variable

⚿ The list of directories mapped in a network

If you want to find a specific copy of a file that exists in more than one location on your hard disk, your best bet is to pass the exact path and file name to ahtGetTimeStamp. Otherwise, you can't be assured that OpenFile will find the copy you care about.

A successful call to OpenFile will fill in the fields of the aht_tagOFSTRUCT structure that ahtGetTimeStamp sent to it. The data type is defined, in the declarations area of basTimeStamp, as follows (see Table 11-14 for descriptions of the components):

```
Type aht_tagOFSTRUCT
  cBytes As String * 1
  fFixedDisk As String * 1
  nErrCode As Integer
  Date1 As String * 1
  Date2 As String * 1
  Time1 As String * 1
  Time2 As String * 1
  szPathName As String * 128
End Type
```

FIELD NAME	DESCRIPTION
cBytes	Size, in bytes, of the structure (use Asc to retrieve this value)
fFixedDisk	Nonzero if the file is on a fixed disk
nErrCode	If nonzero, indicates the error that occurred in attempting to open the file
Date1	Low byte of the 16-bit value containing the file's date
Date2	High byte of the 16-bit value containing the file's date
Time1	Low byte of the 16-bit value containing the file's time
Time2	High byte of the 16-bit value containing the file's time
szPathName	Complete file path for the file located by OpenFile

Table 11-14 Members of the aht_tagOFSTRUCT structure

Calling OpenFile itself is simple, as you can see from the ahtGetTimeStamp function:

```
Function ahtGetTimeStamp (ByVal strFileName As String) As Variant
   Dim typOF As aht_tagOFSTRUCT

Const HFILE_ERROR = -1
Const OF_EXIST = &H4000

   If aht_apiOpenFile(strFileName, typOF, OF_EXIST) <> HFILE_ERROR Then
      ahtGetTimeStamp = GetDate(typOF)
   End If
End Function
```

Difficulties arise from the need to extract the date and time from the aht_tagOFSTRUCT value: They are stored in there as they are in DOS, as packed bitmaps. Though the exact methods involved in the retrieval of these values is beyond the scope of this How-To, the ideas aren't all that complex. To save space, DOS doesn't store file date and time values with separate 16-bit integers holding each of the pieces. Instead, DOS stores these values packed into two 16-bit values, with chunks of the bits holding each of the six values (year, month, day, hour, minute, second). The GetDate function in basTimeStamp does the required bit manipulations to convert these bit-packed values into a variant. Very, very few Access Basic programmers are ever going to need to know how to perform these conversions, so the details of the GetDate function will be left to the reader. (If you're interested, you'll need to find a DOS reference that describes the exact layout of the files' date and time values.)

Comments

The date and time bytes of the aht_tagOFSTRUCT data structure have generally been documented as "reserved" in the Microsoft Windows SDK documentation, though they've been used for the date and time information since Windows 3.0. As with any undocumented values, it's possible that their use might change in future versions of Windows. You'll want to revisit this topic any time you start using a new version of Windows with your Access applications.

11.12 HOW DO I... COMPLEXITY: INTERMEDIATE

Retrieve information about the disk drives in my computer?

Problem

I'd like to be able to gather specific information about the disk drives in my computer; for example, how large they are, how much space is free, whether they're local or remote, and whether they're removable or not. Certainly, Access doesn't provide this information. Is it available using a Windows API function?

Technique

Surprisingly, the Windows API does not provide information about disk drives. To gather this data requires digging into DOS APIs. You can avoid the details, however, by using MSSETUP.DLL, a DLL that ships with every Microsoft desktop product (Access, Access Developer's Toolkit, Excel, PowerPoint, Word, and Office, to name a few). The Microsoft SETUP.EXE uses this DLL to gather information on your hardware, and you can use it too. It is part of the Access runtime, so you can distribute the DLL with your applications as well. This How-To demonstrates a few of the functions in MSSETUP.DLL that will make gathering disk information a snap.

Steps

To test the functions in MSSETUP.DLL, load and run frmDiskSpace from 11-12.MDB. This form, shown in Figure 11-15, contains a list box with information on all 26 possible drives. To fill the list box, Access Basic code walks through all the possible drives, calling the functions in MSSETUP.DLL for each drive.

To use these functions in your own applications, follow these steps:

1. Make sure that MSSETUP.DLL is available and in one of the following directories:

🔑 The current directory

🔑 The Windows directory (the directory containing WIN.COM)

🔑 The Windows system directory (the directory containing such system files as GDI.EXE)

🔑 The directory containing MSACCESS.EXE (or MSARN200.EXE)

🔑 Directories listed in the PATH environment variable

🔑 The list of directories mapped in a network

Drive	Free Space	Total Space	Network	Local	Removable
C	27,049,984	340,746,240	No	Yes	No
D	1,023,998,976	1,023,998,976	No	Yes	No
E	66,387,968	304,996,352	No	Yes	No
F	56,025,088	273,006,592	No	Yes	No
G	55,148,544	150,892,544	Yes	No	No
H	12,976,128	13,066,240	No	Yes	No
I	0	134,215,680	Yes	No	No
J	0	0	No	No	No
K	0	0	No	No	No
L	0	0	No	No	No
M	0	0	No	No	No
N	0	0	No	No	No
O	0	0	No	No	No

☐ Include Floppies

Figure 11-15 The sample form, frmDiskSpace, showing information on all the installed drives

If Access can't find MSSETUP.DLL in any of these locations, it will send you a "File Not Found" error message. Your best bet is to copy it from the ACCESS\SETUP directory to the WINDOWS\SYSTEM directory.

2. Import the module basDiskInfo from 11-12.MDB.

3. To call the functions, use the information in Table 11-15. Each function takes as its only parameter a string expression beginning with the drive you are interested in.

FUNCTION NAME	DESCRIPTION	RETURN VALUE	EXAMPLE
aht_apiFreeSpace	Retrieve the amount of free space on the specified drive.	Long (the amount of free disk space, in bytes)	lngFree = aht_apiFreeSpace("C")
aht_apiTotalSpace	Retrieve the total amount of space on the specified drive.	Long (the total amount of disk space, in bytes)	lngTotal = aht_apiTotalSpace("D")
aht_apiIsDriveLocal	Verify that the specified drive is local.	Integer (1 if the drive is local, 0 otherwise)	fLocal = aht_apiIsDriveLocal("C")
aht_apiIsDriveNetwork	Verify that the specified drive is a network drive.	Integer (1 if the drive is remote, 0 otherwise)	fNetwork = aht_apiIsDriveNetwork("E")
aht_apiIsDriveRemovable	Verify that the specified drive is for removable media.	Integer (1 if the drive uses removable media, 0 otherwise)	fRemovable = aht_apiIsDriveRemovable("I")

Table 11-15 The Access Basic functions in basDiskInfo that call MSSETUP.DLL

How It Works

As with any other DLL, you must supply the necessary Declare statements in order to be able to call external routines. (These declarations are in basDiskInfo, which you imported in step 2, above.) In this case, the functions are not part of the "official" Windows API, but exist in the vendor-supplied DLL, MSSETUP.DLL. To use these functions, you must ensure that Windows can find the DLL by moving it to a reasonable location first.

Even though the functions mentioned here are not part of the official Windows API, you can call any DLL function that is set up correctly to be called from Basic in an Access Basic program. MSSETUP.DLL contains many functions that you can't call from Access and some that aren't of interest to Access programmers. But the functions listed in Table 11-15 can be useful as part of installation routines you might need from within your Access applications, or anywhere else you need information about the storage media in your computer.

Comments

There are two known problems with MSSETUP.DLL. Since the disk space functions return long integers, you can use the functions only with drives no larger than the largest value a long integer can hold: 2,147,483,647 bytes. In addition, the DLL's algorithm seems to have a problem: With drives larger than 1 gigabyte or so, the free space and total size functions return invalid values (perhaps future versions of this DLL will solve this problem). One solution is to use SETUPKIT.DLL, which ships with the Visual Basic Professional Edition (VBPE). This DLL can find the amount of free space on the current drive only, but it has two advantages over MSSETUP.DLL:

- It works correctly with drive sizes up to the maximum value of a long integer.

- The DLL (SETUPKIT.DLL) is significantly smaller than MSSETUP.DLL.

On the other hand, SETUPKIT.DLL doesn't ship with every copy of every Microsoft product, so your users might not have it. If you own the VBPE, however, you have the rights to distribute SETUPKIT.DLL.

To use this DLL, include this declaration in your application:

```
Declare Function DiskSpaceFree Lib "SETUPKIT.DLL" () As Long
```

Since this function can find the amount of free space on the current drive only, you'll need to include code to change the current drive, for example:

```
Dim lngFree As Long
Dim strCurrent As String
Dim strNewDrive As String

strNewDrive = "C:"
strCurrent = Left$(CurDir$, 2)
ChDrive strNewDrive
lngFree = DiskSpaceFree()
ChDrive strCurrent
```

Though slightly less convenient, this method correctly returns the amount of free space on the current drive, up to 2,147,483,647 bytes.

11.13 HOW DO I...
COMPLEXITY: ADVANCED

Collect and display information about the system and the Access installation?

Problem

To add polish to my application I would like to include an About... dialog box that displays Windows information, such as the free system resources and the screen resolution. I'd also like to display the Access user's name and some of the settings found under the View|Options menu. How can I gather this information?

Technique

You can use the Windows API to retrieve information about the system on which your program is running. Access itself also provides a variety of functions to retrieve information about its own internal state. By using these various functions as the control sources for unbound controls, you can present a selection of system information to your user.

Steps

Load 11-13.MDB and open frmSystemInfo in regular form view. The values shown on your screen will, of course, differ from those shown in Figure 11-16, depending on your hardware and the other software you have running. If you like the look of this form, use it as is in your own applications. (You'll still need to import the form, frmSystemInfo, and the module, basSystemInformation, into your application, as directed in step 1, below.) To create a similar form in your own application, follow these steps:

1. Import the module basSystemInformation from 11-13.MDB to your own application. This module contains all the constants, API declarations, and Access Basic wrapper functions that you'll need.

2. Create a new, blank form. Place an unbound text box on the form for each piece of information you wish to display. Set the control source of each text box as shown in Table 11-16.

ITEM	CONTROL SOURCE
Current User	=ahtAccessInfo("CurrentUser")
OLE/DDE Timeout	=ahtAccessInfo("OLE Timeout")
DDE Requests	=ahtAccessInfo("DDERequests")
First Weekday	=ahtAccessInfo("FirstWeekday")
Default Record Locks	=ahtAccessInfo("RecordLocking")
Default Open Mode	=ahtAccessInfo("DefaultMode")
Current Database	=ahtAccessInfo("CurrentDB")
Jet Version	=ahtAccessInfo("JetVersion")
CPU Type	=ahtCPU ( )
DOS Version	=ahtDOSver ( )
Free Memory	=ahtFreeMemory ( ) & "K"
Free Resources	=ahtFreeResources & "%"
GDI Free Resources	=ahtGDIFreeResources ( ) & "%"
User Free Resources	=ahtUserFreeResources ( ) & "%"
Number of Tasks	=ahtNumTasks ( )
Screen Resolution	=ahtScreenX ( ) & " by " & ahtScreenY()
Coprocessor	=ahtWinCoprocessor ( )
Windows Mode	=ahtWinMode ( )
Windows Version	=ahtWinVer ( )

Table 11-16 Control sources used for text boxes on frmSystemInfo

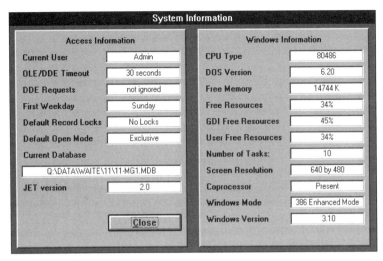

Figure 11-16 The demo form, frmSystemInfo

3. Add a command button to your form. Name the button cmdClose, set its caption to "&Close", and create an event procedure with the following code attached to the button's Click event (see this book's Introduction for more information on creating event procedures):

```
Sub cmdClose_Click ()
    DoCmd Close
End Sub
```

4. Set the Default property of cmdClose to yes. Choose Edit|Tab Order and drag cmdClose to the top of the control order, so it has the focus when the form is opened.

5. Save your form and switch it into form view. The unbound text box controls will display the system information you requested.

How It Works

The functions used here employ a variety of techniques to return the requested information. Access itself returns the Access information, and the functions query the low-level Windows API to retrieve hardware and windows environment information. Each low-level function is wrapped in an Access function to provide basic error checking.

Retrieving Access Information

The ahtAccessInfo function uses a Select Case statement to choose which piece of information to return, depending on a single text argument passed into the function.

- The Access user's name is returned by the CurrentUser function (which replaces the User function of Access 1.x). If security has not been activated, the user's name will always be Admin.

- Most of the other information about Access is returned by the Application object's GetOption method. The Application object represents the current instance of Access itself. The GetOption method allows you to read the state of any of the items normally found under the View|Options menu. To use this method, you have to present the exact text of the option name as an argument.

- The remaining information returned by ahtAccessInfo is read directly from the properties of objects. The Name property of the current database gives you the full path and file name of the database itself. The Version property of the DBEngine object identifies the version of the Jet database engine that is running on the user's system.

Retrieving Windows Information

The example form uses several functions to return information about the current installation of Windows.

- The ahtCPU, ahtWinCoprocessor, and ahtWinMode functions use the GetWinFlags API function to return information about the memory and system state. This function returns a single long integer with each bit indicating a different flag value. The sample database uses symbolic constants for these flag values in order to make the code more readable.

- ahtDOSver and ahtWinver use the Windows GetVersion function to return information on the DOS and Windows versions currently installed. This information is returned as four separate bytes packed into a single 32-bit long integer, and the functions perform appropriate hexadecimal arithmetic to extract the packed information.

- ahtFreeMemory uses the GetFreespace API function to retrieve the size of the global heap. This includes virtual memory space, if there is a swap file on the computer.

- ahtFreeResources, ahtGDIFreeResources, and ahtUserFreeResources all call the GetFreeSystemResources API function. When large applications (such as Access) are running, monitoring free resources can become a critical part of the application. In general, any time your free resources drop below 10 percent, Windows will become unstable.

- ahtNumTasks uses GetNumTasks to count the number of items on the task list. This may be larger than the number of applications running, since some applications spawn multiple hidden tasks.

☞ ahtScreenX and ahtScreenY use the GetSystemMetrics API function to return the size of the screen in pixels. This API function can return many other pieces of information about your system, including the width of the window borders, the size of icons, and whether or not a mouse is installed. You can use this function to retrieve a great number of details about the current Windows installation. To call it, you just pass it one of the constants in Table 11-17, and it returns the requested value to you.

CONSTANT NAME	VALUE	DESCRIPTION
SM_CXSCREEN	0	Width of screen.
SM_CYSCREEN	1	Height of screen.
SM_CXVSCROLL	2	Width of arrow bitmap on a vertical scroll bar.
SM_CYHSCROLL	3	Height of arrow bitmap on a horizontal scroll bar.
SM_CYCAPTION	4	Height of window title. This is the title height plus the height of the window frame that cannot be sized (SM_CYBORDER).
SM_CXBORDER	5	Width of window frame that cannot be sized.
SM_CYBORDER	6	Height of window frame that cannot be sized.
SM_CXDLGFRAME	7	Width of frame when window has the WS_DLGFRAME style.
SM_CYDLGFRAME	8	Height of frame when window has the WS_DLGFRAME style.
SM_CYVTHUMB	9	Height of scroll box on vertical scroll bar.
SM_CXHTHUMB	10	Width of scroll box (thumb) on horizontal scroll bar.
SM_CXICON	11	Width of icon.
SM_CYICON	12	Height of icon.
SM_CXCURSOR	13	Width of cursor.
SM_CYCURSOR	14	Height of cursor.
SM_CYMENU	15	Height of single-line menu bar. This is the menu height minus the height of the window frame that cannot be sized (SM_CYBORDER).
SM_CXFULLSCREEN	16	Width of window client area for a full-screen window.
SM_CYFULLSCREEN	17	Height of window client area for a full-screen window (equivalent to the height of the screen minus the height of the window title).
SM_CYKANJIWINDOW	18	Height of Kanji window.
SM_MOUSEPRESENT	19	Nonzero if the mouse hardware is installed.
SM_CYVSCROLL	20	Height of arrow bitmap on a vertical scroll bar.

Table 11-17 Options for GetSystemMetrics   *(Continued on next page)*

CONSTANT NAME	VALUE	DESCRIPTION
(Continued from previous page)		
SM_CXHSCROLL	21	Width of arrow bitmap on a horizontal scroll bar.
SM_DEBUG	22	Nonzero if the Windows version is a debugging version.
SM_SWAPBUTTON	23	Nonzero if the left and right mouse buttons are swapped.
SM_CXMIN	28	Minimum width of window.
SM_CYMIN	29	Minimum height of window.
SM_CXSIZE	30	Width of bitmaps contained in the title bar.
SM_CYSIZE	31	Height of bitmaps contained in the title bar.
SM_CXFRAME	32	Width of window frame that can be sized.
SM_CYFRAME	33	Height of window frame that can be sized.
SM_CXMINTRACK	34	Minimum tracking width of window.
SM_CYMINTRACK	35	Minimum tracking height of window.
SM_CXDOUBLECLK*	36	Width of the rectangle around the location of the first click in a double-click sequence. The second click must occur within this rectangle for the system to consider the two clicks a double-click.
SM_CYDOUBLECLK*	37	Height of the rectangle around the location of the first click in a double-click sequence. The second click must occur within this rectangle for the system to consider the two clicks a double-click.
SM_CXICONSPACING*	38	Width of rectangles that the system uses to position tiled icons.
SM_CYICONSPACING*	39	Height of rectangles that the system uses to position tiled icons.
SM_MENUDROPALIGNMENT*	40	Alignment of pop-up menus. If this value is zero, the left side of a pop-up menu is aligned with the left side of the corresponding menu-bar item. If this value is nonzero, the left side of a pop-up menu is aligned with the right side of the corresponding menu-bar item.
SM_PENWINDOWS*	41	Handle of the Pen Windows dynamic link library (DLL) if Pen Windows is installed.
SM_DBCSENABLED*	42	Nonzero if current version of Windows uses double-byte characters; otherwise, this value returns zero.
*Windows 3.1 only		

Table 11-17 Options for GetSystemMetrics

Comments

There is a SetOption method of the Application object, which allows you to write to the same set of options that Application.GetOption retrieves. This method is very useful for putting Access into a known state at the start of your application. You should use the GetOption method to read the user's original settings, and restore them when you are done.

GetWinFlags does not distinguish between an 80486 chip and a Pentium chip. When run on a Pentium system, the ahtGetCPU function will incorrectly identify the CPU as an 80486.

There is a bug in Windows for Workgroups 3.11 that causes GetVersion to return 3.10 as the version number. GetVersion also identifies all versions of Windows NT as being Windows 3.1 running on DOS 5.0.

On a Windows NT system, ahtNumTasks will only report the number of tasks being run in the WOW (Windows on Windows) 16-bit emulation layer.

12

Using OLE and DDE to Extend Your Applications

HOW DO I...

No Access application exists on its own. Since Windows is a multitasking operating system, you'll want to link your Access applications with other Windows applications. Windows provides two mechanisms for communicating between applications, OLE (Object Linking and Embedding) and DDE (Dynamic Data Exchange). OLE is easy for users and application programmers to work with and allows for the creation of custom controls. It also accommodates OLE Automation, making it possible for Access to control various applications using Access Basic. (It is also the basis for Visual Basic for Applications, the cross-application version of Basic that serves the entire group of Microsoft Office products.) Since OLE is a new technology, many mainstream Windows applications don't yet (or perhaps will never) include support for it. DDE is more manageable for developers who create the tools you use, but it's far more limited in scope and can be "cranky" to control.

This chapter presents examples of using OLE in each of the ways it interacts with Access. You'll also find a few examples of using DDE with applications that don't offer OLE Automation. You'll learn to activate an embedded OLE object (a sound file). You'll see how to use a custom OLE control, starting with its installation and working through its interactions with Access Basic. You'll get a chance to use the statistical, analytical, and financial prowess of the Excel function libraries directly from Access, as well as to retrieve Word for Windows Summary Info for any selected document. You'll learn to use DDE to control, from Access Basic, Delrina's WinFax Pro and the Windows Program Manager. Finally, you'll dig into OLE Automation, creating a form that allows you to alter properties of Microsoft Graph objects on a form.

> *NOTE: To take full advantage of this chapter, you'll need a copy of Microsoft Excel 5.0 or later, Word for Windows 6.0 or later, and Delrina's WinFax Pro 3.0 or later. Anything else you need you either already have, or it is included on the CD-ROM with this book.*

12.1   Play an embedded sound file from within an application
Sound capability has become an integral part of the Windows environment. This How-To will show how to use the Windows API to play WAV files at any time throughout your applications. It will demonstrate how to activate any embedded OLE object programmatically.

12.2   Use OLE custom controls
Access supports OLE custom controls, and the market for these controls is booming. This How-To will demonstrate the installation and use of a simple custom control. The examples use the Multi-select List Box control. It's freeware, provided by Andrew Miller at Microsoft.

12.3   Use Excel's functions from within Access
Through the power of the new OLE 2 Automation, you can harness Excel from within Access Basic. This How-To will show you the basics of retrieving values from Excel's exhaustive function library.

12.4 Retrieve and set Summary Info in Microsoft Word documents from Access

This How-To will demonstrate how you can retrieve and set the Summary Info for a Word document without ever leaving Access, using the new built-in OLE Automation features.

12.5 Send a fax to WinFax Pro directly from Access

Using DDE, you can easily convince WinFax Pro to send a fax for you, directly from Access. In this How-To, you will see how to make WinFax Pro do your bidding.

12.6 Add an item to Program Manager's Startup group

Program Manager supports a full command set, available from any application that supports DDE. It is the vehicle by which every installation program adds groups and items to Program Manager. This How-To will show you how you can use that same capability from your own programs.

12.7 Modify Microsoft Graph settings programmatically

Microsoft Graph, shared between Access and several other Windows applications, allows you to create sophisticated charts from your Access data. This How-To offers a striking demo of manipulating the objects created with Microsoft Graph from Access Basic code.

12.1 HOW DO I...
COMPLEXITY: INTERMEDIATE

Play an embedded sound file from within my application?

Problem

My application stores WAV files as OLE objects within a table. I'd like to be able to play them on demand. I know that users can double-click on the icon in a form to play the sounds, but I'd like some control over this. Is there some method to play one of these embedded sounds when I need to?

Technique

Access 2.0 gives you substantial control over the use of OLE objects. Using the Action property of the control that's displaying the OLE object you can tell the object to activate itself, copy to or paste from the Windows Clipboard, update its data, close, or delete itself. (The Action property pertains to bound or unbound OLE objects, and to graphs as well.) You can also call up the Insert Object or Paste Special dialog box to place data into the control. This How-To uses a bound OLE field, but it works just as well with an unbound object on a form.

Steps

Load and run frmOLE from 12-01.MDB. This sample form, shown in Figure 12-1, is a continuous form, pulling the data from the table tblOLE. If you click on a Play button, the form will activate that OLE object, stored in the OLEObject field of the table. The sample table includes three WAV files and one Microsoft

Graph object. Clicking on the Play button will either play the sound or activate Microsoft Graph so you can edit the tiny graph object. Click on the Insert button to call up the Insert Object dialog, which allows you to insert any OLE object you like into the table.

The steps involved in creating such a form are quite simple:

1. Create a new table or modify an existing table, adding a column (named OLEObject in the sample) with its Data Type set to OLE Object. (Note that you cannot index on an OLE field, and therefore, it can't be your Primary Key for the table.)

2. Import the module basOLEConst from 12-01.MDB. This contains the necessary OLE constants, so your code doesn't have to refer to OLE actions by number and can use a named constant instead. These constants all come from CONSTANT.TXT, a text file that's in your Access directory. If you'd rather, you can just copy the three constants you'll use here— VERB_PRIMARY, OLE_INSERT_OBJ_DLG, and OLE_ACTIVATE—from CONSTANT.TXT (or basOLEConst) into your own global module.

3. Create a new form. To emulate the sample form, the only property you need to set is DefaultView. Set it to Continuous Forms, so that you'll see multiple rows at the same time. This isn't necessary, but it will make your form look like the sample.

4. Create a bound OLE object (the cactus picture with the XYZ across the top, on the toolbar) on the form. The code in this example is based on a control named objOLE. You'll need to adjust the code appropriately if you name your control something else. The sample form includes the Description field from tblOLE as a text box, but this isn't used in the sample code.

5. Add two buttons, named cmdPlay and cmdInsert, and captioned Play and Insert. Attach the following code to the Play button's Click event (see this book's Introduction for more information on creating event procedures):

```
Sub cmdPlay_Click ()
    Dim ctl As Control

    On Error Resume Next
    Set ctl = Me!objOLE
    ctl.Verb = VERB_PRIMARY
    ctl.Action = OLE_ACTIVATE
    On Error GoTo 0
End Sub
```

Figure 12-1 The OLE sample form, frmOLE, which allows you to play or insert OLE objects

Attach the following code to the Insert button's Click event:

```
Sub cmdInsert_Click ()
    On Error Resume Next
    Me!objOLE.Action = OLE_INSERT_OBJ_DLG
    On Error GoTo 0
End Sub
```

6. Save your form and run it. When you click on the Insert button, you'll see the Insert Object dialog (Figure 12-2). This dialog allows you to either create a new object or insert one from an existing file. Once you make your choice, Access will place the object into the table and display it on the form. When you want to activate the object, click on the Play button. For a WAV file, this will cause your sound to play. For a Microsoft Graph object, it will activate Microsoft Graph. The same goes for any other object you insert; clicking the Play button will activate it.

How It Works

The Action property for OLE objects in Access is different from almost any other property, in that setting its value causes an action to take place. Normally, properties describe characteristics of an object, and methods cause actions to take place. In this case, however, when you set the Action property to the constant OLE_ACTIVATE (the value 7), Access activates the control at the time you set the property. If you set the Action property to the constant OLE_INSERT_OBJ_DLG, Access displays the modal Insert Object dialog at the time you change the property. This is how the buttons work on the sample form: By changing the OLE control's Action property, the code tells Access what action to take at that point.

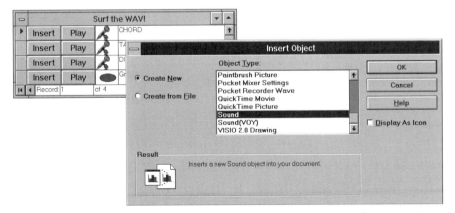

Figure 12-2 The Insert Object dialog allows you to insert any OLE object into the form

Table 12-1 lists the values for the Action property that you're likely to use (the constants come from CONSTANT.TXT). There are others available, but this list will get you started. For more information, see the Access Basic On-line help topics on the Action and Verb properties.

CONSTANT	VALUE	DESCRIPTION
OLE_COPY	4	Same as choosing the Edit|Copy menu item. Copy the OLE object onto the Windows Clipboard.
OLE_PASTE	5	Same as choosing the Edit|Paste menu item. Paste the OLE object from the Clipboard into your control.
OLE_UPDATE	6	Retrieve the most current data for the OLE object from the application that created the object and display it as a graphic.
OLE_ACTIVATE	7	Same as double-clicking the control. You must set the control's Verb property before you can use this Action.
OLE_CLOSE	9	Close the OLE object and end the active connection with its creating application.
OLE_INSERT_OBJ_DLG	14	Display the Insert Object modal dialog, allowing the user to insert an object.

Table 12-1 Some of the Action property's possible values, and their descriptions, from CONSTANT.TXT

Comments

This technique works just as well for unbound objects on forms. For example, if you have an embedded Word document, you could use code to activate the OLE object (named Embedded0 in the following example), set its first paragraph to bold, and then close the object:

```
Dim objWord As Object
' Activate the OLE object, using the primary verb
Me!Embedded0.Verb = VERB_PRIMARY
Me!Embedded0.Action = OLE_ACTIVATE
Set objWord = Me!Embedded0.Object.Application.WordBasic

objWord.StartOfDocument
objWord.ParaDown 1, 1
objWord.Bold 1
Set objWord = Nothing
' Close the OLE object
Me!Embedded0.Action = OLE_CLOSE
```

By the way, if you need to play a WAV file but don't want to embed an OLE object or use OLE at all, you can use the Windows API sndPlaySound function to do your work. (This function is aliased as aht_apiSndPlaySound or aht_apiSndPlaySoundLong, depending on the use.) Just insert the following declarations and constants in a form's module:

```
Declare Function aht_apiSndPlaySound Lib "MMSYSTEM.DLL" Alias ⇒
"sndPlaySound" (ByVal strSoundName As String, ByVal intFlags As Integer) As Integer

Declare Function aht_apiSndPlaySoundLong Lib "MMSYSTEM.DLL" Alias ⇒
"sndPlaySound" (ByVal lngSoundName As Long, ByVal intFlags As Integer) As Integer


Const SND_SYNC = &H0
Const SND_ASYNC = &H1
Const SND_NODEFAULT = &H2
Const SND_LOOP = &H8
Const SND_NOSTOP = &H10
```

Table 12-2 describes the possible flag values for the sndPlaySound function call.

CONSTANT	VALUE	DESCRIPTION
SND_SYNC	0	Play the sound synchronously, and do not return from the function until the sound ends.
SND_ASYNC	1	Play the sound asynchronously, and return from the function immediately after beginning the sound. To terminate a sound once it's started, call aht_apiSndPlaySoundLong, passing a 0& as the first parameter.
SND_NODEFAULT	2	Don't play the default sound if the requested sound can't be found.
SND_LOOP	8	The sound continues to play repeatedly until you call aht_apisndPlaySoundLong with the first parameter set to 0&. You must also specify the SND_ASYNC flag to loop sounds.
SND_NOSTOP	16	Return immediately with a value of False, without playing the requested sound, if a sound is currently playing.

Table 12-2 Possible values for the intFlags parameter to sndPlaySound

Normally, you'll call the aht_apiSndPlaySound function to play the WAV file. If you use the SND_ASYNC or SND_LOOP flags, you'll need to call the aht_apiSndPlaySoundLong function, passing a 0& value as the first parameter. The following code example is the simplest way to play a WAV file using the Windows API. You can try this out by loading the form frmSndPlaySound from 12-01.MDB and pressing the button on the form, which executes the following code:

```
Sub Button0_Click ()
    Dim strSound As String
    Dim intFlags As Integer
    Dim intResult As Integer
```

(Continued on next page)

(Continued from previous page)

```
' You'll need to change the following line for your own
' situation.
strSound = "d:\windows\tada.wav"

' Play the sound asynchronously and
' skip the default sound if the chosen
' sound isn't found.
intFlags = SND_ASYNC Or SND_NODEFAULT
intResult = aht_apiSndPlaySound(strSound, intFlags)
End Sub
```

12.2 HOW DO I... COMPLEXITY: INTERMEDIATE

Use OLE custom controls?

Problem

I've heard about custom controls for Access, but can't find any mention of them in the manuals, nor any way to use them. Are these controls like Visual Basic's VBX files? How can I get some to play with? What's the licensing arrangement?

Technique

OLE custom controls (often called OCX controls, since that's the standard file name extension for them) represent Microsoft's new technology for distributing application "components" that are reusable across many applications, and available in both 16- and 32-bit versions. These controls rely on OLE to communicate with the applications that contain them. They allow you to add new functionality to Access forms and reports that would otherwise be difficult or impossible to create yourself. As other products evolve to include support for OLE custom controls, you'll be able to take the same controls you use on Access forms and use them on Excel spreadsheets or in Word documents. Although they are comparable in concept to VBX add-ins for Visual Basic, behind the scenes they're very different. VBX add-ins are tightly linked to Visual Basic and are only available for 16-bit operating systems. As Windows moves toward a 32-bit operating system for future versions, Microsoft must supply some mechanism for creating distributable, encapsulated tools that will work with many applications. The solution, then, is the OLE custom control, which can be compiled to work in either a 16- or 32-bit environment.

The Access Developer's Toolkit ships with three OLE custom controls: the data outline control, a simple calendar, and a scroll bar. These were the first three OCX files that were commercially available. More controls will become available as existing VBX vendors convert their custom controls to the OCX model and as new vendors enter the market.

This How-To walks you through the steps for using a simple custom control in your application, from installation on. The CD-ROM accompanying this book contains the custom controls used in the examples in this How-To as well as several other freeware or demoware custom controls to try out.

> ### CREDIT WHERE CREDIT IS DUE
> The Multi-select List Box custom control, MSLB.OCX, was created by Andrew Miller, at Microsoft, as were TAB.OCX and SPINLBL.OCX. Andrew has graciously made these custom controls available free of charge. Please read carefully the licensing agreement on this book's CD-ROM before distributing these controls. These controls are distributed as is, and neither Andrew nor Microsoft can provide support for their use.

Steps

To try out a custom control, load and run frmMultiSelect in 12-02.MDB. This sample form consists of two instances of a Multi-select List Box, as shown in Figure 12-3. You can select multiple items from the list on the left to be added to the list on the right, using one of three methods:

⚷   Click and drag over multiple contiguous items.

⚷   Click on one item, then Shift-click on another to select all items in between the two endpoints.

⚷   Click on multiple items, using Ctrl-click as you click each individual item.

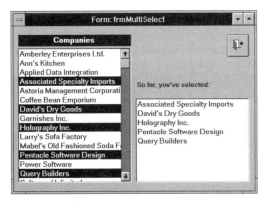

Figure 12-3 The sample form, frmMultiSelect, including two instances of the Multi-select List Box custom control

Using a custom control requires five basic steps, which are listed here and detailed in the following subsections.

1. Ensure that Access is set up to accept custom controls.
2. Install the DLL that supports custom controls.
3. Install the control itself.
4. Place the control on a form and set its properties.
5. Write code, if necessary, to control the object at runtime.

Prepare Access to Accept Custom Controls

1. Before you can use custom controls at all, you must set a flag in your MSACC20.INI file. This file, normally found in your Windows directory, controls Access's settings. Use a text editor (such as Notepad), to modify the file and find the [Options] section. Add the line

```
AllowCustomControls=1
```

so that the entire section looks something like this (paths will be different, of course, and yours may have other values):

```
[Options]
SystemDB=D:\ACCESS2\system.mda
UtilityDB=D:\ACCESS2\utility.mda
AllowCustomControls=1
```

Adding the AllowCustomControls value alerts Access to display the correct options when you attempt to insert a custom control on a form or report. The next time you start Access, it will take note of this change and allow custom controls.

Install the DLL

As with any other OLE application, Access's use of custom controls must be registered with the Windows OLE registration database. To make this step as simple as possible, the sample custom controls that are included with this book include a registration program, MSAREG.EXE.

In addition, the DLL, OC1016.DLL, must be available and registered before you can use custom controls. If you've already installed the Access Developer's Toolkit, you can skip these steps, because its installation program registered OC1016.DLL for you.

2. Copy OC1016.DLL from any of the custom control directories on your CD to your Windows\System directory.
3. From Program Manager (or its equivalent on your system), run the command line, where I: is the drive containing your CD-ROM, and C: is the drive where Windows is installed:

```
I:MSAREG C:\WINDOWS\SYSTEM\OC1016.DLL
```

Install the Control

4. This part's easy. Just place the *.OCX and *.HLP files in a convenient directory. These are the only files you'll need for all the sample controls.

Add the Control and Set Its Properties

The first time you use a custom control, you'll need to tell Windows and Access where it's located on your system. Once that's done, you won't have to do it again.

5. In Access, create a new form. On this form, place an unbound OLE object (use the tool with the cactus picture *without* the XYZ on top). Access pops up its Insert Object dialog box, as shown in Figure 12-4. (If your dialog box doesn't include the Insert Control option, you may have skipped a step. Make sure you enabled custom controls by modifying MSACC20.INI, as indicated in step 1.) Choose Insert Control and click on the Add Control button. This allows you to specify the location of the OCX file you want to add to your system. In this case, find MSLB.OCX and select it. For this sample form, place two Multi-select List Boxes on your form, and name them objLB and objSelected.

6. Once you've inserted the control into the unbound OLE object on your form, set its properties. Unlike built-in controls, whose properties you set using the properties sheet, in Access 2.0 you set the properties of OLE custom controls using the Properties menu item, available by choosing the custom control's name from the Edit menu (or, as shown in Figure 12-5, from the fly-out menu available by right-clicking on the custom control). For the Multi-select List Box, you'll see a form like the one shown in Figure 12-6. If you select another set of properties—Fonts, for example—you'll see the Properties page shown in Figure 12-7. For the sample form, set the

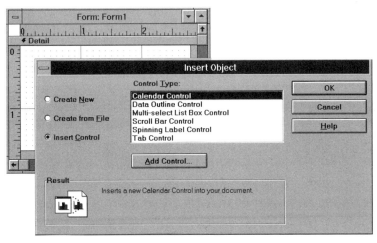

Figure 12-4 The Insert Object dialog box, where you add a new custom control or insert an existing one

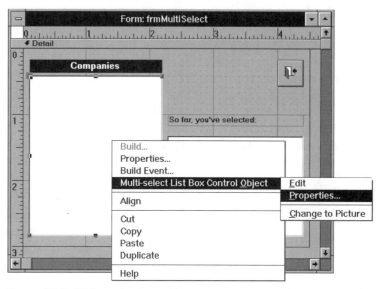

Figure 12-5 Click on the Properties menu item to set the properties for the custom control

MultiSelect property for objLB to be Extended, and for objSelected to be None.

Program the Control

The Multi-select List Box won't do much for you without some Access Basic programming. You'll need to place items from a table into it, and react to mouse clicks, so you can fill in the second list box. The following steps show you the code that's in the sample form, and the upcoming "How It Works" section discusses how it all comes together.

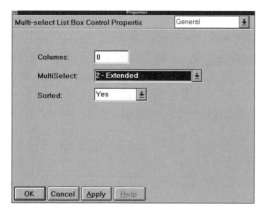

Figure 12-6 The General properties for the Multi-select List Box

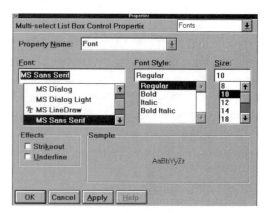

Figure 12-7 The Font properties for the Multi-select List Box

7. Place the following procedures in your form's module. Since Access doesn't directly support all of these event procedures, the simplest way to create the code is to click on the Builder button on the toolbar (or choose View|Code) and start typing in the module that appears.

```
Sub objLB_Click ()
   Dim obj As Object
   Dim objSelected As Object
   Dim intI As Integer
   Dim strChosen As String

   Set obj = Me!objLB.Object
   Set objSelected = Me!objSelected.Object

   objSelected.Clear
   For intI = 0 To obj.ListCount - 1
      If obj.Selected(intI) Then
         objSelected.Additem obj.List(intI), -1
      End If
   Next intI
End Sub

Sub objLB_AfterStartup ()
   Dim db As Database
   Dim rst As Recordset
   Dim obj As Object

   Set db = DBEngine.WorkSpaces(0).Databases(0)
   Set rst = db.OpenRecordset("tblCompanyAddresses")
   Set obj = Me!objLB.Object

   Do While Not rst.EOF
      obj.Additem rst!Company, -1
      rst.MoveNext
   Loop
   rst.Close
End Sub
```

8. As always, be sure to save your form. Since OLE custom controls are a new technology, they can be somewhat unstable. It can't hurt to save your work often.

How It Works

If you need to refer to a custom control programmatically, you do it by creating a variable of type Object and setting that variable to refer to the control:

```
Dim obj As Object
Set obj = Me!objLB.Object
```

Setting obj to refer to Me!objLB is not enough, since objLB is just an OLE container. The object *inside* that container is the OLE control. Therefore, any reference to the control and not the container will need the full name, Me!objLB.Object.

Once you've set up a reference to the custom control, you refer to it just as you do any other control. It has properties, methods, and events, and you can use them all from your Access Basic code. For example, the Multi-select List Box has an AddItem method, allowing you to add an item to the list box. To add an item, use code like this:

```
Dim obj As Object
Set obj = Me!objLB.Object
' Add a new item to the end of the list
obj.AddItem "A New Item"
```

The example form, frmMultiSelect, uses several of the Multi-select List Box's properties to do its job. The ListCount property lets you know how many items are currently in the list. The Selected property returns True or False for each item in the list, depending on whether or not the item is selected. Finally, the List property returns the list box text for any specific item number. Using these three properties, you can walk through each item in the list, adding the selected items to a different list. The objLB_Click procedure, shown in step 7, copies the selected items from objLB into objSelected. The procedure also uses the custom control's Clear property—which deletes all the items from the list—to delete all the items from the second list before it starts adding new items.

```
Set obj = Me!objLB.Object
Set objSelected = Me!objSelected.Object

objSelected.Clear
For intI = 0 To obj.ListCount - 1
   If obj.Selected(intI) Then
      objSelected.Additem obj.List(intI), -1
   End If
Next intI
```

To copy data from a table into the list box, you must walk through the table (or query) one row at a time, using the AddItem method to add each item. The objLB_AfterStartup procedure, in step 7, is used by the sample form to fill the list box.

```
Set rst = db.OpenRecordset("tblCompanyAddresses")
Set obj = Me!objLB.Object

Do While Not rst.EOF
   obj.Additem rst!Company, -1
   rst.MoveNext
Loop
rst.Close
```

The following tables describe the properties, events, and methods of the Multi-select List Box.

Table 12-3 lists the properties of the control.

PROPERTY	DESCRIPTION	VALUES/COMMENTS
BackColor	Background color	Any long integer.
Columns	Number of columns in multicolumn (snaking) list box	0 to arrange items in a single column; 1 or more to arrange items in snaking columns. You can't switch from 0 to any other number (or vice versa) at runtime, but if you design the list box with more than one column, you can change the number of columns at runtime.
Font	Font of the list box	A structure containing the following elements: Name, Size, Weight, Italic, Strikeout, Underline. To set a font size in code, for example, use the Font.Size property of the object.
hWnd	Handle to the list box	(Read-only).
ItemData(nIndex)	Array of 32-bit values associated with items in list box	This array is useful for storing a number associated with each row. For example, you could store the row's Primary Key in this column. It's like an extra, hidden column that can only hold long integers.
List(nIndex)	Array of items in the list box	A 0-based array of strings, containing the items in the list box. Not available at design time, read-only at runtime.
ListCount	Count of items in the list box	Not available at design time, read-only at runtime.
ListIndex	Currently selected item	Not available at design time.
MultiSelect	MultipleSelect behavior	0 to disallow multiple selections; 1 to allow simple multiple selections (click or (SPACEBAR) selects or deselects an item); 2 for extended multiple selection (using (SHIFT)- and (CTRL)-clicks and arrow keys)
NewIndex	The index of the item that was just added	If the list is sorted, this value returns the only way of knowing where in the list the item you just added was added. Read-only at runtime, not available at design time.
Selected(nIndex)	Select/Unselect status for each item in list (multiselect only)	Returns True if the indicated item is selected or False if it's not. Not available at design time.
Sorted	If true, added items will be inserted sorted	Read-only at runtime. See the NewIndex property to know at which index new items are added.
Text	The text of the currently selected item	Not available at design time, read-only at runtime.
TopIndex	Index of item that is at the top of the list	Not available at design time. You can use this property to scroll through the list without ever selecting an item. Just increment the TopIndex property to scroll the list.

Table 12-3 Properties for the Multi-select List Box custom control

Table 12-4 lists the events for the Multi-select List Box custom control. Note that this control can supply events that Access doesn't normally support, such as AfterStartup. To create event procedures for these events, name them as shown here:

```
Sub objName_EventName()
```

For example, the sample form's module contains this subroutine:

```
Sub objLB_AfterStartup ()
```

> NOTE: If you need to copy data into the control when you open the form, use the control's AfterStartup event. The control itself isn't completely created by the time the form's Load event occurs (which is where you would normally load data into the control).

EVENT	OCCURS
AfterStartup	After the list box has been initialized
Click	When the user clicks the list box
DblClick	When the user double-clicks the list box
KeyDown	When the user presses a key in the list box
KeyUp	When the user releases a key in the list box
KeyPress	In between the KeyDown and KeyUp events
MouseDown	When the user presses the mouse button
MouseMove	When the user moves the mouse button
MouseUp	When the user releases the mouse button

Table 12-4 Events for the Multi-select List Box custom control

Table 12-5 lists the methods supported by the Multi-select List Box.

METHOD	PARAMETERS	DESCRIPTION
AddItem	strItem as String, intIndex as Integer	Add/Insert an item to the list box.
RemoveItem	intIndex as Integer	Remove an item from the list box.
Clear		Clear all items from the list box.

Table 12-5 Methods for the Multi-select List Box custom control

As shown in step 7, you can loop through all the rows of a recordset, copying the data to the list box, using the AddItem method. The –1 tells the control to add the item to the end of the list.

```
Do While Not rst.EOF
    obj.Additem rst!Company, –1
    rst.MoveNext
Loop
```

Comments

If you've used Visual Basic, you may be wondering why you must go through such an odd and complex set of steps to place a custom control on a form. In Visual Basic, custom controls appear on the standard toolbar, and you use them just like built-in controls. OLE custom controls are a new technology, however, and Access 2.0 didn't get the interface smoothed out as nicely as it might have. Undoubtedly, in future versions of Access the control interface will become more and more straightforward.

In Access 2.0, custom controls cannot be bound; that is, they can't automatically read and write data to and from tables. If you want to display data in a custom control, as this How-To demonstrated, you'll need to copy the data in and out of the control using Access Basic.

You must be aware of the licensing arrangements for any custom control you plan to distribute with your applications. Since these are retail software, their owners decide how and when you can distribute their work. Most custom controls are intended for runtime distribution with applications, allowing end users to use them, but not to modify them or change their properties in design mode. To this end, make sure that you don't distribute licensing files that enable design-time modifications along with your applications.

12.3 HOW DO I...   COMPLEXITY: INTERMEDIATE

Use Excel's functions from within Access?

Problem

Excel offers an amazing array of statistical, analytical, and financial functions that I'd like to use in Access. I know I can control embedded Excel worksheets, but is there some way simply to call Excel functions from within Access?

Technique

Using OLE Automation, you can ask Excel to use its built-in functions to perform calculations and return a value to your Access application. This requires starting Excel, however, and that can take some time, so you wouldn't normally do this just for a single calculation. But for a number of calculated values, or a single calculation that would be too difficult or take too much time in Access, it's worth tapping into the OLE connections between Access and Excel.

There are many ways to use OLE to link Excel and Access. You can embed an Excel spreadsheet or chart object into an Access form and control the Excel objects programmatically. In that situation, your interaction with Excel would be very similar to the example shown in How-To 12.7, in which you control a Microsoft Graph object from Access Basic. You can also use OLE Automation from Access to create and manipulate Excel objects *without* using an embedded spreadsheet or chart. These methods are detailed in both the Access and Excel manuals. This How-To, however, just uses the Excel engine without creating any specific Excel object, and this technique isn't usually mentioned anywhere.

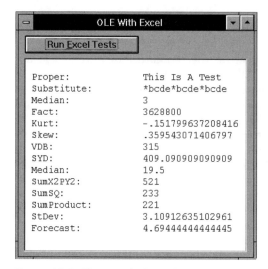

Figure 12-8 The sample form, frmTestExcel, once its series of function calls are completed

Steps

To test the OLE communication between Access and Excel load frmTestExcel, from 12-03.MDB. To start the test, click the button on the form. The code attached to the button will start up Excel and run a series of tests, calling Excel to retrieve the results for a number of function calls. After all the tests, the sample looks like Figure 12-8.

The sample form tests two different types of function calls you can make to Excel from Access: functions that accept simple parameters and functions that require Excel ranges as parameters. The following steps describe how to set up the example form, and "How It Works" explains how to call the two types of Excel functions from Access Basic.

1. Create a new form containing a single text box (named txtResults on the sample form) and a command button to run the Excel tests (Figure 12-8).

2. Import the module basExcel from 12-03.MDB. This module contains the function you need in order to copy data from a column in Access to a spreadsheet column in Excel.

3. Enter the following code into the form's module (click on the Builder button on the toolbar or choose View|Code):

```
Sub AddLine (strLabel As String, varValue As Variant)
   Me!txtResults = Me!txtResults & Chr$(13) & Chr$(10) & " " & ⇒
Left(strLabel & Space(20), 20) & varValue
   DoEvents
End Sub
```

```
Function TestExcel ()
    Dim obj As Object
    Dim intCount As Integer
    Dim objRange1 As Object
    Dim objRange2 As Object
    Dim objSheet As Object

    Me!txtResults = Null
    DoEvents
    AddLine "Starting Excel:", "Please wait..."

    Set obj = CreateObject("Excel.Application")
    Set objSheet = CreateObject("Excel.Sheet")

    Me!txtResults = Null
    DoEvents

    ' String functions
    AddLine "Proper:", obj.Proper("this is a test")
    AddLine "Substitute:", obj.Substitute("abcdeabcdeabcde", "a", "*")

    ' Simple math functions
    AddLine "Median:", obj.Median(1, 2, 3, 4, 5)
    AddLine "Fact:", obj.Fact(10)

    ' Analytical functions
    AddLine "Kurt:", obj.Kurt(3, 4, 5, 2, 3, 4, 5, 6, 4, 7)
    AddLine "Skew:", obj.Skew(3, 4, 5, 2, 3, 4, 5, 6, 4, 7)
    AddLine "VDB:", obj.VDB(2400, 300, 10, 0, .875, 1.5)
    AddLine "SYD:", obj.SYD(30000, 7500, 10, 10)

    ' Using ranges

    ' Copy from a column to a spreadsheet, and get its median
    intCount = ahtCopyColumnToSheet(objSheet, "tblProducts", "Unit Price", 1)
    Set objRange1 = objSheet.Range("A1:A" & intCount)
    AddLine "Median:", obj.Median(objRange1)

    ' Copy two fields to columns
    intCount = ahtCopyColumnToSheet(objSheet, "tblNumbers", "Number1", 1)
    intCount = ahtCopyColumnToSheet(objSheet, "tblNumbers", "Number2", 2)

    ' Create ranges
    Set objRange1 = objSheet.Range("A1:A" & intCount)
    Set objRange2 = objSheet.Range("B1:B" & intCount)

    ' Print out calculations based on those ranges
    AddLine "SumX2PY2:", obj.SumX2PY2(objRange1, objRange2)
    AddLine "SumSQ:", obj.SumSQ(objRange1)
    AddLine "SumProduct:", obj.SumProduct(objRange1, objRange2)
```

(Continued on next page)

(Continued from previous page)

```
    AddLine "StDev:", obj.StDev(objRange1)
    AddLine "Forecast:", obj.ForeCast(5, objRange1, objRange2)

    ' Quit and clean up.
    obj.[Quit]
    Set obj = Nothing
    Set objSheet = Nothing
End Function
```

4. In the properties sheet for the command button, enter the following value in the OnClick event property:

```
=TestExcel()
```

5. Open the form in run mode and click the command button. This will call the TestExcel function and fill the text box with the results.

How It Works

Excel obligingly exposes all of its internal functions to external callers via the Application object. The following sections describe each of the steps necessary to call Excel functions directly from Access Basic code.

> **NOTE:** No matter which Excel function you call, the return value will be a variant. Declare a variable as a Variant if it will contain the return value from an Excel function. In the examples, the return values went directly to a text box, so the issue didn't come up.

Setting Up to Communicate with Excel

Before you can call any Excel function, you must start Excel and create an object variable in Access to link the two applications. You'll always use code like this to create this linkage:

```
Dim objExcel As Object
Set objExcel = CreateObject("Excel.Application")
```

By linking with Excel's Application object, you can request Excel to evaluate any of its internal functions for you. Creating the object will take a few seconds, since it must start Excel. Calling CreateObject will start a new, hidden, instance of Excel, even if it's already running.

If you need an actual sheet within Excel (and you will, for functions that require a range of values as input), you must also set up an object in Access that refers to that sheet. To do that, you'll need code that looks like this:

```
Dim objSheet As Object
Set objSheet = CreateObject("Excel.Sheet")
```

This code starts Excel, if it's not already running, and instructs Excel to create a new sheet. You can manipulate this sheet directly from Access, and you'll do that later in this How-To when you copy data from a table column into a spreadsheet column; but that's not the real intent of this How-To. Of course, Excel must be registered correctly in your Windows registration database for CreateObject to be able to start Excel. If you installed Excel correctly and your registration database has not been corrupted, there shouldn't be any problems.

Calling Simple Excel Functions

Once you've created your Access object that refers to the Excel Application object, you can ask Excel to perform simple calculations for you. For example, to use the Excel Product function, you can use code like this:

```
Dim intProd As Integer
intProd = obj.Product(5, 6)
```

After this call, the variable intProd will contain the value 30.

For example, the TestExcel procedure, in frmTestExcel's module, uses the following code fragment to call four Excel functions (Proper, Substitute, Median, and Fact). Each of these functions requires one or more simple parameters and returns a single value. (The AddLine statement just adds the output of the function call to the text box on the sample form. These four functions are the first four in the output text box.)

```
AddLine "Proper:", obj.Proper("this is a test")
AddLine "Substitute:", obj.Substitute("abcdeabcdeabcde", "a", "*")
AddLine "Median:", obj.Median(1, 2, 3, 4, 5)
AddLine "Fact:", obj.Fact(10)
```

Excel supplies many simple functions like these that Access doesn't have. (You'll need the Excel spreadsheet function reference, available separately from Microsoft Press, to take advantage of any of these functions.) Some of these functions (Proper, for example) are easy enough to write in Access Basic code, but if you've already got the connection to Excel working, it makes perfect sense to use Excel to retrieve these sorts of values, rather than writing the Access Basic code yourself.

To call analytical or statistical functions in Excel, use the same technique shown in the previous paragraph. With the reference to the Excel.Application object, call any function that takes simple parameters and returns a single value. The next four examples on the sample form call the Kurt, Skew, VBD, and SYD functions:

```
AddLine "Kurt:", obj.Kurt(3, 4, 5, 2, 3, 4, 5, 6, 4, 7)
AddLine "Skew:", obj.Skew(3, 4, 5, 2, 3, 4, 5, 6, 4, 7)
AddLine "VDB:", obj.VDB(2400, 300, 10, 0, .875, 1.5)
AddLine "SYD:", obj.SYD(30000, 7500, 10, 10)
```

Calling Excel Functions Using Ranges

Sometimes you'll need to call Excel functions that require a variable number of values, or you'll want to use the data in a table as the input to an Excel function. In that case, you'll need to call the Excel function using a spreadsheet range as the input, and you'll need some method of getting the Access data into the spreadsheet so you can use that data as input to the function.

To copy a column of data from an Access table or query into an Excel spreadsheet column, call the ahtCopyColumnToSheet function, found in basExcel (in 12-03.MDB):

```
Function ahtCopyColumnToSheet (objSheet As Object, strTable As String, ⇒
strField As String, intColumn As Integer)
    Dim db As Database
    Dim rst As Recordset
    Dim intRows As Integer

    Set db = DBEngine.Workspaces(0).Databases(0)
    Set rst = db.OpenRecordset(strTable)
    Do While Not rst.EOF
        intRows = intRows + 1
        objSheet.Cells(intRows, intColumn).Value = rst(strField)
        rst.MoveNext
    Loop
    rst.Close
ahtCopyColumnToSheet = intRows
End Function
```

Given a reference to an Excel sheet, a table or query name, a field name, and a column number for the Excel sheet, ahtCopyColumnToSheet will walk down all the rows of Access data, copying them over to the Excel sheet. The function returns the number of rows that it copied over to Excel. For example, to copy the Unit Price field values from the tblProducts table to the first column of the opened spreadsheet in Excel, use:

```
intCount = ahtCopyColumnToSheet(objSheet, "tblProducts", "Unit Price", 1)
```

> **NOTE:** To keep it simple, this version of the ahtCopyColumnToSheet function doesn't include error checking, but certainly any code used in real applications would need to check for errors that might occur as you move data from Access to Excel.

Once you've copied the data to Excel, you can create an object that refers to that range of data as a single entity. Most Excel functions accept a range as a parameter if they accept a group of values as input. For example, the Median function, used above, accepts either a list of numbers or a range.

To create a range object in Access, use the Range function, passing a string that represents the range you want. The following example, used after the form copies the data from a table over to Excel, calculates the median of all the items in the column:

```
Dim objRange1 As Object

Set objRange1 = objSheet.Range("A1:A" & intCount)
AddLine "Median:", obj.Median(objRange1)
```

Some Excel functions require two or more ranges as input. For example, the SumX2PY2 function, which returns the sum of the squares of all the values in two columns (that is, the sum of $x^2 + y^2$), takes two ranges as its parameters. The following code fragment, also from the sample form, copies two columns from tblNumbers to the open sheet in Excel, and then performs a number of calculations based on those columns.

```
' Copy two fields to columns
intCount = ahtCopyColumnToSheet(objSheet, "tblNumbers", "Number1", 1)
intCount = ahtCopyColumnToSheet(objSheet, "tblNumbers", "Number2", 2)

' Create ranges
Set objRange1 = objSheet.Range("A1:A" & intCount)
Set objRange2 = objSheet.Range("B1:B" & intCount)

' Print out calculations based on those ranges
AddLine "SumX2PY2:", obj.SumX2PY2(objRange1, objRange2)
AddLine "SumSQ:", obj.SumSQ(objRange1)
AddLine "SumProduct:", obj.SumProduct(objRange1, objRange2)
AddLine "StDev:", obj.StDev(objRange1)
AddLine "Forecast:", obj.ForeCast(5, objRange1, objRange2)
```

Closing Excel

Once you are done with your Access/Excel session, you must take steps to close the Excel application. If you don't, OLE will continue to start new instances of Excel every time you attempt to connect with Excel.Application (using CreateObject), eating up about 15% of your system resources each time.

To close Excel, use its Quit action. Normally, you would use syntax like this,

```
obj.Quit
```

but since Access itself includes a Quit statement, Access won't accept this. To indicate to Access that you want to use the Quit method of Excel's Application object, surround the keyword in square brackets instead:

```
obj.[Quit]
```

Access will allow this instruction to pass on through to Excel, which will shut itself down.

Finally, release any memory used by Access in maintaining the link between itself and Excel. To do this, use code like the following, which "closes" the object variables and releases any memory they might have been using:

```
Set obj = Nothing
Set objSheet = Nothing
```

Comments

Each application reacts differently to the CreateObject function. Excel starts a new hidden instance of itself when you call CreateObject using the "Excel.Application" value, but uses the current instance if you call CreateObject with the "Excel.Sheet" value. Microsoft Word, on the other hand, uses the running copy of itself, if possible, when you create an object linked to the Word.Basic object (that's the only object that Microsoft Word exposes, as you'll see in How-To 12.4). If there's not a copy of Word running, CreateObject will start one up, but it won't be hidden.

Since it takes time to start Excel once you call the CreateObject function, build your applications in such a way that all work with Excel is isolated to as few locations in your code as possible. Start Excel, then do all your work. Another alternative is to make your object variables global, and have your application start Excel if it needs to, and then leave it open until it's done. Don't forget to close Excel, however, so you don't reduce your system memory and resources.

When you're done with the OLE application, you'll need some way of closing down. As with the CreateObject command, each application reacts differently to your attempts to shut it down. Excel won't quit unless you explicitly order it to, using the Quit action. If you just set the object variable that refers to Excel.Application to be the value Nothing without executing the Quit action, the hidden copy of Excel will continue to run, chewing up memory and resources. If CreateObject started Word, setting the object referring to the Word.Basic object to be Nothing will automatically shut down Word. You'll need to be aware of how each application you use expects to be closed.

Excel exposes rich and varied inner workings via OLE. Taking advantage of Excel's capabilities is nearly impossible without reference materials. This How-To topic barely scratches the surface of what's available to you in Access from Excel. If you need to use the two products together, invest in the reference materials on Excel's Visual Basic for Applications from Microsoft Press, and/or the Office Developer's Kit, available on CD-ROM from Microsoft.

12.4 HOW DO I... COMPLEXITY: INTERMEDIATE

Retrieve and set Summary Info in Microsoft Word documents from Access?

Problem

As part of a document management system, I need to retrieve and set the Summary Info for Microsoft Word documents. I just can't figure out how to communicate with Word to retrieve the information I need.

Technique

Unlike Excel, which exposes almost all of itself via OLE, Word exposes very little. The only object you can refer to, from Access, is the WordBasic object. However, using this object, you can do anything that Word Basic can do, and that's a lot. This How-To shows you how to use Word Basic to retrieve the information you need, and how, in general, to communicate with Word for Windows.

Steps

To retrieve Summary Info for any Word for Windows document with the .DOC extension, open frmDocInfo in 12-04.MDB. This sample form, shown in

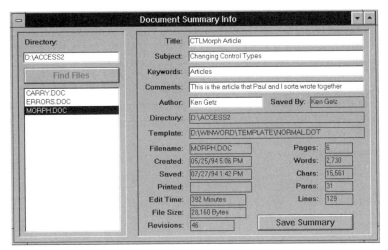

Figure 12-9 The sample form, frmDocInfo, showing a document's Summary Info

Figure 12-9, allows you to view and/or change the Summary Info for Word documents.

To use the sample form, follow these steps:

1. Import frmDocInfo and the module basSortArray from 12-04.MDB.

2. Run frmDocInfo, and type a path name into the text box. Click the Find Files button to retrieve a sorted list of the DOC files in the specified location.

3. To view the Summary Info for your chosen document, double-click on its name in the list box. This will start Word, load the specified document, retrieve the Summary Info, and then close the document.

4. To change the Summary Info, enter the data in the enabled text boxes on frmDocInfo, and click the Save Summary button to store the information.

How It Works

Microsoft Word for Windows exposes only a single object, the Basic object. Once you've established a link between Access and this object, you can use all its capabilities from your Access Basic application. The next few sections outline the steps involved in communicating with Word via OLE.

Starting the Connection with Word for Windows

To be able to retrieve or set Summary Info from Access, you must create an object variable to refer to the WordBasic object. (If you make it a module global variable, it'll be easier to close later on.) For working with a specific form, consider using a module global variable for the form's module—this is how the sample form works:

```
Dim objWord As Object
```

To start the conversation with Microsoft Word, use the CreateObject function to obtain a reference to the Word.Basic object. If Word isn't running, this will start a non-hidden instance of it. If Word is currently running, this function will obtain a reference to the currently running instance. In either case, since you can't control how Word starts up, you may want to minimize it (using Word Basic's AppMinimize command) so that it's out of the way, visually. The DoEvents command (an Access Basic command) gives Windows a time slice before going on, so it can make sure the screen gets repainted after minimizing the Word window.

```
Set objWord = CreateObject("Word.Basic")
objWord.AppMinimize
DoEvents
```

See the OpenWord function in frmDocInfo's module for an example using this code.

Retrieving the Summary Info

To retrieve the Summary Info for a given document open the document using Word Basic's FileOpen command:

```
objWord.FileOpen "C:\TESTFILE.DOC"
```

Once the file is open, you use the Word Basic CurValues object, which maintains the current values of all the dialog boxes in Word, to retrieve the information you want. Set an Access object variable to refer to a Word Basic data structure, a "record" of values from the File Summary dialog box in Word:

```
Dim fsi As Object
objWord.FileOpen "C:\TESTFILE.DOC"
Set fsi = objWord.CurValues.FileSummaryInfo
```

See the lstAvailable_DblClick event procedure in frmDocInfo's module for an example of using this technique.

The object variable, *fsi,* now refers to a live data structure in Word. It acts as a user-defined type in Access, and contains members, each of which contains data. Table 12-6 describes the members of the FileSummaryInfo data structure in the order in which you'll use them when calling the FileSummaryInfo statement. All elements are strings, except for the Update member, which is only used when executing the FileSummaryInfo statement.

MEMBER	DESCRIPTION
Title	Title of the document
Subject	Subject of the document
Author	Author of the document
Keywords	Identifying keywords
Comments	Comments about the document
FileName	File name of the document, without its path
Directory	Directory location of the file (read-only)
Template	Document's template (read-only)

Table 12-6 Members of the FileSummaryInfo data structure

MEMBER	DESCRIPTION
CreateDate	Creation date for the document (read-only)
LastSavedDate	Date the document was last saved (read-only)
LastSavedBy	Name of the last person who saved the document (read-only)
RevisionNumber	Number of times the document has been saved (including changes to the summary information by this program) (read-only)
EditTime	Cumulative time the document has been open, in minutes
LastPrintedDate	Date the document was last printed (read-only)
NumPages	Number of pages in the document (read-only)
NumWords	Number of words in the document (read-only)
NumChars	Number of characters in the document (read-only)
NumParas	Number of paragraphs in the document (read-only)
NumLines	Number of lines in the document (read-only)
Update	Used only when executing the FileSummaryInfo statement; ensures that the summary information is current
FileSize	Size of the document, in the form "12,345 Bytes" (read-only)

Table 12-6 Members of the FileSummaryInfo data structure

To use the members of *fsi*, treat them as any other user-defined type, except that you can only read the values (you'll need to use the FileSummaryInfo statement to change the values). For example, to retrieve a document's keywords, you could use code like this:

```
Set fsi = objWord.CurValues.FileSummaryInfo
Debug.Print fsi.Keywords
Set fsi = Nothing
objWord.FileClose 2
```

This code retrieves the summary information it needs, then "unlinks" the *fsi* variable from the Word FileSummaryInfo structure by setting it equal to Nothing. Finally, it closes the file you opened, using the FileClose WordBasic action. The 2 on the FileClose statement tells Word not to save the file, whether it's been changed or not. See the DisplayFileSummaryInfo subroutine in frmDocInfo's module for more information.

Changing the Summary Info

To write information to a document's FileSummaryInfo structure, use the Word Basic FileSummaryInfo statement. This statement takes as many parameters as there are rows in Table 12-6, and you can use whichever parameters you need. The parameters are position sensitive, so you must use commas as placeholders for any parameters you don't specify. You needn't put trailing commas after the last value you specify, however. (If you want to set Summary Info for a document that is currently open in Word, but you're not sure if it's the current document, you must specify the FileName parameter to indentify the document.) Note that most of the FileSummaryInfo values are read-only.

On the sample form, frmDocInfo, you can only enter new data into the read/write fields. To set new Title and Keyword values, you could use code like this:

```
objWord.FileOpen "C:\TESTFILE.DOC"
objWord.FileSummaryInfo "New Title", , , "New Keywords"
objWord.FileClose 1
```

Note the commas used as placeholders for the Subject and Author fields, which this code is not changing. See the event procedure cmdSaveSummary_Click in the sample form's module for an example of using this code.

Close Word for Windows

Once you're done, sever the connection by setting the object variable that refers to the Word Basic object to Nothing, as shown here:

```
Set objWord = Nothing
```

This will close Word, if you opened it with the call to CreateObject, and release any memory used by the OLE connection between Access and Word. If Word was previously open, it will stay open.

Word Data Structures in Access

Complex data structures, as outlined in Table 12-6, are a part of working with Microsoft Word for Windows. Unfortunately, because of the differences between Word and Access, you won't be able to use one of Word's best features: its use of named arguments instead of positional arguments. For example, to use the FileSummaryInfo statement to set a document's keywords from Word for Windows, you could use a statement like this:

```
FileSummaryInfo .Keywords = "New Keywords"
```

Since Access doesn't support named parameters, though, you accomplish the same task this way from Access Basic:

```
objWord.FileSummaryInfo , , , "New Keywords"
```

As Table 12-6 shows, the Keywords value is the fourth parameter to the FileSummaryInfo statement. This conflict can cause you a great deal of trouble, especially if you don't notice that the Word Developer's Kit lists the parameters in a different order from what Word expects from outside callers. To get the exact positions, you'll need to use POSITION.TXT, a text file that ships with both the Word and Office Developer's Kits. This file lists each statement in Word Basic along with the order of its parameters. Don't even try to work without this file—it's just impossible.

Comments

To refer to an embedded Word document, rather than loading Word and the file explicitly, you must first activate the object, and then you can take whatever action you need. For example, if you want to set the first paragraph of your document to be bold you could use code like the following, attached to the Click event of a command button. This code fragment assumes that the name of your OLE control is Embedded0. See the Word Basic documentation for explanations of the StartOfDocument, ParaDown, and Bold actions.

```
Dim objWord As Object
' Activate the OLE object, using the primary verb
Me!Embedded0.Verb = 0
Me!Embedded0.Action = 7
Set objWord = Me!Embedded0.Object.Application.WordBasic

objWord.StartOfDocument
objWord.ParaDown 1, 1
objWord.Bold 1
Set objWord = Nothing
' Close the OLE object
Me!Embedded0.Action = 9
```

When you use the CreateObject function to start Word for Windows, you have no control over how or where it loads. If it was last used full-screen, it will start up full-screen. If the aesthetics are important to you, take matters into your own hands: Use the Shell function to start Word minimized. You can use the information in How-To 11.8 to find out whether Word is running first. You can use the information in How-To 11.10 to close Word when you're done, since there's no automated way to shut it down if you started it yourself.

As with any cross-application tools, it's imperative that you have the correct documentation if you're going to be using Word Basic from your Access applications: the Microsoft Word Developer's Kit and/or the Office Developer's Kit.

12.5 HOW DO I...

Send a fax to WinFax Pro directly from Access?

Problem
I use WinFax Pro, and I need to print a report directly to the fax/modem. I'd also like to fill in the name and fax number automatically. Is there a way to have Access send the printout directly to WinFax Pro, along with the recipient information?

Technique
WinFax Pro can communicate with Access via Dynamic Data Exchange (DDE). This protocol is gradually being superseded by OLE Automation, but for now, DDE is the only way to chat between Access and WinFax. (Few Windows applications other than Microsoft Office support the OLE Automation technology yet.)

Think of DDE as a conversation between the two applications: Access calls WinFax Pro and attempts to send and receive information. Though this How-To cannot fully explain the details of using DDE with every application, it will

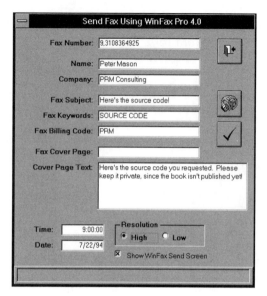

Figure 12-10 The sample faxing form, frmSendFax

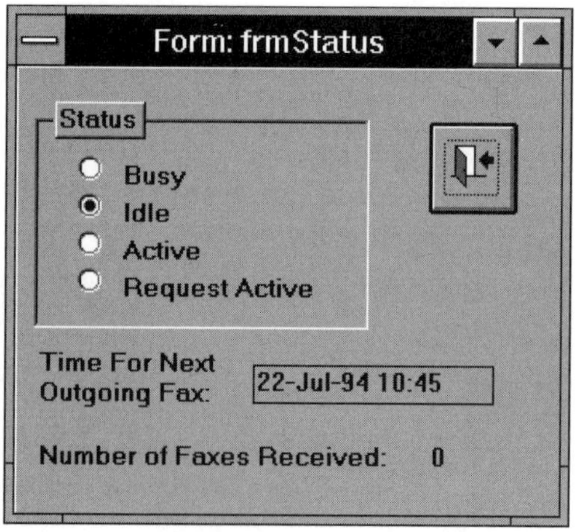

Figure 12-11 The sample form, frmStatus, showing the current WinFax status

cover the WinFax DDE interface completely. Of course, to use the information in this How-To, you'll need to own a copy of WinFax Pro and be familiar with it.

Steps

To get started, load the sample database 12-05.MDB. Open one of the modules in the database in design mode (any document will do, actually) and click on the Fax It button on the toolbar. (The AutoExec macro for this database loads the WinFax toolbar, which includes just that single button.) You will see the form shown in Figure 12-10.

You can request information on the current status of WinFax Pro by clicking on the check mark button on frmSendFax. This pops up a second form, shown in Figure 12-11, which includes all the information that you can request from WinFax via DDE. If WinFax Pro isn't currently running when you call up this form, you'll be informed that you can't retrieve status information, and the form will close.

Once you've completed the form, click on the button with the WinFax icon. This sends the information on frmSendFax to WinFax and starts printing the current document to the WinFax printer driver. When the printing is done, the code sets the current printer back to the original default printer. (None of this will work unless the selected document normally prints to the default Windows printer. See Chapter 5 for information on programmatically setting and detecting the assigned printer for a document.)

This How-To's steps have two levels of detail: First we'll explain how to use the sample forms and code supplied in 12-05.MDB, and next we'll explain how to use DDE to converse with WinFax in your own applications.

Using the Sample Forms

To include the functionality provided by frmSendFax and frmStatus in your own applications, follow these steps:

1. Import the modules listed in Table 12-7 from 12-05.MDB. This may seem like a long list, but each module is small. Small modules are easier to reuse without consuming too many resources.

MODULE NAME	PURPOSE
basDefaultPrinter	Set and retrieve the current default Windows printer.
basIniFile	Read and write values in INI files.
basPrintTypes	Data types for printer manipulation.
basToken	Pull apart delimited strings (for printer handling, in this case).
basUsage	Determine whether or not an application is running.
basWinFax	Send document to WinFax printer driver.

Table 12-7 Modules to import from 12-05.MDB, for support of frmSendFax and frmStatus

2. Import frmSendFax and frmStatus from 12-05.MDB.

3. Import the macro, mcrFaxIt, from 12-05.MDB. This macro contains a single action, RunCode, to run the ahtFaxIt function in basWinFax. Running this macro will print the current document to WinFax Pro.

4. Modify an existing toolbar or create a new one, adding a button to run the mcrFaxIt macro. To do this, select View|Toolbars, and choose the New button on the dialog or select an existing toolbar. Click the Customize button, and from the list of items on the left, choose All Macros. From the list of macros, choose mcrFaxIt, and drag the chosen macro to your toolbar. This places a script icon on the toolbar. To modify its picture or use text instead, right-click on the new toolbar button, and select the Choose Button Face option. Either use one of the supplied bitmaps or enter text in the text box at the bottom of the dialog box. The sample database uses the text "Fax It" rather than a bitmap.

5. Either import the AutoExec macro from 12-05.MDB or modify your existing AutoExec macro, adding the ShowToolBar action and setting it to load your new or modified toolbar when the application starts up.

6. You should be able to select any object, click on the toolbar button you've just created, and have the sample form, frmSendFax, pop up.

7. Once the form has popped up, fill in the information you'd like. All the fields are optional except the fax number. You can specify a fax cover page by giving its file name, or just leave this blank to use the WinFax simple cover page. You can specify a time and date to send the fax, or just leave those fields blank to send it now. If you check Show WinFax Send Screen, WinFax will pop up its Send dialog before it sends the fax, allowing you to alter the address, add it to the WinFax address book, or modify the cover page.

Using DDE Directly

To create your own DDE conversations between Access and WinFax Pro, follow these steps. For details, see the "How It Works" section.

1. **Initiate the conversation with WinFax Pro.** Use the DDEInitiate function in Access to start a conversation with the FAXMNG application (that's WinFax's application name) on the TRANSMIT topic. If you get a nonzero channel back, you're fine; otherwise, you'll need to try to start the WinFax application using the Shell function. If that fails, you're out of luck. If it succeeds, try again to initiate a conversation, using DDEInitiate. If it still fails, quit. Otherwise, move on to step 2. The code to initiate the conversation, from frmSendFax, looks like this:

```
On Error Resume Next
intChannel = DDEInitiate("FaxMng", "TRANSMIT")

If Err Then
   Err = 0
   ' It's got to be in your Path or this won't work!
   hInstance = Shell("FaxMNG.EXE", 6)
   If Err Then
      MsgBox "Unable to start WinFax Pro."
      Exit Sub
   End If
   intChannel = DDEInitiate("FaxMng", "TRANSMIT")

   If Err <> 0 Then
      MsgBox "Unable to start a DDE conversation with WinFax Pro."
      Exit Sub
   End If
End If
```

2. **Send the necessary information.** Once you have a conversation going with WinFax, send it any information you've gathered up from the form. Look ahead to Table 12-10 for all the values you can send to WinFax, using the DDEPoke subroutine, before printing the fax. WinFax supports only a single topic to which you can poke information, SendFax: In the example below, all the information is poked to the SendFax topic. You'll want to send the recipient information (including the required fax number) first, and then any other information you have. Every piece of information you send via DDE must be delimited with quotes, so carefully examine the pattern of quotes and take care when creating your own code. The following code fragment sends the information to WinFax:

```
DDEPoke intChan, "SendFax", "recipient(" & BuildRecipient() & ")"
DDEPoke intChan, "SendFax", "showsendscreen(" & QUOTE & ⇒
IIf(Me!chkShowSendScreen, "1", "0") & QUOTE & ")"
If Not IsNull(Me!txtCoverPage) Then
   DDEPoke intChan, "SendFax", "setcoverpage(" & QUOTE & Me!txtCoverPage & QUOTE & ")"
End If
```

```
If Not IsNull(Me!txtFillCoverPage) Then
    DDEPoke intChan, "SendFax", "fillcoverpage(" & QUOTE & Me!txtFillCoverPage & QUOTE & ")"
End If
DDEPoke intChan, "SendFax", "resolution(" & QUOTE & ⇒
IIf(Me!grpResolution = 1, "HIGH", "LOW") & QUOTE & ")"
```

3. **Terminate the conversation.** Once you're done sending information to WinFax, that's all you need to do via DDE. You must terminate all DDE conversations manually, since Windows supports only a limited number of these conversations. If you don't use the DDETerminate subroutine to shut down the channel, Windows may run out of conversation handles. Here is the code:

```
DDETerminate intChan
```

4. **Store the current default printer and set the new one.** As long as your document has been configured to print to the default printer, you can retrieve the current default printer information, store it, and set WinFax to be the current printer. This is accomplished in the following code from ahtFaxIt in basWinFax. (For more information on setting and retrieving the current default printer, see Chapter 5.)

```
Dim dr As aht_tagDeviceRec
Dim drDefaultPrinter As aht_tagDeviceRec

Const ERR_PRINT_CANCELLED = 2501

On Error GoTo ahtFaxitError

' Get the default printer information and store it away.
If ahtGetDefaultPrinter(drDefaultPrinter) Then

    ' Switch the printing device to be WinFax
    dr.drDeviceName = "WinFax"
    dr.drDriverName = "WinFax"
    dr.drPort = "FaxModem"
    If ahtSetDefaultPrinter(dr) Then
...
```

5. **Print the document.** WinFax is now waiting for someone to tell it to send something. When you print to the WinFax device, you're telling WinFax that it's time to go into action. You set the WinFax device to be the current Windows printer in step 4, so using the Access Print macro action will do the job.

> ✏️ **NOTE:** in the sample application, ahtFaxIt loads the form frmSendFax before it prints the document, in order to gather information about the fax's recipient. The order of events isn't terribly important; as long as you use DDE to send the information to WinFax before you print the document, it should go where you want it.

6. **Reset the default printer.** Once you're done printing, reset the Windows default printer so that the next print job will go to the real printer (unless you go through this particular code again). Since you stored the default printer in step 4, it's simple to put it back:

```
If Not ahtSetDefaultPrinter(drDefaultPrinter) Then
    MsgBox "Unable to reset the default printer."
End If
```

How It Works

When you initiate a DDE conversation with an application, you must specify its application name (which is often different from its executable file name and must be determined on a case-by-case basis), and you must specify a topic about which you want to "talk." WinFax's application name is FAXMNG, and Table 12-8 lists the topics about which WinFax is prepared to initiate a conversation. In each case, you'll need to use the DDEInitiate function to retrieve a channel number. All other communication between Access and WinFax will use that channel number as a reference. For example, to initiate a conversation on the TRANSMIT topic, you'd use code like this:

```
Dim intChannel As Integer
intChannel = DDEInitiate("FAXMNG", "TRANSMIT")
```

TOPIC	DESCRIPTION
TRANSMIT	WinFax's send features: recipient information, resolution, attachments, cover pages
CONTROL	Winfax's control features: idle/active, immediate receive, retrieve status

Table 12-8 WinFax Pro's DDE Topics

Access supports a number of procedures related to DDE, but the four listed in Table 12-9 are the ones you'll use when writing Access Basic code to communicate with another application. In each case, you'll refer to a channel number, obtained through a call to DDEInitiate, using the topic listed in the second column. To use DDEPoke, you must have a channel obtained by a call to DDEInitiate on the TRANSMIT topic. To use DDERequest, you must have a channel obtained using the CONTROL topic. The next few paragraphs discuss the details of requesting and sending information from and to WinFax Pro.

ACTIVITY	TOPIC
DDEPoke	TRANSMIT
DDEExecute	CONTROL
DDERequest	CONTROL
DDETerminate	(Either)

Table 12-9 Access DDE procedures, and corresponding WinFax topics

Sending Information to WinFax

Table 12-10 lists the items about which you can send information to WinFax. The item in the first column is a keyword, representing the piece of information you're sending. Follow each keyword with a comma-delimited list of quoted strings in parentheses, as shown in the third column of the table. The DDEPoke items are case-sensitive and must be used exactly as they appear in the table.

ITEM	DESCRIPTION	PARAMETERS
recipient	Specify recipient details (see Table 12-11).	recipient(*"Fax Number", "Time", "Date", "Name", "Company", "Subject", "Keywords", "Billing Code"*)
setcoverpage	Specify the file name of the cover page.	setcoverpage(*"filename"*)
fillcoverpage	Provide the cover page text (can include WinFax variables).	fillcoverpage(*"Text for cover page"*)
attach	Specify the file(s) to attach.	attach(*"filename"*)
resolution	Set the fax resolution.	resolution("HIGH"|"LOW")
showsendscreen	Tell WinFax to display the send screen before sending the fax.	showsendscreen("0"|"1")

Table 12-10 Items available with DDEPoke

Sending Parameters via DDE

> ### QUOTED STRINGS WITHIN STRINGS
> In most DDE implementations, you must send the parameters to any DDE items as quoted strings. This means that you must create strings that themselves contain quoted strings. This can be somewhat tricky in Access Basic. Be sure to follow the suggestions in this topic on embedding quotes within strings.

Although there are several methods to create strings containing quotation marks, the one used here, the QUOTE constant, results in code that's relatively easy to decipher. You first create a constant, QUOTE,

```
Const QUOTE = """"
```

which creates a quoted string containing a single quote (two quotes inside a string are seen as a single quote by Access). Then, whenever you need to embed a quote within a string, you can use the QUOTE constant. See How-To 7.1 for more suggestions on embedding quoted strings inside other strings. For example, the following pair of procedures build up the recipient string, as defined in Table 12-10, pulling values from frmSendFax in the sample application:

```
Function FixUp (ByVal varVal As Variant)

Const QUOTE = """"

    FixUp = IIf(IsNull(varVal), "", QUOTE & varVal & QUOTE)
End Function


Function BuildRecipient ()

    Dim strVal As String

    strVal = FixUp(Me!txtFaxNumber)
    strVal = strVal & "," & FixUp(Me!txtTime)
    strVal = strVal & "," & FixUp(Me!txtDate)
    strVal = strVal & "," & FixUp(Me!txtName)
    strVal = strVal & "," & FixUp(Me!txtCompany)
    strVal = strVal & "," & FixUp(Me!txtSubject)
    strVal = strVal & "," & FixUp(Me!txtKeyWords)
    strVal = strVal & "," & FixUp(Me!txtBillingCode)
    BuildRecipient = strVal
End Function
```

To send the recipient information to WinFax, you use the DDEPoke command in Access. DDEPoke requires you to specify a topic, and WinFax supports only a single topic: SendFax.

```
DDEPoke intChan, "SendFax", "recipient(" & BuildRecipient () & ")"
```

Remember, the values you send via DDE must be strings, and they must contain strings surrounded with quotes.

Table 12-11 lists all the parameters for setting the recipient in WinFax via DDE. The BuildRecipient function, above, pulls the value for each of these fields from the sample form. Your own application could get them from a table, a form, or from an INI file. Step 2, under "Using DDE Directly" in the "Steps" section above, demonstrates the use of the other DDEPoke items.

PARAMETER	DESCRIPTION	FORMAT OR MAXIMUM LENGTH
Fax number	Fax number to be dialed	47 characters
Time	Time at which to send the fax	hh:mm:ss
Date	Date on which to send the fax	mm/dd/yy
Name	Recipient's name	31 characters
Company	Recipient's company name	42 characters
Subject	Subject of the fax	79 characters
Keywords	Keywords associated with the fax	33 characters
Billing code	Billing code associated with the fax	26 characters

Table 12-11 Parameters for the DDEPoke recipient event

Controlling WinFax's Operational State

You can use DDE to control the WinFax operational state, too. Table 12-12 lists all the options available with channels initiated on the WinFax CONTROL topic. These options allow you to set WinFax to be idle, active, or to receive an incoming fax immediately. For the record, using the GoIdle DDE command is the only way to force WinFax to release its control over your comm port. If you need to share the same port for WinFax and Access auto-dialing, you'll want to include two routines to clear the port and then reset it once you're done. For example, the following procedure will force WinFax to go into idle state (of course, you'd need to add error checking in real code):

```
Dim intChannel As Integer
intChannel = DDEInitiate("FAXMNG", "CONTROL")
DDEExecute intChannel, "GoIdle"
DDETerminate intChannel
```

ITEM	DESCRIPTION	EXAMPLE
GoIdle	WinFax releases the comm port and disables automatic reception. This method represents the only way of forcing WinFax Pro to release the port so another comm program can use it.	DDEExecute(intChannel, "GoIdle")
GoActive	WinFax takes over the comm port again, reenables Automatic Receive, and handles any scheduled activities that took place while it was disabled.	DDEExecute(intChannel, "GoActive")
ReceiveFaxNow	Tell WinFax to receive a fax manually. This is useful if your application detects that an incoming call is a fax call.	DDEExecute(intChannel, "ReceiveFaxNow")

Table 12-12 Items available with DDEExecute

You can request information about the current operating status of WinFax using the DDERequest function and a conversation based on the CONTROL topic. Table 12-13 lists the information you can request. These items are case-sensitive, and you must use them exactly as shown in order to effectively communicate with WinFax. All three of these items are used in the sample form, frmStatus in 12-05.MDB. The following code shows the sample form's Open event procedure, which calls WinFax three times to retrieve all three pieces of information:

```
Sub Form_Open (Cancel As Integer)
   Dim intChannel As Integer
   Dim strStatus As String

   On Error Resume Next
   Me.SetFocus
   intChannel = DDEInitiate("FAXMNG", "CONTROL")
```

(Continued on next page)

(Continued from previous page)

```
    If Err  0 Then
        MsgBox "Unable to communicate with WinFax."
        Cancel = True
    Else
        strStatus = DDERequest(intChannel, "Status")
        ' Get rid of trailing CR/LF
        strStatus = Left(strStatus, Len(strStatus) - 2)
        Me!grpStatus = Switch(strStatus = "BUSY", 1, strStatus = "IDLE", 2, ⇒
strStatus = "ACTIVE", 3, strStatus = "REQUEST_ACTIVE", 4)

        Me!txtNumberReceived = DDERequest(intChannel, "NumberFaxesReceived")
        Me!txtNextOutgoing = DDERequest(intChannel, "TimeUntilNextOutgoing")
        DDETerminate intChannel
    End If
End Sub
```

ITEM	DESCRIPTION	EXAMPLE
Status	The operating status of WinFax (see Table 12-14 for specifics).	strStatus = DDERequest(intChannel, "Status")
NumberFaxesReceived	Number of incoming faxes logged in the WinFax log.	strNumFaxes = DDERequest(intChannel, "NumberFaxesReceived")
TimeUntilNextOutgoing	Time and date of next scheduled outgoing fax.	strTime = DDERequest(intChannel, "TimeUntilNextOutgoing")

Table 12-13 Items available with DDERequest

Table 12-14 lists the possible return values of status requests. If you request the number of faxes received, you'll get a string containing the number of new faxes. If you request the time for the next outgoing fax, you'll receive a string in the format *dd-mm-yy hh:mm*, as shown in Figure 12-11.

RETURN VALUE	DESCRIPTION
"BUSY"	Winfax is currently sending or receiving a fax.
"IDLE"	Winfax is not monitoring calls, so either you turned off automatic reception, or you've used the GoIdle DDE command.
"ACTIVE"	Automatic reception is enabled, but there's currently no activity.
"REQUEST_ACTIVE"	You've used GoIdle, but there's a pending outgoing fax, and WinFax is waiting to receive control so it can send the fax.

Table 12-14 DDERequest Status return values

Comments

The sample form, frmSendFax, would need substantial enhancement before unleashing it on end users. For example, you can use the Windows common File Open dialog, discussed in How-To 4.7, to accommodate the selection of a cover page file. You can use the WinFax Pro phone book files (if they're stored in dBASE format) to retrieve a list of names and phone numbers, rather than requesting that the information be typed into text boxes. The error handling is rudimentary, at best, in the sample forms, and you'd want to make that a bit more robust before using it in an application.

The information in this How-To is applicable to a number of other applications. If you place the code supplied here in a library database, you could supply this functionality for any database. You might store the faxed image file names as information in a table and use DDE to have WinFax provide Fax-On-Demand services, sending the document requested from the Access table.

12.6 HOW DO I...   COMPLEXITY: INTERMEDIATE

Add an item to Program Manager's Startup group?

Problem

As part of my application, I would like to allow users to add the application to Program Manager's Startup group so that my application will start when Windows does. I just can't figure out how to put the information into the Program Manager group. Is there a way to communicate between Access and Program Manager so I can do this?

Technique

Program Manager (and most of its replacements) accepts commands using DDE that allow you to create and delete groups and items within those groups. You can also retrieve lists of the existing groups and items. This How-To answers the "How Do I..." question by explaining most of Program Manager's DDE interface.

Steps

To test Program Manager's DDE interface, load and run frmProgMan from 12-06.MDB. This form, shown in Figure 12-12, allows you to view groups and their items, create and delete groups and items, and show a particular group in Program Manager.

> ## NOT ALL SHELLS ARE CREATED ALIKE
> When you first load frmProgMan, it will attempt to begin a DDE conversation with Program Manager. If you are using another Windows shell, you may or may not have trouble. Most alternative shells either pretend they're Program Manager, intercept the DDE conversation, and handle all the work themselves; or they start up Program Manager for you when you first attempt to initiate the conversation. This sample application was tested with three of the major shell replacements on the market, and it worked fine with all of them.

Once you select a group from the list on the left, the form will display the group's items in the list on the right. If you select the first item in the right-hand list—the group itself—the form will display the information Program Manager has stored about that group. (Figure 12-13 shows frmProgMan with a group selected.) Once you've selected a group in the right-hand list box, you can click the Show button to have Program Manager display that group. The code attached to the Show button tells Program Manager to open the group window using style 3 (look ahead to Table 12-20 for a list of window styles), so the window will be maximized within Program Manager's main window. Program Manager may grab the focus, depending on the previous state of the group window you've selected. (The boxed text, "Switching Focus" in the "How It Works" section describes this in more detail.)

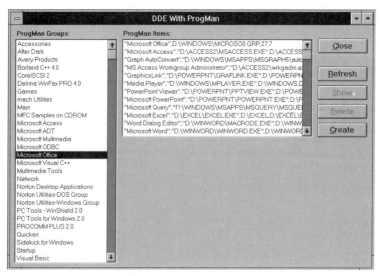

Figure 12-12 The sample form, frmProgMan, allows you to communicate with Program Manager via DDE

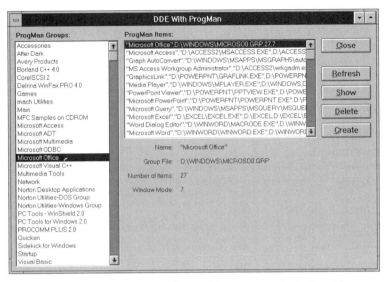

Figure 12-13 The frmProgMan form with a group selected and its information displayed

Select an item in the group (any row below the first row in the right-hand list box), and the form will display all the information that Program Manager stores about that item. Figure 12-14 shows frmProgMan with an item selected.

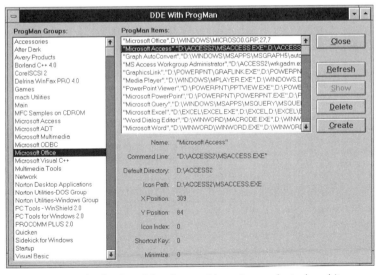

Figure 12-14 The frmProgMan form with an item selected and its information displayed

With either a group or an item selected, you can create or delete a group or an item. If you've selected a group, pressing the Delete button will instruct Program Manager to delete that group. If you've selected an item, frmProgMan will instruct Program Manager to delete the item from within its group. No matter what's selected, pressing the Create button will pop up a dialog asking whether you want to create a new item or new group (just as Program Manager does). Either choice will pop up the appropriate dialog box, requesting the necessary information.

The following steps describe first how to use the sample forms in your own applications. Then they explain most of the DDE interface to Program Manager. Although there are more DDE options available, most common tasks can be accomplished with the tools provided here.

Use the Sample Forms

To include the sample forms from 12-06.MDB in your own applications, follow these steps:

1. Import the items shown in Table 12-15 from 12-06.MDB into your own application.

OBJECT	NAME	PURPOSE
Form	frmNew	Choose new group versus new item
Form	frmNewGroup	Enter new group information
Form	frmNewItem	Enter new item information
Form	frmProgMan	Main form
Module	basProgman	Perform DDE conversations with Program Manager
Module	basSortArray	Sort arrays (list of program groups)
Module	basToken	Pull apart strings (item and group information on frmProgMan)

Table 12-15 Objects to import from 12-06.MDB

2. Load and run frmProgMan.

As described above, you can use the form to manipulate groups and items in Program Manager from your Access application. If you want to use pieces of frmProgMan in your application, but not the whole thing, that's fine too. If you use the group list (lstGroups), you'll also need to include the function that fills it, FillGroups. If you also want the item list (lstItems) from frmProgMan, you'll need its list-filling function, FillItems. In addition, you'll want to place code in lstGroup's AfterUpdate event that requeries lstItems once you've made a selection in lstGroups. So, you'll end up with an event procedure like this:

```
Sub lstGroups_AfterUpdate ()
    Me!lstItems.Requery
End Sub
```

To use other bits and pieces of the functionality of frmProgMan, you'll need to investigate its form module.

To Use DDE with Program Manager

If your main interest is just using DDE to control Program Manager, follow these steps:

1. Import the module basProgMan from 12-06.MDB into your own application. This module is completely self-contained and includes a number of functions that will set up a DDE conversation with Program Manager, do the work or retrieve the information you need, and then terminate the conversation. Because we've hidden all the details of the DDE, you needn't worry about getting all the syntax and parameters correct.

2. Depending on your needs, call one or more of the wrapper procedures described in Table 12-16. All of these functions are discussed in detail (Table 12-21) in "How It Works."

PROCEDURE	PURPOSE
ahtPMCreateGroup	Create a group, given a group name and a path name for the group file.
ahtPMCreateItem	Create a new ProgMan item, given the group name, the item name, the command line, the default directory, and whether or not to run the application minimized.
ahtPMDeleteGroup	Delete a ProgMan group, given the name of the group to delete.
ahtPMDeleteItem	Delete an item from a group, given the name of the group and the name of the item.
ahtPMGetGroups	Fill a dynamic array with all the Program Manager groups.
ahtPMGetItems	Fill a dynamic array with all the items for a particular group.
ahtPMShowGroup	Show a particular group, given the name of the group and the window mode to use.
ahtPMShowMessages	Allow callers outside this module to set the status of message showing/hiding. Send in True to show messages, False to hide them (no DDE involved).

Table 12-16 Procedures in basProgMan to aid in using DDE between Access and Program Manager

How It Works

Program Manager supports two operations: You can either request information using the DDERequest function (Table 12-17 lists the DDERequest topics), or you can execute actions using the DDEExecute subroutine (Table 12-18, later in this section, lists the most useful subset of the Program Manager's DDEExecute command string interface). As described for WinFax in How-To 12.5, DDE conversations between Access and Program Manager involve three main steps:

1. Initiate the conversation.
2. Perform the necessary tasks.
3. Terminate the conversation.

Retrieving Information from Program Manager

Table 12-17 describes the two groups of information you can request from Program Manager. The sample form, frmProgMan in 12-06.MDB, uses both these requests in order to fill its two list boxes.

TO RETRIEVE	PROGRAM	TOPIC	ITEM	RETURNS
List of groups	PROGMAN	PROGMAN	PROGMAN	List of existing groups, separated with CR/LF pair
List of items in a group	PROGMAN	PROGMAN	<Group Name>	List of items in the specified group, separated with CR/LF pair

Table 12-17 DDERequest topics for Program Manager

To retrieve a list of groups from Program Manager using the Access DDERequest function, you must first initiate a conversation with the PROGMAN program, on the PROGMAN topic, requesting information on the PROGMAN item (Program Manager's DDE is a bit single-minded). The DDERequest call returns a carriage-return/line-feed delimited string of group names. It's up to your code to pull apart the list of groups and place them into whatever data structure that is most convenient for you. To simplify this task, you can use the ahtPMGetGroups function in basProgMan. It accepts, as a parameter, a dynamic array to fill in with the list of groups. This function, shown below, performs the DDERequest for you, and it calls the private CopyToArray function to break apart the returned stream of groups and fill the array you've sent it. It returns the number of items in the array.

```
Function ahtPMGetGroups (avarGroups() As Variant)

    ' Fill a dynamic array with all the Program Manager
    ' groups.

    Dim intChannel As Integer
    Dim strGroups As String
    Dim intCount As Integer
    Dim intI As Integer

    On Error GoTo GetProgmanGroupsError
    ' Most replacement shells will start progman for you
    ' if you attempt to start up a DDE conversation with it.
    ' That is, you won't need to Shell() ProgMan.
    intChannel = DDEInitiate("PROGMAN", "PROGMAN")
    strGroups = DDERequest(intChannel, "PROGMAN")
    intCount = CopyToArray(strGroups, avarGroups())

GetProgmanGroupsExit:
    ahtPMGetGroups = intCount
    On Error Resume Next
    DDETerminate intChannel
```

```
    On Error GoTo 0
    Exit Function

GetProgmanGroupsError:
    MsgBox "Error: " & Error & " (" & Err & ")", MB_STOP, "ahtGetProgmanItems"
    Resume GetProgmanGroupsExit
End Function
```

To call this function from your own code, use code like this:

```
Dim avarGroups() as Variant
Dim intCount as Integer

intCount = ahtPMGetGroups(avarGroups())
' If you want the list sorted, call
' ahtSortArray, in basSortArray
ahtSortArray avarGroups()
```

To retrieve a list of items within a selected group, you can use the ahtPMGetItems function, which works almost exactly as ahtPMGetGroups does. This time, however, you pass in a group name along with the dynamic array to be filled in, and the function uses the group name as the topic, rather than PROGMAN (see Table 12-17). It calls the CopyToArray function to move the items into the dynamic array. You generally won't sort the array, however, unless you first store the first item; this first item returns information about the group window itself. All the rest of the rows contain information about the individual items. To use ahtPMGetItems, you might use code like this:

```
Dim avarGroups() as Variant
Dim avarItems() as Variant
Dim intCount as Integer

intCount = ahtPMGetGroups(avarGroups())
' If you want the list sorted, call
' ahtSortArray, in basSortArray
ahtSortArray avarGroups()
intCount = ahtPMGetItems(avarGroups(0), avarItems())
' List all the item information for the specified group
For intI = 0 To intCount - 1
    Debug.Print avarItems(intI)
Next intI
```

Executing Tasks in Program Manager

Program Manager includes a command string interface that you can access via DDE, allowing you to execute tasks involving groups and items within those groups. Table 12-18 lists the commands that are addressed in this How-To. Other commands are available (and they're documented in the Windows SDK documentation), but they're not as useful for Access programmers.

FUNCTION	PARAMETERS	DESCRIPTION
AddItem	See Table 12-19	Use CreateGroup first to select the group.
CreateGroup	*GroupName[, GroupPath]*	Select the group if it exists, otherwise create it.
DeleteGroup	*GroupName*	
DeleteItem	*ItemName*	Use CreateGroup first to select the group.
ShowGroup	*GroupName, ShowCommand*	See Table 12-20 for ShowCommand values.

Table 12-18 DDEExecute command-string interface for Program Manager

In each case, you use the Access DDEExecute procedure to communicate with Program Manager. You must construct a string containing the function name, parentheses, and any arguments for the function. For example, to create a group from Access, you can use code like this:

```
Dim intChannel as Integer
intChannel = DDEInitiate("PROGMAN", "PROGMAN")
DDEExecute intChannel, "[CreateGroup(My Group, MYGROUP.GRP)]"
```

The command string must be surrounded by square bracket delimiters ([ ]). Luckily, Program Manager is far more relaxed about the use of embedded quotes than almost any other DDE-enabled application. For example, WinFax Pro *requires* embedded quotes in command strings you send to it. Program Manager will accept embedded quotes, but doesn't require them.

Some functions, such as AddItem, allow quite a few parameters, almost all of which can be left blank (Table 12-19). To use the AddItem command to add a new item, you must first select a group in which to add the item. To select the group, use the CreateGroup command, which creates a group, if necessary, or selects it if it already exists. The only required AddItem parameter is the command line, and if you specify the coordinates for the icon, you must specify them both. For example, to create a new icon to run C:\EDIT\MYEDIT.EXE with the description "My Editor," minimized, in the My New Group group, you would use code like this (you'd normally include error-handling code, too):

```
Dim intChan As Integer
intChan = DDEInitiate("PROGMAN", "PROGMAN")
' First select the group (or create it)
DDEExecute intChan, "[CreateGroup(My New Group)]"
' Use commas to delimit parameters, even missing ones
DDEExecute intChan, "[AddItem(C:\EDIT\MYEDIT,My Editor,,,,,,1)]"
```

PARAMETER	DESCRIPTION	REQUIRED?	USED IN SAMPLE?
CmdLine	Command line to run the application. Must be at least the executable file name, but it can also include parameters as necessary.	Yes	Yes
Name	Name that appears below the icon in the Program Manager group.	No	Yes
IconPath	Name and path of the icon file to use. If executable file specified, use the first icon in that file. If left blank, use the first icon in the executable file specified in the CmdLine parameter.	No	No
IconIndex	Index of the icon in the specified IconPath file (or the specified executable). Use the first icon specified otherwise.	No	No
XPos	X-position of the icon within the group, as an integer. Both this and YPos required to set the specific position. If left blank, use the next available position.	No	No
YPos	Y-position of the icon within the group, as an integer.	No	No
DefDir	Default (or working) directory for the application.	No	Yes
HotKey	Hotkey for this application (stored as an integer).	No	No
fMinimize	Run minimized (1 = True, 0 = False).	No	Yes

Table 12-19 Parameters for the AddItem function

SWITCHING FOCUS

Using the ShowGroup command with Program Manager sometimes moves the focus to Program Manager, but most often it does not. Whether or not the focus switches depends on the state you request for the program group, and on its current state. Though you could make a matrix of options, comparing current states (minimized, normal, or maximized) against the new window state (1 through 8, as in Table 12-20), the rules are quite simple. If you change the state of a group that's currently minimized, the focus will switch to Program Manager. That means that if you choose actions 1, 3, or 4 for a group that is currently minimized, Program Manager will grab the focus. You can try this yourself, calling the ahtPMShowGroup function, passing it the name of a group and a new window style.

WINDOW STATE	ACTION
1	Activate and display the group window. If it was minimized or maximized, restore it to its original position (normalized).
2	Activate the group window and display it as an icon.
3	Activate the group window and display it maximized.
4	Display the group window normalized and leave the current group selected.
5	Activate the group window, and display it in its current placement.
6	Minimize the group window.
7	Minimize the group window and leave the current group selected.
8	Display the group window in its current placement and leave the current group selected.

Table 12-20 Command values for the ShowGroup function

The Wrapper Procedures

To make your DDE programming simpler, the module basProgMan includes wrapper procedures that handle all the details for you. Table 12-16 provides a description of each of the wrapper procedures, and Table 12-21 describes each procedure's parameters. The procedures that handle each of the commands are described in Table 12-18. In some cases (AddItem, for example), the wrapper functions don't allow you to specify all the possible parameters for the Program Manager command string. If you find these wrapper functions too limiting, you can modify them so they allow you to pass in whatever parameters you like.

PROCEDURE	PARAMETER	DATA TYPE	PARAMETER DESCRIPTION
ahtPMCreateGroup	varName	Variant	Name of new group.
	varGroupPath	Variant	Name of group file (can be null, in which case ProgMan uses a name of its own choosing).
ahtPMCreateItem	varGroup	Variant	Name of the group in which to create the new item.
	varName	Variant	Descriptive name for the new item, appears under the icon.
	varCommandLine	Variant	Command line to execute when this icon is chosen. Cannot be null.
	varDirectory	Variant	Default (working) directory when the application starts up.

Table 12-21 Wrapper functions in basProgMan

PROCEDURE	PARAMETER	DATA TYPE	PARAMETER DESCRIPTION
	varMinimized	Variant	Logical value: Run the app minimized?
ahtPMDeleteGroup	varName	Variant	Group to delete.
ahtPMDeleteItem	varGroup	Variant	Group from which to delete item.
	varName	Variant	Name of the item to delete.
ahtPMShowGroup	varName	Variant	Name of the group to show.
	intMode	Integer	Window state, as listed in Table 12-20.
ahtPMShowMessages	fShow	Integer	Logical value: Display messages during DDE wrapper functions? If True, functions use message box if errors occur and when deleting items from Program Manager. This subroutine sets a module global variable, so you only need to call it once per session.

Table 12-21 Wrapper functions in basProgMan

All of the wrapper procedures (except ahtPMShowMessages) in Table 12-21 end up performing the same set of steps to communicate with Program Manager. To simplify the code and to centralize error handling, those steps have been pulled out into the single private procedure in basProgMan, DDEExecutePM, shown in the following code example:

```
Private Function DDEExecutePM (strCommand As String)

   Dim intChannel As Integer

   On Error GoTo DDEExecutePMError

   intChannel = DDEInitiate("PROGMAN", "PROGMAN")
   DDEExecute intChannel, strCommand
   DDEExecutePM = True

DDEExecutePMExit:
   On Error Resume Next
   DDETerminate intChannel
   On Error GoTo 0
   Exit Function

DDEExecutePMError:
   If Not mfHideMessages Then
      Dim strError As String

      strError = "Error: " & Error & " (" & Err & ")" & Chr$(13) & Chr$(10)
      strError = strError & "DDEExecute Failed: " & strCommand
      MsgBox strError, MB_STOP, "DDEExecutePM"
   End If
```

(Continued on next page)

(Continued from previous page)

```
    DDEExecutePM = False
    Resume DDEExecutePMExit
End Function
```

This code, given a string to execute, initiates the DDE channel, uses DDEExecute to execute the command, and then terminates the connection. If all goes according to plan, the procedure returns a True value. If an error occurs, it displays a message box (unless you've used the ahtPMShowMessages procedure to disable warning messages), and then returns False.

Each of the wrapper procedures (except ahtPMShowMessages) returns True if the function succeeded or False if it failed. Unless you've called the ahtPMShowMessages subroutine to disable messages, you'll be warned with a message box before deleting a group or an item, or if any error occurs.

For example, to use the wrapper functions to add an icon to the My New Group group that will run C:\EDIT\MYEDIT.EXE minimized, with the description My Editor (as in the example above that called AddItem directly), you could use code like this:

```
Dim fSuccess As Integer

' Disable error messages
ahtPMShowMessages False
fSuccess = ahtPMCreateItem("My New Group", "My Editor", "C:\EDIT\MYEDIT.EXE", Null, True)
If Not fSuccess Then MsgBox "Unable to create new item!"
```

This example also calls ahtPMShowMessages to disable error messages from within ahtCreateItem, so the code fragment itself can handle them.

For examples of each of the wrapper functions, check out the code in frmProgMan's module.

Comments

Though this How-To covers a great deal more than the original question, all of the information here will be of use to Access programmers working with the DDE interface to Program Manager.

The sample form, frmProgMan, is not only a good example of using DDE to converse with Program Manager, it's also a useful tool on its own. Since you can see what is in each group without having to open and close each group's window, it's a quick and easy way to clean out your Program Manager groups. For it to be a really useful tool that you could distribute, it would definitely require some extra work. But it's a good start.

Although it's impossible to test every Program Manager replacement, we did test three of the major ones (Norton Desktop 2.0 from Symantec, PC Tools 2.0 for Windows from Central Point, and Dashboard from Borland), and all of these either handled the DDE conversation themselves or started Program Manager automatically at the first DDEInitiate function call. Before relying on the routines here, you should verify that the code works correctly with your own shell program (though it's hard to imagine any full-featured Windows shell program not supporting this feature).

To shield you from the details of the DDE conversation, and to isolate the DDE code in one routine, each of the command-string replacement functions calls the DDEExecutePM function. This makes the code neat and easy to understand, but it does introduce two issues to consider:

- By calling DDEInitiate and DDETerminate each and every time you call one of the wrapper functions, you're adding substantial time and overhead to your application. If you make many calls to Program Manager via DDE, you'll want to reconsider this design. For most applications, though, this shouldn't be a problem.

- DDETerminate has been known to cause memory leakage. That is, after each call to DDETerminate, not all of the memory used in the DDE conversation gets released, and multiple calls to DDEInitiate/ DDETerminate can deplete your free memory. The memory leakage has not been substantiated on our test machines.This shouldn't be a problem unless you perform many calls through the routines provided here. If you do need to make many calls to Program Manager, you might consider rewriting the provided routines so as not to initiate and terminate a new conversation for each function call.

12.7 HOW DO I...

COMPLEXITY: ADVANCED

Modify Microsoft Graph settings programmatically?

Problem
I need to be able to alter Microsoft Graph objects programmatically. Sometimes, I'd like to allow users to modify some of the attributes of a graph before printing it. Other times, I'd just like to modify the size of a graph's title. Is there a programmatic interface to Graph objects?

Technique
When you create a Graph object (using the form design toolbox), you actually embed an OLE object onto your form. The parent application for this object is MSGRAPH5.EXE, which is normally installed in the MSAPPS\MSGRAPH5 directory under your Windows directory. Graphs created by MSGRAPH5 expose a rich and powerful set of objects and properties that you can control programmatically from Access Basic. The only current documentation for these objects and properties is in a help file that is part of Microsoft's Office Developer's Kit (ODK), and a discussion of all of them is far beyond the scope of this How-To. The goal here is to demonstrate some simple manipulations involving pie charts. Once you understand the concepts behind setting and retrieving Graph object properties, you will be able to expand on the sample provided here to create your own masterpieces.

Steps

Load and run frmGraph in 12-07.MDB. This form, shown in Figure 12-15, includes a simple 3-D pie graph and controls that allow you to alter the graph's properties. All of these operations are performed by manipulating the Graph object's properties using OLE Automation. For example, with the Rotation and Elevation group of controls you can rotate the pie graph around the horizontal access (change its elevation) and around the vertical access (change its rotation). With the Position and Size controls you can change the location or size of the title, the legend, or the plot area. You can also explode one or more pie slices a specified percentage by double-clicking on the list box on the right side of the form.

Since the topic of OLE Automation control over Graph objects is so immense, this How-To focuses on creating a simple form like frmGraph. Once you've walked through the steps involved in this form, and armed with the Microsoft Graph help file from the ODK, you should be able to work wonders with Microsoft Graph and Access.

The following steps document all you need to do to create a form similar to the sample form, frmGraph. You might start by creating this form and then expanding on it, adding your own features once you've got it all working. We won't specify exact locations or properties for the controls on your form, since you may want to modify the "look" of the sample form as you create it. On the other hand, we will specify control event procedures, because these determine how the form operates.

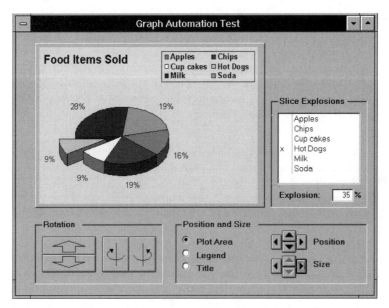

Figure 12-15 The sample form, frmGraph, allows you to alter properties of the 3-D pie graph

Set Up the Form

1. Create the table that will hold your data. In the sample database, you'll find tblFoods, which is the example that will be used throughout this How-To. If you use a different table for your example, you'll need to substitute field names to match those in tblFoods. Table 12-22 lists the structure for tblFoods. Any field properties not mentioned in the table have no bearing on the example, and they can be set any way you like.

FIELD NAME	DATA TYPE	OTHER DETAILS	DESCRIPTION
Item	Text		The food item name
Exploded	Number	Byte	The percentage exploded on the pie chart
Quantity	Number	Integer	The number sold for the given item
ID	Counter	Primary Key	

Table 12-22 The structure for the sample table, tblFoods

2. Create a query, based on tblFoods, named qryItems. This query will be the basis for the graph itself and for the list box showing the list of pie slices. Figure 12-16 shows the query design surface for qryItems. Your own version of this query must contain all the fields you want graphed, as well as the calculated field, IsExploded,

```
IsExploded:Iif(Exploded > 0, "x", "")
```

which controls the display of the "x" in the pie slice list box on the form.

3. Create an unbound form (named frmGraph in the example, but this name can be changed to whatever you like). Set its properties as shown in Table 12-23; these are the standard settings you'd use for any unbound form. Other properties can be set as you like.

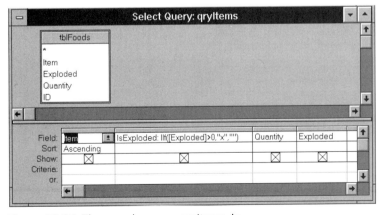

Figure 12-16 The sample query, qryItems, in design mode

PROPERTY	VALUE
RecordSource	
DefaultView	Single form
ScrollBars	Neither
RecordSelections	No
NavigationButtons	No
AutoResize	Yes

Table 12-23 Property settings for your unbound sample form

4. Choose the Graph tool in the toolbox, and create a graph control on the empty form. Then, follow the steps in Table 12-24 for creating your pie chart. Your form will look something like the one shown in Figure 12-17.

PAGE/QUESTION	CHOICE
Where do you want your graph to get its data?	qryItems
Which fields contain the data you want for your graph?	Item, Quantity (or whatever fields you want on your graph)
How do you want to calculate...?	Add (sum) the numbers
What type of graph do you want?	3-D Pie Chart (2nd row, 4th column of the graph type choices in the Graph Wizard)
	Data Series in Columns
What title do you want on your chart?	Food Items Sold (or anything else you like)

Table 12-24 Steps to take through the Graph Wizard

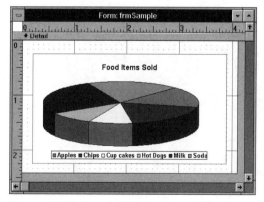

Figure 12-17 Your initial pie chart will look something like this

5. With the graph control selected, change the control's Name property in the properties sheet from Field0 (the default name that Access gave it) to objGraph. That's the control name expected by prewritten code later in this How-To.

6. With your form still in design mode, double-click on the graph control. Access will send you to the Microsoft Graph application, so you can modify any and all portions of your graph's display. For frmGraph, we added percent labels for the pie slices and moved the legend, title, and plot area around within the graph area. Make any changes you like.

7. Go back to Access using the File|Exit and Return menu option, and make sure and save your form.

Create the Controls

The following steps outline how to create the controls that will later be used to manipulate the Graph object. The sample form, frmGraph, lays them out in very specific groups, but you can place them any way you like. For the controls with bitmaps, you may find it easiest to copy them from frmGraph, if you want to use the bitmaps. Otherwise, you can supply your own or use text captions.

8. Create four command buttons on the form to control the graph's rotation and elevation (see Figure 12-18). Name them (from top to bottom and left to right in the figure) cmdElevationUp, cmdElevationDown, cmdRotateLeft, and cmdRotateRight. If you like the bitmaps as displayed, just copy the buttons from frmGraph, rather than creating your own.

9. Create an option group named grpPosSize. Set its DefaultValue property to 1. Inside it, create three option buttons, labeled Plot Area, Legend, and Title, with values 1, 2, and 3, respectively. This option group will indicate

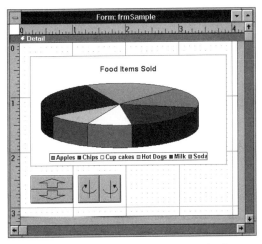

Figure 12-18 Your sample form with the four rotation buttons added

to the form whether you want to move and size the plot area, the legends, or the graph title.

10. Create two "clumps" of buttons, as shown in Figure 12-19, to control the movement and resizing of the graph. You'll probably just want to copy these from frmGraph, but if you create your own, name them as follows: cmdLeft, cmdUp, cmdRight, cmdDown for the top group; and cmdSizeLeft, cmdSizeUp, cmdSizeRight, and cmdSizeDown for the bottom group. Lay them out in any way you like, or use the configuration in Figure 12-19. You may also find it useful to create labels for the groups of buttons, as shown in the figure.

11. Create a text box on your form to contain the percentage of explosion for pie slices. Set its properties as shown in Table 12-25.

PROPERTY	VALUE
Name	txtExplode
Format	Fixed
DecimalPlaces	0
DefaultValue	35
ValidationRule	Between 0 and 100
ValidationText	Please enter a value between 0 and 100

Table 12-25 Property settings for the Explosion value text box

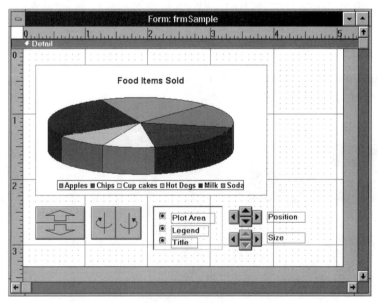

Figure 12-19 The sample form after adding the option group and command buttons for moving and resizing objects

12. Create a list box to contain the list of pie slice items and their exploded state. Set its properties as shown in Table 12-26. You'll need to replace differing field names with your own values.

PROPERTY	VALUE
Name	lstItems
RowSourceType	Table/Query
RowSource	Select [IsExploded], [Item] from qryItems;
ColumnCount	2
ColumnHeads	No
ColumnWidths	0.2 in;0.75 in
BoundColumn	1

Table 12-26 Property settings for the explosion list box

Figure 12-20 shows the new form with all its controls in place.

13. Select all the command buttons on your form, using Shift-click. Then set their collective AutoRepeat property to yes.

14. Select all the controls on your form besides objGraph. (To do this, drag the mouse in the left vertical ruler until you've selected all the objects. Then, Shift-click on objGraph to *remove* it from the selection. Neat trick!) Once you've got them all selected, set their collective DisplayWhen properties to be Screen Only.

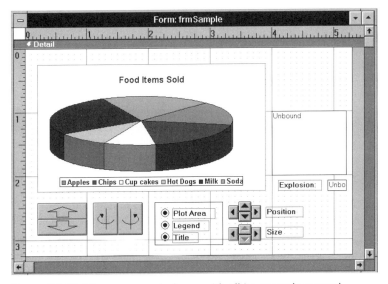

Figure 12-20 The new sample form, with all its controls created

Creating and Attaching the Code

The following steps create the form module that controls the elements of the graph. All the code for this example resides in the sample form's module, not in global modules.

15. Import the module basHandleGraph from 12-07.MDB. This module contains the general-purpose routines that move, size, rotate, and elevate the chart objects. (In the "How It Works" section Table 12-28 describes each of the properties used in the example, along with the procedure from basHandleGraph that does the work.)

16. Open the form's module, and enter the following fragment in the declarations area. This creates the constants used in determining how fast things move and rotate on the screen. Altering these constants can change the apparent speed at which graph parts move.

```
Const MOVE_DELTA = 5
Const ELEVATE_DELTA = 5
Const ROTATE_DELTA = 15
Const SIZE_DELTA = 5
```

OBJECT	EVENT PROPERTY
cmdDown	OnClick
cmdElevationDown	OnClick
cmdElevationUp	OnClick
cmdLeft	OnClick
cmdRight	OnClick
cmdRotateLeft	OnClick
cmdRotateRight	OnClick
cmdSizeDown	OnClick
cmdSizeLeft	OnClick
cmdSizeRight	OnClick
cmdSizeUp	OnClick
cmdUp	OnClick
Form	OnLoad
Form	OnClose
grpPosSize	AfterUpdate
lstItems	OnDblClick

Table 12-27 Objects and their properties that include event procedures

17. Table 12-27 lists the events to which you'll need to attach code. For each object in Table 12-27, set the appropriate property to be [Event Procedure]. Then, enter the procedures shown in the following listing. These are the routines that react to your mouse clicks on the form to move the various pieces of the graph. (You can copy each of these from frmGraph's module, if you like.) Most of these subroutines just call directly to the procedures

imported in step 15. A few of them, though, actually do substantial work.
See the "How It Works" section for details.

```
Sub cmdDown_Click ()
   MoveIt Me, MOVE_DELTA, 0
End Sub


Sub cmdElevationDown_Click ()
   ElevateIt Me, ELEVATE_DELTA
End Sub


Sub cmdElevationUp_Click ()
   ElevateIt Me, -ELEVATE_DELTA
End Sub


Sub cmdLeft_Click ()
   MoveIt Me, 0, -MOVE_DELTA
End Sub


Sub cmdRight_Click ()
   MoveIt Me, 0, MOVE_DELTA
End Sub


Sub cmdRotateLeft_Click ()
   RotateIt Me, ROTATE_DELTA
End Sub


Sub cmdRotateRight_Click ()
   RotateIt Me, -ROTATE_DELTA
End Sub


Sub cmdSizeDown_Click ()
   SizeIt Me, 0, SIZE_DELTA
End Sub


Sub cmdSizeLeft_Click ()
   SizeIt Me, -SIZE_DELTA, 0
End Sub


Sub cmdSizeRight_Click ()
   SizeIt Me, SIZE_DELTA, 0
End Sub


Sub cmdSizeUp_Click ()
   SizeIt Me, 0, -SIZE_DELTA
End Sub


Sub cmdUp_Click ()
   MoveIt Me, -MOVE_DELTA, 0
End Sub
```

(Continued on next page)

(Continued from previous page)

```
Sub Form_Close ()
    CloseObj
End Sub

Sub Form_Load ()
    Dim rst As Recordset
    Dim intI As Integer
    Dim db As Database

    Set db = DBEngine.Workspaces(0).Databases(0)
    Set rst = db.OpenRecordset("qryItems")
    intI = 1
    Do While Not rst.EOF
        ExplodeIt Me, intI, rst!Exploded
        intI = intI + 1
        rst.MoveNext
    Loop
    rst.Close
End Sub

Sub grpPosSize_AfterUpdate ()

    ' After choosing one of Plot Area, Legend, Title,
    ' make sure the appropriate sizing buttons
    ' are available.

    Dim fEnabled As Integer

    ' Only enable the Up and Down sizing arrows
    ' if the Legends are selected (item 2).
    fEnabled = (Me!grpPosSize = 2)
    Me!cmdSizeUp.Enabled = fEnabled
    Me!cmdSizeDown.Enabled = fEnabled
End Sub

Sub lstItems_DblClick (Cancel As Integer)

    ' After selecting an item from the list,
    ' mark it as exploded and do the explosion.

Const QUOTE = """"""

    Dim rst As Recordset
    Dim db As Database

    ' For the sake of this simple app, just
    ' skip errors altogether.
    On Error Resume Next
```

```
    Set db = DBEngine.Workspaces(0).Databases(0)
    Set rst = db.OpenRecordset("qryItems")
    rst.FindFirst "Item = " & QUOTE & Me!lstItems.Column(1) & QUOTE
    If Not rst.NoMatch Then
        rst.Edit
            rst!Exploded = IIf(rst!Exploded > 0, 0, Me!txtExplode)
        rst.Update
        ExplodeIt Me, Me!lstItems.ListIndex + 1, rst!Exploded
        Me!lstItems = Null
        Me!lstItems.Requery
    End If
    rst.Close
    On Error GoTo 0
End Sub
```

18. That's it. Save your form, and then run it. You should be able to manipulate its pieces, just like you could on the original frmGraph.

How It Works

This section first discusses the generic routines imported in step 15, and then it covers the more specific event procedures that call the generic routines (described in step 17).

Referring to Objects

The first step in manipulating an OLE object is referring to it. The SetObject function (in basHandleGraph) sets the global variable, *obj,* to refer to the graph object on your form. The main portion of this simple function boils down to this statement:

```
If obj Is Nothing Then
    Set obj = frm(GRAPH_CONTROL)objGraph.Object
End If
```

This fragment uses a variable of type Object. This data type, used only when referencing OLE objects, allows you to refer to any part of an OLE object. As you'll see, you can set an object variable to point to a section of a graph, or a point, or the legend, or the whole graph itself.

SetObject first checks to see whether *obj* (a module global variable of type Object) is currently referring to an object. If not, its value is the predefined constant Nothing, and you need to initialize it. Otherwise, just use it as it is. (This check can save you some time, as it takes a fraction of a second to initialize the variable. When you're trying to rotate pie charts, every millisecond counts.) If you must assign *obj* to refer to the Graph object, you set it equal to the graph control's Object property. The graph control exposes many properties, just like any other control, and its Object property is just one of them. A graph control's Object property is a reference to the OLE object itself. Once you have that reference, you can treat it as an entity with properties and methods. The rest of this How-To focuses on using the graph object's properties and methods to force it to do what you want.

Manipulating Objects and Their Properties

The generic routines imported in step 15 deal with properties of the graph object—in this case, a 3-D pie chart. Table 12-28 lists the properties of the Graph object managed with the code here. Each of the procedures in basHandleGraph uses these properties to change the appearance of the pie chart on the sample form.

PROPERTY	DESCRIPTION	VALUES	EXAMPLE	USED IN
Elevation	Front-to-back rotation, or the viewing angle for the graph	From 10° to 80° (though documented as accepting –90° to 90°)	obj.Elevation = 25	ElevateIt
Explosion	Percentage explosion of a single pie slice [1]	0% (the pie slice point is in the center of the pie) to 100% (the point is at the outer rim of the pie)	obj.SeriesCollection(1).Points(1).Explosion = 50	ExplodeIt
Left and Top	Position of the left and top edges of an object (in points) [2]	0 to the size of the graph area	obj.PlotArea.Left = 0 or obj.Legend.Left = 0 or obj.ChartTitle.Left = 0	MoveIt
Rotation	Rotation of an object around its vertical (z) axis	0° to 360° (except for 3-D bar charts, where the value must be between 0° and 44°)	obj.Rotation = 300	RotateIt
Width and Height	Width and height of a graph object, in points	0 to the size of the graph area	obj.PlotArea.Width = 100 or obj.Legend.Height = 300	SizeIt
Size	Point size of a specific font object[3]	A reasonable font size, in points	obj.ChartTitle.Font.Size = 12	SizeIt

[1] Not a property of the graph, but of a specific point within a specific collection of points within the graph.

[2] Note that Access uses twips (1/20 point), but Graph uses points. The examples use the PlotArea, Legend, and ChartTitle objects.

[3] The Size property is a property of a Font object, which is itself a property of a Graph object that displays text.

Table 12-28 Sample graph object properties and their uses

Avoiding Overlapping Procedure Calls

Because you have set all the buttons on your form to auto-repeat as you hold them down, there's nothing to keep you from holding a button down and calling the procedure attached to the button's Click event over and over, even perhaps before the previous invocation has completed. This overlapping calling can cause you trouble, since Access only supports limited space on its internal stack for procedure calls. To avoid this problem, each of the generic procedures includes code to ensure that it doesn't get called until the previous call is completed. To do this, each uses a static variable, fInHere, which the routine checks as soon as it starts:

```
Static fInHere As Integer

' Avoid recursive calls into here.
If fInHere Then Exit Sub
fInHere = True


'
' Do the work here
'
' Let Windows catch up
DoEvents

' Clear the flag
fInHere = False
```

If the flag is True, you exit from the routine. If not, the routine sets the flag to True, does its work, calls DoEvents to allow Windows to catch up, and then clears the flag once it's done. Using this framework ensures that you won't run out of Windows stack space while holding down a particular button. (For more information, see How-To 7.4.)

Handling Specific Events

In addition to all the moving and sizing done in response to button clicks, there are two more events that require discussion. When you first load the form, code attached to the OnLoad event property goes through qryItems and sets the appropriate explosions for each of the pie slices. When you double-click on the list box of slices on the form, code attached to the OnDblClick event property for the list box finds the correct pie slice and explodes it, if it wasn't exploded, and sets its explosion back to 0 if it was.

In the form's Load event, the code walks through each row of the query and calls ExplodeIt for each item it finds:

```
Set db = DBEngine.Workspaces(0).Databases(0)
Set rst = db.OpenRecordset("qryItems")
intI = 1
Do While Not rst.EOF
    ExplodeIt Me, intI, rst!Exploded
    intI = intI + 1
    rst.MoveNext
Loop
```

If rst!Exploded is 0, that's fine, since it will just force the graph not to explode that specific slice. Note that this method requires that the graph be based on qryItems, too, so that the items are in the same order in the query as they are on the graph.

The list box, lstItems, is more complex. It pulls its values from qryItems, which, in turn, pulls its items from tblFoods. The table stores the specific explosion values (this allows you, when the form loads, to explode each slice a different amount, as shown in the code just above). The query includes the same information as the table, sorted on item name, plus an extra calculated column ("x" if the slice is exploded, and "" if it's not), which shows up in the list box. Double-clicking on an item in the list box toggles the current value in the table for that slice. If it's 0, it uses the explosion amount in the text box on the form and explodes the slice. If it's not 0, it sets the value to be 0. By setting the value in the table, calling the ExplodeIt procedure, and then requerying the list box, the code attached to the list box's DblClick event both explodes the slice on the graph and updates the list box's display.

```
Set db = DBEngine.Workspaces(0).Databases(0)
Set rst = db.OpenRecordset("qryItems")
rst.FindFirst "Item = " & QUOTE & Me!lstItems.Column(1) & QUOTE
If Not rst.NoMatch Then
    rst.Edit
        rst!Exploded = IIf(rst!Exploded > 0, 0, Me!txtExplode)
    rst.Update
    ExplodeIt Me, Me!lstItems.ListIndex + 1, rst!Exploded
    Me!lstItems = Null
    Me!lstItems.Requery
End If
```

Comments

The examples shown here barely scratch the surface of the capabilities of OLE Automation with Microsoft Graph. You can take these examples, though, and build on them using the ODK's help file as a guide.

> **GRAPH 5: NOT JUST USEFUL IN ACCESS**
>
> Access 2.0 and Excel 5.0 share the same graphing engine. (This explains why the Microsoft Graph help file is geared toward Excel Visual Basic for Applications programmers, since the Excel group put together the help file.) In any case, code you write for graphs in Access should work almost unmodified in Excel, and much of the Excel code in the help file should work just fine in Access. Certainly, learning to program Microsoft Graph in Access is a worthwhile use of your time, if you ever intend to also write applications in Excel (or using Visual Basic for Applications, as it becomes part of more Microsoft products).

The sample form, frmGraph in 12-07.MDB, has been set up so that only the graph itself will print (every other control on the form has its DisplayWhen property set to Screen Only), so it does serve a real purpose. You could supply a form like this to end users, perhaps allowing them to specify a row source for the graph on a previous form. Then, using this graph form, they could alter the characteristics of the graph before printing it. Only the altered graph would print; all the other controls on frmGraph are hidden when you print the form.

Be aware that Graph consumes immense amounts of memory and system resources. When working on this book, it was nearly impossible to run Microsoft Word 6.0, Access 2.0, and Microsoft Graph all at the same time. You'll need to take this into account if you're attempting to write applications that use multiple products along with Microsoft Graph.

One useful addition to the sample form presented here would be to allow for different graph types. Although the mechanics of changing the graph type are simple (it only requires changing the object's Type property), the ramifications for this example are complex, since it would require changing all the limits for the various movement and rotation values. It's a good additional project for you to take on, as you like.

Simpler additions include:

- Allowing the title to be toggled on and off (using the chart's HasTitle property)

- Allowing the legend to be toggled on and off (using the chart's HasLegend property)

- Changing the font style for the legend items—for instance, changing obj.Legend.LegendEntries(n).Font.FontStyle to "Bold Italic"

There are many other variations on item visibility (axis titles, point markers for non-pie graphs, for example) and font/style changes. Have fun with Microsoft Graph! It allows more flexibility than any built-in Access component and is guaranteed to give you hours of tinkering pleasure.

Index

Books have a substantial influence on the destruction of the forests of the Earth. For example, it takes 17 trees to produce one ton of paper. A first printing of 30,000 copies of a typical 480-page book consumes 108,000 pounds of paper which will require 918 trees!

Waite Group Press™ is against the clear-cutting of forests and supports reforestation of the Pacific Northwest of the United States and Canada, where most of this paper comes from. As a publisher with several hundred thousand books sold each year, we feel an obligation to give back to the planet. We will therefore support organizations which seek to preserve the forests of planet Earth.

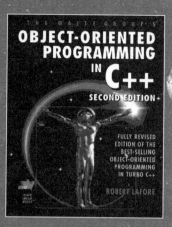

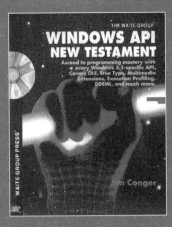
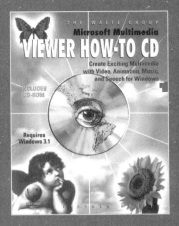
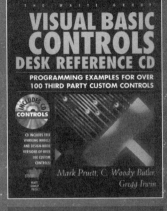

LIMITED WARRANTY

The following warranties shall be effective for 90 days from the date of purchase: (i) The Waite Group, Inc. warrants the enclosed disk to be free of defects in materials and workmanship under normal use; and (ii) The Waite Group, Inc. warrants that the programs, unless modified by the purchaser, will substantially perform the functions described in the documentation provided by The Waite Group, Inc. when operated on the designated hardware and operating system. The Waite Group, Inc. does not warrant that the programs will meet purchaser's requirements or that operation of a program will be uninterrupted or error-free. The program warranty does not cover any program that has been altered or changed in any way by anyone other than The Waite Group, Inc. The Waite Group, Inc. is not responsible for problems caused by changes in the operating characteristics of computer hardware or computer operating systems that are made after the release of the programs, nor for problems in the interaction of the programs with each other or other software.

THESE WARRANTIES ARE EXCLUSIVE AND IN LIEU OF ALL OTHER WARRANTIES OF MERCHANTABILITY OR FITNESS FOR A PARTICULAR PURPOSE OR OF ANY OTHER WARRANTY, WHETHER EXPRESS OR IMPLIED.

EXCLUSIVE REMEDY

The Waite Group, Inc. will replace any defective disk without charge if the defective disk is returned to The Waite Group, Inc. within 90 days from date of purchase.

This is Purchaser's sole and exclusive remedy for any breach of warranty or claim for contract, tort, or damages.

LIMITATION OF LIABILITY

THE WAITE GROUP, INC. AND THE AUTHORS OF THE PROGRAMS SHALL NOT IN ANY CASE BE LIABLE FOR SPECIAL, INCIDENTAL, CONSEQUENTIAL, INDIRECT, OR OTHER SIMILAR DAMAGES ARISING FROM ANY BREACH OF THESE WARRANTIES EVEN IF THE WAITE GROUP, INC. OR ITS AGENT HAS BEEN ADVISED OF THE POSSIBILITY OF SUCH DAMAGES.

THE LIABILITY FOR DAMAGES OF THE WAITE GROUP, INC. AND THE AUTHORS OF THE PROGRAMS UNDER THIS AGREEMENT SHALL IN NO EVENT EXCEED THE PURCHASE PRICE PAID.

COMPLETE AGREEMENT

This Agreement constitutes the complete agreement between The Waite Group, Inc. and the authors of the programs, and you, the purchaser.

Some states do not allow the exclusion or limitation of implied warranties or liability for incidental or consequential damages, so the above exclusions or limitations may not apply to you. This limited warranty gives you specific legal rights; you may have others, which vary from state to state.

SATISFACTION REPORT CARD

Please fill out this card if you wish to know of future updates to *Microsoft Access 2.0 How-To CD*, or to receive our catalog.

Company Name:

Division/Department: Mail Stop:

Last Name: First Name: Middle Initial:

Street Address:

City: State: Zip:

Daytime telephone: (   )

Date product was acquired: Month   Day   Year   Your Occupation:

Overall, how would you rate *Microsoft Access 2.0 How-To CD*?

☐ Excellent   ☐ Very Good   ☐ Good
☐ Fair   ☐ Below Average   ☐ Poor

What did you like MOST about this book?

What did you like LEAST about this book?

Please describe any problems you may have encountered with installing or using the CD:

How did you use this book (problem-solver, tutorial, reference...)?

What is your level of computer expertise?

☐ New   ☐ Dabbler   ☐ Hacker
☐ Power User   ☐ Programmer   ☐ Experienced Professional

What computer languages are you familiar with?

Please describe your computer hardware:

Computer _____   Hard disk _____
5.25" disk drives _____   3.5" disk drives _____
Video card _____   Monitor _____
Printer _____   Peripherals _____
Sound Board _____   CD ROM _____

Where did you buy this book?

☐ Bookstore (name):
☐ Discount store (name):
☐ Computer store (name):
☐ Catalog (name):
☐ Direct from WGP   ☐ Other _____

What price did you pay for this book? _____

What influenced your purchase of this book?

☐ Recommendation   ☐ Advertisement
☐ Magazine review   ☐ Store display
☐ Mailing   ☐ Book's format
☐ Reputation of Waite Group Press   ☐ Other

How many computer books do you buy each year? _____

How many other Waite Group books do you own? _____

What is your favorite Waite Group book? _____

Is there any program or subject you would like to see Waite Group Press cover in a similar approach? _____

Additional comments? _____

Please send to: **Waite Group Press**
                        Attn: *Microsoft Access 2.0 How-To CD*
                        200 Tamal Plaza
                        Corte Madera, CA 94925

☐ **Check here for a free Waite Group catalog**

STOP!

BEFORE YOU OPEN THE DISK OR CD-ROM PACKAGE ON THE FACING PAGE, CAREFULLY READ THE LICENSE AGREEMENT.

Opening this package indicates that you agree to abide by the license agreement found in the back of this book. If you do not agree with it, promptly return the unopened disk package (including the related book) to the place you obtained them for a refund.

MICROSOFT ACCESS 2.0 HOW-TO CD

KEN GETZ

HELEN FEDDEMA

MIKE GUNDERLOY

DAN HAUGHT

WAITE
GROUP
PRESS™

Publisher **Mitchell Waite**
Editor-in-Chief **Scott Calamar**
Editorial Director **Joel Fugazzotto**
Managing Editor **Joe Ferrie**
Production Director **Julianne Ososke**
Designer **Karen Johnston**
Production **Deborah Anker**
Cover Design **Cecile Kaufman**

Printed in the United States of America
94 95 96 97 • 10 9 8 7 6 5 4 3 2

Microsoft Access 2.0 how-to CD / Ken Getz ... [et al.].
      p.   cm.
   Includes index.
   ISBN: 1-878739-93-X : $44.95
   1. Database management. 2. Microsoft Access. I. Getz, Ken.
QA76.9.D3M556 1995
005.75'65—dc20   94-42623
                                                                                        CIP